TOUCHING THE ETERNAL

A BRIEF AUTOBIOGRAPHY OF A LIFETIME OF MIRACLES

1944-2013 AND BEYOND

BY THE ONE HE CALLS "YEDIDAH"

Dedicated to My Faithful Abba Yahuweh

"If we are not faithful, He remains faithful,
for it is impossible for Him to deny Himself."
II Timothy 2:13

THE GREATEST MIRACLE OF ALL IS ABBA'S LOVE AND MERCY!

Copyright © 2013 by Yedidah
Revised Edition (November 5, 2014)
All Rights Reserved

ISBN-13: 978-0-615-89938-1

Dedicated to My Faithful Abba Yahuweh

TABLE OF CONTENTS
Touching the Eternal

INTRODUCTION: LAYING THE FOUNDATION	1
PART I: **THE FORMATIVE YEARS OF MY JOURNEY**	25
PART II: **THE JOURNEY CONTINUES:** **GETTING TO KNOW ELOHIM**	52
PART III: **THE JOURNEY IS SABOTAGED:** **MY DETOUR FROM FAITH (1966-1985)**	86
PART IV: **THE JOURNEY BACK HOME (1985-1986)**	199
PART V: **TRAINING ASSIGNMENTS FOR FULL-TIME MINISTRY:** **LEARNING THE LIFE OF A SERVANT (1992-2001)**	231
• GERMANY (1992)	234
• CHINA (1994-1995)	239
• MONGOLIA (1996)	259
• RUSSIA (1999)	271
• AFRICA (1996-2001)	286
• ISRAEL (1999)	325
PART VI: **THE MIDDLE EAST AND TRAVELS BEYOND (1999-2013)**	339
• JORDAN (1999-2007)	339
• GREECE/PATMOS-ATHENS-CORINTH	366
• SWITZERLAND--ITALY--FRANCE	374
• ISRAEL	386
• WESTERN TURKEY	391
• WALES	442
• U.S. (INCLUDING ALASKA)	485
• COLOMBIA--ENGLAND	504
• IRELAND	511
• PANAMA	517
• EGYPT--BOLIVIA--GERMANY	531
• SCOTLAND (OUTER HEBRIDES)--ICELAND	567
• ROME/VATICAN	581
SHARING GOOD MEMORIES: **A PHOTO JOURNEY THROUGH THE YEARS**	595

A COLLECTION OF MIRACLE STORIES
(1946-PRESENT)

PART VII:
MIRACLES OF PROVISION
HE NEVER FAILS OR FORSAKES US!   **634**

PART VIII
STORIES OF HEALINGS AND
MIRACLES OF DELIVERANCE   **657**

PART IX:
PERSONAL STORIES OF HELP
ALONG THE ROADSIDE   **677**

PART X:
STORM STOPPING MIRACLES   **687**

PART XI:
STORIES OF PROTECTION AND RESCUE   **694**

PART XII:
MIRACLES OF HIS LEADING, CONFIRMATON
OF HIS WORDS, AND OTHER ADVENTURES IN
PERFECT TIMING   **703**

Introduction - Laying the Foundation

TOUCHING THE ETERNAL
A Brief Autobiography of a Lifetime of Miracles

INTRODUCTION

LAYING THE FOUNDATION

One morning in November 2011, I was doing intercession with a family at "Banias" in north Israel--which is in the ancient tribal area of Dan, below the Mount Hermon ridge. "Banias," Arabic for "Panias," was ancient Caesarea Philippi. Banias was once an ancient center of worship of the god Pan, worship of Zeus, and the worship of the Emperors of Rome. Under the temple of Pan was a huge river that flowed from Dan, the source of the Yardan (Jordan) River. Supposedly the opening of the underworld, ruled by Hades, was under this temple. Human sacrifice was performed here, and the bodies of the dead were thrown into the river that ran under the temple of Pan. The opening to the river in the temple of Pan was called "the gates of Hades." Pan was one of the DNA mutates known as "Nephillim" (**Genesis 6:2,4**)--a mixture of man and horse. It was in Caesarea Philippi that Messiah Yahushua (whom the Greeks re-named "IEsous"/Zeus/Jesus) made His proclamation that the "gates of Hades" would not prevail against His assembly of His people (**Matthew 16:13-26**). It was there that the Apostle Shimon Kepha (Peter) made his famous statement "You are the Messiah, the Son of the living Elohim" (God).

The book of *Enoch I* tells us that in the days of Jared, fallen angels came down on Mt. Hermon (called "Ba'al Hermon") to take human wives to produce the Nephillim, and in our day they will return to Mt. Hermon. The Hermon ridge rises above Banias. Seven days after being in Caesarea Philippi, Yahushua Messiah took Kepha, Ya'cob and Yochanan (Peter, James and John) up on the side of Mt. Hermon. There He stood in His radiant esteem, with Eliyahu (Elijah) and Moshe (Moses), revealing His Deity and proclaiming the day when He would take His Bride to Himself with Eliyahu as His attendant, and Moshe as the attendant of His Bride. The Bible has quite a bit to say about Mount Hermon, back to the time of Abraham.

That morning, in 2011, the anointing (Presence) of Yahuweh--Elohim of Abraham, Yitzak, and Ya'cob, Elohim of Israel--came powerfully on me to do intercession for His people right in the entrance-way of the cave of Pan. I proclaimed Psalms of victory and of Messiah's triumph over Satan. Then, I went up a few steps and sat down on a rock next to steps going between the entrance of cave of Pan and the temple of Zeus. I had been proclaiming **Psalms 96-100** at the temple of Pan, which I had also declared in the face of the Dragon in places like Tiahuanaco, Bolivia. Then I opened to **Psalm 86**, which I read. The power of His Spirit came upon me as I praised Him for His great deliverance of me from the "nethermost depths." **Psalm 86:13**: "**For Your loving kindness towards me is great, and you have rescued my soul from the nethermost depths of She'ol**" (Hades).

As I was praising Him, an American tourist came down the steps. She stopped to say to me: "You look like you are one who works in the temple here." (I was simply dressed modestly--long skirt, long-sleeved blouse, wearing a Jewish-style head covering). Her statement numbed my mind. I did not answer her. She leaned over closer to me, and said, "Do you speak English?" I said, "Yes." Then I looked up at her, and from deep in my spirit, I said with a firm, but calm, boldness: "**I only serve Yahuweh, Elohim of Israel!**" She was shocked, grunted, and walked off quickly. As I went down the hill to wait for my friends, I asked Abba what that was all about. He let me know that I needed to make that proclamation right in the face of the gods of the ancient world--the very gods that people all over the world are calling forth to return right now!

Messiah gave this sign of our time: "And as it was in the days of Noah, so also shall it be at the coming of the Son of man" (**Luke 17:26**). The distinguishing mark of the days of Noah was the mixing of human DNA with that of fallen angels, animals, reptiles, birds, fish, and plants. There was only one family left undefiled by this mixing, who still was in the image of Yahuweh – Noah and his family. Today, the trans-humanist movement seeks to create a post-human world. This goal has reached to the highest levels of the intellectual and political world, with experiments of all types going on by the thousands. To be 100% human will be incredibly rare if they are not stopped. Worship Yahuweh! Messiah will stop all the works of the Devil at His coming!

Today, to side exclusively with Yahuweh, Creator of the Universe is contrary to international law. Even the use of His Name is contrary to international law. The Vatican has made it illegal in their churches, and in the homes of their members, to use "Yahweh." He has been thrown out as the Creator by the world's scientific community, and the Roman Catholic Church. Truly: WE ARE IN the days of Noah! The Nephillim are also returning! The earth is becoming more and more violent. (**I Timothy 4:1-2; II Timothy 3:1-7; 4:3-5; Romans 1:20-32**, for examples. "We know this, that in the last days raging insanity shall come!" **Psalm 139:1-8; I Peter 1:2, Ephesians 1:1-3**, and other Scripture, tell us that we were known by Elohim before the foundation of the world. He chose us according to what He saw of our end--not our beginning, not our in-between life--but our end. Thank you Abba!

If you saw my life, a large part of my life, you'd have given up on me. But, He did not give up on me! Therefore, from my innermost depths I boldly said: "**I only serve Yahuweh, Elohim of Israel**!"

He is my precious Father, my Abba. I have left all to be His servant. To get me to this place, He has had to take me through much suffering. However, I consider it my schooling for my eternal position with Him. I do not want to leave His Presence for a nanosecond – not ever! Thus, through this "mini autobiography" you will come to know a little of the extraordinary life of the Yahuweh named "Yedidah." I have had a lifetime of miracles.

A "miracle" is something that only Abba Yahuweh does—something no human could ever do. It is a sovereign act of His intervention. It is something that identifies Him as Sovereign over us.

In his book, *At The Master's Feet*, Sadhu Sundar Singh recorded the words of Messiah, which he heard in a vision: "**The greatest of all miracles is the new birth in man, and to the man who has experienced this miracle, all other miracles become possible.**"

The articles I write, the teachings I give, the life I live, are from the heart of my Abba (Father). I write and speak from experience in my growing to know Him through many very hard years. Progressively He has revealed Himself--His nature, His ways, and His thinking, as well as His preciousness as a loving Father. This is why I have such a strong personal and intimate relationship with Him. I've paid the price for this relationship! Knowing Him carries the highest price tag of all, for the world hates Him!

Everything I am--my boldness, my Elohim-backed authority, my knowledge of His Word, my knowledge of living by His Spirit, my passion to do His will—all has been because He, the Potter, crushed this clay in His loving hands so that He could remold this vessel for His honor. This is why I have had a lifestyle of touching the eternal. He dwells with those who are contrite, humble--"bruised in spirit"--who "tremble at His Word." (**Isaiah 57:15; 66:1-2**)

Only those who understand what it truly means to suffer for His sake, under His discipline and training, for reigning in the eternal Kingdom, will understand His tender but tough dealings with us. He tries and tests, so that we die to self-will, and take up His. (**II

Timothy 2:3-4; I Peter 4:1-2) He wants to make victorious overcoming warriors out of us. He is a Father – a fabulous Father!

In the true new birth, when one is transformed by the Spirit of Yahuweh Himself, He does forty things that change us into a new creation. (**II Corinthians 5:17-21**) He opens the portal of our eternal spirit, which resides in the loins area (digestive/reproduction area) of our body, so that we can reach into the eternal realm of Yahuweh, and He can reach into us! The Spirit (Yahuweh) speaks to us in our spirit to teach, to direct and guide, to show us things to come, to convict, and to comfort. If one is truly born again, He offers us the privilege of asking Him to abide in this body-temple of ours.

Elohim does not speak to the volatile soul. The soul works through the brain. Its reasoning mind and unstable emotions are earth-bound. The soul is our natural life force. Through its " five senses" (sight, hearing, smelling, touching, tasting), we relate to this world. It is the seat of the sin-prone nature of man, the lusts of the flesh that war against the Creator. That portal to the kingdom of darkness was opened to mankind in the Garden of Eden. Unless it is, by discipline and humility, brought into subjection to the spirit, no one can ever know Yahuweh. [Refer to: "The True New Birth"/July 2009] **PLEASE NOTE: All articles referenced to in this book, may be found at comeenterthemikvah.com and/or laydownlife.net.**

Together the soul and spirit comprise the "spirit-man," which is identical in appearance to our outer man. It is this "spirit man" which goes into eternity after death, while the body decays and disintegrates. At the glorious resurrection when Messiah comes, we will be united in a resurrected body, and thus be "saved"--spirit, soul, and body--to live forever with Elohim. The wicked are not so. They will be resurrected 1,000 years after the righteous, but their end is not eternal life, but eternal death. [**Carefully read Revelation chapters 19-22**] "The end of our faith is the salvation of our entire being." (**I Peter 1:1-9; Philippians 3:20-21; I Thessalonians 5:23**)

This autobiography took seven years to write. Now it is July, 2013, and I am preparing to release it. It is a story of one weak woman that Yahuweh calls "Yedidah" – "beloved." I tell it with no pride! On May 4, 2012, while in Israel, I wrote the article "Through" (2012). It is the very nature of Abba Yahuweh to take us through things, as He took the children of Ya'cob (Israel) through the Red Sea. Unless He took me "through" He could not have brought me out. Most look to escape suffering and hardship, yet it is through these things that He can change us and free us from all that keeps us from being truly free, content, and joyful.

Introduction - Laying the Foundation

This is the story of one very human woman, whom He saw from the foundation of the world and chose to join Him in His exploits in the latter days, to bring His life to many. I do not teach from an intellectual mind, but share what He has taught me, so that I give only honor and esteem to Him! Yahuweh is my Abba, Friend, and constant Companion. Yahushua Messiah is my Savior, my Master, my soon-coming Bridegroom, and my Friend who never leaves my side. Their Presence abide with me. The more I love Him, and the more I hate anything of the kingdom of darkness, the more I realize that I have learned the wisdom of fearing Yahuweh.

I don't write from theology, or from my opinion. He took me out of religion a long time ago. He put me in the wilderness of southern Jordan, the Negev Desert, for 8 years, so that He might become my exclusive Teacher. I had to unlearn so much! In the manual "Faith Walk" I give you step-by-step instructions on how to walk by real Scriptural faith, because He has made me walk it out. He makes sure that I live what I write, otherwise I would be a hypocrite--and I am no hypocrite!

Almost every day He gives me new things from His heart, mostly from His Word or by impression to my spirit, but also in dreams, visions, by revelation knowledge to my spirit, or by experiences of His intervention. But, always His constant Presence is ever-abiding. He speaks to His people in forty different ways--each with precedent in the Bible. He is very personal with those who seek Him with all their heart. In writing, He so often flows through me sometimes for hours. Sometimes I lose time, being in the eternal realm, so that I do not even know what I wrote. His wisdom flows out of my spirit like water. Messiah said: "`Out of your innermost being shall flow rivers of living water'. But, this He spoke of the Spirit..." (**John 7:37-38**) The eternal spirit can receive an unlimited amount of information from Yahuweh and retain it all. For the re-born spirit actually has a mind of its own. I tell about how real this is, in my story about Tanzania, 1998. He tells us that to belong to Him means that we submit to being led by His Spirit, taught by His Spirit, filled by His Spirit, and empowered by His Spirit, every moment of every day. This takes dying to self will, to pick up His will. Oh the freedom that gives!

At the end of 2011, He impressed on me to get my own website. My son helped me. By January, we had **comeenterthemikvah.com** fully functional. The articles are organized in ten collections. Under "The Mikvah of the Spirit", are many examples from my own life showing how to live in the Spirit, so that all can live this awesome life!

Along with details of my life, with many miracles interwoven in the story, I also include **six collections of stories** that will build your faith and encourage those of you who are pressing in to know Him with all your heart. This takes discipline and concentrated effort. **"You will seek Me, and you will find Me, if you search for Me with all your heart."** (Jeremiah 29:11)
My life-story is divided basically into four parts
   1) My initial establishment on a firm foundation
   2) My willful tearing apart the firm foundation, resulting in bitter separation from Him
   3) His sovereign restoration of the firm foundation, upon which He has built the "house" to His eternal specifications
   4) And, the result of living on a firm foundation – the assignments of the Master. I know His incredible mercy and love.

"**Though we are unfaithful, He remains faithful, for it is impossible for Him to deny Himself.**" (II Timothy 2:13) HalleluYah!

Psalm 32:8 Abba speaking: "**I will educate you and enlighten you in the proper path to travel. I will advise you with what I have seen.**" (from the Artscroll Tehillim) Oh how I have relied on this verse! He sees the end from the beginning. Though He has to allow us to reap the results of the sin that we sow so that we might learn, He continues to pressure, test, discipline, teach, and lead into the path of righteousness--if we are truly His child, so that we might mature into His nature, ways, and thinking. How liberating to have the Spirit in control, so that we walk in the very nature of our Creator! No stress, only peace...no fear... for He tells us what we need to know. How awesome!

Daniel 32:35: "**And some of those who have insight shall stumble, to refine them and to cleanse them, and to make them white until the time of the end--for it is still for an appointed time.**" I read this, in my spirit I know I am one of "those." That appointed time is upon us. We are in the time of the restoration of all things **Acts 3:19-21**, and the time of purging **Acts 17:31**. As the Apostle Yochanan (John) laid his head on the chest of Messiah Yahushua at their last supper together, and heard His heart beat, so I only want to hear what He has to say, and give it to His people so that they, too, might know Him as a personal precious Companion and Friend. I fear one thing: Losing His Presence.

I want you to know that no matter what has happened in your life, ABBA WASTES NOTHING! He uses everything, even the most terrible things, to form us into a vessel of honor in His House. As you read through this autobiography, I tell "the good, the bad, and the ugly." I don't spare much. But, I tell it as it was to show you that no matter what we go through, He will use it in His hands as an instrument to His honor and esteem, and for ours too. From one who was drowning in regrets, I exhort you to stop sulking over regrets. Stop the self-pity. Stop the whining. Stop the negativity. Submit to Him, die to "self", and He will bring "beauty from ashes."

Jeremiah 9:23-25: "**Thus says Yahuweh, "Let not the wise boast in his wisdom, let not the mighty boast in his might, not let the rich boast in his riches, but let him who boasts boast in this—that he understands and knows Me, that I am Yahuweh..."**

The word "boast" means to twirl around vigorously in great joy. And so I boast that I know Him. That is the only boasting I can do. For without His constant love and protection, I would have squandered my life away and died a long time ago. Many times, Yahuweh had the right to kill me. But, Yahushua told me He would pray for me that my faith fail not, so that when I came back to Him with all my heart, I would spend the rest of my life working to bring His people to know Him. So, my purpose in writing is surely NOT to talk about me or exalt me! Those that know me know I do not exalt myself. He has taken all pride out of me. All that I am is because of His mercy! I am His bond servant, no more, no less.

In articles like "Living From the Eternal Mind"/November 2010, I relate how He has taught me to live. In articles like "Walk the Hard Road"/2005, I relate how He taught me to be totally dependent on Him for everything, while in the wilderness of the Negev. He uses people to do His will, and I thank Him so much for those "helpers" whom He has sent to bless me in so many ways. I am so appreciative of those who pray for me!

Psalm 118:6-7: "**Yahuweh is with me – I have no fear. How can man affect me? Yahuweh is with me through my helpers; therefore I can face my foes.**"

Psalm 73:25-26: "**Whom else do I have in heaven but You? And I have desired no one but You on earth. My flesh and my heart fail, but Elohim is the rock of my heart, and my portion forever.**"

At the end of 1998, after my fifth trip to Africa with one of my daughters and two friends, I asked Him what He wanted me to do next. He did not hesitate. He said: "**I want you to give away all that you have and move to Jordan**" (Aqaba). The joy came, and I did as He said. This is the normal life of a disciple (a taught one) of the Master. We are a disciple of whoever teaches us. We are also a disciple of the one whom we obey. I have one Master and one only, and I serve only Him!

I arrived in Aqaba April 18, 1999. There He had me to Himself. Elohim only deals with servants, whom He trusts to obey quickly. He only rewards servants. The servant is a "bond-slave" who has no life of self-will. He relinquishes His will to His Master, for he loves his Master! But, He has to teach His servants Himself – so that they know the desires of their Master, so that they know the voice of their Master, so that they know the nature, ways and thinking, of their Master.

Deuteronomy 15:15-16 is a picture of the choice that we must make if we are going to follow the Lamb of Elohim wherever He goes. Speaking of the "shmittah" year—and the release of servants: "**And it shall be when he (*the servant*) says to you, `I do not want to go away from you' because he loves you and your house, because it is good for him with you, then you shall take an awl (*like an ice pick*) and thrust it through his ear to the door and he shall be your servant forever**." (Italics mine)

The words "because it is good for him" are special to me. My eternal goal is **Revelation 22:3-5** -- especially verse 4. To dwell in the Presence of my Master forever is the passion of my heart-- no matter what pain the "awl" produces. **Isaiah 50:5-6**, Yahushua speaking of His past and future: "**The Master Yahuweh has pierced My ear and I was not rebellious, neither did I turn away. I gave My back to those who struck me and to those who plucked out My beard. I did not hide My face from humiliation and spitting**."

Being an astute and disciplined business woman and teacher, after two ordinations and the incorporation of a non-profit organization, you can imagine, I became more of a "mover and shaker" in ministry than even before. But in moving to Aqaba in 1999, He took all the human moving and shaking out of me quickly, and left me daily as a little child, asking "Daddy, what do we do today?" As I obeyed Him daily, you will read how He took me from my small beginnings to the worldwide ministry I have today. I wrote articles explaining, like "Daily Flowing in His Perfect Timing", "Led", and "On Assignment." I just did what He asked me to, one day at a time, and He used it to build what I am doing now. I claim no credit for it! He did it! I just obeyed His instructions. It is so simple – just obey every day and He takes our life and makes something beautiful out of it. He is the Master Potter! We are a lump of clay. Only He can bring forth the beauty! (**Isaiah 64:8**)

Introduction - Laying the Foundation

So far, since the mid-1950s, He has taken me to 37 countries; many of which I've visited multiple times. I've flown on close to 400 airplane flights, on 47 different airlines, as well as many trips by train, bus, ship, boat, ferry, and car. To date, I have written approximately 500 articles, studies, and time-dated updates, as well as compiled much research for my own use. Because of my site, **comeenterthemikvah.com**, and the site of my friend in Texas who has posted all my articles and updates for years--**laydownlife.net** -- the articles are going into five continents, into the most major nations on earth. This year (2012) I have reached, as far as I know, close to 100,000 people. In some ways I am a pastor to a large assembly, for almost daily I do counseling of individuals, and other personal ministry. I get weary, but not stressed out. Since 2000, I've worked at the computer between 12-14 hours most days that I am not traveling. My strength is His strength.

Yahushua said: "**Come unto Me all you who labor and are heavy laden and I will give you rest. Take My yoke upon you and learn from Me, for I am meek and lowly of heart, and you shall find rest for your souls.**" (**Matthew 11:28-30**)

In Him, I rest. I have taken HIS YOKE upon me. I have learned from Him. He is gentle, kind, and gracious. Daily, He taught me how to be productive without being "busy." Most busyness is no more than a flurry of activity to carry out one's self-centered agendas, or to work under false mercy or false responsibility, out of guilt, or from driving motivation. But, working for Him is simply my allowing Him to be an open channel for Him to work through me. I obey, but He strengthens me to do it. He provides for me. I do not need to be in stress, worry, anxiety, or fretting. I know Him, so I trust Him. He knows me, so He trusts me. "**I can do all things through Messiah who strengths me.**" (**Philippians 4:13**)

In 1958, when I was fourteen, I was with my parents at the home of my grandmother in Oklahoma. They were all snoring so loudly I couldn't sleep. So, I got off the couch where I was lying, pulled up a chair and knelt to pray. I began crying. I cried out to Father, and pleaded with Him: "Please never let me have a normal life." In my mind a "normal life" was dusting and ironing. I told Him I wanted to be in the middle of everything He was doing. Wow--did He answer that prayer!

Later I asked Him not to send me to Africa or the Middle East, but anywhere else was OK. He didn't answer that one! I spent seven years in and out of Africa, and lived in Aqaba, Jordan, on the Red Sea for eight years. I did well in Africa, and I love the Middle East! I never had a "normal life!" To this day, I stay away from dusting and ironing (smile)--unless it is direly necessary. Never dictate to Father what you want or don't want! He is the Most High, the Almighty Elohim of Creation, not a fictional character of Western mentality!

I did not start out having a writing ministry. I was an ordained minister through an affiliate ministry with the Assembly of God. I had my own corporation in Texas. But, after moving to Aqaba, in 2000, some good friends gave me a computer. Abba was teaching me so much and I wanted to share it.

In 2001, He gave me a prophetic word: "**Pour out, pour out, don't stop! Your vessel will not run dry. Just keep pouring the oil, the wine, and the fire—whatever is needed! Keep pouring out until My Son comes**." He gave me a quick picture of **II Kings 4:1-7**.

Since then, I have not stopped writing, teaching, counseling, warning as a watchman, interceding on His behalf, "gatekeeping", praying, ministering, sharing the Good News of salvation, the baptism into the Spirit, or reaching out to others in some way.

I was always active in ministry since age six – but this was my life-"calling." I never set out to write articles. I started with an e-mail list of 15 in 2000. In answering people's questions about the Word, I was doing an incredible amount of research, for example, going to the roots of Christianity, which became the study: "The Foundation of Deception." Even though I graduated from a major Bible College, He had to do a lot of changing of my theology.

October 25, 2002 I had an all-night dream: I was going outside a city to a place in the mountains to hear a Torah teacher teach His Word. At one point, I woke up and He said clearly: "**Go to HIM outside the camp**!" Isn't that what He says to all of us: **Hebrews 13:12-13**: "**And so Yahushua also suffered outside the gate, to set apart the people with His own blood. Let us, then, go to Him outside the camp, bearing His reproach**."

I had such grief as He taught me, for I had so few to share with. I gave it all to Him – for what could I do with such a small sphere of influence? From 2001, I spent my days mostly alone, researching and writing 12-14 hours a day. His Word was getting into my spirit so much that my mind was getting so sharp that my friends thought I had a photographic mind. I don't! He downloads into the mind that is in our eternal spirit, never into the soul's volatile unstable reasoning mind that so often takes His Word and twists it to make it sound palatable to the sin-prone nature of man.

The mind of our spirit, if born again and filled with His Spirit, can contain huge volumes of information and not forget anything.

Introduction - Laying the Foundation

This is what was happening to me. People have sometimes cruelly mocked me, saying I am the lady who writes long articles. But, all that He was teaching me began just flowing out. From my correspondence with individuals the articles developed. People would ask questions, and I'd often spend hours in answering them. Most never said, "thank you." But, by answering their questions I was building a library of His knowledge in my spirit. I later wrote articles on subjects most inquired about, which saved me hours of writing to individuals, most of whom were just curious to know my answers. Eventually, by His working, my e-mail list of 15 grew to over a 1,000. Much of that came from teaching in meetings.

In 2011, I was in my bank. You know how the credit card and debit bank card folks want you to let them know when you are taking a trip so that they don't cancel your card if they see activity from another country? I went to tell my bank customer service department that I was gone a lot of the year, and to ask them if they could tag my account so that they would not cut it off no matter where I used the card. The lady looked up my account on the screen. She smiled and said: "Well it says here that you are a `world traveler' so you don't need to tell us each time you go somewhere."

Abba had to set me apart unto Him while I was very young. You will read about that miracle at age four. **Again: A miracle is simply something that no human can do, no human can even think of doing! -- Something that is impossible without the intervention of the Creator of the Universe!** Because of being raised in a religion, I was a "religious" child and teen. Thankfully, He took all of that out of me in Jordan. I am definitely NOT a religious person. He also let me go through the sewer of life so that I have love and understanding for humans in general. I know Yahuweh and I know Yahushua. They are NOT a religion! They are Persons! They are Persons, our Creators, Who long for our fellowship!

My father was born and raised on the Cherokee Indian reservation in Oklahoma. He was ½ Cherokee and ½ Irish. He had an Eastern mindset. From early childhood my heavenly Abba began training me in Eastern thinking. From 1966, He began teaching me to "Walk the Hard Road"--an article that tells a lot about my training in Jordan. The thinking of the ancient Eastern world is practical, pragmatic. [Refer to my article: "East vs. West"] The Western world thinks in terms of the abstract, philosophies, concepts, in illusions of the mind and emotions. The Eastern world deals with hard-core tangible reality.

The Hebrew language itself reflects the nomadic culture of the ancient easterners, who became the Hebrews. So, to understand the Word, and Yahuweh Himself, is almost impossible with a Western mind-set. I've realized of late, that He taught me think as a Hebrew. The Word was written to one family group that was given one Covenant with Yahuweh. It is centered on one country within its Scriptural boundaries, from Dan to Be'ersheva.

Yahuweh is the Elohim of Abraham, Yitzak, and Y'acob (Isaac and Jacob). Ya'cob had twelve sons. From these sons came the "children of Israel." "Israel" is the name that Yahuweh gave to Ya'cob. Messiah came only for the lost ten tribes, or family groups, of Ya'cob, whom Yahuweh had to disperse into the nations AMONG the gentiles. Messiah told His Apostles only to go to the lost ten tribes of Ya'cob to spread the message of salvation. (**Matthew 15:24; 10:5-6**) He is an exclusivist and always has been. Of course, He is kind to all, and all can join this family by faith and obedience to the Covenant of Yahuweh, but few outside of this family have done that. The passion of His heart is to restore a repentant remnant of the whole House of Ya'cob – all the tribes – back to Himself in these last days. Hundreds of Scriptures tell us this. [Refer to: "Are You a Gentile?"; "Who Are the Ten?", "The Aliyah Scriptures", beginning with **Ezekiel 37:15-29**] I am very intertwined with this passion of His heart, in much intercession for the remnant of all the tribes, and in teaching on it.

He never ever calls His people "gentiles" (barbarians, heathen, pagans, foreigners, strangers and aliens). He never changed His Covenant or His Word to fit the minds of the Western religion of Greece and Rome that hates His Torah (instructions, teachings of the Kingdom of Heaven). The war is Lucifer/Satan against Yahuweh and His right to rule His Creation. That battle is raging greatly now.

Because Abba trained me in the Eastern mind-set, when I moved to a Muslim country, and began going in and out of Israel, I had no culture shock! I immediately fit in. I smuggled Bibles into Mainland China about forty times. I loved China. I had no problem with the culture. I've lived in several third world nations, most to the east of the Atlantic, but also in Panama. I love the people and they love me. In the practical world of the East, it is easier to learn the Word from His mind, and to know Yahuweh and Yahushua Yahuweh as They are – as Persons – not abstracts. Their Word is not abstract.

But, if we drape a Greco/Roman toga on Him, He is not the same as the Elohim of the Scriptures, and neither is His Son, Messiah Yahushua. Therefore, the church of the West has all sorts

Introduction - Laying the Foundation

of wrong ideas about Their nature, ways, and thinking. Thus their religion reflects the culture and thinking of Greece and Rome, not the ancient nomadic Hebrew culture. Therefore, the reality of "discipleship" (being a taught one of a Master) is not understood, or the cost of being a bond slave of the Master. Conforming to the nature of the Master, obeying Him, fearing Him, understanding the command to lay down one's self-life to take up His will, is not understood. Thinking according to Yahuweh's Kingdom culture is foreign to the ways and thinking of the Western culture.

I always wanted to know the real Elohim of the Bible. Now I do, but He had to take me through much suffering to find Him. By the time I was six I was doing evangelism. By age nine I was doing missionary work, teaching in a Mexican Baptist Church in my town, and playing the piano for services. From my early teens, I began doing evangelism in Mexico and on the Navajo Indian reservation. Beginning in my 20s, I began outreach in many different arenas to bring the Good News of salvation to people, to strengthen faith, and teach the Word.

I stress that every born again believer is called to follow the **Acts 1:8** pattern. "**And you shall receive power after the Set-Apart Spirit has come upon you, and you shall be My witnesses in Jerusalem, in all Judea, and Samaria, and to the ends of the earth**." First we begin at home, then branch out to neighboring cities, our county, state, and nation, and then go from there to the nations of the earth.

The following is an overview of my extensive ministry, demonstrating the Acts 1:8 pattern

He started me out when I was six, leading other children to the Savior. At age 9, I played the piano in a Mexican Baptist Church, and taught Sunday School and Vacation Bible School. As a pre-teen, and teenager, I went on several trips to Mexico. By the time I was in college, and after getting married, I began ministering in about every form of ministry you can imagine, mostly in the area of evangelism, but also in teaching the Word. I preached, and taught, on the streets of Los Angeles' skid row district all hours of the night to the homeless, to drunks, pimps, prostitutes, homosexuals, and gangs, in Rescue Missions, on the street at Hollywood and Vine, to children in churches, in parks, and in housing complexes, to the sick in hospitals, to the elderly in nursing homes, in adult day care facilities, in jails, prisons, half-way houses, and in juvenile facilities. I handed out tracts in public places, went door-to-door to present the Good News, performed in skits, worked as a "Minister of Music " in churches, directed choirs, sang, played the piano and/or organ. I taught in "Children's Church", discipled adults in classes in church, in home meetings and rent facilities. I took one church choir to Long Beach's Queen's Park and had outdoor services, and taught in two Bible colleges. He sent me several times to the Navajo Indian reservation to teach, as well as back to Mexico several times. THEN he sent me out to the nations. This is only a general overview.

Abroad, I did such things as smuggle Bibles into China. I taught English to college students in Mongolia and spread the Good News as I could there. I worked with the Jewish Agency in Russia for the return of Jews to Israel. I have ministered to many in about 32 countries, in healing, in miracles, and in deliverance from demons. I have preached in many open-air evangelistic rallies, and taught in many, many churches and home groups. I taught leadership to ministers in conferences in Africa. The variety has been astounding.

Since 2006, He has been sending me on intercession assignments of different types all over the coastal and river areas of America, to call back the repentant remnant of the House of Israel, and to speak His Enoch message to the spirits of the fallen ones, as in Tiahuanaco, Bolivia, and at Stonehenge, England, and give a message to the gods of Egypt standing by the Great Pyramid of Giza. He has taken me to the Outer Hebrides, to France, and to places all over the world for intercession.

I have ministered in the office of an Apostle, as a youth pastor and nursing home pastor, as an evangelist, and a teacher of the Word. But, He trained me specifically to be an end-time watchman-Prophet, a gatekeeper, an intercessor, a teacher, a counselor, and a writer. All of these besides my ministry in music, in performance, as a choir director, pianist, and Minister of Music.

In the summer of 2012, He sent me on one of the most important intercession assignments of my life – to the Vatican in Rome, to Patmos (**Revelation 1:9**), and to Delphi, Greece to address the ruling hierarchy of the Satanic world. [Refer to: "The Declaration Assignment"]

In everything He has called me to do, He has been the one to instruct and direct. I just follow His leading. I'm tired out just writing that. So, you know all of that had to be His strength, not mine! The amazing variety of ministry led to authority, confidence, and boldness in different countries.

Today, from continuing on to obey Him, as in **Luke 14:25-33** and **Luke 18:28-30**, I now have no home of my own, no car, no lands, and no regular income. I live the life of a nomad. It is hard, but the benefits from His loving hand are amazing! Yes, He's made me live what I write! **Luke 14:25-33** was my springboard: **"Unless you forsake all that you have, you cannot be My**

Introduction - Laying the Foundation

disciple." Messiah said: "**Without Me, you can do nothing.**" Amen to that! **So, to Him go all the honor, esteem, worship and praise forever and ever!** Before I teach, write, or speak in any situation, I first study the whole Word (Genesis to Revelation) on the subjects I will be teaching. Unless the whole Word unites to teach, with the Spirit as our Teacher, we must not teach. To repeat what another says, is useless unless He has taught it to us! So, repeating what man says, leads others into error, and we become a collaborator with false prophets!

I Peter 4:11a: "**If any man speak let him speak as the oracles of Elohim….**" "**As a man thinks, so is he.**" What we think comes out. If indeed we have disciplined the soul by the Word, so that it submits to the "mind of the spirit", then out of our mouth will come only what is pleasing to Yahuweh and Yahushua. And then there is the "fear of Yahuweh", which is mandatory if we are to instruct others. If I cannot repeat what He has taught me, I do not teach or send an article. I do not give out my opinion as fact.

After a lifetime of training, in 1986, while studying the life of Yochanan the immerser (John the Baptist), Yahuweh gently said to me: "**I have called you to the office of the Prophet.**" I was stunned. But, what He had to do to bring me to that point is my story.

Please note: When I say "He spoke to me", or "He said", or "He let me know…", I mean that I heard Him in one of the 40 ways He speaks to His people. [Refer to: "Forty Ways Elohim Speaks to His People"] Think! If your best friend calls you on the phone, do you ask: "who is this?" NO! You know who it is! I am not one of those flaky mystical spooky people. I am very down-to-earth! I just hear from Someone I know! Throughout the Word, His servants heard Him. He talks! It is just that most people are too busy with their own agendas to listen. I know the boundaries of being one of His servants. I know the boundaries of speaking for Him. If I cross them, I will be unfit for His service. The true prophet must only say what He wants said, or else they are a false prophet. [Refer to: "The Message of the True Prophet"] Most big-name preachers teach a mixture of truth and error. But, if someone speaks out of their head, Yahuweh didn't send them. Most in the affluent West want a McDonald's-type fast-food education <u>about</u> God, but few even care to <u>know</u> Him. These fast-food teachers take a verse here and a verse there out of context to prove their nauseous beliefs. And people gobble them up as if they were slobbering over a McDonald's McRib sandwich.

I do not chitchat the world's shallow rhetoric. I do not engage in useless flesh-appealing pursuits, i.e. worldly entertainments that drain the spirit of His power. That is boring to me! Crave Truth! Love His Word-Truth with all your heart--for those who do not love it enough to seek it out from Him will end up being like those in **II Thessalonians 2:8-12.** They will receive deception that will damn them for eternity. And Yahuweh says He is the one that allows them to receive this deception. Pure Truth can only be taught to us by the Teacher Himself! All who are His students understand the same things.

In 2003, He gave me **Ezekiel 3**, and called me as a watchman to America. I have been faithful to give warnings upon warnings. But, now, the battle is at the gate! The nation of America is dying. The great whore of Babylon is rising in power over the earth (**Revelation 17; Zechariah 5:5-11**). Behind her comes Leviathan – son of Lucifer. He has taught me much about the hidden agenda of the Roman Catholic Church. The ancient power of the Roman Empire never died, it just hid in the Roman Catholic Church. Soon they will throw off their façade of religion, and become the world-ruling political force of ancient Rome, once again. From Constantine onward, the papacy is the oldest monarchy on earth. Even now they are flexing their muscles, for they know they have legal power over all the nations on earth. In other words, the woman will ride the beast to world power.

I have studied and taught on the end times for much of 48 years now. What keeps me excited is watching events that point to the coming of Messiah Yahushua, my Beloved! In 1986, Abba renewed my passion for studying and teaching on the end times. I see what is happening so clearly. He has opened my understanding for I live out of my spirit, and dwell in His realm of eternity to hear Him.

In 2005, while sitting on my flat-roof "balcony" in Aqaba, He gave me a prophetic word that I was to be a gatekeeper for His people in America, and in the land of Israel. I began to do intercession around the Gulf, up the rivers of Texas, to all major rivers of America, to Alaska, and on the East Coast. In 2005, I began intercession over all the borders of Israel. [Refer to: "Intercession: Knowing the Basics"] Scriptural intercession backed by His authority is far different than the hocus pocus of most church intercession, which stirs up demons more than anything else, and carries a spirit of pride and arrogance. Scriptural intercession proclaims exactly what He wants said – no more, no less – mostly from His Word, with His authority-backing. [Refer to: "Authority Backing"]

America has the largest concentration of the House of Israel (Ephraim/Joseph), the ten scattered tribes from 722 BCE, than any other nation. Except for Israel, America has more Jews than any other nation. He instructed me to prophesy to, warn, exhort, and encourage the "lost sheep of the House of Israel" – the ten northern tribes of the House of Ephraim.

When I began writing this autobiography in 2006, I did not know about the final cycles before the coming of Messiah. In 2007 Abba revealed to me what the Orthodox Jews have known for centuries, and what the Luciferic rulers have known from eternity past. The founding fathers of America knew this timing in 1776, and wove it into symbols on the dollar bill, in Washington D.C., as well as into their Masonic practices. [Refer to: "America's Secret Destiny"]

Now we are in the last cycle, and things are moving rapidly--Messiah is coming soon. [Refer to: "The Shmittah Year Prophecy", "The Forty-Eight Hour Transition", The September 12, 2007 Report", "Pole Shift" and "What Are the Elite Doing to Prepare Their Ark?"]

In teaching on these subjects, I was propelled forward into my ministry work for Him at a break-neck speed. Since 2007, through teaching tours, and writing many articles on timing, those listening to the prophetic voice of Yahuweh have had their lives radically changed. I've spent much of my last 14 years warning people to sell or give away all they can, and prepare to leave the U.S. – for its destruction is near. Few listened, but more and more are listening now. It surely isn't just me with this message. Secular people know this to be true. But, the Word speaks clearly about America as end-time Babylon, and Abba exhorts us to "flee." For when He pours out His wrath, He does not want to have to destroy His children with the wicked.

If secular people, and a lot of ex-military people, are fleeing the U.S. – why are His people holding on for dear life to things that will perish along with them? Most have a pie-in-the-sky religion, that has no concept of **LUKE 14:24-33**! We must also prepare spiritually. I love being in His Presence more than anything on earth! I am spending more and more time in worship, in speaking and listening to the Psalms being read or sung, in both English and Hebrew. I was a classic Music Major in college, yet the simple melodies that are sung with His Word is the most profound music on earth. In worship, without even realizing it, as we are lost in His Presence, He transforms us, taking from us what has kept us from our peace and joy in Him.

Revelation 4 and 5: He is leading His set-apart ones more into worship. He is calling us into an intimate relationship with Him. Praise and worship fill us with continual joy and peace. In worship the Spirit can remove what is defiled in us, and cleanse us from all unrighteousness—if we let Him. He calls us to humility and repentance. Abba is good – a refuge for those that seek Him with all their heart! I strongly recommend proclaiming the Psalms of victory. This is the most powerful spiritual warfare. [Refer to: "Ancient of Days", "The Power of Praise", and "Worship – the Journey of the Ark"]

Because I had to learn Scriptural spiritual warfare for survival, I teach it with boldness from experience. I know how the enemy thinks and his plans. I know how he works on the mind of Yahuweh's people. He has shown me the "depths of Satan" and his plans for Yahuweh's creation. So, I expose the enemy's plans clearly. I see the workings of the enemy clearly, whereas most people cannot see the evil lurking inside what appears to be good. I expose what is lurking within "good"--things hidden in religion, and cultural tolerance.

I have taught a lot about the "Bridal remnant." The word says that His Bridal remnant, the marked and sealed ones who sigh and cry over the abominations done in Jerusalem, who are blameless, who follow the Lamb wherever He goes, are few and far between--only approximately 144,000. (**Revelation 14:1-5**)

On October 23, 2007, I was in Tiberias, Israel. I sat at a window overlooking Lake Kinneret (the "sea of Galilee"). I began writing on the characteristics of the Bridal remnant. I entered the future in the eternal realm, and hours later I finished the study, but did not know what I wrote. [Refer to: "The Two Witnesses, The Bride of Messiah, The Forerunning Company, and The Fleeing Remnant"]. He will take you as fast as you want to go with Him. But, He is all light, and if we draw back into darkness, He will leave. Like in **Ezekiel 11:22-23**, He will leave, and most won't even know He has left! Yet, He longs to share His secrets with us. **Amos 3:7: "For the Master Yahuweh does nothing UNLESS He first reveals His secret to His servants..."**

Unless a prophecy is witnessed to by **ALL** HIS SPIRIT-TAUGHT SERVANTS the prophets, that prophet is a false prophet. Never listen to a person with a new idea, or a "revelation" that is not 100% backed from the whole Word, in context! The Spirit teaches His students the same thing. But, it takes discipline to learn from Him. I also expose false prophets. I do not expose anything or anyone out of pride or a superiority attitude! I expose to save as many as possible from falling away from Truth!

I raised four children, and I worked in the secular world a lot of my life. I understand having to work and raise children. I understand what so many of you go through in your life. My purpose in writing my life's story is not to exalt me – but to help others to understand themselves, and to desire a relationship with Yahuweh and Yahushua Yahuweh!

Introduction - Laying the Foundation

In 2004, while riding in a truck out in the Midian mountains of the Negev, He spoke to me the words of **Ezekiel 40:4**: "...**See with your eyes and hear with your ears, and set your heart on all that I am showing you, for you were brought here in order for Me to show them to you. Declare to the House of Israel all that you are seeing**." The goal of my life for eternity is **Revelation 22:3-5**! I want to eat of the tree of life and go "back beyond the garden gate." [Refer to: "The Stump", and "Back Beyond the Garden Gate"]

One day, about 1988, I was walking around a room at Grace Temple in Fort Worth, Texas, in June Joyner's prayer class, as we praised Abba with all our heart. I was thanking Him for saving me from a life of sin that could have ended my life easily. He spoke to me this in such compassion and love: "**You could have spent the last twenty years more profitably, but I have called you to this last hour.**"

I exclaimed: "More profitably! Is that all you can say about my horrible years of sin and rebellion against You?" I said: "Do you mean that the work You have for me is within the 7th millennium?" He said: "Yes."

We crossed into the 7th millennium from the re-creation of the earth September 29, 2000/2001, Tishre 1, Yom Teruah--a "shmittah" year. On that day everything changed. I have studied and reported on the mind programming that has been done to the American people that is resulting in their very DNA being changed – so that our humanity is being stolen from us. I have exposed the evil of America. Please refer to these articles: "Eugenics: The Planned End of Mankind"/January 2008; "Digital TV: Beware!"/June 2009; "How To Keep Functioning in Peace and Joy When Project Blue Beam Does Everything Possible to Make Sure Your Mind Shuts Down For Their Takeover"/April 3, 2010; "HAARP Atmospheric Plasma Weapon – What You Breath is Slowing Taking Over Your Mind and Body"/May 25, 2011; "Mind Control, Hidden Manipulation, and the World Brain"/September 2006 and "Quiet Wars and Silent Weapons"/October 29, 2007]

Besides "The Foundation of Deception" exposing the roots of pagan Christianity, I have written: "Exposing the Lies of Monotheism", "Exposing Rabbinic Judaism and Its Link to Rome", "Exposing Kim Clement and other False Prophets", "Religion", "Exposing the Real Agenda of Mary Worship", "Exposing Equinox Observance", and "Exposing the Trinity Doctrine", as well as articles refuting heresies, like "Replacement Theology", "An In-Depth Investigation of the Teachings of Soul Sleep", "Denying the Deity of Messiah"—to free many from heresies. I've also exposed the plans of the Illuminati for a one world order. Abba shows me what the enemy is doing, and I blast it wide open. But, He says to do that--to expose the darkness to His light, to bring out what is hidden and masked. I wrote the article "Betrayal", to warn people about how easy it is to betray those you love. In "Who Will Be Left Behind?", I warn against the incredibly non-Scriptural pre-tribulation rapture hoax, which has kept more people in an illusion state of deceptive fantasy than probably any other false doctrine, with roots in the Vatican.

I don't delight in exposing evil – but I must! I just wrote "Sixty Six Teachings Assumptions Found in Christian Evangelical/Charismatic Churches That Have No Scriptural Foundation"/October 2012. I've taught on Edom--the place of refuge that Abba has given to us. I've reported on what I saw those eight years in Aqaba that has fulfilled much prophecy.

Daniel 2:21b-22: "**He gives wisdom to the wise and knowledge to them of understanding. He reveals deep and secret matters. He knows what is in the darkness and light dwells with Him.**"

From **Mark 4:22-25**: "**Take heed what you hear!...For whoever possesses, to him more shall be given, and whoever does not possess, even what he has shall be taken away from him.**"

I want to know His secrets, not for the sake of knowledge, but to know Him more intimately!

In the early 1990s, He gave me the calling of **Isaiah 21:11-12**. We have now moved into the period of "night." He has given me **Ezekiel 3** and **Ezekiel 33**, and **Jeremiah 1**, as different aspects of my calling. The more faithful I am to do His will, as He instructs, the more faithful He becomes in fulfilling His promises to me!

For years, He instructed me in every meeting to drop the plumb line and quote **Amos 7:7-8**. "**This is what He showed me: See, Yahuweh stood on a wall made with a plumb line, with a plumb line in His hand. And Yahuweh said to me: `Amos, what do you see?' And I said, `A plumb line'. And Yahuweh said: `See, I am setting a plumb line in the midst of My people Israel--no longer do I pardon them'** ." The plumb line divides groups, congregation, families, and friends – quickly. I've seen the results, some with grief, some with shock, and some with joy. The plumb line is His Word!

In January of 2008, He instructed me not to drop the plumb line anymore in meetings, but said: "Now we have moved into **Amos 4:12b**": "**Prepare to meet your Elohim, O Israel.**"

In February, He said: "**The tares are now rising above the wheat.**" And in March He said: "**Wake up and strengthen that**

which remains and is about to die." (**Revelation 3:2**) In June of 2012, in Iowa, He told me to drop the plumb line one more time. I was in the heart of the nation of America. Read my report in: "Dropping the Plumb Line – Separation: The Grief and the Joy", and "The Release of Judgment on the Nation – Shavu'ot 2012 and Current Events"] The dropping of the plumb line is "prophetic action" which releases the Spirit to go and separate and divide. Messiah said He did not come to bring peace on the earth, but division (**Matthew 10:34-39**).

One major focus has been to excite a remnant about the coming of Messiah, but in **doing so, I have to give the message of Eliyahu (Elijah) in I Kings 18:21 "How long will you keep hopping between two opinions? If Yahuweh is Elohim follow Him! If Ba'al, then follow Him.**"

Especially since 2006, He has sent me on many intercession trips to many strategic places on the earth, to call a repentant and humble remnant of Ephraim home, to join with Judah for the final exploits! I praise Him for allowing me to join with others of like heart to do this, in some very unusual places. I love it when I can link arms with others who have a like heart. I joined with a family from Canada in 2011 to go to the Outer Hebrides' northern island tip (the Isle of Lewis) to call home this repentant remnant. I have since done intercession with this family in Israel. They are nomads too – they sold all and came to the Hebrides, backpacked across Europe, and then camped out in Israel. Then in Elul (late August 2011), He sent me to Iceland to proclaim from there. Elul 1 – Tishre 1, 2011, were pivotal dates regarding the return of this repentant remnant. [Refer to: "My Iceland Report"]

Since around 2003, I began traveling and teaching in many meetings throughout the U.S. I am very saddened to see the rebellion in the people--the apostasy spreading so rapidly in America and Israel--denying the deity of Messiah, turning from the Word, even denying Him totally, to follow teachers who are leading people into the lake of fire. Some came to hear me out of curiosity. Some wanted to argue their religious beliefs they got from man. However, more than anything else, their ignorance of the Scriptures, and their not knowing Him as a Person, has really made me suffer.

Many want to tell me what their pastor or rabbi said. Many, out of "plastic politeness" have said they liked my "message", but not understanding that it was Yahuweh's message. Then there have been the horrendous betrayals because of jealousy and jezebel spirits. The enemy continually attacks in a variety of ways. But, some of the attacks from Messianic or Christians people have been satanic in nature. Many hide under a layer of "vanilla frosting", but when their spirit comes up against the Spirit of Yahuweh in me, they attack.

I have grieved so much that people choose to hear human teachers, when the Spirit of Yahuweh longs to teach us. Thus, people cannot know Yahuweh. Some have not heard Him ever speak to them, though they have been "believers" for many years. Perhaps He did speak, but they did not recognize His voice, or they didn't do as He said.

When Messiah baptized me into the Spirit, November 1967, He gave me the nine gifts of the Spirit (**I Corinthians 12:4-11**), including a very strong gift of "the discernment of spirits." I know the difference between the spirit of man, demon, and the Spirit of Yahuweh. Knowing His nature and this gift will save you from great trouble!

He gave me the mandate of **Hosea 8:1 and Isaiah 58:1**: "**Put the shofar to your mouth, like an eagle against the House of Yahuweh, because they have transgressed My Covenant, and have rebelled against My Torah**" ... "**Cry out! Do not spare! Lift up your voice like the shofar. Declare to My people their transgression and the House of Israel their sin.**"

In doing this, it has cost me greatly, because people do not want to face the fact that they are wrong about anything. Pride is a destroyer of Truth. Fear is a destroyer – it paralyzes, torments, drives, and pushes Yahuweh totally out of a person's life. For "without faith, it is impossible to know Him." Faith is NOT a belief system of some religion. Faith is actively obeying the Master, believing Him above everything that is seen, heard, or felt. In the face of horrendous deception those that "know their Elohim will be strong, and do exploits." I teach a lot on "The Exploit People." (**Daniel 11:32**)

A main theme of my writings is to teach people to be set-apart to Yahuweh. **Hebrews 12:14b**: "**...without set-apartness no one will see Elohim.**"

The jezebel spirits (**Revelation 17**) have caused me more grief than anything else, but also I've had people try to use me to get advantage for their own ministry. They feign friendship with me to get into my inner circle, in order to get people to listen to them. The greatest battles have been from those who are jealous of the favor He has bestowed on me. I carry great favor from my Master. But, I have paid the price for it! Some have thought they could just walk in and take it from me, and when they found they couldn't, they have spread lies about me, slandered me, and tried to destroy my reputation. But, Abba has been my shield, my defense, and my hiding place! (**Psalm 3**)

Introduction - Laying the Foundation

As a whole I see people, in general, who have allowed themselves to be immersed into the mind-programming of the Illuminati, rather than in His Word. I have watched people get weaker and weaker in all ways, even losing the ability to receive truth and walk in it. I see the spirits of Lucifer taking over the church. Few humbly repent--most have a "whore's forehead" as **Jeremiah 3:3** describes.

Fear is taking over to an incredibly high degree, as minds are being absorbed into a "world brain", and fear is instilled if they do not conform. I've exposed TV. Most have submitted their minds to the TV, the major mind-programmer of Satan, to the culture's mind programming, public education's mind programming, religious mind-programming, so even their will is being taken over and controlled. The hypnotic e.l.f. (extra low frequency) pulse waves are dulling the mind, and DNA-altering vaccines, and chemicals are being taken into the human body, so that western man is literally being changed, hypnotized, dulled, and reduced to a zombie-like state. But also, we are in the age of Laodicea – the time of the lukewarm.

I do not dwell on these things. I can't! You must not! I have too much work to do for my Master! But, I report on them because the world is turning on His set-apart ones, and it will be the norm for all of those who side with Yahuweh and Yahushua Yahuweh.

I warn you: "**All those who wish to live righteously in Messiah Yahushua will suffer persecution**" (**II Timothy 3:12**). The words of **Matthew 10:17-22** will happen! **These Scriptures define the foundation of my testimony**:

Psalm 113:5-8: "Who is like Yahuweh our Elohim, Who is enthroned on high? He looks down on the heavens and in the earth. He raises the poor out of the dust, and lifts the needy from the dunghill, that He might set him with princes, even with the princes of His people."

Psalm 40:2-3: "He brought me up out of a horrible pit, out of the miry clay, and set my feet upon a rock and established my goings. And He put a new song in my mouth, even praise unto our Elohim, many shall see it and fear, and shall trust in Yahuweh."

Since I jump around a little in this book (smile), here are some reference points to keep you sane!

Early years – Arkansas to California (1944-1974)
North Carolina (1974-1986)
Texas (1986-2006)
Florida (2006-Present)
Aqaba (1999-2007)
Traveling to the Nations for the Master (1992-Present)

Parts I to VI are "loosely chronological" --covering the broad scope of my life. Beginning with Part VII, I share stories that are not chronological. **They are in collections by subject matter.** These miracle stories are from 1946 to present, and ongoing, of course. The miracle stories and stories of His intervention are NOT ALL told in the collections. I scatter them throughout the autobiography. But, the stories in the collections fill in the blanks of the previous six parts that tell of my life and my Abba's interventions.

I want to encourage you! If Yedidah can live this normal life of a set-apart disciple, so can you! I write this for your blessing so that you might have courage to step out and enjoy TOUCHING THE ETERNAL!

THE GREATEST MIRACLE OF ALL IS ABBA'S LOVE AND MERCY!

PART I

THE FORMATIVE YEARS OF MY JOURNEY

If you are truly born again--born from above by the working of the Spirit of Yahuweh--you are on a life-journey. This life is our school to prepare us for our eternal life in the Kingdom of Yahuweh and Yahushua. We have duel citizenship – citizenship in the country of our birth and citizenship in the Kingdom that is soon to come to earth.

Philippians 3:20-21: "For our citizenship is in the heavens from which we eagerly await the Savior, the Master Yahushua Messiah..."

TO BEGIN...

I was born in July, 1944. My parents lived in a tiny little town in the Ozark Mountains of Oklahoma, where my mother's mother and father lived. Granddad was a medical doctor, but he would not deliver any of his grandchildren. So, when I was ready to be born, my mother had to go to a hospital in Fort Smith, Arkansas. Her younger sister, Ahnie, 19 at the time, was in nursing training. In those days, they used ether to knock patients out, and kept the mothers in the hospital 10 days. However, it was war time. The hospital was affiliated with Fort Chaffee and so all the rooms were taken, and beds were out in the hall because of all the wounded soldiers being brought home. But, because my Aunt was an assertive little lady, she got my mother a private room. Ahnie was the first one to hold me.

My precious Aunt Ahnie died on my mother's 100th birthday in 2011. I thought to myself, with a smile, that my mother was probably having a huge family get-together to celebrate her 100th in heaven, and Ahnie didn't want to miss it. I had the strange feeling of being left out.

After the 10 days in the hospital, I was taken back to our little town in Oklahoma. Granddad lived until I was two. He came from a fine aristocratic family. One family member was a signer on the North Carolina original state Constitution, another was Patrick Henry, another was Ty Cobb. His family were successful people in many areas of life.

They tell me I hauled off and smacked granddad across the face one day while he was holding me, which caused a lot of laughter. I sure wish I had known him. He would travel to doctor the Indians, riding in a horse-drawn carriage. They often couldn't pay him in dollars, so they gave him potatoes and other food from their gardens. My wonderful "Nanny"--as I named my grandmother, the only grandmother I ever knew--basically raised me until I was about 18 months old because both my parents worked as teachers in a country school, and were gone from early morning to night. It is said by psychologists that a child's personality is formed by 18 months. Nanny had a small garden next to her little house, and she would set me in the garden while she either tilled the soil, planted, weeded, or harvested. Maybe this is why every spring I have such a desire to get outside, and plant a garden. I love the out-of-doors.

Nanny was a vegetarian because when she was a little girl the family killed her pet calf for dinner. That hurt her so deeply that she never ate meat again. Only one time, for me, she had a bite of a chicken wing. As an adult, for seven years I was a strict vegetarian too. But, to this day I eat only a little chicken with my vegetables, fruit, and grains, and sometimes fish, but rarely red meat.

Nanny influenced my early years more than any other person. She was gentle and kind, and had a super sense of humor. She was also a spitfire when her temper got riled up. She played the banjo. Being a mountain woman, she could also spit tobacco as well as any man. I loved her so much. I miss her! I loved the mountains. So, later in life had my own beautiful home by a stream, in the woods, in North Carolina. But, my love for the sea won out. I got that love when we moved to California in 1946.

When I was about eight years old, Nanny moved to California and got a little house near us. I would go across the street from Lincoln Middle School and have lunch with her in her little bungalow. Sitting on her bed, she taught me how to blow bubbles with bubblegum and to whistle. Those things are very important to a child (smile).

Nanny lived next to a 90 year old lady named Mrs. Mooth. I called her Grandma Mooth. I loved visiting her. Also, living in our little town in southern California were Nanny's two brothers and their wives and children, and grandchildren, Com and Becky, Son and Aunt Annie. I loved going to Uncle Com and Becky's house most of all. They lived in the country and had hunting dogs like Granddad did—"blue tick hounds." I loved Nanny's family very much. She had four children – my mother being the oldest, then Fairy, then John, and then there was the baby Ahnie.

In the early 1940s, unbeknownst to my parents, or Nanny, or most everyone in America, there were things being introduced into the thinking of the American people that most went along with, even though it made no sense. Because granddad was a doctor, Aunt Ahnie became an RN. She married my precious Uncle Charlie and they had four children. Their daughter became a nurse. Two of their sons went into medicine, one became a doctor. My family was medical-minded. So my mother's mind set was: If the doctor said something should be, then it should be. So, as a baby, I became a victim of a couple of the experiments that were part of many experiments continued on after World War II by the Nazi doctors that America brought into the AMA via "Operation Paperclip." Many of the very experiments that were done on the Jews were continued on the American people--like vaccines, experimental medicines, and DNA manipulation. Today those experiments are very advanced – the goal being a post-human world.

But, in the 1940s they began psychological experiments using physical means. For example, doctors told mothers to give their children full fat cow's milk in a bottle, because breastfeeding was bad for them. Because breastfeeding was bad, "formulas" were invented to replace breastfeeding. Because the cow's milk and formulas caused colic, children screamed with stomach pains. But, psychologists and doctors told parents not to pick up their children when they screamed, for this was bad for them.

So, being influenced by the medical world, my mother did what the doctors deemed "right," even though it went against nature and common sense. Then there were the psychological experiments done via Dr. Spock's infamous book on child-rearing, that has produced a generation of rebellion.

I was one who screamed from the colic because of the cow's milk, and was not picked up and held by my mother or father. I don't think Nanny would leave me screaming, but she had to feed me formula. So from the bassinet, a whole generation of children were left with a sense of being unloved--screaming inside with psychological and emotional pain from an unloved spirit--a generation that desperately wanted love but sought it in all the wrong places. In California, I was told my Aunt Annie and her daughters had mercy on me and would pick me up when they came to visit. However, crying alone in a crib--along with a whole generation of other children--I grew up very lonely, with psychological and emotional damage, with an unloved spirit, hating myself. This produced parents of the next generation who did not know how to love their babies as they should.

In the 1980s there was a resurgence of mothers wanting to breast feed. But, believe it or not, in 2011 the U.S. Center for Disease Control made the statement that American mothers should stop breast feeding because breast milk has been found to inhibit the working of vaccines. Isn't this hysterical? It just proves that breast milk stops the destructive defilement coming into the body from what is put into the vaccines. Chemicals put in the vaccines are literally changing DNA, giving children autism, making some crippled and even mentally deranged. The Creator put into breast milk what would fight defilement to protect the baby.

The experiments with DNA manipulation, changing the very human nature basic to mankind, is today being carried out in places like Mexico City--and in underground laboratories in the U.S. American-sponsored scientists, as well as the Pentagon itself, are experimenting with mixing human DNA with that of animals, fish, birds, reptiles, and even plants and robotics. *Jasher* and *Jubilees* speak of this "in the days of Noah." We are truly "in the days of Noah" in every way – even astronomy-wise, as per **Matthew 24:37-39** and **Luke 17:26-33**.

Ladies, breast feed your babies, cuddle them, kiss them, tell them you love them. Fathers hold your babies, kiss them, tell them you love them – and then show it by your living the nature of Messiah.

When I was almost two, my parents moved to California. The only thing I know about that plane ride to southern California was that my mother told me I peed all over her. My parents rented a tiny house behind another house.

Even at two, I had thick auburn-red hair that was very curly. I had big hazel-colored eyes and fair skin, from the Scotch-Irish lineage of my mother's family and my papa's Irish lineage. Papa, was ½ Cherokee and ½ Irish. He was very fair-skinned and almost died from huge blisters he got from a severe sunburn at the beach. He had auburn red hair and light blue-green eyes. He was a tall man--6' 4." My mother was 4' 4."

One day Mr. Pat, the milk man, came to bring our weekly milk supply. I met him at the door. My mother told me that I patted my hair, and said: "pretty curls Mr. Pat." My mother was so proud of me. She dressed me like a little doll. I even had a Hop-Along Cassidy western dress and hat that I wore with pride.

In that little one-bedroom house, I slept on a wide green metal trunk until we moved to our own house when I was five. It was there that the powers of darkness came in a vision over my trunk-bed of a beautiful tiger that just appeared and stared at me. The demons that accompanied the vision brought spirits of the fallen ones that robbed me of my innocence. I woke up having an orgasm. I wanted the tiger to come back.

Those who have been in Satanism will understand how portals are opened in little children and familiar spirits or other demonic influences come in to use that child as a channel of their wickedness. I have tremendous understanding of how portals are opened. I praise Yahuweh that He also opens portals into His dimension. The portal into the mind and emotions (soul) is the only entrance into which the demonic can legally operate. The portal of the spirit (in the loins area of our body) is the only portal that Yahuweh will enter. It is our will that determines the opening and closing of all portals. But, a child, being totally naïve, does not know what is happening to them until it happens, and then the takeover of the enemy begins. Only Abba's intervention can block that, as the will of the person is developed. This is why at the same age, four, Abba intervened. I had a powerful setting apart from Yahuweh, which separated me from this world unto Him.

I was riding in the back seat of my parent's car as papa drove towards the Huntington Beach Pier. I was looking out the window, watching people walking along the street, some carrying surf boards. **All of a sudden, I watched a clear translucent bubble form around me. I heard a voice saying: "You do not belong here anymore."** I knew in my spirit that it was "God." I turned to my mother and said: "The most important thing in life is God." She was surprised. She told me about her surprise when I was older. I went back to looking out the window, but something had changed. I didn't see the world the same way--I was "in the world, but not of it."

The spirit is eternal, located in the "heart" of us – in our loins area. Because it is eternal, it can be far advanced over the age of the body and soul. The soul can only contact this natural physical realm through the five senses. It operates through the brain. We need the soul! It is also our life-force. But, we need to corral it under the disciplines of the Spirit of Yahuweh, until it submits to Him and aligns to the eternal re-born spirit. Then we can be at peace!

So, in actuality, I was drawn into spiritual war at age 4. But, of course, I did not know I was in a war. My church did not tell anyone about the "other side." However, I was in the midst of battle without knowing it. When I finally found out that I was between two powers vying for my eternal life, I was so weakened that it took my Heavenly Father's sovereign power to rescue me and lift me out and deliver me totally. This is why I have such a powerful passion for truth! I was told so many lies and was involved in so much deception that when I was confronted by His truth in 1995, and began to walk in it, He jet- propelled me forward to make up for lost time. Yet, nothing that ever happened to me was not without His knowledge.

He used EVERYTHING through it all, to prepare me for the work He ordained for me to do from the foundation of the world in these last days. He set me on the main path of my calling in 1986, but most of it was still before me. Shame and guilt make a child hide inside, become "introverted." So, as with many millions of little children attacked by "familiar spirits," a portal was opened in my life that affected my decisions that almost destroyed me later on. Familiar spirits attack children at a very early age, and they grow up not knowing what had happened to them, and without a sense of identity, and feelings of shame and self-hatred. And so it was with me. Something also happened when I was about 2 that my mind has blotted out--something that caused deep shame. Papa's brother, Dick, alluded to it once when I was a teenager, and I understood a little of what he was alluding, but couldn't pin point it.

Exodus 20:5 is hard to understand: "**I, your Elohim am a jealous El, visiting the sins of the father on the children to the third and fourth generations of them that hate Me.**" He judges each one of us as individuals. We are not judged for our parent's sin. (**Ezekiel 18:19-20**)

In my mother's immediate family were many 33 degree Masons. The Masonic history went back into Ireland. My father had almost no family that he knew. But in every family the same sins run down through the generations until they are broken by one empowered by Yahuweh.

Neither my father's family, nor my mother's family, hated "God." They were "good" Christians. But, at the root of Greco-Roman Christianity is hatred for Yahuweh and His Torah--Christianity, being rooted in Egypt, Greece, Rome, and Persia. Greece and Rome hated the Torah so much that they outlawed it with the death penalty for anyone who obeyed Yahuweh's Kingdom teachings and instructions. Christians are taught one basic premise: "We are not under the law of the Jews." When "St." Jerome translated the Latin Vulgate, he changed the word "nomos" in Greek to a word for Roman judicial law. The word "nomos" has the same meaning as "Torah' -- the teachings and instructions for living rightly in the Kingdom of Yahuweh. Torah is the good Word of a loving Father for His children, for our peace and joy always.

No matter how the sins come upon little children, they cause shame, guilt, and a feeling of being bad. If not corrected, these feelings cause wrong decisions to be made later on, and often destroy one's whole life. This is because little children think that when an adult does something to them that is wrong, that it is their fault. Adults are like gods to them, and if they are defiled by an adult, then they think of themselves as bad, shamed, and dirty. The guilt is internalized. I learned this later on because of what was done to my children.

PART I - The Formative Years

So I began early to learn about the dark kingdom. But, I did not learn Scriptural spiritual warfare until I was an adult. And, then I had to use it to survive. [Refer to the three-part series: "Scriptural Spiritual Warfare"/2010, written from much personally-learned wisdom]

As a little child, because of growing up alone, feeling that I was not as good as other children, I hid in a fantasy world. I was incredibly introverted. I pretended I had an invisible friend named "Little One." I could not look others in the face, even friends. I kept my head down. I would cross the street if I saw someone I knew coming so that I would not have to talk to them. I day-dreamed a lot, like of being an ice skater, or a famous orchestra director. Because of my flexible joints, I could not ice skate. My constant falling from twisted knees and ankles at age 10 began digging a deep well of hate, which exploded years later. But, I could dream.

So day-dreaming took over my identity. I could be whoever I dreamed I was, and shut out the real world. Shame does horrible things psychologically and emotionally to children. Then they take it into adulthood. If the enemy can get us to think in a fantasy world to escape reality, we will lose our anchor of who we really are. But, Western culture as a whole is steeped in fantasy and illusion, abstracts, concepts, and emotional manipulation. It is the ancient world of the East that is steeped in reality. The Scriptures were written about, and to, nomadic Hebrews--the whole language is about being nomadic, walking a trail, being out in the wilderness, and herding livestock. It was written to one family group, with one Covenant, with One Elohim (God) in one homeland. But, I grew up steeped in Western culture. Yet, without my realizing it, at age 4, He began teaching me how to think like an ancient Hebrew.

A pit began to be dug for me very early. When I quote **Psalm 40:1-3**-- "He brought me up out of a horrible pit and set my feet upon a rock", I say it in gratitude with all my heart. It takes the Mightiest of the mighty to deliver one from other "mighty ones" (demonic spirits). **HE BROUGHT ME OUT! ALL praise to Abba's mercy and love!!!**

The sadism of other children didn't help. Being so withdrawn, the bully-types loved to taunt me. I was born with five under-developed little toes--three on one foot, two on the other--and knees that are not quite straight. I was also born with joints that were too flexible. The expression for this is "double jointed." So, I fell a lot from knees and ankles moving out of place. One day at a Baptist youth camp, when I was around 11, a girl asked me what was wrong with my knees. In bitterness I said: "God made me like this." I felt hatred for a God I did not know. Later I would forsake Him and hate Him. I magnified my "imperfections" in my mind, thinking I was disgusting and ugly. Self-hatred entered in early in life. So, I dreamed of being beautiful and popular. In reality, I was definitely not ugly or disgusting. I am not ugly or disgusting. I am not "deformed." Now that I can look objectively at myself, I like myself. I don't hate myself anymore. I don't run myself down. I have no self-pity. I am an optimist who lives in reality. I am quite normal looking. My family had "good DNA." So, now at nearly 69 I am not wrinkled, nor do I even have dimples in my knees (smile).

The loss of correct personal identity is what has happened to most of the American people. For example, the teaching of evolution in public schools teaches that we are no more than a higher form of the animal kingdom. Thus, our dignity as humans, being made in the image and likeness of a Creator, has been taken from people in general. Promiscuous sex abounds because people think they are no more than a mammal. Because of the teaching of reincarnation, people think abortion is all right because the soul of the child simply goes into another body. The Creator and His boundaries have been rejected by most. But, only in Him can we have dignity as humans! Then the Illuminati mind programming that has been so horrendous in America since the 20s, has told the people what would give them identity, or course nothing on a good foundation. [Refer to: "Mind Programming, Hidden Manipulation, and the World Brain" and "Quiet Wars and Silent Weapons"]

You can imagine my joy, and the freedom it brought, when in 1995, I came to understand that I am a part of the House of Israel, and His Covenant included me. I have since been dedicated to exposing the "Jew-Gentile" lies that have disheartened "the prodigal son." (**Luke 15:11-32**) But, by this time, I had come to respect myself, to like myself, and feel good about myself, so He was already transforming me out of darkness into His marvelous light.

So often, children who are called by Abba from the foundation of the world to serve Him are attacked by evil spirits early in life, even from the womb, so that it is difficult for them to have any sense of identity in Yahuweh. If we live with shame, and think we are bad, holding guilt and condemnation inside, then our decisions are warped. We receive evil from others as a natural course of life. A victim mentality is developed. If a "root of bitterness" sets in, it defiles many. (**Hebrews 12:15**) Bitterness, if not dealt with early-on, leads to hate and rebellion. Also little children are easily traumatized by fear. Once fear gets a foothold in a person's life, it

PART I - The Formative Years

quickly becomes a stronghold. Consequently, when assaulted by cruelty from others, fear bows to it, tolerates it, and allows it to continue. I grew up with a lot of fear, worry, anxiety, fretting, and self-hatred--negative emotions that were a common trait in my mother and her sisters. I know some of you reading this can identify with it. **Keep reading! Yahuweh is more powerful than Satan!!! HalleluYAH!**

A word of warning to those of you who turn to psychiatrists, support groups, and religious leaders who try to delve into your past: It is NOT in rehearsing what was done to you that heals you! Bringing up old memories from the past can cause worse harm. Opening your mind up to negative forces opens a portal to the demonic realm. And, oftentimes, in trying to remember the past, we believe fantasies about what happened. These religious cults of inner healing can be further damaging and open more portals to the enemy. It is in using our will to release the hurt to a loving heavenly Father, whom we trust, that brings the deliverance. As we get into the Presence of Yahuweh and worship Him in the quiet of our own home, reading His life-giving Word, being taught by His life-giving Spirit, He will reveal to us what needs to be corrected, and then He will faithfully remove the thorns from your life. Praying the Psalms also brings peace.

Only Elohim can set you free! The greatest danger of all is in being self-centered. In trying to remember your past, for some psychological manipulation, causes one to center on their own hurts, bringing feelings of self-pity, and trauma to the surface. This is destructive! This is why He sets His children on the **Acts 1:8** pattern right from their new birth – to get them to "die to self" and embrace what is on His heart for their good, reaching out to others.

Abba has come many times, as I sat in His Presence, and moved over me like a giant magnet to remove things that I could never remove by myself. We can help ourselves some, but when things are deeply embedded, things we are even unaware of that our mind has blocked out, it takes His sovereign work to set us free. Reading self-help books puts you in bondage to formulas and to your own abilities. You cannot deliver yourself! The only self-help I recommend is that you submit totally to Yahuweh, stay in His Presence, and to allow Him to do it. Daily, we must allow Him to do as He wills to free us, and to transform us into His image and likeness. **(II Corinthians 3:17-18)**

Psychologists or Psychiatrists may tell you what your problem is, but no matter how much knowledge of the human mind they have, no one can heal you and set you free except your Creator! It is a sovereign work of His loving kindness! What He does in you is permanent! Your past does not return to haunt you. If you get haunted by a past memory that is painful, tell the Devil where's he's going to end up – in the lake of fire.

In my rebellion later on, I questioned "God." I asked Him: "Why don't You do for Your servants what Lucifer does for his?" I was referring to the servants of Lucifer with all their money, their lovely houses and cars, their freedom to do as they please, their ability to go to the doctors as they need to, to get massages for their backs, etc.

One evening in 2006, I was in an apartment in Tiberias, Israel, and I got up in the middle of the night to go to the bathroom, and when I got back into bed I heard that slimy snaky voice that I had heard before--the voice of Lucifer. He said right into my right ear: "Why doesn't Yahuweh do for His servants what I do for mine?" The anointing rose up from my spirit and I told him: "Let me tell you what He is going to do to you..." I didn't get too far with my information before "POOF", he vanished.

As a little child, I was very free and happy, and very inquisitive. I sat up in the backseat of our car and noticed everything around me. I didn't want to miss anything. My life! I also loved big words. One day, Papa had to stop quickly for a pedestrian to cross. I said: "Mommy, that Presbyterian almost got hit." My mother had to explain that the word was "pedestrian." I had a little boy doll named "Butch." I called him "Bitch", until my mother corrected me that his name was "Butch", not "Bitch." I was very upset at signs for the Heliport, asking why would they be advertising hell? I also was upset by the signs for the Dam, since that was a bad word. I didn't miss much! These basic characteristics can be seen in me at 69, though my knowledge has increased greatly. (smile) Do you remember that show with Art Linkletter--Children Say the Darndest Things?" I loved that show.

My New Birth

When I was six--two months before my seventh birthday--I was singing in the church choir on a Sunday morning. It was Mother's Day, May 13, 1951. It is as clear to me today as it was then. I felt strongly that in the evening service, I was to walk down the center aisle of the church and receive Jesus as my personal Savior in front of everyone there. I had known Him since I was four, but it was time to let everyone know of my faith.

After church, at home, I told my mother of my decision to "walk the aisle" that night and receive Jesus as my personal Savior. She was very concerned that I was doing it as a "Mother's Day" present to her, not knowing what I was doing. I assured her that I knew what I was doing, and it had nothing to do with Mother's Day. That afternoon, we went to my Uncle John's house, my mother's brother, in Eagle Rock/Los Angeles. I was so filled with joy that I spent all afternoon telling my cousins that in church that evening I was going to "receive Jesus" into my heart. I shared the basic gospel with them. Their mother was Roman Catholic and Uncle John was secular, so they did not understand being born again.

My joy was bursting. That evening, my mother said I skipped down the aisle at the "invitation hymn." I was so excited. I sat on a pew up front, and a deacon came over to give me a card to sign. I looked at him and told him: "I didn't come down here to sign a card. I came down here to go in there to receive Jesus as my Savior" (pointing to the prayer room). He took me to the prayer room.

Then, I discovered that three of my 6-year old friends, two girls and a boy, also had "come forward" that night to receive Jesus-- one of them being the Pastor's daughter. She later became a missionary. We were baptized on "Children's Day" and welcomed into the church on "Father's Day", in June. My baptism was very important to me. I knew it meant that I belonged to Jesus and everything else was unimportant. [Refer to: "The Mikvah of Eternal Salvation"/2011 for my personal testimony]

One Saturday evening, May 13th, I was in a meeting in Aqaba, Jordan, celebrating my spiritual birthday. Father spoke to me quietly: "My days begin at sunset." I knew what He meant--my real spiritual birthday was May 14th --the day of Israel becoming a nation – the day that Messiah talked about in **Matthew 24** to do with the fig tree. As an addendum to praising Abba for this special day, on May 13, 2010, I was in a room in an apartment in Tiberias, Israel, working to organize my belongings. All of a sudden Father came to me so strong with love for my son-in-law, David, husband of my youngest daughter. I was stunned. I thought: Wow--Abba sure loves David. But, I did not know what that meant. But I began praying for David's salvation. The next day, May 14th, 2010, Abba came to me again with such love for David. I prayed more for his salvation. Then the next morning I read an e-mail from my daughter, who had recently separated from David, and had gone with their two daughters to stay with my oldest daughter. They had a semi-rocky marriage. David, though not a bad man, was emotionally unstable in some ways because of past hurts, and she was tired of crying over him. The subject line of the e-mail simply said "Numb." She said that David had come to see her, and asked if he could pray with her. He had gone and poured out his heart to the pastor, who then led David to the new birth.

She asked me what I thought she should do. I said "do nothing; watch the fruit; look for signs that he is really born again and not just saying so to get you back." So for a few days she watched him. She wrote me: "Mom, he's really born again. He wants to pray. He wants to read his Bible, and he is witnessing to his family and to everyone at work." She went back to him. David was radically born again, and the fruit of it remains. They have a wonderful marriage! HalleluYah! They just took a wedding anniversary cruise to the Caribbean (2013). He is with her "in spirit and in truth", and he has given her liberty to serve the Master in many ways that he blocked before.

On Israel's Independence Day 2012, which they celebrate by the date on the Hebrew calendar for May 14th, 1948 (Iyar 4) my 6-year old grandson prayed for salvation with his parents. He had already been witnessing to me of his faith before he turned 6. All of my children and grandchildren have been born again, one spirit-filled, between the ages of 3½ and 7, except for one grandson at about age 12. Even though our names are written in the Lamb's Book of Life from the foundation of the world by His foreknowledge (**Ephesians 1:4-5; I Peter 1:2**), there is a day when each must make their public confession before people.

My earthly father imparted five things to me that transformed my life:
1) **Passion for the Word**
2) **Passion for the Spirit**
3) **Passion to win the lost to salvation and teach (disciple) them**
4) **Passion to study and teach about the end times/passion for Messiah's return, and**
5) **Love for Israel**
   THANK YOU PAPA!

Interestingly, my mother gave me five foundational platforms, without which the passions Papa gave me would not be worked out in my life:
1) **Passion to study and do research to find truth**
2) **Passion to teach the truth I learned, and to educate all ages of people so that they might be encouraged to seek Elohim with all their heart**
3) **Practical skills in organizing and recording data--"a business head" for office management and leadership**
4) **A love for giving, and**
5) **A love for, and appreciation of beauty.**
   THANK YOU MOMMA!

My mother taught elementary school, mostly third grade, for twenty-six years. Besides her teaching ability, and personal home management abilities, she was a very gifted artist. Her oil paintings are exquisitely beautiful. Her love of beauty was best expressed by them. While I did not inherit her artistic abilities, I did inherit an eye for beauty and color, and so I express my artistic nature in photography. I have had a life-long love of photography. I love bright colors, especially in nature. But, I did pick up my dad's music ability. My mother had a large "plate" collection--plates she got as souvenirs in all the places we visited. My mother would paint pictures of scenes, and I would journal our trips.

My mother was a very elegant and aristocratic lady. One day we asked one of our very southern sophisticated relatives to trace our family history for us because my mother was thinking of joining the DAR – The Daughters of the American Revolution. We had all the credentials. Our relative Jehoshua Taylor was a captain in George Washington's army. But, I was not interested in the DAR.

My grandmother's first cousin was the famous baseball player, Ty Cobb. She even looked like she could have been Ty's sister. When my parents moved to North Carolina after I did, they stayed in Ty's big 14-room house on the Blairsville Highway. Ty would walk from that house, about ten miles, to baseball practice in Murphy. We got milk at Bobby Cobb's dairy, just over the Georgia line. If you line up pictures of Ty, and my grandmother, and Lyndon B. Johnson, they could be brothers and sister. My mother said we were related to Lyndon, as well as Lady Bird. But, I don't claim him!

My grandmother's "Johnson" family was from England, but their parents were from France. They were from the Fox family, which was from the Fuches name, which is Jewish. The Taylor name is also Jewish. Many Jews who were named Snyder, in Germany, took the name Taylor when the Jews fled into England. In late 1998, Abba told me that I was from the tribe of Asher. When He said that, peace came over me, such as never before, or since. I stayed up that night until after 1:00 AM studying the Scriptures about Asher. One of my mother's favorite expressions was: "As your days are so shall your strength be", which is in the prophecy to Asher (**Deuteronomy 33:24-25**). She also said: "This too shall pass", referring to whatever hardship we were going through.

Asher manned the port at Tyre, while others from the ten Northern tribes of Ya'cob (Jacob) went to Sea with the Phoenicians, going around the world to find building materials for Solomon's Temple. Asher's inheritance was above today's Haifa, and up into Lebanon as far as Tyre. In our eternal inheritance (**Ezekiel 47:13-23**), Asher still has coastland.

One day, upon entering a friend's apartment in Aqaba, I saw they were listening to Gwen Shaw's series on the characteristics of the tribes. They said: "We are about to listen to the tape on Asher, do you want to join us?" Of course I did. Everything said about Asher was me, down to the cells in my body.

Around 2006, I did an investigation from Scripture, and from Ya'ir Davidy's book *The Tribes*. In searching for the location of both parent's families, I found that in 1066, when William the Conqueror came into England from France, both parent's families were from the same area, within 50 miles of each other. They were given special land grants by William, because they were aristocratic families. They later migrated to Scotland and Wales, to Ireland, and France, then to America in the early 1600s. William's chief Captain of his army moved to an area of north England named Staffordshire. He liked the name so well that he took it for his own name – Stafford. As I will tell later, it is very likely that Papa's real last name was Stafford. Even Minnie Ballard's family (mother, or grandmother, of Papa) came from the same small area.

One day in June of 2005, as I was on an airplane from Amsterdam to Cardiff, Wales, the Captain came on the intercom and said: "We are now crossing the border from southern Scotland into England." I was sitting in a window seat. I had my camera. We were not flying very high up, so I took a picture out the window of the English countryside below. There was a circle of clouds around the green landscape.

Asher has been found to have settled in southern Scotland and northern England. When I got the picture back, I stared at it numbly. Right in the middle of the picture was a particular cloud. The other clouds formed a nice border for the picture, but this cloud was right in the middle of the picture. It was pointing in the direction of the plane. But, the shape of the cloud was identical to the shape of the logo/symbol of Asher, the olive tree, in every detail.

Though we were what is known as the "struggling middle class" at times, my mother's family came from an aristocratic family with a noble background, even being related to Patrick Henry and one of his wives. Later we nicknamed my mother "Ladybird", after "Ladybird" Johnson (Claudia Taylor)--wife of former President Lyndon Banes Johnson from Texas. One of Ladybird's favorite projects was to plant wildflowers along the highways of rural Texas. My mother told me we were related to Ladybird. Ladybird was half Jewish. My mother was a proper lady. She had elegant teacher friends, too, who came to visit and have tea.

I was more like my Cherokee father, which antagonized the aristocratic side of my family. If I didn't act like they thought I should, they accused me of being like my dad. One day, while talking to one of them on the phone, they started accusing me of being like my father. I finally said: "Thank you very much! He is a wonderful man, and I am so happy to be like him." They shut up once and for all.

I loved digging worms for my pet chicken and duck. I loved climbing trees and camping in a tent in the backyard. We had a huge silver maple tree outside my bedroom. I loved to climb up in it and just sit. I always gravitated to the outdoors. I still do. The term then was "tom boy." I loved strange pets and sports, too.

One day, about age nine, while my mother was serving tea to her elegant teacher friends, I was outside playing. Being the inquisitive type, I saw these little white things crawling all over our garbage. It was a very hot day. I ran in to tell my mother and her friends about the little white worms (maggots) that were all over the garbage. She was horrified, and got me out of there quick.

I will never forget the times the beggars came to our door in the 1950s. At that time, the homeless could come to private homes. She would put lunch on a card table, and set it out under a big tree in our backyard and feed the homeless. I would stare out the window watching them, wondering what kind of person they were.

She loved visiting those in the hospital who were members of our church, but who had to stay in the hospital, or in a nursing home. As a little girl, I will never forget the Sunday afternoons that we took flowers to a lady in her 90s who was in a hospital-type nursing home. Her name was Mrs. Brewer. I loved her. Her children were worldly and didn't want to be bothered with her, so they rarely visited her. One day she gave me a little blue ceramic dish and a little ceramic bear. I treasured those gifts. They were stamped "made in occupied Japan."

When I was in my early 20s, my mother and I went to a charity benefit in Los Angeles. Some of the biggest performing "stars" of the day were going to be singing and performing, like Andy Williams singing "Moon River", and Mahalia Jackson singing "The Battle Hymn of the Republic", and the Beach Boys singing "California Girl" and "Surfin' USA." We got good seats, a few rows back, to the right of the stage. They had sectioned off a huge section in front of the stage for the families of the performers.

The little girl who was the beneficiary of the charity extravaganza had a rare and deadly disease. She was brought in to sit on the front row by herself, in front of the performers, so they could sing to her. The show was about to start, and the whole center section was still empty. No one seemed to be coming to sit there. So, I got up and motioned to my mother to follow me. I went down and sat right behind the little girl. Because I did that, about a hundred people got up and filled in the whole sectioned off space before the ushers could stop them. They tried to get us to move, but no one moved. About ten minutes later, the Jackson family came, and the families of all the celebrities and they had no seats to sit in, so they were put in the balcony. That was me – leading rebellion against properness!

My shyness had worn off. That night, my mother lost her properness. She clapped and sang and bounced around to the Beach Boy's songs. She said she loved the Beach Boys. That was one of the very few times I saw my mother really let-loose. One time she showed me how they did the 1920s "flapper's" dance.

I love to tell this story, and I still laugh about it. In 1958, we were on a trip across Canada from British Colombia. We got into Banff, and found there were no places to stay because Queen Elizabeth and Prince Philip were in town. So, we spent the night in the parking lot in front of the police station, where others also spent the night. My mother was given the backseat in which to sleep. As usual, she had to put her hair in rollers, and cream on her face. She complained all night because she was not comfortable. Papa sat behind the wheel and I in the passenger seat. Papa kept teasing her, which made her mad. I still laugh about it. Because he snored, I didn't get any sleep.

The next morning, we found a cabin at Scratches Cabins, and then went to breakfast. At breakfast, we saw in the newspaper that the Queen and the Prince would be visiting the Buffalo Park about 10:00, and then leave for Calgary from a small train station at Field. So, after breakfast we went to the Buffalo Park and my dad, who loved to take movies with his 16 mm camera, took movies of them as their convertible car passed the Buffalo Park.

Then we took off to catch the royal couple before they got to Field. It was about 60 miles from Banff. As we came up over the crest of a hill, we saw below us the entourage of the Queen. We located her by seeing her little white hat. We followed the procession until it disappeared into the train station. When we got to the entrance, the Canadian police officer said we could not come in. I leaned up over the backseat and looked him right in the eye, and pleaded with him saying: "We've come all the way from California and we want to see the Queen." He let us in.

In those days security was nothing like it is today. My mother, the proper lady, stood by the train behind the rope, with other proper Canadians. The Queen walked between the train and the rope, and my mother tried to get a picture of her but was jostled by someone, and so she got a picture of the Queen with a long extended chin. But, papa and I got under the rope. He started the motion pictures. The Queen mounted the back platform of the train. We were not far from the back of the train. I remember seeing one of the police standing with his arms folded looking at the crowd, pacing back and forth, but not looking at us. The Queen was disgusted with Philip because he was taking his time talking to one of the train crew, which I understand was common for him. So, when he mounted the platform, she turned and scolded him--she was not happy. Then she turned and saw us. We named the movie reel "The Royal Reel." On that film you can see her reaction. She opened her mouth in awe that we were clear under the rope, and not with the proper Canadians. "Come on lady! We're Americans!" For good or bad, that's Americans! Then the train took off, and my mother joined us under the rope, and she and I took off running after the train. I don't even want to imagine what the proper Canadians thought of us. Of course papa got it all on film. Oh the fun of adventure! We had such an exciting trip. Later, I put that reel on VHS along with other movies he took of me as a little girl.

While a member of Community Chapel in Long Beach, California, 1969-1974, I wrote the Queen, sending a gospel tract, and witnessing to her of the new birth, and telling her I was praying for her. I got a nice letter back from her "Lady in Waiting," her secretary, telling me that the Queen sent her "thank you" to me for my letter and appreciated my prayers.

Then sometime during my time of living in Texas (1985-2006) Abba instructed me to go to London, and stand in the area of Buckingham Palace, and He would instruct me, and help me to get to speak to her about the future, and her part in it, and her relationship with Israel. But, at that time, I feared. I didn't see how I could leave my two young girls at home with their father. Sadly, I let the instructions pass. A few years later, in that same house, I was looking over my news clippings of the visit of the Queen to British Columbia in 1956, and as I turned a page, my left hand touched a picture of the Queen of her getting off the plane in Chicago. As I touched it, electricity went up my arm, and I became so stunned that I jumped up and went up and down our hall, holding my left arm, asking Father what was happening to me. He said, "Do what I told you to do."

But, again, I feared. I could not leave my girls with their father. I asked a pastor-friend who was friends with Margaret Thatcher and her son. I asked him to see how I could see the Queen, or get a message to her that I wanted to talk to her about the future. I wanted to talk to her as a mother to a mother. But, he was afraid of getting involved, and so told me he could not do it. Abba had told me to just go, and He would instruct me. I was not afraid to go, but I was very afraid of leaving my daughters. Abba came one other time to try to get me to go, but then He left it. Slowly that assignment left my spirit. I have learned by experience that you don't question Abba, not for any reason, but obey, and He will take care of all the details. Now, I know that I could have left the girls with a friend for a few days. But, I was not thinking straight at the time. Years later I bought a linen towel from a yard sale. I opened it up and saw it was a souvenir towel from the UK. It read: "London Calling."

In 2007, I was given a prophecy about the Queen--a very strong prophecy that included **Daniel 5:25-28**. The prophecy extended to her a chance to repent. It also had to do with her mother's acts against Israel, supporting Hitler in WWII. I had a friend in Aqaba whose son-in-law was one of the Queen's bodyguards. He said he would get the letter to her. My friend gave me the address and told me how to send it. I did not hear

PART I - The Formative Years

back. But, the prophecy was "Thus says Yahuweh..." He told me when to send it – July 7, 2007 – 777 triple emphasis on His number of completion. To follow my Master as a faithful servant, He had to restore my assertiveness, with wisdom and understanding. So, do you see why, even at my age, how I can press into the mob and get a seat on the Sunday bus from Jerusalem to Tiberias, just like the best of the body-to-body jammers? He has made me bold and assertive, yet full of peace in the power of His might--all esteem and honor to Him!

Returning from the rabbit trail: At age 5, in 1949, my parents bought a little two-bedroom pink stucco house in La Habra, California. It was in a quiet, peaceful neighborhood in the middle of an avocado grove. We were surrounded by orange groves that expended towards Brea, and avocado groves all around us. It was a peaceful place to grow up. I road my tricycle, my "skeeter", and later my bicycle. In those days, there was no fear. I loved getting a Coke at the drug store "fountain" for a nickel. Good ole' days!

We had a big backyard with many different types of fruit trees. Mother planted a rose garden. It was here that I later dug worms for my pet chicken and duck. My parents paid $9,000.00 for that house. It was on about ¾ of an acre. Can you imagine how much that house would cost now? I could walk to the Mexican side of the town. They had a tortilla factory, and I would go with my friend Jeanne to get tortillas for our tacos. I grew up on Mexican food. Yum Yum!

I began kindergarten at a nearby elementary school where my mother taught third grade. The schools were within walking distance. So was Temple Baptist Church. I was a leader in Temple Baptist Church. I lived in La Habra until I got married. My parents lived there until they moved to North Carolina, to join us in 1975. It was there in North Carolina that they built their dream house in the country.

From 1949, by age five, I was hooked on traveling. My parents bought me two books, which I still have, with stories that changed my life forever. One was called *The Wonderful Train Ride* and the other *In The Mouse's House*. I had my parents read the train story so many times. It was about two children who went on the train by themselves. I memorized the story. Because of it, my mother, in desiring to visit her sister and family near Green Lake, Wisconsin, decided to take me with her on the train when I was eight. It was a long train ride – from California to Wisconsin over several days. We had an upper birth compartment on the train. But, because I had terrible motion sickness as a child, I could hardly go a block in a moving vehicle without vomiting. So, I spent a lot of time on the train throwing up. But, still, I had my wonderful train ride, there and back.

The story of the mouse's house put a spirit of loving to solve mysteries into me, as well as excitement to hide out from enemies. It was the story of a mouse family who lived under the ground in a field where a farmer was plowing to plant grain. Their whole house was shaken, so they had to pack up and leave quickly to find shelter, or else the farmer would surely plow them down. Wow! Sounds like now. I'm in Israel and threats of war are all around, and also danger from earthquakes. Abba has laid on me to stay in "packing mode" so that everything I consider important is kept from what I can leave behind. I know how those mice felt, now.

Before my scheduled appointment to have my tonsils taken out, at age five, my parents began going on trips. My mother had all three months off in the summer since she taught school. Papa had weeks of "sick leave" time left over since he was very healthy. So we were free to travel at least two months each summer.

Our first trip was to Sequoia National Park. We stayed in a cabin. We had to pump our own water from a pump outside the cabin. At night, bears would come on our porch to find food. My dad snored, so it was hard to sleep, but I loved being there so much. When we got back, I had my tonsils and adenoids taken out. I had such bad bouts with tonsillitis. Early in 1949, I had pneumonia, so our doctor said I needed this surgery. It was performed at his office. I was given ether to knock me out. I was so sick from the ether, but the ice cream was nice. But, since the surgery, I've have few respiratory illnesses.

From age six on, they made trips almost every summer across America. We camped out in Sequoia and in Yosemite National Park, and in other National Parks in California. We went to Yellowstone National Park. That was a thrilling trip. We stayed near the famous "Old Faithful" geyser. We went on good ole' Route 66 to North Carolina, or across Route 40 to Arkansas to visit Ahnie and Charlie and my cousins, or north to Oregon and Washington, and then to British Colombia, Banff, Jasper, Lake Louise, the Colombia Ice Fields, and across Canada to Manitoba. I loved traveling so much. I became the map reader. I only got them lost one time, but it was bad!

Because of papa's pent-up anger from his childhood, and my mother's aristocratic controlling nature, there was a lot of tension, and serious fighting. My peaceful world as a child was torn apart by age seven, because of my parent's fighting. One night during what I perceived as a serious life-threatening incident, I tried to call the police, but in my desperation couldn't get hold of the police; I realized I didn't know how to dial the police. It turned out that it was a ruse by my mother to make my dad scared that he'd lose her. But, the trauma of that night stayed with me. It was not long after this that my parents decided to make a go of it and the severe fighting stopped.

I will never forget the night of their restoration. I had a little hard- bodied teddy bear about six inches long, that I named "One Arm" because his arm had come loose from its inside hook and I lost it. Then I lost "One Arm." I was sad about it. I thought I lost him in the avocado grove across from our house. One night my mother was leaving my dad, so she packed our suitcases and took me with her.

We got across the street by the avocado grove, and she stopped. She couldn't leave him. Being a seven-year old, I thought we were off on a great adventure, and I was disappointed that she wanted to turn back. Since we were by the avocado grove, I asked her if I could search for "One Arm." We looked in the grove and I found him. That had to be a miracle (smile). I have "One Arm" to this day. It was symbolic of the torn apart marriage that was found and restored. A few days ago, my almost 2-year old granddaughter grabbed One Arm and ran around with him. Life goes on ...

My mother and dad built an exemplary marriage. They grew so close and so in unity that they were a blessing everywhere they went. Even after my dad lost his beautiful baritone speaking and singing voice because of aneurisms, and had a scratchy-sounding voice, he would bless and encourage people everywhere he went, especially in our little town of Murphy. He spread cheer. He told merchants: "Have a good day in the Lord." He could not sing in the choir anymore, but he spread such faith and love that some called him their spiritual father.

But, I held onto judgment for many years. Because of my parent's problems, I severely judged papa. I even called him a religious hypocrite, and hated him. But, in actuality, it was me that had the religious spirit. Papa was a very humble man. Because of their problems, he began to drink cheap wine. After being violent with my mother, he would go pick up his Bible and read it. I loathed him for that. Later on, even when I was extremely wicked, he never believed anything bad about me. He had a gift of love that few have. However, in growing up I didn't see it.

On day I wrote him a note that I wanted him to stop drinking. I put the note on a TV tray. He read it, and he stopped drinking. Since his teens, he had smoked Camels (very strong cigarettes) –

a couple of packs a day. But, one day, he just set them down, and never smoked another one, and Abba kept him from withdrawals.

Just before he died, he came to me with tears, and asked my forgiveness for anything he ever did to hurt me. He knew he was dying. He had aneurisms around the aorta valve of his heart. One day they burst, and he bled to death internally. I hugged him and told him he did not need to apologize, but his tears surprised me.

Papa was raised on the Cherokee reservation in Oklahoma by his grandmother, Minnie Ballard. He grew up alone. Minnie was divorced from Swake Miller, and their children, Dick and Dici, were grown and married. Papa's real mother and father were Vaudeville actors in Missouri. He grew up thinking Minnie was his mother, though actually she was his grandmother. He grew up thinking Dick Miller was his brother, but we found out he was really his uncle. Dick was a good man. But, in those days families kept secrets. My dad said Dici treated him more like a son than Minnie did, though Dici pretended to be his sister. Dici was married to Jack Stafford, of the Stafford lineage from 1066 from North England. I have a picture of Jack Stafford, and my dad looks just like him – a tall thin auburn-haired man.

One night, after Dici and Jack Stafford divorced, Dici began dating another man. My dad was a teenager then. He had been born again and had the gift of the "word of knowledge." He told her that if she went out with this man that night, the man would kill her. She laughed at him. That night the man killed her and himself. My dad was so wounded. He had a lot of anger in him because he had no one to talk things out with. Minnie grandmother was rather distant. He said one day while he was a child she got very mad at him and yelled: "You're not my son."

Later when my parents applied to go on a tour of Israel, they sent for my dad's birth certificate in York, Nebraska, where Minnie had told him he was born. But, there was no record of his birth there. They found a page out of Minnie's old Bible, and in it she had tried to erase his last name, "Stafford, Jr.," and replace it with Swake's last name. But, she did not get everything erased, so dimly written was his birthplace in Missouri, where Dici and Jack Stafford were in the Vaudeville show. I still have the original copy of that Bible page.

I was about 1½ years old, before we moved to California. My parents set off to take me to visit my grandpa Swake – Minnie's ex-husband, who lived on the reservation. They got out about five miles from Nanny's house. I was lying down in the back seat of the car. I began to whine: "wanta go home see Nanny." They turned around and took me back to Nanny's house. Swake never saw me. My dad was a school teacher, like my mom. They met at the Tahlequah Teacher's College, in Tahlequah, Oklahoma. He was two years younger than she. He was a lazy student. But, he liked her, so he asked her to help him with his studies. This is how they met. I have their college transcripts. My mother was Valedictorian at her graduation, with an impressive list of A's, and my dad got a lot of Cs and Ds. He was brilliant, just a lazy student.

Papa was a professional musician. In the 1940s he had his own band. He played the trombone. He taught trombone lessons later on. But, while playing in a night-club late one night, a man walked in and shot his wife dead. That ended it for my dad. He got out of the band night-club business. He became a teacher and then the school Superintendent at a Middle School in La Habra. But, he hated disciplining naughty youth, so he quit teaching. He then worked for GM. Then he got the job he loved in the Post office. He carried mail for years, then he advanced to working inside. He was offered the position of Post Master, but he turned it down because he loved working alongside his Mexican friends that lived in our town. He also shunned exaltation.

He had such a beautiful baritone voice. He sang in our church choir. He taught "Sunday School." But, he did not like being a leader. My dad had every right to get privileges and money from the Indian Bureau. He had original proof of his heritage. But, he decided not to do it, but to trust Abba for everything. See my roots?

At age 9, I began ministering in the Mexican Baptist Church as a pianist and a Vacation Bible School teacher. I loved being with the Mexican people. To this day, Spanish is my strongest language outside of English. My best friend was Josie Viagomez. Her family attended the Mexican Baptist Church. I was a part of her wedding. Note the "ez" at the end of Josie's last name? It has been found in Inquisition records in Mexico City, that many of the Jews who fled there to escape the 300 years of the Spanish Inquisition, got caught in the 300 years of the Mexican Inquisition. Most of their names ended in "ez."

Years later, in 1992, after papa died (he died in 1982), I had been out shopping and was returning home with the groceries. As I pulled into the driveway, Abba flashed a memory in front of me of his reading his Bible after a fit of anger, and Abba said: "**He was only getting up**!" In that short distance between entering the driveway and parking the car, Abba healed me of many years of hurt, and cleared up all the misunderstanding I had of papa. He was no hypocrite. The only thing he knew to do after the enemy used him to do wrong was to go to the Word and pray for forgiveness. How many times have I fallen and run to Abba for mercy? I was only getting up!

For years, I judged my parents harshly in bitterness. Finally, one day I got sick of listening to myself whine about my parents and about my rotten life, and I said to myself: "Shut up lady! You're boring!" That ended it – I shut up. Then He was able to show me reality. I look back and shake my head in sadness: I was a far worse parent than they could have ever been. I did nothing to stop things that put my children through years of severe suffering and abuse. I write this with tears. I look back now at my growing up, and realize that my parents did a lot more right than anything they could have done wrong. I have seen them holding hands, smiling, in the "cloud of witnesses" three times. **THANK YOU ABBA YAHUWEH FOR MY PARENTS!!!**

After they moved to North Carolina, I got to know papa better. In later years, we had such wonderful fellowship in the Word about the coming of Messiah. It was the passion of his life to study the Word about the return of Messiah. He was a super grandpa! I have a cassette recording of his voice before the aneurisms attached to his vocal chords, in which he says: "I love my grandchildren." I also made recordings of each of my children as little children. Oh the southern accents--so cute! Papa got to see all four of my children before he died on November 4, 1982. My mother got to see her first two great grandsons before she died--March 30, 1995.

After she died, being the only child, I handled all the affairs of her estate. In going through all her things, I found a collection of letters and notes on Revelation that papa had written. In 2001, I had the joy of taking those notes into the cave on Patmos, where John received the Revelation, and read them aloud. Oh the tears! What a precious man my papa was/is! Abba saw him from the foundation of the world, and worked with him to bring him to a state of preciousness. The journey of his life ended in victory, as did my mother's life.

When Papa died in 1982, in North Carolina, the funeral parlor was filled with so many people, it looked like the town Mayor had died. Papa spread so much joy to so many people. Their church built a special wing onto the building and dedicated it to him. I know that today He is singing in the heavenly choir with the angels.

Papa loved North Carolina. It is so beautiful in those mountains. They bought property, right next to one of our relatives' property. In a large tree trunk, by the house next door, you can still see an iron loop, used for the tying of horses. That was where the stage coach stopped, and my family had a restaurant, and place for lodging. My mother's family can be traced back to that area, and in western Tennessee, to the early 1600s.

They built a gorgeous large home, which sat on many acres. Papa loved riding his riding lawn mower. They planted roses and fruit trees. But, before building, they had to dig a well. For days the drill went down and there was no water. They went down 400 feet, and there was no water. They were so discouraged. But, they said that they would try one more time. I'll never forget that day. They struck so much water that the water shot up to the top of the rig and sprayed everywhere. They tapped into a river. When my husband and I bought our house, the well was no good, so we had to do the same thing. We had the drillers try by our stream. They went down and down and found no water. Then on the last try, they hit a river – enough water for the county. Abba is so good!

Like tapping into the River of Life, we have to dig and dig and dig into His Presence to find Him. This has become the theme of my life – to get people to seek Him with all their heart, for they will surely find Him! (**Revelation 22:1; Jeremiah 29:13**) I am crying so hard now, that it is hard to see the computer, but these are tears of praise to Abba Yahuweh for His goodness!

I was always a naturalist. I still am. I love eating natural foods, and using real essential oils, and living simple. I kept all sorts of animals. I had a pet duck I named Ducky Doo, and a pet chicken named Henrietta, that I raised together from featherhood. When the chicken died of old age, the duck went into mourning. I also had a pet tortoise. We had loads of cats that papa and I rescued. My mother was always wondering where all the cats came from. I even got ringworm on my head from one cat that we called "Ma Kettle," who gave birth to many scraggly kittens. But, that never stopped papa and I from our rescue efforts. I fed baby birds that fell from trees through an eye dropper. But, when a possum came down from the hills behind La Habra and tried to attack my chicken, with the help of papa, we got the possum into the trunk of our car. The next morning, we drove towards the desert, and let it go. I had water turtles and fish too. I've found animals have a special attachment to me, too. Years later when I cleaned houses to prepare to go to China the first time, I often would be told by pet owners that their dog or cat was vicious, and warned to stay away from them. I remember one cat I was warned about that was said to be very mean. The cat was near the dining room table when its owner went into the kitchen. The cat jumped up on the table beside me. So I started petting the cat, and the cat started purring. When the owner saw this, she was very mad at me. I've had "vicious" dogs curl up in my lap while I'm teaching, or lay beside me while talking to their owners. In Africa, the chickens would run around my feet while I was teaching. One curled up at night around my neck.

In North Carolina (in the 1980s) I worked for a veterinarian, and really had the chance to see if I had favor with the animal kingdom or not. I assisted in surgeries, as well as fed animals in their cages. I also was a receptionist, and had to take snarling animals to their cages. My youngest daughter picked up on that and had all sorts of pets-- hamsters, tree crabs, silk worms, cats, dogs, fish, turtles, etc.

I loved to sleep out under our big maple tree in a little tent, especially in the autumn when there were lots of leaves. I wonder how many Sukkots I slept in a tent out under that tree, not knowing the reality. I loved investigating creation. I loved climbing that tree, and just sitting up there on a limb. I found that I could peel the skin off of our "century cactus" and put it on a wound, and my damaged skin would draw together quickly. One year the century cactus bloomed and the local newspaper carried the story. One time when I was a teenager, our Spanish-speaking gardeners came running from the century cactus to tell my mother in broken English that they had killed lots of kitties. She was horrified and ran out there to see what they were saying. They were using machetes to cut the grass around the cactus and had sliced up some baby skunks.

I planted gardens as much as I could, along the sides of our fence. We had a huge backyard with many fruit trees of all types. In that area of Southern California we had the five species of fruit mentioned in the Scriptures relating to Israel--dates, olives, pomegranates, figs, and grapes. We lived in an avocado orchard area, and we had a huge avocado tree in our backyard. It produced about 200 avocados in a season. I grew up eating avocado sandwiches. It is a wonder I didn't turn green. We had apricots, plums, peaches, loquats, pomegranates, and figs. Out in the desert not far away, we could get dates. It was my special treat to get date milk shakes.

I loved to sing. I sang in choirs in church, and in high school. I loved to dance. I had/still have a good sense of humor. I got that from papa – he was such a comedian! And I loved adventure. I started a "Mystery Club." My little friends and I would find things that looked suspicious and contrive all types of possibilities as to what it was all about. I read Nancy Drew novels with a passion. I loved unlocking secrets. Our little group saw an old enclosed van/truck parked behind a grocery store near our movie theater. We saw a cat jumping from the back of the truck and deduced there had been a murder in that truck. Most likely there was no murder committed in that truck, but the thrill of a mystery was overwhelming. I suppose this was a foreshadowing of my love of uncovering real evil by our real enemy, the enemy of Yahuweh, and exposing it. He always let me see things few saw … and under His direction, my love of adventure has been channeled.

I was also a leader from early age. I started several clubs and groups. At age two, while my mother was cleaning in a back bedroom, I took her purse, put it over my shoulder, and set off walking down the street. I was going to buy groceries. You can imagine her panic. I had gotten two blocks from home when she found me. She spanked me! Didn't she know I was going shopping for her? My heavenly Abba started early with my training in leadership. I just needed to learn wisdom! I would also teach my dolls, pretending to be a school teacher. My youngest daughter sent me a precious video of her youngest daughter reading the Bible to my old dolls. They were the dolls I traveled with from age five, so they are old ladies. She is showing the dolls the verses in the Bible.

Up until age seven, when life became too serious at too young an age, I was not too different in nature than I am now – passionate and bold and in love with adventure. But, that didn't totally go away after age seven! I loved to read; I loved to learn. I loved Abba with all my heart. I loved people, and was confident in myself without being proud. Tragically, however, negative forces began to eat away at those qualities that Abba had instilled in me.

Let the journey continue...
THE GREATEST MIRACLE OF ALL IS ABBA'S LOVE AND MERCY!

PART II

THE JOURNEY CONTINUES

GETTING TO KNOW ELOHIM

My parents started early to teach me the path of salvation. I did not know the Elohim (God) of Israel, but I was on my journey to know Him. At six I joined the Brownies, which met at our church. In one of our meetings, we each made our own tambourine out of a paper plate. I colored a picture in the middle, and laced little bells around the side of it using red yarn. I still have that tambourine. My parents would kneel by the couch each night to pray. I brought the tambourine, and as we prayed I shook the tambourine, making the bells sing. My parents asked me what I was doing, and I said: "The organist plays music while we pray at church so I am playing music while we pray." My parents tried to hide smiles, but I detected them anyway. I figured they just did not understand.

In the summer of 1951, I turned seven, after being born again in May. During one of our trips, I had my first baptism into seeing His power, and my faith locked in. My parents and I had been on a long trip across country from California to North Carolina. They drove our classic brown 1949 Hudson. It ate a lot of gas. But in those days, gas was between 15 and 19 cents a gallon because America was pumping its own gas. There were always "gas wars" that lowered the prices. On our return trip, we were about 40 miles outside of San Bernardino and realized we were on "empty." We stopped at a truck stop gas station out in the southern California desert, at a tiny little place called Amboy. There, gas was 15 cents a gallon. My parents had a checkbook, but no cash. They would not take a check. My parents asked if I had any change left. I had about 20 cents. I gave that to them and they bought 20 cents worth of gas. We had to go forty miles through the desert to San Bernardino on one gallon of gas. I stood up in the back seat keeping my eyes on the gas gauge and praying we'd make it. I tell you the truth, that gas gauge never moved. We got into San Bernardino, and with a check, they bought enough gas to get us home. That was my first of hundreds upon hundreds of miracles of all types.

From age six, my heart carried great concern for "lost souls." As I got older, I would be out playing, and papa would tell me an evangelistic crusade or a healing meeting was being aired on T.V. Quickly I would quit playing and come inside to watch. As people came forward to receive Jesus, I would cry. As people were healed of diseases, the crippled walking, and the blind seeing, I cried.

At age seven, when it came to telling my friends that there was no Santa Claus, I did it with great exuberance. I loved telling people the truth, as I learned it. The truth stung for a second when I found out there was no Santa, but at the same time, I loved finding out the truth. Finding Truth has been the passion of my life, because I had learned so many lies and deceptions in my early years, which affected my life adversely later on. And, when it came to proclaiming the Good News to others, I was bold. I was a bold teacher of the Word from an early age, and defended the truth with boldness. It was strange, although I was an insecure child, I was not a fearful child when it came to talking about my Savior.

One day, papa came home from working at the Post Office. A co-worker was upset at me and told my dad that I had witnessed to his daughter about salvation, and she had "received Jesus as her personal Savior." Her father was an atheist. He railed on my dad and told me to leave his daughter alone. I didn't... (smile).

As I developed a relationship with the One the church calls "the Holy Spirit." We developed our own code of interrelationship. If something was "OK," He would give me a blanket of peace or a "joy jump" in my spirit. This little sign is still "our sign." I've depended on that sign many times for strategic knowledge, and for peace. He began early to teach me the eastern mind-thinking and ways. So, early on I began to separate from the Greco/Roman culture of the West, and began to think like the culture of the Scriptures. Today, I thank Abba so much for that!

I wish I had known then that the "Holy Spirit" was really Yahuweh, who is "the Spirit." But, in my church we made a clear distinction between Father, Son, and Holy Spirit. Later I separated Father from the Son and Holy Spirit, picking up the hate spirit of Greece and Rome, thinking that a cruel and sadistic "God" was the cause of all my problems. This is a common problem in fundamentalist circles in Protestantism. I was amazed recently to hear movie producer-teacher, Rob Skiba, say that he had the same problem with God, in his growing up. He is now studying his Hebrew roots. It is also Luciferic/Masonic doctrine, that Yahuweh is the bad God, and Lucifer the good one.

I was a nervous child. I hated loud noises--sudden loud noises in particular. I feared balloons bursting at birthday parties. Things like firecrackers and other types of fireworks on July 4th or any other time, made me very nervous. I had fear also of loud voices--shouting, and angry voices. Negative emotions disturbed me greatly. I cowered from angry voices, and imploded.

Now His authority backing and the wisdom I've learned has taught me how to stand when I need to stand, to do spiritual warfare when that is needed, and to flee the scene as Elijah did, if that is needed. But, more than any other spirit, the jezebel spirit (witchcraft, control, unrepentant cruelty, jealousy, competition) has attacked me from childhood to present. I have learned the secret of spiritual warfare with worship, declaration of His victory, and praise! To be good soldiers in His army, we have to know the ways and plans of the enemy. We also have to know the orders of our Captain and be ready to carry them out!

I've learned that He always brings victory THROUGH the problems, IF we hold onto faith in Him. His silence doesn't mean something bad is going to happen, it just means "wait" and "trust Me." I learned He does not speak through circumstances. He can speak for Himself without us having to play guessing games. The only reason His people play guessing games is because they don't tap into the "mind of the Spirit" to get the "skinny" beforehand. ("Skinny" is a radio term meaning information details)

John 16:13b – hint, hint! He tells us things to come, if we wait for His voice. He speaks in forty different ways to us – maybe that's not enough for most people, but only one way is enough for me! [Refer to: "Forty Ways Elohim Speaks to His People"/2005] I have heard Him in 39 of those ways. I have not yet had the Master use a donkey to speak to me, as He had one speak to Baalim.

In second grade, age 7, it was a hard and fast rule on the playground, "do not throw rocks." But, I had a crush on Curtis Aiken. He was playing with my girlfriend Janet Meyers, and I was jealous. So, I picked up a rock to throw over them to let them know I was there. But, Curtis raised up just in time for the rock to sink into his left temple, and produce blood. I ran to the drinking fountain hoping I'd be undetected. Curtis told the teacher. When we got back into the classroom, the teacher told me to come up front to go to the principal's office, which was in the room next to ours. As I got up, Curtis snidely said to me: "Do you always do whatever you're told?" Yes, I did. That question haunted me for years. I did as I was told, because I lived with so much fear. My mother and her mother and sisters lived with anxiety. That's why now, in my articles, I attack fear so strongly. Along the way, He delivered me from fearing man. He instilled in me fear of displeasing Him, and losing His Presence. Thank you Abba!

The teacher opened the door to the principal's office, and there sat my mother, having her lunch. She asked what I was doing there, and I told her. She panicked. She said: "Get back into that classroom before the principal comes." She taught third grade at

PART II - The Journey Continues

that school, and the principal was a good friend. That night, I really got it from both parents – I was justly punished. Later, from age 9 to age 17, I was in the 4-H club. My leader was Curtis' mother. By that time, Curtis and I had become good friends. I loved 4-H. I became a Junior Leader. I won first place at their regional talent show, and won awards at State Fairs.

I had great respect in my growing up for what my church called "God's house." It agitated me that children whispered to each other in church, even when sitting next to their parents. It disturbed me that older children sat in the back of the church, wrote notes and giggled during church. If anyone of them whispered around me in church, I'd tap the shoulders of the children in front of me and tell them to be quiet. If children were running all over the "altar" (platform where the preacher preached) I would call them down. This raised some eyebrows with their parents.

I saw things in "black and white." There was no gray realm. I did not want to be lied to. I knew in my spirit that when my pastor said that the works of the Spirit were no longer necessary because we had the Bible, I knew he was wrong. Abba showed me clearly, right from wrong in man's teaching. He extends that ability to all of His children.

As a teenager, I challenged my American Baptist Seminary-graduate youth director. I asked him about the 1,000-year reign of Messiah. He made a joke. He said, "I am a pan-millennialist--everything will pan out in the end." His answer was no joke to me. I looked him square in the face and told him he needed to study the Bible.

When I was a young teenager, I went on a field trip with the youth of my church to the Seminary of my denomination--American Baptist--the only Baptist denomination at that time that was part of the National Council of Churches. We each chose a class we wanted to visit. I chose a class about the Bible. I sat in the front row. From early childhood, I always wanted to sit in the front row. I didn't want to miss anything. I still am that way. I sit in the front of the bus, if possible. And if someone is already in the front seats of the bus, I wait until they leave, and then I go sit in the front seat.

At the Seminary, the professor who taught our class began by telling us the Bible was stories and myths, and we needed to learn that it was not to be taken literally. He said the stories in Genesis were myths. My spirit was enraged, but I sat quietly. Before I got back to our van, I went to the office of the Dean of the Seminary and told him what this man said. I also wrote a letter addressing it in no uncertain terms. About a month later, I learned that the professor had been fired. I felt a twinge of guilt that I had caused the ruckus that probably got him fired, but I knew it was the right thing to do.

All of this seeing things that are wrong and addressing them was not because I was a busybody, a know-it-all, or a religious super-spiritual kid. No! It was Abba training me to stand up, reject the wrong, and embrace the Truth. It worked into His training of me for the office of Prophet/Watchman, to which He would call me in 1985. The Spirit began to show me more things that were not right--the youth department was a social club. No one was serious about "God." I became an oddball because they thought I was too serious. I was just siding with right.

When I was in High School, my youth director was going to show the movie "The Birds" by Alfred Hitchcock at the church, in order to draw young people to the church that were not "saved." I told him it was wrong. I asked him what was wrong with challenging them with following the Savior. Why did they have to be lured in by an evil movie? I boycotted the movie.

In the sixth grade, I had a teacher named Mr. Johnson. He asked us to write stories. He said that I would be a journalist one day because I was such a good writer. Through the stories, I told him a lot about my sadness because of my parent's problems. So, he became a kind and understanding counselor. I found out later that he was a born again man, who really had a father's heart.

There was a girl in that class named Peggy Roberts. She went to my church. By the sixth grade I had turned inward. Peggy could laugh and make others laugh. I will never forget walking home from school one day and talking to Father, saying "I want to laugh like Peggy Roberts." Years passed. Then, one Sunday morning, I saw Peggy at church after she had married. She seemed sad and withdrawn. By that time, I could laugh like Peggy laughed in the sixth grade. I give all praise to my Abba, who set me free! I still love to laugh. The next year, while attending Lincoln middle school, I started joining church teams that went to Mexico. My heart was stirred for the "mission field." For me, life was doing His work. In doing His work, my sadness left me.

I grew up reading stories of missionaries. Hudson Taylor became my hero. He was a true man of faith, who walked away from the conventional missionary organizations and from their financial support, to embrace a life of suffering to be with the Chinese people. He dressed like the Chinese and lived in their houses—something unheard of in missionary organizations. Abba taught him faith because he disciplined himself to depend on Him alone. I learned so much from these great men and women of faith, like Hudson Taylor, George Mueller, Sammy Morris, Sadu

Sundar Singh, William Cary, Lottie Moon, Jonathan Goforth, Brother Andrew and Brother David.

These great people of faith took the Master up on His Word and were true disciples, true servants. They set an example in my life that later strengthened me to become what Abba wanted me to be. Of course such books as *God's Smuggler* and *March of Faith* about Sammy Morris, and *The Autobiography of George Mueller*, all came together to make me see life very differently than my peers. I always asked a lot of questions. I wanted to trust God for everything! I saw the materialistic world as a weight, a burden. I wanted to be free to serve the Master like the early disciples. I did not know then that I was the normal one, according to Scriptural culture standards, and that Messiah's requirements for discipleship were far different than anything taught in the western church.

I also developed life-long pursuits that were natural but good. From age seven, I loved to cook. My mother started me out with making meat loaf when I was seven. She would also stand me on a box and let me wash dishes. I love cleaning the kitchen even to this day. The families I've stayed with appreciate that! This started me on the road to becoming a gourmet cook. At age nine when I joined the 4-H Club, I took cooking as my project. I entered cooking competitions at the 4-H Fairs and won ribbon-prizes. One of my favorite things to do at the fair was to curry the horses that were preparing for competition. I love horses.

I was a natural-born leader. But, the enemy did everything he could to make me a cowering follower. One morning, after we moved to Texas in 1986, Abba woke me up at 5:00 AM. He told me to get pencil and paper for He had a "word" for me. I said to Him: "This had better be good." I hated to get up early. He started off: "I train My leaders differently than I train My followers." Then He proceeded to tell me about the training of the leaders and the high price of discipleship. His followers are also blessed, and can have a relationship with Him. Yes it was worth it to get up at 5:00. I now have no problem getting up at sunrise. [Refer to: "The Sunrise Lessons"/November 2007]

I've taught leadership and pastor's seminars in Africa. **A true leader is first a humble follower. Under Messiah, our Captain, we are in training for reigning!** A true leader must develop patience, compassion, and understanding. A true leader is a broken, contrite person--one who knows that there is a Master above them that they must be totally submitted to. A true leader is an example to the followers.

When teaching church leaders at Andrew Womack's Charis Bible College in Kisumu, Kenya, (1996-1997) I had to gently burst their bubble. They wanted titles of importance. I asked them what the meaning of "ministry" was. Then I proceeded to tell them that it was "deaconos" (Greek), from which we get the title "Deacon." It means a "menial servant--one who scrubs floors." I told them that if they want to be His servant, they had to humble themselves and be willing to serve as a menial servant. Then as they were faithful, and He could trust them, Yahuweh would exalt them.

I was a leader in my church from the time I was a child. I was on all types of "committees." I became respected, so I had chances to minister. But, I knew how to make people laugh, so I starred in many skits. It was/is a natural gift. My son has this gift--a natural comedian. Papa had this gift, and also my grandmother. When my children get together, we have a party!

I still have a way of saying things that make people laugh, even when I don't mean to be funny. Sometimes it comes out in meetings. I can be serious, and people start laughing at the way I've said something. I see the humor in things. The joy of Yahuweh also bubbles, even in the face of enemy attacks. Maybe this part of me has been a gift to keep me going, for "the joy of Yahuweh is our strength."

As I told previously how I prayed to Abba when I was fourteen that I would not miss anything, I said I did not want to live a "normal" life, but one on the front row of all that He was doing. He always had me on the front row. I always got to do things others didn't. He always showed me things others didn't see. It was, and is, a pattern in my life. I was the only one who saw the birth of that Navajo boy in the back of a van, out in the desert on the reservation in 1964. I was the only one who walked up the hill of the grape vines to a castle in Switzerland, while my tour companions wandered around town. He has sent me on adventures to places that very few people ever get to see. I say this marveling, because in reviewing my life, I see that it had to be Abba always intervening. I have been highly favored, and it has to be because He has wanted me up front to show me things that He has wanted me to see for my "schooling." In Aqaba He gave me **Ezekiel 40:4**: **"Son of man, see with your eyes and hear with your ears and set your heart on all that I am showing you, for you were brought here in order to show them to you. Declare to the House of Israel all that you are seeing."** [For understanding the "House of Israel," refer to "How Could I Give You Up Ephraim"/2011, and "Who are the Ten?"/2005]

PART II - The Journey Continues

THE CALL CHINA

In 1961, when I was seventeen years old, I went to a movie with a friend. In those days we got into the movie theater for 10 cents. The movie was: "The Inn of the Sixth Happiness." The movie was about the life of Gladys Alyward--an English missionary to China. It was during that movie that He spoke to my spirit, and gave me an overwhelming desire to be a missionary in Mainland China. Gladys proceeded forward, strictly by following her heart in faith. She worked as a house cleaner, a menial servant. She saved from meager earnings each week to buy a one-way ticket to China. But, the fire in her spirit to share the Good News of salvation with the Chinese drove her forward. She got the cheapest ticket, on the Trans-Siberian railroad at a time when there was war in that region. Her life was nothing short of miraculous. I wanted that type of life.

As I left the movie theater that day, I saw several rows of Chinese people sitting across the back of the theater. Before that, I don't remember ever seeing one Chinese person in my town. As I passed by them, I had a powerful "baptism" of love for them that went all over me. I felt like they were my people. I told the girl I was with, Jeanne--a total secular, but my best friend-- that I had to get a copy of the book from which the movie was taken. I did not know the real name of the book was *The Small Woman*. I was looking for a book that was entitled "The Inn of the Sixth Happiness." Jeanne took me all over town, but I could not find a copy of that book. I was so disheartened. We tried one more place I'd never been to--a drug store at the edge of town. I couldn't find the book. She was looking at the book "Peyton Place" – a naughty book in its day. I told her I'd come to the car in a minute.

She left the store and went back to the car. **I stood by the circular wire rack that held the paperback books. It had a hollow center. In desperation, I closed my eyes, stood on my tiptoes, and reached down inside the wire rack where books had fallen into the hole in the middle. I grabbed a book and pulled it out. I opened my eyes and stood there in shock. I had pulled out <u>The Inn of The Sixth Happiness!</u>"** This little paperback was named for the name of the movie! This book, now falling apart and yellowed, became my most precious possession.

In later years, I loaned the book to Chinese evangelist Nora Lam to read on the plane as she went home to California. I had helped Nora put together a conference in Ft. Worth. Thank goodness she sent it back to me. I still have that book to this day, held together by a rubber band. Later, a friend gave me a color version of the movie. I sent a copy to Nora. One day, I watched it to find out what had so inspired me to go to China during my watching it in the movie theater. I saw that this lowly woman, rejected by missionary societies and discouraged by friends, saved up her little bit of money earned by cleaning houses, and bought a one-way ticket to China, and how Father used her mightily for her faith. She is most known for bringing 100 children from the north of China to Canton through Japanese lines during the war between China and Japan.

Later, during the watching of this color version of the movie, I asked Father why He wanted me to go to China. He replied: **"China is your diving board--after that it is the world."** Within the first half hour of the movie, I had my answer. It was her strong knowing that He wanted her in China that caused her to pursue her goal no matter what the obstacles. I did not try to copy Gladys when I went to China years later, however, to earn money to go, I cleaned houses. Read how He provided the money for me to go in Collection VII, "Miracles of Provision." My first trip to China was in 1994. And, indeed, just as He said, after my third trip in late 1995 of taking "illegal materials"--Bibles--into China about forty times, I began going to the nations. The summer before beginning college (1962), I had the opportunity to go to a missionary conference at the BIOLA (**B**ible **I**nstitute **o**f **L**os **A**ngeles) Hotel in downtown Los Angeles. That weekend I had been invited to a friend's wedding, and also was invited to a party. There were youth events going on at my church. I was also invited to spend the night at a friend's house. But, to me, the missionary conference was the most exciting thing--everything else seemed boring in comparison. So, for my college education, I opted to go to an obscure Bible college, that was still being built in La Mirada, California--an extension of BIOLA in downtown Los Angeles. It was considered the college of the "Fighting Fundies"-- the Fundamentalist Evangelicals--so named because of their passionate fighting over theology.

Next to the college, they later built Talbot Theological Seminary. BIOLA was not even accredited until the first year I attended. But, it was where I felt I must go to prepare for the mission field. I was not being led by Yahuweh--I was being bull-headed--led by my Baptist denomination's thinking. I thought that if one was going to serve God, they had to go to Bible College. That is NOT true! I could have done what many of my classmates did and go to Fullerton Junior College for two years, or just apply to a missionary organization and go. But, I was so naïve, so in a box of my denominational thinking that I probably made a wrong

PART II - The Journey Continues

decision. But, at that time, the concept of walking by faith was more theology than practical.

BIOLA University has today become a leading private University, but back then, it was very religious. We were not allowed to go to movies, or use "play cards." The women could not wear pants on campus. Today, it is very liberal, from what I hear. One of my music professors was Richard Unfried, the organist for the Crystal Cathedral. The Pastor there, Robert Schuler, became Rick Warren's mentor. Warren is a big one-world religion guru with Tony Blair. Then there was Rayner Brown – a composer. He had a dead fish personality, but he was a super teacher. Then there was Mr. Swartz, a very good music teacher. My piano teacher was Mrs. Schumacher.

I was a Music Major, with a Bible minor. I reasoned that since I was preparing for the mission field, I needed some type of education that would allow a mission board to consider me. I did not learn from reading the lives of the great missionaries who just trusted Abba. My mother wanted to send me to a fine women's college in the North East U.S. In those days they called them, "Finishing Schools." I was determined to be a missionary. Sometimes being hard-headed is not good! For me, most of my hard-headedness was not good!

Today, by what I've learned about paid denomination/organizational missionaries, I'm sure glad I am not a missionary. I do not like that title. I am simply a servant of my Master--free to follow the Lamb wherever He goes! (**Revelation 14:5**) I am one of His disciples – taught ones. I have laid down my will, to take up His! I have no pride, no religious self-righteousness – I am honest about myself. "Humility" simply means "to be honest about ourselves." I do not put myself down, nor exalt myself. I am realistic!

I love the story about Mrs. Heflin, who sent her daughter, Ruth Heflin, on a ship to Hong Kong at the age of 18, because Ruth was called to be a missionary. She went alone because the missionary she was supposed to travel with backed out. Ruth learned faith early in life, and Abba led her. She ended up going to every country on earth. I have gone to about 40 countries, some many times, to teach and preach, but I am reaching more people by my articles on the web. Now, I live totally by just obeying Him and letting Him care for me. I have no home, no car, and not much of this world's goods, but I am free.

I had developed a passion for archeology, which I could have pursued through Talbot Theological Seminary, who had a "dig" in Israel. I could have done a lot of things, but I held the course I'd set for myself. So, after four years, in 1966, I graduated. I graduated with high grades, a B+ average. If 1966 were not the year of my marriage, I would have graduated at at least Cum Laude. But, in organizing a wedding, I let go of my studies. But, then again, music was just not my thing. I thought it would help me on the mission field--my reasoning was wrong. This is why I plead with people to not go by human reasoning, for it is often so wrong. Only Abba sees our future and will direct us by "what He has seen." **Psalm 32:8, from the Artscroll Tehillim**: "**Let me instruct you and teach you in the proper path to travel. I will advise you by what I have seen**."

Being a missionary consumed me during my college years. I was a leader in the Missionary Society. I got to meet some awesome people, like Corrie Ten Boom. My desire to go to China kept building and building, UNTIL the Missionary Society leaders dropped the bomb on my faith (1965, my junior year). In all that time studying to be a missionary, I just assumed I'd be able to go to Mainland China. I had watched movies about China, but did not notice that they were all about either Taiwan or Hong Kong. I learned in 1965 that I could go to Taiwan, or Hong Kong, but that no missionaries could get into Mainland China--it was closed to the Gospel, closed to tourists, closed to all foreigners. In my thinking, I was not called to Taiwan or Hong Kong. I was called to Mainland China. I did not know that Brother Andrew had, around the same time, counseled Brother David who was called to go into Mainland China, saying that there were no closed doors for those of faith.

While working for the Far East Broadcasting in the Philippines, Brother David began working to send in Bibles along the Nepal border with traders, and when China did open, he was ready and had contacts. I had a leading to the Far East Broadcasting in my spirit, but my reasoning mind kept me away. Later Brother David worked with Paul Estabrooks, another one of my heroes, who worked with "Open Doors with Brother Andrew", to get one million Bibles into China in one night! I met Paul in Ulaanbaatar, Mongolia, in 1996. What great fellowship we had! What a privilege!

Neither my denomination, or BIOLA, taught the walk of Scriptural Hebrew-type faith. They did not teach me the nature of the Elohim of Israel either, so I grew to think He was something He was not. My college, like all religious institutions, taught intellectual knowledge about God. It taught service to God. Each semester we had to choose a "Christian Service Assignment" in which we served God in some way. So even though I had known how to hear Him since childhood, those years in Bible College pushed me into the realm of the intellectual reasoning soul, rather

PART II - The Journey Continues

than into the realm of the Spirit. I did not have the understanding then that if He puts something on your heart to do, no man can stop you. I did not know that Hong Kong or Taiwan could have been my launching pad.

I had a chance to join Vince and Virginia Gizzi, precious missionaries, in Taiwan, but had no understanding of positioning myself, or of timing. No one told me that by faith He would open doors that no man could shut.

I did not know about Jackie Pullinger. As a young woman in her 20's, she had just been born again, and baptized in the Spirit, and she wanted to serve God. Her Bible study leader, a young man himself, told her to get on a ship, and where God told her to get off she was to get off. She took his advice! Abba told her to get off at Hong Kong. Her life is one of the most incredible adventures I've ever heard of. Jackie was a single woman on her own--and He had her go into an area that was so bad, so filled with wickedness, that the police wouldn't enter. For Jackie's story read *Chasing the Dragon*. Being also baptized in the Spirit, she had His power, and through His gifts of deliverance and healing, she reached the "dregs of society" with the message of salvation, and lifted them into heaven. Along with Brother Andrew, later on, she began smuggling Bibles into Mainland China, and then along came Dennis Balcomb with "Donkeys for Jesus" to do the same.

In 1994, I met Jackie and attended her meeting. After the meeting they fed all of us, about 100 people. They piled mountains of rice on a table, and had a large pot filled with chicken broth and a few vegetables. Each picked up their plate, scooped up some rice, and someone poured the broth onto your rice, and that was your lunch. I love the precious ones of China!

Her sermon that morning never left me. She preached on what really happened to Yahuweh's people because of sin in the Garden of Eden--saying that it was our passion for knowing God and walking with Him that the Devil stole from us. I find that to be very true. People can learn ABOUT God, in theology, concept, and philosophical ways, but most people have lost their passion for seeking Him with all their heart, so that they might know Him, and love Him as a real Person.

I worked directly with the persecuted, by going with Open Doors into China. Then, I was a spokesman for the Voice of the Martyrs for several years, especially during the years I spent in Africa. I met Richard and Sabina Wurmbrand and Tom White, attended conferences, and heard many speakers from persecuted countries tell of reality-suffering for the Master. I am not ignorant of what a life of persecution entails. So, who will rule and reign with Messiah in His Kingdom?

In 1962, I began working with the maintenance department of the college. I worked with them for two years. I loved it. I scrubbed bathrooms, but I also had other assignments. In the summer, I often stayed on campus to work. I saved up my money and gave my parents a money tree for their anniversary one year. Even though the college tuition was only $2,000 for the whole four years, including my dorm rent, food, books, and other fees, still, in the early 1960s, that was a lot of money. They paid for it via an insurance policy they cashed in.

In 1964, while in college, at age 20, I found out about an organization called Practical Missionary Training (PMT) that took teams for three months to Guatemala, or to the Navajo reservation in Arizona. To earn money for our trip, we went in small groups to different churches to present our desire to be missionaries. I played the piano some of the time, but in each meeting I gave my testimony of my desire to be a missionary. My favorite verse was **Isaiah 6:8**: "And I heard the voice of Yahuweh saying: `Whom shall I send, and who will go for Us?' And I said: `Here am I! Send me.'"

People gave me money and said they would pray for me. In one meeting, I met a man named Mr. Green. He was a widower. He took a liking to me, and maybe too much of a liking. He sent me a check for $45.00. I was very upset. It was too much money! I could not take such a huge amount of money from this man, so I sent it back. I had a strong sense of integrity with money. I still do. I don't ask for money, and I am quick to thank those who give to me. I think that asking for money to do Abba's work sends a strong message to Abba. It is prostrating oneself as a pathetic beggar. It says to Abba: I trust man, not You! These multi-millionaires on TV that beg for money to promote things in the name of giving to God, are a disgusting bunch of human beings. Mr. Green continued to write me until my senior year in college, when I told him I was getting married. Then he stopped writing. Looking back, I may have had a better life if I had married Mr. Green. But, then again, maybe not...

Walking to a local store one day, when I was about thirteen, I found a $1.00 bill on the sidewalk. I put it in my pocket and told my friend Jeanne that I was going to send it to Billy Graham to help win souls. I had gone to a Billy Graham Crusade when it was in Los Angeles in the 1950s, and I would cry and cry as people came for salvation. If a meeting was televised I would sit there at the "invitation hymn" and cry and cry to see people saved. Though I found out the dark truth about Billy in later years, still, many were born again by hearing his simple presentation of the

PART II - The Journey Continues

Savior. I believe Abba rewarded me for my sending that $1.00 bill. He's always provided for me.

In all my parent's traveling years, we went to several different Indian reservations along "Route 66" - to the Navajo reservation many times, and up into Colorado - i.e. the Pueblo. We went to the Zuni reservation, too. I loved it so much. Because the Guatemala trip was too expensive, and too far away, not to mention my love for the Indian culture, I chose to go to the Navajo Reservation in Arizona. I am glad I chose to go there, for many years later, I would visit their ancestors in Mongolia - feeling right at home with them.

Once on the reservation in Arizona with PMT, I spent three months doing very practical primitive things. I learned a lot! My great joy was sitting on a sheep skin in a hogan (mud and stick house) sharing the Good News of salvation with a Navajo family. I learned how to make rain water stretch; to drink, to wash in, to wash clothes in, and to water plants.

One day, my partner, Lorrine Prosser from Louisiana, was out with other team members and I was alone with the head nurse and a Navajo nurse. An old women who had walked a great distance, came to them and said her daughter was having a baby and needed help to get to the hospital. Like in many Navajo families, the husband was off drunk somewhere. We put the old lady in the van and went and got her daughter. A lightening storm the day before had left cattle struck dead in the desert. On the way to the hospital, swerving to miss a dead cow, we got stuck in sand, and the woman began delivering the baby. The nurses opened the van doors, and I stood there and watched a beautiful baby boy being born. He came out with white skin, but upon beginning to breathe on his own, his skin turned the most lovely light brown. I had never seen such a thing. I held a baby for the first time when I had my own first baby. We pushed and pushed, and the van got unstuck, and we proceeded on to the hospital. The head nurse drove, while the Navajo nurse helped the afterbirth to come out into a bowl. When I got back to the compound that night to report on what had happened, they just looked at me with little response.

I just marvel that throughout my life, I have been privileged to go to places that few go to, to do things few get to do, and to see things few see. I never pray for these privileges – He just arranges them. How easy life is when we just rest in His decisions. He is so personal!

During PMT, we went on a trip down into the Grand Canyon on horseback to minister to the Supai Indians at the bottom. We also went down a cliff along Mooney Falls, where we camped out by the river that flowed from the Falls. Our first night, we camped out along the top ridge of the Canyon until early morning. It had rained that night, and we only had plastic sheeting over our sleeping bags, but, that was OK. As the sun came up, our missionary leader, David, sang the most gorgeous hymn. It echoed in the Canyon. Then our horses arrived. I had never been on a horse before--not like those. When I was a little girl, my parents would take me to Griffith Park in Los Angeles and let me ride ponies, also ponies at carnivals, with someone to lead me around in a circle. We went down a very narrow path with a sheer cliff on the left, and a 100' drop off on the right. I remember looking down between that horses ears thinking, "I am depending on what is between those ears to keep me alive."

Once down into the Canyon, we stopped at a little Supai church, which had been carved into the mountain. I played the little pump organ for the singing. Afterwards, we proceeded down to the cliff above Mooney Falls. The missionary helped us scale down the side of the cliff to the river. Then we walked along the river where we set up camp. I remember waking up in the night to frogs croaking in my ear, trying to jump in my sleeping bag. We were between the cliff and the river, and at night the frogs made their way to the river by hopping over us. I am glad I was a nature girl who was not afraid of little critters. We stayed a week down there. It was quite an adventure.

On one assignment, my team mates and I were assigned to a missionary outpost up near the Utah border. We slept on cots in the hogan. At night, going to the toilet meant going outside among the sheep and squatting. That prepared me for the African bush. We wore Navajo clothing. We went into Utah with huge barrels to get water. We used the same water for washing clothes, for dish washing, bathing and washing our hair, and watering plants. Of course, drinking water was separate. Everything was recycled, and used. Food was also recycled as long as possible. Our rice for lunch became pudding for dinner desert, etc. I sure learned practicality, and how we can live on so little. Navajos, who came to the mission station, often joked with us, pretending to take our picture. They were so disgusted with the white tourists taking their pictures as if they were some novelty. It was during this time, that we got to go deep into the reservation and be with the people who were herding their sheep in high pastures for the summer. They would throw a tarp over the bushes for their shelter, and cook using sage brush for fuel.

We went to Navajo homes. It was there that I met some precious believers, and our dear Navajo lady evangelist, Elsie Begay. We saw the old ladies weaving, and the young ones tending sheep, and babies. The women were so "natural" with their nursing too. It embarrassed the boys of our team. Babies were strapped down to "cradle boards," and the mothers would carry them on their backs while doing chores.

We went to other mission stations, where we worked with different groups of missionaries. At one point, a male missionary needed to take a local witch doctor home. He had joined us for dinner the night before. I had my first lesson in watching someone eat primitive style. It prepared me for China. Long Salt was his name. I was in the back of the truck, which was bouncing over the rocks and hills. I got sick. I tapped on the window for them to stop. Long Salt got out and helped me out of the truck and put me between the missionary and him. He was kind. He even let me take his picture. Thinking back on that, that was very unusual. The older Navajos think that if someone takes their picture, they capture their soul.

I'd often find myself in the back of trucks. One day, as we were bouncing towards another mission post, I looked up at the big sky and told Abba, "**I want to live like this the rest of my life**." I had a backpack and a bedroll, and I was so happy. The nomad life caught up with me in 1999! It is now a serious reality, in 2013.

One day two missionaries and I were taking an old woman home. It began to storm. She was so scared. We began singing, "There's Power in the Blood", and she calmed down. Every day was an adventure. We learned so much about the treatment of the Navajos by the American government. They get free land and free money, and the men are emasculated because the women rule over them. So many of the men stay at the "trading posts" and stay drunk, while the women rule the family. It is very sad. I love the Navajo people. The Mongolians are the ancestors of the Navajos. When in Mongolia in 1996, it was like déjà vu – I felt like I was among Navajos.

I have the picture of a little girl holding a baby in a cradle-board. That baby would be about 48 years old now. In Mongolia, I saw the same things as on the Navajo reservation--the hogans, the weaving, the outdoor life, the wearing of turquoise jewelry, the bow-legged men who rode horses all their life, the basic living of the Navajo, and the faces of the Navajos. We also visited Choco Canyon and the Anasazi ruins. I still have wonderful pictures of life on the Navajo reservation.

Near the end of my time with PMT, they gave us a "personality test." I flunked in their estimation. In Abba's estimation I got an A. They told me that my aggression level ran off the charts. They said I would never make a good missionary with that much aggression, because I would probably not submit well to my superiors. If I did not have the traits Abba put into me now, I would never have been able to do what He called me to do.

The Director of the China Inland Mission told Gladys Alward that she was unfit to be a missionary because she had no formal education. Yet, when all the missionaries left north China for fear of the Japanese, she was the hero. It was that same Director who met her in Canton, with her 100 children she rescued from the Japanese. From one of the last scenes in the movie, as Gladys and the children entered Canton, she recognized the Director, but he did not recognize her. She said to him: "Remember me? I was the one whom you said was unfit to be a missionary." It was Hudson Taylor who founded that mission. They sure were a long ways from his life's understanding of the requirements of a servant of God! It takes faith and obedience to the Master, that's all.

I learned later the truth about missionary organizations, and how they expect their paid missionaries to come under their "corporate will." I found out too, in Mongolia, in Russia, and everywhere else I went with a missionary group, that being led by the Spirit was unacceptable to them. I had to submit to their rule. I could not be under the Spirit's rule. But, I went with the Spirit's orders and got myself in trouble several times – in fact, a lot of times in Russia. And I was an American too, which was repugnant to the Russians.

I am not rebellious. He just started teaching me early in life to know His voice and to follow Him. In the book of Acts, the Apostles were out preaching on the Temple Mount in Jerusalem, and the High Priest and the Sanhedrin were furious. They locked them in prison. An angel got them out and told them to go right back outside and keep preaching, which they did. When they were rearrested, the High Priest asked them why they kept on after being told by the Sanhedrin to stop preaching. They replied (**Acts 5:29**: "We have to obey Elohim rather than men." It is as simple as that. We are citizens of the Kingdom of Yahuweh. He is our ultimate authority. When Satan's kids say we can't take Bibles into China, and Yahuweh says to take them – who should we obey?

"Bopping around" in the backside of the desert with PMT, we saw many ancient Anasazi ruins that had not been excavated by archeologists. As we passed one of them, the missionary stopped the van so that I could get out and look up close. I saw a grinding stone sitting in a large stone bowl. The bowl was too heavy to take, but I have the grinding stone to this day. The grinding stone became symbolic of the work Abba had to do in me before I could embark on the calling He gave me from the foundation of the

PART II - The Journey Continues

world. In 2010, in the ruins of Qumran in the wilderness of the Dead Sea, where the ancient scrolls were found in 1947, as I praised Abba, I looked down and saw a grinding stone at my feet. I picked it up and brought it back with me to Tiberias.

I am no one special. I just wanted to know what it was like to take Elohim up on his demands for discipleship (**Luke 14:25-33**). In 2004, in Aqaba, while bopping around the backside of the Negev desert, He gave me **Matthew 13:16: "Blessed are your eyes for they see, and your ears for they hear,"** and **Ezekiel 40:4**: **"Son of man, see with your eyes and hear with your ears, and set your heart on all that I am showing you, for you were brought here in order to show them to you. Declare to the House of Israel all that you are seeing."** I have been faithful to do that!

My love of archeology, and geology, and other earth sciences began early. My parents belonged to a "Rock Club." We went on fieldtrips to find special rocks. Our traveling adventures always included finding special rocks, and exploring caves. I also loved astronomy very much. My dad got me a telescope to search the heavens.

Later on, after graduating from BIOLA, I took courses in Archeology and Anthropology at Cerritos College. To this day, when off the paved road, I keep my head down to look for artifacts and special rocks. By the stream below our house in North Carolina (1974-1986), we found arrow heads, spear heads, and other artifacts. We also found fossilized remains from an ancient Indian site. I just love adventure! I like discovering things. These "loves" have kept me going through very hard times – so that my focus remains strongly on events pointing to the return of Messiah Yahushua!

I wrestled with my identity from childhood. When I was about twelve, while waiting for my mother to come out of a store, papa, who was sitting behind the steering wheel of the car, without turning around, very simply told me that I was part Cherokee Indian. After that, I chose to identify with the Indians. I made sure there was no hair on my body that showed, except for my head-hair, because Indians are smooth-skinned.

When I was about 15, we went to North Carolina for a visit with relatives where we saw the outdoor play-production "Unto These Hills." I was so angry at what Jackson did to cause the "trail of tears" for MY PEOPLE, that when we later went to Andrew Jackson's home estate in Tennessee, I chose to sit in the car for two hours in the blazing sun, until my parents finished going through "the Hermitage."

I was so at peace when He said to me: "You are of the tribe of Asher." My heavenly Father told me my earthly identity in His eyes – I am a child of Ya'cob. I find it fascinating that after all these years, I have come to understand the scattering, and migration of the lost sheep of the House of Israel--the ten north tribes--who were finally all expelled by 722 BCE for their heinous sins against Yahuweh; driven into the nations AMONG the gentiles. I learned from all of Scripture that He never called His people "gentiles." He never made a covenant with Gentiles.

I learned that there were two branches of the Cherokees. The Missouri branch, where archeologists found Paleo Hebrew tablets in ancient Cherokee ruins. It is believed they are from the 722 BCE dispersion of the 10 northern tribes. The Chickamauga Cherokee, of which my father belonged, the ones who went on the "trail of tears" to Oklahoma. They say they came out from the 70 CE dispersion of the tribe of Judah.

A friend of mine, in talking to a Cherokee Chief on the Cherokee reservation in North Carolina, was told that the Cherokee elders know that those on that reservation are a combination of the twelve tribes of Ya'cob. They long to know their Hebrew roots. So without knowing it, papa set the stage for me to know my identity as one from the House of Israel/Ephraim/Joseph.

Papa loved watching "westerns" on TV. I began watching episodes of "Cochise" with Michael Ansara, and other programs on about Indians. I tried to immolate their lifestyle and thinking, which became natural to me. I was attending Lincoln Middle School at this time. Abba began teaching me to feel at home in the ancient culture of the Middle East--the Hebrew culture--and to feel at home in the Third World. The First World never interested me much. Abba did not forget my prayer prayed on the Navajo reservation. He has brought me back to it. He is continuing the process of stripping me of everything that is security in this life, to pick up the back-of-the truck life again--only this time, bouncing around the world on a big aircraft at 38,000 feet up.

When I was about eleven, my parents and I were at LAX seeing my grandmother off to Oklahoma on a plane. I remember looking out the window at airplanes taking off and said: "**One day, I will go up in an airplane**." I still love to see planes taking off and landing. Since the 1970s, I have been on hundreds of flights, in so many different airports, and STILL I love flying. I love the take offs and landings. There were the exciting landings, like coming into Hong Kong on that little tiny strip of a runway that went out into the ocean. Pilots had to be specially trained to land there. Another was coming into La Paz, Bolivia in 2010, the highest airport in the world at over 13,000 feet. The pilots also have to be specially trained, for the air is so thin that they zoom into the airport at a very fast speed. I thought that was great! I never get tired of going into the wild blue yonder, especially for Abba's purposes!

In taking courses in Archeology and Anthropology, 1968-1969, at Cerritos College, we often went on "field trips." We would camp out in the California desert, and go see Indian markings in ancient areas. Oh what a joy that was – sleeping on the ground under the stars. I learned so much in those courses. One semester, I had a teacher who was an atheist. I learned so much about the Bible from him, and the information in our text book. My love for the Creator grew greatly, and my understanding of His plans grew also.

Before, during, and after college, I had an incredible variety of ministries. In 1966, while working with friends, I began going with them to "skid row" in the heart of Los Angeles, ministering to the drunks, the prostitutes, the pimps, the homosexuals, the gangs, the homeless, and all the down and outers there. I preached in a nearby soup-kitchen--a "Rescue Mission." I ministered in nursing homes. I was a nursing home pastor, and a Word-teaching youth pastor. I visited the sick and ministered in hospitals. I preached in detention homes, jails, prisons, juvenile detention facilities, in homeless shelters, in "half-way houses," in parks, and in a "church on the street" in Long Beach, California. I also ministered in churches of different denominations, and of all different sizes. During this time, I came to know Andre Crouch and his singing group--The Disciples--that became famous.

I loved ministering in "black" churches. I love the African-American believers. This prepared me for my seven times of ministering, 3 months at a time, in Africa. One Sunday, I was playing the piano at a very large African-American church. They did not have a nursery. Our oldest daughter was about seven months old. The ladies assured me that they would take care of her while I played the piano and ministered. I looked out over that huge audience from the stage, and saw my white baby being passed around all over the church. After the service, they brought her to me. Seeing them caring for her was so precious.

Abba led me into doing about every type of ministry you can imagine. I headed up all sorts of out-reaches to win the lost. I handed out tracts on the street, in malls, and went door-to-door to share the Good News in different neighborhoods. I did all sorts of children's ministry--in churches, in parks, and in housing project areas of the Watts area of Los Angeles. You see, I read in the Word where those who know Him obey Him, and are His witnesses, servants, bond-slaves, and soldiers in training for reigning. I read about Sadu Sundar Singh and the life he lived in the Master's service, and I look at the mental and physical slaves of the affluent West, slaves to their idols, and I think – "get me to Tibet!" I had a heart for Tibet and Nepal and Burma (now Miramar) for a long time. I don't know why, but I feel drawn to them.

I not only played the piano and organ, but the accordion. I played the accordion in many meetings on the streets of Long Beach. One song I loved to play, which was not a Christian song, was "The Happy Wanderer." The words reflect my desire for freedom, the open air, and the wanderlust spirit of adventure. After so many years, I am still the happy wanderer for Yahuweh-- following the Lamb, Yahushua, wherever He goes! HalleluYah! As I began having more and more problems with my joints and vertebrae – getting older – I told Abba: "If you will keep me walking, I will keep going for you." Even with all the injuries I've had in the last three years, I am still walking by His mercy. But, even if I cannot walk – I will still minister for Him! Some times I got very discouraged, but I would listen to Steven Curtis Chapman sing "The Great Adventure" a couple of times, and faith would rise to keep me going! I wrote an article—"The Great Adventure"/December 21, 2011.

In 1965, I began working with an organization called "Open Air Campaigners." We preached in Los Angeles mainly, but the hardest was the affluent area of Hollywood and Vine--where intellectuals loudly mocked us. We opened up our van on the street and began singing and sharing testimonies. The couple who ran this ministry were trophies of His grace. Wes had been a successful and well-to-do tennis pro. He was an atheist because of Santa lies told to him as a child. She was a Mormon. One day, they were in separate cars, and each had a devastating car accident. It left Belva crippled for life. They were taken to different hospitals. Finally, Wes got out, and found her. While he was in the hospital, Messiah came to visit him. He was gloriously born again. While Belva was in the hospital Messiah came to visit her, and she was gloriously born again. When they reunited, they found that He had visited them both, and they rejoiced in this great miracle. They dedicated their lives to sharing the Good News with those on the street. It was a privilege to work with them. Belva played the auto-harp for our singing, and he led the testimonies and preaching using us volunteers. I can still see Wes's face – so radiant with the love of Yah. Precious people!

Acts 1:8: **"You shall receive power after the Set-Apart Spirit has come upon you and you shall be My witnesses in**

PART II - The Journey Continues

Jerusalem, and in all Judea, in Samaria, and unto the uttermost parts of the world."

In other words, begin in your home town, then go to your close surrounding area, then go to further places within your country, then branch out to the whole world, as He leads step by step! I have followed this pattern. I understand reality. Few have any interest in the Truth anymore. I found that to be true throughout the Western world, and here in Israel too. But those in Third World nations are crying for Truth. They are crying to be "saved." Many Christians are crying to learn the Torah. Where are their teachers? Who have you shared His Truth with today? "Freely you have received, freely give."

I knew a 6-year-old boy in Kenya, named Moses, who was taken to a U.N. hospital with two broken knees. Moses was such an inspiration to his U.N. doctor, the nurses, and other patients, that they were sorry he had to leave. He witnessed to the salvation of the Master everywhere he went. He was an anointed child. To watch Him work--watch someone transformed by the Spirit, born from above, by His power--there is no greater joy in the world! **The greatest of all miracles is the true new birth! To watch it happen is the greatest of all joy!**

My usual testimony given on the street with Open Air Campaigners went something like this: "**If I had the world on one hand, and Jesus on the other, I would always choose Jesus because the world has nothing to offer, but He offers eternal life.**"

Abba honored that, knowing that the day would come when I would know His Name and His Son's Name. After the testimonies someone would get up and preach. Then after the meeting we would talk to people who had been listening about their salvation. Many came to know the Savior through that simple witnessing.

In 1966, just a few months after I was married, Abba caused me to take a quantum leap into His eternal realm. He did this so that He could come through the portal of my re-born spirit and begin my training in learning about the world of Satan/Lucifer/Dragon/Devil, that I did not know existed. In order to face the enemy, learn his plans, and finally come out unscathed, He had to fill me with Himself, and give me "gifts" that I would desperately need in spiritual warfare.

Here begins the story of Messiah baptizing me into the Spirit of Yahuweh, and my taking that message to other nations

I had been reading Charles Finney's Autobiography. He moved in the power of Elohim. He was filled with the Spirit. Everywhere he went, people cried out in repentance for salvation. One night in

November 1966 when I was 22, I was preaching in downtown Los Angeles--four months after I got married. I was approached by a kind young couple who went to Angelus Temple, and attended the Foursquare Life Bible College. They asked me if I had ever been baptized into the Holy Spirit since I became a believer--the same question the Apostle Sha'ul asked the men in **Acts 19**. I said, "No, but I want Him to fill me." As a child I had listened to my pastor tell us that all the events of Acts didn't happen anymore, because now we have the Bible and churches. I always knew it was not true.

My husband and I went to their apartment. I can still see the details of all of this in my mind. We knelt by their couch. The man put his hand on my husband's back. The lady put her hand on my back and began praying very softly. I put my head in my hands and said to Abba: "I want You Holy Spirit, but please don't scare me." I was a Baptist remember. We were taught that most "supernatural" things were of the devil, especially "speaking in tongues." All of a sudden I felt extremely hot. Then I began to tremble. My first thought annoyed me, "Why is she shaking me?" But, she wasn't shaking me. Two words, I know now are Hebrew praise words, came into my mind, but I remained quiet. Afterwards, I got up, and knew something had happened. But, my husband let me know that he got nothing out of it.

That night, I had a dream in three sections. First, Satan came to me to get me to curse "God." I spoke the two words I'd received that night at him, and he ran away. The second time the same thing happened, and he ran away. The third time, the two words took the form of a javelin that formed in my right hand, and I ran at him with these words, and he fled away, not to return.

The next morning, my life was radically different, and has been every day since. It was like the light had been turned on in a dark world. I had joy like I'd never known before. The fruit of the reborn spirit was enhanced (**Galatians 5:22-23**), especially joy. All sorts of things began happening. All the nine gifts of the Spirit began manifesting. (**I Corinthians 12:7-11**). But, without this empowering and personal infilling of His Spirit, the Spirit of Yahuweh, I would never have survived the ensuing years of living in the enemy's camp. For more understanding on Messiah's baptizing the born again ones into the Spirit of Yahuweh, refer to the articles under The Mikvah of the Spirit on **comeenterthemikvah.com**

One of the saddest times in my life occurred in the next few days. Though my husband was with me that night, he did not receive the Spirit because, as I learned 29 years later, by his own

PART II - The Journey Continues

admission, he was not born again. He proceeded to make up a "tongue" so that I would not "upstage him" in the eyes of people. He claimed to be a Christian, but did not understand the first requirement for being truly born again – repentance.

I learned to recognize the satanic counterfeits of "tongues." I do not fake anything, so he was jealous of me. I was so gloriously happy to have the Spirit fill me. My whole life had been changed. The fruit of the re-born spirit was manifesting to a much higher degree. I was not shy anymore, but His power and boldness was in me.

Here is what was so tragic, and continues to be to this day: The young couple who prayed for us did not have a telephone, but we made a dinner date to meet that next Saturday night at their apartment at Life Bible College, next to Angelus Temple. That morning, my husband announced: "We're not going." I had no idea how to contact them. I had no idea how to find them. All I could think of was their preparing our meal and we did not show up. That has, from time to time, caused me many tears and much grief. One day in eternity I will meet them again. But, if you are reading this and you are one of that young couple, please contact me via **comeenterthemikvah.com**. I so long for that restoration!

Even though we began attending Angelus Temple, we never saw that young couple again. We met some of the remaining family of Aimee Semple McPherson, like her son Rolf. We became good friends with two sisters--Esther and Marie Jensen--who had been in the church when Aimee preached. These were people who were calmly strong in the Word, in love, and knew the power of the Spirit rightly, not as some show, but in reality.

There was a man there that we met who had been in a car accident years before, and his whole body was crushed. I will never forget standing down by the grand piano as he told us his story. His inner organs and his bones were crushed, and he was bleeding to death internally. The doctors sent him home to die. All his family could do for him was mop up the blood, and try to give him water. But, some friends had heard of the miracles of healing at Angelus Temple, and called an ambulance to take him in a stretcher to the church. I talked to people who were there. They said that as they brought him down towards the front of the church, without anyone laying hands on him, they heard bones cracking loudly--the acoustics in that place are awesome. When they got him down front to pray for him, he got off the stretcher totally healed. He went home. The next day the doctors called to see if he had died. His wife told them that he was sitting at the kitchen table having a big steak breakfast. This is the type of people that were mentors to me. This was before the big hype word of faith movement that is so commercialized. This was an extension of the book of Acts.

I met Dr. Hinderlighter. He was 106 when I met him. I remember that he lived to be about 111, in perfect health. His second wife was in her upper 80s. He was so full of the love of Abba and Messiah. I remember him kneeling by the chair I was sitting in, talking to me. His face was so radiant. We were gathered for dinner at the home of Rolf McPherson. I also met Aimee's daughter and her family. Precious people!

I remember Doris Akers and her choir. Do you remember her? Her famous song chorus still carries an anointing: "There's a highway to heaven, none can walk up there but the pure in heart, there's a high way to heaven, walking up the King's Highway." I've walked up the literal King's Highway many times in Wadi Musa. The King's Highway leads right to the entrance of Petra. My very first article was about the King's Highway entitled "There Shall Be A Highway." The information I got was from the Word, and from the consulting engineers who headed the project. The chief consulting engineer gave me engineering maps, and told me many exciting stories.

I met Dr. Harry O. Anderson--a man who was like a father to me. He was a pure-hearted pastor. When he died, they had an open-coffin funeral. Lying there in that coffin, he had a smile on his face that was radiant. No one at the funeral home made his face smile--that's the way his mouth was set when he died. I wonder what he saw as he died that brought that smile.

After being baptized by Messiah into Yahuweh's Spirit, His Spirit began speaking to me more. Demonic spirits began appearing in my apartment, and I would command them to leave and they would leave. I will share just two examples: One day I was making cookies, and was looking for the next ingredient, when I saw a tall man standing in the bedroom doorway, wearing a tuxedo and a tall black top-hat. I felt his presence--evil. I knelt down behind the couch and began commanding him to leave. He left quickly. Another time, I was looking for a good book to read and I went to my bookcase, and while searching for the book, Abba said: "Go into the bedroom and pray." I did as He said. I sat on the bed and began praising Abba and praying. Then I commanded the devil out of the room. I saw off my left shoulder the venetian blinds pulled back about a foot from the closed window, and then loudly slapped against the window. I kept praying. But, as time went along the demonic manifestations increased. As I increased in boldness and knowledge of life in the Spirit, the enemy's attacks increased.

PART II - The Journey Continues

I began to manifest all the nine gifts of the Spirit in **I Corinthians 12:1-13**, especially the word of knowledge and the word of wisdom. Since then, He has increased my authority level against the demonic greatly. He began teaching me about spiritual warfare. I began having dreams and visions that reflected the "word of knowledge," and the "word of wisdom," as well as "prophecy," which increased through the years to this day.

I had to re-read the whole Word and let Him teach me. BIOLA had given me a foundation in the Word, but so much of it was interpreted by my teachers to fit the dispensational evangelical fundamentalist doctrine. I had to re-learn what they told me that was wrong, what they mocked as not for today, and see it as Abba saw it, so that I might apply it in the here and now.

I began moving in the prophetic realm. He has allowed me to move in miracles, in healings, in deliverances from demons, in words of knowledge and wisdom, and more and more into the prophetic realm. One of the gifts He gave me was the interpretation of dreams. It is a powerful gift. I can also discern if a dream is from Yahuweh or from the mind's psychic realm. One of the strongest gifts that we all desperately need is the gift of the discernment of spirits – to discern the spirits of man, of demons, and the Spirit of Yahuweh. So often, religion mixes these three, an example being that man attributes the works of the Spirit of Yahuweh as the spirit of the devil – thus blaspheming the Spirit/Yahuweh.

I have led many in Africa, Mexico, South America, and other places, to the baptism in the Spirit. **Luke 3:16**: It is Messiah who baptizes us into the Spirit. The Spirit is Yahuweh Himself. (**II Corinthians 3:17-18**) He is the one who transforms us into the nature and likeness of Elohim. But, I found that Americans and other westerners have a hard time because they let their intellect (soul/mind, emotions) get in the way, and He only honors child-like faith. This is why there are few true miracles and healings in the U.S., because it takes child-like faith to receive them. In the Third World the people are child-like in their faith, and so they receive easily.

Matthew 18:1-4: "Truly I say to you, unless you turn and become as little children, you shall by no means enter the kingdom of heaven. Whoever, then, humbles himself as a little child is the greatest in the Kingdom of heaven."

June 15, 1967, at 7:45 PM, Thursday evening after prayer, I wrote out the cry of my heart. Here it is from my journal: "**I want my life to count in eternal values, and to carry on the ministry of Jesus Christ. There is nothing else to live for. I want God to be glorified for eternity because I lived for a**

few years on the earth. I want to leave an army of souls behind me, whose one goal it is to glorify Jesus Christ. I'm sick of working and thinking about temporal things. Only eternity can measure what is really worth anything. Souls are what interest God--souls that will live forever--and souls are what interest me. The hour is late. Jesus is coming!"

March 8, 1991 I wrote it this way: "**To rescue souls from the kingdom of darkness, in partnership with the Holy Spirit, and bring them into the kingdom of light, to ground them in the Word and get them filled with the Holy Spirit until they glorify Jesus and bring others into His kingdom is still the burning, overwhelming desire of my heart. Again I cry--Give me souls, use me to Your glory, oh God, or I die.**"

No, I had no idea about His true Names and titles back then, but **Hosea 2** tells us that He will take the names of Ba'al out of our mouth. Today, I call Him by His real Name and use the Hebrew words for Their titles, but He heard the cry of my spirit – and He has answered me more abundantly than I could ever ask or think! [Refer to the study: "The Hebrew Names and Titles of the Creator of the Universe – the Father and Messiah of Israel"/January 2005]

When we are born of the Spirit, forty things happen by His sovereign action. [Refer to: "The True New Birth"] But, one thing that does not happen is His infilling. We must ask for that (**Luke 11:13**). When we are born of the Spirit, and come into the Covenant of Yahuweh, the Spirit of Yahuweh baptizes us into Messiah (**I Corinthians 12:13**). But, when we are filled with the Spirit within our eternal spirit, and get the "mind of the spirit" in operation, then His anointing teaches us (**I John 2:27**). It is Messiah Himself who baptizes us into the Spirit (**Luke 3:16**).

The prayer language, the language of angels, that we receive when this happens, as is consistent in the book of Acts, and from Sha'ul's writings, is for spiritual edification, for intercession, and for spiritual warfare. Also, as He wills, some receive the languages of men, for ministering in other countries. The nine gifts of the eternal Spirit operate from within us. [Refer to: "The Manifestations of the Set-Apart Spirit"/August 9, 2008 and "Living From the Eternal Mind"/November 2010]

When I was in Africa those six years, they often called on me to teach on the baptism into the Spirit, and then to pray for people to receive the Spirit. I always gave a week of teaching from the Word before praying for anyone. The pastors told me that because most of the people had come out of witchcraft, even though born again, the demonic spirit still tormented their mind

PART II - The Journey Continues

and body. So, in praying for them, it was a time of deliverance for many of them--the demons coming out as the Spirit came in. I found this to be very true, especially when praying for people in a remote area of the Serengeti Plain of Tanzania. The demonic was manifesting to a high degree as people were set free and received the Spirit of Yahuweh. You will read about my six years in and out of Africa in Part V.

My experiences in life also helped me set many free in Africa. In fact, it is through encounters with the forces of darkness and our overcoming in our daily life that prepares us to go through the tribulation to the coming of Messiah Yahushua in victory. He gradually increased His authority-backing of me, as He tested and tested and found me faithful. **He has to be able to trust us**! I learned the power of the spoken word. But, without His authority-backing, we'd better keep our mouth shut! [Refer to: "Authority Backing"] Too many people do "intercession" and "spiritual warfare" without knowledge and wisdom, and all they do is stir up demons who retaliate against them. I do not focus on "demons." I focus on my Abba Yahuweh. Yahuweh is El Elyon – the Most High. He is El Shaddai – The Almighty!

I was concerned that I only had two words in my angelic vocabulary. About a month after being baptized in the Spirit, while lying in bed, I was reading a classic of that day: *They Speak With Other Tongues*. I do not remember what portion of it I was reading, but all of a sudden I sat up, threw my legs over the side of the bed, and began speaking in a very clear fluent language. It was so clear and fluent that it sounded like an earthly language. Later He began giving me "warfare languages", and even a language with some Hebrew words that I recognized when I began hearing Hebrew. He has given me several languages. I am never surprised by a new language, for these are His languages, and they are all beautiful. Some sound more beautiful to me than others, but they are all clear and distinctive. In speaking them, I listen to myself, for it is His Spirit using my vocal chords to speak. No one would know I wasn't speaking in an earthly language. This helped in China when I needed a breakthrough to get His work done. I could speak out loud because they didn't understand me. The sound of the demonic languages are ugly, creepy, and have a lot of the "s" sound in them – the snake sound. The enemy cannot produce beauty, only illusions and counterfeits.

The first time I ever went to a synagogue was with a Jewish lady, to attend a Bar Mitzvah. The rabbi was speaking in Hebrew. I had never heard anyone speak in Hebrew before. I kept hearing words that were familiar in one of the languages Abba gave me. I leaned over to my Jewish friend, and told her that the Spirit of

God had given me some of those words to speak in a prayer language. She said: "Well, then, you probably know more Hebrew than I do." I learned that Jews understand the Spirit.

One year, our church team was praying for a Navajo lady on the reservation to receive the Spirit, and all of a sudden she started speaking profusely. We looked at our Navajo translators, and asked if she was speaking Navajo. They shook their heads "No."

The pastor I traveled with for five years in Kenya, dear Vincent Wanyonyi Wabuke, said that after praying for people to receive the Spirit in a remote village, an old woman, who spoke nothing but her native dialect, went over to kneel by a chair. She then began speaking in perfect English "He is coming; He is coming soon, prepare, prepare."

One time in Africa, up in the mountains of Uganda in a remote village, while praying for others to receive His Spirit, I was told by Abba to help a lady who was stammering--not breaking free into her Language. He instructed me to have her repeat the first line of the language that was given to me in 1966. I did so, and she burst forth into the whole language. Vincent was listening and was astonished, because he recognized the language I normally speak in prayer. It is a prayer language that bypasses the enemy's understanding; it is also a powerful spiritual weapon.

Alan Shook, a pastor in Fort Worth, said: "If you do things the Bible way, you will get the Bible results." So true! Moving in the Spirit is not spooky, nor is it a power-show that draws attention to the minister. With Messiah and His disciples, it was simply moving by Yahuweh's command, with His authority-backing.

I wrote a three-part series on Scriptural Spiritual Warfare/June and July 2010, in which I give the wisdom that He has given me, and wisdom from experiences. Don't you know that we are born again with combat boots on! It is through the baptism into the Spirit, by Messiah, that we receive the "weapons of our warfare that are not carnal but mighty to the pulling down of strongholds." We just have to learn how to use them properly. (**Ephesians 6:10-18; II Corinthians 10:3-6; II Timothy 2:4**)

In college, in 1963, I took a class in "Typology" taught by Mrs. Hooker. She compared the wilderness journey, the tabernacle of Moses, and the Levitical offerings, to Messiah. That class changed my life. Mrs. Hooker was a little missionary lady in her 80s, who wore a hairnet, and was all wrinkled up. I got straight "A's" in that class. I began studying the seven Festivals of Yahuweh, and Father began drawing me to teach on them as to how they pictured Messiah, not knowing that many years later I would go to Jerusalem and be part of them. He begins where we are, then

PART II - The Journey Continues

leads us forward. I taught them years later in Women's Aglow meetings, and other places, to introduce our Hebrew roots to Christians.

After college, and after I was married, I became the Minister of Music in two churches. I was a Sunday School teacher, a leader of children's and women's groups, and on and on. At the Community Chapel Bible College--Southern California Bible College--I created the "Old Testament Survey" class. Because of our outreach to people that most people would run from, we led many gang members, prostitutes, pimps, and ex-convicts, to salvation. So, in the College, I taught ex-Hell's Angels, ex-pimps, ex-prostitutes, ex-criminals, as well as "regular" people. It was the "ex" people who were the most enthusiastic to learn the Word. I also taught the book of Revelation (1971) at the Bible school.

His Tenach (miscalled "Old Testament") came alive to me. I've come to know that there is no such thing as an "Old" vs. a "New" Testament. His Covenant is eternal, and Messiah renewed it and made it fresh and alive to all of His people, bringing it into the realm of the spirit and the heart. As I taught the Tenach, Father gave me revelation every day about Messiah in the pages of the Tenach, which I shared with my class. I would go home from teaching, lie down on the couch with my Bible, and He would pour revelation knowledge into me. The next day, I would tell my students to get their pens ready to write because "I had been on the couch." They knew that it meant He had told me something, so they eagerly listened.

I was also the pianist for the Community Chapel Choir and for congregational praise and worship. We had moved from Glendale, California, to belong to Community Chapel in Long Beach. They needed a pianist and I was it. They had an organist. We were a great team. But, I only knew how to read music, not play it "by ear." At Community Chapel, because no one read music, we took the songs off of cassette tapes. The choir director, Kay Mallet, and her mother, pastor Esther Mallet, got involved in my training. They taught me chording. They taught me how to feel the beat of some of their songs, where, for example, the emphasis was on the second beat. I finally learned, and ended up playing what is termed "bar-room piano" – free as a jaybird. Later in teaching piano, I taught students to read music, but also play free by chording. Oh what excitement each Sunday morning was when this rag-a-muffin choir came strutting down the aisle, robes flying in the breeze, singing rallying choruses like "We're Comin' Out of Babylon." Beginning in 2001, I began exhorting Abba's people to literally get out of the system of Babylon (Lucifer's system) and the nation of end-time Babylon--America.

I had the privilege of having the leaders of the most terrifying Hell's Angel's group--the "San Bernardino Chapter"--sitting next to me on the piano bench, as I tested their voices for the choir. Here is something no religion of any man can do: The San Bernardino chapter, known as the "San Berdoo" chapter, of the Hell's Angels was reportedly the most violent and feared chapter of this lawless gang in America. Their "president," Otto Freedly, was feared throughout the U.S., even by other Hell's Angels gangs. But, most feared of all was Teddy Medina of the San Bernardino chapter. They called him the "poster boy"--probably because his picture was on "Most Wanted" posters. When the very infamous Charles Manson was in a Los Angeles prison awaiting trial, the police were on high alert. At the same time, they captured Teddy Medina. It took twelve men to hold down Teddy-- a tall, muscular Mexican man. The Los Angeles sheriffs said that they feared Teddy far more than they feared Charles Manson.

Faith in the death and resurrection of Messiah opens the door for total transformation of someone's life, as in the case of Teddy. In the Los Angeles jail, Teddy received Jesus as his personal Savior and Lord. Teddy was "saved"--"re-born from above." The faithful Spirit of Yahuweh worked in Teddy's life to bring about the forty things that He does when someone trusts in Messiah. I met Teddy a few days after they released him from jail. He was the meekest man I'd ever met--gentle, kind and so grateful for his salvation. I became good friends with Teddy, and his life exemplified the radical change of one who had been born of the Spirit, born from above by faith. The news of Teddy's change quickly got to Otto Freedly and the other members of the gang. Then, Otto was born again.

Two of his top leaders were Gary and Sharon Dix. Sharon was so violent that the State of California took away her thirteen children. Gary was on a very expensive daily heroin habit. Sharon and Gary received Jesus as their Savior too. Gary immediately heard the sound of a trumpet. His heroin addiction was taken from him instantly, and he was healed of any desire for it. Sharon was so changed that the State of California gave her back all thirteen children, whom she raised in righteousness after that. They became born again too. One of the daughters, called Sissy, who had been involved in satanic ritual, became one of the shining members of the choir.

News of their salvation went into the other Hell's Angels gangs all over the United States, and into the prisons. Many others also came to new life in Messiah. Teddy, Otto, Gary and Sharon wanted to join the choir. The choir was made up of ex-gang members, ex-prostitutes, ex-pimps, ex-prisoners, and ordinary

PART II - The Journey Continues

folks that hid their sins under respectability. As Teddy, Otto and Gary and Sharon sat on my piano bench, where I tested their voices for their position in the choir, it was so overwhelming to me that these once vicious gang members were letting me take them through the "la, la, la, la, la" test so that they could sing in a church choir.

I remember visiting Sharon at her house one morning very early. She had been up for hours making bread. I asked her why she was up so early. She said that she had wasted so many years of her life (she was only in her mid-30's) and now she wanted to be a blessing to her family, and so she was making them fresh bread for breakfast. When Hell's Angels across America, many in prison, learned of the transformation of the meanest bunch of all, especially Teddy Medina, they began writing to find out what happened. I was privileged to be able to write to some of them in prison.

During this time, also, I wrote leaders of countries, and many in our Congress and Senate, with the message of salvation. I got a personal letter back from the President of Rhodesia and one from Queen Elizabeth's "Lady in waiting"--her personal secretary. I handed out gospel tracts in malls and on the street. I went door to door with several evangelistic teams, sharing the Good News. I even used Halloween night to go door to door to share the Good News. Unless we give out, we are like the Dead Sea. The Dead Sea takes in fresh water from the Jordan, but does not give it out, so no life can live in the Dead Sea.

Brother Yun was imprisoned many times in China for doing evangelism. In fact, the average pastor in China is in prison for 17 years or longer, and anyone doing evangelism is arrested. Brother Yun's mother knew about 2 verses from the Bible, for no one could get Bibles. She gathered people in her home to hear of salvation, and led many to salvation. She gathered people to pray, always under the threat of arrest. Brother Yun wrote his story in the book *The Heavenly Man* – you should read it. If your brothers and sisters in China, who refuse to submit to the government's control over what the Master says, risk their lives daily to spread His salvation, what's wrong with the lazy people of the affluent West? Persecution and martyrdom are coming to the affluent West very soon!

I led what was called "Church on the Street" in Long Beach, California, down by the Long Beach Pier. Many military men came down there, as well as gangs, the homeless, and others. The choir dressed up in their robes. We had a sound system that boomed the music and the preaching that was heard for blocks away. One night I took a lady I worked with, in Lakewood, to the meeting.

She turned out to be demonized (under demonic control). She took off running across the main boulevard. I ran after her. We ran past a gang of bikers. I finally caught her and took her back to the meeting. But, the bikers asked if they could help me. They were sitting there in the park across the street listening to the music and the preaching. Later I visited her in a mental hospital with another employee. They had her very sedated. She was even kept, as I remember, in a straight jacket. She kept saying in her drugged stupor that I was so pure and holy and so good. I know that the "accuser" had tormented her and it drove her crazy, for she was tormented by guilt from her fornication. What a tragedy. I never had any fear when serving the Master, even when preaching on the streets of Los Angeles at 2:00 AM and nine months pregnant. I had one gang stop me. The leader asked me what I was "high on." I told them boldly, "I'm high on Jesus." They let me preach to them. That was the time of the hippy "Jesus Freaks" movement. I had a lot of friends in the Jesus Freaks movement. I would go to their meetings and share meals with them. It was my greatest joy to preach the good news of salvation to the lost--no matter what their age, or their situation.

TIME OUT: I know! I am jumping around giving stories, in different states and different times, but hopefully as you keep reading the whole picture will fit into place. I am trying to tie together topics that fit together. He never wastes anything – good or bad! He uses everything to prepare His chosen ones for what He has called them to from the foundation of the world. Please do not get bogged down by the next Part. Realize that what happened to me was part of my schooling, under the tutelage of the Master. He warned me beforehand, and He brought me out afterwards. In allowing me to reap the crop of my sowing--He had to stand to one side. But, the lessons I've learned have been, and will be, invaluable as I have, and will again, face the Dragon in Jerusalem! "You will walk into the face of the Dragon and come away unscathed", thus says Yahuweh.

Please know, I am totally free from all negative emotions from the past. Negative emotions draw demonic spirits like a magnet – they feed on negative emotions. I am free! I blame no one but myself for what happened to me, because of my own decisions. However, I don't even carry guilt of my own sin anymore, for He has taken that away. I must focus on helping others prepare for eternity, and exalt and worship Yahuweh and Yahushua Yahuweh!

I have NO ties to hurt, wounds, self-pity, vengeance, bitterness, anger, or unforgiveness. Therefore, I do not gossip or slander anyone in my past. I only report as simply as I can so that you will know the great mercy of Abba for me. I will simply report the events that Abba used to turn me totally around and reset me on the path that He planned for me from the foundation of the world. Today, I walk in freedom and peace, and in the joy of my Abba Yahuweh, and my Messiah Yahushua.

We must never play the "blame game." Each of us is responsible for our own decisions. We must face reality, and let the Spirit reveal to us what we need to do to straighten out our lives. Our prayer must always be: "**Search me, O Elohim, and know my heart. Try me, and know my thoughts, and see if there is any wicked way in me, and lead me in the way everlasting.**" (**Psalm 139:23-24**) Allow the Spirit to search you, and help you to know yourself. No one knows themselves, only He does. Pride reigns in an improper view of ourselves, for good or bad.

Jeremiah 17:9-10: "The heart (*soul: mind, emotions, reasoning, will*) is deceitful above all things, and desperately wicked, who can know it? I, Yahuweh, search the heart and try the reins (*the root of the mind's and emotion's actions*), to give every man according to his works and according to the fruit of His doings." His judgment is on an individual basis. He goes deep, and sees the real intent of our decisions and judges, and rewards us, according to the purity of what He sees. We must always remember that unless we forgive others--let go, and go on--He cannot, and will not, forgive us. (**Mark 11:25-26**)

But, forgiveness doesn't mean we have to jump back in fellowship with whoever did cruelty to us – that's foolishness. However, neither must we hold them in a cage in our heart, so that when we feel self-pity we bring them out in front of us to pour our hurts out, and to wallow in negative emotions, either privately or publically. This nonsense not only wastes time, but energy, when you could be sharing your deliverance from sin with others to help them be free. We stand alone at the judgment seat of Elohim. We will have no one to blame then. So, we might as well stop the blame game now, and face reality.

This next section tells of how I jumped into the pit, and how my faithful Abba and my faithful Bridegroom patiently pulled me out of it. In the meantime, it was my schooling for my future work for Him. He wastes nothing!

THE GREATEST MIRACLE OF ALL IS ABBA'S LOVE AND MERCY!

PART III

THE JOURNEY IS SABOTAGED

MY DETOUR FROM FAITH

(1966-1985)

Psalm 103:8-10: "Yahuweh is compassionate and showing mercy, patient, and great in loving kindness. He will not always strive, nor will He forever bear a grudge. He has not treated us according to our sins, nor rewarded us according to our iniquities."

II Timothy 2:12: "If we are not faithful, He remains faithful—for it is impossible for Him to deny Himself."

Lamentations 3:22-23: "It is because of Yahuweh's mercies that we are not consumed, because His compassions fail not. They are new every morning – great is Your faithfulness!"

Ephesians 1:3-5: "Blessed be the Elohim and Father of our Master Yahushua Messiah, who has blessed us with every spiritual blessing in heavenly places in Messiah, even as He chose us in Him before the foundation of the world, that we should be set-apart and blameless before Him in love, having previously ordained us to be adopted as sons through Yahushua Messiah to Himself, according to the good pleasure of His will..."

I Peter 1:1-2: "Kepha, an Apostle of Yahushua Messiah, to the chosen...chosen according to the foreknowledge of Elohim the Father, set apart by the Spirit unto obedience and the sprinkling of the blood of Yahushua Messiah: Favor and peace be increased to you."

He put into me "the great adventure" from age four, when He wrapped me around with that bubble and said to me: "You don't belong here anymore." He meant that He was separating me unto Himself from the Lucifer-controlled world system. But, I did not know He intended to lift me up into His eternal realm to learn His eternal secrets so that I might be His servant in these days before Messiah Yahushua returns. He reveals Himself and His plans for us as we walk the straight path that He has laid forth for His people, through His Torah.

It took me the greatest percentage of my life to finally understand Him as a Person and His plans for me. He deals with us as individuals. He deals with us intimately as a Father who knows our end from our beginning. Sadly, most do not understand the role of a real father, nor of a home where a father has his role and the mother has her role, and the children have their role, and all flow together in perfect harmony. It is hard to know Him as Father when we have problems with our own earthly father, and our home-life is anything but according to the nature, ways and thinking in our heavenly home.

"The Great Adventure"
by
Steven Curtis Chapman

Chorus
Saddle up your horses we've got a trail to blaze
Through the wild blue yonder of God's amazing grace
Let's follow our leader into <u>the glorious unknown</u>
This is a life like no other - this is The Great Adventure

Verse 1
Started out this morning in the usual way,
Chasing thoughts inside my head of all I had to do today,
Another time around the circle, try to make it better than the last.
I opened up my Bible and I read about me,
(it) said I'd been a prisoner and God's grace had set me free.
And somewhere between the pages, it hit me like a lightning bolt,
I saw a big frontier in front of me, and I heard someone say
`Let's Go!'

Verse 2
Come on get ready for the ride of your life!
Gonna leave long-faced religion in a cloud of dust behind,
and **discover all the new horizons just waiting to be explored**
This is what we were created for.

Bridge
We'll travel over, over mountains so high,
We'll go through valleys below.
Still through it all, we'll find that
This is the greatest journey that the human heart will ever see
The love of God will take us far beyond our wildest dreams.
Saddle up your horses
Come on, get ready to ride!

PART III - The Journey is Sabotaged

It was following my Leader into the "glorious unknown" to the "new horizons" of the eternal world that Satan tried to steal from me. He succeeded, but only for a while.

It was my passion for the "great adventure" that he wanted to take from me, to reduce me to a useless vessel to be thrown onto a garbage dump. That's what Lucifer stole from Adam and Hawwah (Eve) – their passion for the Presence of Yahuweh and Yahushua Yahuweh. He turned their passion for being with Him to a passion to get what their flesh wanted. (**Romans 8:5-8, 13-14**) But, Abba used everything to make a warrior out of me, using all the knowledge I learned of the dark kingdom and its "king" to stand against him. Soon Yahushua will throw Lucifer/Satan/"that old Dragon"/Devil, into the lake of fire. In the meantime, the demonic world keeps trying to take down Yahuweh's set-apart ones. But, as I grow stronger and stronger in the power of the might of my Elohim, Yahuweh of Hosts, I can feel freedom like I've never felt before. He uses every attack of the enemy to make me more of a stronger warrior than before. In many places of ministry, I am known as a warrior, and a prophet of the Most High.

We have our own will. Abba won't override our will unless we ask Him to. And I asked Him to. My stubborn, hard-headed will has gotten me into so much trouble, that I learned to only trust His will! He has more respect for us than we do for ourselves. He asks that we submit our will to Him for our good, but He won't force the issue. But, from the foundation of the world He knew who would receive Him and who would not, and who would ultimately allow Him to make them blameless--even though rebellion and all sorts of evil intervened to make it appear that they will not make it through. He leads us by His foreknowledge. "I will guide you by what I have seen." (**Psalm 32:8**)

The reason it has taken seven years to write this autobiography is because of this part, which covers 30+ years of my life. But, it is this story about how He has dealt with me, that I believe will help others to have hope and be encouraged. A few of you, perhaps, have come out of Satanism. You know how this affects little children and youth, and how evil works to destroy mind, emotions, spirit and body. Today my four children and their children are trophies of His mercy and love. They are miracle children. To different degrees the effects of abuse on them as little children and early teenagers is still evident, but their spirit is alive and well and He is transforming them, and setting them free! All praise to Yahuweh and Yahushua Yahuweh!

Amidst all of my desiring to do His will, I was also a very flesh-oriented teenager. I was strongly self-willed and stubborn. And, I had developed a religious side that later I found disgusting. Abba graciously had to take me into the wilderness of Jordan, into the Negev Desert, for eight years, to remove any vestiges of religiosity out of me. He did with me as a potter must do with a misshapen vessel--He crushed me, and then remolded me, so that I could be a "vessel unto honor."

I was always a free-spirited child. I was always an outdoors girl. I loved to hike. I loved to play sports. I started early with tetherball, jump rope in elementary school, ping pong, and crochet. Later it was baseball, tag football, field hockey, swimming, tennis, and my favorite--basketball. In my senior year of High School I was the school badminton champion. Like with volleyball and tennis, I could place the ball, or the "birdie," anywhere I wanted it to go. In college, I took up golf. That was a little harder (smile). As I grew up, I loved to watch the L.A. Dodgers, the Lakers, and the L.A. Rams. Once Joe Montana entered the picture, I cheered for the 49ers. I loved to watch our High School team play football. We were the "Highlanders," complete with a Scottish terrier mascot. We even had a bagpipe band.

I spent many hours each week at my best friend's house watching sports, playing chess, and 7-card stud poker. Jeanne and Diana McBride were my best friends, though I also had Treva and her family next door, and other friends close by. I was not without "playmates." Because I loved sports, later, when my two youngest girls were in band, and marched at football games in High School, I became a "band mother." I went with the band to help them in any way needed. I loved that so much! My third child was a clarinet player. She made "all city Band" in Fort Worth six years in a row--two years in Middle School and four years in High School. The youngest one played the trumpet, like my son. I went to all of their performances. My girls were in gymnastics and dance classes also, so I was always very involved with my children in their schools, and their performances. I also kept watch on what they were learning in school.

I was a tall, thin girl, with long and thick auburn hair, hazel eyes, and a terrific figure--too terrific for my own good. I attracted boys who hid their "flesh" under a religious mask, like me. My shyness, religiosity, and incredible naivety kept me a virgin until I got married. But, I was also very "backwards" socially. I attracted socially backward boys. My choices in boys was NOT GOOD. My parents had to have some serious talks with me about boys, but it did little good. Too much of the time, I was a mouthy teenager, strong willed, stubborn, and rebellious--a hardheaded redhead. But, at times, I had religious pride that was

PART III - The Journey is Sabotaged   91

off the charts. My mother commented a lot on my stubbornness. And I could be very dramatic--my mother called me "Sarah Bernhardt," a famous actress of her day.

As I grew up, my teacher-mother whipped me with a thin wooden "yardstick." Papa had tremendous restraint, because if he ever whipped me in anger, he knew he'd hurt me. One day, I crossed the threshold of his tolerance. I was about 15, I think. I had gone with my Baptist Youth Group to Greenlake, Wisconsin. I came back with a terribly religious spirit. I just mouthed off to him one too many times. He just quickly backhanded me, and almost knocked me out of my chair before I knew what was happening. I burst into tears, holding my jaw, and ran to my room. He was strong and could have broken my jaw, so his backhanding must have been with much restraint. I knew I deserved it. To this day I know I deserved it! That's one thing I never faulted him for.

The "mouthy" arrogance, plus my deep anger, turned into a cursing problem. Later on, I had a filthy mouth "that would make a sailor blush." Because of so much deep-seated hurt, I lashed out. Oh the schooling He had to put me through to get all that rebellion out! He had to crush me hard and make me face myself. He had to let me know that He was El and I was not. The final humbling from those lessons came as late as January 2011.

Truly, He applied the grinding stone, and the tribulum. Here in Israel, to my left on my table, is the grinding stone I found at Qumran. Also on the table is a symbolic tribulum, and a plumb line. Today I use them to do prophetic-action/intercession. But, He had to apply them to my life before I could apply them to the lives of others, and to nations.

Jeremiah 6:19: "Hear O earth! Behold! I will bring evil upon this people, **even the fruit of their thoughts**, because they have not harkened unto My words, nor to My Torah, but have rejected it."

II Corinthians 10:4-6: "For the weapons of our warfare are not carnal, but are mighty through Elohim to the pulling down of strongholds, casting down imaginations and every high thing that exalts itself against the knowledge of Elohim, and **bringing into captivity every thought in obedience to Messiah.**"

I kept so much sin in my thoughts. But, thoughts create. It is not until later that we see the "fruit of our thoughts." Thoughts project, and later cause action. All sin begins with thoughts. Messiah put a magnifying glass to the Torah and made it very clear, and expanded it. He says in **Matthew 5:27-28**: "You have heard `you shall not commit adultery,' but I say to you that anyone looking on a woman to lust for her has already committed adultery with her in his heart."

The "heart" is the mind, the soul--the core of our self-life, what we are. "As a man thinks in his heart, so is he." (**Proverbs 23:7a**) We are defiled from the inside out. (**Mark 7:20-23**) He had to bring on me the "fruit of my thoughts" to punish me. We think we're hiding in our thoughts, but they do create! Thoughts become open portals for the enemy, because he uses thoughts implanted into our mind to twist us and turn us towards his way of thinking! The enemy cannot touch our re-born spirit, but he sure can implant thoughts that lead us to wrong thinking and sin. He can touch our body if our soul (mind, emotions) is open to him.

We are where we are today because of our thoughts! Persisting thoughts turn to action at some point, for good or for bad. Looking back, all of the sinful thoughts, all the sinful fantasy thoughts, were eventually used by the enemy to create my downfall. It was only the mercy of my Abba that brought me out of the pit, and then began working to change my thoughts. This is why I teach so much on how He can transform us through His Word, through worship, through verbal proclamation of praise and our desire for Him. **For unless our thoughts are changed, we won't be changed**! Outward change can be a sham if the thoughts and intents of the carnal soul remain hidden. Satan masquerades as an angel of light, and so do His servants. (**II Corinthians 11:12-15**)

Oh, the great patience of Abba Yahuweh! Oh His persistent love! But, He has faith in His foreknowledge, so has not destroyed us all. He has emotions, but they are all righteous. He has wrath and anger for the wicked, for the children of darkness. He also has to punish His own children who stubbornly rebel against Him. He is a Father. But it is all His love. How can righteous anger be love? The season of tribulation in its fierceness across the earth will actually be the height of His love for His people--to free His people from the "chaff" that binds them. Like chaff on wheat, unless it is removed, the wheat is no good for food. "Chaff" is our sin, our emotional instability, our foolishness, our mistakes, our wrong decisions, and our down right wickedness. It binds us from being free. He has to use harsh measures to free us, because the chaff clings to us.

His discipline and dealing with us are often in harsh ways, but it is always from His love. A good father must be hard on his children who have a rebellious bent, in order to keep them from hurting themselves, just like a horse has to be broken so that a man can ride it. **Psalm 32:9**: "Be not as the horse, or as the mule, which have no understanding, whose mouth must be held in with bit and bridle, lest they come near unto you." I was like

PART III - The Journey is Sabotaged

the stubborn mule, whose mouth needed to have a bit in it. I was like the wild horse who needed a bridle. He had to break this stubborn mule. I sure did not do anything to change myself – I couldn't. He had to crush me so hard that I finally submitted to His working in me, and He has done the transformation! This is why I have no pride in my accomplishments.

Here I begin the story of my breaking and crushing, so that the Master could remold me into a "vessel unto honor." (**Jeremiah 18:1-6**) Like papa, Yahuweh had tremendous restraint towards me. However, when Abba reached the limit of His restraint, for my own good, like my papa, He had to take His right hand and His right arm and backhand me to the floor. I deserved it! Out of it, because of Messiah's intercession on my behalf, He has transformed me into another person altogether. Without Messiah's intercession on my behalf, as you will see later, He had every right to give me over to death. Did you ever see the movie *The Apostle*? The bottom line was that no matter what the man did that was wrong, he was what he was – a lover of Jesus who was compelled to preach the Word. That was me.

In that personality test I took for PMT in 1964, the test that showed my aggression "ran off the charts," there was one question that was asked that I will never forget. They asked: "If you stood behind a child seated in a grocery cart in the checkout line at the grocery store, would you smile at that child?" I put "No." I did not like children. I gravitated to older people. I found my peers to be hurtful. In fact, I turned my head from looking at little children. A few years ago I remembered that question clearly as I stood behind a grocery cart with a little girl in it, in the checkout line of Walmart. She was smiling at me. I smiled back, waved, and said something to her. I often get tears in my eyes as I smile at children and see their happy responses, for I know that my smiles come from Abba's heart of love.

Now I am the grandmother of an adopted little girl, who is 2 years old. I hold her, cuddle her, and love her so much, and she loves me. I am a great grandmother of a little boy who is almost 2 years old. He is a very loving child, too. The years of being a mother, a grandmother, and now a great grandmother, have totally changed me. I have so much love for little ones! He set me FREE! HALLELUYAH!

In writing this autobiography, I've cried a lot, because of all the goodness of Abba! In my "detour" into a deep pit, though He had every right to, Abba never forsook me! He used everything to educate me in what I need now to carry out His will.

A good soldier must know the ways, thinking, nature, and plans of his enemy, or else he is not a good soldier. He must also know the nature, ways, thinking and plans of His Commanding Officer. **(II Timothy 2:3-5**) I think, at times, that He went overboard with my education of the plans, ways, nature, and thinking of the enemy. He had me thoroughly cover the subject--that's for sure! Often I would be reading another book on the plans of the Illuminati, martial law, and the takeover of America, or about Satanic rituals in the Vatican, and ask Abba: "Why do I have to keep learning about these things?" He always responded with something like: "Keep reading."

I know what is coming--from where, from who, for what purpose, and how it is to be done--and still He wants me to learn more. Why? Because over and over He has told me He will take me through it. [Please refer to my article "Through"/May 4, 2012]

It is not His nature to zap His people out of hardship and trials. It is **through** "tribulations" of all types that we become strong, mature, disciplined, toughened, and prepared for Kingdom business. It would be like putting a lollypop-sucking 8-year old on the front lines of battle and expecting them to do well. He has to train us. Read **Hebrews 12**! We have to grow up!

Wisdom comes from knowing the enemy well, but knowing the will of our Captain even better. In all my studying on the plans of the enemy, the one thing I have learned is **Isaiah 40-46**: Yahuweh is El Elyon (The Most High) and El Shaddai (the Almighty), and there is none else!

THE INTENSE SCHOOLING BEGINS

From early 1965, because I was so disheartened with finding out that Mainland China was closed, I fell into hopelessness. I felt that I lost my direction, so I fell prey to deceptive thinking that led to many years of detours. My stubborn mind had locked into going to Mainland China, and no amount of wisdom penetrated. The Proverb says: "**In a multitude of counselors there is safety**." I sought no counsel, and I was offered no council. But, being the headstrong person I was, I would probably have rejected council. At times people tried to warn me of possible danger, but I didn't listen.

All my friends were either getting married, signing on with mission boards, or preparing for jobs, and I was left, so I thought, on the roadside with no direction. I had wise alternatives but I either rejected them because of stubbornness, or because I was so naïve.

I had been dating a man for three years, beginning in 1963, whom I met at BIOLA. David had become the president of the Missionary Society. But, there were things he did that were not right, so I later broke up with him. He continued to be a friend, to this day, even though we live on two different continents.

PART III - The Journey is Sabotaged

One night, in my senior year of college, while ministering in my "Christian Service Assignment" with Open Air Campaigners, a man came from Florida to join us. He, and his Florida friend Ronnie, were bold preachers. The man I was dating was passive and not bold in proclaiming the "gospel" like these two men. I was impressed by loud passionate preaching. These new preachers wowed me with their boldness. I thought loudness and bold talk were signs of spirituality and fervor for "God." Wow, did I ever fall for deception! I was infatuated with Ronnie. He was very kind to me as a brother, but showed little interest in being my boyfriend. The man who became my husband was aggressive in pursuing me. He would make sure that I sat next to him at our fellowship table after the meetings. He was a flatterer. But, there were things in his personality that turned me off, to say the least. He was a good flatterer, and I fell for it. One day as I was leaving our group meeting to return back to college, I was talking to him and some other people. I said that my mother wanted to send me to Southwest Baptist Seminary in Fort Worth, Texas, to get my Master's Degree, (strange, but when Abba moved us to Texas in 1986, we lived not far from this Seminary). I thought my mother had a good idea. Too bad I didn't go to Texas! My to-be husband blurted out: "You can't go to Texas; I want you to stay here." I was flattered. Someone "liked me."

He said he had been a Baptist minister in the Air Force, and in Florida. He wrote a column for the Orlando Sentinel where his mother was the Editor. She was a good writer. His dad was a White House reporter under Truman. Both were successful people.

In Florida, after losing her third husband, his mother was left very poor. He worked as a bag boy in a grocery store to help pay their bills. Because of poverty, and his feeling that he was responsible to care for his mother, he was unable to go to college. He was very bitter over that. He worked hard to keep his mother from losing her house, car, and etcetera. Ronnie had also come from the same area of Florida, however, it wasn't until the group meetings that they met. Ronnie also had a tumultuous background.

The flatterer moved to California to stay with his dad, who had just gotten re-married. After my to-be-husband came to California, there arose problems between he and his dad, and his dad's new wife, so he moved to the BIOLA Hotel in downtown Los Angeles. This Hotel was a dormitory for students attending the nursing college of BIOLA. BIOLA had moved the main campus to La Mirada, and it was new and developing when I began to live on campus in one of the new dormitories. The campus was about 30 minutes drive from my home. So, I chose to stay in the dormitory. I went home on weekends and holidays. I had four wonderful roommates those four years.

In my sophomore year, I began working for the maintenance department cleaning bathrooms. I loved my job! I saved up $100.00 and made a money tree and gave it to my parents for their anniversary. In those days, my whole college education was about $2,000.00 for four years, so $100.00 was a lot of money.

In my junior year, working for maintenance, I was assigned to clean the office of the Dean of Talbot Theological Seminary, which was on the same property as the college. The Dean's last name was Feinberg. He was so particular that once he found a fly in the bathroom across from his office. He called maintenance to come get rid of it. I meticulously dusted his office, and he never once complained. I also dusted around manuscripts when Dean Feinberg and his associates were at lunch. Those manuscripts were the translation of the "New Testament" of the *New American Standard Bible*. Dean Feinberg and his associates were the translators. I considered that a high privilege.

The Dean spoke fluent Hebrew, Greek, Latin, and of course English. He was as Jewish as they come! Wow, was he brilliant! The Talbot Theological Seminary had a "dig" in Israel. I loved archeology and geology and the "Old Testament," particularly the Prophets. I often dreamed of going with them on the "dig." I even thought of going to the seminary to study archeology. I did study archeology and anthropology at Cerritos College years later, but I wonder what my life would have been like if I had stayed at BIOLA or at the seminary. Who would I have met and married? If I had gone to Taiwan, or Hong Kong, who would I have met or married? How would my life have been different? By all rational thinking, it would have been better. But, Abba had His plans for me, and taking me through hell and back out was part of them, so that He could break this vessel and remake it in His image and likeness. We reap what we sow. The only way to get out of that cycle from bad seed sown is to destroy the old crop, plow the field afresh, then replant it with good seed. **Galatians 6:7-8**: "**Be not deceived. Elohim is not mocked: for whatsoever a man sows that shall he also reap. For he that sows to the flesh, shall of the flesh reap corruption, but he that sows to the spirit, shall of the Spirit reap life everlasting**."

I thank Abba for seeing the end from the beginning: **Psalm 139:1-18; I Peter 1:2; Ephesians 1:4; Psalm 32:8** Hebrew Tehillim) "**I will educate you and enlighten you in the proper path to travel – I will advise you with what I have seen**."

I loved being on campus. I was happy. I had friends. But, my bubble would burst before I left. I dated Ronnie for a short while,

PART III - The Journey is Sabotaged

but in my confusion, thinking Ronnie didn't want me, and having broken up with David, my life took on a meaningless directionless course. There was a college retreat in the mountains that I went to in order to be with friends and try to clear my head. David was there. Though we had separated, we were still friends. I later found out from a friend that David probably wouldn't have married me, because he wanted lots of children. He figured since my mother only had one child, that I might not be able to have children. What a joke! I could have had twenty+ children easily. I am one healthy lady!

At this retreat David asked me what I had in mind for my future. He really believed I was called to be a missionary. He had been in the Marines for four years, so he was four years older than me. He had been in Taiwan, and met Vince and Virginia Gizzi, who were missionaries. I met them, and had a chance to go work in Taiwan with them. But, my heart was set on Mainland China. At the retreat I told David that I was in despair, **and I would probably marry the first man who came along**. I cursed myself with those words! **One day and one wrong decision can change your whole life**!

One weekend I stayed on campus. I was horribly bored. My friends had boyfriends, some were engaged, and my life had fallen apart in learning that I could not immediately get into Mainland China upon graduation. I walked by the pay phone in the hall of my dorm and thought about calling him. Finally, I decided "what the heck--what did I have to lose." I had the greater part of my life to lose, but I didn't know that then. I did not have a dime, so I borrowed one from my roommate, and called the flatterer. I can still see in my mind, standing there at that pay phone inserting the dime, and dialing the number he had given me. That was 1965. I learned much later that he had decided not to pursue me anymore. He figured I loved Ronnie. So, that phone call brought him back into my life.

I so strongly emphasize that we must not go by our own reasoning, or our emotions, but only ask the Spirit His opinion about everything. But, Abba knew, and Abba was watching. NO, I do not think that my downfall was His perfect will for me, or even His will for me at all. But, He had to let me reap the "fruit of my thoughts." He had to break my stubborn will.

At that time I also held deep hate for my father because I considered him a hypocrite. I judged him cruelly. I was proudly religious. And because of my lack of "honor" for my parents, He had to "take me down a notch, or two", or three – all the way to the bottom of the pit. I came out with tremendous love and understanding for my parents!

I'm sure Abba had some wonderful plans for me to teach me what I needed to know without my going through so much hell. He had to let me reap what I sowed. He had to break my headstrong bent. He had to humble me to the dirt. He had to let what was hidden within me run its full course. So, I am a very objective thinker today. I look back on all of this and am amazed that Yahuweh didn't throw me away. I am amazed that I can look back and realize that it was my decisions that caused my hell on earth. I could have escaped so many times, but was driven by almost paranoia, taking the form of a traumatic gripping fear of loneliness.

So I officially started seriously dating the one I'd marry. He did things that embarrassed me in front of other students, like the shabby way he dressed, and his depressed demeanor. I noticed that other students avoided him. He always looked so sad. He also had a "lazy eye," which made him look more sad. In the course of dating him, I found out that he had a very dark side. Students who lived at the BIOLA downtown L.A. dormitory told me that he was bringing prostitutes into his room, and they were heard screaming. Instead of listening to them, I was hurt by what they said. I took it that they were meddling in my life. My PMT leader-friends whispered among themselves so I could hear, saying that in dating this man I was on the "rebound from my breakup with David." That was not true. But, because of their gossip, I became defensive.

Later he told me that what the students said was true. He told me in detail what he did to these prostitutes. He also told me the stunts he pulled in the Air Force that almost caused them to give him a dishonorable discharge--trying to get his friends to feel sorry for him. The enemy without and the enemy within is either proud of what he does, or he hides it. He chose to be proud of it.

Before marrying his second wife, he told her everything he did to me, and even added more. She phoned me before marrying him and asked me if what he said was true. I told her "yes," but that he added things that were not true. She took him to her psychologist, who pronounced him very loving, and very normal. So she married him.

In the 60s, 70s, even 80s in some states, the laws were very flimsy on prosecuting husbands who abused their wives and children, unless the wife had bruise marks. I sustained every type of abuse you can imagine, all affecting me mentally and emotionally, which dehumanized me. The children were abused mentally and emotionally, but later I found out about other types of abuse carried out in secret. Today, I could have put him in prison for what he did to me and to our children. But, back then,

PART III - The Journey is Sabotaged

there was a covering of respectability that caused many hurting wives and mothers to remain silent, with little to no recourse for their abuse. The façade of religion also hides a lot of wickedness in Christian pastors, and other church leaders. The now uncovered history of Popes, Cardinals, Bishops, priests, and nuns, is so satanic that it would make the average person sick just to know of it. Abba once told me: "**Christianity is the mask of Satan.**" Truly **II Corinthians 11:13-15** is reality.

In dating him, I noticed that he was always making puns, telling jokes, and saying things that were nonsensical, even saying weird things that were beneath normal intelligence. I didn't like that. I had teacher-blood in me. But, he liked me. I felt sorry for him. I felt I could help him. Oh my, so many women fall into this pit.

The more I dated him, the more I was ostracized from my friends. He was very controlling. I didn't want to offend the one who "liked me." But, other people did not like that. He spoke to me often to demean me in public, even in front of my parents. So, I really did not like him a lot of the time, but he offered direction that I didn't have. It was the fun times that made me stay with him--he did have a delightful side.

In growing up, I did not learn self-respect. I did not learn to stand up for myself. I was prone to draw within myself around strong controlling personalities and just do what they said, no matter how angry I was inside. It may have been a result of the loud fighting my parents did at times. Up until just about 7 years ago, I cowered when people would yell at me, and I would make excuses for myself.

I made up in my head that perhaps God was arranging this relationship for me. I've come to understand that He did not arrange it, but He allowed it. He respects our will; He won't override our will. Truly, He uses everything to break us and re-shape us, so that our outcome is "a vessel unto honor." (**II Timothy 2:20-21**)

In college, because of my intellectual pursuit of knowledge about God, I had let go of my relationship that I had as a child with Him. He taught me to **know Him**, but religion taught me to seek **knowledge about Him**. Therefore I lost my personal relationship with Him. This is the trap of western mind-programming--knowledge is a god that takes the place of knowing the Elohim of the Scriptures personally, and being led by His Spirit like a little child. "A little knowledge puffs up" and brings pride, and Yahuweh won't dwell with our pride! I had a lot of knowledge, a lot of it from religious deception, but no wisdom.

Oh, yes, I was a straight "A" student in Bible. But, I substituted learning about God and the Bible, for knowing Him in simple faith. I had a fundamentalist Christian concept of Him--a theological understanding. I had faith, but it was the Christian variety--rooted in western culture--not in the culture that the Scriptures were written in. Oh the unlearning I had to do before He could start really teaching me! It is impossible to know the real Elohim of the Scriptures, the Elohim of Abraham, Isaac, and Ya'cob (Jacob) through western culture. Western culture thinks in abstract terms. Eastern culture thinks in tangible, real, concrete terms.

In early February, 1966, he asked me to marry him. I did not respond right away. I was confused, directionless, and empty of heart. But, using his manipulative and controlling personality he kept pressing me to make a decision, until one day, at my parent's house, he said that either I told him I would marry him or he would leave me right then. That panicked me. I saw nothing ahead of me but a gray empty swamp of nothingness. So, I sat with him on the couch, and he held me. I felt mental torment by demonic spirits. I became so confused. I thought that if I said "yes" the tormenting spirits would go away. I said "yes," but the tormenting spirits increased to my surprise.

To this day some people still tell me that they cannot be around him, because of the tormenting spirits that assail them. To this day some people still tell me that they cannot be around him, because of the tormenting spirits that assail them. To this day, if he comes into the home of one of our children where I am staying, after he leaves, it is at least a week of demonic manifestations, coupled with not sleeping well. Only after spiritual warfare, are we able to return back to normal. I did not know then what I know now, or I would have run away fast! But, then, I have self-respect now.

Years later Abba gave me a dream to let me know what really happened the night he gave me the engagement ring – February 19, 1966. The only friends I had were either secular, religious, or flighty Christians, and I never thought about going to my college counselor. Literal terror of loneliness went a long way to affect my decisions.

To show you how far back the loneliness went, by age seven, my mother would stand me on a footstool and let me hang up clothes outside on the back clothesline. The clothes pins were wooden, shaped like a rough human form with two thick legs, and with a knob-like head at the top. I would make sure that all those not used on clothes were in twos or threes on the line, for to me, even at that young age, for one pin to be by itself was something I would not allow.

PART III - The Journey is Sabotaged

Also at seven, I watched seven reruns of the movie "Heidi." I pretended I was Heidi. I would sit out on the back porch at dawn and pretend I was shepherding the sheep on the mountainside. That movie had a profound impact on my life. I identified with Heidi's loneliness. In 1996, I went to Switzerland on a tour, and we went to the Heidi memorial. It closed a door for me.

I had a friend years later, who had gone through a divorce, tell me: "You have to make friends with loneliness." I never made friends with loneliness, but I grew to appreciate times of being alone. I also love being with my family, and with Abba's people.

As I grew up, I was a "latch-key" kid. Because my parents both worked, and the fact that we didn't live very far from the elementary school, middle school, and the high school, I would walk home from school to an empty house. Upon getting home, the ice cream man would come with his singing truck. I would buy ice cream. One day I came home from school and felt that there was someone in the house. I was scared. The "ice cream man" had stopped outside the house and I asked him to come and help me. I gave him one of my dad's guns. Of course, there was no one there, but I lived with a lot of fear.

Needing affection, as a child and even into my teens, I "kissed the faces off" my dolls and stuffed animals. I am an affectionate person. I kissed my babies a lot. Now I love cuddling my grandchildren! Now I have a great grandson to cuddle! You that know me now see how I am towards my children and grandchildren, and how they love me. How great is Abba's mercy! How great is His patience. Without Him I would hate to think where I would have ended up. So I owe Him everything!

<u>**My testimony**</u>: **Psalm 40:2-3** <u>The Scriptures</u> version: "**He drew me out of the pit of destruction, out of the muddy clay, and He set my feet upon a rock, and He is establishing my steps. He put a new song in my mouth--praise to our Elohim. Many shall see and fear and put their trust in Yahuweh**..."

Psalm 113:7-8: "**He raises the poor out of the dust and lifts the needy from the dung hill that he might set him with princes, even the princes of His people**."

In 1984, I had reached such a state of despair I cried out amidst sobbing to Abba: "Pity me, pity me." His response was strong: "Pity you! No one will pity you! I will set you among the princes of My people." And I am happy to say that He has abundantly done that! No one pities me, and I do not pity myself!

After reading how I allowed the enemy to dig a deep pit in my life, you will praise Abba to learn how He brought me out. **He not**

only brought me out, He used the deep pit I dug with hate, to fill it up with His love.

The story of Richard and Sabina Wurmbrand is amazing. Richard started the Voice of the Martyrs. Richard was in prison for 18 years and Sabina for 14 years in Romania. Their crime was being a believer in Messiah, and being Jewish. At one point, Richard spent a long time in solitary confinement. After being released and Romania became free, Richard bought the solitary confinement prison, and used it to store Bibles and Bible-teaching materials in for distribution.

I also heard about Ulf Eckman. His Bible College in Sweden once was the warehouse used by Voltaire to print his blasphemous atheistic materials against "God." **Genesis 50:20**, Joseph speaking to his brothers: "**But, as for you, you thought evil against me. But, Elohim meant it for good, to bring to pass, as it is this day, to save many people alive**."

It is the nature of Yahuweh to take what the enemy does, and turn it to His esteem and honor, and the good of His people! The famous expression that came out of Joseph's statement is: "What the Devil meant for evil, Elohim has turned to good." So it was with me! You will marvel at His goodness to me! You will also marvel at how I tied his hands from helping me too. But, He never gave me over to death. He had the right to kill me many times for I crossed His boundary lines over and over, but He saw the end from the beginning. **Praise Him forever and ever!**

What is also so awesome is that He has delivered me from deep wounds in my spirit, mind, and emotions--from anger, bitterness, hate, despair, and deep depression! Today I live in peace and joy! Every day I get up with expectation of good. And, I respect myself. I have no more self-hatred. So as I report these things, I want you to know that I hold nothing against my ex-husband! I see him occasionally at family get-togethers, and we talk as civil people talk.

On the day of my grandson's wedding (2010), the family was later assembled at my oldest daughter's house. I sat on the couch, and my ex-husband sat at the other end of the couch. A man had driven he and his wife to Tennessee for the wedding, since his wife recently had surgery. This man began asking me questions about the Bible. I quickly began talking about the need to observe Torah. The anointing was very strong on me. Our children were sitting across the room with their spouses. They stopped talking. They listened. Father gave me His Presence so strongly, and what I said was powerful. But, my ex-husband said that he didn't believe we had to guard Torah. Afterwards, my

PART III - The Journey is Sabotaged

youngest daughter came, hugged me, and said: "Mom, we were so proud of you!"

At times, I pray for his deliverance. So, in reporting these things I have no negative emotions. I am just reporting facts. The only emotions I have come from deep in my spirit – because of my love for Abba Yahuweh and Yahushua.

When he forced me to flee from him in early 1996, my children were upset for my sake. One of them asked me if she should continue to see her father, or if I thought she should not see him. He had told her to leave the house after graduation from High School, after years of terrible inhuman abuse of her mind and emotions. She had done nothing but try to find his love for her, but he was brutally sadistic with her. He began at age 5 with cruel mind control to bring deep seeded negative emotions in her. So, as you can imagine, I was at a crossroads with her question. If I told her to not see him anymore, would I be violating the 5th Commandment? If I told her to see him, would he continue his cruelty to her? I said it like this: "He is your father. You must honor him as your father. You must not hate him. But, it is up to you if you want to see him. I won't tell you what to do." She was almost 19 at the time. She, and the other four continued to see him, and the portals are still open. I still wrestle with this question. Did I do right? The ensuing years show I did not. In telling her not to hate him, I did right, but their seeing him kept portals opened that almost caused the death of two of them, and has bound them emotionally and mentally to different degrees.

Some of you may have been married, or are still married, to Christian ministers who are hiding their deep sins under a cloak of false spirituality, so you know what I went through. Some of you may identify with some of my life in different aspects, and so my hope in telling these things is to give you hope and perhaps direction. Abba will deliver you, but first you have to want to be delivered, and you have to do your part in getting your freedom. I wrote "Homes Put to the Plumb Line," and "Family," in which I give wisdom to those bound in hurtful marriages.

I often wonder if the length of time I stayed in my situation had to do totally with my being mind-programmed into a submissive victim, or if it wasn't Abba holding my head underwater a little longer until I developed a strong enough desire to be delivered. I entered my marriage with a ton of my own baggage--that made me vulnerable to being controlled, manipulated, deceived, lied to, a "victim" of ritualistic satanic torture and abuses of all types. But, really, I always had an open door of escape. Truly **II Corinthians 10:13** is true: **"No trial has overtaken you except what is common to man, and Elohim is trustworthy, who shall not** allow you to be tried beyond what you are able, but with the trial shall also make the way of escape, enabling you to bear it."

I was a bird in a cage, but the cage door was always open! That's so hard for me to face at times, because I played the blame game so well! Yet, in 1985, when He finally showed me by a dream, the reality of what I'd done, saying "it has always been your own hand," I had to stop the blame game! Most of the time it is our own emotional disturbance that makes us think we are victims, and so we do nothing to get out of our situation. It develops into a "victim mentality," which is dangerous. I was also horribly insecure and terrified of being alone. I only knew the Christian world of my upbringing. I had little to no counsel from my parents, from my pastor, my youth director, my teachers, or my college Women's Dean either. So, I just went by what I thought.

In teaching now, I tell people "I do not think"--meaning that I only go by what my Abba has taught me, not allowing my human mind to dictate to me. In obeying Him, I have avoided so much trouble! My parents, without meaning to, often cut off communication. I tried sharing with my mother some of my feelings about things, but she reacted with some light-hearted statement that shut me down. I tried later in college to talk to her about a very serious problem that I was facing in my own life and I needed counsel, but my mother got indignant as I brought up the subject, and shut me down.

I do not remember my parents cuddling me, except for my dad when I was a little girl. I loved for him to carry me. He was 6'4" and I felt so tall in his arms. But once, when I was ten, we were approaching Dodge City, Kansas on a trip, and there was a terrible lightening storm. The night sky was lit up with streaks of lightening. I was so scared. I was sitting in the front seat of the car between my dad who was driving, and my mother. I cuddled up next to her for safety. But, I do not remember her hugs. I never doubted my parent's love however. Some people are just not the affectionate types, but that does not mean they are without love. And, then, I know that adults often do not remember affection from their parents. I am sure I had more affection from them than I remember. They were wonderful parents! But, even as a little girl, I craved hugs very much. That craving most likely went back to the doctors telling mothers not to pick up their children in the crib, if they were crying or screaming.

So, for whatever reason, I grew up not knowing how to express real love towards others--compassion, tenderness, caring towards others—even though I had love in me. I was often amazed how others could go to someone who had lost a loved one, for example, and put their arm around that person and talk to them in comfort. I could not see myself doing that. Now it is natural to console people who are hurting with hugs and prayer.

My roommate, in my third year at BIOLA, made pretty cards for sick students, and for lonely ones too. I was amazed that she did that. As a child I was called an "introvert." It took radical changes in my life to turn me into a balanced person – one who loves quiet times, but one who loves people too. I am one also, who, when need-be, can be an "extrovert." But, I tend to be quiet. I like my alone times. Yet, I love being a part of a family too.

I try to understand people. I don't judge. I try to see what is good and build on that. I am no psychiatrist or analyst, but Abba has taught me to understand the heart of people, to see behind their façade, or masks, if they have any. He gave me a strong "discernment of spirits" to understand not only "normal" human nature, but the activity of demons in people who appear to be normal. As the Spirit has grown stronger in me, I sometimes cause demonic spirits to manifest openly. It is often shocking when this happens, especially when I am with people I considered friends.

For our good, we must not live in the past, though I did for a long time. We can't live by "IF only," or "what if." The past is past, and Abba is a forward-moving Elohim. The past is our schooling for what is ahead. Sometimes people carry unforgiveness against someone in a little box that they keep in their heart. When they are feeling bad about themselves, they pull out the box, remembering all that someone did to them. By doing so, they renew emotional memories, and end up in despair. Many times in the middle of the night, upon awakening, the enemy would fill my mind with what someone did to me, or what I allowed to be done to my children that harmed them. I went through "the regrets" for years until Abba delivered me, especially over my mistakes with my oldest daughter, and allowing all my children to go through so much abuse.

My mother was a brilliant woman, but held bitterness inside until her death. She was ultra-talented. She wanted to be a linguist, and involved with politics, in Washington D.C.. But, her High School counselor in North Carolina, advising her about college, told her that women could be nurses, teachers, or Christian missionaries, but that politics was for the men. So, she chose to be a teacher. My dad said that in later years, while she was dreaming, she would wake him up in the night, beating on him saying something about disciplining naughty students. She quit teaching in the early 1960s because of discipline problems.

My mother condemned the Apostle "Paul" for being a chauvinist, because he put women down. I defended "Paul." Truly she was one "born out of due season." I learned something not long before she went into a nursing home that explained the deep-seated crying in my heart to be loved, held, cuddled, and accepted for me. I asked her, if when she was carrying me, she did not want me. I saw anger fill her face. She said that having me, ruined her career. In a way she did what I did--gave up what was in her heart to conform to what someone else said, and deeply regretted it. I have no box in my heart! Abba's big eraser has erased my sin, and forgiven me, so I cannot hold un-forgiveness against anyone else!

I remember one time at BIOLA I was very sick, and sick for a long time, with no sign of improvement. I prayed for healing, but it felt like God had gone on vacation--there was no indication that He heard me. He led me to read **Mark 11:25-26**. I realized that my un-forgiveness towards my father was blocking my healing, and His forgiveness of me. So, I went down the hall to the chapel. It was late at night and no one was there but me. I knelt down and spoke words of forgiveness over papa. The next morning I was totally well again.

One day, in 1987, while in mamma June's prayer class, she gently told me that there was someone I had not forgiven. I was hurt. I had no un-forgiveness against anyone. After the class, I got in my car and pondered what she said. I asked Abba: "Who is it that I have not forgiven?" He said to me: "It is you." I had not forgiven myself for what I had allowed in bringing on my own hurt and hurt for my children. He began healing me of self-hatred.

After getting engaged on February 19, 1966, just four months from graduation, my grades plummeted. I could have graduated magna cum laude. But, in preparing for the wedding, I just gave up studying. My to-be-husband was poor. He could only afford a $19.00 diamond ring. After giving me my $19.00 ring, he told me that he had given the girl he was going to marry, back in Florida, a very expensive diamond ring. He said she broke the engagement in order to be a missionary. Wow, that really hurt. I had given up being a missionary to marry him, and all I got was a $19.00 ring.

One morning I was making my bed in the dorm room, and Abba spoke to me the words of **Isaiah 54:17**. Later that day, I had to see the women's counselor, Ms. Hart, for approval to wear the ring. It was college law that if a woman got an engagement ring, she had to wait a month before she could wear it on campus. But, that morning, Ms. Hart told me I could wear it right away. Then she said: "The Lord has given me **Isaiah 54:17** for you." To

PART III - The Journey is Sabotaged

this day, I wonder what that really was all about, except perhaps it was prophetic of His plan for me, as He saw it in my future.

"'**No weapon formed against you shall prosper, and every tongue that rises against you in judgment you will prove wrong. This is the inheritance of the servants of Yahuweh, and their righteousness is from Me', declares Yahuweh.**"

So, I wore the ring, and word got around that I was engaged and was given the right to wear the ring. Some of the students wanted to see the ring, even students I did not know. One morning at our Chapel service, some were asking to see the ring in the row ahead of me. So I took it off to give it to them. They passed it around and snickered among themselves about the diamond being so little. Great Christians huh! They did not like my fiancé. That added to my bitterness, and drove me more to my decision to marry him.

One evening, about 25 years later, on the anniversary of our getting engaged, I had a dream--a "word of knowledge" from Abba about what really happened. In the dream I was entering a restaurant. I was looking for the hostess to seat me. A young man came up to me. He was a "skin-head." He had a semi-open shirt, and a swastika hung from his necklace. I followed him, and sat with him. At one point, he got up and sat by me, grabbed my left hand and shoved a ring on my left ring finger so hard that it hurt me. There were other aspects to the dream that told me what really had happened that night in 1966, but later, my husband would confirm the dream.

My husband later told me that he thought he was the incarnation of a Nazi torturer and it was his delight to carry out his "assignments." He also told me that he was the incarnation of a Catholic Inquisitor in the Spanish Inquisition, who delighted in torturing Jews. It is curious. His grandparent's and father's last name was Gross. I found out that this was a name taken by Jews who had fled to Germany, escaping the Spanish Inquisition. The Germans made them take a name that described their family. "Gross" in German means large. His grandparents said they were Germans. If so, they were very aristocratic Germans. They were wealthy. But, in all of their decisions, and their decisions for their son, they acted Jewish. After divorcing my husband's father, his mother changed his name to the name of her new husband. In the Air Force he had a chance to change his name back to Gross but he didn't, and his grandparents cut him out of their inheritance.

My mother planned the wedding with me. We did have fun together. She did not approve of my choice in a man, to say the least. But, if she had given me her counsel, would I have received it? Most likely not! She had tried to give me counsel about a college, but I strongly opposed it. She had wanted to send me to a fine ladies "finishing school" in the Northeast U.S. That sounded boring to me. Wondering again: What would have happened to me if I had gone to a lovely women's "finishing school" in the north east, as she wanted? Who would I have married? What would my life have been like? Oh how easy it is to lapse into "what ifs." But, this is why I am so submissive to the direction of the Spirit, and have been since the early 1990s, growing ever more submissive in Jordan. I trust His judgment and wisdom for my life! He has done nothing but be kind and good to me!

I chose an expensive wedding gown. In those days it cost $100.00. It was gorgeous. My mother and papa had saved up $2,000 dollars for the wedding, cashing in insurance policies. My mother never let on, but she not only disliked my fiancé--she had grown to hate him. She saw too many signs that he was "not right." But, she respected my will. Unfortunately, Abba respected my will, too. Papa liked him because my to-be-husband had a fine façade of spirituality that fooled a lot of people, including papa. After my mother died, my Aunt Ahnie said that my mother hated him. She said my mother was very full of pride, and he embarrassed her.

My church had never taught me about the "depths of Satan," so my naivety was incredible. (**Revelation 2:18-25**) The "depths of Satan" are connected to Jezebel. The spirit of Jezebel can be in women, and in men. The python/anaconda spirit of Apollo/Apollyon, the coming "Beast" (anti-messiah) of **Revelation 13**, is also associated with the Jezebel spirit. This was the principle spirit that sought to destroy me, and took me into the "depths of Satan." She hides (as a "mystery") but is the "mother of harlots." (**Revelation 17**)

After I was forced to flee from him in early February of 1996, my husband told me that he would send his spirits after me to "dog my steps the rest of my life and I would never escape him." From 1996 to this day, everywhere I have gone I have encountered his spirits in other people. So I continue to encounter and do spiritual warfare over Jezebel spirits, to this day. Jezebel is also the mother of witchcraft! The practice of witchcraft against me has been great. I have been attacked many times by witchcraft almost to my death. I will explain a little about this further on.

The spirit of witchcraft has risen over the earth to a high degree, and it will increase. There is an insanity that accompanies witchcraft--a person will do anything to get what they want, with no shame--just as Jezebel had Nabot killed to get his small vineyard. As one man put it, behind Jezebel comes Leviathan (the Great Dragon from the sea – the Beast). Twice now, once in 2006 and once in 2011, I was at the ancient ruins of Jezre'el where Jezebel lived. I saw the area where Nabot had his vineyard, and where Jezebel was thrown by her servants off the palace wall and eaten by her own dogs. Unfortunately, I learned all too late that the Christianity of my growing up and early adulthood was so backwards in understanding anything beyond John 3:16 and pot-luck suppers, that they had no concept of the realities of the kingdom of Lucifer. The façade of false spirituality has blinded so many to the truth.

II Corinthians 11:12-15: "...Satan himself masquerades as an angel of light! It is not surprising, then, if his servants also masquerade as servants of righteousness..."

In 1995, the worse year of all, I thought I could confide in a long-time friend who told me she thought her husband was having an affair with a lady in their church. So, I gave her a miniscule few sentences about what I was going through. She later called another one of my best friends and told her what I said. Then they called my husband to tell him what I said. You cannot imagine my punishment for that! What the enemy has hidden is now gushing out publically, being proclaimed from the housetops – on T.V., in movies, in books, in magazines, etc. Human sacrifice to Satan in the Vatican? -- Oh yes! Ministers having affairs? -- Oh yes. Pedophiles and homosexuals, in the ministry – Oh yes! Witches and warlocks hiding in the churches, even in the ministry – Oh yes! I take comfort that Messiah has said that in our day everything hidden will come to light!!! (**Mark 4:22**)

In 2001, Abba began my research on the pagan roots of Christianity. He brought me the research material in most unusual ways. It took months to pull it all together, but in the end, the study "The Foundation of Deception" was completed.

While driving a borrowed truck one day, going to teach at a home in Texas, Abba spoke to me: "**If the root is defiled, the tree is defiled, its branches and leaves are defiled, its fruit is defiled, and everyone who eats of it is defiled**." The word "defiled," from the Strong's Exhaustive Concordance, Hebrew Dictionary, #2930: "to be foul, contaminated, defiled, polluted, to be utterly pronounced `unclean" as a leper. Impurity, filthiness, vile ..." I had to realize that Yahuweh and Yahushua Yahuweh have NOTHING to do with religion. All religion is defiled, its roots going into the mind of Lucifer himself. [Refer to my article:

"Religion – Lucifer's Detour to Ignorance and Damnation"/September 28, 2009]

In 1989, I furthered my education by returning to my study of the end-times through studying with an ex-Satanist friend of mine, Ken. He gave me a book that was very deep in the occult, written by Scottish Rite Masonic guru, Manly P. Hall - a book that sits by the Satanic Bible in bookstores. He had hexed it on both ends. I had asked this man, who became my friend and encourager in the study of end-times, why Satanists copied the Mass of the Roman Catholic Church. I will never forget it. He leaned back in his chair, folded his arms, and got a "Cheshire Cat" grin on his face, and said: "It's the other way around."

Ken had been a powerful Satanist, a leader of many covens. His voice was so deep and powerful that it caused many to tremble. He was preparing to receive the incarnation of a principle demon. In preparing his speech, he mistakenly whispered the words of the Invocation outside of the pentagram, and, as he said, he smelled the demon before he saw him. I know that "smell" – the smell of sulfur/"brimstone." That week Pentecostal preachers had been at his door preaching the "gospel" through the door, and he heard some of it. In smelling that demon, he knew he was about to be torn into shreds. He called out "Jesus" and fainted. Ken told me that in Satanism, the name "Jesus", is used to dispel demons, but also to call them. But, in this case he was thinking of the "Jesus" preached by the Pentecostal preachers. When he awoke, he crawled on his hands and knees into the bathroom to see if he was intact. Then he humbly repented and found salvation.

He offered his assistance to the Fort Worth Police Department to help them find missing children who were being kept in cages for sacrifice at Halloween. He wrote a booklet exposing Halloween, and the human sacrifice that goes on. This is why as a service to parents whose children were in my youngest daughter's class at school, I took their children home after school rather than their walking home alone, especially during the time of Halloween.

Ken and his wife attended our church. He began an end-time prophecy class in his home, which we diligently attended each week. Our pastor allowed me to teach an end-time prophecy class in the church which lasted two years. From his answer about the Catholic Church, I began studying. There were many 33rd degree Masons in my mother's family. My oldest daughter's father-in-law was a Scottish rite Mason, and her husband was considering joining the Lodge. I tried to tell her how to talk to him to discourage him from doing it. I prayed. He didn't join. But, all of

PART III - The Journey is Sabotaged

this is tied together--the occult, the Vatican, Satanism, and the Masons. They're all in bed with each other.

Ken loaned me Manly P. Hall's book: *Masonic, Hermetic, Qabbalistic and Rosicrucian Symbolical Philosophy – An Interpretation of the Secret Teachings concealed within the Rituals, Allegories and Mysteries of all Ages*. These secret teachings inspired Madame Blavatsky, who inspired Hitler. These stolen "secrets" go back beyond the Flood of Noah's day at a time when Lucifer and his fallen angels gave Yahuweh's secrets to fallen man. Yahuweh's secrets were then perverted and twisted to fit into Lucifer's plans to destroy Yahuweh and His people – plans that now exist in the forefront of the minds of Luciferic world leaders. The book of *Enoch I* tells about these stolen secrets, which His enemies have used to pervert His people. Know this: His wrath will come upon the earth, and His enemies will be chained in the depths of the lake of fire forever.

Abba has also made sure that I got information from psychiatrists explaining what happens to children who are demon possessed at a very early age – how they split into many personalities, lose their own identity, and open portals for demonic activity. Some children "freeze" at an early age because what they see is too terrible for them to handle. Thus, they split into other personalities to defend themselves. The tragedy is that unless delivered they continue on through their life like that. Their "powers" in the demonic realm often become their security, even their identity, including their power to control others. He made sure I also got information that explained naturally and spiritually what I was going through, like Bobbi Jean Merck's book: *Spoiling Python's Schemes*. Wow, it told the story of my life. When I finished the book, I was so angry at the python/anaconda spirit that had controlled my life, that I began doing spiritual warfare against it. That was a stupid thing to have done. It was like I was taking a table knife to the tail of a sleeping T-Rex. Within half an hour, two of my children were almost killed in car accidents, and my daughter-in-law lost her baby. She said she went into the bathroom, and everything became dark. She heard evil laughter. Then she felt a tight band go around her waist, and she miscarried the baby. In spiritual warfare, we stay within the boundaries that Abba has set up for our protection, and only do warfare if He backs it with His authority – otherwise, we're out there on our own.

My friends at church were so terrified at my exuberance in studying such material that they told the senior pastor and an evangelist pastor (both dear friends). These two men trusted me--that I knew what I was doing--and told my lady friends so. It is amazing now, that the writings of Manly P. Hall are being studied by many Christians, and the truth about the purposed destiny of America is being exposed as well as the plans of the secret societies and its Illuminati backers. I wrote an article using one of his books: "America's Secret Destiny"/January 25, 2009.

In the 1990s, it was as if the lid came off the hidden things of darkness, and the light began shining and exposing things. It was in the late 1990s that so many of the House of Israel, trapped in Christianity, began throwing off the darkness of religious deceptions and coming to the true knowledge of the Covenant Torah of Yahuweh.

Before understanding the truth about Halloween, which I learned one Halloween night from a teaching by John Jacobs on TBN, followed by a booklet from Ken, Halloween was one of my favorite holidays. I dressed up a lot as a witch. I even used Halloween to go door-to-door and hand out Gospel tracts. I put Gospel tracts in trick-or-treat sacks. I took my children "trick-or-treating."

In my sophomore year at BIOLA I was the organizer of the sophomore Halloween party. It was a big success. I even had a haunted house set up in the hall of the home we met in. I put my face into cold cream, then put it in flour, drew black circles under my eyes, donned a white cape, and went to the party as a ghoul. That was before I lived in a haunted house. So, I can understand why naïve people keep celebrating it. We just were never told it was real. I learned how real it is from Ken who was able to tell the police about the kidnapped children kept in cages all over Fort Worth. Halloween is a high witches' "shabbat" in which they do human sacrifice. It is over three days- until the night of November 2nd.

Ken gave me a copy of a booklet he wrote exposing Halloween and giving his testimony. This was all part of my finding out what I had been living with all those years. I took Ken's booklet to my youngest daughter's third grade teacher. She read it and stopped all Halloween celebrations with her class. Good for her!

Right now, I am writing this part and it is October 30, 2012. I am in Israel. Tomorrow morning is October 31st. I am going to Jerusalem to celebrate the opening of Abba's Sukkot by His ancient timing. This Sukkot, which begins at sunset on October 31st, is a historic turning point in the history of mankind.

One day, after studying Manly P. Hall's book that Ken had given me, Abba spoke gently to me: "Put the book down." I set it on the floor. He then asked: "Now, what did you learn from your study?" I replied: "I learned **Isaiah 40-46**. I learned that there is no God

PART III - The Journey is Sabotaged

but You – that You are the Creator, and You are all powerful, and I must not worship any other God but You!"

In 1966, after my graduation from BIOLA, we got married in a fine church wedding at Temple Baptist Church. The church was filled with family and friends. I did not know until later that my husband had contemplated running from the wedding that morning. We had a good honeymoon, going to San Francisco for a week. I was so hopeful that we could serve God together. But shortly after we were married, the bubble popped, the naivety left, and I realized what a horrible thing I had done. I so wanted to be a good wife. I tried very hard at it. I wanted to be loved, but found only sadism and cruelty in return. I gave in to his control, and the psychological and emotional wounds began to multiply.

I continued to preach on the streets and do evangelism. I handed out tracts in shopping centers; and places like China Town in Los Angeles. I did door-to-door witnessing. I did "children's ministry." I ministered in healing and deliverance services. I taught the Word in churches, in women's groups, and in homes. I played the piano and directed choirs.

My dear mother! At age 10, my mother started me on piano lessons. I was lazy in practicing so often she'd "whop me" with the yardstick -- that's old fashioned American slang! But, I did end up playing the piano, and teaching piano for 25 years. Thank you momma!

In November of 1966, I was baptized in the Spirit, as I have related above. Initially, we moved into an apartment near where my parents lived. My husband had no money, so I paid for it with money I had saved from working at the Post Office. I was highly disciplined even back then, in some things. I knew how to save money. I was always very frugal because of some years of poverty that my parents went through.

We continued to fellowship with Ronnie, and our new friend David Reimer. I loved Brother David, but he hurt me--he made fun of us living in such a luxurious apartment. It was not luxurious at all, but he lived in a trailer. After three months when the money ran out, we moved to Glendale, and got an apartment. My husband got an office job right away. I asked him if they wanted anyone at his office to empty the trash cans. I was so bored. I had a college degree, but a Church Music Major and a Bible Minor were useless in the secular world. So, I went to a job-finding agency. They wanted $300.00 to get me a job. I agreed, and they found me one as a file clerk in an office.

To my horror, after finally getting me away from my parents, my husband began to practice, what I now know was ritualistic sadistic sadomasochism on me. Nothing in my Christianity had prepared me for that. I have learned that what I went through was "ritualistic satanic torture." It began the slow process of dehumanizing me. Until I got married, I had never even seen a naked little boy, let alone a naked man. I did not even know what a male penis looked like. On my wedding night, I was really shocked. There was no love involved on both parts. I just knew that I had direction for my life--I was married to a minister.

No one told me I had a will that I could use to choose things that I wanted. My mother dressed me as she wanted me to look. I just went along with it. I grew up pleasing my parents, my teachers, my church leaders, my friends, and a church-created God. By pleasing others I thought I had "peace." No one taught me that I should stand up for myself, or that I had the right to choose what I liked. I had a perverted understanding of giving myself to God. I thought that meant doing what everyone wanted me to do. I figured my calling to serve God on the mission field was over. My husband had no desire to go to the mission field.

In 1988, in an evening church service at Grace Temple in Fort Worth, a minister came to speak to us – a former pastor of my Aunt Ahnie and her family. His topic: "God gives us back our dreams." Abba restored my calling to the mission field that night. Thank you David Shibly!

Ignorance is NOT bliss! -- What you don't know can really hurt you! Getting me alone away from my parents, my husband began to release the darkest of his many personalities. After the first horrifying session of torture, I knew I had to do something. I was not totally dehumanized at that point. So, I seriously thought of an annulment. But, then, I thought of all that money that my parents had spent on the wedding, and I did not want to hurt them, or shame them in front of their friends. I did not get the annulment because I respected my parents. Looking back, it would have been a small price to pay for freedom. I never told my parents what was happening to me. To the day of his death my dad thought my husband was a righteous and good Christian man, and could not understand why I was so hostile towards him. My mother knew a few things, but I never told her.

As time went on, I became frozen in my mind. There was no sanity in what I was experiencing. But, since he mixed it all so well with Christian spirituality I stayed confused. I thought he was born again. But, I soon found out he had many personalities. So, actually, I never knew who I was living with. One moment he might be a wonderful man who was good to me, and the next moment, quite the opposite. It was the good days that kept giving me hope! I knew he did not love me. But, I did grow to love him. Maybe I experienced the "Patty Hurst Syndrome," I don't know.

PART III - The Journey is Sabotaged

Maybe part of it was I felt so sorry for the little boy that had been so rejected from birth. Later I will tell what happened to him as a little boy that caused the splitting of personalities. But, because of the good times that were interspersed with the very bad, I had consigned myself to staying with him. I saw no way out without hurting someone else. Yet, in trying to please others, I hurt myself more than anyone else.

I found out years later that he married me because I had everything that he didn't, and he wanted to take it from me. He was insanely jealous of me. I had two good parents, a stable home, a college education, friends, and favor with people. He knew I was genuine, so he tried to copy me so that others would think well of him. It is the spirit of Jezebel that carries an insane spirit of jealousy and competition. Just like the story of Nabot's vineyard at Yizre'el, those with the spirit of Jezebel want what others have, and if they can't get what they want, they take extreme measures to get it. Jealousy rides this spirit, to the point of driving people insane to get what they want!

One of the main characteristics of a Jezebel spirit is that a person has no remorse for what they do. In **Jeremiah 3:3** Abba calls that a "whore's forehead." Years later I asked him if he ever felt any sorrow for anything he ever did to me, or to the children, and he mockingly sneered at me, and said "NO!" I became my husband's "front man." He hid behind my favor with Christian leaders, and so assured himself a place in that favor. You would not believe how many women, and men too, have tried to do that by feigning friendship with me to advance their own ministries. I call it "piggybacking"--riding a successful person to get a hidden agenda fulfilled. They don't want to pay the price required for Abba's favor, so they try to usurp from those who have paid the price!

It is the spirit of Mystery Babylon Mother of Harlots (**Revelation 17**) who "rides the Beast" – the spirit of religion has always ridden politics and economics, and well-thought-of people to get what it wants. In 1995, he applied to get a PhD from Letourneau University. By writing a thesis and paying $3,000.00 he could get a PhD. We owed back rent, but he used our rent money to buy the PhD. The majority of the thesis was from my writings on the end times. When they sent his certificate with the PhD, they wrote in a letter saying that his wife should be getting the PhD, because almost all of it was my writing. He had given me credit for the information. So, I became the front-man--the one who held the mask in place.

While I was dating him, early 1966, he was asked to speak at our Baptist church. He had memorized a sermon by a famous

Scottish minister--Peter Marshall. He delivered it word for word, with a Scottish accent. My mother and I were so ashamed. To this day, he memorizes sermons and teachings from popular ministers, and then repeats them as his own. It is called "plagiarizing." In all the years we were married, I only saw him read the Bible one time, and that was to find a subject to preach on.

One day in 1996, after having fled from him, I was out walking and listening to a sermon by Joyce Meyers on my headset. In getting back to the apartment I had rented, I found that someone had sent me a copy of a sermon that he had written out. It was identical to the message, word-for-word, that I heard on my headset while walking, yet he signed his name to it, as his own writing.

About three months into our marriage, my husband told me that he wanted to join "Club Wow" – a sadomasochistic club in Los Angeles. I was so hurt. I prayed that he wouldn't. In dismay, I kept all this inside. At this time, also, he told me he wanted a divorce. I should have done it! But I didn't do it. So, again: "What if?"

About four months into our marriage, his mother came to visit us from Florida, with his half brother, Patrick. The woman was very strange to me. She said strange things. She told my dad that she loved cigarettes so much that she could eat them, and she demonstrated that with her hands. She had so spoiled the half-brother that he delighted in being sadistic with me--even lying about things that I said, making his mother angry with me. Finally, they packed up and left. Ronnie drove them to the airport. He said that the reason she gave for leaving was that I left "good milk out on the counter." He said she was in a hysterical state when she left. Before she died, we became friends, for which I am grateful. I am glad that before the brother died, we became friends also.

Before getting married, the only birth control method I heard of was "the pill." It was the latest popular method then. I went to my Catholic doctor and asked for a prescription for the pill. He was angry about it. He told me what the pill did to a woman's body. He also warned me that if I went off the pill my chances of getting pregnant quickly were very high. I was very upset at what he told me, so I went then to a secular doctor to get the pill. But, in questioning the secular doctor, he sheepishly admitted that what my Catholic doctor had told me was true. Of course the secular doctor prescribed the pill for me.

After being married six months, I got very uneasy about the pill, remembering what my Catholic doctor had said. I later

PART III - The Journey is Sabotaged

learned it was really an abortion pill. I stopped taking the pill, and as he had warned me, very quickly I got pregnant. Because of stress, I had gotten down to 115 pounds. In Glendale, I went to a Seventh Day Adventist doctor, associated with the big Seventh Day Adventist Hospital. My new doctor, Dr. Gaspar, knowing I was underweight, didn't say anything about my craving for tuna sandwiches, salads with Green Goddess dressing, and of course onion rings and chocolate malts. I got up to 150 pounds. I was 5' 7 1/2" tall, with medium bone structure. So, my doctor felt it OK for me to gain the weight. I had been too thin.

My husband delighted in throwing me on the floor on my belly, tying me up and torturing me until I screamed. I cried and cried-- what would become of this child? I was afraid to tell anyone what I was going through. Only those who have been through such things would understand. Today, as a whole new person, I would not have even dated him once. In my Baptist mind, however, he had "prayed the Dear Jesus prayer" to go to heaven, so I figured he was born again. I learned years later that praying a prayer means nothing unless the Spirit does those 40 things in us to transform us into a new creation – it is a sovereign act of Yahuweh. (**II Corinthians 5:17**) Yet, interwoven with all of that, there were so many miracle stories of His intervention. This is what kept me with him – hope. You can read about some of the amazing miracles of provision in Part VII, Miracles of Provision.

It was the spring of 1967. I could not stand that boring file clerk job anymore, so I got a job working at the Forest Lawn Mortuary Hollywood Hills Park. Our little baby girl was born on November 18, 1967. Forest Lawn gave me two months "sick leave." I felt the responsibility to work. I had the idea that if I didn't help to make money, I was useless. I know now that this came from the subtle mind-programming of the American youth, for the goal of the Illuminati mind programmers is to create a Feudalistic state worldwide of the ultra rich and their slaves.

So, I returned to work when my little girl was two months old. It was during the Vietnamese War. Many dead soldiers were brought to us for burial. One day, I was taking a "first call" up to the third floor, to give to the men who would pick up a body. It was in the embalming area. I walked past many dead bodies. But, there on a table, was a baby. Its little face was turned away from me. I saw what I thought was a little braid across her head. I went over to look at this baby. I stood there numbed. She looked identical to my little girl--both about the same age. The braid was not a braid at all, but stitches from an autopsy. For some reason, she had not been named yet - so they called her "Baby Sunquist."

I never forgot baby Sunquist. I was so distraught anyway that my little baby had come into a very bad world.

We were horribly poor. But, my husband was good about working. I have to say that he was not lazy. However, he seemed obsessed with keeping us in debt. He loved to borrow money to do things that were unnecessary. He loved giving people money that we needed, to make himself look good. So, we were in a state of dire poverty. I had hope for our marriage until the day I had to sign the divorce papers because he was marrying someone else. But, Abba was faithful through it all. No one can rightfully judge Yahuweh unfair, unjust, or unfaithful!

In 1966, my husband got a job as a funeral attendant at the famous Forest Lawn Glendale Park – the one where all the stars are buried. One day Walt Disney died and his funeral was to be at this Park. He was cremated, and put in an urn. The funeral was to be blocked off except for a few friends and family. My husband was asked to be an attendant on this funeral. It was while he worked at this Forest Lawn Park that he met some wonderful people who became good friends.

One night, after I was baptized in the Spirit, I went with Ronnie and David by myself to preach on the street since my husband didn't want to go. I was on the verge of telling them what my husband was doing. I know they would have intervened and my life would have been very different. But, I held back. In those days, you didn't tell what others did--it was not socially acceptable. I was also so ashamed. At this time, I became a children's Bible teacher through the religion department of the public school. If a family wanted me to teach their children the Bible, the school would let that child out early one day a week, and I'd go to their home.

So, I see His hand in everything, even the most horrible things. I know now that it is His love that allows the "tribulum" to be raked over us, so that the chaff (our own sins "that so easily beset us," our fleshly desires that keep us in bondage to the Devil--and keep us from Yahuweh) must be broken off the wheat so that He might gather His wheat into His barns at the coming of Messiah (**Matthew 3:11-12**).

I loved working for Forest Lawn--never a dead, I mean dull, moment! I worked arranging funerals, dealt with the family counselors, and even worked, like Lily Tomlin, answering the switchboard. Remember her on Saturday Night Live? -- "Is this the party to whom I am speaking?" Those were the days when comedy shows were funny. Back then, even that show was good fun.

PART III - The Journey is Sabotaged

It was at this Park that I worked with an older Mormon lady named Maude Zendell. Her view of family showed me a life that I wanted so desperately. She and her husband loved each other and so closely worked together on everything--and it was genuine. They had such a lovely family, too, that was so unified.

I also worked with a very sweet Jehovah's Witness lady. In my growing up I would usually not talk to them, and if I did, it was in anger. But, she confided in me that she thought she was one of the 144,000 born again ones. In that religion only 144,000 can be born again. I thought she might be born again, but was trapped in that demonic religion of Judge Rutherford--33rd degree Mason. She longed to know God. We became friends.

After I was baptized in the Spirit, and our daughter was born, we started going to a little "full-gospel" church in Glendale. Our Pastor was Leroy Hux. He, and his wife Katy, and their daughter Molly, became close friends to us. Molly was in her 20s when she got cancer from a wound on her leg, and decided not to have an operation. Abba showed me in a vision that she would die. I love these precious people! They were so pure of heart. Molly was a testimony to her faith to everyone in the hospital and to those who came to visit her.

Now that I know the Elohim of Israel, I realize that though she was strong in faith for her healing, she had not heard from the Spirit. He often gives us alternative means of healing. Sometimes He even uses doctors and medicines. So, she did not have to die. Today cancer, heart disease, and doctor/nurse "fowl ups" are the three main causes of deaths in America. But, these things can all be treated by natural means. And Abba expects us to be wise and astute--always learning from the Spirit, and listening to His wise and good direction.

Later I learned another lesson that cleared up false charismatic religious teaching. Just because a promise is in the Bible for someone else, or in general, doesn't mean we can claim it for ourselves anytime we want to for our own purposes. The Spirit has to tell us that it is for us – then we hang on to what He says to us. But, because people do not know Him, they listen to their own head and presume on Him to do for them what they want. I have to have the Spirit tell me what to do, or I won't do it. He turned my stubbornness into a good channel. He finally led me to the ultimate submission to His will, in which I said: "You are Elohim and I am not." You'll read the story of that serious encounter in Part VI.

From the first of our time in Glendale, from 1966, we had friends who helped us, who brought us groceries or put money in our mailbox. But, then, we played "the game" with Him. The more we gave, the more He gave back. We called it "the game" because we would put our last $5.00 in the offering, and the next day, someone would put $10.00 in the mailbox. So, we put $8.00 in the offering or gave it to some other poor person, and He would have someone give us $15.00. It brought joy in the midst of so much chaos.

In giving birth to our first baby, I was in hard labor with her for 17 hours. I remember they kept me sedated a lot. Upon awakening one time, so that the nurse could poke me to get blood, she said she had a message from my husband. My husband had said: "The Lord has been to the mail box." I remember smiling, for I knew what that meant. Through the years, my husband misused money a lot. But, his final dealing with me regarding money set me free to follow the Master. For what he did in 1996, I still bless him, and still have hope for him.

When I went into labor, my doctor had gone on vacation, so his brother, and the hospital team, took over. They kept putting their arms up inside of me to turn her to get her into birth position. She was lying sideways, doing leg kicks. Finally they used "forceps" on her temples to pull her out. Nowadays they won't do that. Too many forceps slipped and caused brain damage or neck injuries. Now, they just order a "C-section" which, except for rare needed emergencies, is not good! Because my doctor was on vacation, all of that special assistance was free. My total bill for the doctor, and the hospital, was $300.00, and my parents paid that.

After she was born, and they cleaned her up, they wheeled her into my room in a little glass crib, and placed it near the end of the left side of my bed. She just stared at me. I wondered in sorrow what would become of that little life. At that time, breast feeding was still not accepted. So I bottle-fed her with an awful cow-milk formula. Cow milk is designed to grow a baby calf up into a 300 pound cow quickly. It was never meant for humans. Sheep and goat milk is fine. I wish I had known the joys of breastfeeding, cuddling her and loving her as a good mother should. She also had a bad case of colic from the formula. I had to read a book to find out why she was crying. I knew nothing about babies. The book was Dr. Benjamin Spock's infamous book on raising children, but it was good for what I needed it for.

My mother came to help me. One day, I was trying to take a nap while she slept. My mother was cleaning the kitchen. My husband came into the bedroom, which was just off of the kitchen, and began slapping my stomach. It made a loud noise. Then he would laugh. I was so tired. He kept on slapping my stomach and laughing. I kept saying "stop it." My mother heard, and thought he was beating me.

PART III - The Journey is Sabotaged

When my little girl was 5 months old, like her dad, she had a "lazy eye." So, my mother and papa took her for a few weeks to their house, and kept her under a lamp, where she stared into the light, and it straightened her eye. My daughter has always had such a special love for my parents, whom she named "Nana" and "Gramps." Today, she is the mother of my oldest grandson, and the grandmother of my great grandson. She has chosen to be called "Nana." In Hebrew, "nana" means "mint"--a fragrant, life-giving herb that is pleasant to be around, used in cooking and teas.

Because of the stress of graduation from college and my wedding, I was a nervous wreck. I dropped between 114 to 120 pounds. Because of all the stress after my daughter was born, I dropped from 150 to below 120 pounds again. I was so tired all the time, and only 22 years old. But, after a couple of months, I thought I had to get back to work at Forest Lawn. I did not know I had options. I tied my breasts up with a towel to stop the flow of milk, and bottle fed her. Something happens psychologically to both mother and child when a mother does not breast feed. The baby needs the cuddling to develop security and confidence, as well as the nutrition. The mother needs the joy of feeding her own baby. It is a time of bonding. I know some women can't breast feed, like my second daughter, after adopting her little girl. But, she made sure she cuddled that baby up very tightly and bonded with her.

Yet, even as a tiny baby, lying in her crib, my husband's incredible sadism was practiced on our little girl. He would hold his hand over her face, and press down, until she screamed. By the time she was five, my little girl had been set for a life of suffering. My husband told her at age five that if he and I ever got a divorce, it was her fault. He filled her with such overwhelming accusations, and left her dehumanized. She went from a happy little girl to a very sad little girl. I did not know how to be a compassionate mother. As much as I cuddled and kissed my stuffed animals, I had never cuddled a baby. To me, a baby was added responsibility, not much more. I had not been cuddled as a baby. I did not realize until later that being a mother is being a part of Abba's creation process, to envelop that new life with love and tenderness – the highest privilege that any human can have.

As a baby, she had serious colic, and cried very much. At least I knew to pick her up. But, I was so nervous and stressed out. The ritualistic sadistic torture--verbally, mentally, emotionally, sexually and physically--added to the stress. I had no peace. I tried to please my husband and obeyed all the rules he set. But, he changed rules so often, and never told me they were changed, so I was always guilty of not obeying. So, I transmitted my nervousness, my stress, and my unhappiness, to my baby. I screamed at her also when my nerves got bad. She began to be traumatized by both parents by the age of 1. I did not know how to show love, even though I loved her very much. One day I knelt by the couch to pray for her, and Abba gave me **Psalm 91:14-16** to pray over her.

After she was born, we had a short time before we had to get out of the apartment we were in because of rules against children living there. So, we moved to another house--a little old cottage-style house behind another house in Glendale. I took a job as a second grade school teacher at Village Christian School, a private school, in Sun Valley. I learned about the position from friends at our Assembly of God church in Sun Valley. Because of my work, I left her with babysitters. At that time, since she was not yet a year old, they came to our house. One day, just before leaving for work, waiting on the babysitter to come, I got a call from the babysitter saying that she knew who my daughter was – a midget that had been in a circus, and that she could no longer babysit her. I was so horrified. I had been leaving my baby with a mentally deranged woman. I desperately called another lady whom I did not know, who said she would watch her. The whole first year, she had many babysitters, and some were not good. One day I went to pick her up from the babysitter and I was told that she had taken her first step. I was so hurt. I had the joy recently of seeing my little adopted granddaughter take her first steps.

Because of my music background, at Village Christian School, I wrote and directed a Christmas play for 700 children, and played the piano too. "Christ Was Born to Save" was the title of the play, taken from an old hymn. Today is December 25, 2012, Christmas Day for the Christian world. I am happily not celebrating it. I am content to edit this autobiography. The afternoon of the play, it began to rain. The weather man said it would keep raining all night. Knowing that the auditorium would be packed with parents, grandparents, children, and friends of the families, I prayed all afternoon that the rain would stop while the people came, and the 700 children were coming and going from the outside to the inside, and not start again until they got home. You can read the conclusion to this story, about my initiation into learning how to command weather, in Collection X – Storm Stopping Miracles.

One day, leaving school, I was so stressed out that I left Sun Valley Christian School and began driving home on the freeway without picking my daughter up from her babysitter. I had to turn back around and go get her. Because I was teaching phonics, I

PART III - The Journey is Sabotaged

taught her as we would go home each day, and she learned to talk very early.

At about five months of age, she got bronchitis that stayed on and on, and we had no money to get her to a doctor. I had no understanding of clinics. Also, that little house we lived in for about 3 ½ years was haunted with demonic spirits. We would see things moving around. The spirits tormented our baby a lot. At times, we would hear her, as if she was being suffocated. All I understood was trying to survive. It was here that horrible things happened, and she saw some of it. Traumatic impressions on the minds of little ones shape their future.

In that Assembly of God church in Sun Valley, my husband was the assistant pastor, and I was the Minister of Music. I directed a nice-sized choir, and played the piano. But, as we learned about a large church in Long Beach from our good friends Donna and Howard – Community Chapel – we started going there for their Thursday night services.

We bought an old car for $200.00. It took us down the freeway to Long Beach. We met many friends there who tried to help us find a place to live, but because we had a child, most places didn't want us. I began teaching my choir in the Sun Valley Church the songs I learned at Community Chapel. The pastor was furious. He did not like those songs. He liked classic formal church music. But, my choir sure loved the joyful songs from the heart, and so did the people. He was a gruff old guy. After we left, I heard his church dwindled down to very few. He was the type that stayed aloof from the people. It was in that church that I tried to find healing for my knees. Because of neglect, and an injury I had when I was eleven--falling backwards over a tree limb--my back was deformed, and my left leg from the hip to the knee was numb.

I was becoming more and more bitter and angry at "God." When being prayed for, I could feel the power of Elohim going through me. But, at times, I felt the power go into the floor between the minister and I. Then I would go back to my seat, feel my left leg, and it was still numb. The numbness remains to this day, as a testimony to me not to go by what I see or feel, but only by faith. It was a progressive learning process about real faith. That's why I could write the truthful manual on faith: "Faith Walk – A Lifestyle of Overcoming"/January 25, 2007. I tell about this healing in more detail in the Collections Part VIII. Years later, in relating this testimony in Saltillo, Mexico, many in the congregation were healed as I spoke.

Being so discouraged, I asked my pastor why God would not heal me. His answer set me back for years. He said: "Because you have no faith." I was so devastated by his statement. I had loads of faith. I saw others being healed, why not me? My anger at "God" grew. I did not understand the nature and methodology of the Elohim of Israel. Now I understand it, but it took many years to learn.

Next we moved to Long Beach to attend Community Chapel. Pastor Esther told us to give our little girl high doses of vitamin C for the bronchitis. We did, and she got well within days. I think that the air in Glendale--very highly toxic with industrial fumes--was the culprit. While carrying her in the womb, our friend David Reimer came to visit, and brought his son who had chickenpox. I had never had it. But, I got it at age 22, pregnant with her. It affected my baby's eyes early in childhood. So, she had to wear glasses. She hated glasses, still does. My ignorance of practical things was incredible! I was a neglected child in many ways, so I neglected many of her basic needs. I just had no idea of how to care for a child. Only by receiving the love of our Creator can we really love ourselves, and love others! Today she is a miracle! Abba has done so many miracles in her life! I am so proud of her! She has such a heart to win the lost to the Savior's love. She prays much, teaches His Word, and witnesses to His salvation every chance she gets. She is doing what so few so-called "believers" will do – obeying the Master who died to redeem us.

Our little girl was such a sweet little child. When she was still a baby, we went to Baja, California, down to La Buffadora – the "blow hole" -- on the sea. We camped out. I remember a donkey coming to lick the baby food off her face. I remember a pig grabbing a loaf of bread out of our tent. I ran out of the tent, chased the pig, and scared it so bad that it dropped the bread. Oh the joys of Mexico!

As she got to be 5, she became more and more withdrawn. I did not know that sexual abuse from her father had begun--not penetration, but open exposure that shamed her. This kept up for years. She did not tell me until sometime after she was married. I confronted him with it, but he acted like it was nothing. Other youth in high school, preying on her sadness, tried to get her to take drugs, but she said she had enough problems already and did not want to add any more. I am so thankful for that! She had some boyfriends that were losers, but wow, she finally married a prince! I do not judge her for her reactions to her abuse. She never purposely did anything to hurt any of us. She was always, and still is, a very compassionate and loving woman, showing consideration even to those who hurt her deeply, like me. Since our restoration in January of 2011, I love her more now than ever before.

PART III - The Journey is Sabotaged

We moved to North Carolina when she was six. Her brother was three. When she was 16, she began running away. Children do not run away from love and security. I never faulted her for running away! She and a girl friend who went with her hitched a ride with a trucker going towards California on the famous Route 66. She called me from Louisiana to tell me where she was. She was a good girl, but horribly hurt. All she knew was to go to meet her father who had left us during a brief separation and moved to Pomona, California. I alerted the sheriff's department to try to find her. I was so panicked. I did not know that the girl she was with was hoping to sell her into "white slavery" in Colorado. The trucker was so precious. He told her that her friend was bad. He let the friend out in Colorado. But, my daughter continued on with him. She said he slept behind the wheel, and let her sleep in the cab. He took her right to her father in Pomona. To this day, I bless that man and pray for him. Then, the social services got involved and paid for her to be flown back to me. But, her running away continued.

One night, after her dad came back, at 3:00 AM, she wrote us a note and slipped out of the house. She caught a ride going to the Ocoee River road into Tennessee, heading towards Chattanooga. A Tennessee highway patrol officer found her and brought her back to Ducktown. He called us. We went to Ducktown to get her; it was just over the North Carolina line. When we got there, we saw a young policeman "writing her up." The patrol officer, who was the senior officer in Ducktown, being a good father himself, told her horror stories of women who were raped and killed on that road. After this incident, the social service took her from us and placed her in a foster home. The people she lived with were good people. I praise Abba for them.

She began dating that police officer who wrote her up. I got a lying report on him from a jealous police officer who worked with him. But, she had her foster parents check on him. They gave him a glowing report. He came from a good family. But, I was against the marriage. She was just 17, in 1984. He was 20 or 21, I think. She was only in her junior year of high school. They tried to find someone to marry them, but she was underage. They even went to states close by, but they were denied the right to marry without a parent's OK. So, while I was working as secretary at the Catholic Rectory one day, she called me. She said they'd tried to get married, and came up to the Courthouse in Murphy. The lady in the Courthouse told them to get ahold of me. I told her I'd go see the lady. So, I went to the Courthouse and saw her. She was a sweet lady, a motherly type with compassion. She sweetly said: "The best thing you can do for your daughter is to sign the papers, allowing them to get married." I bless that lady for her wisdom.

I called my daughter back and told her that I signed the papers. It is hard to write this … I am crying. She said they would live in his grandmother's old house. It was just across the road from his parent's house. I thought to myself that any man who would move close to his parents must be a good man. Well, to this day, he is a wonderful son-in-law. He is a hard worker, and has done very well for himself and his family. He was a police officer for some years. But, then he got out, which I am thankful for. He quickly advanced in his work and become a boss with a marble mining company. He has been a wonderful husband and father. He loves Jesus and is a teacher in their church--so is she. Abba is also teaching him many things that the church does not teach – bringing him closer and closer to Abba. They are both highly respected. Their son is a miracle son. Today he has a wonderful wife and little boy. He is also a policeman with a very good reputation. My mother requested that *Amazing Grace* be sung at her funeral. When she died in 1995 I asked my son-in-law to sing "Amazing Grace." In his heavy southern accent, he played the guitar and sang. It was beautiful!

She went on after marriage to graduate from Hiwassee Dam High School. I was/am so proud of her. Today, as I am editing this portion of my autobiography, it is May 2nd, 2012. It is their 28th wedding anniversary! Congratulations! They still live in that little house, which they've fixed up like a doll house. I was privileged to be a part of my grandson's wedding to a fine girl. I am so blessed. My tears are of gratitude to Abba. For good stories during the time of her growing up, read the Collections: Parts VII-XII.

The things that crushed my daughter from infancy opened portals for the enemy to touch her body. She was only able to have this one son, and he is a miracle. She lost three in the womb. She has had many ailments, some very severe and life-threatening. She has been in car accidents that by all reality should have killed her, but they didn't. She just recently had serious back surgery, with complications. Yet, Abba's hand is on her. She is a trophy of His grace!

At one point, because of the witchcraft power of projection, such evil was done to her that she almost died. She told me she saw an apparition of my dead mother calling her to come to her in heaven. I told her to think: Nana could not return, she was happy in heaven with gramps. Out of her mouth came: "Oh, that's right, it was a demon." This broke the power of the witchcraft before the enemy could take her life. But, the enemy's attempts at her death

PART III - The Journey is Sabotaged

sure came close to manifesting. She was born again at about age six. Abba's hand has been on her since "before the foundation of the world!" The evil one wanted her dead, but Abba wants her to live! She has always been a pure-hearted person, who loves other people.

Because of trauma that began with babyhood, her memory has been blocked out to a great degree. In fact, a great part of the memory of the past has been either erased, or dulled, in three of the children. Because the oldest could not remember clearly, my ex-husband lied to her about me, telling her such cruel things that I never did, and she believed him. He actually told her that I did all the things that he did to her. He told her I never loved her, but only loved her brother. One time, because of deep hurt, she drove from Tennessee to Texas, while very sick, to confront me with some of the things she was led to believe. I was devastated. None of it was true. I left her hotel room, pounded on the steering wheel of the truck I had borrowed, and cried loudly: "Devil, you're not having my children!"

Today, I am learning more of the miraculous deliverances of Abba for my children. No, the Devil will not have them! The Devil will not have their spouses! The Devil will not have their children, or their children's children! HalleluYah!

As was my pattern, confronting someone with truth was not something I could make myself do. So, all those years, I did not clear up miscommunication with her. I had not said I was "sorry" for what I let happen to her. But, my regret was kept inside and I cried in solitude. But, as you'll read later, the miracle of January 22, 2011 restored us.

One day, a year ago, while crying out in prayer for Abba to deliver my children and save them, I had my Bible open in my lap. I looked down to the only underlined phrase on that page. It was **Isaiah 49:25**: **"I will contend with him who contends with you, and I WILL SAVE YOUR CHILDREN**!" That was Abba's personal word to me. I am seeing Him bring that to pass before my eyes.

We moved to North Carolina in 1974. For incredible miracles of that trip, read Part IX: Miracles of Help Along the Roadside.

When we lived in California, from 1973 to 1974, we attended a Russian Orthodox Church. But, when we moved in 1974 to this little town in the Blue Ridge Mountains of western North Carolina, they had no Eastern Orthodox churches. Upon arrival, the Roman Catholic priest, Father Bob Rademacher met us at the cabin we'd rented, and we decided to go to St. Williams.

I played the organ. There were born again people there, who were even Spirit-filled. It was at a time when Rome gave its blessing to "the charismatic movement." These were some of the most truly born again people I've ever known. Later most of them left the Catholic Church.

At St. Williams I was the social director, organist, children's Catechism teacher, and secretary of the priests at the Rectory office. We had such good friends in that church. We were like a family.

I met beloved Pam Brinke. She had been in Israel with her husband, Norman, many times. After he died, she kept going to Israel, working with the International Christian Embassy at their Sukkot festival. I met her by "accident" there one year after I moved to Jordan. I was having lunch in the dining room of the Crown Plaza Hotel in Jerusalem. On the way to my table, I passed by this lady that looked so familiar. I thought to myself: "she looks just like Pam Brinke." So I snuck over to the table to read her name tag, and saw it was Pam. I spoke to her, and she was in shock. What a glorious reunion!

After Father Bob came Father Del Holmes, then Father Bob Healy, and then Father Tom. These were men from the Glenmary Fathers from Cleveland, Ohio. Father Del was also a trained psychiatrist. I worked for him as his secretary. He became a good friend to my family. He was such a jolly man, and his sermons were very profound. He was also very wise. He increasingly became very upset at what he saw in my husband's behavior.

One Halloween night, I think our oldest daughter was 7, and we took her trick-or-treating. She wore a skimpy fairy costume. By the time we came back to the rectory to get candy, my husband, a pedophile in one of his personalities, was acting out. He came into the rectory, grabbed a broom in the entry way, and put it between his legs, making some embarrassing joke.

The next day Father Del told me that it was a sure sign of something awful happening in our family. So, Father Del, on his own, took the case to a friend of his in Louisiana. This friend was one of America's most famous psychiatrists. This man was initially made famous by one of his cases, which became a movie--"The Three Faces of Eve." Father Del told him of his observations of my husband. This psychiatrist diagnosed him with multiple personalities, schizophrenia, sadism, cruelty, a sadomasochist, a pedophile, a homosexual, and one who was dangerously insane. Father Del knew it was true. The doctor told Del to tell me to get those children away from him right away immediately. But, I didn't, even though I knew well that what he said was 100% true.

I learned later, and had it confirmed by others, that he was truly demon possessed, from his Satanist background during early childhood. I knew he was demonized (under the control of demons). I learned that he was analyzed by the Air Force psychologist, after he was caught doing harmful sadistic things to get attention, and make people feel sorry for him. I do not know the extent to which he was actually involved in Satanism, but it began very early.

I learned that people demonized, and demon possessed (inhabited by demons), cannot "change"--they must be delivered. Demons are the disembodied spirits of the Nephillim. They seek a body to work through. They are real tangible beings, not mental fantasies. They have to be cast out. The only problem, as I even discussed with my husband, is that most do not want to be free of their "friends", which give them their identity, power, security, and control over others. Once, I referred to the demons in my husband as his "friends," which he did not deny.

I see the American people now almost reduced to a zombie state where most are almost unable to use their will to function positively. This is similar to the state I was in. Most are in a survival mode because of not only the mind-programming, but because of the mind and DNA-altering chemicals in food, water, air (chem-trails), vaccines, medicines, the hypnotic "sound of silence" through the TV, the mind-altering hypnotic e.l.f. (extra low frequency) pulse waves, HAARP rays, and on and on, bombarding the American people daily. This zombie state is spreading to most of the population. It is not all induced by man's evil tampering with our DNA. The "powers of the air" are coming in greater force now, i.e. witchcraft, so people are being manipulated and taken over without knowing it. They just know something is very wrong, but they don't know why. I understand what is happening to people, that is why I can compassionately plead with His people to get out from under that canapé of evil.

I was mentally clouded so much of the time while being married. But, I also feared going to a woman's shelter and taking my children. I hid behind false hope, false mercy, and false responsibility. I did not want to go back to my parent's house. I just wanted my freedom, but kept ending up "bound and gagged" and in a prison-house of my own making. I could not think much beyond daily survival.

Desperate for some identity of my own, while secretary to Father Del, I decided to become a "nun," a married affiliated with a convent. So, Father Del led me through my dedication vows to Mary. I began corresponding with a nun in a convent. She was a very precious older lady. I remember telling Father Del that I wanted to take this vow because "I have nothing else to do with my life." He cautioned me of the seriousness of the vow. I did want to be "holy." After returning to Abba, I denounced my vow to Mary. But, all of that, too, was used for my schooling.

I understand that within the Catholic system are some precious people, trapped by deception, who really want to know God with all their heart. I knew some wonderful born again, Spirit-filled nuns. I knew some very wonderful priests and "Brothers." One very kind Brother, Ken Woods, who was a helper to Father Bob, told the children the story from **Mark 4:35-41** about Jesus calming the storm. My young son heard the story, and it became his favorite Bible story. Then there was Brother Marion, who came with Father Healy. He was a hard worker! He was too fastidious for Father Healey. Father Healy was a rough old Irish priest--blunt and caustic. He appeared to be heartless. During one lunch break, from the retail store I worked in, I went by the Rectory to get some information from Father Healey. I saw that there was a straggly cat crying at his door to get food. He pushed the cat away with his foot. After work, I went back to the Rectory, to get things I had left. At the door, there was the cat, licking milk from a bowl. Father Healy opened the door, and I let him have it – "SO! Your true nature has surfaced!" He grinned. I took the cat home and named it "Bobby" after Father Bob Healy.

Yes, I know full well the corruption of the Roman Catholic system, the rising of the Jesuit Vatican to world power, and what's in the future for those billion people still bound by loyalty to the pope/Roman Caesar. But, within that system, Abba has His eye on His people.

My dearest friend, Dorothy Weatherington, went to St. Williams. She was so devoted to the Church, and to Mary. We were such close friends. When I finally left the church, she was very hurt and has masses said for me. But being her friend was a great blessing! She and her husband, "Whitey" lived on a farm. She raised goats. My children loved her so much. Jimmy was their autistic son. She was so full of compassion and love. I miss her very much.

I also miss Mary Helen Allen and her family in Texana, a suburb of Murphy set aside for "black people." She went to St. Williams. We had so much fun together! Maybe my relationship with her paved the way for my love of the African people. My children loved to play with the black children in Texana. The famous book, *Walk Across America*, by Peter Jenkins, tells more about his time in Murphy and Texana than any other place.

Mary Helen watched my children at times at her house. One day, we went into town to Hardee's for lunch. I was holding my blond blue-eyed fourth baby, who was about three months old. Mary Helen said: "Give her to me." So I passed her to Mary Helen.

PART III - The Journey is Sabotaged

This is so funny! As she entered the room with the tables and chairs, I heard her saying over and over "momma's little baby." I got our food and sat down. She was laughing. She said: "You see that old man over there? He looked up and saw me with this white baby, and about dropped his hamburger!" Oh I loved her sense of humor! When we'd meet downtown or in a store, we'd stop and hug each other just to get reactions from the "white folks." It was so funny. My mother was big prejudiced. She did not like Mary Helen and I hugging in public.

But, during the Civil War, in General Sherman's march through the south, he killed some of our family because we had black folk who worked for us. We never considered them slaves. We treated them like family. When the Proclamation was given by President Lincoln, my family told the black folk who worked for them that they could leave, but they didn't want to leave. It was kind of like the **Deuteronomy 15:13-17** scenario. Sherman was a cold-blooded killer. My cousin Jess Wingate was sick in bed when Sherman came through, and Sherman's men shot him dead. While Murphy wasn't against black people living there like some surrounding towns, still the black people only lived in Texana.

My family continued on to help black folk. To this day, it is the same. Mary Helen's husband worked for some of my relatives in Murphy for over 30 years. When he died, they paid for his funeral and every month gave Mary Helen money for her living expenses. Mary Helen became a Catholic because Father Bob had been so good to her family, and she died a Catholic. I understand how good humble people who seek to know God personally can get caught up in Catholicism because of its hidden mysticism that makes one feel "holy" and good about themselves.

While still in California, we attended Loyola University charismatic meetings. It was when the charismatic movement became so popular under Pope Pius in the 1960s. The pope's sister had become part of the movement, so he gave his blessing on it. The main auditorium at Loyola always packed for those meetings, with many priests and nuns attending. There was so much unity and love among the people. They had Bible studies in "cell groups." Later, I learned that there was a basic message of the new birth that was accompanying this movement, along with the message of the "baptism into the Holy Spirit." Some Catholics left the Catholic Church after studying the Word for themselves. Most people, however, went from the charismatic Catholic movement back into Mary worship, since in the pagan world of Nimrod, the Holy Spirit and Mary are considered as one in unity.

I will never forget one Sunday morning at St. Williams. I laid the third child down in the Rectory to sleep during the service, and she kept screaming. I went over to the church in such a stressed mode. I saw Bill Block. I told him my baby would not stop screaming. I had to play the organ and the service was about to start. He told me later that he went over, put his hand on her, prayed for peace over her, and she instantly fell asleep. He was such a gentle kind man.

In Part VII, Miracles of Provision, you will read about my attending the Spirit-filled nun's prayer meeting at the hospital near St. Williams early in the morning, and the faith-building "famous nickel story." Abba met me where I was at and helped me, even in my state of despair. Abba did many wonderful things during our twelve years at St. Williams. As long as Abba sees that people will continue on their journey towards Him, towards truth, no matter how many ditches they fall in, He will protect them and work with them, because He sees their end. Some of our friends just kept coming forward on their journey, and today guard the Torah of Yahuweh.

We had good friends at St. Williams who had escaped from Cuba. The husband of the family was a medical doctor. Their children became friends of our children, and they became our dear friends too.

Through my husband's selling radio advertisements, we met an Indian family--Paul and Minnie Kumar, and their son. They were Methodists from South India. Their son looked so much like our son – only with black hair, brown eyes, and a tanned complexion. I loved them. Their son became one of my son's best friends. Then one day Minnie called me and told me that they loved me, but they could no longer see us because of problems with my husband. It was a crushing blow, but this happened all too much during our marriage.

By this time, some of you may be very disgusted, and critical of me. But, your day is coming! If you remain alive during the tribulation, you will be subjected to "the depths of Satan," and then you will understand. I wish better for you. But, those who are self-righteous and think themselves proudly superior to those who have gotten themselves into tragic circumstances they can't seem to get out of, will find out shortly what the evil one has power to do over the mind and the will. But, I choose to think that most of you understand, and will bear with me as I tell you how Abba pulled off massive miracles to set me free!

Our little daughter was dedicated to "the Lord" when she was about a year old. She had learned the word "book." All during the little ceremony, she kept calling out "book." What a cute kid! When she was nearly 3, we decided to plan another child. I prayed for a boy. Our son was born in 1970. He was the only one

PART III - The Journey is Sabotaged

of the four that was planned by us—but all four were planned by Abba! I was pregnant with him when I taught school at Village Christian School in Sun Valley, California. I quit my second grade teaching job because we had decided to move to Long Beach. He was born in Long Beach, in December, 1970.

Read the miracles that Abba did to help us get a little house in Long Beach, when no one wanted to rent to us in Part VII – Miracles of Provision. There were good memories. We were at our little Andy Street house in Long Beach. The night before he was born, I was playing the piano at Community Chapel, and was dancing before "the Lord." The next night, my husband was driving our old car home from work on the L.A. Freeway. It was raining. The car could only go about 25 miles an hour, and was on "its last legs." I was beginning hard labor. I wanted him to be born before Christmas because I did not want to be in the hospital during Christmas. I could not reach my husband – that was before the days of cell phones. I could not reach my parents. I tried to call Howard and Donna, but they did not answer their phone. I did not think to call the police. Our daughter was taking a nap. It was about 5:00 PM. The pains had gotten to one minute apart and one minute long. So, I did the wrong thing, but I did not know it was the wrong thing – I took a bath. Then I went and lay down on the couch. While lying there, Abba gave me a whole song--music and words. It is lovely. Being a Music Major in college, I wrote the song on music paper, which I have to this day:

When I trust Him, when I trust Him there is peace.
When I trust Him, when I trust Him there is peace.
No matter what I see there is peace
No matter what man says there is peace
When I trust Him, when I trust Him, there is peace.
But, when I doubt there is confusion, and where's peace,
I can't find any, and my way is dark and muddy as the sea..
But, when I trust Him, when I trust Him there is peace

Finally my husband came home, and he "rushed" me through the rain to the hospital. For some crazy reason we brought the cat, which kept walking over my belly. I suppose it was for "comic relief." I've always loved cats. When I got to the emergency entrance, they quickly examined me and immediately took me into the Delivery Room. His head was already starting to come out. My doctor came flying into the delivery room, washed his hands and got ready. He had been to a Christmas party. I told him I was sorry I got him away from the party. I asked him: "Are you going to circumcise him right away." He said: "You're awfully sure you're having a boy." I said "Yes, I am having a boy." I knew I was having a boy.

At that time I was the pastor of a nursing home. On one Sunday, while visiting the people in their rooms, one lady called me over, put her hand on my belly, and said: "How nice that your first one will be a boy." I felt really spooked about that. But, she was wrong – he was my second one.

In those days there were no sonograms. I had a spinal block, and out he came. But, the doctor used forceps. To this day, he has problems with his neck, as does his older sister. Then, instead of waiting for the eighth day, the doctor circumcised him right away. My mother said, when they finally got to the hospital, that he looked blue, shaking from the cold and the circumcision. But, my little boy was included in the Covenant of Yahuweh with Abraham! I brought him home in a Christmas stocking that the ladies in the hospital had made. Exactly like his sister, he was 7½ pounds and 21 inches long.

The first one was born in November, the second one in December, the third in October, but the fourth--May. The first one was born at 6:33, the second at 7:33, and the third at 8:33, and the fourth at 11:15 at night. That fourth one broke the mold – always.

At Christmas he stared at the lights on the tree. I had him home. Poor little thing--I never had a baby boy before! The doctor told me to put medicated cream to heal the circumcision and alcohol on his umbilical chord. I reversed it, and wow did he scream. I was in tears.

It was at that point that I told Abba that he would NEVER go into the military because I didn't want him to die in war. I was very protective of him even from birth. Years later, when he was a senior in High School, we had no money to send him to college. I then told him about the benefits of the Air Force. The Army recruiter did everything he could to try to get him into the Army, but he joined the Air Force. He told his recruiter that he wanted a job in avionics, working on F-16s, and he wanted to leave for his assignment in October (1990). She told him that was impossible. He most likely would work as a mechanic and would not leave until the following March. We prayed. The next Saturday morning, I went to do my usual grocery shopping and prayed that he would get the job he wanted at the time he wanted it. When I returned from grocery shopping, he said his recruiter called and was very stunned. She had been looking for jobs for him on the computer and all of a sudden up popped an avionics job on F-16s, and he was scheduled to leave in October.

He was always highly favored. One time he had no shorts or jeans, and it was summer. I was working at St. Williams and a Floridian came in with a box full of clothes and told me to take

PART III - The Journey is Sabotaged

what I wanted. The box was filled with Nike shorts, and other expensive name brand things--all his size. Then my mother called me the same day and said she felt to buy him jeans. She asked what brand, and I told her he wanted Levis. So she got him Levis.

After going through his training in Denver, he was given sealed orders. That was not the norm. He thought it was his "remote tour of duty," assignment to either South Korea, or Alaska. They hinted it might be in the Far East. He was planning on getting married between graduating in Denver and going on his assignment. They got married. And then they went to Carswell AF Base in Fort Worth to get the orders unsealed. He wanted to go to Germany. The officer at Carswell was surprised at the sealed orders. It said it was highly unusual. He came back and said: "You're going to Germany." Then he said: "the bad news is that you cannot go together because there is only one seat left on the plane." My son said: "We are going together." So the stunned officer went back to check again, and he came out and said: "One more seat has opened up."

I'll never forget the day he left for Lackland Air Force Base. I watched he and his wife, holding hands, walk away from our car, back to where he would be transported, south to Lackland. I cried. He was my buddy. He was the only one who enjoyed my gourmet cooking. He loved to cook. He still cooks the most awesome gourmet meals! Only my youngest daughter had any desire to cook. He was the only one who was interested in joining me on archeology trips too. So, I knew my life would be different after he left. Upon visiting him in Lackland, I went to the main desk to ask the man to call him, and he said they couldn't. I said I was his mom. The man said: "Oh, you're an Air Force mom." He called my son.

My son was so powerful in miracles. In Part VIII, you will read that at age 14 he did spiritual warfare over me regarding my serious migraine headaches, and Abba healed me totally. He had a passion for studying the Word before he went into the service. Upon getting to Germany, Abba did more miracles to get them a lovely upstairs apartment in a little village where St. Bernard of Clarviox had built his monastery. It was there that Abba brought him back on track. He was a high achiever. He was a superb trumpet player. He wrote skits and plays, and directed videos that were amazing, even in High School. Now he's working on videos to promote the Torah and the truth about Israel.

Even his manager of the McDonald's, where he worked during High School, wrote him a special high recommendation. From that he continued to get awards and commendations in the Air Force that would fill two walls. After he returned to the U.S. from

Germany, he was stationed for 2 years at an AF Base near Macon, Georgia. He then moved back to Fort Worth, Texas where he transitioned into the Air Force Reserves at Carswell AFB. After a total of eight years in the military, he was ready to work in the civilian world.

The first day on his first job he came to see me, and I went out to meet him as he pulled up in his car. He looked as if he had been crying. I asked if something at work had made him upset. He said: "no, it's all the cigarette smoke." He quit that same day.

There was one job he really wanted. There were 50 applicants more qualified than he. He applied anyway, by faith. He didn't even complete the test they gave him because there were things on it he had not learned in the Air Force. They gave him the job anyway. His work in the Air force had helped him to land a superb job in a major avionics company near the Dallas/Fort Worth airport. He advanced well in that company and became a manager over many. He worked on the computer systems in the cockpits of commercial airlines. He said that when he got an El Al Israel plane part in, he would pray over it. He also became an FAA inspector for both commercial and Government airplanes, responsible for ensuring the safety of the repaired part. He even trained some pilots in how to use their new computer system. He was honored greatly in this job.

At his dedication to "the Lord," at age 6 weeks, a true prophet, named Wally Wilcox, had a vision and a prophecy regarding him. My son's name in Hebrew means "the way, the journey, the conversation, the way of life, the road well-trodden." His name is in the Tenach about 600 times. In the vision, Wally saw him walking up a long dusty, well-trodden road carrying the staff of authority at a very young age. That has proved true. In later years, when I found this out, I told him his name was in the Bible about 600 times, and what it meant. This started him on his journey to find his Hebrew roots. He's found them!

As he got to be three and four, we went everywhere together. I would hold his little hand. He was always so beautiful. He had platinum curls, and big blue eyes. His is still very handsome. At that time there was a song that was popular called "You And Me Against the World." I applied it to my son and I.

He was terrified of his dad. His dad would reach out and try to grab him, and he would run away. I don't know what happened to that precious little boy from his dad. But, he was traumatized at an early age, as was his sister. He did not talk until he was about 4. He would point at things, and say one word, but no sentences. He knew to point, and say "Donald's" and "fries" – for he loved McDonald's french fries. One day, we were driving down the main street of Palm Springs. We were on a mini-vacation. I heard singing from the back seat of the car: "Jesus loves me this I know, for the Bible tells me so..." I did not turn around. I said to our daughter: "Honey, your singing is so nice." She said: "Momma, it was not me, it was him." I turned around and our little boy was singing "Jesus Loves Me." It was the first time we had heard him say anything beyond one or two words.

So, you can imagine how I felt last October, 2011, when he came to Israel with me – the first of my children to join me in the Middle East. It changed his life. He told me he came to Israel to find direction for his life. I said: "No! Seek what is on Abba Yahuweh's heart, ask what is the passion of His heart, and align to that, then you'll have your direction." He took me up on it. He found what was on Abba's heart, and he immediately began doing all he could to join with Abba in His passion. He guards the Torah and has a passion for the Word, and for the return of the whole House of Israel to the Covenant of Yahuweh. He is working on spreading this good news. In October 2012, he came to Israel with his new wife, one that really loves him and respects him, and we had a wonderful time together!

At Community Chapel, I was considered in the "in-crowd" with the pastor and her daughter, Esther and Kay Mallet, and with the elders. Besides playing the piano, I also prophesied in the church. Later on Wally tried to council me in wisdom, but as much as I respected him, I could not follow through with his wisdom. This is why I understand what is happening to so many of the believers in America – though they know truth, they are almost incapable of following through on it because of the severe mind-programming done to them from childhood. So, I have compassion, though it is my job to do everything I can to shake them lose from their stupor.

Tomasa, a humble Mexican woman, went to sleep one night and dreamed she went to a village in Mexico and led a lady to salvation at her house. Two weeks later, Tomasa got a letter from the lady thanking her for coming and giving her the "Gospel." Peggy Rood was also one of the elders. I dearly loved her. Lori Scott was another leader there. We were close friends. That church moved in the Word and the gifts of the Spirit. I've never known a church that reached out to those people that others were afraid of, like the Hell's Angels, prostitutes, pimps, ex-convicts, and etc. They sure had a heart of love for the lost.

I worked with Sylvia Millhouse at Lakewood Savings and Loan-- a large Real Estate, Tax and Insurance Company. She was a divorced Catholic girl. One of her two young sons, Danny, was dying of leukemia. I had been witnessing to her about Jesus. She thought the Bible taught that Mary was immaculately conceived and rose to heaven to become the Queen of heaven. I had to tell her that was not in the Bible. She came to Community Chapel and was born again. The elders, including Wally Wilcox, prayed for her son, and he was instantly healed. She became quite an evangelist. She later married a man in the church.

It was near our son's 1st birthday that I had my first nervous breakdown. He was born December 21, 1970, so it was early winter of 1971. I was working at Community Chapel as a pianist, a teacher in the Bible College, which I helped start, was head of "Church on the Street," was a nursing home pastor, and worked in many other ministries through the church. I bought my little son a hot dog from Der Weinersnitzel, put him in the nursery bed cage at church, and went to hospitals and jails, and juvenile homes, etc., to evangelize. Amazing that years later he met a girl in Texas that was in the "cage-crib" next to him at Community Chapel. Small world ...

But, because of the severe abuse I got from my husband, one night after teaching my class on Revelation, I felt weak. The world began to spin around me. A friend took me home. The nervous breakdown took over. For the most part, I went through it alone. One of my best friends in the church was Peggy Weebee – we'd pal around together. Peggy kept my son for me for a while, so that I could rest. I had to stay lying down, for I could not raise my head without getting very sick. Of course, going to a doctor was out of the question--we had no money and no insurance.

Sadly, though they reached out in love to others, when I could not go to the church anymore, no one came to visit me. Peggy Rood came one time. Lori Scott came. Later on, Teddy Medina and Wally reached out to me. Slowly a few of my friends came to visit, but only after I began improving. So, in despair, and in my great weakness of body, I began going across the street on Sunday mornings to Mass at a Catholic Church. They never asked me to minister. They asked nothing of me. This was wonderful. I could go and come as I willed.

From there I thought I would try another Catholic Church about two miles from us. It was in there that I was amazed to hear the foundational Good News. The priest said that it was not by works, not by church attendance or even baptism that saved us, but only through faith in the death and resurrection of Jesus. I went back there. I found peace. I didn't have to produce to please people. And, it had to be because Abba was overshadowing me with His care.

It was also during the time of the "Charismatic Renewal" movement within Catholicism. This, too, was part of my schooling.

PART III - The Journey is Sabotaged

I guess that's why when we got to North Carolina, and Father Bob came to visit, it was not hard saying "yes" to his invitation to join the Catholic Church. Because I have always been an insider, I learned the good, the bad, and the evil. I also learned to separate the religious system from the individual. If someone had seen me going to a Catholic Church after I left Community Chapel, they might have judged me. But, Abba didn't. As a baby, my son was sickly with colic, and so was always throwing up his formula. I got little sleep. One morning, about 6:00 AM, I got up to feed him, and was so exhausted that I could hardly feed him. All of a sudden the whole house began to shake, things fell off the shelves, and I could have cared less. It was a major earthquake (1971). Yes, I remember those California earthquakes.

After I regained my strength, I worked for the big insurance and tax complex in Lakewood, not far from where my son was born. Like with the Forest Lawn jobs, I got to handle accounts of well-known people. I handled a property sale for Christine Jorgenson. "It" was the first sex change person that hit the public news--a man who became a woman. Another one of my cases was handling the insurance for apartment buildings that Carol Burnett and Lyle Waggoner had bought. At this time, I had a good babysitter for my two children--the daughter of Howard and Donna Phelps. I became much more conscientious as a parent. I made sure my children were well taken care of.

Here's an example of how conscientious I had become: I went to pick up my oldest daughter from Kindergarten. I was going about 5-10 mph through the street because older children had gotten out of school and were running around on the sidewalks. All of a sudden a boy, chasing another boy, came out from between cars, and I hit him in the stomach. He grabbed his stomach and ran to the curb. I yelled out the window to the witnesses saying I would be back in a minute because I had to pick up my daughter from Kindergarten. I got her hastily. I was so traumatized. I went directly back, and found the boy with his mother and the police. I parked the car and ran over to the police telling them I was the one who hit him. His mother told me she was mad at her son because he ran out in front of me. The police man asked: "Are you all right." I thought I would go to jail. The police were scared because they thought I was going into shock. But, at least, I had picked up my daughter.

Even though we both worked, my husband kept running up the credit cards more and more. Finally, he felt he should leave us. The peace was incredible. I put my son's playpen in the living room, brought out the ironing board, and made it a home. I love things out that I use all the time. I don't like putting them away and then having to get them out again. I suppose you could call that "organized clutter." We had so little monetarily, but I could have sustained us on my salary. One day, while I was at work, a man called me from a loan company. My husband wanted to borrow more money, but they needed my OK. I told him not to loan it to him. But then, pity for him, mixed with fear, crossed my mind. I called the man back and told him to go ahead. Then my husband wanted to come back. I let him, thinking I was doing right, even though Wally had said to not let him back in. The first thing he did was take down the playpen and the ironing board, and my heart sunk. The peace was gone.

Years later, he decided to put me on an allowance. He gave me $5.00 a week. I saved up the money for a month, then went down to a sale at Mervyns Department Store on Hulen Street, and bought three skirts. I showed him what I bought with my allowance. He was furious, and cut out my allowance. With my husband, I had almost no right of choice. One time, I had bought a special wine at a winery that was in a little heart-shaped vase. I tried to put it one place, and he kept moving it. So, one day I got super glue and glued it to the counter. He went to move it, and wow was he surprised!

Abba opened so many doors to my cage so that I could have flown free at any moment, and taken my first two children with me. What kept me caged was what was still inside of me. Abba was not finished reshaping me! I didn't totally lose my will – I just wanted "security" – and an end to loneliness, no matter the cost. I understand Israel. Most Israelis want security no matter how much land they have to give away to get it. I understand Americans! After 9/11, Americans laid down many personal rights that were guaranteed under the Constitution for the sake of security.

Now in 2013, the American people have almost given up all of their rights for security. I was deceived. The American people are deceived, and Israel is deceived--giving up the rights to property, and to personal justice, so that life can continue as usual without interruption. This is not freedom. It is not security--it is slavery in disguise. In **Exodus 14**, the Israelites wanted to return to Egypt as slaves rather than face the wilderness of the unknown across the Red Sea. I was not unique in my fears – I craved security no matter what I suffered. I just didn't know until later to what extend my children suffered.

I know about mind-programming. When I write about it, it is personal as well as factual. It takes away the will. [Refer to: "Mind Control, Hidden Manipulation and the World Brain"/September 2006, and "Quiet Wars and Silent Weapons/October 29, 2007]

PART III - The Journey is Sabotaged

Why do you think I plead so much with people in my articles, telling them how the Beast will come to power? It is because I know... at times, my mind would shut down. At times, I slept behind the couch with a knife under my pillow, in terrifying fear. I would wait until he fell asleep, and then sneak out of bed and lie behind the couch. Sometimes, the trauma got so bad, I lost the ability to think or speak. Other times, I'd fly into rages of hate. I became filled with so much anger and rage. He loved to incite me to rage. Demons feed off of negative emotions. Abuse in families is on the rise. Parents fight with each other. Evil spirits torment the mind until they get emotions of anger and frustration, self-pity, or hate, and then they feed off the negative energy. They want to take our energy from us!

Now, to stop chaos around me, I play real worship music, like the Sons of Korah singing the Psalms, or Kent Henry's "Seeking the Sanctuary", or the reading of Psalms, like Kent Henry's "The Sword of the Spirit" CD. I also listen to praise music by Paul Wilbur, Chris Tomlin, and others, including music that is sung in Hebrew. The wisdom of Rav Sha'ul in **Philippians 4:4, 6-8** is so profound--it admonishes us to close all portals to the negativity that rides on falsehood that drags the spirit down: "**Rejoice always, again I say `rejoice'! Let your gentleness be known to all men. The Master is near. Do not worry at all, but in everything by prayer and petition, with thanksgiving, let your requests be known to Elohim. And the peace of Elohim, which surpasses all understanding, shall guard your hearts and minds through Messiah Yahushua. For the rest brothers, whatever is true, whatever is noble, whatever is righteous, whatever is clean, whatever is lovely, whatever is of a good report, if there be any uprightness and if there be any praise – think on these things**!"

So many years of so many nights I would wake up feeling like I'd been beaten up. I called this "the demonic beatings." Demons can torment to the point where the mind makes the body feel like it has been beaten. Even to this day, if there is a jezebel spirit anywhere near me, when I try to sleep, the tormenting spirits are present, and make me incredibly nervous. But, now I know how to do quick and powerful spiritual warfare to run them off. How does anyone really learn anything? I didn't even learn during suffering. A pastor-friend once said that it was only in <u>crisis</u> that most people really desire to change. So, Abba allows crisis. We sometimes have to get desperate, or "to the end of our rope," so that we make decisive decisions that will change our course positively.

My husband only once beat me physically. We were living in the little house behind our landlady's house in Glendale, before moving to Long Beach. Because I had said it was impractical for him to hock his watch to buy a dog for $75.00, he became enraged and beat me terribly in front of our little daughter in her crib. She was one year old, standing up in her crib screaming. I was covered in black and blue marks. That afternoon, Ronnie called. He had married Carol. They wanted to take us for a ride in their "new" Oldsmobile convertible. Of course, my husband said "yes." I covered myself up to hide the bruises and pretended to have a good time. Deep shame wounds the spirit, causing us to hide truth, and so we continue to suffer. Later Ronnie divorced Carol and married an Italian lady. I found out that he was very emotionally messed up, so life with Ronnie would have also been bad in a different way.

Once dehumanized, a person just lets anything happen--they give up. I gave up. I've talked to enough people who have been through things like this. Yet, like I said, I was a bird in a cage of my own fears and insecurity – the door was always open. Abba was always there to help me escape – but I did not know Him like I know Him now. To dehumanize me further, he called me the filthiest of names, and mocked my physical problems, also. So, I began calling myself the same filthy names. I would pound on my head with my fist, and curse myself as being the stupidest person who ever lived, using the same filthy words. He kept repeating that I was bad, and had to be punished. So, the words "you're bad" kept going in my head for at least two years after I got my freedom. This is why it is such a miracle that my self-hatred is GONE!

In 1974, we moved from California to North Carolina. We had so many miracles along the way--incredible stories. For these stories refer to the Collections under "Stories of Help Along the Roadside," Part IX. We had rented a tiny cabin near Murphy, before we left California. But, upon arrival, our possessions would not fit in the cabin, so we took them to a cousin's house that was being built. It had a foundation and a few standing posts. That night it rained. Our things had been barely covered, and were exposed to anyone who might want to steal them. We went to talk to the owner of the tiny cabin and told her of our plight. She said there was a friend of hers that was going to rent a big farmhouse down the Blairsville highway. She called this lady and we met her. She said that there were several people wanting to rent Glen and Ruth Owenby's farmhouse. She was a sister of Ruth, I remember. I told her that my Aunt Fairy and Uncle Lyle had lived in Andrews, up the road, and my mother had grown up

PART III - The Journey is Sabotaged

in Murphy. She went into shock. She and my Aunt Fairy had been the best of friends from childhood. So, we got the house. Glen and Ruth became our friends. I'll never forget the first night in that house. I slept so wonderful. Glen's Chemise cows had come through the back fence and were making cow noises near our bedroom window. The next morning Glen came to meet us and apologized profusely for the cows. I laughed, and told him that I slept so wonderful. We had come from the city, and the peace of his house was wonderful. I loved the cow noises – moooooo. We lived there for two years.

I was not used to country life. It was too slow for me, so I had a hard time with the slow drivers on the two-lane winding roads. But, after a couple of years, I slowed down too. In the meantime, my anger at slow drivers caused me to take many dangerous risks with my car, even with my children aboard. At one point, I went into a curve too fast, and rolled the car over and over, with two children in it. If it had rolled to the right, we'd all have been dead. But, no one was hurt. I had deep anger. Abba has delivered me from that too. He has had to totally renovate me! But, then, HE GETS ALL THE PRAISE!

Glen's house was a big farmhouse with a huge garden plot out front, and a field in the backyard. It had a big fireplace in it. The spring before we came, a terrible tornado had come through town, and along with other damage, took down the Big Six radio tower just out of town. They had just gotten a new tower put up. My husband had a choice of a job as the manager of a local drug store, or to work for this radio station--I encouraged him to work for the radio station, and he took it. He sold advertising, did broadcasting, sportscasting, and covered Hayesville Band competitions.

One night, a tornado was projected to come through Murphy. He volunteered to go to the station and broadcast until the tornado alert was over. I was so proud of him. Many people were proud of him. I laid on the couch listening to the tornado go over. It roared like a freight train moving across the sky. I kept the radio on to make sure he was all right. That put him in very good stead with the owners, and it was not long before we were very good friends with them.

I began my own gardening at the Bellview house. In front of the house was a huge garden plot. So, I planted huge gardens. But, wow was I ignorant. I threw gasoline from a can onto the corn stalks, then lit it with matches and kept throwing the gas. I could have been burned up. One day, I came back from town, and saw that the big-horned bull of the cattle herd of our landlord had gotten loose and come through the gate into my backyard. I got mad. I didn't notice my red blouse until later. I just ran after that bull screaming. He looked at me, got scared, and charged back to his own pasture.

Then there were the cute little brown worms crawling in the front yard that I thought I would keep for fishing. There was a huge lake across the Georgia line from us with 106 miles of shoreline – Lake Notla. We went fishing quite a bit. Our two oldest children loved fishing--so did I. We would rent a small motorboat and go out on the lake. But, I had to draw back my hand quickly when those cute little brown worms raised their heads and their tongues flicked in and out. We had lots of copperheads around there, and these were baby copperheads. I did some stupid things in learning country life. Our two oldest children loved it so much there.

Our daughter was eight and our son was five. He loved gardening with me. He planted "tators." When his "tators" became edible, he had so much fun digging them up (that's "potatoes" to you Yankees). Pearl Anderson, who lived up the hill, stopped on her way back from town. She could not believe some of the things I was growing in the garden, for she'd never seen snow peas, and other unusual things that were common to Californians. She invited me to come visit her, and that's how I met my precious friend. I helped her in her garden also. She rewarded me with vegetables.

Those mountain people practice a basic Torah. For example, when they are through with harvesting, they leave green beans, okra, and other crops un-harvested so that the poor can come and get it. I got a lot of our food that way from the neighbors. We became friends with Clyde and Wilma McNabb, who lived down the road in a 100-year-old house. She was a well-known weaver in that region. We're talking precious people who are 100% genuine. I loved to go visit them, just to be around them. I began doing investigation of my family there, for that was the heartland of our family who had moved to Tennessee and North Carolina from England and Ireland in the 1600s. One of them was a signer of the original North Carolina Constitution.

In 1976 my parents moved to North Carolina. Before my mother left that area to move to Oklahoma, where she attended college, one of her teachers said: "You'll be back; they always come back." Well, she came back with my dad, and they loved it. When they first arrived, and while waiting for their house to be built, they stayed in the old Ty Cobb Plantation home at the time. They built their dream house on family land in Ranger. I think I already told about the old house next door, and how the old stage coach line stopped there so people could get food on their

PART III - The Journey is Sabotaged

journey--the big iron hitching post ring still in the tree. So much history in that region! My mother's cousin Ragina (pronounced Rag-ee-na) lived there at the time, and we loved her. When I sold my mother's house after she died, another cousin bought it and the property around it, including Ragina's old house, for by that time Ragina had died, too.

We had other cousins – like Tom and Juanita Ferguson and her family, whom we visited when I was a teenager. They'd take us out on their boat on the lake near their house. They were quite rich. Then there was Aunt Myrtle, whom we visited when I was a teenager. She had been to a ladies "Finishing School" and was quite proper. She lived in a big house that sat on the top of a hill at the entrance to Murphy. Now a big Baptist Church is on that hill. I remember going to her house. It was a dark house with lots of old pictures everywhere. Her son Tom lived there after her death. One night he fell asleep smoking a cigarette, the bed caught fire, burned the house down, and burned him to death. So much tragedy happened there.

On December 7th, in the late 1970s, my son's best friend's mother, and her sister, were coming through the stop light just below the Baptist Church, just below where Aunt Myrtle lived and Tom burned to death. A drunk, who was coming from a Christmas party, ran the light and hit their car, killing them both. I was due through that stop light that very day at that very time, to get to an appointment on time. But, I was late. When I got to the stop light, the crash had just occurred. I took Gary into our home and adopted him as a son, until his grieving father wanted him back. Today, my son and Gary are still communicating, and Gary still refers to me as "mom." He wished me Happy Mother's Day this last May. That brings tears to my eyes.

It was 1974. I got a job at the Ranger Elementary School as a substitute teacher. I worked full time for a while because I took the place of a lady who was having a baby. I taught seventh and eighth graders. It was like the story of *Christy*. Some of my students came to school barefooted. I taught thirteen-year olds in my class that could not read. But, they liked me so much that they got excited about reading. When the homeroom teacher came back and saw the progress of her class, she got jealous. So, I lost my position as a substitute.

It was a snowy winter. Few people in that area had indoor plumbing. While I was still teaching, I left the children with a mountain Baptist lady who had an outdoor toilet. The children had to walk through the snow to go to the toilet; something they were not used to. The lady was very good to the children.

Going up the dirt road next to our farmhouse in Bellview, to a hilltop, sat a house in a large field. It was the home of Pearl and Willard Anderson, and their son Charles. Pearl Anderson became my life-long friend. Her daughter Evenell had married Doug Anderson, and they lived down the road. I'm talking country roads. Her husband Willard had what is now called "deep depression." It was a "familiar spirit." Their son had depression, too. Willard would sit, head down, in his chair all day. Pearl had to do all the gardening and housework. She had learned to drive a car when she was 70, and had bought an old car to get her to town and back. Their son, Charles, was in his 40s. He had gotten himself into trouble from drinking too much and taking drugs, so he was not much help either.

Pearl was part Cherokee, so she got free medical for herself, Willard, and Charles. Charles wanted to find salvation, so he went to the little country church with his mother. But, the self-righteous religious folk there were very cruel and told him he could not be saved because he smoked cigarettes. I encouraged him a lot and gave him the message of salvation. Pearl was one of those simple people who lived the life of a true believer. She manifested the fruits of the Spirit of Yahuweh. She never complained. She was always cheerful. At times she would babysit my son. Evenell became a good friend too. She was also a friend to my third child. She fed her well, and offered her "used" corn husks to chomp on when she was teething. Between the simple, but good country cooking, and Dorothy with goat milk, she was very healthy.

We went to visit her after we moved into our own house at Hickory Hills, just one country lane down the road. One morning it had snowed and the two long driveways between our house on the bottom hill and the top hill had iced over. But, I put my daughter in the car and got up the hills. I got part way down the steep hill leading to the main road, and the car began to slide. It slid into a ditch. Then a truck started sliding from the top, and almost hit us. But, the trucker got me out, and I proceeded to Evenell's house. I stayed until the roads were cleared. Evenell suffered from what is now called "Bi-polar Disorder." Then it was called "manic-depressive" disorder. She was also very overweight. One morning, while preparing to go teach Bible School at her church, she just dropped dead of a heart attack in the bathroom. So sad! I attended Willard's funeral, and then Evenell's funeral.

Charles went into deep depression. One day Charles took a gun and went to Doug's house. He pretended to be crazy and pretended he was going to kill Doug. Doug snatched the gun from Charles as he pretended to attack Doug, and Doug shot him dead.

PART III - The Journey is Sabotaged

It was a staged suicide. The police figured that out, and Doug was not prosecuted. Pearl was alone, except for the youngest daughter named Marilyn. Marilyn and her husband lived near Atlanta. She and her children and my third child were friends. Marilyn was a good daughter. Because of the manic-depressive disorder that came on Willard and the two older children when they got near age 40, Pearl was very concerned that Marilyn might have it. But Marilyn never got it.

Finally, Pearl got up in her 90s, still sharp, but needed help, so Marilyn took her to a good nursing home near Atlanta. I went to visit her there. Pearl had gone blind by the time she reached 100, but she stayed in good health, and her mind was as sharp as could be. She still had a great sense of humor. She told me that when she was watching my son, she saw him playing with the toilet paper he had torn off the roller, and was putting it in the toilet. When she saw him, he got scared and threw the whole roll in the toilet. She would laugh at that story. I miss her! Marilyn and I kept up with each other for years. Pearl considered me her best friend. Looking back, even though she had friends and relatives, I guess I was her best friend. I was loyal to her. I loved her. We would visit other friends of hers in the area, and we always had a good time, but I was the one who kept her company and encouraged her through the years.

While in the Owenby's Bellview house, I met people down the road – Joan and Jim Vance. Joan and I became good friends. Our family had been to Cherokee, the Indian reservation, to Ashville, and all along the mountain road through the Nantahala Gorge, and Bryson City. It is a gorgeous area. It attracts a lot of tourists.

One day Joan and I decided to go to Gatlinburg, Tennessee, up in the Smokey Mountains. Her children were in school. I took my oldest daughter and son. My son was four and a half. Joan and my daughter went shopping in one store, and I went to another with my son. My son saw a pop gun and wanted it. I bought it for him, but told him, DO NOT OPEN IT. I told him to sit on a bench while I went into the store for a minute to look for one of those antique irons. I was gone about 2 minutes. When I came out, he was gone. The streets were packed with tourists. I panicked. I mean I panicked. I nearly lost my mind, I was in such a state of terror. We had come from California were there were reports of kidnapped children all the time, and I was terrified out of my mind. There was a policeman in the middle of a large intersection. The cars were backed up four ways, and he was directing traffic. I didn't care. I went out in the street, grabbed him, pulled him over to the curb, and told him my son was lost. He motioned to another policeman to take over, and he came over to the sidewalk with me. About that time, Joan and my daughter came up and wondered what was going on. I told them he was lost. His sister clapped her hands in glee and said "yeah – good!" Then she realized it was true, and she panicked too. The policeman called his Captain, who told him that a little lost boy had been found and taken to "The Trading Post" – a shop down the street. I went there, and there he was behind the counter, playing with his pop gun. I couldn't get mad at him. I just hugged and hugged him. The shop owner said that a nice young man had brought him in.

Years later I had been praying with all my heart about protection over my children. One morning while driving out of our driveway in Fort Worth, going to get groceries, Abba flashed that scene in front of me-- and I heard the words again of the shop owner: "A nice young man brought him in." By the time I got onto the street, He said: "**He was an angel**." That "nice young man" was one of Yahuweh's messengers! In Part XI of the Collections, I tell about how He protected my children at different times when they could have been killed.

In 1976, I was pregnant with our third child. We wanted to buy our own home. There was one for sale in Hickory Hills. One of our relatives, Louise Bayless, the one who tried to help me get into the DAR, told us about the house. The real estate agent was Margaret Warner, another relative, whose husband built the house. We went to see it, and wanted to buy it. It was a miracle we had the down payment. The house cost $35,000.00. The monthly payments were about $325.00. But, we struggled to pay that.

It was a brand new house that sat up on a hill, with steps going up to it, and a large garage below. It had three bedrooms, a big living room and dining room, a big kitchen, and a large balcony that faced the woods and the stream. Eventually, we closed off the garage and carpeted it, making a big family room out of it. Below the steps to the garage, just inside the garage, was a separate room, which we turned into a fourth bedroom. The house sat on a little over an acre overlooking the woods and a wonderful stream. There was a well on the property, but it was too shallow. Sand kept pouring into it. So, we hired a well-digging company and they dug close to the stream. They tapped into an underground river. We were so very blessed!

We had a walk-way cemented under the balcony that ran the length of the house facing the woods. Into the wet cement we had the oldest daughter, our son, and the third child, put their hand prints, and the paw print of our precious dog, Colombo. We wanted a dog. We went all the way to Chattanooga to the "Pound" and got our part Boxer, part Hound. That dog was such a part of

PART III - The Journey is Sabotaged

our family. When one of the cats had kittens, Colombo stood guard so that they were not eaten by the possums. We had possum, bears, mountain wildcat, deer, rabbits, owls, and snakes, along with other woods animals. So, Colombo was our guard dog.

Then there was Glenda down the road. She was the same age as my oldest daughter, but wow was she mean. She acted more like a boy than a girl. She shot our neighbor's dog. Glenda was so mean to my children. I got her in trouble one day with her dad because of it. She got a well-deserved whipping. Colombo ran off with a pack of wild dogs, but finally we got him back. Then he totally disappeared. We suspected Glenda shot him.

We were about 1/2 mile from the Georgia line, going towards Blairsville. Just up the hill, out to the road, and down about 1/4th mile, was the old Ty Cobb plantation home. My parents moved to North Carolina when my dad retired from the Post Office in 1975. At first, as I said above, they stayed at the Cobb plantation until building their own home. It was a huge 14-room house, with a big corn field out front. Ty had walked from there 10 miles into town every day for baseball practice. Bobby Cobb had a dairy just over the Georgia line, where we'd go and get fresh milk out of the cows. I made yogurt, and cheese, and butter. We were very healthy.

I remember when Ty died. I was in my late teens. There was a big news story on him. I learned that before he died he received Jesus as his savior. I well remember going to watch the L.A. Dodgers play at Dodger Stadium, and before the game, the announcer told us to stand as they had a minute of silence for Ty Cobb. My friend Jeanne, the one who took me around my hometown to find the Gladys Alyward book, was with me. She told me I should shout out that he was my cousin, but I kept quiet.

In February of 1976, we went on a trip to Washington D.C. with the first two children. It was a good trip. It was after that that I found I was pregnant with our third baby. It was in that spring that we moved into our new home in Hickory Hills. I was working in a retail store in Murphy – at Sky City. I then went to work for Big 6 selling advertisements. This baby was my inspiration to stop working and begin to be a real mother.

There was no room for a huge garden like I had in Bellview, but I had little gardens in specially laid out garden beds to do organic gardening. I had learned much from my class on Organic Farming at Tri-County College in Murphy. I also bought produce from our local markets in bulk--like boxes of "cull tomatoes" (tomatoes with imperfection). I used the tomatoes to make homemade spaghetti sauce, which I froze for use on my homemade pasta. I also loved to "can" things in glass jars, which I stored in our basement cupboards. It hurt me when my husband took his wealthy friends, who bought advertisements from him at Big 6, down to the basement and freely gave them things I had canned.

Gourmet cooking, gardening vegetables and herbs, archeology, and photography, were my greatest outlets - and living in the country in North Carolina provided me with all of those joys. At our lovely house, I had fifty different herbs that I had planted – a few from the woods, but mostly all were purchased at a gardening store, or through a mail-order catalogue. I got my many rose bushes from a mail-order catalogue.

Each Christmas I would buy a small live tree and then plant it after Christmas. We had some gorgeous pine and fir trees in our front yard. One day my little son brought me a few sprigs of Lemon Balm squished in his little sweaty hand. I planted it, and it was one of my biggest herb crops. I took some to Texas when we moved, and it made hedges. Abba blessed it most likely.

I used the herbs in cooking and medicine. I was a regular "Granny Clampett," except I never cooked possum for dinner (smile). One day I had a bad headache. I took four of the common dried herbs, put them in a cup of hot water, and sat down to relax and drink the tea. I took one sip of the tea, and it was like someone shot me with a tranquilizer gun. Whatever was in those herbs caused such total peace to rush through my veins that the headache left. Yes, I still have the "recipe."

My husband loved his job at the radio station. The owners were a prominent family in the region. We were friends. I referred to my husband as "a large fish in a little pond." He later became a small fish in a big pond. He was also a sportscaster for local sports teams, but also for college teams in Chattanooga. He covered school band competitions. He was so good at that. But, he finally left Big Six and took a job in Chattanooga with a Christian television station. This helped him get a good job with a Christian television station when we moved to Fort Worth, Texas in 1986.

This is funny: While working for Big Six we sometimes hosted celebrities. One time, Junior Samples came to one of our Big Six dinners. Remember him--BR 549? He was very popular on "Hee Haw." That night after the dinner, my husband and I, and the radio station owner's son, went to his motel room to talk some more. Junior had an itch on his back. So, I scratched it. I thought: "This is crazy -- who would believe it? Here I am in a motel room with Junior Samples, scratching his back" – heehaw. He was a nice guy.

Earlier that night we also enjoyed the sky entertainment. In those mountains we had a special type of entertainment, whether from humans or aliens. I'm telling the truth! We would sit outside at night and watch the UFOs in the sky. They would come in groups of three and hover, then shoot out at odd angles. It was almost every night. They were close too--not way up in the sky. One night we went to have dinner across the Georgia line with our skeptical radio station owner and his wife. She had tried to get him to believe in the UFOs but he laughed her off. That night here they came. We pointed at them. Max stared at them in wonder. He looked at us like a deer in headlights and said: "I just saw a UFO." We laughed...

I had joined a community choir in Brasstown. One night, about 9:30, I was returning from choir rehearsal. I was driving on a narrow two-lane road through nothing but forest country. There were no street lights—so it was very dark. I rounded a curve in the road and saw this huge saucer-shaped vehicle in a field right by the road. I mean it was huge. It was round with lights glowing out of its "windows" with a large cap on the top out of which a bright red light was flashing. Being me, I went to pull over on the shoulder of the road, and in that four-five seconds, those cowards took the ship straight up, and it hovered about ½ mile above me. I yelled at it: "Chicken!" I wanted a "close encounter of the third kind." I really think it was human-powered. I had no fear of it, but whoever "manned it" was afraid of me evidently. I've known that the Germans, Russians, and Americans, have had anti-gravity technology for at least 50 years, and have built such crafts – some as big as a mile wide. But, there are also crafts driven by aliens (fallen angels) from whom man got this technology, after World War II especially.

Then there was the classic: My husband and I were out driving down the Blairsville "Highway" to eat at a restaurant near Blairsville. We were all alone on this country 2-lane road. As we crossed the North Carolina line into Georgia, we saw off to our left a large saucer-shaped lighted vehicle, known as a space ship, rising slowly from behind a tall hill. It slowly began to parallel us on the highway. It went along beside us for about a mile. I just told my husband "keep driving." We were concerned because we had heard that they could shut down the engines of cars. But, this one just moved with us, then all of a sudden, it shot in front of us across the highway and into the field across from us to the right. We just kept driving. It was numbing, but it made life in the country a lot more fun.

A couple moved to the Brasstown Folk School area. He had been a Professor at the famed Fuller Theological Seminary. She was a musician. They set up a workshop and built instruments that were typical of the old mountaineers of the Appalachians.

They had a little class for my oldest daughter, where she learned to play the recorder. Then they had a class for younger children, which was kind of like a "music appreciation" class. I enrolled my son in that. One day I went to get him early from his class, and the children were all lying on their backs, and the woman was coming around touching them on the forehead. I felt really wrong about that. I never took him back. But, I learned later they were strongly New Age people, as were so many who had moved into the Brasstown area. She was teaching them to receive their "spirit guides." Oh the protection of Abba!

My husband was/is a brilliant man, a writer, and a tremendous actor in stage productions, as well as a stand-up comic. He tried to break into show biz as a comedian while we lived in California, but it didn't fly. He was/is highly gifted. Most of his jobs through the years have been in sales. He is an expert in sales, both in advertising sales, and product sales. Because of the job with Big Six, we had lots of high-brow friends. We were in the inner circle of our town. We were "big shots." We would party with the best of them. I threw some "whing-dinger" parties, too.

I loved to dance, from my days in bebop rock-and-roll, to the music of Elvis Presley, Nat King Cole, Fats Domino, Chubby Checker, and Bill Haley's Rock Around the Clock. So, the 1950s were truly "Happy Days." Little did I know then what was being hidden from the American people while President Ike played golf in Palm Springs.

In North Carolina, I became a mixture of a mother, gardener, gourmet cook, school teacher assistant in my children's schools, organist at church, children's catechism teacher, cashier in a retail store, public school teacher, a veterinarian's assistant, advertising sales lady for Big Six, secretary to priests, a voice for radio advertisements, and party-organizer. On top of that, I took three courses at Tri-County Community College – in archeology, organic gardening, and photography. I started the camera club that became so well known throughout the region.

During the photography class, the teacher expressed his desire to have a camera club in our area. I raised my hand and said: "I'm the secretary at St. Williams' Catholic Church, and we can meet on Friday at 7:00 PM in our social hall." He was delighted. The class had so many Floridians in it, and all were excited. It developed into such a thriving club, going on many field trips and entering into competitions with other clubs in the region. It was an example of Abba's favor, even then. For everything I have put my hands to, and my efforts behind, has prospered.

We took most of our field trips in the spring and fall. The Floridians would come in autumn to see the leaves turning colors,

PART III - The Journey is Sabotaged

enjoy the gorgeous dark blue skies, the sunshine, and crisp fall weather. I had my mother's eye for beauty in context, my son too. My son came on the field trips. We would get down on our hands and knees and take pictures of the tiniest mushrooms, and flowers. In one of the competitions, he beat me. He never let me live that down (smile). My son would go with me on the college's archeology field trips, and chalk the Indian markings. The teacher loved him.

My son loved to cook like I did. We watched cooking shows on TV. Julia Child's cooking show was our favorite. One day my son did something that deserved punishment, and it must have been really serious, because I dealt out the maximum punishment on him: I denied his right to watch Julia Child. To this day, he reminds me of my extreme cruelty to him in denying him the right to watch Julia Child. We watched Jeff Smith of "The Frugal Gourmet" too. I loved watching Jeff because he had scenes of his shopping in different exotic places in Europe. That was before my traveling days. I day-dreamed that one day I would go to Italy and Greece, and all those exciting places that Jeff went to. To date, I've been to those places several times and I have really enjoyed them!

I cooked foods from around the world. I remember hosting friends of my second daughter, her school mates who would come to spend the night. I would serve them stir-fry, complete with bean sprouts. Those little mountain kids would look at it, and pick at it--probably wondering if they were worms. I took a picture of my youngest as a baby in her high chair with a big smile on her face, and bean sprouts hanging out of her mouth. That area had so many multi-millionaires that dressed like hillbillies so you couldn't tell them from the local farmers. There were famous singers, like Dolly Parton who came from just down the Brasstown Road. Her cousin told me she had red hair and was covered in freckles. They bleached her hair, and bleached her freckles.

When we first moved into the Bellview house, I remember it snowed not long after we got there. I had never seen it snow in my life. I grew up in southern California. I went to places where there was snow, but I never saw it fall. I was wearing a short-sleeved top, because it was warm in the house. We had a fireplace. But, I ran outside and took pictures, and just let the snow fall on me. The children loved to make snowmen and play in the snow. The biggest snows would come in March sometimes.

I loved baking bread for our family. I subscribed to *Bon Appetite* magazine, and bought all kinds of vegetarian cookbooks, besides Julia Child's classics. I was a vegetarian for seven years there, but cooked regular meat dishes for my family. I made fresh pasta almost every day for seven years, and made sauces from natural ingredients. I picked greens from the woods. Pearl had a big patch of poke greens behind her house, so each spring I'd gather poke greens and cook them for dinner. We also had "fiddle ferns" that I found in our woods. They taste like green beans. I gathered water cress and Joe Pye weed. I studied the edible plants around us. I learned how to pick the good sumac, which tastes like lemons, and make it into tea. (There is a poisonous sumac.) At that time, I didn't know it was an important spice in the Middle East. My family and I were very healthy. Later, when we moved to Texas, and I could no longer afford to buy natural foods, I ate cheap processed food. The first taste of it was canned Ravioli. It was horrible! Later, I returned to my discipline of nutrition.

In North Carolina, I loved studying about the natural plants that grew in the woods, and about healthy eating. I joined a Co-op, and got wonderful natural products each month. Even when we were on food stamps, and had to stand in line for government handouts, I collected good things from the woods to eat. I loved getting roles of empty tea bags from the Co-op and putting in herb blends. Then the tea bags were sealed with a hot iron.

I had joyfully come to North Carolina hoping to leave my rebellious years behind me in California. But, shortly after moving to North Carolina, the ritualistic torture began again. My husband had not come to North Carolina to put the past behind him. So, in despair, it didn't take long before I lapsed back into sin. Talk about a mixture! In California, sin had become comfortable to me. Usually people do not sin because they are forced into it. They use excuses, blaming sin on someone else, but it all comes from within a person. Messiah said that well (**Mark 7:20-23**) Familiar spirits manifest. They are demonic spirits that make sin comfortable. Because of deep anger at "God," and bitterness at what I'd allowed to happen to me, I had become comfortable with sin. It challenged me. I felt justified in doing it, but also used the suffering as an excuse to continue in it.

I could have left my husband at any time. I could have done a lot of things through the years to change my situation. The cage door was open. It took major upheaval to get me out. Once out, I wondered why I had ever stayed in. Humans! We are so complex! Abba never left me, but He let the "fruit of my thoughts" and my actions run their sinful course. When He called a halt to it, it was over! "Hear, O earth, Behold! I will bring evil upon this people, even the fruit of their thoughts..." (**Jeremiah 6:19**)

Abba has shown me that my life paralleled the House of Ephraim/Joseph/Israel– the northern ten tribal groups of Ya'cob.

PART III - The Journey is Sabotaged

In the beginning, there was innocence. But, later, there was the breaking away, and the sin. He had to drive the ten northern tribes out of His Land into the nations AMONG the gentiles, where they remain to this day, even though their punishment of 2,730 years ended September 12, 2007 on that historic Sukkot. Few wanted to return – captivity has been all too nice. But, He promises to bring back a remnant.

From innocence, to living in flesh, to sin, to punishment, to restoration, and forward to victory and honor – this is the history of the House of Israel/Ephraim/Joseph, and this has been my life story. In 2011, I wrote about this in the study on Hosea, written about His love for the ten "lost" tribes: "How Could I Give You Up Ephraim?" The "lost tribes" were not lost to Judah, and today men like Ya'ir Davidy and his team of Jews and Ephraimites, men like Steven Collins, and John Hully, have discovered where the individual ten tribes settled, as in his classic book *The Tribes*.

In intercession for the return of a repentant remnant of Ephraim to the Covenant of Yahuweh, I often use **Hosea 11:8-9**: **"How could I give you up Ephraim? How could I turn you over Israel? How could I make you like Admah? How could I set you like Tseboyim? My heart turns within me. All My compassion is kindled. I shall not let the heat of My wrath burn, I shall not turn to destroy Ephraim. For I am El and not man, the Set-Apart One in your midst, and I shall not come to you in enmity.**"

Admah and Tseboyim were two of the five cities of the plain, along with Sodom and Gomorrah, that Abba destroyed to ash. (**Genesis 19**) Abba had every right to reduce me to ash. But, He saw me now – and "His mercy endures forever!" When about everyone gave up on me, my earthly father thought I was as pure as the virgin Mary, and said so, and my heavenly Abba, knowing the truth, still never gave up on me! My mother did not turn against me either, though she was more realistic than papa. My mother's family gossiped a lot about me, but never turned against me. They knew my husband too, and were very leery of him.

My Baptist church did not teach that the God of the Old Testament was mean and cruel. They never ever alluded to it. But, the spirits of Greece and Rome live within Christianity. I had many 33rd degree Masons on my mother's side of the family, who were high up in politics in North Carolina. In Albert Pike's *Morals and Dogmas*, the Masonic "Bible," he teaches that Lucifer is the good god who illumined Eve, and Yahuweh is the bad god, the god of darkness, who kept illumination from Eve. Masonic/Illuminati hierarchy says that Lucifer is good, Yahuweh is bad. While I never called Lucifer good, I did come to the point of calling "God" all sorts of filthy names, and hating Him. I remember praying as a young teenager, with anger in my spirit, because God told Joshua to kill men, women and children, and His LAW was cruel. I saw Jesus and the Holy Spirit as being good. I could not reconcile how Jesus and His Father were the same... though Messiah had said: "I and the Father are One." I knew that Jesus never told anyone to kill other people. So, even as I prayed, the hate spirits of Greece and Rome--the spirit of the Christian religion--against the "LAW of the Jews," surfaced. I kept these thoughts tucked away. But, when I went through years of ritualistic satanic torture and abuses by one who was respected as a Christian minister, all that questioning surfaced, and my hate for the evil God of the OLD TESTAMENT came out full front in vengeance.

In 2012, I was watching a Rob Skiba DVD, and he related the same thing happened to Him – a hate for the God of the Old Testament because He killed people, and ordered people to be killed. He wondered where that idea had come from in his mind, because it was a conscious thought processing. I wonder how many children who have grown up in the church system, as adults, have this thinking, either on the surface, or latent in their subconscious. Oftentimes, when people hear that we must guard the Torah, their response comes from deep hate of "the LAW."

THE "PSYCHOLOGICAL REVERSAL"

In my fifth year of marriage, in July of 1971, while living in Long Beach, California, there came the wound that was so powerful that it caused what psychologists call "a psychological reversal." It was as if one day I wanted nothing more than to serve God with all my heart, and have a good marriage and loving family, and the next day I started my downslide into the pit, though the transition between those two took a few months. The wound was so deep and so damaging, that I almost died spiritually, mentally, emotionally, and even physically. In reporting these things now, I have no emotion. These events happened so far back in the past, and they are under the blood of Messiah. Yahuweh and Yahushua have forgiven me! So, I report from total objectivity.

With Sha'ul, who called himself "chief of sinners," I can say: "**I am crucified with Messiah, nevertheless I live...and the life which I now live in the flesh, I live by the faith of the Son of Yahuweh, who loved me and gave Himself for me**." (**Galatians 2:20**) He did for me what I could not do for myself!

It was our fifth wedding anniversary, July 23, 1971. I had come home from work. I was hoping we'd go out for a nice dinner. As I entered the house, my husband was sitting on the couch, leaning back casually, with a sadistic smirk on his face. I asked him if we could go out to eat on our anniversary. But, he said nothing. He just handed me a piece of paper with a phone number on it. Then he said that he had set up a "wife-swapping" night for us, and for me to call the man I would be having sex with. I was numb. I took the paper and started to dial the number. My mind had gone into total shutdown. I got halfway into dialing and I hung up the phone. My mind shut down. You could say that after five years of ritualistic satanic abuse and cruelty of many types, and a nervous breakdown, too, that this was "the straw that broke the camel's back."

The psychological reversal began. I had given my life to the service of ministering to others, to evangelism, to teaching the Word. It was this trauma that caused me to snap. It didn't manifest right away, but it was as if a cancer had entered my soul, and was eating away at me. Deep anger surfaced that turned to bitterness, to hate, and then to revenge. It also led to deep depression. Once the hate began to manifest, I took great delight and comfort in it, thinking I was getting revenge on the God who had betrayed me.

I have no problem being honest. Abba has totally transformed me. But, to do it, He had to let my hate-filled vengeance run its course. Demonic spirits that came to me as a little child began to manifest and take control. It was as if all barriers came off my mind and emotions, and I felt I had been freed to be as wicked as I could possibly be. It took a few months, but the psychological blow from someone I wanted to love me, who wanted to turn me over to another man for sex, while he had sex with his wife, caused me to die inside.

While pregnant with our son, the abuse was making me so nervous and terrified, that I was on the verge of the nervous breakdown that took over after he was born. So, I asked my mother if we could go to visit my Aunt Ahnie and their family. While there, I was so weak that often I could not stand up. While at Nanny's house, I collapsed on the couch. Nanny was fixing dinner, but I was not hungry. My mother did not know what was wrong with me, so she accused me of being lazy. I grew up being falsely accused of things, but that hurt. I had not told her anything I was going through in my marriage. It must have been Abba, for I began craving my Aunt Ahnie's salty, briny, pickles. I ate just a few, and within minutes I felt strong and healthy. One day in Texas, I was talking to a former M.A.S.H. doctor, and told him about the pickles. He confirmed that there were properties in the pickles that would have healed me.

I continued at Community Chapel until the nervous breakdown in 1971, then I was too sick and weak to do any ministry. I took shelter in the Catholic Church for a while during the nervous breakdown, but because those I loved at Community Chapel did not come to visit me, I felt justified in dumping the whole of Christianity.

Before the above tragedy, I had purchased a new Bible at Community Chapel. One morning I picked up the Bible, while lying on the bed and opened it. It opened to **Luke 22:31-32** (KJV): **"And the Lord said, `Simon, Simon, behold Satan hath desired to have you that he may sift you as wheat, but I have prayed for you that thy faith fail not, and when you are converted, strengthen thy brethren."** The passage was underlined in green ink. I had a pen with green ink that I used to underline favorite Scriptures. I rolled over on my right side, with the Bible next to me and cried and cried. Then I went numb. I realized it was a new Bible. I had never written in it before. I rose up on my right elbow to look at the passage again. It was not underlined in green ink.

It was a message from Yahushua Himself. He knew what I was about to do, and He personally said He would pray for me, and that after I was delivered, I would help others be free. And when I was delivered, my faith was much stronger and more pure. So, do you see that even in the worst of things, Yahuweh brings eternal good? It is because of His foreknowledge (**I Peter 1:2; Ephesians 1:4; Psalm 139:1-18; Jeremiah 1:5**) I look back and deeply thank Yahushua for praying for me. He interceded for me when His Father had every right to execute the full judgment of the Torah against me. But, because of His foreknowledge, He let me punish myself.

The enemy began to stir thoughts that far exceeded the sin-filled thoughts of previous years. Familiar spirits descended! I went to the grocery store across the street to steal very explicit sex novels. I didn't care. When we first got married, we had been so poor that I had felt justified to steal food from the supermarket. I did not do it that much, and many times I went back to the store, bought the same item, then left it inside the store – to make up for the item I originally stole. Thankfully this didn't last long--my conscious caught up with me.

All my life, my mother bought my clothes, until I got married. And, then I had no money to buy clothes, except at thrift stores. But, when I worked for Forest Lawn Cypress, and we lived in Long Beach, I went to buy clothes of my liking – skirts up to the thigh and tops down to the middle--the sexier the better. Abba knew it all had to surface. Only when that which is within surfaces, can it

PART III - The Journey is Sabotaged

be skimmed off, as dross is skimmed off of gold once the temperature is hot enough to melt it. Our thoughts create--good or wickedness. Sin doesn't just happen. Yet, my spirit had been born again. I knew that. In all of it, I never denied my Savior! That was also His great mercy! I cursed Jesus and the Holy Spirit, too, at the peak of my hate, but I feared denying my salvation. This, again, shows the difference between the soul (carnal, fleshly mind and emotions-seat of the sin-prone, earth-bound nature that can be manipulated by Lucifer and demons) and the spirit, which is perfected at the new birth. The spirit sets boundaries when it comes to eternal matters.

I had never known a man to love me, for me. So, I set out to get someone to hold me, whatever it took. I let hurt bury me in depression and despair. I lost the will to care anymore about anything except getting revenge on a God I did not know, whom I thought had failed me, and who I thought was incredibly sadistic, who got pleasure from torturing me.

But, what we are is what we are. As an example: Even in a drunken state, I'd sit on a bar stool and cry and tell the guy next to me about how Jesus loved him and wanted to save him. This is why I understood the main character in the movie *The Apostle*. That's a good movie. **I did all I could to carve a deep cavern within me that would contain my hate, bitterness, and anger. When He delivered me out of that pit, He filled that deep cavern with His love, so that I was filled with passionate love for the Elohim of Israel whom I now really know! The depths of hate became the depths of love!**

I began doing everything I could to match the image of the *Cosmopolitan* magazine woman, who proudly proclaimed the right to be a "classic bitch." I really did not want to hurt anyone except God. I knew I could not hurt my husband. He was very pleased with my rebellion. So, the more I sinned, the more my husband loved it – he encouraged it. By bringing me down, he felt justified in everything he did to me, and to our children.

My makeup was so professionally applied that I had people ask me if I was an artist. With my long thick auburn hair, hazel eyes, great figure, sexy clothes, artistic make-up, and incredibly rebellious personality, of course, I attracted a lot of the wrong types of men. But, that was the idea. I prided myself on my collection. I was a huntress with no shame. That demon spirit of the tiger, which appeared to me when I was four, put a spirit of the huntress into me.

I understand **Jeremiah 3:3**! I had a "whore's forehead." I even tried to get a job as a night club "go-go" dancer, and as a masseuse for hire, but I knew that was going too far. I was hired, but I didn't take the jobs. The Spirit of Yahuweh stopped me from a lot of things that could have been eternally disastrous. I don't mean to be offensive in saying these things. I just want you to know the depths I went to, so that you will rejoice when you read of what He did for me! **How can you appreciate what He did for me, until you realize what He had to do for me**?

My life of sin peaked in California when I worked for Forest Lawn Cypress. It was a wonder they kept me employed there. But, I did my work well. It was while working here that I saved enough money for us to move to North Carolina. I thought my life of sin was all over when we left California, but it was not long before I continued it in North Carolina. All the while, I tried to be a good mother. I always loved my children. I did not know about "portal openings" to the demonic world back then. I did not know what was happening to me, either. I was trying to survive.

In North Carolina, because we were part of the social "in crowd," I got myself into a lot of personal trouble. At parties, I ruined any good reputation I had left. At times I'd drink too much moonshine, which they made into a punch called "purple Jesus." I'd get wild and very "loose." My high falootin' friends loved me. I was FUN! But, of course, it was only a cover for my inner pain.

The county we lived in was a "dry county" – no liquor was sold or allowed in public. So, we just went into Georgia. There was a makeshift night club there, and our radio and political friends went there almost every weekend. I loved to dance. So, I'd drink, eat pretzels, and dance. I did not know I was pregnant with my third baby. One night I drank 21 glasses of wine and ate lots of pretzels, potato chips, and crackers, and danced and danced. I was one who could "hold their liquor." I was so scared when I found out I was pregnant. But, thanks to Abba's intervention she was a perfectly healthy baby. But, I did the exact same thing with the fourth one. And Abba made sure she was perfectly healthy.

The Methodist minister and his wife were under scrutiny by the religious factors of our small town. Sometimes they would come to this "night club," but leave early. Finally they were found out, and dismissed. It was the favorite place of the sheriff and his top men-- bankers, doctors, and politicians. You know--the secular crowd. Being Catholic no one cared if we went or not. We were "big wigs." Some of my Catholic friends were also friends of those in the insider club.

But, in the midst of it all, I have some good memories of my times with my children. Our family went to the Cherokee Indian Reservation near Ashville, to the Biltmore House in Ashville, on mini-vacations, and to fish on Notla Lake. Then there was the "trestle tracking" that my son and I did along old railroad tracks, and our digging for arrowheads and spearheads in our stream. I did research on our family, interviewed people, and even wrote articles for Catholic magazines, which were published. I got a little scared, however, when a monastery of Italian monks asked me to come to Italy to talk to them. I had written in a magazine on Fatima, about my new birth. I wrote different articles for our local newspaper, *The Cherokee Scout*. Every January, for the January 22nd edition, I wrote an article against abortion.

I was involved with our children--in their schools, and extracurricular activities like sports, band, gymnastics, karate, and in special classes in other things. I was a school "room mother." I was involved with their friends, and tried to include my children in all the good things I was doing too. I tried to make a family. I had wanted so bad to be a good wife, and have a happy home. I wanted so bad to be a good mother. Today my children love me! It is a miracle of Abba's redemption!

I took thousands of pictures of my children's growing up, especially in the days in North Carolina, because it was so beautiful there. About age eight, my parents bought me a box-style Brownie camera. I began taking pictures of our trips. During the years, I took priceless pictures of special people, like Rolf McPherson, Dr. Hinderlighter, the Jensen sisters, as well as multitudes of family pictures and friends. I took pictures of Junior Samples, friends at St. Williams, Mary Helen, of many other friends, my parents, my grandmother, and my mother's family too – the old Dickey cemetery, and on and on--thousands of pictures in nearly 20 large albums. I do not have those pictures today.

My husband had/has almost hypnotic power to manipulate and control people, exerting such pressure on them that they give in to him, and then forget what they've done. He exerted this power over the child I trusted with all those pictures, until they simply "cracked" and gave them to him. To this day, they don't remember doing it. I found out quite by accident that this had happened. I was at my oldest daughter's house in Tennessee. She got a large package from her dad. In it were many pictures of herself as a child growing up. I saw that and realized they were pictures from the 16 large albums that I had another child keep for me. I called them in hysterics. They said that my husband had put extreme pressure on them, so they gave in. I considered those pictures my most precious possessions. No, I don't fault them. This type of hypnotic pressure is satanic!

This same type of hypnotic pressure, whether by pulse wave technology, or by lying spirits, will be used by the false prophet and anti-messiah to bring the world's people into subjection to them. It is a power similar to the "sound of silence" pulse waves coming off the T.V., which were used in Iraq in 2003. When America's ground troops came face to face with Saddam's finest troops, the sound of silence was used. Saddam's troops simply laid down their guns, began to cry, went and put their heads on the shoulders of the American soldiers and kept crying. This is what will be done to the American people when the Beast's takeover begins. I tried to get my husband to allow me to see the pictures, but he said "NO!" Now, he says he does not have them. Maybe they are in a storage shed, or maybe he threw them away. But, pictures are often used to do witchcraft and voodoo on people. We've seen enough of that in our family, even to this day.

It was one of the greatest heartbreaks of my life, since I considered them my most precious possession. Yet, I now question the need to collect "images," in the name of "memories." Perhaps Abba did me a favor! But, this opened a portal for the enemy to barrage me with hurt for years. However, honestly I ask: "If I had them today, what would I do with them?" I can't take them with me. I'll lose all of my pictures at some point, for Abba is preparing me to go with one suitcase. I never know when He tells me to go somewhere, if I will return to my home-base in the U.S. Since 1996, I have taken thousands of pictures of my adventures in many countries, and of my family. In trusting another child with some of my most precious possessions from my childhood, they were sold without my permission, or thrown out. But, I have to consider that if Abba allows something, it is for our good in the long run. He is fair in His dealings with us!

After so many years of the enemy bringing those hurts back to me, especially in the middle of the night, Abba taught me a principle to reverse the attack: When the enemy begins bringing those memories back, I throw my hands up into the air, and begin to loudly praise Yahuweh, and the enemy quickly leaves. Wisdom comes slow, but finally Abba gets His point across, one way or the other.

Shortly after I got married, I had a dream of living in a trailer alone. I was living in a remote area, so I did not lock the trailer door when I left. I came back home one evening to the trailer, and saw that the door was open. Someone had violated my trust and entered my home. I had kept what was most precious to me in a dresser that sat along a wall. I opened the drawers to see if my precious things were still there. But, in their place, ever so perfectly arrayed, I saw costume jewelry set in rows – all cheap fakes. I ran to the open window and looked out into the night. An enemy had stolen what was precious and replaced it with what was cheap and worthless. That was a perfect picture of so many things my life.

In 2011, to consolidate all the years of travel pictures, and lighten my physical load, I threw out hundreds of them by my own will, with about 70 pounds worth of albums. Though good memories are precious, they can be obstacles to our going forward with our Master!

In October of 1984, my son and I were on one of the Camera Club's fieldtrips into the mountains. I've never seen the sky such a dark blue. My son came and sat with me overlooking a river below. A member of the club, Ian, took a sneak picture of us sitting there, facing the river. He gave the picture to me. Talk about precious! I still have that picture!

Our third child was conceived in the Bellview house, but she was born in 1976 after we moved to our own house in the Hickory Hills subdivision. Because we were $1/4^{th}$ of a mile from the Georgia line, and it was ten miles into Murphy, my doctor and the "hospital" (a very tiny facility) were in Blairsville, Georgia. This baby was twenty days overdue. Ten days before her birth, I was hurrying across a parking lot to avoid an on-coming car. I had to get home to fix dinner because Father Del was coming to dinner. In my haste to avoid being hit by an oncoming truck, I tripped and I fell into a bank's shrubbed entryway. Hardly anyone was around, but finally someone found me. An ambulance was called and I was taken to the hospital. I had cracked three bones on the top of my left foot--I was wearing sandals, and because of my flexible bones, my left foot bent backwards and cracked the bones. So I was put in a cast. The cast was only removed a few days before she was born. I also had bruised my pelvic bone by my right foot coming up when I fell. I know that sounds weird, but my flexible joints cause a lot of weirdness. Still this baby hung in there another ten days.

Papa always said that rain was a sign of blessing. The first one was born while it was raining, the second one, too. But, we were experiencing a drought--it had not rained for several months. Because it had been five years since my son was born, I had forgotten what labor pains felt like. The morning of October 20th, 1976, I got up at 4:00 AM because I felt some strange pains. I sat on the couch and wondered what to do. I did not want to wake up my husband. Then it started raining. It rained very hard. The pains got so bad that I finally got him up and he took me to the emergency room at the hospital. A nurse put her hand on my belly, and they quickly rushed me into delivery. I didn't know I was in labor (smile). I had told Dr. Van Robinson that I wanted my tubes tied so I would have no more babies. He said that I should wait and tell him on the delivery table if I wanted my tubes tied. She was born at 8:33 AM. He asked me if I wanted my tubes tied. I told him "NO." That was one of the best decisions I've ever made, or we would not have our powerhouse blond. You got it-- the blond with the big blue eyes was born when it was raining too--in that, she did not break the pattern. As I am writing this (2012) her family visited me in Florida yesterday – she's still a powerhouse blond, a powerhouse for Yahuweh and for righteousness!

In North Carolina, I had been selling advertisements for Big Six. I had hired an old lady to watch my third baby while I worked. She was a nice old lady, but one time I went to pick up my daughter, and she said that she fell with my baby in her arms. My little girl was OK, but that convinced me to stop working and begin to be a real mother. I had so much fun "playing dolls" with her. She became my little buddy. She was so much fun, and quite mischievous. She went with me everywhere. Sometimes, she'd pull stunts--like running out in front of cars and trucks. One time she ran through the beach area at Vogel Lake until she floated face down. I thought for sure she had drowned. But, she was delightful--she still is. But mischievous – oh my! Now, her little adopted girl, age 2, is just like her. They have to lock the front door just to go to the mailbox, or else she'll open it and run out. She is a "live wire" – and I love it! It is amazing too, that this little adopted girl looks so much like my daughter!

All four of my children are mischievous, love to tease, and have a super sense of humor. You can imagine what it is like when we all get together. They love each other, and they love mom. But, where did they get that mischievous nature? They blame me! They're right! When she started school, I was working in the Catholic Church as a secretary to the priest, but also I taught Catechism to prepare seven-year-olds for their first communion. I really taught the children how to be born again. So, before receiving her first communion, she received salvation by personally confessing that the Savior had died and risen for her, and that she trusted Him for salvation. That was May 1982. But, long before that, she loved to talk about Jesus and heaven. Later she was gloriously baptized into the Spirit, and became a real witness to Elohim. Today, she and her husband guard the Torah also.

On Israel's Independence Day, April 15, 2012, she and her husband prayed with their precious six year old son who wanted to ask Jesus to save him and take him to heaven. Shortly before that, the youngest daughter of my youngest prayed for Jesus to save her. They are five months apart in age. In January of 2012,

PART III - The Journey is Sabotaged

the three youngest children went together to Haiti, on their first united missionary trip. It impacted their lives very much, and brought them into such unity of spirit.

This is funny now, but it wasn't then. One day while working as secretary/social director for Father Del, I let this third child go outside to play in the big front yard of the rectory. She was about four. I had fixed up a used tricycle for her to ride. The church was on the main highway, 64, between Murphy and Andrews. It was a two lane highway. A good friend and neighbor of ours, John Gorecki, came to visit Father Del. After pulling into the driveway, he came running in and told me that my daughter was riding her tricycle down the middle of the Andrew's highway. I went out and there she was. The traffic was backed up in both directions. She was riding right down the center line of the highway. I panicked, but later on we all had a good laugh. No one was honking.

She was/is such a loving child. From the time I stopped selling advertisements for Big Six and stayed home with her, I pampered her with lotions and powders. She loved "Family Feud," and every time she heard the music she would come running to the TV. At that time, Richard Dawson of M.A.S.H. fame was the host of Family Feud. Years later, my husband in the duties of Big Six, interviewed quite a few stars and political figures in person. He also met Richard Dawson. This led to our trying out to be on Family Feud, however we didn't make it. One day, at my husband's request, Richard called our house to talk to her. She was so excited.

My husband had a way of getting in with big named people – he had unusual favor with them. The famous actress, Myrna Loy, not only let him come visit her in her private cabin near Murphy, but wanted him to stay for several hours to talk to her and her secretary. He interviewed many of the famous Nashville singing stars, since he covered the Georgia Mountain Fair each year for Big Six. Danny Thomas had come to Chattanooga to do a benefit at a hospital, and my husband was determined to get an interview. There were many reporters waiting to interview Danny, but he refused them all. But, my husband asked him for an interview, and he gave it to him. My husband even talked to the White House Press Secretary via phone in Washington D.C., early the morning after Jimmy Carter was elected, and got an interview.

The children developed a fear of my gift of knowing what they were up to. If my oldest daughter slipped out to go meet her boyfriend at night, I'd wake up and go lock the door. She'd come back and pound on the door, then I would let her in, and tell her what she did. One day my son, about age 11, was walking down the street in town with his friend Chris Burnell, and Abba spoke to me: "They are going to the pool hall." When he got home, I asked him how he liked the pool hall.

My oldest daughter and my son, being three years apart, fought horribly. They even told me later that they'd chase one another around the house with knives. I whipped them with the belt so many times, but wow they were stubborn. I wonder where they got all that stubbornness? Hum...they're all like that! OK, OK--from me again! However, as with me, I find that instead of rebellious stubbornness, they have developed strong steadfastness for righteousness, and resolve to follow Yahuweh. HalleluYah! The last two responded to my rebukes quickly. I only remember spanking the youngest once, and it was just a gentle swat. I said that the last two made up for the first two, as far as discipline that is. But, as the years have passed, they all love one another, are very close, and stand up for each other. My son just recently said in an e-mail: "I love my sisters." So, the plans of the enemy just keep getting foiled!

Like I said, my husband had become a celebrity in Murphy for his radio announcing, but also he was a sportscaster for teams in Chattanooga, and covered Hayesville band competitions. People would ask for his autograph. When the movie *Steel Magnolias*, starring Sally Fields, came out in the 1980s, one of the main actors looked so much like my husband that no matter where we went, people would ask for his autograph and we would have to tell them that he was not the actor.

We did have fun with that. I did have love for him, and there were areas in which I respected him very much. It was the mixture that kept me in constant confusion – between hope and despair. Human beings just don't become psychologically fragmented. Something has to happen to them to make their mind break into pieces. It usually happens between the ages of 2-5, like with my husband.

So, to cover this story fairly, I must report on what happened to him as a little child. This is why I still have hope for his deliverance! This is why I still have compassion on him. I keep asking Abba to save him if it is possible. At the same time, I keep praying that his demonic influence on my children and grandchild will come to an end. For him, a portal was opened to the demonic realm at about age three. He "froze" in correct development--mentally, emotionally, socially, and spiritually. So, here is this brilliant child with so many talents, emotionally frozen, and taken over by demons, before he had any choice in the matter, or knew what was happening to him. I grieve so much because so many hundreds of thousands of children, just in America alone, are

PART III - The Journey is Sabotaged

abused, exposed to horrible things, and demonized - even from babyhood.

In the Islamic world, the violation of children is a "norm." Most Muslim children grow up mentally and emotionally disturbed, even demonized. But, there are Arabs that are not like this--some are even Christians, though most who call themselves "Christian" are Roman Catholic, Greek, or Syrian Orthodox. Again, Yahuweh deals with individuals. Muslim children, as young as two, are being sodomized. By age two they are taught to throw rocks and fight, or their older brothers or other older boys will beat them up. Because they traditionally marry late, boys in their early teens are taught homosexuality. The Arab glib expression is: "A woman for children, a boy for pleasure, a melon for ecstasy." Nasty, I know, but that's general Arab male thinking. I lived among them for eight years, so I know. The word "love" is not in the Koran. They think of love, compassion, righteousness, and goodness as laughable weaknesses, unfitting for a Muslim male. This is the "spirit of the Medes" of **Isaiah 13:17-22** that is inside America now. Is it any wonder that Abba's love has warned and warned Americans in "end-time Babylon" to get out before He has to come in His wrath? A demonic spirit can open a portal of entrance into a little child, if there is a familiar spirit in its parents that attracts the demon. But, now, the demonic world is coming into our earth to such a huge extent because we are so near the appearing of the son of Lucifer/Satan as the "Beast," world ruler. As we entered 2013, the time of darkness has come, and is descending on the earth quickly.

I knew from my husband's mother that from age six he had been diagnosed by the school psychologist as having serious psychological problems. The school psychologist suggested that his name be changed to the name of her new husband, since she had a son by him and her six-year old son was jealous of him. So, his name was changed. Tragically, his grandparents, very sophisticated people from Germany, cut him out of their will, when in the Air Force he rejected going back to his birth name. His grandparents controlled his parent's lives. They forced his mother at age 19 to have an abortion, which they paid for. In her dying state, she asked me if my husband, her son, was the reincarnation of the baby that Grandma Gross had forced her to abort. At that time, I had a New Age bent, so I told her that he was the reincarnation of the baby she'd aborted. She ended up hating her husband because of his parents' control over him, and so she separated from him. But, he loved her so much. She contrived a scheme. She pretended to take him back in order to get pregnant. After getting pregnant, she divorced him. He never got over it. My husband looked like his mother. I really liked Dad Gross. I understood his pain.

One night after our son was born, I had a "spirit" visitation of his mother holding out her hands to us and pleading. Pat was a Wicca witch, so projection was something she did. I told my husband about it, and he called her. She had been in surgery at the time, and almost died. She asked us to come to visit. It was not until 1974 that we were able to go.

After her marriage to my husband's father, she married a man named Hack. It was Hack's last name that my husband inherited when he was six. Then after her divorce from Hack, she married an older man named George, but he had died. When we got there, she was married to Mike Handy. It was there that I began to like her, and have compassion on her. It was there, also, that I began to like my husband's ½-brother, Patrick, and his new wife. Sadly, it was not long after we got there that Pat died. We attended her funeral. She was such a brilliant woman, but her life was a tragedy. Her sister Joan was older than she was. Joan was a very wicked hard-core witch. She vowed to ruin her sister's life. Joan attended Pat's funeral, with her two sons. Spooky lady!

Before Pat died, I had to stay on heavy doses of valium. Things were in such turmoil that even my husband and Patrick got into a fist fight right in front of me, and our two children. It was not long after, that Patrick contracted leukemia and died at age 30. I draw no conclusions. But, from his own admission, my husband got his witchcraft powers from Aunt Joan. It was rumored that Joan killed her husband by cancer. My husband could also heal people who had cancer by his prayers. When I had many violent headaches, he would pray for me and the headache would be gone. Like with HAARP, it can create hurricanes, typhoons, cyclones, earthquakes, tornadoes, snow and ice blizzards, wildfires, droughts, and floods, but it can also prevent them. It depends on who is using the technology, whether it is for good or bad.

In 1980, our third child went to kindergarten. I had opted out of the tube-tying after she was born, so I could still have babies. I was 36 years old. I was lonely for another baby. But, I didn't want to tell my husband I wanted another baby. I had bottle fed the other three, and I wanted to breast feed. I had done so many things wrong with the first three, I asked Abba to let me have another child so that "I could do everything right." For about four months I tried to get pregnant. Finally I did. But, I did not tell anyone. When I was five months pregnant, and showing very much, I still had not told anyone. People at church were asking me about it. I told everyone I was eating a lot. It was just before Christmas. My husband and I were on our way to a Christmas party. He began telling me about holding a newborn baby that day, and that he wanted another baby. That night I told him – your wish has been granted – I am five months pregnant. He was happy. I was so relieved!

My parents came over for Christmas day, and I was wearing a bathrobe with a tie around the waist. My belly was quite large, so we had to tell them. At this time, my back was in such terrible condition that I was going to the chiropractor about three times a week. I slept on the living room floor. I kept my weight down-- only gaining her weight, as I did with the last two. I laid on the floor dreaming of what it was going to be like to do everything right by this child – and Abba gave me revelation of what it meant to really be a good mother! I had stopped my sinning, and began my climb out of the pit, with His help of course.

The evening of May 31, 1981, I was about to slice cheese cake for my husband and guests, and all of a sudden sharp pains hit me, and he rushed me down to Blairsville to the hospital. The same doctor that delivered the third child delivered her. She was born May 31, 1981, at 11:15 PM. She was 9 pounds and 4 oz., 21 inches long – my biggest baby. My doctor let her stay in the room with me, so I could breast- feed her. My son was so disappointed--he wanted a brother. But, she made up for not being a brother many times over. I was so sure I was having a boy that I only picked out boy names. At midnight, the night before she was born, I lay in bed thinking that maybe I should pick out a girl name just in case. Abba gave me her name – it is beautiful. It means "the tenderly beloved, like unto El" (God).

She was so good. We went many places with her, and she was so content. I let her breast feed as long as she wanted to. About two weeks into breast feeding, I got so sore that I thought I'd have to stop. But, the mother of a friend of my son was a leader in La Leche League – a support group for breast feeding mothers. She had me use Vitamin E to heal me. I could take her anywhere – even to a New Year's Eve party at a big hotel--nurse her, dance, and enjoy the evening, without her even making a sound. She was my easiest baby to care for. Sadly, when my baby was 18 months old, my dear Nanny died. My mother and I went to her funeral in Oklahoma. When I returned my daughter did not want to be breast-fed anymore, she was happy with her cup.

Shortly before Nanny died, we took the children to see the Indiana Jones movie: *Raiders of the Lost Ark*. I put my baby under a blanket, nursed her in the theater, and she never made a sound. But, going to the movie, my son was totally disgusted. He thought we were taking him to see a "western." But, quickly, he became so fascinated with the movie, that it led to his fascination with all the Indiana Jones movies. It fired up my spirit of adventure, and his too. I sometimes call him "Indiana," and during my Petra exploration days, he called me "Indiana Mom."

That little blue-eyed blond was a light to our family. After she was born, because of my breast-feeding her, my husband stopped having sex with me until she stopped breast-feeding. Being bi-sexual, my acting like a real woman disgusted him. Breast-feeding makes a woman very desirous of sex. So this was a suffering for me. But, because I was getting so strong in Yahuweh, He sustained me, and I was OK. As with each of my children, after they were born, my life took on happiness. I loved being a mother! I love good family life! I am so blessed to stay with my third child, her husband, and the two little ones, when I am in America. They are such good parents, and the children are my delight. Abba is letting me enjoy them very much! I get to see my youngest granddaughter daily, and my two other granddaughters as much as possible, since they live in another state. Now my son, and his new wife, live four miles from me, so I get to see them a lot while I am in the states.

Tragically, after her little sister was born, when our third child was five, my husband began seriously to open portals in her life, by which he could use her as a channel through which to project witchcraft. He began seriously to mind-program her into deep jealousy for her little sister. He would sadistically dehumanize her, while praising her little sister. This programming went on for a long time. But, it did not take long for it to manifest. When the last child was three months of age, I was lying with her in the bedroom to nurse her to sleep. I heard the third child screaming and pounding on the doors, and making all sorts of confusion outside the bedroom door. I was furious. I got up and opened the door, and there was no one there. I went and checked, and under orders from her dad, she was at the other end of the driveway pulling weeds. She learned the power of "projection" of her emotions. He began working to open a portal so that she would be his "lackey"--an extension of himself. But, he never figured the Yahuweh factor! Abba told me several times as she got older that she was His child, and I was not to interfere with His dealings with her! By sixth grade, her teacher told me that she was the most morose and sad child he had ever taught.

We were very poor. In the sixth grade she was taunted cruelly by her peers because of such trivial things, like her tennis shoes were not the Keds brand. We didn't have money to buy Keds, so we bought her $5.00 tennis shoes. It caused her to withdraw within herself. Demonic spirits feed on negative emotions, so they keep their victim in a state of misery. Things like joy, peace, love, and happiness are often things to be rejected. Misery brings pity, and pity can be used to manipulate and control others. This is the basic "jezebel spirit." As a child gets older and learns to use these powers to control others, they move into witchcraft. There has to be deliverance by the power of Yahuweh. Demonized people, or demon possessed people, just don't "change" because of counseling, or psychology. Demons are fallen angels--real beings--not mental disorders! Many demonized people, like those with jezebel spirits, hide easily in either Christianity, or the Messianic mix of Christianity. It is easy to hide in these religions, for they are almost blinded to evil.

When our son was a year old, we planned to go visit Dad Gross and Penny. It was Christmas 1971. We had bought and wrapped some nice presents for them. That morning, he called us and said for us not to come. He said "I have a monkey on my back" – an expression meaning a hidden problem. He and Penny had a son of their own, to whom they left all of their inheritance. So, my husband was cut off from all his inheritance, which made him determined to get mine. Penny died of cancer, too, after a long time of suffering.

In taking Scriptural healing classes with Charles and Francis Hunter I learned that things like stroke, crippling diseases like MS, and cancer, are mostly all demonic-induced. Cancer is brought on by traumatized cells. By calling off the demon the disease leaves. The Hunters would have a crippled stroke victim in front of them, for example. They could see in the spirit that the demon was pressing on the brain to cause the crippling. They could see that as they cast out the demon, he left. Then they would massage the crippled limb and it would straighten out and be healed. Because of their simple childlike faith, and their mild manners and calm ways, Abba honored their methods and He healed people. Many diseases, are spiritually-based, as men like Henry Wright, and doctors, have found. Many are sick because of stress from false responsibility, as well as from un-forgiveness, deep-seated anger and bitterness, grief, bad memories, or demonic activity.

I had a horrible case of Fibromyalgia. I learned from Wright's book, *The More Excellent Way*, that the muscles store memory, and grief. I released my years of grief to Abba (2008), and within 24 hours the Fibromyalgia was gone, and it has not returned. Some essential oils, as Dr. Charles Stewart points out in his book, *The Healing Oils of the Bible*, can actually take the trauma from cells, thus causing healing—even from cancer, so that the cancer does not return.

After my husband's mother separated from Dad Gross, and gave birth to my husband, she took her little son, and went with her sister Joan to Arlington, Virginia--headquarters of python/Apollo worship in America. They lived there about three years. Pat was a tarot card reader – a Wicca witch. Walt Disney was a practicing Wiccan warlock. It was in Virginia that something happened that opened a portal for the demonizing of my husband, before he was six years old. He later said that he saw satanic things there, which led him into Satanism. Interestingly, my husband's mother's maiden name was "Henry." She was a direct descendant of Patrick Henry. Since our family was also a direct descendent of Patrick Henry, and one of his wives, that made my husband and I distant cousins.

His mother had supposedly received Jesus in the same tent revival the night my husband said he was saved. The evangelist was E.J. Daniels. Like so many old-time evangelists, he had a lot of zeal but little wisdom, so he presented the Gospel in a fear-producing way. Both were scared of going to hell so they went forward to "pray the prayer." But, Pat went back to tarot card reading, and he to his satanic perversions.

Joan was a hardcore witch, who practiced "black magic." So, what my husband saw as a little child must have been awful! He perhaps saw human sacrifice, was used in sexual orgies, was sodomized, or abused terribly in some way, because he began splitting into many personalities before he was 6 years old.

I lived with mocking spirits. One Easter Sunday morning, about 1992, there was particular upset in our house. He was mocking the way I looked, and the girls chimed in, too. I went back to my son's room and he was putting on his shoes. I asked him what he thought of the way I looked. He said something that makes me cry every time I think of it: **"You're just mom to me**." Meaning that no matter what anyone else said, I was loved by him for myself. He's still that way today!

Another Easter morning, I walked in to see how the third child was doing in her preparation for Easter Sunday, and there was my husband with his hands around her neck, digging his fingernails into her neck so hard so that blood was running down her neck. I called him off, and he simply left the room. She told people at church that the cat had scratched her. As we entered church on our way to our Sunday School class, I asked him if he was a warlock. He turned, faced me, and with a smirk on his face, told me that he was a warlock (male witch). Whatever happened to him, a portal to the enemy's world was opened in him, and he split into several personalities at an early age. To survive he also became a master at lying, manipulation, and drawing pity. Thus he survives.

PART III - The Journey is Sabotaged

The infiltration of witches and warlocks into the church system is an incredible phenomenon. Many pretend to be ministers. By witchcraft many cause divisions, arguing and turmoil within the church. The attacks are always directed against those with pure hearts, and against Truth. Heresies abound. Personality cults are also of this nature. If a preacher or teacher is so "charismatic" that people obey them without question, you have a jezebel-demonic situation. I've had a thorough education! This is why I have been a good sounding board for dismayed pastors, rabbis, and elders of congregations who have problems with jezebels. Evil is just not perceived by most Christians in the Western world. If anyone says "God bless you," or holds a Bible, they are accepted as a nice "believer." So it is easy for "every unclean and evil bird" to nest among Christians and Messianic groups, under the shadow of end-time Babylon. (**Revelation 18:2**) Because man worships man, and God is an abstract THING to learn about, most have no clue that evil is right under their nose. This situation is pointed out in **Revelation 2:18-28**. I don't think the members of the Thyatira congregation thought of this "prophetess" as Jezebel, but she was. She led them astray into sin, just like all of these snakes. [Refer to: "Evil – Crossing the Threshold"/February 7, 2010]

I learned that sadomasochism is not just a type of sexual perversion--it is a mental lifestyle. A person bound by this spirit has to create pain and suffering in others. Peace, joy, and love do not create pain, so those things are rejected and even hated. He despised "joy." He loved misery. He used it to get pity. It worked on me, and it works on many others. But some were discerning. I lost some precious friends by their discernment. The goal of a sadomasochist is to get a negative reaction by inflicting pain. Once the negative reaction comes, this justifies their continued whipping, torture, and sexual abuse of their victim. There is a satanic joy/pleasure that comes in this type of perversion. But, real joy is an enemy to them. Demonic spirits feed off the negative energy--misery, hate, bitterness, anger, and violent emotions. This is why young girls, going through their "periods" each month, are so attacked by demonic spirits, because of the hormonal changes that produce negative reactions. The same things happen with most women going through menopause.

With this lifestyle, there can be little to no peace. Peace is an enemy to them too. So, daily, for some reason, big or small, the peace was disturbed. Jealousy was at the root of much of it. If one of the children, or me, got a phone call and he did not, he began raging. He had the habit of screaming at the two youngest children every morning for some small thing they'd done, like leave their toothbrush on the bathroom counter. He would scream so hard that he'd turn red. So, the children were almost daily mentally and emotionally wounded. Before my son applied to join the Air Force, I had a dream of him in camouflage fatigues and military boots. Father would make a warrior out of him! At the same time, I had a dream of the two youngest girls brushing their teeth and getting ready for school. Next to them on the bathroom counter were hand grenades, and other weapons. They also have had to learn to battle for themselves, and Abba has strengthened them. We all have to learn to fight the enemy on his own grounds as a part of our normal life, like brushing our teeth.

The third child had so many severe sinus headaches, and terrible bouts of PMS each month. The air in the Fort Worth-Dallas area is polluted with so much garbage that many people live with headaches. As a result of the mind programming, his screaming made her go rigid like a board. I would have to hold her until she melted in my arms. Oftentimes, because of turmoil in the morning, she would not get breakfast. So, as she left the house, I'd give her some breakfast to take with her. That made trouble for me.

One day she threw herself on the floor in front of him and said: "I just want you to love me." His cruel response was bitterly cold – "NO!" This daughter is one of the most compassionate, tenderhearted, caring, loving persons I've ever known. She is loyal and faithful, and stays to help people as long as they let her. She is loved by many. Because of a wonderful family, and the love she gets from those she ministers to, she knows she is very, very blessed. She and her husband are very generous givers. They love Israel! She is a servant of Yahuweh. She and her husband guard the Torah. I am free to teach their children the Torah. There were so many times that I wanted my say in her life to "straighten her out." But Abba always said: "No! Keep quiet! She's mine!" I really believe that she has an awesome destiny with Him.

One day, after my husband ordered her out of the house upon her graduation from high school, I was returning from visiting a friend. I was stopped at a red light near our home. It was raining. I looked up, and had a vision of her walking away from me. Then she turned and looked at me and smiled so sweetly. Then she turned back and walked away. I knew she would find happiness, and she has. Abba has given me so many dreams and visions through the years, of "word of knowledge," what is, and "word of wisdom," what will be and how to handle it.

I do not want you to get bogged down reading what the enemy did, for in everything there was the hand of Abba giving miracles.

PART III - The Journey is Sabotaged

He sees our end from our beginning. He treats us according to what He sees of our end. She was chosen before the foundation of the world to be a blessing to the world, and so she is. It is clear to me that the more a person has been chosen, from the foundation of the world, to serve Abba, the more He puts into them at an early age. So, of course, the more the enemy is aroused to try to stop it. When the enemy sees a little child being doted on by Yahuweh, he takes note and moves in to destroy. He did that with me, and with our four children. BUT HE FAILED!

In Texas, she worked to put herself through college at UTA. It took her six years to do it, but she did it! I helped her out some from my mother's inheritance, but mostly she did it herself. During her last year in college, a friend of hers introduced her to a man who was finishing up a double Engineering Major at TCU. They fell in love. He is the most wonderful son-in-law! He is a great husband and father. He gives her the love she always craved. He is also her best friend. HalleluYah!

Just before the wedding, I was at their house, and the phone rang. It was the Personnel Director at Lockheed. He wanted to talk to my soon-to-be son-in-law. They were considering hiring him after he graduated. I told the man he had graduated and was about to marry my daughter. I told him what a wonderful man he was. The Director was so impressed that he told me to have him call him. My son-in-law got the job. I tease him that it was me who made it happen (smile). But, when it comes to someone's eternal life, I learned not to intervene in what the Spirit is doing with a person. He taught me not to "play Holy Spirit." Yahuweh will not cross our will. We tie His hands from helping us by our own mental and emotional confusion, fear, insecurity, and all that negativity that blocks faith. I am not a controller!

As time went on, Abba slowly but surely brought me understanding of what I was living with. He began showing me Scriptures that described my situation. He also gave me dreams. One morning, during the time of the usual screaming at the girls, I was still asleep, and I had a dream. I saw a huge snake coming through the bedroom door, right by the door handle. I watched as it began to wrap itself around me. I looked at the markings and said to myself: "Oh my God, it is a python." I heard a voice say to me: "No! It is an anaconda." Then through the same door where the snake in the dream had entered, my husband burst into the bedroom with anger, and woke me up.

Later that day I looked at a nature card set that my youngest daughter had, and saw that the markings of what I saw were indeed those of an anaconda. The card said that the anaconda was the longest and largest of the snakes, a type of python. It kills its victims by first hitting them in the head to stun them, then coils around them, and drags them into the mud, where they are slowly devoured. A Satanist will tell you about the snake spirits. I learned that the anaconda/python spirit is the highest of the snake spirits, under the Serpent himself. Today, "serpent power" is entering the church in disguise. Even cartoons for children are introducing them to "serpent power." Oh Come Messiah Yahushua, Come!

Today, the Hindu Kundalini spirit has invaded the church. This spirit wraps itself around the spine and controls the nervous system of a person. It is manifesting incredibly in meetings like the Toronto and Lakewood "revivals." In 2011, I wrote an article exposing this spirit that has ruined true revivals in America clear back into the 1700s.

In Texas, at our rented "Wind Chime house," things got worse. The stress grew so great that I had panic attacks for about two years in the early 1990s. Then I had heart pains so badly that they did not totally let up for about two years. My left arm would ache, and I could not breathe except in short gasps. I kept dying, literally--my spirit kept trying to leave my body, but I'd call it back. This wrestling with Abba to let me live and finish my course went on into about 2006. I almost died alone in my apartment in Jordan. I wrestled with Messiah many times to let me finish my course. I had many dreams during that time. In one, He was walking up the side of a mountain. He turned to see me. I was struggling to catch up with Him. He smiled, took my hand, and we walked up the mountain together.

The near death experiences continued in Aqaba, and back in the U.S. There were several times in Jordan that I thought I was dying – my spirit was leaving my body. I would always plead with Him to let me live so that I would finish my course. He had shown me so many times that I would live through the tribulation to the coming of Messiah. [You will read about my 8 years in Aqaba in Part VI]

But, back in Texas, during the two years of heart pains, I kept vacillating between wanting to die and wanting to live. One night when the chest pains were so bad, I got up to go to the bathroom, and the Spirit said very harshly: "Do you want to live, or do you want to die? TELL ME NOW!" I was sure awake by then. I said "I want to live." He healed me of the chest pains. But, one time I did die. I descended to the bottom of a canyon. I saw Yahushua, from waist down, holding out His hands to me. In the dream, my husband was there also. He asked me if I wanted to come "home," as He asked so many times after that. I evidently opted to live, because then I woke up. The next morning, my

PART III - The Journey is Sabotaged

husband asked me if we went somewhere in the night – for he said that he was with Jesus and I. It was real.

I've only heard the audible voice of Yahuweh twice. His voice is deep and powerful. The first time was in 1990, after our ordination. I got up to go to the bathroom at 3:00 AM, I heard the booming voice of Yahuweh say: "You shall be called Word Fellowship." The next morning I told my husband. He said it should be called Word Fellowship International. I went along with that, but that's not what Yahuweh told me. Later in Africa the ministry was known as simply Word Fellowship, as it is today. But, we quickly proceeded with incorporation--a 501 C. Abba gave me so many dreams and "words of knowledge" about it! It finalized so quickly that we were amazed, it was just before Christmas. Even our CPA, who was associated with the organization who ordained us, was shocked at how fast it happened.

We were both ordained together in 1990. I was ordained a second time through a church in Burleson, too. The corporation was finalized in 1991. But, when I went to Jordan in 1999, I dissolved both the ordinations, and the corporation. Abba had changed my life, and the hype of church ministry meant nothing to me anymore.

After our dramatic separation in January of 1996, my husband tried to take over Word Fellowship, but I blocked him. I had finally gained self respect. Still, I had hope for our marriage. After about 5 years of separation, we legally divorced.

I sometimes met him for breakfast, or lunch. One morning I was having breakfast with him and he seemed so free. His eyes seemed clear, not glazed over as before. I went out to my car and asked Father: "Has he been born again?" My hopes went up. As I got into my car, all of a sudden over the top of the steering wheel, I had this vision: I saw an old dilapidated farmhouse. Outside was a well. It had light coming out of it. In the vision, I saw myself walking to the well. I looked down through the shaft. There were broken timbers. I could see the bottom of the shaft. There at the bottom I saw the back of an anaconda. I was so let down. Abba let me know that he had only hidden more deeply, so as not to be detected. I understood.

Later Abba gave me another dream. My youngest daughter and I were living together in an apartment. I came home from work and went to my electric skillet to start to fix dinner. When I opened the skillet, I saw a huge black snake in it. I clamped down the top and turned the heat on high. Then for some reason I left the apartment. About three hours later I returned. I thought the snake would probably be mushy. I slowly opened the lid on the skillet, and to my surprise the skillet was perfectly clean, except in it was a small brown snake – a copperhead, which is deadly poisonous. Abba spoke to me: "He has not changed; he has only changed his outward appearance."

Later, when in Africa in 1997, I was reading a book on faith, lying in my bed in Kisumu. I had been thinking of going back to him. But, while reading the book, my husband was not on my mind at that moment. All of a sudden, Abba flashed that dream of the snake in the electric skillet before me, and said: "Beware! He still has the heart of a snake."

I never wanted a divorce. I wanted a happy home. I wanted an old fashioned marriage with a man who was kind to me. I've never asked for much. All I wanted was for someone to love me, be kind to me, and show me respect. But because I had never learned to respect myself, I drew disrespect. Yet, through it all, to me, divorce was something to be avoided. Abba says: "I hate divorce." But, He had to divorce the ten northern tribes, and send them into punishment. Sometimes it just has to be done. Satan will not have my children, their spouses, my grandchildren, or their families. Yahuweh has promised me: "**I will save your children**." (**Isaiah 49:25**)

Yahuweh has followed through: I received salvation – or at least made my public confession of faith – at age 6½. My son was 3½. My youngest daughter was 4. My oldest daughter was 6. My third child was 7. Three of them have been baptized in the Spirit at an early age, and began moving in miracles and other gifts of the Spirit. My oldest grandson was about 10 when he was born again, the second grandson under 10, the oldest granddaughter about 8, her sister at 6, and now the third grandson at 6. I have one more granddaughter, our little adopted girl, who is almost 2, and my great grandson is 1.

I know that most of the House of Israel came to salvation by the One in Matthew, Mark, Luke and John, via the church. **But, no matter who does the delivering of the baby from darkness to light, it is Abba who guides the growth**. And as each child is ready for promotion in knowledge of truth, He takes them further on. We can grow up into Him as fast as we want to, for the spirit of man is ageless!

Maybe you never learned anything about Satan's world beyond TV horror movies, but it is not an illusion – it is real, and evil is increasing. Lucifer was a created being. He was so elevated in Abba's court that he was actually the "angel that covered" Yahuweh in His throne room. He was the most beautiful of all the angels. He was given much authority and power. But, that was not good enough for him. He had a will, and he became jealous. So he used his will to attempt to destroy Yahuweh and set up his

PART III - The Journey is Sabotaged

own kingdom. Using human beings, he has worked his way into this world to the point where mankind feels comfortable with him. (**Isaiah 14:12-20; Ezekiel 28:12-18**) Great darkness is now covering the earth. Lucifer/Satan and the fallen ones have tremendous power. Don't mock them or take them lightly. **Jude 1:9**: "**But Micha'el, the chief angel, in contending with the devil, when he disputed about the body of Moses, presumed not to bring against him blasphemous accusation, but said `Yahuweh rebuke you.'** " In **Zechariah 3:2**, we find the most powerful of all rebukes of Satan. Yahuweh Himself uses His own Name to rebuke Satan: "**And Yahuweh said to Satan `Yahuweh rebuke you! Yahuweh who has chosen Jerusalem rebuke you...'** " He spoke the end of all things to Satan--that He would rule Jerusalem. [For a thorough study on spiritual warfare refer to Scriptural Spiritual Warfare Parts I, II and III/June-July 2010]

There are powers given to those who submit to evil. Their powers are greater than that of any natural human. But, their power is not greater than the power of Yahuweh! "...**greater is He who is in you, than he who is in the world.**" (I John 4:4) To learn wisdom, one has to submit to Yahuweh's training before they can take on the powers of evil (**Ephesians 6:10-18; II Corinthians 10:3-6**). Unless you know well how to use the "weapons of warfare" rightly, you are totally exposed to being taken over by evil.

My life and experiences were all just a part of my training. In 1993, while still attending Grace Temple, we were invited to join a family from India, Prafel and Minnie Martin, and their children, who had attended Grace Temple. Prafel sought my advice regarding moving to New York, and I felt the Spirit wanted them to go. So they moved to Schenectady. They asked us to come visit them. They had arranged a meeting in the New York area for us to speak at. We had a wonderful reunion with them, and they took us to Albany for an outing.

In the meeting the next day, I was to have ½ the speaking time, and my husband would have the other ½. The meeting was on July 24th, the day before my birthday. The Indian family who hosted us lived in an old brownstone in the Bronx. They put on a huge spread of food in honor of my birthday. The table was so long because of all the people they invited. They had every type of Indian food you can imagine. It was wonderful! That night I slept on a mat on the floor, and Abba gave me the message He wanted me to give the next day--a message about salvation. There were many Indian people coming that were not born again but who were very wealthy and attended the Methodist Church of

India. I knew that this might be the only time they would hear the Good News of salvation without churchianity. The Spirit's anointing was on me to preach once again.

That night we went to a large home. There were at least 100 people packed into that home. The women wore their saris – they were lovely. There was music before the speaking. We each had 30 minutes to speak. My husband asked our friend if he could go first. Of course he, being a male, was allowed to go first. He got up and did a comedy routine mixed with a humanitarian message. He told jokes. He talked about everyone being "one in spirit" – a New Age message. He went on past his 30 minutes and then into an hour. By the time he finished, I had no time to speak. It was such a disaster that Prafel put his head in his hands and would not look up. He was so embarrassed. But, of course, the polite Indian people thanked my husband for his nice message.

It was near 10:30 PM. Friends of our friends wanted us to come to Queens to their house to pray for them to receive the baptism in the Holy Spirit. That was my gifting, and I was excited about it. But, my heart was broken because I saw those lost souls going home still lost. It took us about 35-40 minutes to get to their house. My husband and I sat in the back seat. I stayed very quiet. I was so grieved. My husband kept poking me in the side, saying in a low mocking tone: "You're jealous of me aren't you? I took your speaking time and you're jealous." I was not jealous. I was grieved over those lost souls. We got to their little house in Queens. Not only their relatives, but others had come to be filled with the Spirit. The ladies all wore saris. I began ministering to them. It was midnight EST. It was, then, July 25th --my birthday. What a birthday present from Abba! This little group was being filled with the Spirit, and ladies in saris were falling on the floor under the power of the Spirit. I thought that was a super present. We stayed with them. The next morning, after breakfast, but before we left to return to Texas, they pulled out a cake with my name on it and ice cream. That was so sweet of them!

In 2005, I was sitting on my roof top (flat tiled roof) in Aqaba, and Abba reminded me of that July in 1993. Years before, I asked Him why He let that happen. I'd ask: "Why, after giving me that powerful message did He allow my husband to do that dirty work?" It was a question that troubled me. But, that day, as I was preparing to go to Israel to teach, He told me "why."

Please learn from this! He let me know that He had given me the message, and the authority to speak it in His Name. I could have gone to our friend and told him that I had been given a message from God and had to speak it. He knew I moved in prophecy. I had given him a word from Father about their moving to New York, which they followed, and were glad they did. So, Abba would have opened that door for me, because it was not my message--it was His!

In 1993, I did not know about authority levels, or what He backed and my right to be bold under His command. While being shut away with Him for six weeks during the summer of 2001 in Aqaba, much to my shock, He told me that He had given me the authority of the rod of Moses, and the mantle of Eliyahu. I did not receive that easily. Many manifestations from Him took place during those six weeks. He was preparing me to go to Jerusalem for Sukkot. Understanding my identity in Him has been very slow coming. I still wrestle with it, even after all these years of His confirmation. He had given me the message. It was up to me to go forth to give it!

During my almost 30 years of marriage, I still did many different things to serve the Master. I continued my study of end-time prophecy, taught the Word, and ministered to the needs of individuals. I also continued to do evangelism. My time of rebellion covered about 12 years: 1972-1984. And, even during that time, there were times of service to Him.

Before setting out to ruin my life, and after returning to Abba, I moved a lot in prophecy. Abba gave me powerful prophecy for individuals and for the church. I worked for five years also, 1987-1991, with Women's Aglow Night Chapter in Fort Worth. I taught in different chapters at different times. I learned during these years how to minister to individuals, in healings, in miracles, in deliverance, and in personal counseling. I had learned wisdom! When my youngest was in high school in Fort Worth, she was asked to be on the counseling team, since her wisdom was incredible to them. All four of my children have a gift of wisdom! They have helped me many times over hard times.

I also learned that you do not tell Abba "No! Get someone else." I was singing in the choir one morning at Grace Temple, and Abba gave me a powerful prophecy to give to the church. They had been manipulating the working of the Spirit, which is very common in charismatic churches in general. The prophecy was so powerful that as I took the microphone, I leaned over under the power of the Spirit. I saw in my spirit, a form of a man standing in front of me. I believed Him to be the "Holy Spirit." Jerry and Carolyn Savelle were in the audience. Meadowlark Lemon of the Globetrotters was there too, and the church was packed. I stepped up to the microphone 5 minutes before noon. Pastor Harold made sure church was dismissed at noon. There were several influential people, including rich Masons in that church, who wanted out by noon. So, when I went to take the microphone, it was almost noon. I noticed that Pastor Harold was shaking. His prophecy was not a short message. But, it was so powerful that I heard weeping throughout the auditorium. I handed the microphone back to the pastor and he quickly dismissed the church. But, during the week, those who had been weeping came to him for counseling.

One man was on the verge of going back to drugs, and the prophecy had shaken him so much that he rededicated his life to God. Later that man and his wife became Messianic believers. I saw them at Rami Gabrielli's assembly in Hurst. I saw this couple again at an anniversary party for Pastor Nichols years later, around 1997, and we had good Messianic fellowship. We were surrounded by Kenneth and Gloria Copeland, the Savelles, and other celebrities of the Christian world.

I found out that my son-in-law attended their Bible studies in their home after his work. It was there that he learned some of his Hebrew roots. Later he was used of Abba to instruct my daughter, who was not speaking to me because she thought I was "trying to be Jewish" and had forsaken Christianity. Actually, I had forsaken Christianity, but I sure was not trying to be Jewish. Today, both of them are guarding the Torah.

Strange how people keep getting recycled into your life. I was at a funeral in north Israel in November 2012. Before the funeral, the wife of the deceased took me to the home of friends who would be having a lunch for us after the funeral. It was the home of Rami Gabrielli and his family. Several were there from Fort Worth. Small world!

Getting back to "never tell Abba "NO, get someone else," the next week I was in the choir and it was nearly noon again, and He asked me to go down and take the microphone and give the identical message. I told Him "get someone else." I had had too much flack from that prophecy during the previous week. Within about 30 seconds, a dear sister/friend came down from the top row of the choir to take the microphone and she gave the same message. I talked to her later. She said she was so scared because she had never prophesied in church before. But, she gave the same message. Jeanne is still a friend. She and her husband really knew how to hear from Abba. Because I told Him "NO," it was a good five years or more before Abba restored the gift of prophecy. "The gifts and callings of Yahuweh are without repentance." He never withdraws the gift once it is given, but the one who has the gift can turn from Him--even into hell, because He respects our free will.

Even this last year, I have had those "get someone else" words in my mouth a few times. When those words start to come out of my lips great fear grabs me, and I keep silent. I am terrified to tell Him "NO, get someone else" because I know He will, and I will lose my position of trust with Him. "**Let Him be your fear and let Him be your dread**." "**The fear of Yahuweh is the BEGINNING of wisdom!**" (**Isaiah 8:13; Psalm 111:10**) I am terrified of being out of His will! The more we can be trusted, the greater the punishment if we become rebellious!

When the youngest was in the third grade in southwest Fort Worth, I saw the need to take children home from school that walked home by themselves. It was so sad for me to see so many little ones, from age 5 up, walking home by themselves. I was a latch-key child, but in my day it was so much safer than now, when little children are the targets for so much evil. I had a large white station wagon. This is how I met one of my dearest friends – Janet Chang. Her daughter, Susan, and my youngest daughter became the best of friends too. I took Susan home. I also took some of the children to church productions, and some of them were born again. At this time the two youngest watched Gospel Bill and Nicodemas on TBN. They even went to Gospel Bill's summer camp in Oklahoma. One evening, Grace Temple hosted Nicodemas, and I took a car full of children.

My youngest was always witnessing to salvation from age five. She led many of her friends to salvation. She'd bring them home and we would pray with them. One day in Texas, I was practicing my Hebrew dance steps in the living room, while my little girl and her friend, Jessica, were in her room. (I took Hebrew dance lessons at Shady Grove Church in Plano two to three years in a row.) My daughter came out and said: "Mom, we have a new little sister." Years later I asked Jessica if she had been born again, and she said: "Don't you remember I prayed to receive Jesus at your house?"

One day in taking home a little girl, I led her to salvation. Her mother belonged to the Church of Christ, and worked at Carswell AFB. The little girl was so excited. I gave her a little Bible in which I wrote her spiritual birthday. She told her mother. Her mother said no one could be born again, and she took the Bible away and told her daughter she could not read it. Later the little girl let me know that she knew she was born again no matter what her mother said.

To give one last example of the power of demonic projection: After I was forced to flee from my husband, I got a job working in my church's pre-school Day Care Center. I had been in an accident and my white station wagon was wrecked. I hated that. I had it fixed up with the insurance money. Then my youngest daughter wrecked it. So, I bought a used Honda Accord from a good dealership in north Fort Worth. Because of my nervousness, I couldn't work with a room full of preschoolers. But, for a while I tried. The church was a long ways from my house. This particular morning, on my way to work, I had gotten the mail and saw an 8 X 10 manila envelope from my husband. He loved to write long letters that were damaging to my spirit, because they were just plain mean. I opened the envelope and there was another letter that had words that were devastating. I was on my way to work so I threw the envelope onto the floor of the passenger's side. When I got off work, I got in the car to drive home. I got off the 820 loop, and as usual there was a traffic jam down I-35. I looked down and saw the red light, indicating that I had an engine problem. I remember smelling oil. I prayed and prayed. I got home by His mercy, and had the car hauled to a Honda repair place. My son knew the owner. The owner had been in business working on Hondas for over 40 years. When I went back to get the car, he told me that in all the years he had been working on Hondas, he had never see this problem. I asked him where the problem was. He said: "directly under the right floor of the passenger's side." Projected spiritual evil takes form in the natural to do physical damage.

II Timothy 2:3-4: A naïve and ignorant soldier is a dead soldier. A good soldier lays down his own will to obey His Captain. He is neither ignorant of the enemy's plans, nor of His orders from His Superior Officer. We are soldiers in Yahuweh's army. I had to learn to recognize the enemy. I had to get rid of all the fantasy frosting of my church. I had to learn the real world of battle between good and evil. I had to grow strong so that the evil was not only recognizable, but was conquerable also.

NO! I DO NOT DWELL ON what the Devil does. But, I engage in the battle with wisdom, because I understand fully what I am up against. We have entered the time of **Revelation 12** and **Daniel 12:1**. Soon Micha'el will stand aside and allow the forces of evil to overtake Israel. I am in Israel again. Talk of pending war is all over the nation. But before even that, Micha'el will fight the Dragon and throw him into the earth. The Dragon/Devil/Satan/Lucifer will immediately go after the set-apart ones to try to overcome them. That is in **Daniel 7** also and **Revelation 13**. It is a reality! To deny it, or ignore it, or put it off into the future, is foolish. We are inside the last seven-year cycle before Messiah returns. We are in the season when the Dragon will be cast into the earth, when his son Apollyon will rise to world power, and when the set-apart ones of Yahuweh will enter into tribulation. Yahuweh's chosen watchmen are sounding the shofar

PART III - The Journey is Sabotaged

of warning. We have entered the time of deep darkness that will cover the earth.

Our children literally grew up in haunted houses. It was true of our gorgeous North Carolina house too. We had so many manifestations. The haunted house scenario was common--cold wind on our faces, lights moving, voices, sounds to jar our emotions, things flying across the room, ghostly appearances, things disappearing, etc. One day we heard a huge crash in the dining room. We went running in there, and my 40 gorgeous potted plants, which had been on a special set of shelves in ordered rows, went flying across the room and landed clear across the room near the doors to the balcony. Another time we heard scratching and noises under the stairs in a little closet that we never used. That time we called Father Bob Healy and he came and did an official exorcism. The noises stopped. The words of the exorcism are very powerful.

One of the imps' tricks is to hide things. The hierarchy of Satan goes from the top levels of principalities and powers down to the "imps" – the little guys that love mischief. I had an opal ring that my mother had given me on my 21st birthday. My dad had given it to her. She wanted my oldest to have it on her 21st birthday. One morning, getting ready to go to church, I looked for it, and could not find it. I looked all morning. I was very distraught. The next day, upon taking off my oldest daughter's pillow case to wash it, the ring fell out of it. I confronted her with it. She said "Momma, I did not put it there." She was no liar; I believed her. Demonic spirits were always trying to stir up controversy between us all. On her 21st birthday, I gave her the ring.

I learned so much about the antics—the nature, ways, and thinking—of different levels of demons, from the orbs, fairies, and leprechauns, to the hierarch evil principalities and powers over nations. I've learned about the orbs, and had experiences with them. I learned the boundaries of the different ranks of spirits, but also their perimeters of power. They are legalists, and stay within their authority backing by their leader. I learned my boundaries and the limits and non-limits of my authority backing by Yahuweh. So, I do not overstep my boundaries, but I do not limit His power either.

If you have noticed, PBS has orbs coming out of buildings between cartoons, as part of their logo – at least they do in Tampa. I have taken pictures in different places of the world and wherever there has been a demonic stronghold, I have perfectly formed orbs in my picture. I remember talking to a pastor at Christ Church in Jerusalem. He showed me pictures he took of the night sky the night before. It was filled with these orbs.

One night in August 2011, at 4:00 AM, I awoke to see a green light (the color of crayon green, same color as the Muslim minarets at night) in the upper corner of my closet. I got up to look at it and try to find the source of the light. It was an orb whose rays extended out about 2 feet. There was no source for it. The light faded. I laid in bed wide awake. At 4:15, there it was again. I did all I could to find a source for it, but there was none. It faded. I laid wide awake again. At 4:30 there it was again. This time, I just told whatever it was to get out and not come back. I laid down. I saw a light go across the top of the closet to the door and exit.

Even in my worst state, I was disciplined about TV, and especially taught my youngest about it. To this day, she is very astute as to what she watches, or allows her children to watch. One day, in her early teens, she turned to the Oprah Winfrey show. Back then it was not too bad. But, they had a guest, one who was going to demonstrate the powers he had. He called up six women to put their hands lightly on the top of a rectangular table, which he was going to levitate. My daughter got up to turn off the TV. I asked her why, and she told me. I said: "Leave it on. I want you to see something." A man was about to levitate the table, when he stopped, he went over to one woman, and told her to go sit down. Then he called another one up from the audience. I said: "That woman that he dismissed was a born again Christian. The table would not have levitated while she was there." But, then the table levitated. I told her: "I wanted you to see how pathetic the enemy is to levitate a table, when our Savior has all power in heaven and earth."

Back to the story of life in North Carolina: My husband had gone to work in Chattanooga, and only came home for weekends. But, this weekend he did not come home. I put on a slumber party for my third child's 9th birthday. I invited about seven children. The next morning, one of them asked me: "Who were those little short people in the hall last night?" Duh … I acted ignorant. But, I knew about the short "people"--the ones with the big heads and long spindly arms and legs. In her teens, in Texas, when this daughter was emotionally upset, we would see black cloud-like masses moving around the baseboards of the house. If she really got upset, the clouds rose to 4-5 feet.

Even with his abuse, Abba spared my husband over and over, so I still hold onto His mercy for him. One time when he was on his way back from Chattanooga, a speeding driver forced him off the road. He swerved into a parking lot, and ran the car under an 18-wheeler truck. He fell to the side. People came pouring out of the restaurant. They said: "He's dead." But, he got out and began praising God, to their astonishment. I still have hope that before he dies, he will be free. Abba has spared him over and over, so He must have some good purpose in the future. **I John 3:8b**: "...For this purpose the Son of Elohim was manifested—to destroy (loose the power of) the works of the Devil."

Today my two youngest daughters, in different states, are home schooling their children. They are close friends and love one another. Their children are very close. Abba is a miracle worker! The enemy tried every way he could to keep those two from loving each other. The Haiti trip in January 2012 was such a joy to my heart, that those two, and my son and his future wife, would join together to bring Good News to that devastated nation. The two youngest went to the Navajo Indian Reservation several times with us, and also to Saltillo, Mexico, several times, to do missionary work. They got to minister. They also got to pray for healing and miracles, with results. I took my youngest to Africa with me in 1998, and we ministered together. It was a blessed time. She has a love for the African people. So, Haiti is very dear to her. She's gone there twice now, and desires to go again.

John 16:33: "**These things have I spoken to you that in Me you might have peace. In the world you shall have tribulation. But be of good cheer – I have overcome the world.**"

I know this story is a mixture of the good and the bad. But, that's life! In all of this, I want to show how Abba takes us through schooling with a purpose – so that when it is over, we will come out with strength, and knowledge, that has been used to prepare us for what He called us to from the foundation of the world. I thank Abba for this schooling. I will need all this education in the coming days! But, I am no fool – I wouldn't go back a day into the past! I never would have chosen this school! No sane person would have chosen this school. He used my weaknesses to allow me to go through this school, so that on the other side, I would know the enemy so well that I could warn others. He has trained me to blow the shofar of alarm for His people.

I Corinthians 1:26-29: "For look at your calling, brethren, that there are not many wise according to the flesh, not many mighty, not many noble. But, Elohim has chosen the foolish things of this world to put to shame the wise, and Elohim has chosen the weak of this world to put to shame the strong, and Elohim has chosen the low-born of this world and the despised, and the ones that are nothing, that He might bring to nothing those that are, so that no flesh should boast in His Presence."

II Corinthians 12:9-10: "And He said to me, `My grace is sufficient for you, for My power is perfected in weakness.' Most gladly then, I shall rather boast in my weakness, so that the power of Messiah rests on me. Therefore, I take pleasure in weakness, in insults, in needs, in persecutions, in distresses, for the sake of Messiah. For when I am weak, then am I strong!" In all of my callings from Him--**Isaiah 21:12, Jeremiah 1, Ezekiel 33:7, Ezekiel 3; Ezekiel 40:4**--He appointed me as a watchman. I have to know the enemy to sound a clear sound of alarm.

Abba has a good sense of humor! Years before, I had a dream. I was in an auction. I was sitting on fold-up chairs like the others. There was a small stage in front of the room. The man conducting the auction came to me and asked me to get a man's watch and a woman's watch out of the cabinet behind me and take them up front to auction them off. I was just observing. But, I got the two watches and took them up front and showed them to the people. Then I heard the voice of Yahuweh: "YOU ARE A WATCH-MAN – TELL MY PEOPLE TO WATCH." Not only was He preparing me to be a prophetic watchman, but also a wise gatekeeper! I know well what to shut out and what to let in! I know the voice of the enemy; I know the voice of my Father!

In the Fall (Autumn) of 2005, while sitting on the roof of my apartment house in Aqaba, just resting and watching the border with Israel. Abba spoke to me: "**I have made you a gatekeeper**." For the difference between the watchman and the gatekeeper [refer to: "The Watchman and the Gatekeeper"/September 1996.] He led me to do intercession for the House of Israel/Joseph/Ephraim over all the borders of Israel with other countries, land and sea borders, borders of the PA within Israel, all around the Gulf of Mexico from Key West to Corpus Christi, to the main river-mouths of Texas, to Anchorage, Alaska, and to rivers all over the U.S., in the UK, the Outer Hebrides, Iceland, and Israel.

You can read "Intercession: Knowing the Basics" but here is a quick example of real intercession: One day in Aqaba, I was waiting for a shop owner to open his shop at 10:00 AM. Others were waiting too. At 10:00, some came and rattled the door and looked inside, but it was locked. Then about 10:05, here came a jolly Palestinian man with a ring of many keys. He found the right key, opened the lock, and we went in. But, Abba spoke to me sitting there waiting on him to come: "**Prayer can be done anywhere; intercession must be done on site**." Intercession is taking the Scripture-key that Abba gives us to use to either <u>lock</u> the portal of the gate of hell, or to <u>unlock</u> and open something for

PART III - The Journey is Sabotaged

His entrance to fulfill His Word. Intercession loosens the grip of hell against His people. The man had a lot of keys. But only one key fit that particular lock. This is why everywhere I go, He has to give me my set of keys – Scriptures – to proclaim and declare. Each place is different. Sometimes there are a general set of Scriptures, but often times just a few Scriptures that are pointed only for that lock. He also has given me messages, for gods, for fallen angels, and for Satan himself, the great whore of **Revelation 17**, and the Nephillim. [Refer to reports like: "My Iceland Report"/ 2011; "The Declaration Assignment"/2012] Unless I had all of this training, I would not understand the heart and passion of my Abba, nor the reason for His wrath! I clearly understand His wrath, and why Light has to destroy darkness so that the light continues to shine in its purity.

Here I relate the dream that finally caused my husband to say (1995) that he was not born again. I was confused all those years about his salvation. But, this dream cleared up the confusion. In the dream I saw a man wearing a suit and tie, who walked into a hotel lobby carrying two very heavy suitcases. He could hardly lift them. He got to the reception desk and asked for a room. The bellboy was there to take his luggage to the room. But, instead, without waiting for his room assignment, or getting his key, the man picked up the heavy luggage and proceeded to walk back out the front door. The receptionist called after him: "Sir, Sir, you can't take the ticket unless you give the luggage to the bellboy." The "ticket" was his door key. I told my husband this dream without explanation, though Abba had given me the explanation immediately. Without apparently even thinking, he replied: "IF IT TAKES REPENTANCE TO BE BORN AGAIN – I AM NOT BORN AGAIN." The truth is, that without repentance there can be no new birth.

Not long after this, I had asked him if he ever felt any remorse at all for anything he had ever done to me, or to the children, and he replied with an emphatic "NO!" I also learned that he was a homosexual, as confirmed by several, including a wife regarding her husband, parents regarding their son, and a daughter-in-law regarding her father. He was registered in California as a pedophile. He was caught molesting a couple's little boy.

We need some "comedy relief", so here is one story: One quiet Saturday, I was working in the Cypress Park. We had a "skeleton crew" (smile) because it was the weekend. It was storming terribly. Then the electricity went out. We got a "first call." I typed up the papers, and went to take them down the long hallway to the embalming room where the limo-drivers picked up the papers to go get the body. I lit a candle, put it in a candle holder, and proceeded to walk down the long hallway. I got to the room where there were rows of dead bodies lying on gurneys. As I passed the room, upon seeing so many dead bodies, all of the horror movies I loved to watch as a youth, came back to me. The lightening was flashing, the thunder was crashing. Here I was with a candle in my right hand, the papers in my left hand, walking down a long hall. Oh my--it all hit me. I was terrified. I ran into the embalming room and threw the papers on the desk, for there was no one there at the time. Then I ran out back to the office in panic. Oh how I loved scary movies! I watched all of the ones in the 1950s and 1960s. But, as a child, you don't realize that all those movies, and the ghost stories you hear at "slumber-parties," lodge in your memory, and at some point will produce fear.

At Forest Lawn Cypress, I often drove a limousine all over Los Angeles county to get death certificates. I worked with the Coroner's office, and the police at times, about the distribution of cremated remains. They would bring the little boxes of cremated remains to my desk. The burned flesh was often so fine that it would sift out onto my papers. This was before the remains were put in an urn or scattered over the sea or a lake. I had to arrange those things too. But, I still think it bizarre that I often would have to blow some of the fine remains onto the floor that had sifted onto my papers, and I always wondered what affect that would have on resurrection day. I suppose it won't matter. I even arranged the funeral of Gene Hackman's father, and of other celebrities. I arranged funerals with the help of the family councilors. Great job! But, my rebellious sin-nature manifested strongly. I took weekend trips with one of the limousine drivers who was a policeman on the side. He had a motorcycle, and loved to ride out in the desert. I loved riding motorcycles.

These were my days of maximum "collecting." Each new boyfriend was a trophy of my rebellion. In their giving me the freedom to drive a limousine, I took liberties with my time. It was at this time that I was going to night clubs, and staying away from home a lot. I kept my aggression inside, but once something triggered it, it all came out. An example is that while working for Forest Lawn, I often went after death certificates in one of the limos, if the doctor had been negligent about signing it. One day, I was in a busy office, waiting for the doctor to sign the certificate, and I had waited 30 minutes. All he had to do was sign it. So, I got up, with the office full of people, and said very loudly to the officer workers: "Has the doctor signed the DEATH CERTIFICATE yet? I'm from FOREST LAWN, and I'm in a hurry."

PART III - The Journey is Sabotaged

The office staff froze, then panicked. Everyone in the waiting room looked at me. Within a minute I had the signed certificate.

While still at Community Chapel, before moving to North Carolina, I had my second nervous breakdown. During my second nervous breakdown, I would lie in bed for 16 hours or more and not sleep. I could hardly move. For no apparent reason, my husband decided to take a rag and jam it down my throat. I know the strength of the tongue! But I almost died. That morning was the funeral of a good friend, Marian Lease. Her husband Don, and Marian, were very close friends. I had so wanted to go to the funeral. But after almost killing me, he went to the funeral and told them I was too sick to come.

One night at Community Chapel, I met a man named David. He was a chiropractor. He came around behind me and quickly adjusted my neck. I was surprised, but it felt great. He became my chiropractor. It was he that saved me from a lot of further damage to my back due to neglect, and deformities of the spine that came as a result of neglect. At this time I was about 27 years old. I had such horrible pinched nerves of the sciatic nerve that my leg, from the hip to the knee, had become numb. After David's began the adjustments I never had any sciatica pain.

David became a Russian Orthodox priest later on. After I left the Catholic churches I had been going to in Long Beach, I joined him at his meetings. My son became his altar boy, as he had at St. Williams under Father Del. David never forsook me, even during my worst rebellion. He was a true friend. Through it all, he took care of me. David was a homosexual. His "friend" Ralph was an organist, and big in the "Organ League." The Organ League is full of homosexuals. But, they were good to me, and to my two children. They never harmed me, or the children. I never condoned their homosexuality. But David was a compassionate friend when the "straight men" hurt me. I had prostitute friends to who were kinder to me than the religious bunch who gossiped about me behind my back. Messiah said that the prostitutes and tax collectors would go into the Kingdom before the religious. I understand that very, very well!

I learned to understand real people. I learned to see behind religious masks. I am NO hypocrite! With me, what I am is what I am. Messiah was the hardest on the religious hypocrites. But, in **John 8** He forgave a prostitute. In **Luke 19:2-10** He forgave a tax collector (they were thieves). But, in **Matthew 23** He rebukes the religious leaders harshly for their hypocrisy. In **John 8:44**, He says they are of their father the Devil.

Like I said before, all those years I felt justified. I figured God had failed me, so I felt no shame It was not until one night in

Uganda, Africa, in an old border town with Kenya, that He granted me the gift of repentance. My self-justification was finally gone forever.

During a period of separation from my husband, while working at Forest Lawn Cypress, I lived with a lady my age named Sherry. She had two children, Crystal and Brian, who were about the same ages as my first two. She was also a friend of David. Her little house she rented was close to David's. She had been divorced, and was also going the promiscuous route. We did a lot of nightclubbing together. We stayed together until she got re-married. She married a man whose last name was Martini – Sherry Martini. What a mix! There were times we would cry and pray together. We wanted better for ourselves, but only a few times did our longing to be free from our sin break through to the surface. She was spontaneous. One morning she'd wake up and say "Let's go to the beach," and within 15 minutes I was ready. I am still that way. I can roll out of bed and be ready to go in 30 minutes--I'm a little slower than I used to be (smile).

It was during this time that despair almost led me to take my life. I had a bottle of sleeping pills by my bed. I poured a few into my hand, and then put all of them back into the bottle but one. I had thought of suicide before, but I just couldn't do it. Believe me! The accuser of the brethren accused me night and day for years after I returned to Abba, especially in the middle of the night when I'd wake up with horrible memories. I had to learn to turn the tables on him and remind him of his future. Abba deals with us by what He has seen of our future, not our past or what we are going through now. NO! Yahuweh does not tolerate sin! "The wages of sin is death…" When we sin, we die in some way. We reap what we sow! But, when all the smoke clears, Abba's will is still done!

One prime example: One day at David's, while he was in the kitchen fixing us coffee, I was sitting in his living room. All of a sudden, I heard the voice of Yahuweh: "Get a piece of paper, and a pen." Knowing His voice, I reached for a long legal-sized yellow paper near me, and was ready to write. He began: "**You are Moses. Deliver My people now with My pure love. My pure love is the only thing that will take my people across the sea of confusion to My freedom**." He went on with more of it. This was February of 1973. I still have that paper with me today.

I did not know until years later, that in February of 1973, a Jewish Man from Washington State, who wrote the faith-building *Operation Exodus* and *Operation Exodus II*, Steve Lightle, was in Eastern Europe with a pastor from Sweden. They had been told by Yahuweh to begin to pray that He would raise up those like Moses to deliver His people out of Russia. I became part of the fruit of their prayers. When Abba says in **Isaiah 55:8-9** "...for My thoughts are not your thoughts, neither are My ways your ways"...wow was He telling the truth! Did He condone my sin? Of course not! He had to stand back and direct me by what He had seen from the foundation of the world. (**Psalm 32:7-8**) In other words, **He had faith in His own ability to bring to completion that which He started**! "He will perfect that which concerns me." HE has to do it!

From 1986, He has driven me crazy with showing me 33s in the most incredible places, and ways. I finally asked Him WHY? The number 3 stands for 1) beginning 2) middle 3) end, or completion. He said this to me: "**What I began, I will complete**!" It is His message to us! **Psalm 138:8**: "**Yahuweh will perfect that which concerns me. Your mercy O Yahuweh endures forever! Forsake not the works of Your own hands.**"

I Thessalonians 5:23-24: "**And the Elohim of peace Himself set you apart, and your whole spirit, soul, and body be preserved blameless at the coming of our Master Yahushua Messiah! He who calls you is faithful, who shall also do it**!"

To show you the depths to which I fell, one night my hate grew so fierce against God that I told Him to get out of me. I told the Holy Spirit to get out too. I cursed Jesus, and even Mary. But, I did not tell Jesus to leave me. I feared losing my eternal life. I was screaming, throwing things, and cursing bitterly. I felt the Spirit move like a baby in the womb. I stopped for a moment, but then kept on cursing. I know now that He was letting me know that He heard me. But, He did not leave me. I am crying even now, because His mercy was/is so great.

In 1989, I was telling this to my ex-Satanist friend, Ken. I asked him if he thought I was damned to hell because of what I said. He asked me: "What do you want to do with your life now?" I said: "I want to serve my Father. I want to see souls saved for eternity." He said: "You would not have that desire if He had left you." I am transparent. I am totally committed to allowing Him to do any remodeling He wants to. My prayer is from **Psalm 139:23-24**: "**Search me O El and know my heart. Try me and know my thoughts. And see if any wicked way is in me, and lead me in the way everlasting**." I prayed with tears today, "**Please Abba, anything it takes to get me blameless before you so that I can live in Your sight forever, do it!**" I trust Him. I know He won't hurt me. He won't betray me. He is so faithful that it brings me to more tears. Sarah "judged Him faithful." (**Hebrews 11:11**, KJV)

In rebellious sinning, did I presume on His goodness? Oh no! I wanted Him out of my life. He was good because He is good, and because before the foundation of the world He made His plans, and they included me. Do you see why now He is my life! You know, you really get to know someone when they go through hell with you and don't leave you. That's love! So I got to know my Father and my Savior very well! They never left me!

One day in 1986 I told Ken that I had gained psychic abilities while exploring the occult world. I knew who was calling when the telephone rang, for example. He had wisdom. He told me I could not hear from two masters. He told me to go home, stand in the middle of my living room floor, and tell the Holy Spirit that I only wanted to hear from Him. I felt let down. Like others I've talked to in this condition, I liked my supernatural powers. But, I knew he was right. So I went home, stood in the middle of my living room floor, and told the Spirit that I only wanted to hear from Him. Then the phone rang. I did not know who it was. From that time forward, I lost all psychic abilities of the occult world. He delivered me from all of it.

While in California I got into New Age teachings. I loved the teachings of Analee Skarin – of whom Gwen Shaw was a disciple, and from whom she got much of her teaching. But, when I read Skarin's last book, where it said that Messiah was not deity, I threw them all out. I got into yoga and meditation in yoga position. I continued with these "bents" in North Carolina. I even played the Ouija board once or twice with my New Age friends, but I knew that was of the Devil. I also smoked marijuana with them. A lot of top quality marijuana is grown out in the woods in western North Carolina – so it was easy to get.

When I smoked cigarettes, I never inhaled. So inhaling the marijuana was not my thing. That didn't last long. My New Age friends were good Catholic members of St. William's. But ya know what: When my husband left for California, when I needed help with my baby in 1981, when I went through a third nervous breakdown and could not even lift my head off the floor where I was lying, and had to crawl on my belly everywhere I went, it was these "pot" smoking people who helped me. Linda came over every morning and got my baby out of her crib, cleaned her up, and brought her to me to nurse. They took me to the doctor to get my medicine, and to the chiropractor to get my adjustments on my back. They got food for me from the store. They helped me with my 5-year-old, too.

PART III - The Journey is Sabotaged

That's why Messiah said that the tax collectors and prostitutes would go into the Kingdom before the religious. These people were not religious, just kind. All I got from the religious was judgment. I was gossiped about, and slandered. I cried out for help, but they stuck their noses at me. I am thankful, because it pushed me out of any association with organized groups or religions, and into the arms of my loving Father!

While in North Carolina, early 1980s, I became a serious "Trekkie." I was obsessed with Star Trek, especially with Spock. I started collecting all the books and collectables I could find. I sent away for collectables. I had a huge collection of Star Trek things, from the TV series and movies. It was probably worth about $400.00--quite a lot for that day. It was an obsession. The enemy tried to take me down another road of destruction and open more portals for demonic activity. Finally, seeing what a hold it had on me, I gave it all to a man at St. Williams who was also a Trekkie." Then I wanted it back, and he wouldn't give it back. The enemy tried so many ways to keep me from breaking loose from his grasp, but Abba blocked his every move.

During the third nervous breakdown, because I am a high producer, I would crawl into the kitchen, sit on the floor, take dishes from the dishwasher, dry them, and put them back on the counter. One day the dishwasher broke. I got out my handy "how to do it" book, and went in there, sat on the floor, and took a flat-head screw driver and fixed the dishwasher. During those years in North Carolina, I learned basic plumbing, and even some car repair. I was like my dad, who could look at something, see what was wrong, and fix it. Papa was like that. My son is like that too. At about age four, I took my son with his sister to her pediatrician appointment. I left him with his new little tool kit in the waiting room. It was OK in those days. When we came out, he had taken the table apart and it was lying on the floor. I made him put it back together before we left.

When my son was 14, Pam Brinke, and other Spirit-filled friends, prayed for my son to be baptized in the Spirit. He surely was. He began studying the book of Proverbs. At this time I was inundated with migraine headaches. Nothing got rid of them. I would always have to go to the emergency room of the hospital where they would pump Demurral and Morphine into me, and I would get up and walk out still in pain. I was in the throws of a terrible migraine one night. My son came against Satan, and Abba healed me of migraines forever. The fantastic details of that story are under Part V of the collections. You'll also read about the miracle in Texas one day when the enemy tried to bring the headaches back onto me, and what Abba did, using the hand of Yahushua.

After the last nervous breakdown, as soon as I was strong enough, I went back to work as a secretary to the priest at St. Williams. We had bought an old upright piano, and I had "antiqued" it. I taught private piano lessons. I worked as a music teacher part of the time in a public elementary school in Murphy. As He began restoring me, more and more miracles happened that you will read about in the Collections. Because I wanted to do everything right with my last child, in carrying her, I made drastic changes in my life. That meant no more wild parties, no more heavy drinking--no more moonshine--no more smoking cigarettes, (I had smoked cigarettes for about 6 years), and no more "grass." So, in 1981, Abba began the process of taking me back.

In 1985, Abba spoke to me while studying the Prophets: "**I have called you to the office of a Prophet.**" I was so stunned. But, now, I have no shame, no self-hatred, no regrets, and no unforgiveness. I walk free! When I went to Africa, and different countries, they'd send runners to the surrounding villages crying "Come hear! A Prophet's on the mountain." I've had people in many nations tell me that they saw an anointing of Elijah on me. I do not bill myself as that, but Abba has told me that too. It was here that I got my commissioning.

My return to peace: One day in 1985, I was sitting in my favorite chair, and Abba said to me: "**Go get the Bible; I want to talk to you**." I got it off the shelf and it opened in my lap. I looked down and there was the story of Peter walking on the water. He said to me: "**From now on you will walk on the water!**" And so I have ...

Some of my longer-term boyfriends had given me some expensive gifts. I took them to Father Del and told him to give them to his nieces, which he did. In returning to Him, I lost all desire to be rebellious against Him. To solidify my return, He gave me a life-changing dream, which I relate in the next section, which caused me to see clearly that all of my suffering was from my own hand. Yes, I asked His forgiveness. I returned like I'd been shot out of a canon. It was the same with the psychological reversal, one day I was bitter with sin, and the next day I was home in His arms. But, it took several years before His giant eraser healed my emotions totally, for the wounds were very, very deep. He took my repentance and restoration in stages, as I could take it.

His timing is sometimes really strange. In 1998, I was on a mountain top in Uganda, in a small village, at the home of Dr.

Steven and his wife. It was the middle of the night. I was to teach in a church the next day. I woke up suddenly, and the "gift" swiftly came down on me--the "spirit of repentance." I could finally repent of my sin of whoring. That night, my justification for sinning was taken from me and I repented of what I DID against myself, against the men, against my parents, against my husband, and against Him. Repentance is a gift. Remember, it was not granted to Esau. I cried and cried. That finally began my repentance for my life of sin against my Abba. It was not that I had not asked His forgiveness before that, of course, but true repentance comes deep from within.

In 2003, on Shabbat during Passover, I was with a young girl named Trisha, who bitterly despised me out of jealousy. She later admitted to it, saying it was because of my relationship with Abba. I invited myself to walk with her around the gates of the old city of Jerusalem. We got to the Lion's Gate, and I asked if I could go to St. Anne's Church, where the ruins of Bethesda were. I wanted to take pictures for my son who attended Bethesda Community Church in Ft. Worth--the same church I had attended before leaving for Aqaba. She was disgusted with me, but she said "OK." We came into the garden area, and I heard the voice of my Bridegroom saying: **"AFTER 38 YEARS**!" Thirty-eight years before was 1965 – the year my world collapsed, which led to my marrying my husband.

I began sobbing my heart out. Then we proceeded to the area where the ruins were. We saw the sign that started the trek through the ruins of this ancient Roman "bath" pool. She pointed out that it was a pagan place. I said, yes, but Messiah came here to heal one man. (**John 5:1-15**) I was still sobbing with all my heart. I'm glad we were alone. As I stood across from the sign, all of a sudden I saw Him. I was face to face with Yahushua. I can still see Him in detail. He just stood there. All my pea brain could think of was: "He's the same age as my son." With all those horrible religious paintings of Him, I finally saw a 31 year old Jewish man, with curly brown chestnut hair--Levite length--a nicely trimmed beard, wearing a white belted robe, with brown eyes, and a big wonderful smile. He bowed graciously, then took His left hand and made a sweeping gesture towards the entrance, and said "WELCOME," in His lovely baritone voice that I knew so well. I cried harder. His smile was so lovely. He looked so sweet. Yes, He was nice-looking, but the only way I can describe Him is "sweet."

I proceeded through the ruins. Upon leaving, He spoke to me the words that He spoke to that man whom He healed there: "GO AND SIN NO MORE." After 38 years I was free. The man that had been lying by those pools for 38 years, needed His help. But, after 38 years he was set free. In 1995, I had lost my direction, and like that man by the pool, I had no one to help me be healed.

I was writing articles, I was teaching, I had been sent to many countries, and I was pure of heart, studying the Torah and set-apart. But, He used that day, in the presence of one who hated me because of my relationship with Him, to finally finish the healing that caused me to sin against Him.

To know that our sin is "under the blood of the Lamb" brings peace. All of my past sin is covered by the blood of Messiah Yahushua, my Savior, my Redeemer--my Bridegroom. He died to restore me. I took Him up on **Luke 14:25-33**. I owe Him everything! All praise to Abba Yahuweh and Messiah Yahushua! Now, for the joyful journey back home...

THE GREATEST MIRACLE OF ALL IS ABBA'S MERCY, FORGIVENESS, AND UNFAILING LOVE!

PART IV

THE JOURNEY BACK HOME

(1985-1986)

In 1985, before Abba totally, and finally, snatched me out of the pit I had dug for myself, He gave me a life-changing dream. In the dream, I was standing at the bottom of some stairs in a concrete slab basement, next to about five stairs. The whole basement was dimly lit, and all I saw were white walls. I grabbed hold of my left wrist with my right hand. I began running up and down the hallway, screaming: "The hand of God is on me; the hand of God is on me." Finally, exhausted, I stopped by the stairs and looked down. I saw that my wrist was being held by my own hand. A voice gently spoke to me: "**It's always been your own hand**." I woke up stunned, saying to Him: "I'm sorry; I'm sorry", and asked for His forgiveness. All those years I had hated Him, and it was always my own "hand" – my own decisions that kept me a prisoner. He did nothing but patiently and tenderly watch over me!

It has been incredibly hard to write these things. And to be honest, I left A LOT out! To go into more details of my abuse, and the children's abuse, or details of my gross sinning, would not be a blessing to you--it would only bless and honor the enemy! I want to concentrate on praising and exalting the Creator, not in making the enemy smile. Part III is the reason why it has taken me nearly seven years to write this autobiography. I do not mean to hurt anyone by what I say in this autobiography. I am just reporting facts. My children have forgiven me. That is one of the greatest miracles of all!

About a year ago Abba gently asked me: "Did I, or My Son, ever do anything to hurt you?" I cried. I said "NO!" Then He said: "When you thought I was "God" and My Son was "Jesus", did they ever do anything to hurt you?" I had to pause and think that through. Then I answered "NO!"

Jeremiah 12:7, Yahuweh speaking in grief: "**I have forsaken My house; I have left My inheritance. I have given the beloved of my soul into the hands of her enemies.**" **In Hebrew, the words "beloved of My soul" is yedidah nephish.** As He grieved over the ten northern tribes that He had to expel from the land (722 BCE), so He had to expel me from the peace I could have had with Him. Yet, He said that He called me "Yedidah"—"Beloved." He called me that from eternity past.

In 1986 I was still working as Father Tom's secretary. I had been taking my Bible to read between work assignments at the

Rectory. I was alone in the office one day and the phone rang. It was a lady from the house next door. She said that the man who lived there, a young Baptist minister, had shot and killed himself, and the ambulance had just taken him away. The family had arrived and was in great distress. She asked if the priest was there and if he could come to minister to them. Some of that family was Catholic. I said, "No, he is not here--but will I do--I am a minister." She said: "Yes, please come." I went over there with my Bible. Blood could still be seen splattered on the ceiling. I sat there for two hours presenting His love, His salvation, His deliverance, and His comfort, and praying with them. I went back to the church office, sat down, and heard Him say in my spirit: "**WELCOME HOME!**" Oh the mercy of a loving Father! To Him be all the esteem, all the honor, all the praise and worship!!!

So, you see, there is no praise that should ever go to me! The praise and worship is due only to Abba Yahuweh and Messiah Yahushua!!!

The deep well that my hate had dug became the well that holds my love for Him.

I sometimes get long e-mails from women who tell me how righteous and spiritual they are, and how unspiritual their husbands are. They rant and complain about their husbands, but when I pin them down about their husbands, I find they are not bad at all – just natural human men doing the best they know how. Women who complain about good husbands need to shut up! They need to humble themselves before Elohim. If they get their lives submitted to Elohim, maybe their husbands will see the good fruit and find Elohim too. Nowadays, there are women who are divorcing their husbands because they do not keep the Torah. If a woman keeps the Torah but does not manifest the fruit of the re-born spirit--love, joy, peace, faith, long-suffering, kindness, gentleness, meekness, humility, and self control--no wonder her husband doesn't guard Torah. So many women are so prideful and self-righteous that their good husbands have no example to follow. Many women are so controlling and so judgmental of their husbands, that they drive their husbands away. My heart breaks-- I wanted one of those good husbands. But, I wait for the One to come!

No one who knows Yahuweh and Yahushua personally would call themselves "spiritual!" Yahuweh looks at people differently than man looks at man. Moses murdered a man, and hid him in the sand. King David conspired to have Uriah killed so that he might take his wife, Bathsheba. Saul murdered in the name of religion. Rahab was a prostitute. And yet Abba had His hand on these people for good. Rahab is in the lineage of Messiah.

PART IV - The Journey Back Home

Religious spirituality is an empty shell. Abba appreciates people who are real. He can deal with a person who is genuine. He can't deal with those who hide under a mask, because these people are deceiving themselves above all. He can work with a King David who repented.

He put me through eight years of the literal wilderness of the Negev Desert, and I came out of it "leaning on my Beloved" (**Song of Songs 8:5**). He stripped me of all religion, pride, and desire for anything other than to serve Him. So people who have been jealous of my relationship with my Abba are sickly pathetic. It took most of my life to develop that relationship! Are they prepared to pay such a high price, allowing Him to empty them of all "self" so that that a relationship might be built?

1995 was the hardest year of my life to date. We lived in Fort Worth, Texas. In all, we lived there about 23 years. During 1995, my husband tried to kill me more than once, and also tried to get me to kill myself by setting up situations that left me feeling totally hopeless.

Papa died November 4, 1982. My mother died March 30, 1995. Both were extremely traumatic experiences for me. When papa died, I was living in deep sin. When mother died, I was free, breaking forth to serve the Master. Being the sole inheritor of her home and property, I had to go to North Carolina regularly as the Executor of her will. I had to sell the house, and go through all her possessions—a huge task since she was a collector! I had to make the decisions of what to throw away and what to keep, what to sell, and what to store. It was hard and there were a few things I threw out that I wish I had not thrown out.

After papa died in 1982, my mother became a semi-recluse and got more and more feeble. She had many ladies whom she paid to stay with her to help her. So, the majority of my inheritance went to paying for their services. She just gave up after papa died. He was her motivator. I must say that she had some good women helping her.

My oldest male cousin--cousin Paul--was out to steal her estate, as he had stolen his parent's money and estate by trickery. His mother, my Aunt Fairy, was very feeble before she died, so she signed everything over to him. He did some wicked things. He tried to get my mother to sign over the house, and all the property. At that time she owned quite a bit of NC mountain property. She sold it off a little at a time to pay for the lady helpers. So, I lost at least $100,000 of my inheritance. Paul tried to get my mother to give him the key to the safety deposit box. But, she had her right mind, and would not sign anything he put before her. When I came there to visit one day, the lady on-duty took me aside and told me to get the power of attorney out of my aunt's name and into my own name, and to take my mother's wedding ring, and everything out of the bank drawer--deeds, etc. She told me that my cousin had gone through my mother's desk to find the deeds. I consulted with my mother about it and she agreed. So I quickly got the power of attorney in my name. I made sure he got nothing. My aunt died in great grief one month before my mother died.

Finally the helpers all left. My mother's needs were getting too much for them. When the local Social Service found out she was alone, I was contacted. They said they were going to sell her house and put her in a nursing home, and use the money from the sale of her house to pay for her care. I contacted my lawyer immediately. He was terrific! He got someone to rent the house quickly, which, by law, stopped the Social Service from taking the house. He was the lawyer that helped me sell the remaining land.

We found a lovely nursing home to take her. It was in the hills of Andrews, North Carolina--next town north of Murphy. Many of the nurses and attendants were relatives related to my Aunt Fairy's husband--my uncle Lyle. They loved my mother. She said she wished she had come to the nursing home sooner. She was peaceful there. My mother's family were/are very sharp people. My aunts and uncles were very successful people, and Fairy was a business-minded lady.

But, what a sweet Aunt. I hated eggs. I will never forget, as a little girl, sitting in their home in Wisconsin, Fairy put egg on a spoon and pretend to fly it like an airplane into my mouth. My uncle Lyle was brilliant. He ran with a football 96 yards to make a touchdown for his Andrews High School team. He worked with Lockheed Martin all of his working life. He ended up at Cape Canaveral, Florida, working on the Titan missile project. I really loved him. Before Aunt Fairy died, she got my mother on Medicare. My mother only had her teacher's insurance. So Medicare paid for her care.

My mother died in peace with loving people around her. What a blessing! She maintained her sharp mind up until her death. I signed a living will. She had a stroke, a broken hip, was going blind, and wanted to die. So, they kept her on pain medication, but let her go as she willed. Seeing that she would have no good life of her own with all her physical complications, she stopped eating, and it led to her death. The last time I saw her alive was 10 days before she died. The story of the funeral is both good and bad. It was a sweet funeral with many family members and loving people. I had told my husband it was OK for him to preach at the funeral.

While making the arrangements for the funeral, we stayed in the motel next to St. Williams. The funeral was the next day. That night, while trying to go to sleep, my husband shook me. He began his ritualistic sadomasochistic torture on me, the torture of mind and emotions, and the dehumanizing using my body. I could not wrap my mind around it. I said, please, it is my mother's funeral. He said it didn't matter. The next morning, after all of that, he preached her funeral, and I had to pretend all was well.

In going over her tax returns, I discovered that her CPA had not done his job well. At least part of the money she had paid out for those ladies who cared for her should have been subtracted from her income tax. I took the problem to my CPA in Texas, a good friend in our church. He got it straightened out and I was sent a check from the IRS for a little over $3,500.00. When I got it, my husband was furious. He wanted the money. I sold much of her furniture in an auction for over $4,000.00. It was an exhausting year. It was a mixture-year of the very good, and the very bad!

In the summer of 1995, Abba put it into my spirit to go to Mongolia. I was not being belligerent, or rebellious, I just knew Abba wanted me to go. Being jealous, my husband tried to block my trip. He even called the ministry – the English Language Institute – and tried to slander me. But, the woman whom he talked to was spiritually perceptive and told him he needed to get his own life right with God. It was in my pursuit of going to Mongolia, that I was finally set free. 1995 was his all out ditch-effort to destroy me, in mind, emotions and body.

During 1995, one afternoon, I was getting ready to go to a meeting at a friend's house. He and his wife were missionaries to Germany. It was so peaceful at their house. Ken D. (not the ex-Satanist Ken) taught the Word, then our little group fellowshipped.

One afternoon, my husband called me from work and said that a couple in our new church, Emmanuel Christian Fellowship, wanted to get together for a prayer meeting that night, and to "talk to me." I said I was going to our regular fellowship meeting. But, he pressured me so hard, I gave in. I was angry with myself, but I went. In my spirit, which had come alive and was growing stronger, I knew something was very wrong.

We got to their house, and they took us to the little old church building next door, that they were custodians of. They put me in a straight-backed hard chair, while my husband sat in another chair. They stood over me, the man on my right, the woman on my left. For five hours they screamed at me and told me that everything was my fault, and that I was filled with demons. I knew the only "spirit" I had outside my own was the Set-Apart Spirit of Abba, so I kept resisting. They got in my face and kept screaming, accusing me of terrible things that were not true. As my husband had accused me, and evidently told them, they said I had killed my father, and ran my oldest daughter away. They made it sound like everything I ever did was inspired by demons. I was in numb with shock, but did not condone the abuse. It was just that we were in a part of Dallas that I did not know, in a shabby neighborhood. Also, it was late at night, and I did not want to try to hitch a ride.

Through all of the interrogation and accusation, my husband sat bent over with his head in his hands most of the time. Finally, after five hours, I cracked and began screaming. They were delighted. They said, finally, the demons are gone. It was about 2:00 AM. We went to the car to go home. I could hardly walk. I felt like I was having a breakdown. My husband stopped at an all-night pharmacy and bought a big bottle of sleeping pills. He gave them to me, and told me to take them--that he would tell everyone it was menopause that drove me to suicide, even though I had no menopause symptoms. I went home and made a bed for myself on the floor.

A few days later, I realized I was going into a fourth nervous breakdown. I knew I had to talk to someone. I trusted my pastor and his wife. The next Sunday night I went to the church. I found the pastor's wife in the kitchen area. She took one look at me and called her husband. The next day he sat down with me at the church and listened to what I had to say. He helped me a lot. He understood!

I never had menopause symptoms. In 1981, my mother had gone through so many menopause symptoms that I proclaimed to Abba that I would not have one menopause symptom other than the stopping of my periods. Abba put me on an Asian diet. I did not know until later what that was all about. But, I had lots of tofu (back when soy was not GM), and fresh vegetables, and little meat. I was so healthy! When the time for menopause came, I had not one symptom that was negative. I took Black Cohosh to prevent hot flashes. Five years later, I was in a grocery store line and saw the Prevention Magazine in the rack. Across the front of it were the words in bold print: "Asian Diet Found to Stop Menopause Symptoms." I laughed. I found out that in the tofu is a false estrogen that the body picks up as the real thing. My mother had estrogen shots, pills for hot flashes, and was always at the doctor for something about it. She had huge mood swings. I wasn't going to stand for it. But, mood swings, i.e. depression to giddiness – almost a bipolar situation – is common in many women during menopause. Well I had no mood swings. Abba was beginning to align my emotions to His nature. To this day, I have no mood swings. My children are amazed at me. But, who would have believed I'd be so stable back in 1995?

Before going to Mongolia, my husband had said that since I married him, he was my master--Jesus was not my master. I knew that was not right. After the next church service, as my youngest daughter and I were heading home, I was pondering what my husband said. I turned the car around and went back to the church and asked this pastor if what my husband said was true. He put his long skinny finger in my face and said: "YOU HAVE ONE MASTER AND ONE ONLY!" Meaning Jesus...

I slowly recovered without a nervous breakdown. I was getting stronger, and my focus was on Mongolia. We were still going to the church together. One morning my husband told me that I could not give any more testimonies in church. We had a time each Sunday morning when people could tell what Abba had done for them that week. But, during the testimony time, Abba was stirring in my spirit to the point where I couldn't stand it anymore. I had to tell what He had done for me that week. I stood up and told it. I sat down, and my husband got up in front of everyone and walked out.

My husband wanted my mother's inheritance, and when he saw that he was not going to get it, he went berserk. He told me the only reason he married me was to get that inheritance. There was no love from him towards me, or the children. So, I did not get upset at what he said. I just accepted it as true. He had asked me for a divorce about 4 months after we got married.

In late January 1996, my husband did me the ultimate favor. He cornered me, and said: "Either I am your master or Jesus is your Master—CHOOSE NOW!" He knew what I would say. I was set up. I had no problem answering: I said "Jesus." He lunged for my throat, only pretending to kill me. I grabbed my purse, ran and got in the car, and left. I watched him come to the garage door and just stand there with his arms folded and a smirk on his face.

The next day, he sent out letters that he had already written, to all of our friends and family telling them I had abandoned him, and our children. Knowing what was coming, about a week before that, I had taken some of my mother's inheritance and paid for an apartment for a year. It was 2 miles away. It was also in my daughter's school district. So, when I fled, I fled to my own peaceful 2-bedroom apartment. During that week, while he was at work, I went back to the house to get our things. I hired movers to move the beds, and a few other things that were heavy. I left a lot of things for him however, things I had to replace in the new apartment. Through it all, I continued to have compassion on him.

My youngest and I lived in that apartment for about 2½ years. When the rent went up, and the money started running out, I got a nice 1-bedroom apartment in the same complex, and friends helped me move. So, this daughter and I were together until Abba led me to Jordan. She was almost 16 then, in her sophomore year at Southwest High School.

Because my husband had run up tens of thousands of dollars in debt on credit cards and not paying the IRS for years, he had expected me to use my mother's inheritance to pay all that off. I only had about $65,000.00 when the smoke cleared. My CPA, who had gotten me the $3,500 back, advised me to get another bank account of my own so that the IRS didn't take the money. So, I followed his advice, and did that also with the ministry account. Thus my husband was unable to get any of my mother's inheritance. She still had the land in North Carolina that she and her brother had bought together. But, Abba kept it unsold for seven years, so that North Carolina law would change, and he would not get any of the money. The miracle story of that sale is in Part VII of the Collections.

From February 1996 on, it was like getting shot out of a cannon. Abba led me into so many awesome adventures: First to the Voice of the Martyrs conference in California, then to Mongolia for 3 ½ months, then to Switzerland for a fantastic tour, and then to Africa to start my seven years of ministry there. From that starting place, He has kept me on the move to this day, increasing my work load over and over.

I am happy to give this good report of what my husband did in 1996. My husband had run up our 8-10 credit cards to their maximum. We owed over $30,000.00 to credit card companies. He had stopped paying the IRS, so we owed $40,000.00 to the IRS. That was my mother's whole inheritance money. I prayed so hard. I begged God to make something happen so that the IRS and credit card companies would not take my mother's inheritance. Then one day my husband called me. He said that he felt he should take out a loan and pay the credit cards off and the IRS. He sent me the paid off receipts. I was overwhelmed. For what reason he did that, I don't question. But, I thanked him with humility.

Like I said, the man was a good provider, and there was a good part of him that took responsibility for taking care of his family financially. However, I am sure he didn't want to chance any stain on his good reputation. His greatest fear was that his dark side would be exposed. To show his integrity to provide for us: In early

1986, before we left for Texas, he had no job. After the car wreck coming home from Chattanooga one evening, he quit his job in Chattanooga. Our friend Pam Brinke told him he had to do something to put "beans on the table." That's when he took a job as a bag boy in a supermarket until we moved. I respected that! Here was the big shot of Big Six bagging groceries. I still worked at St. Williams part time.

There were so many miracles that happened to get us to Texas. To build your faith, read about them in Part VII "Miracles of Provision." It was during this time that whatever was good in him, came out. There was one loving, peaceful personality he had among all the others – IF all of him was like that, he would have been such a wonderful husband! May that surface and the rest be removed! He had discovered **Ezekiel 12:26-28**: "...There shall none of My words be prolonged any more, but the word which I have spoken shall be done." So many days, he would come home from work and say: "The Lord gave me Ezekiel 12." It would be the highlight of our days at times.

So many wonderful miracles of His intervention happened during those days of our preparing to go to Texas. It was like Abba was excited for us. We joined with believers who left St. Williams, and others believers, who had formed a prayer meeting once a week. We also fellowshipped with them at other times. We also began going to a little charismatic church. The pastor was an elderly man, and we found peace there. Later we began going to Tommy Field's church, which turned out to be a great blessing in our lives.

In 1996, my biggest extravaganza was to go to Switzerland. I had pretended to be Heidi at age seven, and my dream was about to come true. So, in October of 1996, I knew I had to sandwich in my trip to Switzerland in between my trip to Mongolia and my first trip to Africa. It was a good thing I did it then. Even though I've been back to Switzerland three times, it was always for ministry work. I picked October to go with Trafalgar Tours out of England. The travel agent said there was one place left with that tour--so I booked it. The only problem was that there were no seats on any plane for me to get there. I believed that Abba wanted me to go.

It got close to when I had to be in Switzerland, and still not one seat on any plane into Zurich. One week before I had to go, my travel agent called and said there was one seat on Swiss Air that had opened up to Zurich, but I would be there one day before the others arrived. I said: "Book it!" What a good decision! I was booked into a hotel in Zurich. I spent a whole day walking around Zurich, seeing important sites, and relaxing. The next afternoon, a bus arrived with others going on the tour. They were exhausted. I was sitting at an outside table near the entrance to the hotel eating Swiss chocolates and drinking coffee. I greeted them. Wow, was that a marvelous tour. I paid $300.00 to go on all the special tours not included in the general trip. So when about 2/3 of the tour group was stuck in town, I was off on all the adventures with the other 1/3. What a blessing!

The Scottish tour guide would say something like: "this is Geneva, be back on the bus in 2½ hours." This was the way the whole tour went. I don't think I could handle a tour where the tour guide makes people stand while they talk about the history of a place – BORING! I had my *Lonely Planet Travel Kit* (book) on Switzerland. It gave me details of what to find in each place. So I set off on my own and found all the main sites. Finally, we got to the wine growing area, and stayed at a hotel in Sierre. The next morning we were going to Zermatt, at the base of the Matterhorn. There were fields of ripened grapes everywhere around the hotel. But, the *Lonely Planet* book said there was a castle on a hill above the town, with hundreds of acres of grapes around it. My tour friends all went into town. I set off for the castle. I had to ask the locals for directions at times, but they were all nice to me. I had a lovely time walking up the side of a hill through all those acres of ripened grapes to the castle. Yes, yes – I tasted a few grapes on the way! When I got back to the town my friends asked where I had been, and I told them. They grabbed the book from me and my secret was exposed. Some of the Asians were staying after the tour, so my book helped them make plans. I got samples of the Swiss Dole and Fendant wines to take back to my children. I had just moved into that big Savoy apartment and had no furniture, so we sat on the floor with sheets as "tablecloths" and enjoyed spaghetti and the wine. I returned to Switzerland two more times, and stayed in Montreux with a friend, right by the Castle of Chillon. More in Part VI.

I loved adventure! My son, as a young teen, had adopted Indiana Jones as a hero. So, in about 1997, during one stormy day, while in Ft. Worth, my son took me to see the movie, "Indiana Jones and the Last Crusade." Because it was storming outside, we were the only ones in the movie theater. The movie showed Indiana going by horseback through a winding gorge. At the end of it was a great structure, carved out of rose-red rock. I was enamored with that place. I told my son that we had to stay and watch all the credits because I had to see where that place was. At the very end of the credits were the words: "The Hashemite Kingdom of Jordan." Little did I know that I would live 75 miles south of it for eight years, near the King's Highway of

Numbers 20-21, and take many people to Petra, fulfilling part of the question of **Psalm 108**: "Who will take me to Edom; who will take me to the city of habitation." Isn't that awesome!

My papa studied Revelation, over and over. He was studying **Revelation 4-5,** his favorite Scripture, the night he died. Papa kept notes on Revelation, some of them with deep understanding of truth. In the notes, he asked a question: "Who will take people to Petra; how will they be fed, and by who?" I cried, "It's me papa." At that time I believed I'd be in Petra during the tribulation. I may be. It is the only world-area designated by the U.N. for refugees, famine and disaster relief. If I go there, I will have unusual neighbors in those caves, which they are preparing to enter soon – **Revelation 6:12-17**.

In being forced to separate from my husband, then having to sign divorce papers five years later, I was very wounded. One of the most painful things about interacting with people is their questioning me. Without knowing me, they just blurt out things like: "Where is your husband?", "Are you married?", or "How does your husband like your traveling so much?" I consider it very cruel for people to pry into someone's private life with no respect.

One of the most painful experiences was when I was meeting a group of about 15 people for lunch, in Jerusalem. Next to me sat a man whose wife was on my e-mail list. He did not read my articles, but she did. He and his wife came to Israel from Switzerland to be on a tour with Avi ben Mordicai. The first thing he said was to ask if I was divorced. His wife was upset and tried to shut him up, but he kept talking. I told him I was divorced. Then he asked me if I went to Jordan because of my divorce, implying that I was like so many missionary women, who, after losing a fiancé, or thinking they'd never marry, went to the mission field in despair and loneliness. Nothing could have been further from the truth with me! His questions hurt deeply. Everytime someone asks me personal questions that are painful, it takes many days and lots of prayer to stop the hurt. It is because they are prying for their own hidden agenda--a power-play.

Here's the real story: At the end of 1998, I had come back from a trip to Africa--a wonderful trip. I had taken two ladies; a school teacher, and an x-ray technician, and my 17 year old daughter. As I leaned back in my chair in the living room, relaxing, I asked Father, "Now what do You want me to do?" I did not expect His immediate reply. But, He said clearly to me: "Give away all that you have and move to Jordan." He gave me that familiar "joy jump" in my spirit, and I began thinking of who to give my things to besides my children and cousins. I had a friend there whom I had gone to church with at Emmanuel Christian Fellowship who was part of a little Messianic group. I would not be there alone. I gave away all to my children and cousins, except for a few things I kept in a storage shed for the time being. I also kept clothes and shoes, my Bible, etc. – things I'd need in Jordan. I left for Jordan April 18, 1999. Without planning it, I bought my ticket to leave Aqaba, to move out, at His insistence, on April 18, 2007. I did not want to give up my apartment in Aqaba. I had lived in one large apartment for six years, then moved to a smaller one in the north district of Aqaba for two years.

Jordan was a mixture of many miracles, studying to unlearn falsehood and to learn from Him as He taught me truth, signs and wonders, dreams, visions, revelation knowledge, visitations from His realm, and the feeling of home, along with the crushing, the hurts, the betrayals (by Americans Christians and Messianics, not the locals), the learning experiences, the emotional upheavals, the downright cruelty, but it was all schooling for the rest of my life.

It was in Aqaba, in 2001, that He began my writing on what He was teaching me, and my work for the Master took off like a canon blast. It was in Jordan that I formed a relationship with the real Elohim of Israel and the real Messiah Yahushua. It was there that They revealed Their intent for me. I was alone most of the time, but it was quality time. I did not go back to the U.S. much. I went from there to other nations at times. I spent every Festival of Yahuweh in Israel. I met friends that are eternal friends. I had experiences that few have.

Those eight years were very hard, but without them I would not be where I am now, nor would I have the renewed mind-set I have now. He taught me His Torah, His way! I became "Spirit-taught." He knew I needed confirmation and research material, so HE brought it as He willed. It was amazing to see His intervention in everything He asked me to do! It was there that He showed me His timing for the end times. He fine-tuned my education. It was like getting my Masters Degree and several PhDs. But, the price for that education was extremely high! Because of the favor I had with the Jordanians authorities in the Aqaba Special Economic Zone (a European resort, and a headquarters of the U.N., U.S., and E.U. hierarchy), I got my residency without all the requirements that others had to have. So, the jealousy once again raised its ugly head. I had to battle jezebel spirits, and mind-boggling betrayal, mostly from jealousy. I still battle those things, but not as much now. I've gotten incredibly stronger and wiser!

It was a continuation of my marriage in some ways. Those familiar spirits hang on hard until forced to leave. My husband had

PART IV - The Journey Back Home

promised to project his spirits at me wherever I went. So, some did all they could to lie, to slander, to try to destroy my ministry, and my reputation with those in Jordan, in Israel, and in America. Some even admitted to it being jealousy. Their wickedness worked to a small degree. But, oh the education! So I say heartily: Thank you Abba!

April 18, 1999, I left my family, my home, my job, my parent's inheritance, and all that I had in the natural. The scene at the airport was awful. I did not know if I would ever see my children again. My daughter-in-law hated me--the very one I thought of as a daughter. And, for my son's sake, I had to apologize to her for things I never did wrong. I did not return for a year.

Around 2000, I dissolved my evangelistic corporation, a 501C non-profit organization, and my ordinations. I cut ties with everything that was attached to the government and to the church system. I had only $4,000.00 to get settled. I rented the large apartment for a year. It was a three bedroom, two-bath apartment, with a large living room, and kitchen. I made the large bedroom into an office. It had a balcony. Though I came in from the ground floor and only up about four steps, because it had a deep basement, the balcony was like I was on the second floor. It overlooked Eilat, Israel, and the Red Sea. I was told by my wealthy friends that it would take me $4,000.00 just to buy appliances. I bought all my needed appliances, new ones, for $400.00, which left them indignant. Some people gave me things, like ceiling fans – oh the blessing of that! One lady tried to give me a T.V., but I declined taking it.

In 1997, He had very sternly called me to cut soul ties. He told me to stop watching TV except the "700 Club" News. That might seem silly, but it was the only news cast, about 15 minutes daily, giving truthful news. I loved to watch murder mysteries. I grew up reading Nancy Drew novels. I watched "Murder She Wrote" starring Angela Lansbury, and "Diagnosis Murder" starring Dick Van Dike. They were nothing like today's explicit blood and guts crime dramas, which are satanic in nature for the most part. He gave me **Isaiah 33:14-17** as His reasoning. If He was going to prepare me for the Kingdom, I could not look on evil willingly, let alone enjoy it as entertainment. You know from my articles now how hard I am against the TV, which has now become not only a Satanic mind control device, but a portal throughout which the "sound of silence" pulse waves can come through to shut down a person's mind, emotions, and will.

It was also 1997, when I had my experience of the "marking." I hesitate to share this, for it is extremely personal, yet some have asked me about it. But, I give it here as a part of His teaching me.

He did a lot of changing me in 1997. I was sitting watching the 700 Club News. There had been a bus bombing in Jerusalem. It showed the Prime Minister, Benjamin Netanyahu, walking among the beds of the wounded in a hospital. They showed one young man who had his head bandaged. While cameras rolled, the Prime Minister picked up the phone and called the young man's father in the U.S., to tell him that his son was all right. While watching this, I burst into deep sobbing for the evils done in Jerusalem. During sobbing, I felt something move across my forehead tangibly, as if tracing a line. I stopped crying. Since I had taught the Tenach for so many years, and read it so many times, my first thought was: "This is like the verse in **Ezekiel 9:4**." I ran to the bedroom to get my Bible. I sat on the bed and opened to Ezekiel **9:4** and read it. Then, as is my custom, I grabbed a pen to write the date next to the verse. Then I went cold and numb--the date was **9/4** (September 4, 1997).

In the text of Ezekiel 9, six men came from the direction of the north gate with battle axes in their hands. One man, dressed in linen, with an inkhorn and pen, came afterwards. Yahuweh told the man with the ink to put a mark on the foreheads of all those in Jerusalem who had sighed and cried over the abominations done in the City. Then He gave instructions to the six to kill all in Jerusalem who did not have the mark of Yahuweh on their forehead. To the man with the inkhorn: "**Yahuweh said to him, `Pass on into the midst of the City, and you shall put a mark on the foreheads of the men who sigh and cry over all the abominations that are done in it**."

We have now entered the season that begins the tribulation time. [Refer to: "The Shmittah Year Prophecy" and "The Forty-Eight Hour Transition"/2007 for starters] The prophecy of **Ezekiel 9:4-11:23** has not happened yet. Today the north gate of the Temple Mount is the main entrance gate for the Muslims. I have no doubt but that the slaughters that Yahuweh sends are Muslims. The man with the ink was one of His true "believers." He wore linen, "the righteousness of the set-apart ones." Yahuweh will use Islam as part of His judgment, in Israel, in America, in the UK, and Europe--"the spirit of the Medes" (Read all of **Isaiah 13**)

In 1998-early 1999, I worked in a large Christian bookstore in Customer Service. I began preparing for Aqaba, saving all the money I could. I had $4,000.00 left from my mother's inheritance, and a little from this job. It was a hard job. There was one manager who kept me under surveillance. He spied on me. He wanted to find something wrong with me so that he could fire me. It was a spiritual thing. I don't even think he knew why he did that. But, he arranged some trick to get me fired.

PART IV - The Journey Back Home

It was here that I saw the helplessness of the America believers, especially the white men. When the other cashiers went to lunch, I covered for them at "Customer Service." I had worked in retail stores before, and so it was natural for me to run the cash register. Almost every day at noon I would have this scenario: As African, Chinese, Mexican, and Asian Americans came to the front of the store to check out, they would look to see if there was a cash register open. Upon seeing me, they would come right to me. Mostly the white males, often with children, and a few females, would go stand on the other side of the entrance from me at the empty cash registers and look around with the most pathetic lost faces. I would motion them over, but most of the time, I would have to literally go around the service desk and walk to the other side of the entrance doors and go right to them and say "follow me." I never could understand this phenomenon until I went to live in a "third world" country. The people with third world country backgrounds were survivors. They had it in their DNA. They knew how to look and analyze and move quickly. But, the mind-programmed American whites were so insecure and fearful, that they needed someone to hold their hand and lead them. This is why I write so much to Americans and appear to be so hard on them, because I see what the mind-programming has done. I want to try to help them break free!

It was during this time that a Baptist missionary from Nigeria came to visit one of the managers in her office. She wanted me to meet Karen. Karen and her husband had a bad experience with their mission organization and both were sent back to America. Karen was in tears over it. I told her about my experiences in East Africa, and she shared her experiences in West Africa. We became friends.

One day we went out to lunch. Karen was a "market place" evangelist and it was natural for her to talk to people she didn't know. Near our table were two ladies talking about a prayer meeting. One lady was named Dee Ann. They were leaving the restaurant at the same time we were. So, Karen struck up a conversation with the other lady, and I began talking to Dee Ann from Flower Mound. She invited me to join them. She said their prayer meeting was not about everybody praying, but about listening to the Master and sharing what He said. I began attending these meetings.

This is where I met my dear Ethiopian Jewish friend, Golietha, dear Gezelle, and also Christie, who would betray me in Aqaba. I will talk about these people later. But, that prayer meeting each week opened doors for me in other places to teach and share. I attended them until I left for Jordan, and then when I was in the U.S. in 2001 and 2002.

On April 18, 1999, I went to Aqaba with three suitcases. When I arrived at the Aqaba airport, I saw nothing but dirt and rocks – brown with blue sky. Upon getting my luggage, I found that two of the three suitcases had not arrived with me. I was so let down. My friend met me and took me to her house, where I stayed until I got my own apartment. Others there looked down on me for "imposing" on her, but it did not take long to get my own apartment. She took me to show me where the grocery store was. On returning, we had to cross dirt and rocks in a field. As I was walking along, I looked down and a child's toy was at my feet. It was a little plastic camel, with two humps. Abba spoke to me that those two humps represented my two suitcases. He said, "the suitcases are on their way." In about two days, we went to get them at the Aqaba airport. I don't regret moving to Aqaba at all. I would not have missed its lessons for the world. I embarked on eight of the hardest years of my life, facing reality as never before, but I learned to trust Him, and Him only. My Elohim have proved Themselves faithful to the maximum. Truly **II Timothy 2:11-13** is true!

"Trustworthy is the Word: For if we died with Him, we shall also live with Him. If we endure, we shall also reign with Him. If we deny Him, He also shall deny us. If we are not faithful, He remains faithful, for He cannot deny Himself."

He sees the end from the beginning (**Psalm 139:1-18**). He has His plans set for each of us before the foundation of the world. Thus, He remains faithful to fulfill His own plans--for that is His nature!

The first night I was there, so overwhelmed with loneliness for my children, not knowing if I would ever see them again, the attacks of the enemy began. I was still crying very hard. At dinner, the leader of the group said to me: "I've been given a bad report on you." My pastor at Emmanuel Christian Fellowship had told her not to trust me, because I was unstable and not loyal. I had noticed things very wrong at that church after a while. There was some very spurious teaching, and some very wrong teaching. Also, I thought it strange that the two pastors were very big in Washington with Presidents, and helped shape nations in Africa to cause them to be pro-West, and turn away Communism. I never said anything bad about the two pastors. But, Abba literally told me to flee.

One day Abba spoke to me to get out of it and go right away to Bethesda church in the north of Fort Worth and meet with the

PART IV - The Journey Back Home

mission's pastor. I did not want to leave Emmanuel, but Abba told me to do it. I obeyed. I sat in the parking lot at Bethesda thinking that I was not doing right by just leaving my old church without talking to the pastor who had helped me during the time of my separation from my husband. However, Abba insisted. I went in and met with Vic – head of the mission's department. He had some business in another room. I looked around his office, and there at my feet were missionary posters for China and Africa. He came back in, and before I left he sent me to sign up as a member of the church, and sent me to meet with the Intercession Pastor. I met with him, and before leaving, I was made a part of the inner circle intercession team. So, within about two hours, if was like I had moved from Earth to Mars – a drastic change. Bethesda was a very large prestigious church in North Fort Worth. I was allowed to come up with the elders and minister to the people in the front of the church after services.

About the time I was preparing to go to Jordan, my former pastor from Zimbabwe left Emmanuel Christian Fellowship and started his own church. I went there when I was in the U.S. I had so many friends there. But, one day, I was preparing to go to church, and Abba said: "You will never go into another church again." I was shocked. I was only going for social reasons – to have lunch with my friends after church. Abba was teaching me the Torah. This Pastor was also an insider in Israel.

After He told me not to go, I was stunned. I went into the bedroom looking for something, and for some reason reached into a backpack I had used on my last trip to Israel. I pulled out a small white rock. I looked at it wondering where I got it. Then I remembered – I got it in the Garden of Gethsemane in East Jerusalem. Abba then spoke: "You have just gone through Gethsemane."

He broke me from the church system totally. I had two months of teaching scheduled in Africa. I e-mailed the host pastor to tell him I could not come. He wrote back that something bad had happened (I don't remember what it was) and he could not host me, so it was if Abba worked on both ends. I would have been ministering in churches. That was 2002.

I loved Bethesda. On the very day, April 18, 1999, that I was to leave for Jordan, that very well known senior pastor, Des Evans, preached on Petra. I told him I was leaving that afternoon for Petra. They prayed for me. My son went to that church for many years. His little son went to their school. I worked in their nursery school for a short time, as I reported in Part III. Later, when I could no longer fund the orphanage and school that I started in Kisumu, Kenya, they took up the tab. They sent a team in 2001 to the orphanage with medical supplies. Several ministers came, including Cindy, who dressed like a clown and entertained the children. There are more stories of the orphanage, and many things that happened in Africa later in this part of the autobiography, as well as in the Collections. You probably figured that in seven years of going in and out of Africa, I had a lot of stories. Many were born again. Many were Spirit-filled. And, many were delivered from demons, and healed. There were miracles, too.

Attacks of the enemy have been a big part of my life, but since reporting on the last seven-year cycle in 2007, and the soon-coming of Messiah, the attacks have increased, many of them voodoo, witchcraft, slander, with much betrayal from supposed friends, and attempts to ruin my reputation and destroy the work He has done through me. Through 2008, 2009, December of 2010 and January of 2011, the witchcraft increased greatly. In May, 2011, there were so many attacks from the enemy in my body, my mind, my emotions, and in my family, that I wondered, at times, if I would make it through alive. As I go further, I will fill in a lot of blanks, so that you can more fully understand the high cost of turning your back on the evil one, and giving your life 100% to Yahuweh and His will.

LEARNING TO ENDURE THROUGH
--IN THE CRUCIBLE OF SUFFERING--

Matthew 10:22: "**But you will be hated by all men for My Name's sake, but he that endures to the end shall be saved.**"

This was spoken by Messiah to every one of His followers individually. Right now many are being put through the crucible of suffering, because of their stand for His Truth. A good friend in Florida calls this "endurance training", and so it is. [Refer to my article "Through", written in 2012] Remember, you can find articles on **laydownlife.net**, or my website: **comeenterthemikvah.com**

Here, I give you just a speck of that training. But, so often He allows it to go on, and on, and on, and on -- until we get it right, and learn to praise Him with joy from our spirit, no matter what happens. If we don't get it right, He knows that we will fall apart in the days to come, and forsake our faith in Elohim. So He works hard on us to get it right! He ALWAYS takes His people THROUGH so that they will mature and learn to know Him, trust Him, and fear Him, and obey Him! It is not His nature to cause us to escape tribulation – for it is in the raking of the "tribulum" over us, that the chaff (our own sins and human failing) are broken off so that He might gather His wheat into His barns at His coming (**Matthew 13**). It is His love for us!

PART IV - The Journey Back Home

The constant twisting of knees and ankles and falling, then learning to get right back up and go on, has taught me how to do the same thing with all of life's hurts. I learned to get right back up and back in the game... going forward. Learning this principle has saved me from a life of defeat! Unless we can rebound quickly to the blows that life gives us, we will stay "down for the count"--knocked out of what Abba has for us. He had to rebound me from a lot of depression from regret, and wanting to give up. But, that was one lesson I learned that has kept me going.

Even a year ago, spring of 2012, I fell in the street while walking in our neighborhood in Florida. The cartilage behind my right knee shifted, throwing my weight onto my left knee, which was bandaged, but it tried to go out of place, and I fell in the street. No one was there to see it, and no cars passed. I laid there looking up at the sky, and laughed, thinking, "I'm lying here in the street, looking at the sky." I painfully got up and walked several blocks back to the house. It took a few weeks to heal up, but it had to heal fast because I was going back to Israel. February 3, 2013, I fell and twisted my right ankle, hurt my foot, knee, calf, and hip. I pulled myself up. It was the worst compounded injury of my life. But, I had booked a trip to visit two daughters in Georgia/Tennessee. Four days later, walking with two canes, I went. It took six weeks to heal up. But, I booked a ticket to Israel based on Abba's assurance: "It will be alright." **Micah 7:8**: "Rejoice not over me, O my enemy. For when I fall, I will arise. When I sit in darkness, Yahuweh is a light to me." **Proverbs 24:16**: "For a just man falls seven times, and rises up again..."

Because of poverty and no insurance since the 1970s, Abba has taught me how to depend on Him for everything. He had to toughen me up for what He has called me to do now. I am only alive to serve Him. I am not alive to settle into the good life here on earth, for that is fast passing away. I am alive to help save as many lives as possible because of the wisdom He has allowed me to learn.

In 2007, when I left Aqaba to do more in Israel and go to the nations more, He gave me **Hebrews 11:8-10** and **13-16**, and also **Luke 18:28-30**. It was a miracle of Abba, sending me to the wilderness to live in a Muslim country for eight years, mostly alone. I had to make friends with aloneness, knowing my Father and Bridegroom will never leave me alone. This verse describes how I came up out of the wilderness: **Song of Songs 8:5**: "**...who is this that comes up out of the wilderness, leaning on her Beloved**?"

Since 2001, when I began writing and ministering via the computer, I've spent an average of 10-12 hours or more a day on the computer. My eyes have paid a high price. My driver's license was expiring, so I went to the driver's license bureau in the town I was staying in, in Florida. When it came to the eye test, I read off the left column perfectly. The lady said that I failed to read the right column. I said, "There are no letters in the right column." She turned up the intensity and I saw letters, which I barely read. It is a wonder that they even gave me a driver's license, but it is good until 2017. I figure by that time, if Messiah returns, I'll have a set of new eyes. I went to have my eyes checked and to get new glasses. The doctor said I had a small cataract in my right eye.

In the last year, a pinched nerve developed in my right hip that makes it very painful to walk, and sleep. For about three years, I got dizzy spells, coupled with quick flashes of unconsciousness, that would make me almost fall to the left side. I am thankful for my cane. I am thankful for wheelchair assistance at airports. But, I sure don't use these things as excuses for not obeying my Master. I DO NOT WANT HIM TO GET SOMEONE ELSE to do my assignments! I keep telling Him that if He will keep me walking, I'll keep going for Him – but even if I don't walk, I won't stop writing and teaching and ministering daily as He leads. I have heard too many stories of Christians who are infirmed to the point where they can not move but a finger, yet they still do things to reach out to others with the Good News of the Savior's love.

So many times through years, I felt my spirit leaving my body, and I have begged Him to let me live to complete my course. The more I worship and praise Him, the stronger my spirit is getting, and the more I feel release from the attacks of the enemy. Even last night, as I was in worship, I felt His power coming into my up-raised arms.

In Jordan, I had a vision of my riding a horse at break-neck speed, racing a train, in which Yahushua was the conductor. I was all alone. I thought of stopping for others who were behind me, but I knew I could not break pace. As I sped forward, I looked ahead and saw what looked like an old western town in the U.S.-- people standing on the wooden sidewalks, appearing to be opaque, cheering me on. I've seen the cloud of witnesses three times, and there they were. So, I sped up towards them. **Hebrews 12:1-2** is so vivid to me!

Then there were the lessons of poverty, from 1966 until present day. I remember having to get food stamps. I remember standing with my youngest daughter in a government food line, holding her little hand while I waited to go through the line to get our monthly ration of cheese, butter, dry milk, and a few other staples. I remember all the miracles of provision. Each test was to prepare me to depend on Him for everything. There are many stories of His provision, for me and my family, in the Collection, Part VII. All of our "training" will pay off!! For Father allows us go through some things so that we can help others as well as help ourselves. When we were using food stamps, I would use the food stamps to buy groceries and staples, which we tithed to a pastor less fortunate than us. Because we shared, others shared with us.

Truly **Psalm 40:2-3** is my testimony! "**He drew me out of the pit of destruction, out of the miry clay, and He set my feet upon a rock. He established my goings. Then He put a new song in my mouth, even praise unto our Elohim. Many will see and fear, and put their trust in Yahuweh.**"

Truly **Psalm 86:13**: "**For Your loving kindness is great towards me! And you have delivered my soul from the lowest hell.**" (KJV)

FILLING IN SOME BLANKS REGARDING TEXAS

Shortly after arriving in Texas, even though Abba had said for me to immediately seek Him in (1986) to begin the ministry He had for me, I thought I had to make money, or I was useless. So I got a job as a receptionist/secretary at a radio station in Fort Worth, run by a father and his daughter. All was well until I started witnessing. Because of that, at one point, the daughter of the owner, who was my boss, set up a scenario that made it look like I did not do my job. I caught her in it, but she fired me anyway. I had not done what Abba said to do – and that was the result. I appealed to her father, saying that I did not do wrong. But, he upheld his daughter, of course.

So, I began attending praise, prayer, and teaching classes each Tuesday at Grace Temple, led by June Joyner. I became part of their ministry. It helped "birth" my ministry, and jet propel me into the channel Abba had carved for me. It was here I learned to personally minister to people using the gifts of the Spirit. From 1987, for five years, every Tuesday, I attended June's class. June had been mentored by Venetta Copeland. Like Venetta, June Joyner is a full-blooded Cherokee woman who was a quiet and deep woman of Elohim. To start the class, we walked around the room praising Him for about an hour then there was ministry to individuals. We saw some mighty miracles. It was at this class that I experienced a creative miracle that I tell about later in "Miracles of Healing and Deliverance." Without that miracle I would not be walking today. I learned how to minister like Messiah and His Apostles ministered. I learned the power of the declarative in His Name. I learned how to operate in all the gifts of the Spirit. June had simple, but powerful, child-like faith.

Momma June, as she was called, worked as the night hostess for the Old South Pancake House in Fort Worth. She worked all night then came to the class on Tuesday. The Old South Pancake House was a very popular restaurant, open all hours of the night. But, it was not in a very good area of town. One night she was in the warehouse at Old South Pancake House in the middle of the night, and a demon possessed man came in. He had a makeshift torch in his right hand, which he lit when he came in. Then he saw her. She saw him coming, and she stood her ground. He advanced slowly towards her and told her he was going to light her on fire. She never moved. She stood silent and just looked him in the eye. She took her stance and trusted Abba. When the man got right in her face, she looked right in his eyes as he lifted the torch to burn her. All of a sudden he dropped it and ran out. June told us that she knew that if she backed up one step, she would show fear, and in doing so he would have burned her up. Do you have that kind of faith in the One who loves you and cares for you?

Ephesians 6:10-14a: "**Finally my brothers be strong in the Master and in the power of His might. Put on the whole armor of Elohim that you might be able to stand against the wiles of the devil. For we wrestle not against flesh and blood, but against principalities and powers, against rulers of the darkness of this world, against spiritual wickedness in high places. Therefore take unto you the whole armor of Elohim that you may be able to withstand the evil day, and having done all to stand, stand therefore ...**"

It was during one of the Tuesday meetings that June, whom I call my "ministry mentor", told me there was someone I had not forgiven, and that I needed to forgive them quickly if I was going to go forward with my ministry. I was upset. I searched my mind as to who it might be. I had learned to live in instant forgiveness, and I didn't hold anything against anyone. He had taken all the hate and bitterness out of me. As I was leaving the parking lot of the church that day, I asked Father "Who is it?" He replied gently: "It is you."

I had never forgiven myself for allowing myself to remain in abuse, and dragging my children through it. My regrets went so deep regarding my children. For years I suffered with regrets. The enemy would bring it up to me in the middle of the night, night after night. I am so thankful that my children love me, and are close to one another. It is a miracle of Yahuweh! HalleluYah!

Pastor Nichols asked me to teach the popular series by Larry Lea: "Could You Not Tarry One Hour?" on prayer. I taught it. I had many students. I kept to the curriculum. But, I longed to teach the Word from my spirit. I got that chance. When I asked Brother Nichols if I could teach on prophecy, He agreed. He thought I meant the gift of prophecy. But, I surprised him by saying, "I want to teach end-time prophecy." He was one of my students.

I studied with Ken McBride, and on my own. It was what kept me going – studying and teaching on the coming of Messiah. When Hilton Sutton, the famous charismatic end-time teacher that so many in that movement go by, the one that teaches seven raptures, came to teach at Grace Temple, Pastor Harold introduced me as "his prophecy teacher." That was humbling. Even years later, after I had gone to Aqaba, Harold's wife, Lou Nichols, in hearing me talk about Israel and Jordan, said: "I don't always agree with you, but you're still my favorite prophecy teacher." For Lou to say that was a big compliment. She's adorable!

I began taking Hebrew dance classes at Shady Grove Church in Grand Prairie. My mother told me that by age 40, because of the osteoporosis that ran in our family, that I'd start shrinking in size like all the women on her side of the family. However, to this day, I have not shrunk. I can't dance like I used to, but I sure love praise and worship. Being a musician, I joined the Grace Temple choir. I loved it!

Since my husband thought he was the incarnation of a Nazi torturer, I compared his nature to that of Hitler's. So, I hated Germans with a passion, thinking they were all like him. Wow did Abba change that rotten attitude. In the church we met a young man who was a fireball evangelist and missionary to Germany. My son would go with him to carry a large cross when this man would preach on the street. Wow, you can't do that anymore. But, my son and Ken grew to be great friends. Ken married one of Jerry Savelle's secretaries. They continued to minister in Germany and America.

One morning, before I got to know him, the pastor called him up to report on his recent trip to Germany. I was so mad inside. I sat there in the choir disgusted. But, as I listened to this very precious, loving, and kind young man speak of salvations in Germany, my heart melted, and Abba baptized me into love for the German people. Then we became friends with this young man, and later with his wife Becky. This is the couple who had the meeting I wanted to go to when my husband coerced me into meeting that other couple (1995) who screamed at me for five hours.

Not long after that, when Albania got its freedom, his minister friend, Pastor Allen Shook, and his Albanian wife Beverly, went to Albania to preach the Good News. He brought me a cassette tape of German believers singing, and I was shocked at how they had such a personal relationship with Abba, and were so pure of heart. Later our missionary friend went to Albania with Pastor Allen. They said the people would sit on the sidewalks of the town reading their Bibles.

In 2011, upon leaving Israel to go to Berlin, I sat next to two Germans who told me that they loved Israel, and that there would be a big pro-Israel rally and concert in Berlin when they arrive home. In the in-between years, I went to Germany many times, going through Frankfurt via Lufthansa Airlines.

Our son was in the Air Force there, and in 1992, we went to be with our new grandson, born at Bitburg, Germany, on the Air Force Base. I loved it. So, Abba has His ways of taking out of us misconceptions about others, even hate, and replacing it with love.

We became friends with many wonderful people through Grace Temple. For a long time, I was invited to be a part of Jerry Savelle's Bible Study with his staff every Friday morning. They were good meetings. I got to be friends with his wife Carolyn and their two daughters.

In 1993, my husband and I co-taught an adult Sunday School class at Grace Temple. By this time, I had a longing to go further with in-depth teaching on the Word than what was being taught at Grace Temple. It was hard leaving. Pastor Nichols and Lou, and their children and grandchildren, were our friends. They were like family. But we did leave in peace.

It was a strange miracle how we found Emmanuel Christian Fellowship. We had gone to so many churches. I would like one, but my husband wouldn't – and vice versa. One day, someone we'd known for a while invited us to their church. Others had invited us, but this time we felt we should go, and we did. That first morning our youngest daughter met Margaret—Pastor Jim's daughter. They were the same age. They struck up a friendship, and we ended up telling Pastor Harold that we loved him but we had to move on. He blessed us. We are friends to this day. The third child and her husband stayed on until they moved to Florida. I hated leaving so many friends, but my spirit needed more. And the pastors at Emmanuel Christian fellowship were confirming so many things that Abba was showing me.

PART IV - The Journey Back Home

After fleeing in February of 1996, after almost 30 years of marriage, my African pastor told me that the glory of God would come down on me in my new apartment. Just after moving in, His power came down on me so strong that I had to get down on the floor. Pastor Robert also knew I had a passion for China. He gave me two points of advice: **"You can't have your heart in China, and your body in Ft. Worth."** He said: **"Protect yourself."** I listened to the first one. But, not until recently have I understood "protect yourself."

Pastor Jim taught classes every Tuesday at Joy Witherspoon's house in north Fort Worth. I never missed them. His teaching was awesome. Sometimes, in telling us truth that he knew from his inside sources, he would tell someone to turn off the recording. One day he told about the world conference of unaligned nations in Cairo, Egypt, and how he and Pastor Robert had been asked to write the key-note speech for it. They wanted to know what will happen when Jesus returns.

Those men knew owners of national football teams, presidents, and heads of other countries. They were good friends with President Chiluba of Zambia. I'll never forget when the coffins were brought onto the football field in Zambia's Capital city. Their Olympic athletes had been murdered. Chiluba stood watching. He then made a speech that sent chills down my spine. He dedicated Zambia as a Christian nation – the only country in the world that was a publically declared purely Christian nation until the last few months. In 2012, Ugandan President Museveni dedicated Uganda to the God of the Bible.

Texas was a place of mixtures. I had many friends. I taught a lot in home meetings. I had many open doors to me. For five years, I worked with Women's Aglow. I taught a lot on how Messiah fulfilled the first four festivals of Yahuweh, and how He will fulfill the other three at His coming. And they loved that teaching. I also did personal ministry a lot among them.

At one point, the President of the Night Chapter of Women's Aglow, a woman I thought was a good friend, asked me to teach a class on the Holy Spirit in a home of another member. She also taught a class in her area of Fort Worth. My class was very successful. Ladies came, and heard, and wanted to be filled with the Spirit. Some were born again. I prophesied to some, and lives were changed. I did not go by the outlines of the Women's Aglow, I taught on the Spirit from the Word and my own experiences. I had heard that the meetings, taught by the President of that chapter of the Women's Aglow, had few in attendance. She was going by the outline. One day, she came to my house. We had moved to Wind Chime Drive. She said that the Holy Spirit had told her to stop the house meetings. She went to her Board and they agreed. I was so shocked, and deeply hurt. I told her of what the Spirit was doing in my meetings. She very coldly said: "The meetings are over." Jealousy!

This is what I went through with so many women, and men in ministry, as well as individuals. Their jealousy of Abba's favor, and my success because of His favor, drove them to try to shut me down. I've gone through this over and over, i.e. women trying to piggy-back me to advance their own ministries, or jealously trying to get rid of me if I threaten their control. It really hurt bad. The woman who was hosting me was also an officer in Women's Aglow, so she couldn't host the meetings without reprisal from "the Board."

In 2000, I was living in Jordan at the time in my own rented apartment. I had no home in the US. When I first started coming back to the U.S., I stayed with my son and his wife. But, after a while, his wife did not like me there, so she had my son tell me to leave. I asked "why?" I was quiet. I cooked, cleaned, and looked after their son, and did nothing out of line. I wasn't there that much. But, as he told me, I breathed in her space, and so she didn't want me there. I found out after they divorced that she was jealous of me. I felt so deflated. WHY? What is this useless spiritual sickness that is so common in America and other western nations, especially among Christian and Messianic ministers?

Right away, my college-grad daughter said I could live with her. She got married in March of 2001, so I took up residence with them. She married a fine man who had just graduated from TCU with two engineering degrees. He went to work at Lockheed. She later worked there too. Then she left to get a job teaching all four grades in Social Studies and Geography in the Burleson High School. She said that she spent most of her time trying to bring order to the rebellious students, and she came home every night stressed out. So, she said she wished she had taken a major in business because she's really gifted in that.

They just celebrated their 12th wedding anniversary, and I'm still staying with them--when I am in the U.S. of course. But, they have let me know that they love me to be with them. My son-in-law grew up with his mother's mother in the home until she died. So having a grandma in the home was not unusual for him. Now, I have two grandchildren there to love.

One time when with them in Texas, preparing to return to Jordan, I got an e-mail from someone living in Aqaba saying I should stay an extra two weeks because there was danger in Aqaba due to Ramadan. I asked Abba, and He said to stay. I asked my son-in-law, saying: "I'm sorry, is it all right if I stay an extra two weeks?" He smiled. He said: "Stay as long as you want, this is your home too." I praise Abba. It was hard for her seeing me guard the Torah. She thought I was trying to be Jewish. I remember when she first looked through my copy of *Fossilized Customs* by Lew White. She was furious. I told her that she and I were going to the same place for eternity. Otherwise, I said nothing. I just quietly lived the life before her and loved her.

Abba told me to say nothing to my grown up children – just to live the life before them. In doing that, my three son-in-laws love me. Also, it gave room for the Spirit of Yahuweh to do what He does best on the inside of my children. I told her I would wash her dishes every day of the week except Shabbat. The dishes piled up on Shabbat, and Sunday morning I washed them.

She said they were going to have a garage sale on Friday and Saturday. I had a lot of things to sell, and so did they – big things. I told her I would put my things out on Friday but not Saturday. She said "No one comes on Friday." I told her I would pray that people came on Friday. Early Friday morning, about 6:30, my son-in-law put signs out on the main road about the garage sale. We put everything out. By 7:00 AM the lawn was covered with people. We sold about everything that Friday. On Saturday morning at 9:00 AM, I was sitting in my easy chair, still in my bathrobe, drinking coffee. She came in from the front yard and looked so upset. I asked her how the sale was going. She said: "Not one person has come!" I reminded her that I had prayed they'd come on Friday. She said: "From now on we'll have our garage sales on Thursday and Friday, or Friday and Sunday." I just nodded.

In the meantime, my son-in-law told her what I believed, for he had attended a Messianic Bible study. So she told me she understood. I will never forget the day they told me that they were looking for someone who was consistent in living what they believed. They were so tired of hypocrites. They said they'd been watching me, and because I lived what I believed, they said it was "right to keep Shabbat." I was numb for a week over that!

During our time at Grace Temple, our family went on mission trips with the mission's pastors, Tommy and Carol Lovette, and with Dwaine and June Main – assistant missionary pastors. We went to Lazell Powell's compound to stay, about three times. She had a teaching mission in the "Four Corners" area, in New Mexico. It was on these trips that we bonded with some precious people. We also went on trips to the Navajos with other missions. On one such trip, both of our youngest daughters did some real ministry, leading children's groups. I ministered to women on the Holy Spirit. Some of them received the baptism into the Spirit. What precious times we had. One Thanksgiving, we went with Tommy and Carol and Dwaine and June, and Dwight Cox. It was snowing heavily. Yet we provided a big Thanksgiving dinner for the local Navajos. We rented a huge warehouse that was the meeting place for the local Navajos. It was during this time that I preached the salvation message and some were born again in that place. I learned the Indian ways. We went out to their hogans. It was wonderful. It prepared me for Mongolia and living in the Middle East.

Cory Cox, a friend of my son's, went with us on a trip with Tommy and team to Saltillo, Mexico, to work with Carl Lupnitz and his family. They were missionaries that Grace Temple supported. His father was former top military brass. But after being born again, he set off to do missionary work in Mexico. We stayed on the mission compound in Saltillo. We took our two youngest daughters. June Main also ran the used clothing division of our church's ministry to the poor. Old ladies in the church complained to her about our taking our children into such horrible places. June told them that the girls would rather be going on a mission trip to those places than to Disneyland.

Both girls moved in the power of the Spirit, in healings and miracles. It was in a meeting in Saltillo that the youngest, age 11, led so many to salvation and prayed for that little boy's healing and a miracle occurred. It was a creative miracle. [You can read this in Part VIII of the Collections]

From Saltillo we went high up into the Guadalupe Mountains to minister. We stopped at a little church on the side of the mountain. We had a service there, and prayed for the sick. It lasted until midnight. Then on leaving, a pastor asked us to come up to their church to preach on Sunday morning. So, in the total dark, except for the moon, and in the lights of their truck, our group of about 17, with Cory driving the church van, went up the side of a mountain on very narrow one-lane dirt road. At the top of the mountain, some of us stayed at "momma's house", and some at the pastor's house.

Our family stayed with "momma" and her husband, who gave up their beds for us. They were pure Indians. The next morning, momma made us fresh tortillas from fresh corn, and cooked them on a wood stove. Her husband had made us real Mexican coffee – coffee grounds and water, and cinnamon, all boiled together. On her little radio, we heard Christian music. We went to preach in their daughter's little church. There was a big, big bull next to the house in a pen, which we respected. My youngest daughter saw what she thought was a dog hiding in a bush. She went to pull the "dog's" tail and it grunted. It was a pig. We kidded her about her dog.

Everyone in the team got to speak in the meeting, and our daughters sang. After the meeting, we prayed for people. One man who was deaf, received his hearing. One of the ladies on our team was Wanda Mingus. She was a close friend of June Joyner. They both had studied under Venetta Copeland. Wanda was a good friend to me too. One time, while at Grace Temple, I had bronchitis so bad in my left lung that it hung on for months. One Sunday morning before the service began, as I stood with our praise group on the front row of Grace Temple, as usual, Wanda simply came over, laid her hand on my left chest and spoke healing into my body. I was healed immediately. Like June, she never made a big production of her ministering to people, she just had Abba's authority-backing. Unless we have His authority backing, we had better not do any warfare against the enemy – for if He has not told us to do it, we'd better not do it. We must fear Yahuweh and obey only Him – not what we think in our head! The next morning we drove down the mountain. We saw where we came up, in horror. There was at least a 100' drop off on the side of the road, and here we were following only tail lights on the truck ahead of us all the way up that road. Cory's driving, to say the least, was awesome.

It was on that trip, at the compound in Saltillo, Abba gave me **Jeremiah 1**--the first of my prophetic Scriptures regarding my calling. We went on trips to the Navajos and into Mexico with just Dwaine and June Main as our leaders. It was on one of these trips that Abba gave me my final vision of the three trees. He showed me what He was doing in me because of being in June's class and going on these trips; to establish me firmly as a trusted servant in His house. The final tree was shaped exactly like the symbolic olive tree of the tribe of Asher. He said to me: "Groomed."

Dwaine was an architectural engineer at Lockheed. He was one of my most faithful students in my end-time prophecy class each Sunday evening at Grace Temple. One day his boss came to work tired, and disgusted. He told Dwaine: "Your God kept me up all night." The boss was an agnostic. He said that a voice told him to get a book he had and give it to Dwaine. He searched the house, but finally found the book in his attic. It was a copy of a book, actually. He said that this voice told him someone Dwaine knew needed the book. Dwaine smiled. He told him he knew who it was for. It was for me. The author was a geologist. The book told about the Great Rift Valley Fault line that runs through Israel, which is now giving way. He told about what will happen when the

Mount of Olives splits at the coming of Messiah, and how the account in **Zechariah 14** is extremely accurate.

I learned so much from that book. In doing his awesome video (2013), which has gone around the world -- *Two Sticks Become One – The Final Deliverance* -- about the return of Messiah, my son used information from that book. I later taught from that book on the Navajo reservation to the missionaries. The anointing on me is always so powerful when I teach about it.

While living at the Wind Chime house, I did a lot of walking throughout Candleridge Park in our large housing area. I love to get out and walk. One morning I was walking down the sidewalk, and was thinking about the walls of the New Jerusalem. The foundation stones are Peter, James and John. I thought about Peter and John. But, I mumbled a statement saying that I wondered why James would be included since he didn't do much. All of a sudden, the power of the Spirit came down on me with such love for James. It was so strong that I thought I was going to have to sit down on the grass by the sidewalk. I started apologizing to James and the Spirit. Then He let me know how precious James was to Him, and why. I had forgotten that he was the first of the Apostles to be martyred. I had forgotten that he led the Council in Jerusalem. I had forgotten a lot.

In that house, before we got much furniture, I was lying on the floor with the three youngest children, watching T.V. We had the lights turned off. We decided to make popcorn. So, we went towards the kitchen, through the open dining area, and there in the middle of the dining room floor was a large snake, coiled up sleeping. My husband got a stick and hauled it out and cut off its head. To think that thing came through our patio door, slithered past our heads, into the dining room. The next day our wonderful cat, Sylvester, was playing with some little things moving on the carpet by the patio door. They were baby snakes. We lived near open country, at the outskirts of southwest Fort Worth.

OK! I will take a break from talking about Texas for a while here. I lived there for 23 years, so it was a big part of my life. I wish I could tell about all the wonderful people that became friends, and the opportunities that opened up to us all. Our children did well in the schools. They were successful in many arenas! Fort Worth was good!

ONWARD AND UPWARD TO VICTORY
He called me "Daughter!"

Before going to Aqaba, in April of 1999, after moving to a small one bedroom apartment to save money, I was sitting in the apartment writing out a check to pay off my credit card. I was so thankful to be able to go to Aqaba debt free. All of a sudden,

PART IV - The Journey Back Home

Abba's presence came into the room so strongly that I could hardly move. I stopped writing my check and said, "Yes, Sir, You want to talk to me?" His Presence came close to my right side, and said, one word "**Daughter**." Then His Presence slowly left. I did not realize how important it was for Him to call me "**Daughter**" until later on.

In 1999, my friend from Emmanuel Christian Fellowship, who moved to Aqaba, was taking me on a tour of Jordan. We were going around the big gorge called "the fords of Arnon" in the Bible. It is the dividing line between Moab and Amman. The river going through the gorge flows out into the Dead Sea. It is at this place that **Isaiah 16:2-4** is so important to do with our near future. As she drove, I told her about the word He had spoken to me. She was so shocked that she almost ran off the cliff. She said: "When He called you `daughter', He was saying that He will take care of your every need, and protect you, until the day of your marriage." That will be my marriage to Yahushua.

It was while in this apartment that someone gave me a newsletter from "Lion and Lamb Ministries" - Monte Judah. I had heard Monte speak in a meeting and liked him. In the newsletter was an article on YHWH. Monte said they were the consonants of God's Name. I sat in my chair, and slowly said the Hebrew letters as Monte had written out the Hebrew pronunciation. After about a minute of speaking them over and over, His Presence filled the room so powerfully that I was numbed from it. I thought: "I guess He likes me saying these letters." Now as I look back on it, it was the beginning of my research on His Name, which I have put in the study "The Hebrew Names and Titles of the Elohim of Israel."

My mother's inheritance ran out. I had used it wisely over 3½ years. I even helped out my third child with her college tuition and books. I took the last of it to Aqaba, plus what friends had given me--a total of $4,000.00. Since then, I have had no income to count on. I only get money from offerings/gifts from people who believe in my ministry. I get no government freebees, either. I opted out of Social Security when I was ordained a second time by a church. I opted out of my right to money from the Indian Bureau too, even though I have original documents from the 1800s from the Cherokee reservation. I lived on my credit card in Aqaba, until He gave me another "miracle of provision", which I tell about in part VII of the Collections. He brings what I need, when I need it! I never have had any fear of loss either. From 1966, during all the years of marriage, I have had to depend on Abba for everything. So, walking by faith in finances has been a lifestyle. I learned that to ask for money or to sell a product to do with the ministry was against the Scriptures. So, I just trusted Him. And found Him to be 100% faithful!

In Part V, I share about the years 1992-2001 in detail-- especially ministry in the U.S., and five training missions overseas that prepared me for life in the Middle East. I also tell of the final locking in of the reason for all the training all my life in these last days before Messiah returns. From here on, my story is slotted into definite times and countries.

PART V
TRAINING ASSIGNMENTS
FOR FULL-TIME MINISTRY
LEARNING THE LIFE OF A SERVANT
(1992-2001)

GERMANY (1992) -- CHINA (1994-1995)
MONGOLIA (1996) -- RUSSIA (1999)
AFRICA (1996-2001) -- ISRAEL (1999)

As I say over and over in my articles, I am simply a bond servant of my Master, in training for my eternal position in Yahuweh's Kingdom. I flow daily in His perfect will. He taught me to fear Him, for which I am very grateful! The degree of my obedience and faithfulness is the degree to which He can trust me. Notice in Romans 1:1: The Apostle Sha'ul put being a servant of Yahushua above his calling as an Apostle! As you will see in Parts V and VI, He has trusted me with some incredible assignments. I am simply His servant! He knows I will only do and say exactly what He has told me to do and say. I fear getting out of His boundaries, because they are my protection. They keep me under His tallit – in the "secret place of the Most High." It is my shelter, my security, my safety, and where He can speak to me without hindrances. He knows I keep the portal of my spirit open to Him at all times. I have to! I do not want to miss one thing that He says. Like John the Apostle, I want my ear to His chest, so that I hear not only His words, but His breathing, His sighs, the rise and fall of His emotions, and feel the warmth of His Presence. Most Western believers give lip-service to an illusionary sentimental idea of Him they have in their head, yet go on to disobey Him day in and day out. My relationship to Him is not illusionary.

From early childhood He began raising me with an Eastern mentality. I always dealt in tangibles. Abstracts never interested me. I never went along with the Greco/Roman crowd mentality. It just was not me at all. What was important to those absorbed in Western culture, for the most part, was boring to me. So, as an adult I never felt comfortable around other women who were gushing over what worldly women gush over. I just never fit into the mold of Western society.

So, upon going to the Navajos, to Mexico, to Central and South America, to Africa, to the Far East and the Middle East, I had no culture shocks. Attacks from other people have come almost exclusively from those in America, or the UK--and strangely, mostly from people who call themselves Messianic. I have had few to no problems with the people of foreign cultures, Christians yes, but not the average people. I do not do well with people who have hidden agendas and selfish ambitions, who are masked to others but not to me. But there are those who are unmasked, and we have such a good time together!

He has shown me what life is like outside of His sheltering tallit. Therefore, with fear, I serve Him faithfully, for I never want to leave His side – not now, not in eternity. These assignments taught me much. In these training missions, I went with teams from different Christian organizations. I could not be led by the Spirit, for man controlled my actions. When I stepped out to obey the Spirit, man clamped down on me with disdain, and reprimanded me. So, I had a choice presented to me. I could continue to serve under man's control, and reject what the Spirit of Yahuweh was telling me to do, or I could break with man's control and be free to have one Master and one only. I chose the latter option.

My trip to Russia was my last trip of submission to man. Because I was an American and Abba favored my work for Him, the Russian Orthodox leaders loathed me, and let me know it. But, I usually work well with the leaders who invite me to minister with them or for them, because I submit to them for Yahuweh's purposes. I am not controlling, nor do I push myself ahead. All that aggression has been channeled into passionate pursuit of pleasing my Master, because of my love for Him. I am now aggressively submitted to Him!

These stories are miraculous in themselves. **A miracle is no more than Yahuweh simply being Yahuweh. A miracle can only be done by Him. Man can't do miracles. It takes outside intervention from One much higher than man for a miracle to take place**.

Satan's world is called the "supernatural," but the eternal realm belongs to Yahuweh. Satan performs stunts to wow people into thinking he's great. **Revelation 13:13-14**: Satan will perform through the false prophet to do signs and wonders and wow the mindless idiots of the human race, which accounts for almost all of the human race. When one is born again by the transforming power of Yahuweh's Spirit, the portal of our eternal spirit (in the loins area of us) is opened to His eternal realm. It is in the spirit, not the earth-bound soul of mind and emotions, that He speaks, teaches, convicts, comforts, instructs, guides, leads, and warns us.

It is in this realm that He has taught me to live. Now that I understand His nature, His ways and His thinking, I have come to passionately love Him with all my heart, mind, and strength. So, I submit to Him. These accounts are like the final polishing of my learning before setting me off on my own to do His assignments as His servant.

In working under religious people who set themselves up as gods, I had hurts, and was stifled. But, He used it to bridle me and put the "bit" in my teeth, so that I learned what was of man and his ways, and what was of Him and His ways. To be under the bondage of controlling religious people is imprisonment indeed. For religion in itself is a harsh and often murderous regime. [Refer to: "Religion"/September 28, 2009; "Led"/October 2007; "On Assignment/November 1, 2009] The freedom of letting Him control my life, even my thoughts, is the most thrilling life ever!

Thank you for your patience with my back and forth stories above. I wrote in context as the memories came. But, from now on, for the most part, I will keep things in chronological order. From this point on, you will see the result of my restoration to Abba.

FIRST TIME OVERSEAS GERMANY
(1992)

After High School, my son joined the Air Force. He married a girl from Everman, Texas. I have related some of the miracles of his Air Force training days above. They were able to go to Germany together. They soon found an apartment in a little village in western Germany, Himmerod, not too far from Trier, that was so small that it was on the curve of a road. Except for what buildings used by the landowner, there was only one extra building that had three apartments. It was not far from his Air Force base--Spangdahlem. Himmerod was famous because its Capuchin Monastery and Abby, built by Bernard of Clairvaux. The entrance to the monastery was just a few paces from the front door of their little apartment building. They were on the top floor. The area was gorgeous – fields for farming, with a river coursing through pine trees. Herr Graff was their landlord.

Before too long, my daughter-in-law was pregnant with their son. He was born in October of 1992 on a neighboring Air Force Base--Bitburg. Bitburg was larger than Spangdahlem at that time. We went to visit in December, and stayed through Christmas. Our girls were left with a family of church friends. I will never forget when the plane flew over Scotland --it was sunrise. I was so awed by that – sunrise on the other side of the Atlantic. We landed in Frankfurt. They picked us up, and we went to their home. From there my son drove us to nearby Trier about three times before Christmas, to shop and see the historical sites. The famous Roman "Porto Negro" is there. Trier is on the Mosel River, and pre-dates Rome by 1600 years.

It was a real adventure. Kris Kringle was there, too--tall, skinny, and dressed in a wizards robe and hat. My son let him hold the baby, and I got pictures. European Christmas is different than American Christmas. They decorate trees with white lights on the outside of their houses. Many of the gifts for sale in Trier were hand-carved wooden things, like the famous Nut Crackers. Of course we were in a big open area --the "fussgangenplatz" (phonetic spelling) -- the foot walking area where no cars went. We ate lunch at the two story McDonalds. Trier had its own amphitheater, which was used for sports events, and later for the killing of believers, like at the Coliseum in Rome.

On our first visit it was cold, but sunny and clear. But, on our second visit it had been drizzling rain, and there was a cloud cover. But, I wanted to see where the prisoners and lions were kept that opened onto the coliseum grounds area. So we paid a little money and went down into the grotto where there were cages with iron bars. It was so oppressive, especially with the rain drizzling in. I could imagine the horrors of that place 2,000 years ago. As we came out, being totally mindless, I thought out loud, mumbling: "I wonder if the spirits that were in there 2,000 years ago are still there." They heard me! Instantly my legs felt like they were turning to jelly and I was going to collapse. I grabbed onto a hand rail. My heart was pounding so fast that I could see it moving my shirt up and down. My whole body went into a panic attack. I could hardly speak. My husband turned and saw me, but did nothing. But, my son, having gone a little up the hill ahead of us, turned and saw the look of horror on my face and ran down to me, and began casting the devils off of me. Instantly I was 100% well.

We walked up the hill and went into the famous Roman Catholic Cathedral at Trier, just above where the prison was. This church supposedly contains the robe that was taken off Jesus at His crucifixion, at least that's what Helena, mother of Constantine, said. The Cathedral was built by the Emperor Constantine – creator and founder of organized Greco/Roman "Churchianity." We went to see the encasement, behind glass, where the "robe" was kept. What a massive Cathedral! In the 1930s, Adolph Hitler went there to that church, and used the robe as his symbolic battle cry to kill the Jews. No wonder I was attacked by demonic spirits!

We took several trips to neighboring countries. Trier is near the borders of Luxembourg, and France. We went to Thionville, France the day after Christmas. In Europe they celebrate the 26th too. So when we got to Thionville there was hardly anyone on the street. We were so hungry. So we went to the police station. They did not speak English, but they figured out by our gestures that we needed a restaurant. They took us to the one restaurant that was open. It was a large one that served buffet style. It was wonderful! Everything was so fresh and clean. The food was fantastic. It was there that I had kohlrabi for the first time. I remember seeing dogs, nicely resting at their owner's feet. But, in Europe you can take your dog inside the restaurant with you, on a leash of course. My grandson was in a little carrier, and he was so good. He just rested like the doggies.

Before we got to Germany, my son had bought his first car--a BMW. One night, coming back from the base, after picking up his wife who worked at the Officer's Club, it had been raining. They came upon an accident. In trying to go around the car that was in the ditch, they slid into it. They "totaled" their car. He called me very upset. He said they'd been in an accident. I asked: "Are you all right?" He said: "My car." I repeated my question. He said: "My car." Then he finally said they were all right, but that their car was totaled. So, when we came, they were driving the car of an Air Force friend who had gone back to America for Christmas. I taught my son to drive. It was amazing being with him, especially on the Autobahn.

On December 27th we headed for Belgium. We went through Liege, then on to Maastricht. In studying and teaching on the end times, of course I had studied the ramifications of the Maastricht Treaty. I felt like I had to stand in the very place where that treaty was signed. Being December, the sun went down at near 4:00 PM each day, so it was getting dark when we got to Maastricht. We pulled up in the parking lot of the building where it was signed, and there was no one there. I spotted one car by the front door. So my son pulled up by the door, and my husband and I got out to go in. There was one security man there. He did not speak English. I said in a French accent: "Informacion?" He understood that, but no more. Just then, we heard a door open and then slam shut. In walked a dignified-looking man. He spoke English. We asked him if we could see where the Maastricht Treaty was signed. Hans just happened to be the public relations director for the entire building. Just then our son came in. Hans was delighted to take us to the room, and show us where it was signed. Of course I got pictures. I love being a part of what is happening that affects world history. As usual, Father put me on a front row seat.

The next day we returned to Luxemburg City, where we visited the E.U. Parliament Building. That was quite an experience, but what happened on the way home was a frightening experience. We got out on the Autobahn to return home. It was about 2:00 PM. The car broke down. It is illegal to stop on the side of the road on the Autobahn. But, Abba kept the police away. It was a serious breakdown. We tried to get the car started. People stopped to try to help us. An elderly couple came by and said they would call a wrecker when they got to Luxembourg City. The sun was going down. All I could pray was "thank you Father." Nothing else would come out of my mouth. It was getting colder and colder. The baby slept. Then here came the wrecker! They towed us into Luxembourg City to a Texaco Station. About two hours later, here came one of my son's superior officers, and a couple of other soldiers/friends from the Base, all believers, to take us back to Spangdahlem. We went back to the officer's house where his wife fixed us dinner. I had never known anyone who would do such a loving favor for us like that. The overwhelming feeling of their being so "Christ-like" never left me.

My husband and I had each spoken in their church. So, when the automotive company in Luxembourg City called to tell us that the car was ready, the pastor and some officers went to get it for us. They paid for the repairs. I just couldn't get over the pure-of-heart kindness of these men. The officer and his wife, A.J. and Caroline, and their daughter Marisha, became very good friends. We stayed in contact with them for years. Carolyn is a wonderful musician--a vocalist who has made several CDs, and a pianist.

We went to Wiesbaden, and to several small villages in western Germany. We went to Cochem Castle. These areas were so quaint, so very old-world European. I loved it so much! I took so many pictures, which I still have. The narrow little walk-places, the food, the people – we sure did pack a lot in two weeks! So much education! We went to Koblenz, where the Mosel River and the Rhine come together. It was a wonderful introduction to my near future. And, I learned that the German people were just like other people. To me, they were very pleasant, gracious, kind, thoughtful, and helpful.

I've found most people around the world to be pleasant. But, there are some exceptions at Immigration and Customs, like in Russia. I've had good treatment onboard most of the 47 airlines I've flown on. I've found that Delta has been the most gracious American International carrier. The European and Asian International carriers have always been gracious overall. I've had free flights overseas with Delta, KLM, and Lufthansa. [If you read "Training Mission: A Day in the Life of Yedidah", you'll see how precious the crew of KLM was to me on one flight, helping me not to miss my flight to Panama.

The Asian Airlines are very gracious. The small regional airlines get me there--no problems--inside Africa, to north Panama, around China, and to Mongolia. Even Aeroflot was not as bad as expected (smile). Smaller local U.S. carriers like Southwest, Allegiant, and Vision air, have been very kind.

To conclude the first trip to Germany: It was winter, it was snowy, and it was gorgeous! We attended Christmas midnight Mass at the Monastery Abby. It was like going back to the Middle Ages. The monks sat on hard benches that faced each other in the front of that huge church. They sang acapella music that was ancient, like Gregorian chant. Their voices echoing through the huge church was haunting. People came from as far as Cologne. It was a special meeting place for people all over that region of Germany. Quite an experience! I had been there several times, walking on the grounds, going through the church with its many alcoves decorated with artwork and scenes for Christmas. After all, the entrance was just outside their door. I went on walks through the forest, down by the river, across the field. We visited the village of Rudesheim on the Rhein River, and other small villages in Western Germany. We visited Spangdahlem, and got food and souvenirs from the BX (Base Exchange). We met several of their friends.

CHINA
"CHINA IS YOUR DIVING BOARD AFTER THAT, IT'S THE WORLD."

I had been given a color copy of "The Inn of the Sixth Happiness." I watched it one day to try to learn why Abba used the movie to call me to China. I found my answer. It was Gladys' dogged determination to do what God had told her to do. No matter how she had to get there, she got there. Her adventures are incredible! One little lady from England, who worked cleaning houses as a menial maid, called by Abba to serve Him in a very harsh and hard land, yet she went, and lives were changed for eternity.

She was so favored. She stopped a prison riot, and got basic human rights for the prisoners. She was asked by the ruler of China to go to mountain villages, to begin the process of unwrapping the bound feet of girls who were suffering from the ancient rite of foot-binding. She led many to salvation. Gladys is most famous for taking 100 children from her area in the north down to Canton to safety through the war zone of Japan's attack on China.

While watching that movie, Abba spoke to me: "**China is your diving board – after that, it's the world**!" Before even considering going to China, I had a dream. My son was in the dream. We watched as Gladys unwrapped the feet of the little girls. I explained it to my son. Then Abba revealed to me that He was unwrapping my feet, so that I could go forth and spiritually unwrap the feet of others bound by sin and bound by the lies of the Devil, so that they could be free to go forth for Him.

In 1993, representatives of Open Doors with Brother Andrews were speaking at a church in Fort Worth. We went to hear them. They talked about the opportunity of being a "courier" – to take Bibles into Mainland China from Hong Kong. Of course it was, and still is, a smuggling process, to get Bibles into the hands of the persecuted believers, who are being denied rights, imprisoned, tortured, and killed for their faith.

I took one of the applications to be a courier. I filled it out and met the requirements. I had waited since 1961 for this open door. It was such a precious gift from Abba. I knew I had to go alone. My husband heard me talking to the ministry in California, and said: "I'm called to China, too." That was the first I heard of it.

During 1994 and 1995, we attended a lovely Chinese Evangelical Church, and entered into their festivities, and heard speakers like a disciple of Wang Ming Tao. It was wonderful to be with them. There were also people from other Far East Asian nations. When we had our pot luck dinners, the variety of foods were wonderful! Some things were very strange, like the shredded jelly fish cold salad. But, I loved it. I was not Torah-guarding at this time.

Through much struggle, I went alone in late March of 1994. While in Hong Kong, my husband kept phoning me. The demonic spirits from his phone calls were so powerful that I thought I was going into another nervous breakdown, and would have to go home. I began having panic attacks. To stop the incredible barrage of attacks, I told him that he could go with me the next time. I understand how someone could be pressured to the point of almost losing their mind. It produces a deep fear that if you do not do as you are told, there will be punishment. This mind programming is being done on the American people. It will be used in the near future to make them submit to martial law.

I stayed in an apartment on the 15th floor, with other ladies from Norway, England, and Australia, in the Kowloon area of Hong Kong. From there we went in teams of 2-4 on assignments to take Bibles across the border at many different locations, traveling sometimes for hours, or a whole night, just to get to remote borders where they did not have the surveillance with the conveyor belts.

My first trip was for three weeks. Being my first trip, it was ministry policy not to send anyone on long trips. It was ministry policy not to fly any new recruits anywhere within China. New recruits only could take trains, boats, taxis, or buses. Hong Kong was a modern city under British rule. Its transportation services were excellent. Building was done by first-class machines. Its port was considered the International Port of the world. In Mainland China, the work was done by laborers using hammers to break rocks, and pick axes. The transportation was something to marvel at – that it was so good at times, and so bad at times.

During my three visits to Hong Kong and Mainland China, I was stopped four times in approximately 40 times of taking Bibles into Mainland China. The first time was not long after I got there. We were on our way to Brother Lamb's place through the Lo Woo border at Shen Zhen to Guang Zhou (Canton). The Lo Woo border was heavily guarded. I had two very heavy suitcases on pull-trolleys. I was a "greenhorn." As I pulled my trolleys from Immigration through the Customs area, I looked like I was pulling a heavy load. One short fat Chinese official pulled me over. He took me to an inspection area and opened the suitcases. I thought I was watching an old black and white comedy movie – the man was hilarious without meaning to be. He looked down and exclaimed very dramatically: "OHHHH BIBLES!" They confiscated my Bibles. While he wasn't looking I handed one to one of the inspectors. I had heard that many secular Chinese people wanted a Bible--their spirits reaching out to their unknown Creator. She quickly hid it under the counter. But, I was so discouraged. However, encouragement came as I met with Brother Lamb, and other Chinese believers, in his little upstairs room on Da Ma Zong Street. What a high privilege! Read his book: *Bold As a Lamb*.

"Lamb" was not his real last name, but he had taken that name to describe his life for the Master. He was an accomplished pianist. He had an old upright piano on the second level of his flat, which the renown pianist, Dino, came and played. He had such celebrities as Billy Graham and the Astronaut Jim Irwin visit him. He had been in prison for 20 years for his faith. They tried to break him, but like his friend Wang Ming Tao, who was in prison for 23 years, they couldn't. When they released Brother Lamb, he went back home and found that his wife had died and his ministry was gone.

But, quickly it built up. When we were there, some 1,600 people would gather to hear him teach each week. The police established one of their headquarters on the lower level of his building. Brother Lamb was kept under "house arrest." I'll never forget him coming out and standing in the door of his building to wave goodbye. It is estimated that the average pastor in China who refuses to register, and come under the control of the government's "Three Self Church," spends 17 years in prison.

Brother Lamb's large meeting room upstairs had benches that opened up. He stored Bibles in them and copies of his sermons. While there, there was a blind school teacher who was folding his sermon notes. She had been with him and praying for him for years. A young girl was there. She looked no older than 20. She was helping to staple the sermon notes into booklets, and do other tasks. She had been denied the right to go to college because of her faith. These are joyful people. They do not complain. They take their suffering to be their "schooling." From time to time the police would raid his meeting room and take the Bibles and sell them on the "black market."

I'll never forget, on another visit, when Brother Lamb grabbed my hands and smiled a big smile and said, "God has released me to teach on America in prophecy." I asked him what chapters God gave him to teach on: Right away he said: "**Jeremiah 50 and 51**." Our Father always confirms! He, Himself, teaches those that know Him. Therefore no matter where you go in the world, you find a tiny remnant who is Spirit-taught! I gave him other chapters – **Isaiah 47, Revelation 18, Isaiah 10, 13, 18**. Since then I have found more.

Though the rules were, that anyone who was there less than a month could not fly anywhere, I was asked to work with Miri from England. She and I had such a good time together! We had about 300 pounds of Bibles between us, plus our own gear. There was bad weather in the north of China, remember this was March, as I said earlier. So we had to wait four hours for our plane to be able to take off. It was about 10:30 PM when we boarded our China Eastern Airlines flight, and bumped our way through the skies to Beijing. We arrived near midnight. I prayed the whole way.

Abba gave me **Isaiah 41:10 and 13: "Do not fear! Do not look around in dismay, for I am your Elohim! Yes! I will strengthen you! Yes! I will help you. Yes! I will uphold you with the right hand of My righteousness...for I, your Elohim, am holding your right hand saying unto you, `Do not fear! I will help you'."**

We got through Immigration and went to get our luggage off the conveyor belt at Customs. There was no one there but us, and one woman standing behind a desk--a Custom's Officer. We proceeded to walk to the exit, staring straight ahead. As we did, someone came up to talk to her, and she turned around with her back to us. We went fast and made it out. Perhaps Abba allowed that storm so that we'd have no problems getting through.

We took a taxi to the Cherry Blossom Hotel, a clean 3-star hotel, and slept well. The next morning I learned about Chinese breakfasts – boiled nuts, boiled cucumbers, and boiled eggs. About 10:30 AM, we took our suitcases with us to McDonalds. It was at this McDonalds that we did a suitcase switch. We sat our suitcases by us at our table. Then our contacts, insider Chinese men, came with the same-looking suitcases, but they were empty. They sat the empty ones down, and picked up the ones full of Bibles to take to their warehouse for distribution. We took the empty ones back to the hotel. Then we went to the Forbidden City and Tiananmen Square. The Forbidden City was amazing. Tiananmen Square is the largest public Square in the world. After leaving the Square, we even went into the underground shopping area beneath Tiananmen Square, where silk shirts were about $2.00 each. Miri was a "professional shopper!" She had to buy an extra large suitcase to take back her souvenirs when she returned to England. Back in Hong Kong, we went to Stanley Market on Hong Kong Island, with Tone from the Netherlands. We had such an awesome day together--real sisters!

The next day, Miri and I went to the Ming tombs, where the emperors of the Ming Dynasty were buried. Then we went to a Ming vase factory. On the morning of March 22nd we got up early and went into Beijing. The streets were filled with people pulling carts and riding bicycles. Big pots of steamed noodles were on the side of the road, with baskets filled with steamed dumplings.

We then went to Badaling, north of Beijing, to go up onto the Great Wall of China. I had seen a booklet of the Great Wall, and planned on buying it on the way back. But, this short old Tibetan man came up with the same booklet and kept pestering me to buy it for quite a bit more money. I put him off, and walked on further up the Wall. On the way back here he came again. He was so cute! I told him what they were charging for the book down below the Wall, and he sold it to me for that price. As I left he grinned a toothless grin and waved.

There were other trips, too, with Australians, British, Dutch, Norwegians, Canadians, French, Americans, and one girl from Japan. This one from Japan had such a heart to see Chinese people born again. She wanted to be a missionary to China. A couple stayed with us, Ken and Marian Sinclair, from Australia. We were discussing end-time prophecy, and at that time I was a teacher of the pre-tribulation rapture nonsense. Ken said that Messiah would come "at the last trump" (**I Corinthians 15:51-52**). He pointed me to **Revelation 11:15-18** and explained it. I was skeptical. Today I proclaim that truth boldly. [Refer to: "Who Will Be Left Behind?"]

In the small women's apartment, we slept on bunk beds. In our tiny room were three bunk beds. There was not an inch to spare between the bunks. Akiko, the Japanese girl, came in the middle of the night and slept above me. But, it was good – we all were joined in unity.

Then there was Hainan Island. I was teamed up with the Dutch lady – Hans. We had about 200 pounds of Bibles in two suitcases each, plus our travel gear. We crossed the Lo Woo border, and were scheduled to fly out of Shen Zhen, not out of Hong Kong. But for some reason we missed the plane. The next one to Hainan was scheduled to arrive four hours later. We were on standby. Our contacts had gone ahead of us on the plane we missed. It was 10:00 PM. We saw people lining up to get seats on the plane. It looked like there were hundreds of people in line. When we got up there, the lady was very rude to us. She said there were no standby seats. I walked around speaking loudly in tongues. My Dutch friend didn't speak much English, so she sure didn't understand my angelic tongue.

When the last of the line began boarding, the lady left. A young man took her place. I threw myself over the counter a few inches from his face, and began gesturing for him to find two seats for us. He was so shocked; he quickly found us two seats. The plane was leaving in 15 minutes, so they threw our luggage onto the conveyor belt without checking it. We paid our exit tax and ran for the plane. There was that lady, taking tickets. She was really disgusted when she saw us. We got to Haikow, and our hotel reservations had been cancelled. So, once again, I threw myself over the desk and pleaded. They took us to the top floor. The next morning I was brushing my teeth and the water shut off. I ran outside to see workman. My friend went downstairs to find out what was happening. They had put us in a construction zone. The manager was so apologetic that he came to move the suitcases to another room on the second floor.

I'm laughing – this is so funny. He was short and of small frame. He was lugging those suitcases into the elevator and finally he said: "These suitcases sure are heavy." Well, we got the Bibles there but our contacts had no way of knowing where we were, and we had no contact numbers for them. My friend stayed downstairs to call the ministry to ask them what to do--as she did, in walked the two contacts from Hong Kong. I was upstairs praying. The doorbell rang. In their hotels, you don't knock, you ring the doorbell. I opened the door and there was my Dutch friend and behind her too grinning Chinese men. They got the Bibles to the waiting believers before the day was over. So, she and I went walking. We were the only white folks on the Island – at least we didn't see any other ones. Children tried touching our hair and giggled. I was a strawberry blond at the time.

We went on one of those incredible buses to an old Buddhist monastery that had been turned into a museum. On those buses, the people are jammed body to body, with chickens, and other interesting creatures that people had bought for dinner. Believe me, if a critter moves, they eat it--from land or sea. Merchants put them in large plastic tins, or cages, like the snakes, or in big fish tanks. They'll skin your snake right there for you, or cut the head off of your chicken of choice. I never saw so many unusual creatures.

We went through that museum – fascinating place! They had skeletons of monks from the Ming Dynasty in glass coffins. But, after going through the museum, we were hungry, so we started back towards the hotel. My friend wanted to go down this dismal looking street, and I wanted to go to the hotel. But, she insisted. Good for her! We found a large lily pond. In the middle was a small platform with two tables. It was a restaurant. For 10 yuan each (less than $1.00), we had a lovely fried rice dinner, with tea. No critters in the fried rice – only eggs and vegetables. The cook and the waiters wanted their pictures taken with us – which we took.

Then I had combined team efforts with men. Men came from all over Europe, Australia, New Zealand, Canada, and the UK. Two black ladies, Vera and Ruby, came from Los Angeles. They were so much fun to be with! We took the Star Ferry over to Hong Kong Island and had a fabulous day together. We took the tram to Victoria Peak also. I was assigned to work with a team of Norwegian men. These men were terrific. One morning I walked to the Kowloon Train Station at 5:00 AM with my load of Bibles on my trolley. That was before the days of suitcases on wheels. I remember a large bucket with a hog's head in it, and the chicken feet lined up on a window ledge for sale--no chicken, just their feet.

On one joint team effort, several teams of four went separately through the Lo Woo border, and we met at the Shen Zhen train station. Our Chinese guide worked for Open Doors. All total, we had 26 suitcases full of Bibles. We're talking large suitcases. When we all got there, our guide led us to a large hotel where there were waiting cars of believers who had come for the Bibles. In the process of going to the hotel, a couple of police cars pulled up and stopped near us. Our guide began acting like he was our tour guide--pointing out buildings and talking loudly--and we acted like tourists. When we got to the hotel entrance, there were the cars waiting. They loaded all the suitcases into two cars and took off. They were scared, but they did it! While working with one of the Norwegian men, we got lost in Shen Zhen, but because I knew hand gestures, and some Chinese, I got back to the train station all right. It was fun shopping in Shen Zhen!

I learned so much of the Chinese ways and thinking. The ministry later trusted me to get the tickets for the trains, planes, and the best prices for mini-van "buses," and taxis. I did learn the money system early on. After China, I took classes in Fort Worth to learn Chinese. Our teacher was from Shanghai.

Two examples stand out. My team got out at a ticket booth outside the train station. I went up to the little tiny window, but men started pushing into my space. I bent my elbows out on either side of my body, and stared at them--on the right and on the left--with a very stern expression. They smiled and backed off.

I learned to act like a Chinese. I pounded my hands on the counter, and said "hard seat train" in Chinese. The windows are so tiny, they can't see who is talking to them so they always gave me Chinese rates. The Chinese are infamous for tripling or quadrupling the price for foreigners. But, I fit right in with the locals! This training paid off well when I had to pay bills in Jordan.

The East is a male-based society and a woman has to walk a tight rope between being assertive and being too aggressive!

The other example was with taxi drivers. At one point, I had about 20 taxi drivers around me yelling at me to get in their taxi. I had to pound on my hand and yell prices and do my gestures until finally one decent guy was singled out.

In getting across the border there were many obstacles. In 1994, I relate this one. We were crossing into China on the day where they worship their ancestors – and so the border was jam packed with Chinese crossing from Hong Kong into Mainland China to be with their families. It was confusion piled upon confusion. Everyone was pushing and shoving (which is typical in China). At Immigration, people were putting their Passports over the heads of others to get ahead in line. One lady did that to me. She also pushed her luggage in front of mine and blocked my way. The Immigration Officer saw that, and did not take her Passport, but took mine. A policeman saw it and came over and took my suitcases to the exit door for me. Now wasn't that nice?

We had to learn how to tell the truth without saying anything. Often they would ask if we had Bibles in our suitcases. Instead of saying "yes," and compromising the whole trip, we pulled out our own English language Bible and showed it to them, and said: "you mean like this? I just have one like this." Not wanting to "lose face," because most of them did not speak English, they would wave us on. We had to learn a complete code language too, because spies were everywhere from Mainland China to catch Bible smugglers. It would be five years before Hong Kong would be transferred back into Chinese control, and they had their men at all public places, on trains, listening on phones, etc. to catch people smuggling Bibles. We had to talk about our Boss and our Books, and our touring trips, etc. What an education for my future work for Abba!

I also learned "people power" in crossing streets. In China there are few traffic signals, like in Africa and Mexico, so if people want to get across the street they have to amass in one huge group and just start walking. I always made sure I was on the inside, as far away from oncoming traffic as I could get, just in case no one wanted to stop. Let's talk about Chinese toilets. I should write a book entitled "Toilets I Have Known and Hated." The toilets in China were nasty. I remember one American who had just come from New York. We had met in Shen Zhen at a hotel to eat, and proceed on to our assignment. Teams were generally 1-4 people. But, this time we had about six. I watched her go into the toilet – her first experience in Mainland China. I watched her come out. Oh I wish I had taken a picture of the look on her face. She had her head down, and a blank expression. I asked her how she liked the toilet – she said: "No comment!"

I went a second time with a team to visit Brother Lamb. This time our team was large, consisting of the Sinclair's from Australia, a young man from England, Miri, the girl from Japan, Tone from Norway, Bas from Canada (the director of the Hong Kong ministry), Hans from Netherlands, and Marlene from Australia. We went by train two hours from Hong Kong's Kowloon Station to Guangzhou. We had quite a load of "Books" to take to Brother Lamb. The fellowship with him was wonderful! This time I got my Bibles through with no problem. But, even when I got lost in Shen Zhen, I thought to myself, "drop me off anywhere in China, and I will make my way back to Hong Kong." I felt so at home there for some reason. I had read Peter Jenkins book *Walk Across China*. His trek inspired me so much.

I met so many there who were there because of the movie "The Inn of the Sixth Happiness" (from the book *The Small Woman*). I learned that Gladys Alyward was very upset by the movie because it showed her having a romantic relationship with a Chinese officer. She said none of that happened--they were only platonic friends. But, that movie changed a lot of lives! It changed mine! Ingrid Bergman, the famous Swedish actress known for staring in sexually-oriented movies, was chosen to play the role of Gladys. It affected her life so dramatically that she went to China to find Gladys. Gladys died just before she got there. But, she never performed in any movies after that, I was told.

CHINA (TWO TRIPS)
(1995)
TRIP #1

I returned to America in late March. My three weeks had been packed solid with trips and experiences and miracles. After waiting from 1961 to go to China, Abba made up for it. I began planning a trip for my husband and I to go in October. But, he kept stalling. He did not tell me clearly that he wanted to go. I had booked the "couples room," which at that time had moved to the men's apartment. But, because he kept stalling, we lost the couple's room, and the trip was put off until the next spring (1995). I was very upset. I found out that he really did not want to go. He was jealous of me and didn't want to be left out.

As I said above, because my husband put so much pressure on me, phoning me in Hong Kong, in 1994, I promised him that he could come with me when I returned in 1995. Wrong decision! We went in February of 1995. We stayed in the couple's room. Our first trip was to Brother Lamb's. Then we crossed the bay to Hong Kong Island at Tsim Sha Tsui, and went to Stanley Market. The ministry had rented a new ladies two-story house and a new place for the men. They were not very close to each other. The women's house was called Hebron House, and was in Tai Wei. There were ladies there from England, Singapore, New Zealand, Australia, Tasmania, and Holland. Some came for two weeks, some for longer periods of time. My favorites were Trudy and Mary from England. They were there because of the movie about Gladys Alyward.

The couple's room was in the men's apartment. There were men there from Holland, Canada, England, New Zealand, and Australia. On his first trip to China, my husband pulled so many wicked things on me, and on others with the ministry, it was part disaster and part preparation for more disaster on the second trip. I loved working with Martin from Holland. He was there for three months. He had his own room, where he displayed his butterfly and nature collection. He was a happy guy. He played the guitar and sang.

I was the leader of the next trip to Brother's Lamb's. Martin and another man came with us--so our team was four. My husband was so openly cruel to me, and openly pulled so many tricks to try to make me look like a fool, that one day Martin said to me: "Some people just need to be free" – referring to me. Bless him! We were assigned to go with a team to Macau. It was a Portuguese country like Hong Kong was an English country. But, because both were on a "lease" with China, each went back to China as per the lease. We went by fast boat to Macau and I loved it.

On one trip, we were sent by train into GuangDong province to take Bibles in, but also to get a load of Bibles out that had been confiscated, and bring them back to Hong Kong. It was February 12, 1995. On that day, Li de Xian and his team were taking Bibles into the north of GuangDong province. Upon getting to the hidden place of meeting, believers came to get the Bibles. But, they had been followed by the cadres, and so all were beaten and the Bibles taken. Li was beaten so badly that they broke several ribs. He went back home and healed up, then went back again.

The work of Abba does not stop. The enemy scores a victory, but at the same time Yahuweh scores another victory, so that when the smoke clears, Yahuweh always wins! We had many short trips, and even worked with some from the "Three Self Church" who helped Open Doors' work. I was trusted with the money, and made team leader several times. That is what caused so much jealousy and competition against me, along with sadism and cruelty, from my husband.

While staying in the men's apartment, he got Bas to reveal his innermost thoughts. Bas was single, a lonely man, and so had private thoughts, even sins. Why he opened up to my husband can only be understood by those that know the power of witchcraft. My husband did all this in the name of "counseling." This put Bas into such despair that he ended up leaving the ministry. My husband did this undercover work at Grace Temple too, to undermine the leadership there, with results. He loved to move in and bring division and chaos out of order. Before leaving, we were alone in the couple's room one day, and my husband took the opportunity to practice his ritualistic sadomasochism on me. I was so ashamed.

TRIP #2

In October 1995, when we returned, I feared staying in the couple's room with him. One of the main directors, who organized the teams and their assignments, was Carolyn - a woman from Fort Worth. I had met her mother Helen in Fort Worth before she joined her daughter in Hong Kong. They were friends of my pastor at Emmanuel Christian Fellowship. They became friends of mine.

Even Carolyn was amazed at my 1994 itinerary. She organized some of our teamwork in 1995, and even went with us on one assignment. I was accountable to her for the money I spent for each assignment. So, I confided in her that I needed to stay in the women's Hebron House in Tai Wei. She put me in a large room by myself. Of course, I got questioning as to why we were separated, but I could not go through again what I went through the first time.

There were ladies there from Australia, New Zealand, England, Holland, Singapore, Switzerland, and four from Tasmania. There was even an elderly lady there from Florida, and an elderly lady from Los Angeles. The four from Tasmania did not know each other before they came (amazing). Hebron House and the men's new house area were rather far apart. It was so peaceful there in that room.

In the men's house there were Oola and Sverre from Norway, Cyril from France, and Adrian and Simon from Switzerland. Later, a couple came to stay in the couple's room from New York. Then there came Allesondro, Gacama, and Ettare, from Italy, and then John and Joyce Broom from England.

As time went along, people came and left. Our teams doubled up at times, and the work of getting the Word to the true believers in China was continuous. We went through Tai Wei station to Shekou with some awesome people. In coming back through Shen Zhen, I went shopping with Marianna and Hazel from England.

On another operation we had more people. We went to Shantau. We had Muriel from Wales join us, and Del from Australia. To date, Del had been with Open Doors 17 times, taking Bibles into China. She was such an inspiration to me. After her husband died, she began selling everything she had to pay for the trips. Because I had so much favor with Open Doors, they told me I could come any time and did not have to re-apply. They gave me the money bag for expenses, and made me the leader on many trips. We flowed together so beautifully. What a wonderful family group from all over the world, working together in such unity! The favor Abba poured out on me caused me more problems. It was bad enough that the ministry put my husband and I on the same teams most of the time. He questioned every request I made, and tried to make me look like a fool with my team members many times. But, most were too smart to fall for the tricks.

One day Carolyn came and got me out of a meeting to give me a special assignment by myself. Those meetings were so awesome. We learned a special code language and all sorts of covert ways of getting our "precious cargo" through to its destination. If you ever get a chance to hear the story of how Paul Estabrooks and Brother David got one million Bibles into China in one night, it is astounding. The story is told from Brother David's prospective in his book *God's Smuggler to China*. But, I heard the story from Paul and met him in Mongolia. I highly recommend Brother Andrews' *God's Smuggler*. A friend of ours in Fort Worth had worked with them, and it was Bill who got me excited about applying to go as a courier.

I was in a meeting, when Carolyn came to me and said they needed me to take teaching materials across the Lo Woo border for a young Chinese girl. If she were caught with them, she would be arrested. I got them across-HalleluYah! Once across, I met her at a restaurant near the train station. She spoke good English. She said that she and her husband had been married for eleven months. At that time, he was riding a bicycle into the north of China to take Bibles to remote villages that had never heard the message of salvation. It was very dangerous because they were very primitive people and leery of "strangers." She taught new believers in Shen Zhen. She said they loved each other very much, and wanted to have a home, and children, but the work for the Master was calling them to be apart at that time. What a precious young woman! So many stories, so many miracles in China!

For some reason, my husband was not with me on one assignment, and I got to go on another part of the Great Wall.

PART V - Training Assignments

Because I did not have the money to go to the top on the lift, I walked it – hundreds of steps straight up the side of a mountain, and all the way down. This time it had been raining, and the stone steps were slick. I was coming down an incline on the Wall, holding onto the side of it for support. I looked over and saw four youth with arms around each other, running down the incline. I started laughing and they were delighted. We met at the bottom of the Wall and through gestures and smiles, we kind of communicated. I love the Chinese – even under the oppression of Communism, they have their simple joys of life. Along the way up and down, Tibetans tried to sell me water. On the way back, my face was so red because it was hot, that one Tibetan came out to offer me a cane. We laughed! I loved those people!

On one trip, they sent us up the Pearl River from Hong Kong to a remote entrance port into Mainland China, on the "night boat." It was one of those "oooooh no, you got assigned to the night boat?" But, I loved it. Everyone slept in bunk beds in one huge room in the boat. The next morning I went down the hall to get hot water for my tea and noodles. I have no idea why I took to China so well ... but it sure did prepare me for "the world" beyond, especially the Middle East. We docked at a remote port up the Pearl River, and everyone got their Bibles through with no problems.

Talk about comic relief – here's a funny one: We were to join a team from Hawaii who had loads of Bibles to get into China. They were not with Open Doors but were friends of the ministry. We met in this hotel, but not openly. My husband was sent down the hall to one room, and I was asked to go next door and meet with two men to transfer my Bibles to them. I knocked on their door and one man opened the door. The other one was asleep on his bed in front of the TV. Now in China the hotel rooms are all "bugged." The TVs reverse signal and there is NO privacy. They listen to all conversations of foreigners. As soon as the other man opened the door to let me in, he went over and turned up the volume on the TV very loud. He got down on his hands and knees behind the TV and motioned for me to join him on the floor. Of course the other man woke up from the noise and laid there as if he was alone in the room. We discussed plans to get the Bibles out of the hotel and on their way to the believers.

You know, when you join with people of like mind for such a monumental project that will affect thousands of lives, you have to be secretive. You have to learn wisdom. You need to know when to shut up and when to talk and how to talk. Talk about an education! I would have 18-hour days. Sometimes I'd fall asleep sitting up on the hard-back train, but Abba gave me such strength. I don't know how I did it with my flexible joint problems. That is a huge miracle!

This one is a BIG story with many miracles. I was asked to be the team leader of a team going to Shanghai. They flew us up there, but we took the 36-hour train trip back. The team consisted of two Swiss young men, Adrian and Simon, my husband, and I. We each had two loaded suitcases with Bibles, plus our own luggage to pull.

We took the plane from Hong Kong to Shanghai. The airport at Shanghai was a long ways from the city. We had to go through Immigration, of course, then board a bus to the city. The Swiss boys and I pulled our luggage through Immigration and then got onto the bus. We left our luggage on the lower level, and went on up to the upper level and sat right in front of the big windows at the head of the bus. My husband didn't come out of Immigration. We were getting nervous, since we were the only non-Chinese people anywhere around. We saw him go with policemen into a room whose entrance was just in front of the bus. Then he came out without his two suitcases of Bibles. Right in front of the police, he got onto the bus and came right up and sat by me. The Swiss boys and I were numb. He had tried to carry some of the luggage, and they saw him struggling, and they pulled him aside. It was a miracle they even let him into the Mainland. All I could think of was that they were letting us go so that when the bus got to Shanghai the police there would take our luggage and send us back to Hong Kong. But, when we got out in Shanghai no one arrested us. Talk about one huge miracle!

What is more amazing is that at that time they had put on 150,000 more police in Shanghai to catch Bible smugglers... and arrest any from the unregistered church. They were on a mad search for warehouses where Bibles were stored. The Three Self Church, that was government sponsored, printed a small amount of Bibles that they distributed to their people, but beliefs were controlled and pastors could not preach on the second coming of Messiah – especially from the books of Daniel and Revelation.

I find that fascinating, since Rabbi Akiva almost left *Daniel* out of his canonization of the Tenach, and the Church almost left out *Revelation*, for they said that the Apostle John emphasized the Torah too much. These two sister books are out guideline for not only knowing the timing of the first coming of Messiah, but the second. If the enemy is so staunchly against these two books, shouldn't His people allow Yahuweh's Spirit to teach them the secrets, now not secrets, of these two books? Yet, lazy ones of Western religion avoid these books, except when listening to intellectuals discuss them. Brother Lamb said that if he stood to teach, the police would consider that preaching and he'd be arrested again. But, if he sat to teach, that was all right. Strange! So he sat and taught a lot on the coming of Messiah!

We got to our hotel room in Shanghai and the Director, Bas, called me from Hong Kong to alert me. He said: "Abort Plan A." This meant that the "Books" must not be taken to Brother Lamb. When we got back to Hong Kong, we learned that the police had made a "purge" of Brother Lamb's meeting place and taken all the Bibles. So we couldn't take them back there, and there were no contacts in Shanghai who would risk coming to get them. Bas said he would try to find someone. I had phone numbers of contacts, but none would answer their phones. We prayed hard that our "precious cargo" would get to the believers who were scattered all around Shanghai.

Later that afternoon we heard a knock on the door. The man at the door said his name was Bas, as a code name to let us know that Bas from Hong Kong had sent him. So we let him in. He attended a "Three Self Church." But, he was born again, and helped the persecuted believers. He told us that there were many born again believers in the Three Self Church, but that the government taught the members to be spies against the unregistered believers. On another mission, we worked with two others from the Three Self Church who aided Open Door's operations.

You see, the unregistered stayed free to obey the Master and His Word. Those bound under government control are watched, and restrictions are put on them. They can not witness to anyone under 18 about Jesus. Few have Bibles. There were severe restrictions on what the pastors can teach. And, because China has the one-child law, the members are watched. The free ones, who are hunted and killed, give a second child to those who are unmarried, or to an older woman, to raise. They will not abort or kill a child. The free ones witness to those of all ages who will listen. So often they were gunned down in the baptismal waters, or hunted down later to be beaten, imprisoned, tortured and/or killed.

This man was a friend of Open Doors. He said after dark a man with an Open Door's identification card would meet us downstairs at 8:00 PM. So, we went out about 7:45, pulling all that luggage. We walked right in front of the reception desk to the street curb. There were police cars everywhere. I never saw so many. We stood there and waited about 3 minutes. Then from an alleyway came a tall, thin, very scared man. He came up to us and handed me the Open Doors ID card. I asked him to hail us a taxi, which he did. I asked the Swiss boys to both go with him. They reported back that the "precious cargo" got to the warehouse safely.

The next morning we had a whole day to see Shanghai. We went to the most classic and famous of the Shanghai gardens - the Yu Yuan Gardens. It was built during the Ming Dynasty (1388-1644). After that we went to the famous Bund area where the Yangtze River flows out into the East China Sea.

I've never seen so many people on bicycles – almost as many bicycles in their lanes as cars were in their lanes. We had a wonderful day! The next morning we boarded the train for Hong Kong. It was a 36-hour trip. I got a bottom bunk across from Malcolm. He was a man, maybe in his late 30s, from Ireland, who got tired of being a computer programmer, and put a backpack on his back and set out to walk across China. He was delightful. I loved the trip! It went through the Chinese countryside. Whenever the train would stop in a city area, we'd get off and get more Ramen noodles. They gave us a hot water flask, which they kept filled for us. I had packets of coffee too. I saw so much of the real China. There were two sets of bunks separated from another two sets, and on and on throughout the car. Malcolm was on the bunk opposite me, my husband above me, and the Swiss boys on the other side of the partition. No one smoked cigarettes on our side. The aisle was in front of our bunks. In the morning I went to get food, and coming back I smiled at the Chinese in the area just ahead of us, and they smiled back. I felt at home for some reason.

As told earlier in this story, when I was a little girl my mother bought me the children's book *The Wonderful Train Ride*. I loved that book so much, and had my parents read it over and over to me. I told above about going on the train when I was seven and being so sick. But, this was indeed "the wonderful train ride."

At least twice a day, a lady would come down the aisle with a broom and sweep up all the trash into large plastic bags. I thought she was going to leave the bag at the next stop outside the train. No! She would open a window a throw out the trash – not the bag, but only the trash inside. I saw people along the tracks picking up the trash. I suppose she only had one large bag and had to keep it. But, everyone has to have a job under Communism. I've seen 5 people lined up to take one plane ticket.

There was a young couple on the train a few sets of bunks away from us. The man was an army officer and his wife was in the medical field. I felt to give them a little booklet in Chinese, which had testimonies by Chinese people who had been born again. I did not know at this point that he was a military man. But, obeying the Spirit, I went and sat down across from them and gave them the booklet. He took it. He looked at it, and then he and his wife got excited. He kissed the booklet and put it to his heart and thanked me profusely for giving it to them. They became our friends on the train.

There was the time I had 100 pounds of Bibles in my suitcases. I stood in the Custom's line and saw a long row of police officers standing, waiting to go through luggage that was suspect. I prayed. I got to the front of the line, and looked up, and not one police officer was there. Abba had removed them. I saw many miracles like that.

I conclude this section on China by telling about the last three times my Bibles were taken from me, which was in 1995. A lady in Fort Worth had written gospel tracts for children, with drawings. They were small – in booklet form. I told her I would try to get them into China. She had them translated into Chinese.

I had a load of Bibles. I was in a province far from Hong Kong. My friends had made it through Customs and were waiting for me outside. But, my Bibles were discovered, and I was sent with them to an inspector in a small tent-like structure outside the Immigration hall. The officer was going through other people's luggage. He saw I had Bibles. He turned his head away. So, I took them one at a time and stuck them in my coat, in my pants, down my shirt, and also the children's tracts. He acted like he didn't see me, but he did. Another officer came in and was angry with this man because he had not taken my Bibles or the children's tracts. We went outside. The two men were loudly screaming at each other. I said to them: "Please, they are for children." They kept yelling. Finally, they took the Bibles that were exposed and I was able to get all the children's tracts out along with the few Bibles that I had stuffed on my person. I came back in to get my backpack, and thanked the man who had stood up for me. But, I was a little too vocal and he panicked and scolded me. But, I prayed for that man a long time, because he must have been either a secret believer, or one in sympathy with the persecuted assemblies.

Another time I was stopped bringing Bibles through another border. They confiscated the Bibles. The officer spoke English, so I asked him: "**I thought you had religious freedom in China**?" He replied: "**Yes, we do, but that has nothing to do with Bibles – Bibles are counter-revolutionary materials!**" WOW – what a statement! Jack Nicholas came into Shen Zhen to play golf, but it was illegal for people to bring in Bibles. Yes, the Word of Yahuweh is against the communist revolution, and all revolutions of man that control man. Yes, the Word of Yahuweh has the power to start revolutions and stop revolutions! Brother

Andrews once said: "**We have to be more revolutionary than the revolutionists, in order to win the revolutionists.**" Messiah used a few revolutionary disciples/Apostles to "turn the world upside down." He doesn't need many, just those that are totally sold-out to Him.

To Brother Andrews there are NO closed doors – only open doors that await His people to go through and take the Good News to a lost and dying world. Brother David wanted to get into Mainland China when it was closed due to the regime of Mao. But, in meeting Brother Andrew, he learned that He could get the Word in, in printed form, via Tibetan traders until he could go in with it himself. So he started smuggling Bibles in through Tibet, using mule team drivers. Abba waits for someone to forsake all to follow the Lamb wherever He goes, THEN AND ONLY THEN will He direct their path.

We had such a good time with Allesondro, Gacamo, and Ettore, from Italy. The comedian was Allesondro. We were talking about end-times one day, and he blurted out: "The Popa, he's a Mafia" (Italian accent).

One day a very important assignment was given to my husband and I, to take Bibles into Shen Zhen, via Lo Woo, to people who had come a very long way for them. My husband got through all right, but I didn't. I was leaving China in about four days. I was nervous for some reason and kept running my right hand through my hair. They are experts in psychological profiling. They were waiting for me. I had to put my suitcases through the x-ray machine, and of course they pulled me out. They told me to open the suitcases. I slowly stalled in opening the suitcases, pretending that my key didn't work. But, they took my Bibles. The officer I dealt with spoke some English. He took my passport and put it on the desk of some people nearby. I never had them take my passport before. But, I had heard of Dennis Balcolm being arrested for smuggling Bibles. He is the man who started "Donkeys for Jesus."

So I was really afraid when he took the passport. I walked over and took it back. He grabbed it from me and put it further onto the desk. I told him I was leaving China in four days. He walked with his hands behind his back, and I walked with him everywhere he went. I kept snatching the passport back telling him I was leaving. Finally, he gave me the passport. He stood there with his hands folded behind his back in true Communist style, rocking back and forth, with a grin on his face. He raised his right hand and gave me the thumbs up with a smile. I broadly smiled back at him, and put my thumb up. He had won the battle, temporarily. I had won the war.

I knew that my Italian team members would come and get the Bibles, and take them back in, which they did. And Allesando told me they all got through all right. But, that Lo Woo border into Shen Zhen is the hardest of all the borders, since it was the main smuggling point for Bibles. But, I was so in despair. My husband and I took the Bibles that we had to those waiting for us. We had a long talk with one of them over lunch. It was a sad time for me, since it was my last trip into China.

Not too long before we left China, my husband and I took a trip to Cheung Chau Island. We visited all the tourist places, and all the back alleys, too. It was a gorgeous day, and we had a wonderful time! It was here in an open-air market that I found a copy of Hudson Taylor's autobiography. The mixture of good and bad was so interwoven, but this was a very good day.

Two days before leaving Hong Kong, my husband and I were asked to be a part of a spy mission to Macau. Because Hong Kong was being transferred back to China, Macau would become the main port for smuggling Bibles. They had just built a million dollar airport and had two planes. We took the fast boat. When we got to the airport, we told them that we wanted to learn about the airport because we planned to bring many tourists through Macau, which was true. We asked for a tour of their airport. They were so proud. They gave us special badges. They showed us all the security measures, the check points, the Immigration hall and Customs. We took pictures, and left with smiles.

Macau became the major smuggling center for Open Doors, for Jackie Pullinger, for Dennis Balcolm, and others. Then Macau went back to Mainland China. It was the last of the European settlements on the Continent. Then things got harder, and operations got more strategic, ending up on the inside of China with long-term workers. The work goes on, but much more in secret within China.

On our way back, my back was so out of place that I was in great pain. The flight attendant on Korean Airlines, a very good airline I might add, let me lie down in a back set of chairs. My husband was so furious at me. When we got to Los Angeles, LAX, after going through Immigration and Customs, we went to a room to await our flight to DFW. He began yelling at me in front of everyone that he wanted a divorce. I was so ashamed. Some people hid their faces behind newspapers; some got up and left the area. I'm sure they were ashamed too.

I remember the day, July 1, 1997, when Hong Kong went back to Communist China. I watched it on T.V. Prince Charles delivered a speech. Before he even got back to his yacht, something horrifying happened. The cameras panned the faces of the people.

I saw their expression go from peaceful to terror. Through the Lo Woo border came rolling tanks, like the ones they used to crush the people in Tiananmen Square in Beijing. I cried for days.

MONGOLIA
(SUMMER OF 1996)

Leaving Mongolia was hard. We flew on Mongolian Air to Beijing. We had three days in Beijing before flying back to America. As we were on the bus going from the airport to our hotel in Beijing, I saw shepherds standing with their flocks of sheep. It seemed so peaceful. I leaned my head against the bus window and asked Abba: "Please let me feel the heart of the persecuted believers in this nation." I expected to be overwhelmed with grief and sadness. I was surprised! All of a sudden, I saw in vision, and felt the spirits, of 100-million persecuted believers marching through the streets, singing victory songs. I felt the power and the victory, the joy and the freedom of these people... it was so overwhelming that I began to cry. Even now I am crying. You see that no matter how hard they tried to stamp out the news of salvation, it has been estimated that for at least 30 years now, that at least 20,000 a day have become born again through the witness of these triumphant ones.

It has been said that the end-time remnant of His people would not come from the West but from places like China, like Indonesia, like Cambodia, Burma, Nepal, and North Korea, where to be a believer costs a person everything. I agree! What rewards do lazy, selfish people get? For all their intellectual knowledge it is obvious they do not know Elohim, nor His nature ways and thinking. For most are virtually useless to the Kingdom of Elohim. They are so bound to their self-created boxes for their security, that most won't even tell a neighbor about salvation in fear that their reputation might be sullied. I hear reports of Americans, Australians, Canadians, those from south Asia, Africa, Central and South America, who are on the move outside their native countries to bring the Good News of salvation, and instruction in the Torah, to people in other nations. Their adventures sound like the book of *The Acts of the Apostles* repeated!

Daniel 11:32! What is the ONE main characteristic of the real remnant? "...**They that know their Elohim...**" They "**will be strong and will act.**"

Yahuweh is Spirit, and by His Spirit they are taught, led, convicted of sin, comforted, strengthened and anointed (empowered by His Presence). They walk in daily miracles--as I wrote in "Daily Flowing in His Perfect Timing." As they go forth to "act" in faith on what He has said, Abba brings the needy to them so that they might be saved, delivered, healed, and taught the Truth.

There is a real remnant on the move throughout the Communist ("second world") and third world (developing nations).

The West has wallowed in satiating their flesh and what pleases their mind and emotions, and they are extremely fearful of being outside their security cages. [Refer to: "The Cage"/February 18, 2007, written from a vision I had in Aqaba]

While in Beijing, I visited the famous Beijing Zoo. The pandas are incredible animals--of the raccoon family. The Chinese sure do love their pandas. They had a special section for them. The zoo was so clean and the animals so well taken care of--quite the opposite of what I had heard.

Mongolia! I told above about the struggles I had to go through to get to go, and how it turned out to be the open door for me to finally break free of my marriage imprisonment, and my own mental imprisonment, and come alive again in mind, emotions, spirit and body. That was 1995-1996...

Abba told me regarding Mongolia: "**You will meet a leader of the country and you will open up the whole country to the Gospel.**" I told Pastor Jim about this "word," and he encouraged me. In my mind, I thought that I would meet a government leader, but that's not how Abba worked it out.

I went for a week of training at Azusa College in southern California, with the English Language Institute China. Most were assigned to go to Ulaanbaatar to teach 300 Mongolian college students. They divided the teachers and gave each a small class of about 10 students each. Others were sent in teams of two to different remote "imogs" all over the country – small tribal village areas.

Mongolia only has a population of about 200,000. Ulaanbaatar is the only city. In the very north, tribal people live in tee-pees, just like the Sioux and Cheyenne Indian tribes of America. They live with the reindeer. The Mongolians are the direct ancestors of the Navajo Indians of southwest America. I felt like I was back on the reservation. The men had that bow-legged walk from riding horses and camels since childhood. They looked Navajo. The women wore the turquoise jewelry, and in the Gobi they lived in hogans, just like the Navajos. Their language is similar, and their ways similar. So it was like déjà vu. The families were very close-knit. The mothers openly breast-fed like the Navajo women. The men were so proud of their children, and were kind and loving to them. The children played, like the African children, with rocks and sticks, and made up their games. Even as little children, like in the African children, they were given tasks to do, like bringing water in jugs from a central source. Happy and delightful children! I remember the Palestinian children in Jordan putting fallen palm branches between their legs, pretending they were horses. The creativity of children is stunted when all they have is man-made toys. That's why they set man-made toys aside and play with the boxes.

The winner from our crash-course English teaching--the one who gave the best speech in English in the final competition--would be awarded by getting an all-expenses paid scholarship to study English in America at the Church of God College in Cleveland, Tennessee. When I lived in western Tennessee, I'd pass that College many times traveling through Cleveland.

My roommate at Azusa College was assigned to be my roommate in Ulaanbaatar. Jenny and I did well together. The English Language Institute started out exclusively in China. Because the teachers were Christians, they did not try to seduce the female students for sex like so many other teachers did. So ELIC had a good reputation throughout China. When Mongolia got their freedom from 70 years of Russian rule in 1991, they wanted to join in with world trade, which meant learning English. So they contacted the head of the Education Department in China to ask them who they recommended to come and teach them. They recommended ELIC. So Mongolia contacted ELIC and asked for 100 English teachers. I was one of the first 100 to come. Some who came for the summer session stayed on to teach a full year or more. The summer sessions were called Summer English Olympics. ELIC worked with the Mongolian Ministry of Education, so were bound by their rules of conduct, which meant no witnessing about Jesus, and no Bible teaching! Various colleges sent their top students to us for this crash course. So we had "the cream of the intellectual crop." They came from different majors.

A little background: When the Kubla Kahn, grandson of Genghis Kahn, wanted to make Mongolia a Christian nation, he consulted with Marco Polo. The wife of Genghis Kahn had a copy of each of the four Gospels. Marco Polo went back to Italy to persuade the Pope to send 100 teachers of Christianity. He went to the Pope, but only two priests volunteered to go. When they got into the snow-covered mountains of Eastern Europe they turned back because of the cold. Ulaanbaatar is the second most northerly and coldest of the world's capitols in winter. Because no Christians came, the Kubla Kahn adopted the religion of Tibetan Buddhism – a very mystic and demonic religion.

We were there from early June to late August and the weather was lovely. It is so far north that looking out of our dorm window at night, we saw the "Big Dipper" so huge that it filled the whole sky. It didn't get dark until after 11:00 PM.

We flew to Beijing, China. Then we got a Mongolian Airlines flight into Ulaanbaatar. We went to our dorm-home. The dorm was built next to the school that we used. Jenny was a born again

Spirit-filled woman. In the room next to us was another born again Spirit-filled woman. They kept the three of us together. There were only three of us that were Spirit-filled. The rest of the teachers were Christians like the ones at BIOLA. They were wonderful people, but they did not know how to hear from Abba, so they set rigid rules that got in the way of what Abba wanted done. We were on the 5th floor. Out our window, below, was a Buddhist Monastery. Tibetan Buddhism includes witchcraft and incantations to bring evil spirits against enemies. Going through that monastery museum I kept sensing unseen entities stationed everywhere watching.

I had a dream before going to Mongolia that I was outside of a Buddhist monastery preaching. The angry monks came running out to stop me. But, I asked if I could give one more verse from the Bible to the people, and they agreed. I very slowly went over **John 3:16**. I woke up as they proceeded to attack.

About two weeks into my being there, after returning from the monastery museum, I was lying down on my bed in the afternoon, and all of a sudden some unseen force began pinning me to the bed. I could not talk. I was being drained of energy. I remembered hearing a missionary friend, who worked for Jerry Savelle's ministry, telling of a similar situation that happened to her in Africa. I knew that whatever was holding me down came from the monastery. Jenny ran and got Sharon, the other Spirit-filled friend, next door. Sharon was bold. She got down by my ear and I forced out the words – "call off the Buddhist spirits." She did! Within a few minutes I rose off that bed with incredible energy praising Abba.

During our first week in Ulaanbaatar, the ministry took us on trips to see the surrounding area. On one such trip we went way out into the countryside. The bus stopped and we all got out. There in the fields were yaks grazing – big black hairy cows with super strength. I wanted to take a picture of the yaks. The grass was in mounds. It had been raining and the grass tufts were slick. I had my camera in my left hand, and I was carefully making my way as close to a yak as possible. I was told they were gentle. But, I slipped on one of grass tufts and, as if in slow motion, I fell forward into the mud. I held the camera up so it did not get ruined. My glasses hit the mud, and my blond hair and all the front of me too. The team members came running, expecting me to be hurt. I lay there in the mud assessing the situation. As with falling in the street in 2012 and lying there by the curb looking up at the sky, in both cases I started laughing so hard. I think my team members thought I was delirious. I said to myself: "Well lady, here you are face down in the mud, out in a field in Mongolia surrounded by yaks." It was so funny to me. I had to convince them that I was all right. A Japanese girl wanted her picture taken with me – covered in mud and smiling ear to ear.

We visited museums where they had stuffed wild animals on display, and other examples of Mongolian natural life. We went to remote areas to see how the "gers" were constructed. The Mongolian gers, which the Russians called "yurts", are round wood-framed houses covered in goat-hair felt. The Mongolians are called "the people of the felt tents."

In the Gobi Desert, the Mongolians build their housing out of sticks and mud – exactly like the Navajo hogans. About three years ago, I felt strongly to work with a project to bring Mongolian gers to Israel, for housing of refugees in the days to come. Tragically, because of the sin of one of the leaders on the project, the project was scrapped. But, I learned that there was someone in the north of Israel who knew how to build them. A friend of mine from Wales also said that in his "hippie" days, he had learned to build them. Abba knows!

My students were awesome! I was told that Mongolians were lazy. Not my students! We won the attendance award, and two of them joined the final ten in the ending contest. I challenged my students, and they responded to the challenge. I was so proud of them!

Early on, we were invited to the Mongolian circus. It was amazing. For the event, I had a Mongolian lady make me a "del." A "del" is what they call their traditional costumes worn in the imogs for regular dress, or made especially beautiful for special occasions. This one was gorgeous – dark blue silk with silver design. She even made me a purse to go with it. My students dressed up. I got pictures of them hugging me. What precious young people! -- So pure and innocent in their thinking. I ask some of the young girls if they had a "boyfriend," and they giggled. The marriages were arranged by parents.

For my birthday, these students really made a special surprise. It was near the time to prepare for the contest. They were supposed to be in the room by 9:00 AM for a special session to present their speeches. But, at 9:00 they were not there – not one was there. I was really getting panicky. About 9:15, I heard them on the steps coming towards the room. They came in with smiles, bringing me gifts. They brought flowers. They brought decorations, which they hung up in the classroom. One of the two art majors, Sarnai (Rose), had drawn a large picture of me, and they had all signed it. They brought me a cake. It was hard getting down to working after that. It was probably the most special birthday I've had in my 69 years. They brought me presents that they had never had themselves, like flowers, and the cake. Those young people worked so hard for me. They protected me, too.

I loved dying my hair different colors, from back in my late 20s. I did not like my auburn hair. Now I wish I had it back. But, I was a blond at this time. Before going to Mongolia, I was at a store and went to get a kit for re-dying my hair. As I reached to pick it up, Abba said: "No! You will not dye your hair again." I jerked back my hand. But, then I said: "Just this one more time, please." He did not respond. My overriding his command with what I thought was a good idea was like when I returned from that British Israel meeting in California where they taught about the dietary laws of Leviticus 11. I had just bought a pound of Oscar Meyer lean bacon. After reading Leviticus 11, I knew it was wrong to eat pork. But, I told Him that the next morning I'd cook it all up, eat it, and then never buy bacon again. However, the next morning I found that fresh bacon was blue with mold.

So, with that mentality, I bought it and dyed my hair ash blond. I went to Mongolia. The boys went with me everywhere holding my hand and protecting me. Many times we'd be trying to cross a street, and people in cars would throw rocks at me, or try to push me down stairs. I learned from other teachers that my hair color was identical to the hair color of the Russians who had occupied Mongolia. I went before my class and asked them if my hair color was that of the Russians that had oppressed them. They all hung their heads and nodded "yes." Is Yahuweh smarter than we are?

On July 4th, we went to the American Embassy for festivities. The Ambassador to Mongolia read a speech from the President. I bought a sweat shirt with the official U.S. Embassy Seal of Mongolia on it. We got to attend a drama. I have pictures of the lawn mowers on the lawn of the State Drama Theater downtown Ulaanbaatar--two cows. Being summer, we got to attend Naadam – the three manly sports events – horseback racing, archery, and wrestling competitions. People came from all over the country to the area not far outside Ulaanbaatar. Many families came riding on horse-drawn carts. Gers were put up all over the area for people to stay in.

Young children rode those awesome little Mongolian horses for about 35 miles. It was a long-distance competition. I have pictures of the winners, who got paper crowns. The grass covering the hills and plain was a blue-green color, and not one tree to be seen. It was with those little horses that Genghis Kahn conquered more land mass than any other conqueror in the world. Each of his riders had two horses, so one horse was not worn out by its rider. The archery competition was amazing. We did not see much of the wrestling. We got to visit the famous Tbogt Hann Winter Palace. In there was the King's ger, covered with 150 snow leopard pelts.

My students were: Sarnai Bold (University of Art and Culture/painting), Jargal (Technology University/Physics Major), Tomorbat (Technology University), Khasbaatar (Technology University), Tsengelmaa (University of Art and Culture/graphics), Byambadulam (Technology University/chemistry), Ganchimeg (Technology University/ mathematics), Amgalan (Asian Study in the Technology University), and Erdenetsetseg (Technology University/physics/math).

In preparation for the final speeches for the contest, we joined classes. My class was joined with Walt Rivers' class. We did some things together and some separately. Our two classes went on a picnic in the woods. We had to ford two rather wide and vigorous streams. My Mongolian "angels" got on either side of me and helped me over and back. Jargal, the physics major, brought me Mongolian Edelweiss. We had games and contests and good food. It was a lovely day.

Some of the rules of ELIC were too strict, without mercy. I understand that they didn't want to get out of favor with the Minister of Education, but some of their adherence to rules was cruel in my estimation. There was no room to hear Abba and administer kindness.

Tomorbat was a tall thin young man who worked harder than anyone else in the class. He wanted to be in the finals. He was so precious. One day after school, Tomorbat came running in all excited. He forgot his English and began talking Mongolian. I did not understand. He then grabbed a piece of paper and drew this primitive goat shape on the paper. The tail was up, and from under the tail he drew three balls. I wondered why he was excited about a goat going poop. He motioned for me to come. We looked out the window of the classroom next door, and there below was a mother goat giving birth to her third kid. That is what I mean by innocence and purity.

He confided in me that the West was destroying their country. He told how the families were breaking up and the old traditions that kept them together were being taken away. He told about the gambling, the prostitution, the night clubs, the drugs, the violent movies and violent music that America was bringing in. I learned about the "American package." Unless a country took the package, they got no financial support. This happened in Albania, too. It has happened in Israel. It happened in Russia. If a nation wants American help, they have to allow America to bring in their drug trade, their "white slavery" and pornography industries, their child pornography industry, their violent movie, and violent music industries, and use both adults and children in their fields working on an average of twelve hours a day, being paid 10-30 cents an hour. This is pure evil.

One day Tomorbat, during the time of finals, was on his way to class. He had to ride the bus. The bus came early, and he missed it, so he got there late. The director found out about it, and disqualified him from being able to participate in the finals. To me that was wicked. I did everything I could to persuade her to change her mind, but her words were "those are the rules." It was not his fault. It devastated him. He never came back to class. I saw him after the finals. He was waiting for me outside the building. I kept apologizing to him, but what could I say to make his hurt go away? That young man had worked harder than all the rest.

It was August. My third child had gone to Atlanta with YWAM to share the Gospel at the Summer Olympics. They passed out tracts, and talked to people about salvation. There was only one telephone and it was at the one hotel in Ulaanbaatar, so except for an emergency, we had no way of contacting our family. Of course, no one had a computer. I tried to get news on my short wave radio, but could only find programs in Russian, Chinese, or Mongolian. But, one night late, I got the BBC Europe news. The headlines were that a bomb had gone off in a park in Atlanta, at the Olympics. The second headline was that a passenger jet had been hit by a missile while taking off from New York, over Manhattan, and blown up. I asked Abba if my daughter was all right. He assured me that she was fine. When I got back I asked her about it. She said she had been in that park just an hour before the bomb blast. It is so practical to hear from Abba, who can tell us what is really happening, so that we have peace, and wisdom, and act on what He has said. However, so many are too busy to hear Him. I wrote a very profound article entitled "Too Busy to Hear."

In training in Azusa, I met Mary from Atlanta. She had done quite a bit of missionary work in other countries. She had never married, but was a lovely lady – maybe in her mid-40s at that time. She wanted to come back and work with ELIC full time. She became my prayer partner. She was another teacher assigned to Ulaanbaatar.

We began attending "Orten Geggie." [phonetic spelling] It was at Orten Geggie, one Sunday morning, that I met Paul Estabrooks. He had a team there from Open Doors. He invited me to have lunch with them. I met one of the Open Doors directors too. Paul was a hero to me. He orchestrated the plan to get one million Bibles into China in one night. They submerged the Bibles under a barge and sailed it to a remote beach near Shanghai, where Christians were waiting to get them. At the right time, they loosed the submerged Bibles in their plastic containers, and they floated on the top of the water, where the waiting Christians could go retrieve them.

After lunch, we met with the main translator, at that time, of the Bible into Mongolian. He was from New Zealand. I got a picture of Paul, and he together. I listened as they planned to get Bibles into the Gobi, which was ruled by hostile Buddhist priests. I could not believe what I was hearing. I was in on plans to smuggle Bibles into a very dangerous area. Paul and his team were staying at a hotel that I did not know about. This information was later used by Abba to help a team come in to give Bibles to every home in Mongolia.

A precious young Mongolian man, Batbaatar, who had been attending the Baptist church and had been born again, was a student in the ELIC program. He came to talk to me. He said his heart was broken. He had become a Christian, but he saw all the different groups that had come into Mongolia--all sparing with one another, no unity, and yet the Buddhists had unity. A lot of the young people wanted to become Christians but because of the fragmentation of the different groups they turned to Buddhism.

The first to come in were the Mormons, then the Evangelical Free Church, the Baptists, then the Charismatic churches of varying types. But, none spoke to each other and each did their own things to advance their own church causes. But, there was South Korean Pastor Hwang and his assistant, Pastor Badamdorj, a Mongolian, who came and started "Orten Geggie." They had no other agenda than to spread the Good News and teach the Word, gathering the people for praise and worship, and prayer. They had a fantastic missionary program. When a person was born again, they would teach them in the Word. They would then take them to their imog, if their family was outside Ulaanbaatar, to speak openly to the entire village of their new birth and about the salvation of Jesus.

I had heard that the owner of our dorm building had been born again. Walking back to the dorm from a Sunday service at Orten Geggie, which means something about light, this man wanted to walk with me. He could speak no English. I knew almost no Mongolian, but he was so excited. He had been to his imog and told them about his new birth. He kept pounding on his heart with his right hand and pointing up to heaven. The joy in that man was incredible.

Sharon had led the maid who cleaned our rooms to salvation. She was glowing with joy. I had my picture taken with her. She gave me a Genghis Kahn pin for my blouse. They were very proud of Genghis Kahn, whom they called "Chengus Hahn." Mary and I attended Orten Geggie. One day the pastor asked me to teach his Bible class, which met one day a week for three weeks. They were studying *Ecclesiastes*. I told him I would. I had forgotten that ELIC was totally against such things. They worked with the Minister of Education and part of the deal was that we did not evangelize. Mary reminded me of the rule. The first meeting fell on the anniversary of my wedding, July 23. I asked Abba if I should go. I saw it as a gift from Him. He reminded me of **Acts 5:27-29**.

The High Priest had ordered that Peter, and some of the other Apostles, be arrested for preaching about the salvation of Messiah Yahushua and thrown into prison. But, in the middle of the night an angel from Yahuweh appeared to them, and unshackled them, and led them out of the prison right in front of the guards. While unshackling Peter, the angel had said: **"Go and stand in the Set-Apart Place and speak to the people all the words of this Life."**

When the High Priest found out that Peter and friends were back preaching, he was livid. How did they get out of prison? "And they brought them and set them before the council and the High Priest asked them `Did we not strictly command you not to speak in this Name? And look, you've filled Jerusalem with your teaching'...And Peter and the other Apostles answering said, `**WE MUST OBEY ELOHM RATHER THAN MEN.**' "

Smuggling Bibles into China is illegal. I broke their law. But, Yahuweh said to spread His Word. Who do I obey: Yahuweh, or the Communists who hate Him and His Word? I am not a law breaker. I am very astute to observe the laws of the lands I live in! But, I am also a citizen of the Kingdom of heaven. Should I obey the laws of man if they conflict with the laws of Yahuweh? NO! The Christians of China do not obey the One-child Law--they do not kill a second baby. So, in obedience to Abba, I put my Bible in my backpack and set off for the meeting area, which was closer to the Dorm than the church. I hoped no one saw me. But, they soon found out because some in the meeting knew I was not supposed to be teaching the Bible, so they told the ELIC staff. I went the second week. But by the third week, there had been action to shut me down. But even then, I taught a few.

Abba always confirms His will! After the second teaching session, the assistant pastor came to talk to me. He said he had a vision for reaching the whole of Mongolia with the Gospel. He shared it with me. My spirit was electrified by his zeal. I told Mary about it. Her reaction was surprising. She about dropped her coffee. She said that she had dinner with Dick Eastman, founder and director of Every Home for Christ, in Colorado Springs. He had said to her: "If you find a contact for us, we want to begin going door to door throughout Mongolia giving the Gospel." This organization went to every home in a nation, giving out the message of salvation, the Bible in their language, and set up meetings for teaching. They had just finished with Nepal and wanted a way to get into Mongolia. She was so excited and so was I. I told her what Abba said about meeting a leader in the country and his opening the whole country up to the Gospel.

When I got back to Texas, I phoned this ministry and talked to one of their directors. He called their associate Enoch Tan in Singapore. Enoch called me. By this time, I had more information. I gave him the name of this assistant pastor, the name of hotels, and places they could work out of. I talked to Mary about a year later, and she said that Every Home for Christ had just finished going to every home in Ulaanbaatar, and were moving on to the imogs.

I did nothing but obey Abba, and in doing that, I had to disobey man. I did not want to rebel against my Father, and He honored that. He knew I'd do it. He knew I'd obey Him. Later on, the lady over our teams in Mongolia gave me a piece of her mind about my sneaking disobedience, but damage to the kingdom of darkness had been done. I remember flying out of Mongolia overwhelmed saying to Him: "You did it, didn't you."

On the first day, when I met my students, I first met Jargal. He hung his head and said he was not good at English. He was about 22, a junior in college studying physics. By the time the course was over, he gave a speech to Japanese physicists in English!

In studying for the finals, they had a speech to write and speak in English under the subject, "If I could have anything I want, I would like…" We did some brain storming and I wrote their ideas on the chalkboard. That wasn't easy – I mean writing on the chalkboard. The Russians had left them with little of any value.

One said: "I want a bunch of flowers." Remember they gave me a bunch of flowers for my birthday. Jargal said: "I want a book of my own." Another said: "I want a bottle of perfume." A young man said: "I want eternal life." A young lady said: "I want to give eternal life to every child." It was this one, Gonchimeg, that I led to salvation. I wasn't supposed to do that either. But, while coaching her on her speech, I wrote on her paper, "eternal life has been bought and paid for, do you want to know more?" She did. I took her outside her dorm room into the hall and we sat by the door of her room, and I led her to salvation. She began attending Orten Geggie.

I remember a Mormon girl that I took there. She came out saying, "I have never heard anyone pray to God like that and expect an answer. It seems like they know God." If you've ever seen South Koreans pray, you'd understand her awe. They "davon" all together like the Orthodox Jews in prayer. They also all pray at the same time. I love that so much! So, as we walked, I was able to speak into her life too. Of course, in all of these reports, I am just giving you highlights.

Jenny and I pulled a ticket sitting next to each other on the way back to Los Angeles. She had been a student at Elim Bible College in New York State. She later went to be a missionary to Kirghizstan. We kept up with each other through the years. I sent her gospel tracts. I kept up with Sarnai for a while. She had gone to Japan for further education, but sadly I lost contact with her. I wish so much I could see my students again. Abba assured me that Amgalan would be saved.

RUSSIA
(SEPTEMBER THROUGH MID-DECEMBER 1999)

In September of 1999, from Jordan, I went to Far East Russia during the winter, to work with Operation Exodus, also called Ebenezer, to bring back Jews to Israel. I was the first American to go to that remote part of Russia with Operation Exodus.

It was a time of one trial after another and one miracle after another. But, as I remember, this trip contained more miracles than any other trip I've ever made, because of all the obstacles that were in my path. His daily leading and the enemy's attacks went one right after the other. The enemy would attack, and Abba's forces would counterattack. [Refer to miracle stories on this trip in the Collections]. My journal of this trip reads like the book of Acts.

At that time, Russian President Yeltson hated America, and was even threatening war. He also hated Jordan, because Jordan was being accused of sending terrorists into Russia. At one point, I was concerned because of the shut down of the Moscow Airport after the terrorist bombing. I kept up with the news in Russia, on my shortwave radio. I actually got Russian news in English each evening.

I had to go to the Russian Embassy in Amman to get my visa for Russia. I had to have an entrance visa and an exit visa. I went with two American friends from Aqaba who wanted to shop in Amman. We stayed overnight. They went to the Russian Embassy with me the next morning. I was so afraid I would not get the visa. But, an old song came to me that I sung over and over: Chorus: "We've come this far by faith, leaning on the Lord. Trusting in His holy Word, He's never failed us yet. Oh, oh, oh, we've come this far, we've come far by faith." Verse: "Don't be discouraged. Think of all the things He's done. Things thought impossible, He has already won." (Repeat Chorus) The only thing that bothered me about this song was the phrase: "He's never failed us YET." That leaves open the chance that He might fail, so I changed the words to: "He'll never fail us, NO!"

When I arrived in the Embassy, I saw a Jordanian in one booth and a Russian in another booth. I did not want to talk to the Russian, so I waited to talk to the Jordanian. The Jordanians are gracious. All went smooth, and I got the visa.

Because of Yeltsin's stance against Jordan and America, when I got to Russia, the woman at Immigration in Moscow saw that I had an American passport with a visa from Jordan, and she started screaming at me in Russian, pounding my passport. Finally she took the big inked stamp and pounded my entry visa into the passport. Then she threw the passport at me. That was my welcome into Russia. Even though I had an exit visa, I was concerned that I might not get out. And as it turned out, I almost didn't.

The Russian Orthodox couple who ran the office for Ebenezer in Khabarovsk were very prejudiced against Americans. It caused me suffering. I had just gotten there. I asked the lady if there was some way to contact my children. She spoke very angrily at me: "This is not America, or even Jordan--this is Russia! You Americans think you can have anything you want." In their eyes, I did one thing wrong after another.

They let me teach on Israel in one of their staff meetings. I taught on the Eastern Gate. But, later I made the horrible mistake of saying that Jesus was born at Yom Teruah, in September or October. How did I know this Greek Orthodox couple had their trip booked for Bethlehem for Christmas? They were going to introduce me to a pastor in town so that I could speak at his church, but after that, they refused to introduce me to any of their friends.

I soon ran into Russian morality, or immorality, and got the man of the couple mad at me. I was lying on my bunk the first night there, trying to go to sleep. The bathroom door opened, a male staff member went in. Then a female staff member went in. They were in there about 20 minutes together. Then they came out together. I told the director about this. He said: "I trust my staff totally!" I kept quiet.

Before going to Russia, Abba had told me that I was to proclaim "Let My People Go" into China, from the Russian border. But, Khabarovsk was at least a 2-hour trip south towards Vladivostok, to the China border. I just left it with Abba. They called me in to give me my assignment and told me they were sending me to Kamchatka – the frozen peninsula northeast, on the Bering Sea towards Alaska. I just left it with Abba. It was His business.

They gave me a translator, Claudia, a Russian Christian, member of the Baptist church, who was fluent in English. At first she did not want to be my translator. They had no one else to go with me, so she finally decided to go with me. She had been a performing ballerina, and was very elegant. As we went into Russia, for the most part, she was the only one who spoke English, so I was dependent on her. But, before they sent us by train to Kamchatka, they brought me in and told me they'd changed their minds. First they wanted to freeze me for 3 months on a frozen peninsula, then they wanted to send me into what they thought was an impossible situation. It appeared they were trying to put this American somewhere to "humble me."

A German woman had come before me and was still in Blagoveshchensk. They were very open in their despising of Susan. They said that because of her, the militia hated them, the Jewish Agency in Blagoveshchensk and Birobidzahn hated them, and the Russian Social Service hated them. So they sent me to Blagoveshchensk. They told me that IF I did any good there that they would return and put an office there again. Blagoveshchensk means: "Good News!"

I learned that other volunteers who had been there before me, and before the German lady, had been lazy and done almost nothing. They paid for two train tickets and sent Claudia and I north. They gave me $2,000.00 for our expenses during the three months. We headed out to the very place Abba told me to go. The whole time I was in Blagoveshchensk I had access to the Amur River that separated Russia from China. I shouted loudly over the river, which soon froze – "Let My People Go!"

Years later, I wrote Prime Minister Ariel Sharon about petitioning the Chinese government to release the Jews. I got a precious letter with a message from him, saying that Israel has been petitioning the Chinese government for years to let the Jews return to Israel. I learned that about 22,000 Jews lived in China between Harbin and that border with Russia – at He Hey (phonetic spelling).

On Thanksgiving Day, 1999, I was with some staff members at a buffet in Blagoveshchensk. One was Chinese. He told me about all the Chinese Jews that came from China to trade in Russia, across the Amur River. I asked him how he could tell the Jews from the regular Chinese people. He said: "They have Chinese eyes but Jewish noses, and they have the Star of David, and don't eat pork." Sounds like they guarded Torah!

I spent three months in hard conditions in the dead of winter with one obstacle after another, mostly from the main office wanting me to go home. The temperature dropped to 30 below Fahrenheit at night, with snow and ice. By morning the roads had been cleared. The days were sunny, clear and lovely. Like I have said, from my 20s He taught me to command weather conditions so that His work would not be obstructed. So, I told Claudia right up front that every day while I was there it would be sunny and clear. She thought that was ridiculous. She lived in Far East Russia. Every morning for three months, I got up and would say to her: "Another beautiful day!" She got so mad at me. You can see my pictures – clear skies, sunny, with snow deep on the ground. By Abba's mo'edim, I overcame all obstacles, and accomplished so much--including everything they told me I would probably not accomplish--that they hated me all the more.

At the end of the three months I returned to Khabarovsk with some money left over. I submitted loads of lovely pictures and incredible reports from Jews wanting to go to Israel, and stories of miracles. From all evidence, I don't think they sent the pictures or stories to the main office in England. I never heard from them again.

Ebenezer had an office in Bournemouth, England. It was through this office that I applied and was sent to Far East Russia. They had an intercession group that prayed for those in different parts of Russia who were helping Jews to return to Israel. Because of things that happened to me, at least twice, damaging my knee and getting arrested (Claudia told the main office about what happened to me) the intercessors told me to come out, and go home.

I asked Abba about it, and my new friend – the German lady (Susan) – and I, prayed about it and He said: "STAY." I know why they didn't like the German lady. Perhaps for the same reason the leaders of ELIC in Mongolia didn't like me. Susan followed the leading of the Spirit! I told them I'd stay, and they were NOT happy. But if Abba gives me an assignment, I'm going to finish it!

Later, when I went to Wales the second time, I was once again asked to speak at the Rees Howell's Bible College of Wales in Swansea, at their prayer meeting for Israel. They had invited a lady to lead the singing and make a report on Ebenezer. Guess who that was? You're right! The same lady who ordered me out of Russia, who wished I'd shut up.

When we got to Blagoveshchensk, we had to register with the militia. How did I know I wasn't supposed to leave Blagoveshchensk without their permission? We rented space from a lovely Christian lady named Svetlana who had a downstairs apartment. She had a very respectful 11-year old son named Jenya. The apartment had two bedrooms. She stayed in one, the other one was occupied by two college students, and we stayed in the living room on couch pullout beds. There was a long hall, a bathroom at the end of it, and a tiny kitchen. Within about three days, the police came to visit. They'd been told by our neighbors that two strange people were staying in that apartment. They checked us out and left. Talk about throw backs from World War I and II!

One day one of the college students came back all bruised and bloodied from being beaten by a gang. That is such a huge problem in Russia – so many gangs, so much prostitution, so much violence. Children in orphanages are released when they are 16 years of age, and so many of them turn to prostitution and violence to survive.

PART V - Training Assignments

It was 30 below zero at night, at least. Our space had large windows that faced outside. It was also the meeting room for Jews who came to us for help in returning to Israel. Twice a week the milk truck pulled up and sold milk and other dairy products across the snow and ice from us. Claudia and I loved fresh air. At night we opened the window a little, and snuggled under layers of blankets and thick "comforters." Far East Russia is old Russia--but then, what wasn't old Russia! On our street, besides tall apartment buildings, were quaint little wooden houses that had no indoor plumbing.

In all my travels, the only farm equipment I saw looked like the 1940s. The cars were old; the stores had few products on the shelves – typical Russia. I bought a small clock – I had three choices. I have it to this day – it was German-made. How Russia got to be one of the five permanent members of the U.N. Security Council, along with Communist China, is a marvel to me. About 40% of Russia's economy goes into weapons of war.

I visited a retired teacher in her apartment near ours. She made about $12.00 a month while working, and upon retiring she also got $12.00 a month pension. She and her mother lived on the top floor of their building. On the landing just below their apartment was spray painted on the wall: "Death to Jews." The rise of the Nazi movement had begun seriously in Siberia, and spread to the Far East. Her mother was mischievous—a little white-haired lady. She had a cute little dog that laid on the couch under newspapers. She showed me pictures of her famous author-son, and told stories of the persecution of Jews in that area. When we got ready to leave, she pushed the coffee table against our legs so we couldn't move. She did not want us to leave. I had to use diplomacy. She told us to come back.

I visited another man close by who asked me what Israel was going to do for them, and if it was worth his time going there. I found out that most Russians were so used to the Communist government doing everything for them, that many were spoiled. So, they expected the government of Israel to do the same for them.

While walking along the river one day, I talked to a young Jewish man. He was a doctor--a specialist in treating asthma and other respiratory diseases. He said he made about $25.00 a month working in a hospital. He said he did not understand why his country treated its citizens so poorly. It was into the Far East that Stalin sent the Jews to the "gulags." Many stayed in that area, or were sent to Kamchatka to the east. Some had heard that Israel had become a nation, but knew no way of returning there. I was able to help many. But, the obstacles grew and so did the power of Yahuweh!

We ate well! Svetlana kept us full of soup and Russian black bread, which we covered in butter and fresh garlic. She grated baked tofu, and added carrots and lots of garlic. Garlic is called "Russian penicillin." No one got sick! I remember all the canned pickled vegetables, relishes of all types, and jams too. I remember Claudia putting jam in hot water to make "tea." Oh a breakfast of buttered black bread and two to three cloves of garlic on the top. It is true, a lot of Russians smell like garlic and Vodka. It makes it hard when you're on the airplane, however.

I flew to Russia on Aeroflot. A young man in Aqaba who had flown on Aeroflot told me about Uzbekistan Air. He said the plane shook so bad that the oxygen masks fell out as they were taxiing down the runway. Aeroflot didn't do that, but the seat in front of me broke and the man fell in my lap. I remember the dogs and birds on board too. From Moscow, there are eleven time zones we had to go through before we got to Khabarovsk. Wait till you hear the story of my plane ride out.

Claudia and I put advertisements in the newspaper and on the radio with the phone number of our hostess. The phone was in the hallway. It rang all during the day and into the night while we were there. We got lots of phone calls – some from Russians who wanted to move to Israel but they were not Jewish. I remember one morning, getting up and staggering to the bathroom near the front door, about 7:00 AM, and there was a Jewish family waiting for me to help them get to Israel.

For a short time, Susan stayed with us in the living room on another pullout couch. She snored loudly. But, as far as I could tell, that was her only fault, and I had good earplugs. Susan's translator also stayed with us--Nadia. Not long after we got there, the four of us decided to walk down to the river. I felt Abba warning me not to go, but I was bored and wanted to investigate my area, so I dismissed the warning. **NEVER DISMISS ABBA'S WARNINGS**! When we got to the river, I went along the bank by myself. I looked down at the raging water, which would soon be frozen, and said quietly, under my breath: "Wow that thing is powerful." Just like I mumbled when in Trier, the demons heard me. My left knee immediately not only twisted out of place, but stayed out of place a few seconds – long enough to tear the ligaments very badly. The others came to my rescue and hailed a taxi to get me back to the apartment. I put ice on it and wrapped it. Claudia got me a cane with a spike device that could be released by pushing a button on the cane. The spike went into snow and ice, and kept me from falling. I learned later that the

Chinese called the river "the Black River." The year before, 1998, in Tanzania, Africa, Valerie and I had gone into a very remote area of the north Serengeti Plain, where they sacrificed goats to the "black river god."

The Amur joined the Zeya River. Both rivers froze over. Police were stationed on the ice to keep Chinese from sneaking across the river into Russia. People sat out on the river in chairs doing ice fishing. I asked Father what to do, and He told me to stay. Slowly but surely, I was able to go out and visit Jewish people in their homes. At times I would have to walk up to the 7th floor of apartment buildings because the "lifts" were so unreliable. For the most part, Abba brought the people to me. The work went on every day! The German lady told me that a young man had been there before her, and had only visited a few people in three months. Susan was a high producer. I am a high producer – and by obeying Abba one is always a high producer.

I began attending a very large evangelical church in Blagoveshchensk. Pastor Anatoly of Good News Church let me preach every Sunday I was there. There were hundreds in the congregation. I taught on being led by the Spirit. The pastor said he'd never met anyone who had such a life as me, following the Spirit. I told one story after another of His miracles.

I was invited to visit the Russian Social Service early on, even before the knee injury. They warmly welcomed Claudia and I, and gave us a special book about the city. I made friends with the Social Service. They invited us to attend their yearly luncheon of Russians who had survived the Russian holocaust under Stalin, some were Jews. Some of these Jews had survived not only the Holocaust in Germany, but once back in Russia, they were imprisoned on charges of being German spies, and put to hard labor in a Russian holocaust. Susan got up and talked to them in a wonderful speech of repentance for what Germany did to the Jews. That was on October 20, 1999 – my third child's birthday.

Then the Jewish Agency in Blagoveshchensk invited us to come. I attended an Ulpan class (Hebrew language class). Students were learning Hebrew so that they could return to Israel. Susan got up and gave a speech that astounded them--repenting for Germany's treatment of the Jews. Students came up afterwards to thank us. Some were wondering why we cared so much for them. So, I made friends with the Jewish Agency. "Two down and one to go"--and all in less than a month! They were not happy with me back in Khabarovsk. I was doing what they said I probably would never do. I have favor with Elohim and man – isn't that typical for His servants! It is a gift from Elohim!

I met another ministry there. They let us use their office facilities. They were not too far from where we were staying, but out in the country. Every week we went there to their little office, to use their computer and fax the couple in Khabarovsk about our progress. It was there, too, that I was able to communicate with my children!

I was invited by an Elementary School Principal to come speak to their English class. The class was for 10-12 year olds. They were very respectful. After the class, they stayed around and asked questions about America. Their teacher and the Principal also stayed to ask questions. I felt there was something "different" about the Principal. The next Sunday at the church there she was - leading the congregation in worship. She became a fine friend!

I met a young girl named Lena who attended Good News Church. She had taught in China. She spoke fluent Chinese. Because I had taken Bibles into China, she confided in me that there were teams from the church who took Bibles into China. However, I found out that they took them to the Three Self Church groups. I warned them about that, since there was so much deception in the government church, and perhaps they were spies.

I found out from this young girl that members of the persecuted assemblies in that area of Northeast China were coming across the border with the other Chinese, and meeting in a warehouse on a back street not far from where I was staying. She took me there. I met with Chinese and Mongolian-looking believers. They were so filled with joy. My friend translated while I spoke a little, then also translated while they taught from a copy of the Bible. I have never attended a secret meeting of the underground church, or heard what they taught. But, in this meeting it was all about loving those who persecuted them, praying for their salvation, and diligently sharing with them the message of salvation. I have pictures of them in that warehouse. I went there about three times.

Ebenezer gave me a Xeroxed copy of a very thick book from the Ministry of the Interior in Israel, with instructions for Jews wanting to return to Israel – telling them what Israel will do to help them. I read through it, and when I got to the very middle, there, separated from the material before it and after it, was one paragraph by itself. It said that within six months of getting to Israel, they were required to get a gas mask. I laughed out loud! After being told all the things Israel would do to help them, there in the middle if it were instructions in case of war. Welcome to your new home--get a gas mask!

PART V - Training Assignments

Some young Russian Jewish soldiers came to talk to me. They said they thought that the State of Israel was being used by the evil leaders of the international community to draw Jews into one place, so that they could kill them easily. They said that no country in the world would do for them like what Israel was saying they'd do. Israel was making it too easy. I tried to tell them otherwise, but they got mad and left. But you know what? – That scenario has been the plan since at least 1871. Communism, Fascism (Nazis), and the Holocaust, was planned, funded, and directed, principally by government and financial leaders of America, by U.S. Corporation bosses, by England, and the Vatican. The plan was to bring about Part II of the Mazzini/Pike Plan-- to force Jews to want a State of their own. Once in a country of their own, Part III of the Mazzini/Pike Plan would be executed--to pit Arab Muslims and Jews against each other, to wipe each other out, with Russia, China, North Korea, and America, assisting with weapons. This is so that enough chaos would be created that the world's people would cry for a New World Order and one to govern it. Their plan is working isn't it? [Refer to: "Launching the Chaos"/February 2011]

I felt like I'd done all I could around Blagoveshchensk, so we got a driver to take us south to a little village area near a town named after Emperor Constantine--Constantenovka. On the way we met with other Jewish families, one with four generations of Jews, and began helping them to return to Israel.

Ebenezer is a screening organization. They locate Jews who want to return to Israel, give them information, and send them to the Jewish Agency, giving financial help if needed. Many Jews had a problem because they were baptized as infants into the Russian Orthodox Church, or their parents had been to save their lives. Some wore crosses. The only document one girl had was her grandfather's baptismal certificate, saying he was Jewish. They denied her right to make aliyah. I tried to counsel them about it. I told them to tell the Agency they had no religion, or to put that they believed in the God of Abraham, Isaac and Jacob. But, they thought they had a right to proclaim their Christianity to the Agency.

The Jewish Agency at Birobidzahn said that no matter how it happened, if a person was baptized into the Russian Orthodox Church, or belonged to any Christian church, they could not make aliyah to Israel because they had forfeited their Jewishness. That hurt a lot of Jewish people. Making aliyah should be only on the basis of family record for Jews and Levites. But, the Agency let secular Jews, or Buddhist Jews (like Ben Gurion), etc., make aliyah--just as long as they were not Christian or Messianic Jews.

Ebenezer helps them with money for the train to take them for their visit to the Jewish Agency in Birobidzahn. That Agency was the screening agency for the Far East. It was/is a Jewish center.

In 2005, I met a Jewish man in Tiberias who was a believer. He told me that the agency in Birobidzahn was the one that helped him get to Israel. If a person has the required documents proving they are Jewish, the Agency flies them to Israel free – a one way trip! In order to leave, they had to get rid of all their possessions, except for one suitcase per person.

On our journey south, towards Constantenovka, we stopped in Tamboofka at the home of a family with three generations who wanted to return to Israel, and helped them. Before getting to Constantenovka, we stopped near the Russia/China border. The river separating China from Russia in that area was also frozen. I had the driver stop. I got out and took pictures through the fence on the border. How did I know I was caught on camera?

I met Pastor Victor Maimontov and his wife, Lena, in that area. I never thought anything about his last name. But, since 2007, I've stayed in Israel near the tomb of Maimonides- Rambam – the greatest of the Jewish sages. Of course "tov" in Hebrew is "good." I've got pictures of him – yes, he looks Jewish. Victor invited me to speak at their church. I spoke on the Covenants that God made with Abraham. They were young, maybe mid-20s, and had zeal. They knew how to worship! Victor took me to the "daucha" of a fine Russian family. A "daucha" is a farm out in the country, and/or a summer home. This family attended their church. At that time, it was a farm covered in snow. They raised big pigs too. I remember their little kitchen – with the wood fire stove. Their two cats would sleep on the oven door for warmth. Yes, I have pictures of that too. Victor played the guitar and sang, and so did Alexey, the man of the house. It was so wonderful being with them. We visited several homes of Jewish people who lived out in the country, to tell them about our help to get them to Israel.

Then we got word that the police were looking for me. So Victor took me in his old car into town to the police station. He stayed with me and prayed while they told me that I had broken two laws and was arrested, facing a huge fine and imprisonment. Victor prayed; I cried. I told them I had no idea I had broken a border law in taking pictures at the Chinese border, or that I had broken a militia law by leaving Blagoveshchensk without their permission. I pleaded on the grounds that I was an ignorant American, which was true! They took my case to the police chief who was in his office somewhere in the building. They came back and told me he had granted me pardon, and that I had to return to Blagoveshchensk immediately. I thanked them profusely and went back to get my things. Victor took us a long way north to our apartment.

The next morning I went to the border police headquarters. The man was so nice! He apologized for having me pay a fine – it was such a small fine. He sent me to the militia. The militia was kind too, but they explained the law to me. I told them that I had to go north. They said to come back. I kept going back and they kept telling me that no decision on my case had been finalized. I was getting discouraged. Abba had told me to go to Svobodny, located north of Blagoveshchensk, and Tambooffka which was to the south. These were areas where Stalin had sent Jews to the gulags. It was a frozen area for sure!

One morning, I was continuing my reading of *Jeremiah*. I read the words that Nebuzaradan, Nebuchadnezzar's military Captain, said to Jeremiah when he loosed him to go free after the burning of Jerusalem. **Jeremiah 40:4**: "**AND NOW TODAY I LOOSE YOU FROM THE CHAINS THAT WERE ON YOUR HAND**. IF IT SEEMS GOOD FOR YOU TO COME WITH ME TO BABYLON, COME AND I WILL LOOK AFTER YOU. BUT IF IT SEEMS WRONG FOR YOU TO COME WITH ME TO BABYLON REMAIN HERE. **SEE! ALL THE LAND IS BEFORE YOU. GO WHEREVER IT SEEMS GOOD AND RIGHT FOR YOU**." The words in red jumped out at me. Abba spoke audibly to me: "**As Nebuzaradan did to Jeremiah, so the militia will do to you. Go to the militia NOW!**" I told Claudia to get a taxi quick. It was about 10:00 AM. When we walked into that familiar office area at the militia headquarters, a man came out with a smile, and handed me a piece of paper written in ink, in Russian. He told me that he had listed all the towns that I told him I wanted to visit, and then added that I had the right to go anywhere I wanted to go! I made friends with the militia. I did all three things that they told me at the home office in Khabarovsk that I probably would not do. I still have that paper today and a picture of me holding it, too.

Now to tell you about their starting an office in Blagoveshchensk! Abba is so wonderful! There was one family in particular that I worked with to go to Israel – a husband and wife and daughter. I got very close to this family, but after leaving Russia I did not hear from them. I helped them get to the Agency, coached them, saw them through selling their things, and encouraged them. I have a picture of their daughter looking at the Israel picture book that I brought with me. All she could say over and over with each picture was: "Israel, Israel."

The Ebenezer directors in Khabarovsk sent two of their men to join us, and work with a local pastor, to take us to the north. Claudia bragged all the way up there about what she did, and nothing was mentioned of the miracles that Abba did. We stopped by a large frozen river. Claudia took my picture. I walked with a cane, but I made it up the snowy hill to see the river below. These men took Claudia and I to Svobodny. It was an old mining town, a former gulag, and there were many Jews still there. One of the two men who were with us, knew the local pastor in that area. As we entered Svobodny, he directed us to the church – New Generation Church. Wouldn't you know it! They were having a meeting in the church and a luncheon, and we were hungry. The Pastor, Constantine Ostapchook, and his wife, Tamara, had come from Latvia to take over a church there. They were a newly married young couple. He loved it there; his wife did not.

They were just fixing the buffet lunch when we arrived. They warmly welcomed us. I ate so much. I sat next to this nice young man who was asking me questions about Ebenezer. I asked him who the pastor was because we needed a place to stay. He said: "I am the pastor." He introduced us to a lovely lady, Luda, who had a nice apartment that we could stay in.

Then he said: "There was a woman from Svobodny who used to work with Ebenezer, but her unsaved husband got another job in a remote village a long way away, and they did not know what had become of her." Ula Semenkena was her name. The pastor said that she had many lists of contacts with Jews who wanted to go to Israel in that area. I told him I had to talk to her.

Our hostess, Luda, was a lovely lady. It was late December and she let me use her phone to call my son in Texas to wish him Happy Birthday a few days early. After wishing him Happy Birthday, he told me that John had died. John was the Director of my orphanage in Kisumu, Kenya. What a sad blow. He was in his 30s. He died of cerebral meningitis. He left a wife, lots of orphans, an elementary school named after me, and a church.

In Russia it is tradition to eat a lot of raw pork fat during the winter to stay warm. Our hostess made us fine meals, but this afternoon she put out a plate of pork fat. Then she went back into the kitchen to finish serving our lunch. Claudia started eating it like it was candy. She offered me some. I told her that the Word said for us not to eat pork. She said that the Russian doctors said it was good for them in winter. I asked her how she could violate the Word so easily. And then I saw it – her eyes, which were dark green, turned bright green. She stared at me with a mocking grin on her face, and started eating more pork fat. I knew I was looking at a demon. Here I was in a remote village in Russia with one translator, one person anywhere that spoke English, and she was demonized.

Pastor Constantine asked me to speak in his church. I preached there two or three times. There was a man there who was from Uzbekistan, who had just been born again. He was like a little child in his enthusiasm. He came over that first evening to bring me a wooden carved dog, about seven inches tall. It was cute – a terrier dog. One ear was up and the other was down. One ear had red coloring on the inside of it. I asked him what that was and he said it was blood. He had wiped his cut finger on his ear. He said that Kazak had been in a fight (teasing of course) He said: "It is time for Kazak to go to Jordan." So he gave Kasak to me. Kazak was the name of a high mountain in Uzbekistan close to Kazakhstan. Then we talked about his new birth for a few minutes. He gave me a big soupy kiss on the cheek and went home. Maybe you think that is not "normal"--but it is normal for Russia (smile).

In Middle School in California, there were two tall blond Russian girls who came from Russia to live in America with their parents. The other students avoided them, saying they were stupid. They had heavy Russian accents, and did not yet relate to American culture. They also had the Russian "morality" attitudes, and dressed accordingly, even back in the mid-1950s. But, because the other students were cruel to them, I befriended them and we became good friends. Maybe what I sowed I reaped when I went to Russia.

In the early 1950s a man came from Russia to our church in La Habra. He told the plan of Khrushchev's Russia for the takeover of America. He said that Russia would take over America from the inside by bringing in the "mini skirt", the "bikini" and other immoral types of dress. This would cause the American people to be so filled with sexual lust, that they would become weak, allowing the Russians to overtake them. Today I see that Khrushchev's plan has worked. Even "good" women dress like prostitutes and dress their daughters like prostitutes--it is called FASHION!

Right now, there are about 100,000 Russian troops stationed in America with one goal – takeover. There are Russian subs with nuclear capabilities in the Gulf of Mexico, and off the east coast. There are Russian fighter planes off the east coast and ground soldiers within. They are on all borders – the Alaska border, the sea borders, and the Mexican border.

Our sweet hostess worked in an office. She asked one of the drivers if he would take us in the direction where Ula moved to. He agreed. Early the next morning we met him. He started driving north. We knew the village that Ula lived in was named Sereviancha, meaning "little silver village," but the driver did not know which village it was along that road. Now the miraculous hand of Elohim is shown more than ever! We drove through a snowy forest on a two lane road that had been cleared of snow the night before. I saw a village on the right. I asked him to stop there. He drove across a wooden bridge and I told him to stop at the first house. I would go and see if anyone knew her. I knocked on the door. A lady answered. I said: "I am with Ebenezer and am looking for a woman named Ula." It took her a split second to start screaming. She told me to come in, so I motioned for the others to come in too.

It was Ula. She said that morning she had prayed that if someone came from Ebenezer she would ask her husband if she could get back in the work of helping Jews. She called her husband and asked if she could go with us to Blagoveshchensk. He said she could go. We went back and Ula brought all of her lists. The next morning we headed out. She took us to many homes of Jews who wanted to return to Israel. One old lady and her husband had been through both the German Holocaust, and Stalin's Holocaust. Another, very high class lady, had a daughter who had already made aliyah, and she and her crippled daughter wanted to go too. Ula's husband gave his approval for her to get back into the work. It was so amazing meeting all those people. Ula turned her lists over to the man from the Khabarovsk office, and she was able to get back in the work. The Jewish people loved her.

Then we went on to a village further north. I was just being led by the Spirit because I only had one name of a lady in that village that was from an old list Ula had. I asked around and someone directed me to a business where they thought she worked. Yes, she worked there but had gone to lunch. They directed me to where she was having lunch. I sat down with her and told her about Israel. She began to cry. She said that she and her sons HAD HEARD that a state of Israel for Jewish people had been established. She did not know if she had a right to go there. They wanted to go there but had no one who had any information to help them. I started them on their journey.

We had been using the same taxi driver that we met about ½-way through our three-month stay. He was a married man, but Claudia ended up having an affair with him. She had gone through a very sad divorce recently and was very lonely. She told me her husband had been cruel to her; she felt justified in having the affair. Oh the twisting of the mind to make excuses for what we want to do anyway... If anybody should understand her reasoning, I should. But, I was hard on her because I knew the backlash from having affairs!

This taxi driver took us back to Khabarovsk through the frozen countryside. I think it took about eight hours. We hardly saw anyone all the way back. When I got back I turned in the remaining money. It was late December, and the directors were in Bethlehem. I left a whole album of pictures with stories on each one of the Jews we worked with – which was a lot of them! I had diligently worked on it, and it was lovely. The ministry usually published reports in their monthly magazine from reports of volunteers, but nothing I shared was ever reported, that I knew of.

My last night there, I was given the couch in the staff's dormitory living room to sleep on. One of the staff came in and asked if he could sleep on the couch across the room from me. By this time, I was so upset by Russian looseness that I just blasted him to get out. On my way to the airport the next day, I was asked if Ebenezer did anything to hurt me. I couldn't speak. I just shook my head "no." The organization did nothing to hurt me, nor their helpers, but the attitude of the Russian Orthodox couple in Khabarovsk, and the intercessors in England, had really hurt me.

Yet, I did everything that Abba told me to do. Mission accomplished! I left there with a heavy heart. Claudia and I said "goodbye" to each other, each with a heavy heart. Abba spoke to me: **"This is the last time you will ever have to work under a man-controlled ministry.**" What awesome words!

AFRICA
KENYA/UGANDA
(1996-2001)
TANZANIA
(1997-1999)

1996 was like being shot out of a canon. It was my door-to-freedom year. As I stated above, I had to flee from my husband, who pretended to try to kill me, in February of 1996. In April of 1996, I took my daughter-in-law and young grandson to a Voice of the Martyrs Conference in California. I drove all the way from Fort Worth, Texas, to California. The Conference was held in an area close to where I grew up. So, after it ended, I took them on a tour of the coastal areas between Capistrano and Laguna Beach. We went to Balboa Island--also a favorite place of mine. I even showed her my old stomping grounds – Huntington Beach. The pier was still there, and a lovely 1950s-type burger bar was at the end of it, where we had lunch. The Conference was wonderful! I heard speakers from all over the world. I met others who had smuggled Bibles with "Open Doors with Brother Andrew," and we had fine fellowship. We heard speakers who had been smuggled out of their countries to testify of the horrendous human rights violations there, imprisoning and killing of believers. From June through August, I was with the English Language Institute in Mongolia, as I tell about above.

In October, Abba opened the door for me to go on my dream trip to Switzerland. I had waited for that trip since I was seven, and played "Heidi." It was marvelous. I even got to see the Heidi memorial monument at the base of the hill to "grandfather's house." Later, I even bought that wonderful black-and-white version of the movie *Heidi*, which was made in Europe about 1950--the one I watched seven times in one week on our 19-inch TV. I flew out of Switzerland to America over the Alps. Two weeks later, November 1996, I was flying to Nairobi, Kenya, and flew over the Alps again.

Now I will cover my seven times to Africa 1996-2001, even though I went the last three times from Jordan--1999-2001. While at Emanuel Christian Fellowship in Fort Worth, during 1995, my husband and I met a missionary, Ruth Potter, from Canada, who ministered in east Africa. Her headquarters was Kisumu, Kenya, on Lake Victoria. We attended her meetings in her home, and she invited us to join her in Africa. After our separation in February of 1996, I felt led by the Spirit to take her up on her offer. So in early 1996, I began planning my trip to Kenya. I became an insider in her inner circle. I did not know that it was because I had my mother's inheritance, and she wanted some of it. I have since

PART V - Training Assignments

lost naivety, and learned to be "wise as a serpent and harmless as a dove."

I did not know that she was like so many others I would come into contact with who fain large and productive ministries in poor countries, yet they either had no ministry, it was miniscule, or they claimed to be part of someone else's ministry. I watched this very devious phenomenon with other women, and men, but by the time I figured it out, I always had suffered a lot from their manipulative jezebel spirits. Ruth had incredible ideas for orphanages, hospitals, and schools, for the poor. She sought out wealthy people to share her goals with, who gave her money for the projects, which went into her pocket. Her home was elaborate, her car, her clothes, and her ability to go where she willed, and eat at expensive restaurants.

Her one "orphanage" was run by a negligent man who had a few children, but who did not care for them properly. She had no schools, hospitals, clinics, or anything else. She would come to Kenya, spend three weeks to a month at the most, then return to the U.S. or Canada with all sorts of stories about things she was doing. She also had connections with some of the most devious and deceitful Christian and political leaders in Kenya. They were after the same thing – money. But, I was still naïve at that point regarding Christians and missionaries.

I arrived in Nairobi in the evening. It was late October. I was by myself, so I paid a large fee to stay at the Sheridan. Despite the roaches running around in the bathroom, I slept well. The next morning, I flew to Kisumu on Kenya Air (good airline). Ruth's maid, Rose, picked me up. Ruth was not there. From the first day, my suffering began, which only grew worse.

Darlene was the Leader of Women's Aglow for all of Connecticut. She applied to go stay with Ruth at the same time as me. She had corresponded with me a little beforehand. She got there a week earlier than I did. She later told me she got there early because she was afraid of my "Word-level." Later she admitted to being jealous of my "Word-level" and feared that I would take all the good speaking engagements and leave her left out. She was a charismatic-style preacher. She picked out all the best meetings for herself, and left me with only the Bible College. She had made sure that the pastors knew of her preaching abilities. So, I began teaching in Andrew Wommack's Charis Bible College. I had a fine class of pastors and other church leaders. I taught the Tenach mainly. There had been drought in that area of Kenya for months. We joined together to pray for rain. The next day it rained and rained for days. The news said that nowhere else in all of Kenya did they have rain, but in the Kisumu area. We rejoiced.

In this class was Vincent Wanyonyi Wabuke, Godfrey, and John Aloss. Godfrey became like a son. I worked with his ministry some, until I found out in later years, that he was a lackey of Ruth's, and out for money that was gained in very devious and deceitful ways. That broke my heart.

John Aloss was a pastor. He and his wife Margaret had started a small orphanage, gathering children in two rented rooms, with one kitchen the size of a closet. There were two bedrooms, each also the size of a closet. He put down mats on the floor--one room was for the girls and one was for the boys. The morality among believers in Africa, for the most part, was opposite of the Russian mentality. Girls and boys did not hold hands until after marriage, and then never in public. This was also the cultural understanding in China and Mongolia.

John and Margaret had rented a building in Kisumu with several rooms for their church. They also started an elementary school of about 80 students, which met in that building during the week. I worked with them in 1997 to get their own facility that could be used for the orphanage, the school, and the church.

Then there was dear Vincent. He became my African Director for five of my seven trips to Africa. He took me to Uganda. I introduced him to Tanzania. His wife Lydia and their four children, Dorcus, Lucus, Peres, and Betty were like family to me. Later Lydia gave birth to a daughter they called " Shalom." The other pastors and their families that worked with Vincent also became like family.

Vincent worked with the Water Department of Kenya as a micro-biologist. He was also a wonderful pastor and family man. He was from Bungoma north of Kisumu--quite a long distance. But, he was attending the Bible College while working in Kisumu. He had come to Kisumu to work with his colleagues to find what was in the water of Lake Victoria that was causing so much disease. At the other end of the lake were a lot of dead bodies from Burundi floating in the water. I will tell that story later of how I got involved with Burundi and Rwanda, through Pastor Simeon. The diseases came from that.

There was always some humor to lighten things up. I loved working with the African people. I remember before going to the college one morning, I opened the pantry door to get some breakfast food, and I looked down and there was a chicken in a box on the floor. I talked to the chicken, asking it what it was doing there. It clucked. I love animals! It reminded me of Henrietta, my pet chicken. Nicholas, our cook, said the chicken was for lunch. I told him I never ate what I had talked to. I got back from the college and there was the chicken all golden brown – just out of the oven. I did not eat it.

I met the local pastor, Mark Kegohi, and his wife, Joyce, who had the largest church in Kisumu. What a delightful man--I loved his preaching. He asked me to preach in one of their open-air meetings in a park one afternoon. I preached on the coming of Messiah. People came up to be prayed for, to find forgiveness of sin and eternal life. But, while waiting for the meeting to start, I walked around behind the people, who were sitting on the grass, taking pictures of them from the back, as they faced the area where the microphones and podium had been set up. When I got the pictures back, I saw that in all the pictures taken facing the podium, there were four large pillars of fire – about 8 feet high. I took the pictures from all different angles. There were trees behind the podium, and there was no sunlight coming into my lens. In each picture the fiery pillars were identical. I believe they were Abba's angels. **Psalm 104:4**: "Making His messengers the winds, His angels a flame of fire."

I went out to mud huts in areas around Kisumu to teach women. Of course Darlene had picked that too, so she was the principle speaker. I remember the hugs, and the two-cheek kisses. I love that about the African women--they love to hug, and then they giggle. But, other than that, during the three weeks I was there, I taught in the Bible College, while Darlene preached all the other meetings in true demonstrative charismatic style, which played on everyone's emotions. As I shared with Darlene about what was happening in the Bible College, and about the men I had met, I saw dark spirits moving across her eyes. Periodically she would become violent in her yelling at me, saying I was crazy. When my students came to visit me, she would take over my conversation with them. She would try to discredit me, even lying about me to them while I sat there listening. However, my students were loyal to me. She organized a Pastor's conference in Ruth's house, gathering all the local pastors, with Mark Kegohi as the principle leader. She had a day-meeting with many pastors there. But, overall it was a total flop. I cried most of the three weeks I was there. One evening before going to bed, I remembered that I needed to tell Darlene something. Her door was partially open, so I called her name, and then went into her room. There she was with Rose, all cuddled together in the bed, Rose rubbing her back. I was shocked. Rose later said she was in love with Darlene. I am not accusing them of anything, but they acted like lesbians.

John and Margaret invited me to see their little orphanage, in two little tiny rooms. I knew I had to help them. In early 1997, I sent them a large package with lots of clothes and toys for the children. They sent me a picture of them with the children holding their toys, and of the boxes of clothes. I have that precious picture today. That was the beginning of a long and productive relationship.

Joyce Kegohi arranged for both Darlene and I to both speak at the Redeemed Gospel Church's Women's Conference, held November 16, 1996. It drew women from many congregations in the whole region. We each ministered to individuals afterwards, too. It was a powerful conference – attended by many women.

We packed so much into those three weeks. Near the end of our time there, Ruth had arranged for us to go to visit Julius Osilo and family in Mbale, Uganda. Though plans changed, we still went into Uganda for two to three days to stay with Julius and Grace Osilo, and their family. What a lovely family!

Julius was a business man, as well as a Bible teacher and pastor. Grace had her own shop in the local market selling cloth to the Masai tribe--those tall warriors from the Serengeti Plain of Kenya. I met some of them in Jerusalem at the Christian Embassy during Sukkot. The men stood way over 7' tall, wearing their traditional Masai clothing. They were joyfully born again, Spirit-filled, and loving Abba. I got to talk to some of the women later. They invited me to come teach them. I have my suspicions—"Masai" is very close in sound to "Messiah." Are they more of the House of Ephraim/Joseph/Israel? Maybe! They love Israel. I still have a lovely bright lap blanket of hand-woven wool, woven by the Masai that I bought from Grace's shop.

Julius and Grace took care of 35 orphans besides their own children. I also met Grace's mother--what a lovely lady. We stayed at their large house outside of Mbale. I remember one of their sons, who was in the 5th grade, was doing his homework. He told me he wanted to be a doctor. Their children worked so hard at studies, and had such high aspirations for their lives.

Darlene and I both were to speak the next morning at Julius' church. I could not sleep. The jezebel spirits were so bad that I was tormented by demons all night. After midnight, I saw Darlene get up and go into the living room. I went to find out what she was doing. She was talking to Julius. I sat down and listened. Darlene told him that she taught pastors, and wanted to gather his pastor-friends from Mbale, and teach them. Julius said he'd think about it, but I'm sure he was savvy to her deviousness. That meeting never happened, but I sure was angry at her deviousness.

The next morning we went to the church. Darlene spoke first. I was exhausted. I could hardly stand up. How was I going to preach? Their lively singing helped. But, then it was time for me to preach. I was going to preach about the children of Israel crossing the Red Sea and their freedom from Pharaoh--a type of Satan—comparing their deliverance with Messiah's resurrection, and our delivery from Satan. I got to the microphone. But, before saying a word, the power of the Spirit came down on me to strengthen me. He gave me a prophecy for them, and for the nation of Uganda. It had not been too many years since Idi Amin had come to destroy Uganda – bullet holes were still in downtown buildings in Kampala. There were some at this meeting who had suffered from his tyranny.

As I gave the prophecy, the anointing power of the Spirit of Yahuweh was so strong that I felt like I was lifted off the ground. The interpreter became electrified. He was terrific! He stayed right with me. I preached; the people jumped and shouted in joy. They were right with me. Because Yahuweh's Word is in my spirit, when under such an anointing I never have to think about what Scriptures to use – they just come flowing out of my mouth.

When I was through, I felt like a limp dish rag. I walked over to where Darlene and Rose were standing. Darlene looked at me and said that she and Rose were wondering how I knew so much Scripture. Isn't that ridiculous! I spent most of my life learning the Scriptures. She was NOT happy with me. The next day, we got on the bus to Kisumu, and then we went our separate ways. That ended my exciting 1996.

RETURN TO EAST AFRICA
(MARCH 1997)

In February, I received a wonderful letter from Julius telling me that he would take me all over Uganda from one end to the other. He said that Jesus was coming back soon, and we had to reach as many souls as possible for His Kingdom. Talk about precious! The man's heart was on fire with passion to spread the Good News of salvation. I was very excited. I still have his letter.

I flew into Nairobi. Ruth and her husband had just come in from Canada. Her husband met me at the airport. The next morning he was to take me to Kisumu. He introduced himself. I quickly said how excited I was to be there because Julius was going to take me all over Uganda. He said very coldly: "Julius is dead." I was numbed with shock. He said that he had been ambushed upon leaving his country village one night, and was shot in the head. The authorities thought it was a jealous cousin who shot him. There was one young man in the car with Julius who jumped out into a ditch when the gun fire began. He lived to tell the story.

The very day that Julius was shot dead is the very day I received his letter telling me that Messiah was coming and we had to go all over Uganda with His message. What a tragedy! He and Grace had worked hard, and were doing well financially. Do you see how evil jealousy is? **Song of Songs 8:6b**: "...**jealousy is as cruel as the grave, the coals thereof are coals of fire, which have a most vehement flame.**" Jealousy is at the core of Lucifer's nature. It is the core of the nature of the jezebel spirit. All those who act in this spirit will end up with Lucifer and his fallen angels, in the lake of fire. Later, I went with Vincent to Uganda. Then Abba raised up Pastor Bethuel Dongo to take me all over Uganda, after Vincent Wanyonyi Wabuke died of tuberculosis (2000).

In early 1998, Bethuel and three other pastors had come to speak at a church in the Fort Worth area. Someone told them about my going to Africa. I invited them to come to my apartment after they spoke. Bethuel has an awesome wife, Florence, who is a school teacher. Their four awesome children are named: Thanks, Worship, Glory, and Ezra. They had one little girl who died at about age three, named Victory--she was already an evangelist, and healer, by then.

In Kisumu, I taught some at the Bible College again. I helped John and Margaret get their large facility for the orphans, the school, and the church in Kisumu. I spoke at John's church, and to the students. By this time they had named the elementary school after me. It had about 80 students. The orphanage had about 40 children.

I worked with Pastor Godfrey, and taught in his church, Nanga Village Church. He had rented a large classroom in a school. There were quite a few in his church. I went to his home several times for dinner and fellowship. He had a wife named Francesca, and a few children. I ate my first tilapia in their home.

I went with Vincent to his village near Bungoma. I met his wonderful wife Lydia and their children – Dorcus, Lucus, Peres, Betty, and later baby Shalom. They lived in a very clean area – in a mud and cow dung house, which they also used for a church. Their little kitchen was a round cow dung and mud structure with a thatched roof. There they cooked on a jiggo – similar to a Japanese hibachi.

The staple diet in the village areas of Kenya is "ugali" (oo-gah-lee) – well-cooked corn grits, which is either eaten by itself, or formed into a spoon for dipping up chicken broth or vegetables. I remember the first time my youngest daughter tasted it. I have it on my son's video camera that he loaned me. She ate it, and even liked it. Lydia would put out big bowls of it for visitors. They would throw the crumbs on the floor. When they left, Lydia would let in the chickens to eat the crumbs. The chickens slept in the house at night. The next morning, Lydia would sweep out the chicken poop.

They had a nice grove of coffee trees on his property, as well as pineapples, passion fruit, and a strange large fruit that hangs down from tree branches. I think they called it "jack fruit." To get to this strange fruit, you have to cut through really thick pulp. In the morning, Lydia would also bring me a tub of water, with about one liter's worth of water in it, for my bath.

One morning I woke up to a very strong smell of cow dung. I peeked out the door or the little room the pastors had made for me. I saw a man spreading cow dung on the mud floor. Just then Lydia came in and saw my expression. She smiled, and said: "It's kind of like mopping." I had to cross that cow dung to get to the outdoor toilet, and to brush my teeth. It was OK ... The hardest thing for me was to get over the lack of privacy. But, I finally learned.

Their children were awesome. Dorcus, a young teenager, was taking 13 subjects in school. Their school was next door to Vincent's property. After school, Dorcus came home to do a lot of homework. Lucus also had many subjects and much homework. They were top students. I held several meetings in that school.

At about 18 months of age, Shalom had malaria but Abba healed her. But, she was so weak that they made a habit of carrying her everywhere. They were getting concerned because she was also not talking. The day Vincent died, Lydia told me that she began talking, and when they put her down she would run. It gives me chills to think about it, as if Vincent reached heaven and his first request was for Shalom. I remember her sitting on the floor during meetings in the house. I was teaching them to sing "Shabbat Shalom." She kept looking around to see why they were calling her (smile).

Later I taught them Abba's Name and Messiah's Name. I will never forget the next morning, as I was sitting outside their house drinking coffee. I heard Ronald Kuta singing their favorite songs inside the house, which they also used as a church, changing the names for Jesus, and God, to Yahweh and Yahshua.

Vincent introduced me to Ronald Kuta Wabuke, a cousin, who also pastored a church not too far from them at Natima. Ronald was the Principal of a large elementary school of about 800 students. I ministered in Ronald's church several times, and had special meetings for the youth. In 1998, my team of four, including my youngest daughter, ministered in a large open-air meeting to the children at the school. I loved Ronald and his family. Ronald arranged a pastor's conference for me in Teremi. It was in a school. I tell about this later.

After arriving at Vincent and Lydia's house, spring 1997, Vincent told me he would take me to meet with the pastors of the Holy Ghost Assembly churches, which were north of Mbale. We planned to meet at Grace's house. I took the bus to the border, crossed into Uganda, then took a bus to Mbale. I met Grace at her shop and she took me to their house. I was there about two days, and I was bored. My mind moves at lightning speed, so to sit for very long without being productive is very hard for me. I did not know when Vincent would arrive. So I got up from where I was sitting out in the large open porch area, and walked to the gate of the compound. As I did, I saw two men walking alongside the gate. They saw me and rejoiced. Talk about a "mo'ed"--Abba's to-the-nano-second appointment! It was Vincent, and Pastor Edward from the Holy Ghost Assemblies. They came in and met Grace, and I prepared to go with them.

Already I was having cultural withdrawals – no white people, no English, no familiar food, no familiar ways of doing things--nothing familiar. It prepared me for another three weeks of the same. Remember, I was still a "mover and a shaker" – an ordained minister with a corporation. Vincent became the African Director of Word Fellowship International.

We went by bus high up into the mountains that separate Uganda from Kenya to meet with people at Edwards' village. We then went to Pastor Tom Jimmy's village to preach in his church, and then traveled onto Bumbo. At Bumbo, rows of coffee beans were laid out on thin cloths. Children freely rode bicycles through them. Men made bricks in the same manner as the Hebrews made them in Egypt – straw, mud and cow dung. There were bananas everywhere, put on bicycles to be taken down to market in Mbale. Coffee trees were everywhere too. I even saw albino Africans along the road--quite amazing!

I preached and taught in so many places. I had a week of meetings in Pastor Edward's church, not far from Lwakhakha. It was very remote, on top of a mountain, among a few mud huts. It had been raining, and the streams were rivers. Logs flew down these rivers that went through villages. If anyone got hit by them, they'd die. I had to ford several streams. What amazing adventures! It was here that Pastor John came down from a very high mountain, with men who had been witchdoctors. He wanted me to pray for them to be filled with the Spirit. He was an evangelist and pastor. He only had a New Testament. What a fine dignified man! He told me that every day they prayed "for the peace of Jerusalem." I asked him how he knew to do that. He said, "It is just in our heart to do it." I asked him if he knew that it was a verse in the Psalms. He said he did not know that. I made sure he got a copy of the whole Bible in his native language. I prayed for the ex-witchdoctors. What humble men. They receive Abba's Spirit freely, having previously been born again and delivered from demonic spirits.

It is amazing to me that as poor as these people are, living in mud huts, they dress so beautifully for the work of the ministry, and to attend church. John came to Edward's church from way up in a remote village high on a mountain. Yet, he wore a nice suit, clean white shirt, and tie. Lydia had about three outfits of clothes – two for every day work, and her nice dress for Sunday church. The women dressed very Israeli, without realizing it. Vincent always wore nice slacks, a clean white shirt and a tie. That is the way ministers dress. Women ministers dress lovely too. Their clothes are hung on hangers via a string strung across a room.

It was at Pastor Edward's little family village that a man in his 70s came down from a very remote village in the mountains to see me. He was not saved. But, he "had heard" that there were white people on the earth, and he wanted to see one. I gave him the Good News. I don't know if he received it or not, but he found out there were lots of white people on earth. I met other pastors that I would work with in Uganda, like Tom Jimmy and his congregation, and Jimmy at Bugobero Spiritual Church, which was in a beautiful jungle clearing. I preached in their churches. Later I held week-long conferences in their churches.

Vincent and I crossed back into Kenya, and took the bus back to Kisumu. As we came into Kisumu, I saw two white people crossing the street. I said to Vincent: "Look at those mazungoos" (phonetic spelling)--Swahili for white people. They looked out of place to me. I got used to about 10 people being stuffed into a normal-sized taxi. The matatus (mat taht toos)--trucks with covers over their hauling beds, and with benches on either side, were also packed body to body with people. I also got used to riding on the buses. Almost everyone had a seat, but that was about all the benefits. It was a wonder they got from one destination to another. If people needed to go to the toilet, they would stop by the roadside and the women would get out on the right, and the men on the left.

On one bus ride through Uganda, baboons were everywhere on the road. In going from Uganda into Kenya, we crossed the equator. At times, I was shoved into vans by the men who owned vans. They were trying to get as many people into their van as they could. Being jammed bone to bone with Africans became common. But, there were times I had to get angry at those who tried to shove too hard, or who were yelling at us to shove harder. I had learned in China how to stand my ground and not let others bully me. If only I had that training when I was a child, life would have been so much better! But, all this training served to make life so much better in the male-dominated country of Jordan, where a woman is considered only ½ a person.

In 1998, when my youngest daughter was with me, they were trying to shove us too hard into a small van. I got mad and they stopped shoving. She said: "Wow mom, you're scary." I told her I had to be scary sometimes to survive.

In crossing into Kenya, there was so much corruption at the borders. For example, people were cheated trying to change their money, and the buses were horribly overcrowded with no order to the seating. Statistically, the three most corrupt countries in the world are 1) Nigeria 2) Kenya, and 3) Pakistan. It was so bad in Kenya that AT&T had to pull out, also McDonald's, and every other American business. But, crossing into Uganda was another story. President Museveni ruled the country with tighter laws. No cheating at the border, no overstuffing the buses, and much better conditions. His wife, Janet, I was told, is a born again Christian who stands for social justice, along with her husband. Of course, corruption in government is so typical in Africa that I would not be surprised if even Museveni had his hands in the till. I learned recently (2012) that President Museveni led the nation in repentance for their sins, and dedicated Uganda to the "Almighty God of the Bible."

But, Uganda is a cut above most African countries. Many Jews live there also. In 2000, I was on a bus from Kampala to Kisumu with Bethuel Dongo, and a Jewish man was sitting in the seat in front of me. The whole trip we fought over the window – he wanted it closed and I wanted it open. How did I know he was Jewish? -- He was reading a book written in Hebrew. In 1906, the international community wanted to make Uganda the homeland of the Jews. But, Theodore Hertzel and his pastor-friend said "No."

On that trip, I was bored. Dongo was reading an African newspaper. I asked him if there was anything in it about Israel. He said "No, just African news." Then Abba spoke to me: "**Read Psalm 83.**" I had my Bible with me, so I read it. Then I shook Bethuel and told him that I had just read the latest news about Israel in Psalm 83. Remarkable!

While in America, I not only went to Robert's church, I went to his monthly meetings. The meetings were held in a large auditorium that was set-aside for him where he spoke on end-time prophecy to large gatherings from many different churches. Twice he hosted Mayor Ron Nachman from Ariel, Israel. One time, Mayor Nachman brought several young people to Fort Worth for a special performance, and Pastor Robert rented a very prestigious theater for that performance. For another meeting, he invited his good friend Simeon from Burundi to speak to us and show pictures of the slaughter of his assemblies in Burundi.

Simeon was the Bishop over several congregations in the capital city. He married Mary of the Hutu tribe, whose brother became the President of the country. A rival tribe, the Tutsis, rose up against him and killed her brother, then set out to kill his whole family. Mary, and I think one or two of her children, fled across a raging river into Rwanda where they lived with the Pigmy's for some time. Simeon was a Bishop over several churches, and this rival tribe set out to slaughter the members of Simeon's churches. Some fled into Tanzania, where they stayed at a U.N. refugee camp. Bodies floated in Lake Tanganyika. Of course, with all these dead bodies in the lake, disease developed. Finally, Simeon arranged for Mary and the children to be smuggled out of Rwanda to Nairobi, Kenya, where he joined her in Athi River (near Nairobi).

I stayed with Simeon and Mary and the children several times. Because he was well known, he opened doors for me to speak in several large churches in Nairobi. Mary was going to college, working on a business degree--very brilliant people! I loved their children, but Esther was my favorite. On one visit, Esther, about 9 or 10 years old I think, had picked up a hot jiggo and the coals fell out onto her hand, arms, and legs. She had third degree burns. What a precious child! They were all precious!

During this visit Simeon was in Tanzania. He was visiting his pastors who were still in the U.N. refugee camp on Lake Tanganyika. He often went to visit them, but this time the Kenya government was giving him a hard time, not wanting to let him back into the country. But, finally they did. They were Burundi citizens. But, he poured out his heart to me about his love for his people. He returned before I left, and took me to the airport. They had always taken me to the airport at unusual times of the night.

AFRICA
KENYA--UGANDA--TANZANIA
(SEPTEMBER - DECEMBER 1997)

Once again, I stayed at Ruth's in Kisumu. It was not long before my friend Katy from Fort Worth came. She had also attended Emmanuel Christian Fellowship. Later she started her own ministry in Africa, but this time she had come at Ruth's invitation. I tell the following story in the Collections "Miracles of Provision." One morning we went out to see property that Ruth said she hoped to buy for a school. That day we had also gone to visit Mark Kegohi. Ruth proceeded to invite him and his wife Joyce to dinner, however later in the day, she invited more people-- about 15 others to her house for dinner. She had forgotten to tell Nicholas, our cook. Before we went out that morning, she told Nicholas to fix us four pieces of tilapia, a bowl of corn, a bowl of mashed potatoes, and a small salad. So she called Nicholas, but he had gone home. He had to ride a bicycle to her house each day from a long distance. When we got back to the house, he had prepared exactly what Ruth told him to prepare.

So, what to do? The people, 15-17 of them, were coming in an hour. When they arrived, they looked at what we had put out-- enough for four. Ruth asked me to pray over the food. I asked Messiah to multiply it, since I knew He'd had a lot of practice in that arena. I got a small plate of food and went to sit down. I kept noticing people coming with large amounts of food on their plates, then getting seconds, and thirds. I did too. We had food left over. Later when pondering the coming days of famine, He let me know that He would multiply the food of His set-apart ones. HalleluYah!

That evening, for some unknown reason, Ruth wanted to shame me in front of everyone. Rose was still her live-in maid and caretaker. She served, cleaned, washed the dishes, took care of an orphan girl named Rosie, whom Ruth had "adopted" unofficially, and did all sorts of odd jobs in her service of Ruth. For several days, I noticed that Rose was not washing the dishes after we ate. So for several nights I washed the dishes. Rose and Ruth both saw me washing the dishes. That night there were a lot of dishes, but Rose had left them. While everyone was talking, I went into the kitchen and washed them. Then, I went to sit down to fellowship with those who had come. Ruth came up to me, and with a loud voice she said: "I am so tired of you being lazy and not helping around the house. Rose had to wash all those dishes by herself tonight." I was numb! Right in front of all those people she was lying about me. I said: "I washed the dishes tonight." She said: "You're a liar." The guests were very quiet. That was not the only time she tried to shame me in front of others.

I paid her to stay in her apartment. In successive years, she always came two to three days ahead to get my money for the next month. She would accuse me of things I did not do. She would also say things like: "Jesus came and sat on my desk in my room, and we just had a nice conversation." I knew that wasn't true. She was not crazy, just very devious.

At the time Katy came, I had been sleeping in a room with two beds in it. I slept on the only bed in the house that didn't make my back ache, and throw my vertebrae out of place. The other bed, in the corner of the room, had a board under the mattress which made it too uncomfortable to sleep on. After one night on the couch, she came into my room and said I had to give her my bed for she had a bad back. I was in my 50s; she was in her 30s. She brought all of her things into the room, and I was stuck in the corner on the bed that was uncomfortable and painful for me. Finally, she took over the whole room with her things, and I had barely enough room for my suitcase, which I put under the bed.

Katy had "adopted" a young man who had been born again. She was mentoring him in the Word. He was a college student near Kisumu. He had a brother who had been in prison and was very violent. The brother was soon to get out of prison. Her "son" wanted to stay with us, for he was afraid of this brother who might track him down and kill him. So, we put him on the couch in the living room. About 1:00 AM that night, Abba woke me up. He pressed on me to pray hard, for I was in extreme danger. He showed me a vision of the brother coming to the door, banging on the door, and the young man opening it. The criminal-brother then killed the young man and came with his knife to slit our throats. Oh I prayed hard! Then He let me go to sleep. The next morning, we learned that about 1:30 AM, the brother had come and banged on the door. The young man said he was almost going to open it, but felt he must not open it. Finally the brother went away. We made sure that the young man had other lodging after that.

Later, Katy and I became good friends. We did teaching together in some places, and worked well together. In November, we went to Vincent's home to have a Women's Conference. Women from the whole region came. It was Thanksgiving Day. Two turkeys from a nearby house came for a visit. I told them that they sure were blessed, because in America they would probably be on someone's table. (As I write this, in four days it will be Thanksgiving Day in America, 2012)

It was a powerful meeting. Women were asking how they could minister. Most had lots of children. One woman said her husband was not a believer, and that he made life difficult for her. Several had husbands who were pastors. I told them to work it out where some kept the children while others went to minister--then the ones who went to minister would watch the children while the others went to minister. They were happy with that, and so were their husbands.

At one point during this conference, I asked the ladies to line up if they wanted prayer. That meant almost all of them. As I began to pray, demons were manifesting. One woman said that when she went to pray, a demon would move her stomach up so high that it cut off her breath. I commanded the demon out, and told her to go kneel beside a chair behind me and pray. I went on to pray for another lady, and I heard low-pitched growling behind me. I went to the lady by the chair, and I spoke to the demon again: "I told you to get out!" It left and she began praising God with all her heart – totally free.

Then there were four ladies in a row with strange symptoms of affliction, but not disease. Each was delivered. Some of the spirits I recognized, and they recognized me, because of my life with a warlock. Deliverance for people who understand the workings of Satan is very easy. Our authority is built as Yahuweh can trust us with His power! If He trusts us, then He just flows through us to do all types of miracles to set people free, and so it was at this conference.

We invited the men to come for prayer. Some wanted the baptism into the Spirit. (**Luke 3:16**) One man at the end of the line was not receiving His Spirit. So, I asked him if he had been born again. He said "no." I led him to salvation. I found out later that this was the husband of the woman who said her husband had given her so much trouble. I found out later that he had been doing some very demonic things. But, he was saved and delivered on that Thanksgiving Day. The lady, from whose house the turkeys came from, was a market-place evangelist--her name was Marisella Simiyu. She lived in the mud and cow dung house behind Vincent and Lydia's house. About four times a week she would dress all in white, put a very large round drum over her shoulder, and with Bible in hand, she went to the market place, about a mile away, to preach. She was so joyful--a precious lady. I wonder why believers of the affluent West won't even make friends with those in their neighborhood, or apartment complex, in order to share the Good News of salvation with them. I guess they are too busy making money and running their kid to soccer games. So, who then will the rewards in the Kingdom of Messiah go too?

Transportation in and out of Vincent and Lydia's home was not easy. I remember many times walking to that market on the roadside. It was where we'd get the bus into Bungoma. But, there were other times that I would ride on the most common transportation – the back of a bicycle. That was also how you got from one side of the border between Kenya and Uganda, to the other side--on the back of a bicycle. You could walk also, and put your luggage on the bicycle. Those with bicycles for hire would cry out over and over: "Border, border." Each time, leaving Vincent's home, two of the local youth would put a suitcase on their head and walk all the way to the bus. Along this road between Vincent's housing area and the road to Bungoma, was a High School. I was invited to speak there in 1998, with Valerie, Jean, and my youngest daughter. More later...

Katy got along fine with Ruth. I tried to. I did nothing but be led by the Spirit. I never pretended to be "spiritual"--that was just my nature. I am not a fake, nor a hypocrite! I found out that by being led by the Spirit, as in Mongolia and Russia, I was under His control and not under the control of other people who had latent demonic powers of witchcraft/jezebel spirits. So many have tried to control me for their own purposes, and/or to take advantage of me for some reason.

Even though I received much education in reality, I thought it would be nice if, after getting my mother's inherence money, I paid for Ruth's plane ticket from the U.S. to Africa--early 1998. She told me she would be gone three months. I found out she never was gone more than 3 weeks. But, because I paid for her ticket, I was treated like royalty for a short while. On the way back from Kenya, after three weeks, she met her husband in London for dinner, and they flew back together.

During this time Ruth said that my husband (we were not divorced yet) had called her and wanted to meet with her. It had something to do with him trying to get money from her. Her daughter also met with him. The daughter was wicked like her mother. My husband called me, begging me to believe that it was Ruth who called him. I told him: "I believe you." It was some manipulation she was pulling, and wanted to blame him for some scandal. But, I knew my husband's nature. He had his problems, and also lied a lot, but I knew his nature, and that was NOT his nature. He had integrity in many ways, and I respected him for that.

Her daughter called me some time in 1998, and said her mother was in dire financial straits and needed to borrow $1,700.00, as I remember, maybe more. I balked. But, I said that if the money was returned within a couple of months I'd loan it to her. I was promised I'd get it all back within two months. You

PART V - Training Assignments

guessed it! I never got it back. I've since learned the power of "NO."

Ruth was not happy with me because I kept asking for the loan to be repaid. When I took a team to Kenya later in 1998, I phoned Ruth and asked her if I could take them to her apartment for two weeks. She was very cold, and said that if I paid her whole rent I could stay. Her whole rent was $200.00 a month. The others were willing to pay their part, so it worked.

I even went by car with Ruth all the way to British Colombia, to the Banff area, thinking she needed a traveling companion. It was the winter of 1997. We had a good time actually, but there was much deceit under the rug. I met her husband and several of her friends. But, I must say that Abba did use Ruth to launched me into Africa to do His will, taking me on adventures that few have. Darlene never returned to Africa. Before I returned to Africa in early 1997, Darlene called me to apologize. She said she had been jealous of me. That's crazy! Her ministry with Women's Aglow in Connecticut was far more extensive than mine. I was just getting started. I told her I forgave her.

According to U.S. standards, I live below the poverty level. I have very little worldly goods. I am not famous or popular, or have anything else going for me besides Abba. But, that's it! The spirit of jealousy, jezebel, python, and on and on, are spirits of Lucifer, who hate Yahuweh. Anyone serving and worshipping Yahuweh and Yahushua are his enemy. I am just a bond-slave of Yahuweh, but evidently he thinks I am dangerous to his plans. I plead "guilty!"

Vincent met me at Grace's house in Mbale. I preached at Grace's church. I also preached in a larger city church in Mbale. The people had heard the big American evangelists and teachers teaching the "word of faith" doctrine, and they were all hyped up to get the good life. During the offering time, the pastor asked the people to come up with their offering, which was typical, and put it into baskets laid in a row on the stage, and say: "I will never have to suffer." So here was this chanting going on all around me: "I will never have to suffer."

This American thinking is taking hold in Africa, and the people want money and possessions. The pastors want power and money. TBN had come into Kampala. I met those who were running the station. They were very nice people. They had come from Calvary Cathedral in Fort Worth, so I knew of them. But, they were so excited because the people wanted to be like T.D. Jakes. T.D. Jakes makes about one million dollars a month. His personal banker testified to how he sent at least a million a month into Swiss bank accounts. I thought that surely TBN would not show the wealth of America in their Kampala broadcasts. Those people were poor. But, yes, they showed all the big name preachers with their $700.00 suits, $300.00 alligator shoes, and big diamond rings, preaching on luxurious stage sets. The American lifestyle allows things that most African believers consider immoral. The Director was telling me how the pastors were patterning their churches after that of T.D. Jakes' The Potter's House.

The pastors were becoming arrogant, proud, and haughty. Even though the Word specifies that if His people live righteously they will be persecuted, still they wanted to be like their big American heroes. But, the real pastors, like Bethuel Dongo, saw the evil in it, and would not even let his children watch TBN. The Christian music industry is not much different than the secular industry. On TBN, singers wore American "fashions." Their countenance looked hard and mean. Their body movements are considered indecent among real African believers.

In Tanzania, because of big-name Americans coming there, pastors who used to walk through the jungle at night to preach in dangerous areas under witchdoctor control, having seen many miracles, told me they had to have sound equipment, a stage, a van, and on and on, or they could not go and preach.

In Mwanza, a major city in the north of Tanzania, the Christians had become so soft that they feared going to the villages to preach. They had lost their faith and turned to humans who would "tickle their ears" with soft doctrines. Thus they lusted after material goods and personal gain. Everywhere America goes it corrupts--politically, economically, and spiritually. Everywhere they go they spread lust and sin to the people. They hold out money to the nation, then demand that the nation submit to their vile and filthy "industries." Thus nations worldwide are corrupted and brought down morally by America.

We went through the border village of Lwakhakha near Edward's property. There I met Doctor Steven and his wife, Mary. Steven ran a small clinic—Lwakhakha General Clinic. It was there in their home, that Abba woke me up, the spirit of repentance fell on me, and I was able to cry and repent for the sins that I had committed, against myself, and against Him. There He set me free from my past.

The next morning, we had a big meeting in a local assembly hall. Afterwards, I was praying for people to be filled with the Spirit, as was my usual in all meetings, as well as leading people to salvation. Vincent was helping those who had been filled, but who were stammering. Dr. Steven was assisting me. One woman was under the power of the Spirit, but because she was

PART V - Training Assignments

emotional, she too was stammering. Abba instructed me to do something I had never done before, or since. He said for me to stop her, and tell her to repeat after me the first few words of the tongue that I had since 1967. She repeated the words, then went fluently into the same full language. Vincent was standing behind her, and was shocked. She was pregnant. Dr. Steven was her doctor. He told me that she had been pregnant for twelve months – just like Nora Lamb was with Joseph. I laid my hand on her belly, and it was as hard as a rock. I spoke to the child and commanded that it begin to come out. She was most happy. They took her down the mountain.

The next morning, I was having coffee, and a runner came into the hut where I was, and told me that her baby had been born, and she named it after me, using my middle name that I went by all my life. How precious! Two years later I asked how the little girl was, and was told she was doing well. I suppose this was practice for commanding my first granddaughter to be born-- because grama had come back (from Jordan), and it was time for her to come.

In preaching on that mountain, they sent out runners to all the villages for miles around saying: "Come hear! There's a prophet on the mountain." I never billed myself as such, but my words were prophetic, and they knew. They have no modern ways of communication, so they send runners to deliver messages – reminds me of **II Samuel 18:19-24**.

In 1999, while spending a week with Grace in Mbale, she asked if she could take me to her tribal village way up into the mountains above Sipi (phonetically see-pee) Falls. Talk about rugged terrain. I hear from His Spirit when making any plans; He guides me in timing exactly. He prepared me for my watchman duties a few years later, by making me very time conscious and date conscious. I found a friend in Ezekiel who did the same thing – dated everything.

I was always amazed that along this road, out gardening in their rich-earth fields, were men wearing the Jordanian head wraps – the red and white checkered cloth that looks like an Italian tablecloth. There are many Muslims in Africa. The morning we were to go to her village, Abba told me to tell her that we had to leave by 9:00 AM. I did, but she messed around until about 1:30. I was very upset. I told her it would be storming on the mountain. She had hired a flat-bed truck. I was on the passenger's side on the left (English driving conditions). The window of the truck was broken. We got up near Sipi Falls and it began hailing. The hail balls were large, and they kept coming in the broken window into my lap. At the same time, we had lightning, thunder, and RAIN. The road was dirt and went straight up the side of the mountain.

In that area, there were waterfalls everywhere on the side of the mountain. The rain made mud. The truck kept sliding. At one point, I was a few inches from the mud, because the truck was slowly turning on its side into a ditch. On the other side of the narrow road was about a 100' drop off. Men from the area came running to help the truck stay upright. As we slid towards the drop off, more came, about 30, to hold the truck so that we did not slide down the mountain. Then another vehicle was sliding down the hill above us, and almost crashed into us. I was really mad, but tried not to show it. I knew this would happen. We had left too late. But, somehow, by human muscle, and probably by miraculous intervention, we got to the top.

I saw signs with Bible names everywhere – Mt. Gerazim School, for example, and El Shaddai something. I found that this was a Hebrew tribe that lived amongst warring tribes all around, and we were on the border with Kenya. We got to a house made of boards, with spaces between some of the boards. I did have a private room, but the bathroom was outside--as usual--in a mud hole. A tall old man whose legs were so tiny, came walking in, leaning on his staff. Grace introduced me, saying I was from Jordan. The man said, Grace interpreting: "How is Israel? They are our people! We hear about them on our short-wave radios." Then the pastor of the church came in and said: "If you tell us anything, tell us about Israel." I had such a lovely time with them.

That evening I took my water bottle, tooth brush, and toothpaste, out to brush my teeth. Grace broke a small branch off of a tree, peeled back the bark, and proceeded to clean her teeth, which were beautifully white, and all there. Case in point: We need about 2%, or less, of what we think we need! Up there, I felt like I was with family!

Vincent took me back to Tom Jimmy's, where I met his family and preached at his church. Then he took me to Bumbo to preach. Then I went to Jimmy's church, Bugobero Spiritual Church, way out into the lush "bush." Those people were so awesome! Their pastors were all so awesome. I loved going there.

That was the beginning of many visits, and meeting many precious people. During one visit, I was told that a deaf lady had been born again. She was sitting just below the preacher's platform. Before the meeting started, I went down and laid my hands over her ears, commanding the spirit of deafness off of her. I went back and sat on the platform. I looked at her and saw her eyes wide with amazement. She came and threw herself over my lap saying, in her dialect: "I can hear!"

PART V - Training Assignments

It was in that wonderful place that I led many children to salvation. Messiah baptized many into the Spirit (**Luke 3:16**). One boy, who had come to salvation, told his pastor-father: "I want to be a pastor and serve God." In 1998, I took my youngest daughter here with our little team from Texas. It was such a blessing in that place.

On every trip to Africa, where I stayed 3 months each time except for the three weeks in 1996, there was never a day in which something didn't happen that led to people's lives being changed. Ministry is constant. There are always people with needs--especially spiritual needs. But, stopping to pray for someone with malaria was common. Holding dying babies with malaria was part of ministry too. With their childlike nature, the Spirit was able to do a lot in a short time, because I was not dealing with the gods of humanism--intellectualism, the worship of reason, man's ideas and opinions, teachings, and theories. They are just pure of heart and childlike, so they receive miracles easily. I found this true over and over, in Mexico, in Central and South America, and in Asia. If they are deceitful, it is so obvious that it is laughable.

One time, I was with Vincent in a very dirty border town. A young man came up and asked for money to go to the US. I told him I had no money, and if I did I would not give it to him. He said: "But I'm your brother in Jesus." Some brother! He pestered me a little more until Vincent ran him off. Same in the Arab world--they are so obvious. But, they sure fool the fools! Because some Africans are such con-artists, there have been many western missionaries hurt by their skimming money off of the offerings sent to help the poor, and the orphans. Missionaries who run orphanages often trust their helpers to run things well, so they go back to America, the UK, or to Europe. Then they find out that their helpers are keeping back part of the offerings and the children are suffering. I was taken in a scam by one group of pastors in Uganda, which cost me a lot of money.

In 1997, I ministered at Pastor Meshak's church. What a fine man, with a fine family. His wife's name was Beatrice. She and Lydia were good friends. Another was Pastor Joseph, Electina, and family. Another was Pastor Walter, and his wife and family. Walter's church was not close to Bungoma. His church was way out many miles down a long dusty road. In 1999, when I had hurt my ankle so bad in Israel that spring, Walter asked me to come teach at his church. I could hardly walk. But, he put me on a very big tractor, and got me there and back. I spent several days with Walter and his people. I really met so many fine pastors and people in their churches. Many gave me offerings, no matter how small they were; for they were poor people.

On Sunday morning, I was on the stage at Meshak's church, standing next to Lydia. Just below me I saw what I thought was a midget. He had the face of an older man. He was obviously crippled, which had stunted his growth, but he was clapping and dancing to the music with perfect precision. He was so caught up with the music, and his face was radiant. I asked Lydia who the little midget was. She was surprised. She said: "He's not a midget; he's 6 years old." I was surprised--six years old! She told me his name was Moses. His father was a school superintendent and his mother was a teacher. He had several sisters and brothers. But, he was very different. I learned over the next few years how different!

Ronald Kuta wanted to buy property to put up a larger church near Bungoma. He was allowed by the land owner to have an open-air church under some trees, where there were rocks for the people to sit on. He called it the Rock Church. I went there with Vincent and Lydia, and their children. When I got to the area where people were sitting on the rocks, Moses came up to me with a big smile and extended his hand in greeting. He was so mature! I learned that he had such an anointing that he would often tell the pastors what God said about things. He reminded me of myself at age six. I was so bold when I saw things wrong.

Back at Vincent's one day, I overheard Moses telling the pastors what Father had said, and some of the pastors began laughing at him. I did not mean to be disrespectful to the pastors, who were also friends, but I went ballistic. I told them to shut up. They did. I told them that he heard from Abba, and was much more developed spiritually than most of them. They humbly agreed. At times, that child scared me, because he was so anointed. He even directed the choir at his church.

I went back to Jordan, and returned in 2000. I heard that Moses had slid on water in his house, fallen, and broken both knees. His parents had done nothing! The knees set wrong, and yet he continued to walk and dance. But, he'd fall down, get up, and keep going. He never complained. He sat by me at one church, and turned towards me to say something about how good God was, and the look in his face made me afraid--the Presence of Abba was so strong with him. I prayed for him, of course. But, I felt so helpless otherwise.

His parents came to visit me. I don't remember why. Here were these "educators" who were as ignorant spiritually as any dead-head secular. I asked them if they knew that their son was a prophet. They said they'd heard that. I really let them know how angry I was that they had not taken him to a doctor as soon as they knew he broke his knees. They were shamed. After I left Africa, I found out that they had taken him to a U.N. hospital, to be helped by a retired U.N. doctor. The doctor had dedicated his life to helping the people without pay. This doctor was also a surgeon. He said that he would have to re-break the knees and re-set them. So Moses was admitted to the hospital. His presence changed lives there--including the doctor's!

I am crying now, remember him. Moses had been born with a hip deformity, and his growth was stunted because of it. All who came near him at the hospital saw his radiant little face, always praising God, never complaining. The doctor re-set his knees, and also realigned his hips, so that when I got back, Moses was several inches taller. He was about 8 years old then. The doctor said he had never met anyone like Moses in his whole life. Moses had a profound effect on that doctor's life. I took Moses some new clothes in his new size.

Ronald Kuta held a week-long Pastor's Conference at Natima, not too far from Bungoma. It was the most wonderful conference, with quite a good group attending. It was held at a local school that was not in use at the time. I stayed at the school, as did most of the pastors. I would start teaching about 9:00 AM. We took a break about 2:00 for lunch. Then I taught until about 8:00 PM. Then we'd have dinner. After that, they would gather to ask me questions. We sat outside, using kerosene lamps.

One woman pastor to my right said that they read in the Word that God had very, very long legs, because the earth was His footstool. She asked me about that, so I explained. Another pastor to my left, asked me: "Jesus says in Matthew that we are to baptize people in `the name of the Father, the Son, and the Holy Ghost.' It says in Acts that Peter baptized in the name of Jesus. Now tell us, who are we to believe--Jesus or Peter?" That question took a little longer to answer. But, they were so eager to learn. They are intelligent people, they just had no one to answer their questions.

Abba gave me such revelation knowledge on how the pastors were to shepherd their sheep, and the responsibilities of the pastors, and other elders, that I wrote a book entitled: *The Good Shepherd*. The wisdom in it can be used by anyone in the ministry, adaptable to each one's calling. Vincent and I made one more trip to Uganda before leaving for Kisumu.

TANZANIA
(1997)

Vincent and I left Uganda for Kisumu. The bus ride to Kisumu was about eight hours. We had to cross the border, and go through Kenya Immigration. Vincent could be so funny. He was very "proper"--a gentleman. I remember, we got on the bus in Mbale to go to Kisumu. We were the first ones on. The second one on was a woman, who sat behind us. All of a sudden water started flowing down the aisle of the bus, from her. Vincent kept making sounds of disgust, turning around and looking at her. It was so funny. I said, maybe she's pregnant and her water broke. He kept up the sounds of disgust, smacking his lips loudly. She obviously had peed.

Vincent had never been to Tanzania. I learned about Joshua Mdachi, pastor of Victory Christian Center, and his wife Elizabeth, in Musoma. Joshua invited me to speak at his church. I said I would come. Vincent and I stayed in Kisumu about three days to prepare for our trip to Tanzania. The bus ride from Kisumu to the border of Tanzania at Sirari was eight to nine hours. By the time I got to Kisumu, I thought I was coming down with a horrible case of the flu. I was aching all over so badly. I had been bitten by quite a few mosquitoes in Uganda, but never thought of malaria. I had prayed for others who had malaria. I had held dying babies who were dying of malaria, but it did not enter my mind. I knew nothing about the 15 symptoms of malaria, or of the progression of them. I took Ibuprofen for the aching. But the aching got worse, with no other flu symptoms. I was growing weak, but we had to leave for Tanzania the next morning.

After eight hours of traveling by bus to the border, as we got out to cross the border, I was so weak that I could hardly walk. I had a severe fever by this time. At Immigration I just wanted to lie down in the grass by the roadside and not move. The Immigration officer wanted a bribe, and I had to deal with that too. He didn't get one! We got a bus to go further into Tanzania to Musoma. The bus stopped at a village so people could get something to eat and go to the toilet. The toilet was in a park in the center of town. It had a few holes drilled into concrete, and had only some concrete pillars to block the view from the whole town. But, I had to go.

By the time we got to Pastor Joshua's, it was evening. It was a wonder I was still alive. I tried to act cheerful. Joshua, and the other pastors, saw I was weak, so I laid down on the couch in the living room. They went into another room to begin to prepare the 27 meetings I was to teach in. That's right--27 meetings awaited me, and I could hardly lift my head. Finally, I had to admit to myself that this was not the flu--it was malaria. It was not cerebral malaria or I would have been dead already. I crawled off the couch and went in, leaned my head against the doorway and said: "I think I have malaria." You'd think I had told them I had been shot--they moved so fast. They got me "Metakelfin" – but it was too late for that. Metakelfin is a tablet that is made in Italy. If I had taken it before I had the fever, it would have caused me to sweat out the disease, much like the American Indians knew to do in cases of smallpox. They would wrap a person in a tight thick blanket and put them next to a fire, so they'd sweat out the disease.

When I was 17 years old, we were required to get a smallpox vaccination. I got one. But, for about 10 days I had a mild case of smallpox. The vaccine ate a hole about $1/4^{th}$ of in inch deep into my left arm. I still have the scar to this day.

By this time, I was moving fast into the "black-water stage" – blood in the urine. Malaria destroys white blood cells, attacks the liver, and erases memory. I lost the ability to even remember my own name. I could only function through "the mind of the spirit." My brain-mind (soul) shut down. They couldn't keep enough water boiled for me.

Vincent, being a micro-biologist, made sure that everywhere we went the water was boiled 18 minutes to kill typhoid germs. Only once did I get intestinal bugs from polluted water--but not typhoid. The hole in the floor toilet was in the house where I was staying, and the substances from the toilet mixed with the water – to be discrete about it. It was a bored well--a very shallow well. I had constant diarrhea for about six weeks, and went back to the states with it. It took two cups of vanilla yogurt with live acidophilus culture, from Braums on Hulen Street in Fort Worth, to cure it.

Vincent began teaching in "my meetings!" He'd come back each evening to tell me how good the meetings were going. At one point, I wanted so much to hear healing Scriptures in English. They kept cassette tapes going of praise music in English – songs and choruses I knew from my charismatic church past. My spirit desired to hear healing Scriptures, and within a minute of my desire, they changed the cassette. I heard a man with a southern accent reading healing Scriptures. He had a Texas accent. Then a woman, who also had a Texas accent, read them. It went on for about 45 minutes. I asked Joshua who was reading those Scriptures. He smiled and said: "You know them; they are from Fort Worth – Kenneth and Gloria Copeland." I was so surprised. It was such a good tape. Even though I had no memory, I could talk because there is a mind of the spirit (in the loins area of us) that contacts both the eternal realm and this one. [Refer to: "Living From the Eternal Mind"]

I was growing agitated because Vincent was teaching my meetings. One evening, I heard the voices of witchdoctors who were walking around the house chanting. I asked Vincent what they were saying. He said they were putting curses on me. I heard the voice of the enemy saying I'd never leave Tanzania alive. I cried that I wanted to see the youngest daughter again, the one who was living with me. She won't let me forget that! (smile) Joshua tried to get me what I asked for to eat, but I wanted soda crackers and Ginger Ale, grapes and cheese. But, they had none of those things. But, he did his best. I just was not hungry. I had grown so weak that I could not sit up for more than a few seconds. The members of the church came to pray for me several times. They knew I was dying. Many told me that they were fasting and praying. Yet over me, I tangibly felt His Presence hovering over my bed -- His Presence never left me for a second.

It got down to where Vincent had taught 25 of my 27 meetings, and it was almost time for us to go back to Kisumu. I was eager to preach. So, I told Joshua to carry me to the church, get a chair with arms on it, and pillows to prop me up. I was going to preach. That was Saturday night. The next morning, the church was full of people for Sunday service. They got me into the chair and propped me up. Joshua was my interpreter. I opened my mouth to speak, not being able to remember anything, and I heard the voice of Yahuweh's Spirit speaking in my spirit. He began telling me what to say, one sentence at a time. I repeated what He said. Joshua was quick to interpret/translate into the local dialect.

Strength poured into me. I was gesturing, and animated. I spoke rapid-fire, and he interpreted rapid-fire. I spoke on the coming of Messiah for two hours. When I was finished, I was so weak. Then they carried me back. That evening, I went back to the church and taught another two hours by His strength. I was in the final stages of malaria. My urine was black with blood. Yet the next morning they put me in the front seat of a large truck, and I rode for eight hours back to Kisumu. When I got to Ruth's apartment, I wanted to make sure that I looked OK. So, when she opened the door, I smiled and said: "We're back!" She and Rose both gasped. Ruth said: "You almost died didn't you?" I had a relapse, but this time the Metakelfin worked. It took 2 weeks and then I was strong enough to throw off the disease. A miracle!

I went to the airport in Nairobi very sick, still sweating from malaria. I told personnel at Lufthansa that I had malaria. They were so kind to me. They made sure I had a place to lie down. They helped me with my luggage. They couldn't have been nicer.

When I got off the plane in Dallas, my son was waiting for me. I fell into his arms and cried. I told him I almost died. The incredible weakness continued for some time.

I asked Abba: "You have always healed me; I am a spoiled brat. Why did you let me go through that and not heal me right away?" His response: "**I wanted you to know what it was like to go through that with just My Presence, so that you can go through the tribulation with just My Presence, to the coming of My Son.**" Wow – I still ponder that with awe.

Now, I seek to be in His Presence daily, and feel Him with me. He says: "I will never leave you or forsake you." By the Spirit of Yahuweh abiding in our re-born spirit, He does not leave us. The word "forsake" means to "strand along the roadside with no help." I've had cars break down, or run out of gas, many times along the roadside – but within a few minutes there was always help.

AFRICA
KENYA--UGANDA--TANZANIA
(1998)

I felt strongly in early 1998, that I was to take a small team to Africa. I took Valerie, a school teacher from Dallas, Texas, Jean, an x-ray technician from Weatherford, Texas, and my 17-year old youngest daughter. My daughter and I were living in our two bedroom apartment in southwest Fort Worth. I had prayer meetings every Sunday before we went. We were in such unity. When my hot water heater broke, and water dripped down to the apartment below, I went to apologize to whoever was in the apartment. An African-American lady lived there. I apologized for the water. I also apologized if we were too loud on Sunday afternoons with our prayer meeting. I told her we were going to Africa. She smiled. She said she heard it, and she loved it. I would play Kent Henry cassettes of worship music on my little recorder. Each of us was free to pray anyway we wanted. I paced. My youngest daughter laid on the floor on her back with hands up, praising. Others were quiet. Some prayed out loud and we joined them. I love the freedom that He gives us to be in unity in our own different ways.

A church in Fort Worth had invited some African pastors to come and speak. Someone there told them about me, and they wanted to meet me. They were on a preaching tour. I invited them to my apartment on Sunday afternoon. So, we met Bethuel Dongo, Michael Lutalo, and another pastor. They invited us to come to Kampala, Uganda, where their churches were, to speak. Michael asked me if I wanted to stay in a hotel, because their food was more western. I told him that I stayed with the people in their houses wherever I went, and I ate their food. Michael was surprised. He said he had never heard of an American who wanted to stay with the people. Isn't that tragic? Bethuel invited me to his house.

I preached in Kampala at Michael's Appointed Harvester's Church many times, and also ministered as an evangelist in open-air meetings with him. It was in his church that I gave my first baby dedication. During the open-air meetings with Michael's church, there were several young Muslim men who came forward to be prayed for. I asked them: "Are you tired of sin?" They had their heads bowed. They were crying. They nodded their heads "yes." I made the Good News plain. They prayed; then they lifted their heads, and their faces radiated with His peace. **The greatest of all miracles is the new birth! It is the highest expression of the love and mercy of Yahuweh, and Yahushua Yahuweh.**

Before leaving America, I heard there was a cholera epidemic in East Africa. I asked my team to pray about whether we should get the vaccine or not. I knew that the vaccine was virtually useless. I learned from pharmacists that all I needed to take was Pedialyte or Gatorade to replace lost electrolytes until I could get antibiotics. The next week we met and all said that the Spirit had said "NO" to the vaccine. No one got sick at all on that trip. We also used plenty of anti-mosquito spray!

Here's a funny story: We got on the plane in Dallas to fly to Nairobi. We had one layover in Frankfurt. My daughter had a problem with motion sickness, so I bought Dramamine. I had used it for years. I gave her two tablets. All during the trip, every four hours, I faithfully gave her two more tablets. She slept the whole trip. Even in Frankfurt she was so groggy that she was staggering. That was sad, because she had taken three years of German in school and could speak it well, but she remembered none of it. After getting to Nairobi, I looked at that bottle of Dramamine I had bought. How was I to know they had a new formula! With the new formula you only had to take two tablets EVERY TWELVE HOURS! She will never let me forget that I almost "OD'ed" her. We laugh about that today. Now Dramamine has a non-drowsy formula. Oh the advancements of medical science!

We stayed at a hotel. My daughter felt much better by morning. We took the Kenya Air flight to Kisumu. She said she was not interested in taking pictures, though she had brought her camera. As we were landing in Kisumu, she looked out the window and saw mud huts below, and started snapping pictures.

Upon first coming to Kisumu, my daughter did so well in ministering to children. She put on a puppet show, and ministered to the children at the Soon Orphanage and Elementary School, run by John Aloss in Kisumu. After settling down for a day or two at Ruth's apartment, which she rented to us while she was gone, we set off for Vincent and Lydia's house area. Vincent met us in Bungoma. My daughter loved Vincent, Lydia, and the children, and all the pastors there, and they loved her. One of her favorites was Ronald Kuta. Of course my daughter stood out, with her blond hair, big blue eyes, and white complexion. Ronald invited us to put on a presentation of the Gospel at the elementary school, before about 800 students. We had a huge audience. My daughter and I did puppet shows. All four of us got to minister. We ministered in the churches around Vincent's also, as well as in his church. I never hogged the show. I always gave the other three lots of chances to minister.

Then we went with Vincent to Uganda, through the infamous Lwakhakha "back border." The immigration officers threw our suitcases on the dirt, and went through them in open view of everyone. The officers asked me for "chai." Yes, Chai means spiced tea, but in their lingo it meant bribery. I would not give them a bribe. So they went through my suitcase, pulling things out. Onlookers stood around and gawked. But, they stamped our passports. We stayed in a concrete block house with a dirt floor. All night my daughter kept the flashlight on a very large spider on the wall. The outdoor facilities were also spider-covered.

We spoke at a church near there. All night we could hear the drums of witchdoctors. We learned there was a ceremony performing female circumcision. That's right--female children are circumcised as well as the boys—around the age of 12 or 13--a rite of passage into adulthood. Primitive to the max, yes, but how did these primitive tribes know to circumcise the males? You would not believe how many of those African tribes have Israelite forefathers! Most came from the Bantu people of Ethiopia, from the son of Solomon and Queen Sheba. Look at **Acts 8:26-40** – that high official, the Ethiopian eunuch, was reading **Isaiah 53** when Philip intercepted him.

The Baganda tribe in central Uganda, was living such a high culture when the British took over Uganda, having a King with a Parliament, that the British left them to govern themselves. Michael Lutalo looked so Israeli, though a very black African. While in Lwakhakha, we went up to Edward's village to minister. Back in Lwakhakha, Dr. Steven took us through his clinic. Then on to Mbale. We went to Grace Osilo's house. We ministered in churches in that area too. Then we got transportation from someone in one of the churches, who took us high up into the mountains of Sipi Falls. Grace's niece ,Margaret, was my daughter's age, and she went with us. So it was Vincent, Margaret, Edward, and us four American's.

Before leaving America, Valerie's parents were very worried about her. They were afraid she'd get the dreaded Ebola virus. She had to really calm them down, telling them she'd not go anywhere near where the Ebola was. This is so funny: We stopped in front of the Elephant Caves on our way to the Sipi Falls area, and got out. I told Valerie not to tell her parents, but the source of the Ebola virus had been discovered in the Elephant caves we now stood in front of. She promised she would NOT tell her parents! It was so gorgeous up there. I took pictures of our group in front of the falls. It is like nowhere else I've ever seen on earth in its primitive beauty.

We then went to Bumbo. To get to Bumbo, we had to cross two planks across a stream. If the van missed the planks by one speck, all would be dumped into the stream. When it rained the stream became a rushing river. They put us up in a very large wooden house with many bedrooms. They do not put ceilings in their houses, so the roof beams are high up, and only planks cross the house as supports... where a ceiling would be in a western house.

The next morning we were to hold an open-air meeting, then go back down the mountain. That night, a chicken flew up on one of the beams, and then flew down. I woke up to find it resting, pushed up against my head. I slept with nesting chickens in the corner of houses almost all the time in the bush areas of Africa.

About 3:00 AM it started pouring rain. I woke up, my daughter woke up, and we prayed. In a few minutes, we heard one of the people in the house begin to pray loudly too. The rain stopped. In the morning it was cloudy but the rain had stopped. We got to the meeting and it began to sprinkle a little. But, we held the meeting anyway. There were some there who found salvation. My daughter preached. She used the puppets part of the time to give a message.

Then it was time for us to go. We had a full load of people in that van. The stream was now a small river. We sure prayed, and we got across on those planks all right, but it was scary! I remember Jean, talking to people in our local market place about their salvation. She was so gentle and kind. I have a picture of her bandaging an injury on Vincent's leg. They nicknamed her: "Dr. Luke." She and Valerie were such assets to the trip! Of course, my daughter and I flowed together beautifully.

This is really funny too: I have this on video tape: During our time in Kisumu, Vincent took us to a wildlife refuge park outside of Kisumu on Lake Victoria. All types of hurting animals were rounded up and brought there. While looking at the different animals in their cages, a mischievous spider monkey, sitting in a tree close to my daughter, ran down the tree and began chasing her. She was screaming and running. To escape it, she ran around the back of a large cage, and grabbed onto it. She stuck her nose into the cage and felt a wet nose against her nose. To her shock, she was nose-to-nose with a hyena.

We also went to a resort area on Lake Victoria to have dinner. As the sun was setting we were taken by car to a remote area, which was known to have many hippos coming from the lake onto the land at night. Of course, hippos in the wild can be very aggressive. As the sun set, a family of hippos was coming in, but they saw us. They were still out in the lake a ways. The big one, the daddy, opened his mouth and full blasted us with a warning cry. I took a lot of pictures before it got too dark. But, the ones in the car were scared and warned us to get out of there – which we did.

Africa was quite a culture shock to Valerie and Jean, but not to my missionary seasoned daughter. On the first night at Vincent's, Valerie was kept awake, listening to drumming by witchdoctors. But, I had told them I would hear of no complaining about anything, so she kept quiet. But, she told Jean, and my daughter heard it and told me. I called Valerie over and told her that asking questions was not complaining. My daughter had teenage attitudes a couple of times, but she has always been teachable and pliable. It was a delight to minister with her. She's the little one who was preaching the Good News and doing spiritual warfare at age five, and at 11 in Mexico, moving in healings and miracles.

Another funny story: My daughter went to Africa with blond hair. She returned to the states three weeks later as a brunette. No, she did not dye her hair. It was turned brown by African dirt blowing through it. We went to one village that was way down at the bottom of a mountain in Uganda. It had rained, and we almost turned over getting down there. But, then the wind began whipping. Her hair was so dirty, but she did not want to have them bring water from the river to pour over her head to wash her hair.

Another funny story: About 2½ weeks into her stay, we were back at Vincent's place. She was drinking a cup of chai at least once a day – tea with sugar and milk. Off the wall, she asked me: "Is this milk low-fat?" I laughed, and said: "Do you see that cow out there in their front yard? Lydia milks it twice a day, and I assure you it is not a low-fat cow." She freaked out. She thought she'd at least gained 100 pounds.

Vincent and Edward took us to Bugobero to Pastor Jimmy's (James Wepukhulu) Bugobero Spiritual Church. Tom Jimmy was there, too. Pastor Godfrey from Kisumu went with us, as he did on several of our Uganda excursions in 1998. I have a picture of Pastor Godfrey carrying my son's video camera down that long dusty road to Tom Jimmy's church. He carried it for me everywhere we went.

In ministering at Bugobero Spiritual Church, with Pastor Jimmy, we stayed in a house that had room for all of us, except my daughter. They put her in the shed. It was where they kept their grain and other foods. The next morning her face was covered in flea bites. She has such a lovely creamy complexion. She was so distraught. She was crying: "What will my friends think of me when they pick me up at the airport?" I took them into areas where few white people go, but they were areas I knew well. I never do sissy stuff--I go for the real! I confiscate all lollipops from those who go with me, too.

Back at Vincent's, just down the road was a high school. It was a very nice high school. They asked us to talk to the students. The staff took us on a tour of the school. They wanted to hear from my daughter. She gave a terrific sermon, even including saying that she wanted to be the President of the United States, to which the students all laughed. I honestly think that if she was the President, America would be a lot better off!

Godfrey confided in me that in their public schools they taught that they all came from apes--evolution. He was so sad about that. He said they taught that man evolved from apes in Africa. He said that he never heard an ape tell a joke, or reason out a problem. It made me sad to hear him tell that.

At the end of three weeks, my daughter and Jean had to go home. Godfrey went with us to the airport. He saw Jean and my daughter get on a little domestic Kenya Air plane that probably held 20 people. I told him that the planes I flew on held about 400 to 500 people. His eyes got so big. He had never seen a plane bigger than that little Kenya Air "puddle hopper." He said: "Oh! That is terrible overcrowding." I tried to keep from laughing out loud. All he knew was taxi, bus, and matatu overcrowding. I told him on the big planes, everyone has a seat. I stood there at the Kisumu airport crying as the little Kenya Air plane took them off to Nairobi with my baby in it. I watched until it was totally out of sight.

In November of 2011, she went to Haiti to work with Mission of Hope. In January of 2012, she took a team of three others with her – two siblings, and a lady who would soon be the wife of my son. She longs to go back, but in the meantime she works on projects for worthy ministries to help the poor, in her own hometown, and across the globe. The **Acts 1:8** pattern! Unless you're on that path, you're in a ditch, doing nothing towards your eternal reward!

TANZANIA
(1998)

After they left, Valerie, Vincent and I headed into Tanzania. It was so wonderful crossing the border at Sirari without being sick unto death. We met with believers in the border-crossing town of Sirari, where I spoke in a church, and we met our wonderful intercessor-friend Susan. We went on to Musoma, and stayed with Pastor Joshua and his family. We also ministered in his church.

We went to a small village a ways from Musoma to stay with families there, and taught the Word. It was here that I heard how believers from their area would walk for twelve hours at a time through the jungles at night to go to villages ruled by witchdoctors, to bring "the light of the glorious Gospel of Yahushua ha Machiach" to the people. Those areas were very dark--strongholds of demonic spirits. They would see miracles along the way as Abba kept the snakes, the cougars, and other wild animals from attacking them. In one village they preached how Jesus opened the eyes of the blind. The witchdoctor ran up with two blind people, and said: "Tell your Jesus to heal them, or I will kill you." Yes they were scared, but they laid hands on the blind eyes and commanded them to be opened in the name of Jesus, and they starting yelling "we can see."

Please understand, that ignorance of His real Hebrew Name does not stop the mercy of Yahuweh!

Needless to say, the whole village, including the witch doctor, gave their hearts to Jesus, and then ran to other villages to spread the Good News. Isn't this real life? Isn't this the norm for a person who has received salvation? YES! So what's wrong with their lollipop-sucking Western counterparts who are so cowardly that they won't even share with their neighbor? They kindle the wrath of Yahuweh!

I held children in my lap. They would rub and rub on my arm, because they believed that I only had white paint over my black skin. Some feared me because they thought I had been skinned-- the black cut off. There was so much love between the believers there. We really enjoyed it.

We hired a jeep to take us to the North Serengeti Plain to the home of a pastor. The area is called Nakatoma. They lived not far from where the wild animals roamed. In fact, we found out that they had to corral their sheep and goats and chickens at night because of roaming wild animals, especially packs of hyenas. This pastor and his wife had fourteen children. They lived in a concrete block complex. There was one lady in their church who did most of the cooking and caring for Valerie and I. We stayed in one room together.

Another funny story: There was one outdoor toilet facility--pit latrine. Of course, it was too dangerous to go out at night. As is a must in Africa, I always carried 4-gallon Ruffies scented garbage bags, which come in nice pastel colors. I learned that cavers do the same thing. So at night, we did our business in the garbage bags. But, we were collecting too many--hiding them under the bed. We had to get rid of them, and the pit latrine was almost full. One evening we gathered them up and went outside, hoping no one would see us. We saw a bunch of underbrush out a ways from our compound. We covered the bags over with the brush. We thought we hid them well. But, the next morning, we got up to find the bags torn open and scattered all over the ground.

We were to have a week of meetings. I was going to teach on the Holy Spirit, and then conclude with the baptism into the Spirit of those who had been born again. There were quite a few pastors that were working with us. We met in a rented school that was about one mile from where we were staying. It was a school with several classrooms, and a small auditorium where we held the meetings. Along the way we saw children carrying big jugs of water on their heads--water taken from a stream nearby. We were in the Serengeti Plain, and the villages were scattered and remote.

While teaching at the school, the chickens were everywhere, running around my feet. I did not mind; I like chickens. About the third day while I was teaching, a few people in the class got up and ran around the building screaming. The others told me they were full of demons. I didn't doubt that!

During a Sunday morning service, five young men walked in who were obviously not a part of our seminar. By their body language they were very haughty and appeared to be there to cause trouble. We were still singing when they came in. They sat in the back row. When we finished singing, before I started the message, I walked back to them, got right in their face, and began talking to them about their eternal lives. The one who was obviously the ring-leader broke down in tears, then the other ones. The anointing of the Spirit was strong on me. When His Spirit empowers us, we are bold and without any fear. This is normal for His servants! They came up front with me, and confessed that Jesus was their Savior, in front of everyone. Such joy lit up their faces!

Then it came time for the big day when those who had prepared would be baptized in the Spirit. This is normal for those who have been born again. [Refer to the articles on **comeenterthemikvah.com**, under The Mikvah of the Spirit] The pastor we stayed with gathered all the pastors of the area, including one Moravian pastor. He was terrific! That was a day I will never forget forever.

We were near what was called "the black river." Remember my story of the Black River between China and Russia, and how, when I gave acknowledgement of its power ever so flippantly, my left knee twisted so terribly? In this area, the witch doctors sacrificed black goats to the black river god. As far as I knew, all who attended our meetings had been born again (their eternal spirit perfected), but after coming out of witchcraft, they had not been delivered of the demonic spirits that lingered in their body and soul (mind and emotions). So, they were still under the control of demons (demonized). We moved all the wooden benches to the back of the room, and lined the people up in rows, as was my pattern, on the stage at the front of the building. Each pastor had a row to be responsible for, to personally minister to individuals.

But, as they warned me, when the Spirit of Yahuweh comes down, the demons begin to manifest. And so that happened! As I called for the power of Yahuweh's Spirit to fill the people, some ran outside and threw rocks at people and cars. There were some that ran outside screaming, and attacking other people. At this point, the pastors broke rank and began running outside to get them delivered so that they could come and receive the Spirit of Yahuweh. When the Elohim of Light meets the god of darkness, Light wins out! HalleluYah!

One quite large man was going berserk. About four pastors were trying to hold him down. He was coming to attack me. I had my son's video camera in my left hand. With my right hand, I pointed at him, rebuking the demons in him. I kept it up, but he kept coming towards me. He backed me into the benches at the back of the building. All I could think of in my pea brain was: "If anything happens to this video camera, my son will kill me." Just as he was about to attack me, he dropped to the floor. He came up totally delivered.

After this part of our meeting was over, they wanted to take up an offering for me. They were very poor. I got a few coins, which was a sacrifice from each giver. But, one gift placed into the offering plate was priceless. I still have it. The woman who was our cook, who cleaned our room, who was our helper, who led us each day to the school and back, put her "wrap" in the offering. To an African woman the wrap is very important. It is a large scarf that can be tied around the waste, used as a sweater, as a head-scarf, for wiping ones hands, to swaddle a baby, and other things. She gave it to me. I wear it around a denim skirt with great humility, because it was all she had to give me. But, it brings tears to my eyes. The only drawback to the school was the bat that slept upside down in the bathroom, but we worked around it.

What an awesome week! Valerie and I did not want to leave! I want to give credit to wonderful Lydia – who allowed her husband to be my guide and helper for five years. She loved me dearly. I've lost contact with her. We'd walk down the road to her house holding hands, which in Africa and Asia is common for friends. Valerie, Vincent, and I, and a couple of other pastors, left in our safari jeep. Our radiator was leaking, and we broke down along side the road. Right away, there was a man who stopped to help us. He was a safari guide in the Serengeti. He was an Australian. What a character! But, he helped us get on our way.

As we were going along, Valerie and I both saw this huge bird flying alongside the jeep on our left side. We both said at the same time: "It is a Pterodactyl." It had a massive wing spread. No feathers. It had that crested head that it held high, with an attitude. It looked exactly like all the pictures in dinosaur books. We were so shocked that we forgot to take a picture, even though our cameras were in our laps. Then it flew on.

Valerie returned back home to Texas while Vincent and I returned to Uganda. Edward Buey (Boo-ey) had picked out about an acre of property on which he wanted to build his church. I had money from Michael and Theresa to pay for it. I have a whole video recording of that transaction, and the laying off of the boundaries of that property. They wrote up a deed on a legal-sized paper, and all the pastors signed it, as well as the one selling the property. I have that deed today! I kept the property in my name--kept the deed in my name. I was there long enough to see them measuring off the property for a church. But, I never went back there to see the church that they built.

We met Michael and Theresa in Fort Worth, around 1992. We became close friends. After my fleeing from my husband, they remained close friends of mine, and to my son. It was Michael who gave me my first computer, which I used to launch the writing ministry that Abba gave me in 2001. Michael was a computer genius. I had so much fun with these people. We attended Pastor Robert's church. Theresa was a business woman. She had a fabulous job, but later went to work with Pastor Robert.

When I got back to the states, I called the Creation Science Museum in Glen Rose, Texas, and asked to speak to the Director, Dr. Carl Baugh. He was not there. Three days later I returned to Jordan. About six months later, when my daughter picked me up at the airport, for some reason, the first thing she said was: "Some man called you right after you left who wanted to talk to you about a Pterodactyl." She thought it was a joke. I said, "NO – it is no joke." So, the next day I called Carl and we talked about 45 minutes. I met him about a year later at their dinosaur dig on the Paluxy River near the Creation Science Museum. Just down the road were the evolutionists who also dug around that river, because there were so many dinosaur foot prints there. But, Carl found human footprints next to the dinosaur footprints. I was there to see the footprints and to watch them uncover more and measure them. I saw a Brontosaurus footprint, and a T-Rex footprint. That poor old T-Rex was missing his center toe.

Later I attended Dr. Baugh's July 4th celebration with Bob and Boo Summers. Boo and I were ordained by the same people in Burleson. That night I was interviewed about the "bird." Bob said that one had been sighted in Papua New Guinea when he was there with Carl, but it was so damp that their film equipment was ruined so they could not photograph it. Anyway, it made for an exciting trip back to Musoma.

INTRO TO AFRICA
(1999)

I had moved to Aqaba, April 18, 1999. In June, Valerie joined me in Jordan, and we went together to Africa from Aqaba, via Amman. But, I wonder to this day if I should have gone to Africa in 1999 or 2000, because of happenings that left me devastated. At that time, because I had an open door to minister in Africa, I thought it was my "reasonable service" to go. But, what is logical to the human mind is often illogical to Yahuweh's mind. He has to tell us what to do by His Spirit in us. We must never go off on our own because something looks like the right thing to do! Yes, there can be good that comes out of it, but unless He has called us to do it, the enemy also has a right to get involved with our devastation.

ISRAEL
THE MAIDEN VOYAGE
(1999)

Here I will interrupt the storyline to give an introduction to Aqaba, from April to June, that relates to Africa in the summer of 1999. I arrived in Aqaba, Jordan, on April 18, 1999, to live there. It was a rude shock from the first night. I cried a lot and stayed in a fetal position a lot too. Early on, a friend, from Emmanuel Christian Fellowship who lived there, took me on a mini-tour of Jordan. We went up to Shobak Castle (a headquarters of the Mamlukes), to Karak Castle, to Bozrah, then around the great canyon of the Fords of Arnon, and along the Dead Sea. It was a two-day outing. Then in May she felt like I should see Israel. I did not feel led to go. In fact, I did not want to go, which surprised me. I felt it was not Abba's timing for me to go. Yet, at her insistence, I went. Oh how I have changed. I should not have gone unless I heard Abba say "GO!"

We took the bus from Eilat to Jerusalem. We arrived in Jerusalem at night. But, as tired as I was, when I got off the bus I felt an incredible force of energy going through me. It was tangible. I learned that was normal. Jerusalem has a force of Abba's energy that rises from the ground, and fills the air. We walked to the guest house where we stayed on Jaffa Road.

She had lived in Jerusalem, yet she had not been there for a while, so she kept getting lost and getting confused as to where things were, even how to get to the HaKotel (Western Wall). We walked past the Damascus Gate and were right in front of Zedekiah's Cave, and I felt something push me from behind. I fell and twisted my right ankle so badly that I could hardly walk. I am double-jointed. As many times as my ankle has turned out of place in my life, it has always gone right back into place without tearing any ligaments. But, this time it really tore ligaments and tendons badly. We got a taxi back to where we were staying and I got some ice on it. She asked me if I wanted to go back to Aqaba--I said "no."

The next day, I rented a car on my credit card. She drove. She wanted me to see the Garden of Gethsemane. She drove up past the gate, and parked facing down the road, facing the Kidron Valley and the Eastern Gate. The Garden area was closed for another two hours. I got out of the car and looked straight at that Eastern Gate. It was worth all the fortunes of the world just to see it with my own eyes. The gate that is shut now, will be the gate that Messiah will come through – **Ezekiel 40-46, Zechariah 14:1-5**, after touching His foot on the very Mount of Olives I was standing on.

From there she drove us to Tiberias. We stayed at the Scottish Guest House. We walked to a beach on the Sea of Galilee. I put my feet in the water – it felt so good on my hurting ankle. Being there was so wonderful. But, on the way back to Jerusalem, I said: "I'm driving." I will never forget driving along the Sea of Galilee, called Lake Kinneret from ancient times. I drove down highway 90 until we began the ascent to Jerusalem. At this point she panicked. She said that I had to pull over and let her drive because I knew nothing of driving in Jerusalem. Later I realized it was no different than driving the freeways around Los Angeles. I drove a limousine for Forest Lawn Mortuaries for years on those wild and crazy freeways. She really panicked, and said I'd gone too far, and there were no more pull-offs. But, just ahead was a pull-off. I let her drive. But, the thrill of driving in Israel never left me. Within a month, I was scheduled to go to Africa. To add to the ankle pain, some emotionally traumatic things happened to me because I left my youngest daughter in America.

PREPARING TO LEAVE

In preparing to leave the U.S. to move to Jordan, I did not know what to do, or who to leave her with. I do not know how my mind got so deceived. Abba had impressed on me to go in September to Jordan. But, for some reason I decided He wanted me to go in April. If I had gone in September, I could have seen my daughter graduate from high school. I would have had a room in an apartment near others from Fort Worth, and many of my wrong decisions would have been thwarted. The mind is so deceitful – and so often leads us into confusion and fear so that we make wrong decisions.

In March, I met Sharon Crow. She worked with my daughter-in-law. She said she would stay in the apartment with her until the apartment lease ran out. She came to talk to me. She appeared to be an average Christian woman. However, I did not feel good about this lady. But, feeling desperate, I said she could stay there until the lease was up. After that, my son and his wife took her in; then the third child, her sister, took her in. I was gone a whole year that first year in Aqaba.

How did I know that Sharon was very mentally and emotionally unstable? I also did not know the deep trauma that my daughter was going through because I was leaving. So, as I prepared, showing signs of leaving, she got in with some bad friends she knew in high school. She did not know if she'd ever see me again. At the airport none of my family, or I, thought we'd see each other again. After I left, she and my son oversaw putting my remaining things in a storage barn. My son took some of the things for his house. I threw a lot away, gave loads of things away, a lot to my children, and sold a few things. But, still, the things I left were important to me. I had a 14-shot rifle registered in my name, and it "disappeared." Sharon had a brother, or a boyfriend--forget which--and I have no trouble believing that he stole the gun.

In her confused state, my daughter threw a lot out, left the oven black with grease, and the apartment in a mess. So, I was saddled with a fee. I was also saddled with about a $900.00 phone bill that she ran up calling the psychic hotline. For me, that was astronomical. But, what hurt the most is that my sterling reputation had been ruined.

Then there was the trauma with my daughter-in-law before I left. I had taken Michael and Theresa out to dinner as a thank you for giving me a large sum of money for my trip, and just to relax. We were friends, and they'd blessed me in so many ways. But, I needed to spend about 2-3 hours talking to my son and his wife about my business and other responsibilities that they said they'd do to help me. So, for our dinner I bought the finest frozen pizzas I could find for us to eat while we talked. I had never bought such good pizzas for myself. But, my daughter-in-law found out about my taking Michael and Theresa to dinner. She and my son came for our meeting, but she sat in the car and would not come out. My son said she was upset about the pizzas. I tried to talk to her, but she shut the door on me. She was so angry that I did not take them out to dinner. So, my son got instructions from me. I felt so bad for him because he understood me. There were so many hurts over her handling of my business. People would send me cards, letters, and offerings. I'd not hear about them sometimes for 6-8 months, even though some needed urgent attention, like tracts I'd ordered for Ginny, my Mongolia buddy. For a while

Michael took over my business, but that didn't work out well either.

So, since 2001, it has been so wonderful to have the third child handle my business, and have my Power of Attorney. She checks my P.O. Box regularly. She immediately alerts me to everything that comes in, tells me what people write, and asks what to do about things that need attention. I appreciate her very much!

BACK IN AFRICA

I knew nothing about what was happening with my youngest daughter until soon after my arrival at Vincent's house. Valerie and I were sitting outside Vincent's house when a runner came with a special delivery message for me from my son's wife. I was so far from civilization, and further yet from Kisumu. The message was brutally cold. It told of the $900.00 bill, and other things my daughter was doing wrong. I went into trauma and panic. They helped me get the bus to Bungoma, and I sent a telegram to my daughter. Later in Kisumu, I called her from a special phone center. She quickly repented, and her whole life turned around. But, still, it was overwhelming to me emotionally and mentally. She had not even graduated from high school – she was 17. She was in advanced classes, so she could have graduated that December, but I encouraged her to graduate with her class the next June, which she did. She rebounded quickly. But, I didn't. It took a long time. My ankle was in so much pain, along with the deep hurt in my spirit. I fought depression and despair.

Valerie and I started out by doing ministry in churches around Vincent's house. When we got back to Kisumu, we stayed with Katy and a friend of hers, who helped me with phone calls to my daughter. Then Valerie, Vincent, and I, went to Kampala, and met Bethuel Dongo and his family. I noticed that Vincent was growing very weak. He had no outward signs of anything being wrong, but he had been growing weaker and weaker for some time. Later on, he went for a test for something he thought may be wrong with him, and in their tests they found out that he had a form of tuberculosis in which there was no coughing, just an eating away of the lungs. Dear Vincent! I had tried so hard to get him a visa to come to the U.S. I wanted to bless him. But, the U.S. would not grant him a visa.

I began my many times of ministering at Bethuel's church – Kansanga Pentecostal Church in Kampala. The people there were wonderful. His elders were also wonderful men with lovely families. After we were there a few days, Bethuel took us to a remote village area--Namungo. Pastor Elijah was the pastor there. It was there in that little board church with a tin roof, that I had some of my most wonderful experiences with believers. I loved those people. It was a good-sized church. About a hundred attended the conference. We stayed in a house not far from the church. Their singing and dancing was wonderful. I had to play the bongo drums. They loved it when I played the drums. I loved the matoke--cooked plantain bananas--with peanut sauce. Matoke was their staple food.

The ladies cooked our lunch outside in huge black pots over a fire. Everyone ate so well all week. Some of the ladies wrapped their babies and tied the wrap so that the baby hung tightly from their backs. They had asked me to teach them in a week-long conference on the baptism into the Holy Spirit. I asked Valerie to teach also, which she did, but I learned later that she would rather have been a quiet intercessor. On the next to the last day, we had a glorious meeting where people were filled with the Spirit.

Again, I had to instruct the pastors how to minister as Messiah baptized people into the Spirit of Yahuweh. One woman was obviously demonized; she was punching the air and yelling. I had the pastors carry her out bodily and get her delivered, then bring her back in. I always lined the people up in rows with space between the rows, so that the pastors could get to the people to minister to them. I also ministered to the women because I would put my hand on their bellies when I prayed. Messiah said: "...**out of your belly shall flow rivers of living water. This He said concerning the Spirit, which those believing in Him were about to receive**..." (**John 7:38-39**) Your loins area is where the "belt of truth" is wrapped around, and the "sword of the Spirit" hung from that belt. (**Ephesians 6:10-18**) The "armor" for battle mentioned in this Scripture is referring to the garments of the Levites and the High Priest (**Exodus 28**)

After this, a group of men came in from a cult that taught that we can sin all we want, because Jesus paid the price for us to sin. They sat and listened as I finished up the week's lessons. Those at the church knew what these men believed. But, when I finished, the leader asked me a question. I do not remember the question. I just remember what happened. This had happened before to me, and it goes beyond any control I might have. The Spirit takes over my mouth. This time, He gave the most scathing rebuke to that man with a boldness that was NOT me. Afterward, the bold anointing lifted. I looked at my audience and they were obviously paralyzed in their chairs. I said quite calmly: "All week you have seen my teaching anointing. This is a demonstration of the prophetic anointing." That cheered them up. I expected these men to walk out cursing me. But, quite the opposite happened. Valerie and I, Vincent, Bethuel, and some of his pastors, got in the van for our return to Kampala. The cult-man came over to talk to me. He said, "thank you for hearing from the Spirit for us." We talked for a few minutes. He was such a humble man. I hope they stopped spreading that blasphemous doctrine.

Something happened during that week that was amazing. One day, after lunch, I was about to teach. Florence Dongo and her ladies group from their church in Kampala had come to give some special music and join with other pastors from that church in the week's teaching. It began pouring rain. The tin roof made the rain sound like we were being bombed. They tried using a microphone and the rain was still too loud. So, we waited a little for it to stop. As we did, we saw a motorcycle pull up and two very drenched white people got off and came in. Bethuel introduced them as Stewart and Donna. They had come from Washington State and were working with him to establish an orphanage in that area. They were all ready to move to Uganda, but just had to finalize the plans for the orphanage.

After the meeting that day, Bethuel took us to meet with a missionary-nurse from England named Margaret. She lived in a nice compound house and property in Mityana - a town that was not too far from the church. Stewart and Donna were to stay with her. We sat at her wooden table. I will never forget this scene. Stewart and Donna sat across from me. I was going on and on talking about Aqaba. I told them about top secret things I'd learned about the plans for Aqaba with the U.S., the U.N., and the E.U. Stewart had his arms folded, listening. After a while, I got the idea that maybe I should ask them what they do. Stewart simply said: "I just quit my job with the CIA." I had been giving all sorts of detailed information about our group. I imploded, trying to not look too horrified. He then told us their story. He knew some things that were not right within the CIA, and they knew they had to get out. They had heard of Bethuel in Kampala, and so they gained his help to get out to the bush, where no one would know them, to start an orphanage and stay in Uganda.

Later I would meet with them at Bethuel's church in Kampala, and have an in-depth talk with Stewart. He had prophetic gifting. I wish now I had taken notes on what he said. After this, they made a horrible mistake--they went back to Washington State to get their things. Within 2 weeks of their return, Bethuel e-mailed me with the news: Stewart, a healthy 43-year old, was walking in his apartment and just dropped dead. I figured he knew too much and they got him. What a tragedy!

I was still in so much pain with my ankle. I kept it tightly wrapped because it kept popping out of place. So, I asked Margaret about it, and she surprised me. She said there is a time after the injury that you should keep it wrapped, but there is a time to stop wrapping it, especially tightly, because it won't heal properly. So, I took off the wrap and it got better. A year later, my knee, from the fall in Russia, and my ankle, from being twisted in Israel, still had not healed totally, and were giving me much pain. Upon returning to America, my son took me to his chiropractor, who helped missionaries for free. It was very painful, but he broke up the extra cartilage that had formed around my ankle, making it stiff. He did the same with my left knee, which was also stiff. This chiropractor also gave me a bone density test. My bones are strong!

What a story this is! It is repeated out of context in the Collections, but I wanted to tell it here also: Bethuel put me up with some people from his church that had a home in Kampala. I had a bed in a room of my own. The only problem is that the mosquito netting had holes in it. My ankle was still in great pain. It kept popping out of place at night. I could not walk up the wooden stairs to the platform they had built for the preachers, or stand to preach. So Valerie went and preached in my stead. On the second afternoon, after they left for the meeting, I was so discouraged that I just stayed in bed. The couple who was hosting me both worked, so I was there alone. But, to make matters worse, through the holes in the mosquito netting were coming an army of large roaches. I was being covered with roaches, and I did not care. I began feeling like I was sinking into a pit. I felt my spirit literally begin to leave my body and start to descend downward, even though I was not sick or dying. I'd been down this route before. But, this time, I had no desire to call my spirit back.

All of a sudden, I looked up and saw the "cloud of witnesses" that I had seen twice before (**Hebrews 12:1-2**). I saw my mother and father holding hands and smiling at me. Then a man came out from the group above me, and came and knelt down by my bed. I had quite a few visitations from people in the Bible before, so there was no emotion over this. It was a "normal" thing to me. I knew he was the Apostle Sha'ul (Paul).

He knelt down by my bed, and began explaining **II Corinthians chapters 4 and 6** to me. He let me know that in going from point A to point B in the service of the Master, there were often obstacles, even to near death. It was "PAR FOR THE COURSE." He told me about being in the ocean for three days and nights, about being beaten in the head almost to death, about enemies, loneliness, almost being eaten by a lion, and a few other things. He told me that what happened with my ankle is just something that happened, and I'd get over it, that life with the Master is not easy.

Then he went back into the cloud of witnesses and it lifted and disappeared. As it did, energy poured into me so strong that I felt I could run around a football field--an American football field. And, just then, Bethuel and Valerie came back. I got up and hobbled into the living room and told them: "Get me a place below the platform--I'm going to preach!" They did. I preached on the second coming of Messiah. Once again, Muslim men came forward with repentance and humility to receive salvation. I couldn't witness to Muslims in Jordan, so I guess Abba had me witness to them in Uganda. I still stayed at the family with the roach-mosquito net. After finding I had gone through that situation, they got me a new net.

I was invited to preach at Saint's Gate Church in Kampala. It was a very large church. The pastor had been to America and gotten the T.D. Jakes fever – to be rich and famous. He proudly spoke the "Word of Faith" message! He had shown me his radio facilities in a huge building his church had bought, which they were going to turn into a T.V. studio. Before I spoke to the church, I had a small meeting with some of his people. Some asked questions about the "word of faith" teaching, because it was so different from what they read in the book of Acts. I learned later that the pastor had hidden himself to listen to what I said. He called them to a special meeting that evening, and refuted everything I said.

I preached at his church on my birthday. Vincent was with me. He was so weak, I was worried about him. The message Abba gave me that morning was one of pending judgment, and exhortation to fear God and obey Him. Of course, the church was all caught up in the "Word of Faith" movement, more commonly called the "blab it and grab it" movement. The message I brought certainly didn't fit. They had a lively choir singing before I spoke – all jumpin' and jivin' and shoutin' and proclaiming the loose-goose message of western Christianity.

After this meeting, the pastor invited me to a week's conference in an area far from Kampala. I said I would go. He was about two hours later in coming to get me, and I was upset and let him know it. The whole week he undermined everything I said. I did not know that in his translating my messages, he was mocking me. I wondered why the people kept laughing while I was saying serious things. It was a devastating time for me.

After this, I went back with Vincent to his home. I loved going from Mbale to Kampala and back, by bus. At Jinja we crossed the headwaters of the Nile River. The Nile flows from the south to the north, which is not normal. Lower Egypt is north, and Upper Egypt is south. Crossing the dam at Jinja is awesome. The powerful waters of the Nile at Jinja generate the hydroelectric power to the region. Its power as it pours through that dam is like Niagara Falls.

While Valerie returned to Texas, Vincent and I went back to Joshua's and Elizabeth's house in Musoma, Tanzania. When we got there, they fed us lunch. During lunch Joshua asked: "Did you know you came through a tribal war?" I answered, "No, we did not." He told us that the warring tribal factions along the way to Musoma were waylaying buses, robbing and killing the passengers. We just went on through. We did stop at Sirari, and met with Susan, our intercessor. I also taught in some of the churches there.

It was here that I taught in other local churches, not just at Joshua's. While at another church in Musoma, something else happened that gave proof of the difference between the soul and the spirit. I have already told about Tanzania 1997, and the malaria, and how I could still preach, even though I could not remember my own name.

In this meeting, I was standing preaching with my Bible in my left hand, gesturing as usual with my right hand. Truly the first finger of the right hand is the "Torah finger." The word Torah, while meaning teachings and instructions, literally means in Hebrew: "to shoot out the finger in teaching." It was on the first finger of the right hand that the mosquito bit me in Uganda, that almost caused me to die of malaria in 1997. During this teaching session, as usual, I was very focused on what I was teaching the people. All of a sudden, the Spirit begins talking to me in the mind of the re-born spirit. I heard Him talking. He was giving me a revelation to give to the people. I never stopped preaching. But, I listened to Him in my spirit, and even spoke with Him. When He was finished, I stopped and told the people, "I just had a revelation from God." Of course the revelation went along with what I was teaching. When I gave it, the people jumped and shouted in joy, because it was just for them – for the women in particular, that they carried their babies over the area of the spirit, and what that meant. They understood!

I flew out of Entebbe Airport, Entebbe, Uganda, through Cairo to Amman, then to Aqaba. Flying into Cairo, at about 8:00 AM, I looked down over the plain of Giza, to see three pyramids. One was the Great Pyramid. I went there in 2010 on an assignment from Abba.

AFRICA
(2000-2001)

Earlier this year, I will never forget the phone call from my son, who was living in Texas at the time. I was in America, just before leaving to go back to Jordan. He said a man named Ronald Kuta Wanyonyi had called him to tell him Vincent had died of tuberculosis.

I had a vision while he and I were on a long bus ride in 1998 that he was dressed in a choir robe and singing a solo part with the heavenly choir. I heard the music--I've never heard music like that on earth. That vision and hearing the music kept up, on and off, for several days. When I got to Vincent's home in 2000, it was very strange not having him there. The other pastors took care of me, and kept me busy with ministering in their churches – Pastor Meshak and Beatrice, Pastor Joseph and Electina, Pastor Ronald Kuta and his wife, and others.

In 1999, when I was at Vincent's, I saw how they mounded up dirt and then put tree branches inside and lit them, and then covered them. They let the fire burn the branches into charcoal. Then they used the charcoal for the jiggos. When I got to Vincent's in June of 2000, I saw a mound of dirt next to the kitchen – right where Vincent used to brush his teeth in the morning. I remember one morning, I went out to brush my teeth using water in a thermos, and I saw him brushing his teeth. I pretended to make fun of him--he laughed.

After being there for a couple of days, I asked Lydia if we could go to Vincent's family village, so that I could see where he was buried. Julius had been buried in his family village, and Grace took me to the village to see his grave, and visit with his parents. Lydia motioned to the mound by the kitchen, and said he was buried there. I was so shocked. He had a proper burial with friends, and he was home. Ronald and the other pastors with Vincent fought tribal tradition to allow them to bury Vincent by his home, without him being cremated. They also fought for Lydia so that she did not have to marry one of Vincent's relatives, nor participate in any pagan traditions.

In June of 1999, I flew from Amman Jordan to Entebbe Airport, Entebbe, Uganda. Bethuel picked me up. I stayed with Bethuel, Florence, and their children a few days and ministered in Kampala, then Bethuel went with me by bus to help me get safely to Kisumu. He returned to Kampala, while I stayed with Katy, who had her own place with a missionary friend. Then I went to Vincent's home place.

In coming this time in 2000, I also flew from Amman to Entebbe Airport. Bethuel was supposed to pick me up, but he was

PART V - Training Assignments

not there when I landed. I had to use someone's cell phone to call the church. They did not even know I was coming. They did not know where Bethuel was. But, eventually he came. That's Africa! He took me back to their house. I fell into such a deep sleep on my bed, that later he tried for about 10 minutes to wake me up-- he shook me, yelled at me, poked me, and shook me some more, but I would not wake up. Finally I did, of course. I've had that happened only about three times in my life, but it shows the depth of exhaustion. He not only had me speaking at his church, but opened up places for me to speak in several other churches in the city. I met many new pastors.

I spoke in one large church on my birthday. This church had a precious pastor who was not into "blab it and grab it." A lady gave me a plastic red rose for my birthday, which I kept for a long time. At that church, there was a young white man who was working with the pastor. After I spoke, he sat down with me and very quietly said that he saw the anointing of Elijah on me. I thanked him. I knew from Abba that He had given me that anointing back in 1985, but that it was slow in developing. Of course, I spoke at Michael Lutalo's church again--Appointed Harvesters – and in another open-air meeting with him.

Bethuel took me back to Pastor Elijah's wonderful church. It was then that I taught quite a number of youth, from early teens through early 20s. I had a National Geographic magazine of the landing on the moon, complete with takeoff pictures. I asked them if they knew that humans had landed on the moon. They shook their heads, no. I asked them if they had ever seen a computer? They did not know what a computer was. They knew bicycles, cars, and buses. So I encouraged them to study hard to become the best in their chosen fields.

My missionary friend, Karen, from Fort Worth, who had served the Master in Nigeria, had given me a large quilt with a map of the world on one side, and the other side was blank for signatures. I had the pastors sign the blank side, which delighted them. I did this in many places, and so my quilt's other side is covered in names of pastors. It is lovely!

I stayed with Bethuel and Florence. I remember one afternoon seeing Florence sitting on the concrete floor of her porch with their jiggo, making chapati. It is the most wonderful bread. Years later my pastor-hostess in Colombia gave me some of their local traditional bread – it was Colombian "chapati."

Bethuel took me to a church where people gathered during lunch time to hear the Word. I taught there several times, always giving a message from one of the Psalms. Right outside the side door of the church was a brothel. The people in the church cared for the women who were sex slaves, to bring them to salvation, to find them jobs, and help free them from their life of sin. A few women had been helped, but there were so many problems. For a woman to find a job in Africa is very hard. They taught the women to do some basic skills like sewing, so that they can make clothes and sell them.

I went one day after the meeting to talk to some of the women. The madam of the brothel allowed me to do so. It was very strange for I was sitting outside the door to the brothel, knowing that inside some of the women were having sex. But, I told them how to be free, even with the madam sitting there listening.

Bethuel set up meetings for me in a remote village to teach in a pastor's conference. I believe it was his home village, as I remember. It was a wonderful week with wonderful people. The young man who took me out there had borrowed a friend's car. As we went along, he asked me what I thought of the pre-tribulation rapture of the church. I gently let him know the truth. He said: "My pastor teaches that, but the Holy Spirit in me told me it is not true." I rejoiced!

On returning from there, he was driving along the road and we heard screams coming from the top of the hill. We looked up the hill to our left and a raging bull was charging down the hill towards the road. He was BIG. The young man tried to stop but it was too late – we clipped the bull on his right flank. It really damaged the front of the car. I helped him pay for the repair.

Bethuel had been to the U.S. two or three times, but he wanted to take Florence. I tried to help Florence, but for some reason the U.S. Embassy would not give her a visa. Later she was able to go to the U.S. for a women's conference, as a representative from Uganda. I set up a place for Bethuel to stay in America with a family in Houston. I had meetings in their home in Houston several times. He also stayed with my son for a few days one time.

During the last two weeks before leaving Kampala, for some reason that I forget, but I remember it was for a very valid reason, Bethuel put me up in a hotel. It was during this time that I had malaria AGAIN. But, as soon as the aching started, I asked Bethuel to get me Metakelfin. He did, and I laid there sweating under heavy blankets from the Metakelfin, but I did not get the fever, and thus the malaria was stopped. But still, I was very weak.

I still had two more pastor's conferences scheduled-- one in Uganda and one in Kenya—before I left. I didn't know how I could do that, being weakened from the malaria, but I was going to go anyway. I went to Bethuel's church office to get e-mails. I got an e-mail from the leader of the group I was with in Aqaba. She was in America, but she had "inside information," that something was happening in Aqaba that she could not tell me about, but that I must not return to Aqaba. It was August. Aqaba in August is between 100 to 120 F. I sat there in front of the computer and asked Abba: "What do you want me to do?" He immediately answered: "I want you to cancel the pastor's conferences, and go right now to the Egypt Air office and change your ticket to fly to Jordan right away." I said to Bethuel: "Could you take me to Egypt Air right now?" He took me, and I got booked on a flight the next day to Amman, then to Aqaba. He took me to Entebbe airport about 3:00 AM. My flight went out at about 5:00 for Cairo. I was so exhausted. The director of the airport put me in his office to lie on the couch to sleep. I could not sleep, but it was nice to lie down.

I got back to Aqaba, and sat on my balcony drinking ice tea. I was looking right at the border with Israel. I just sat there speaking in tongues and praying. I did not know what was happening, or what He wanted me back there for. There was no one from our group there, because it was too hot for them in the summer. I went to the market and was amazed at all the new large-sized men in Aqaba with big fluffy beards. But, I thought nothing of it. I just interceded for whatever Abba wanted. How did I know that on that very border, Ariel Sharon had lined up missiles to "wipe Aqaba off the map" IF King Abdullah didn't get all those thousands of terrorists out of there?

The terrorists had lined up missiles pointing at Eilat, so Sharon countered it. If one of Sharon's missiles had fired straight forward, it might have landed on my balcony. I'm just obedient. I found out also that at the same time, Russia moved 60,000 rockets into Lebanon for Hezbollah to shoot at Israel. I learned also that at the same time, the finest troops of Saddam Hussein had moved into the "west bank" and Sharon had sent in tanks to counter that. The world's news media had a field day with that-- Sharon sends tanks into Palestinian land.

The situation was serious, so evidently, Abba needed me there to intercede more than He needed me to teach in pastor's conferences. But, the malaria had weakened me so much that I felt I could not go to Patmos in September. More on that: September 29, 2000/2001 –Yom Teruah, a Shmittah year, the second of the last three cycles before Messiah comes. I will pick up this narrative in Part VI.

I was in Africa seven times in six years, staying three weeks the first visit, but three months each time after that: 6 X 3 = 18 months, plus 3 weeks. So, all total, I was in Africa a little more than a 1 ½ years. About 80% of the time, I was out in the bush - staying in mud huts, or concrete houses, or housing made with homemade bricks. I was out on the road preaching in many places, or riding buses long distances (some through dangerous places)--of course it would take a book just by itself to tell all about Africa.

THE GREATEST MIRACLE OF ALL IS ABBA'S MERCY AND LOVE!

PART VI

THE MIDDLE EAST

AND TRAVELS BEYOND

(1999-2013)

JORDAN -- GREECE/PATMOS-ATHENS-CORINTH
SWITZERLAND -- ITALY -- FRANCE
ISRAEL -- WESTERN TURKEY -- WALES
U.S. (INCLUDING ALASKA) -- COLOMBIA -- ENGLAND
IRELAND -- PANAMA --EGYPT -- BOLIVIA
GERMANY -- SCOTLAND (OUTER HEBRIDES)
ICELAND -- ROME/VATICAN

JORDAN
(1999)

I previously told the story about how Abba told me to go to Jordan at the end of 1998. I sure didn't think that up in my head. That was the furthest thought from my mind. It was November 1998, and I had returned from a wonderful trip to Africa, as you can read above.

I was resting in my easy-chair. I simply asked Him: "What do you want me to do now?" I did not expect an immediate answer – certainly not the one I got! He said: "I want you to give away everything you have and move to Jordan." He immediately implanted joy in my spirit. He is always so good to make His shocking instructions palatable (smile). I am a servant. I am used to instructions from my Master, but this was a shocker. I began thinking of who to give things too – it would be so much fun! And it was...

He wasn't saying anything more to me than He already said to us all in **Luke 14:25-33**. **Verse 33**: "**Unless you forsake all that you have, you CANNOT be My disciple**." He just gave me the specifics of where and when, why, and what for. He expects a nomad attitude and lifestyle in His servants. Western thinking that is flesh-serving is unacceptable to Him!

By this time I had left the two bedroom apartment because the rent kept climbing higher and higher. I had gotten a one bedroom apartment in another building on the same property. My daughter put her bed in my bedroom. I was working at Mardel – a big, and I mean BIG, Christian supply store in Fort Worth. I asked off just before Christmas to go to visit my Aunt Ahnie and Uncle Charlie in Fort Smith. The roads in Fort Worth had iced over; then it snowed. The roads were slick, so getting out of Fort Worth was difficult. But, I had the strongest sense that it would be the last time I saw my Uncle Charlie–and it was.

The money I made barely covered expenses for my daughter and I. My mother's inheritance had dwindled to almost nothing by this time. Precious Michael and Theresa gave me $4,000.00 thousand dollars, and all together I went to Jordan with a little over $4,000.00. I thought I was very, very rich.

I had a scare before I left for Aqaba. In March of 1999, King Hussein died. They were all expecting him to name Prince Hassan, son of Queen Noor, as his heir to the Hashemite throne. But, to the shock of the Jordanians, he named the son of the English wife he divorced, the son who had studied in England and was then a commanding officer of the Jordanian military--Abdullah II. Most likely it was because of the political clout he has with the world community, but for Abba's purposes as well, he was a good choice!

I was told that I should not come to Jordan at that time because of the potential for civil war. But, Abba assured me it would be all right. I got there and found out that the Jordanian attitude was: "We have to trust the decision of King Hussein, and support him as our new King." The transfer of power was totally peaceful!

Not long after my arrival, I learned that I was considered the "poor kid on the block," and looked down on by the affluent Americans in our "group." I had not come to Aqaba for any other reason other than my Master Yahushua told me to come. I never felt a part of "the group." I had not found an apartment right away, so I was invited to stay with my friend from Emanuel Christian Fellowship. We had a good time sharing the Word and fellowshipping. She was precious, she still is. I was able to teach in her apartment several times. She actually had rented two apartments side by side, which she decorated beautifully. I had the other apartment for myself.

One night, not long after arriving, I was lying on my back trying to go to sleep, when all of a sudden this huge over-sized man appeared in my room. He had long greasy-looking hair, a thick beard, and wide face. He was one ugly dude! He did not touch me, but as with the Buddhist spirits in Mongolia, he pinned me to the bed. I could not move anything except my lips, but not very wide. I did spiritual warfare, commanding him to let me loose, for about 45 minutes. Finally he let me loose and left. I had learned Abba's Name by then and was using it. But, he was determined to keep me pinned down as long as possible. I had no fear. I just thought it was an amazing situation that I wanted out of. The next morning, the leader-lady of the group had come to visit my friend next door. I joined them. I told them what happened. The leader-lady casually said: "Oh that was Chedorlaomer; he pinned Hank to the bed twice; but then, you and Hank have a similar calling." She said: "Let's go and pray so he doesn't return." He never returned.

But, in looking at Scripture (**Genesis 14**), he was in that very area. He was the King of Elam (Iran/Persia) who gathered twelve kings of nations from the Midian Mountains to attack the kings of the Dead Sea area, as in Sodom and Gomorrah. In doing so, he took Lot captive into Damascus, and Abraham went and rescued him. I wonder if his visit was a compliment (smile).

As I wrote under Africa 1999, this friend took me on a tour of southern Jordan. When we got to Shobak Castle, something else assailed me. She went on up with the Arab guide to the top of the castle area, while I wandered around below. I walked through a narrow stone hallway, with rooms on each side, and all of a sudden demonic spirits began attacking, and I felt them trying to take my breath away. I ran out of there. She came down the hill with the guide, saw me in distress, and I told her what happened. She asked the guide what happened in those rooms. He said it was a teaching center for the Mamlukes who taught the Koran in that place. She said to me: "Because of your stand in the Word, the spirits of the Koran attacked you."

It was on that trip that another significant thing happened. I told earlier about how, as I wrote the check before leaving Fort Worth to pay off the last of my credit card bill, the Presence of Abba moved into the room so strongly and I stopped writing. I said: "Yes Sir?" He said softly: "**Daughter**." Then His strong Presence departed. I did not know what He meant. As she drove on that narrow road around the big canyon of the Fords of Arnon (**Deuteronomy 2; Joshua 11:18**), the border of Moab and Ammon, I was praising Abba joyfully. Then I told her about what He called me – "**Daughter**." She about ran off the road. She told me what that means in Hebrew cultural understanding: **He was telling me that He would assume total care of me in all ways, protecting me, providing for me, being my counselor--like a Daddy--until the day of my marriage**. That explained His relationship with me until my marriage to Yahushua.

How relevant is the Fords of Arnon today? **Isaiah 16:2**: It is extremely relevant. That very place where the Arnon River flows into the Dead Sea is now called the Wadi Mujib. It is where people will come who will be fleeing out of Amman, out of Damascus, out of southern Lebanon, and out of north Israel. **Isaiah 16:1-5** is talking to some group of people positioned on the straight highway (also mentioned in Isaiah), where the Arnon river flows out of that huge canyon into the Dead Sea. In about 2003, as I was taking a bus to Amman, we stopped at this place. I looked out and saw military huts all along the Dead Sea. It was a military post. They came on the bus to check everyone's ID. I had my residency card by then. But, it put chills all over me because **Isaiah 16:1-5** is talking to the Jordanian military!

Our group was about 40 people. But, I learned that several large groups had come, then left out of discouragement, and some out of anger at the way the "group" was controlled. But, this group was close-knit. I tried to fit in with everything, but sometimes I couldn't. I attended whole meetings where all they talked about was getting a lawyer to help them get residency. At that time, they had to have $100,000 dollars each in the bank. So, they passed the money around so that the bank statements read $100,000 in each account. Early on, the husband of the leader-lady told me bluntly: "If you don't have $100,000.00 we don't want you." That was a big hurt. Welcome to Aqaba! But, he was like that. He loudly condemned me in front of our group, saying things that were not true--things against my very nature-- but others believed him. Can you imagine the shock both he and his wife got when I went to visit them in Fort Worth, pulled out my residency card, and handed it to them to see? Talk about a moment of poetic justice! They were too shocked to speak!

I always prayed two Scriptures when dealing with the ASEZA – **Psalm 5:12** and **Psalm 57:1-3**. An allegorical word for "favor," is "grace." These words simply mean: The empowerment of the Spirit to carry out the assignments of the Master!

Besides the money requirements, they had to get yearly blood tests, then a yearly spit test. They were so angry when they found out that I did not have to have any more blood tests other than the first one, and no spit test. **ASEZA – Aqaba Special Economic Zone Authority --** is controlled by the U.S., U.N., E.U., but mainly by the U.S. in that it set up the ASEZA and the banking system.

The Jordanian Dinar (JD) is always stable: $1.42 U.S. = 1 JD. If I gave the cashier at the bank $100.00 U.S., she gave me 70 JD. I asked a man at the bank why the JD never fluctuated in relationship to the dollar. He motioned for me to lean over so he could whisper in my ear. He said it was because the JD was based on the dollar. I also learned in private, from a man who worked at the ASEZA, that it was the U.S. who set up the whole structure of the economic zone, and the ASEZA itself.

I arrived the evening of April 18, 1999. As I said, two of my three bags did not come to Aqaba with me, but He gave me that little plastic camel I saw in the dirt – with two humps, and said they represented my two suitcases that were coming. It gave me such peace. I could have gone with one suitcase! My little camel "disappeared" with all my moving, but on January 6, 2013, while going through a large plastic container that held some of my rock treasures from Jordan, there it was. It bought back good memories of Abba's continual demonstrations of His love.

The night I arrived, there was a gathering at the home of one of the three leaders. It was a Friday night. I was crying all the time; I couldn't stop crying. I missed my children so badly. I was so worried about the youngest one, and as you read in my Africa report, I had a reason for being worried. I cried for the daughter I was living with. I wanted to go home. I thought I was crazy to have ever gone there. I sat down at the table. The leader-lady sat to my left. I kept getting up and going to the bathroom to wipe away the tears. But, before I even started eating, she said: "We received a bad report on you." That was so cruel! She proceeded to tell me that my former pastor Jim had told her I was not to be trusted because I was unstable and would leave at any time. I told her the story of how Abba led me to Bethesda and that He told me not to tell him I was going. I don't know why He told me to do that, but I have my suspicions. Sadly, that was my "welcome" to Aqaba! I tried entering into the social life and religious life there. They had about three meetings a week – Torah study on Thursday night, a pot-luck meal together on Friday night, and then a re-cap of Shabbat on Saturday night.

In May, I was at my friend's house with some other ladies in our apartment building, and she said: "Let's have some tea and watch CNN world news." So she fixed us tea, and then on the hour, she turned on CNN Europe. Immediately James Reuben, chief spokesman for NATO, came on the screen in his NATO uniform, with the American flag behind him. Large words appeared over the screen: "**One World Government**." He said: "**I am here to announce that the one world government has now been established**." He proceeded to say: "What you are seeing in Kosovo is a demonstration of the power of NATO as the core military of the one world government." We were stunned. He kept talking. He said that the United Nations had better back down and accept the fact that they were in power and the one world order was a reality. After he finished, we waited to see the U.S. News. We listened to 45 minutes about the latest Steven Spielberg movie, and 15 minutes of an update on the Jon Benet Ramsey case. Then the leader-lady called and asked if we had heard the news. She said she had been watching BBC Europe when they announced that the one world government had been established. NATO was the "core military," the G-8 was the economic leader, and the head of it all was Clinton and Blair.

In December Tony Blair stayed with the King of Jordan ten days over January 1st. Then Prince William came for a visit, stayed a week, and went to Petra. In November 2000, Prince Charles stayed with the King several days, and went to Petra. These visits did not hit the world news media, or even the news in Jordan, but we knew all about it from those who were involved with their itineraries.

1999: I went to Africa for three months--June, July and August. Then the big trip--Russia--during September, October, November and December. Reports are above in Part V. Before I went to Russia, I met one of the American directors of Ebenezer (Operation Exodus) who had just moved to Aqaba with his family. They joined our group.

Before I went to Africa in mid-June, the leader-lady took me to see a new apartment building that had been built for the engineers, surveyors, consultants, and project managers with Condote Roma, a major company from Rome that built concrete dams, bridges, conduits, and the like. Their first highway rebuilding project was to rebuild the King's Highway. This is the same highway that Moses and friends walked on to go to Esau's Mt. Seir – Petra. (**Numbers 21:22-23**) It is still called "the King's highway." Condote Roma re-built the very old historic King's Highway all the way from the Port of Aqaba northeast to Ma'an. Then another company took it to Amman, then across northern Iraq to Afghanistan. Then another company took it into the Silk Road of China, which is a military road. So, without break, the King's Highway actually goes from the Port of Aqaba into China.

I was able to rent an apartment in that building. I really loved that place! The apartment had three bedrooms, a big office area, big living room, kitchen, two bathrooms, an entryway as large as a small room, and a balcony, for only $350.00 a month. I stayed there six of my eight years in Aqaba. The rich of our group told me that it would take $4,000.00 to buy just the appliances. As I tell in the Collections, I got my appliances that I used for the eight years I was in Aqaba, for $400.00. I got a small Japanese-made refrigerator, a 3-burner hot plate that I set on the kitchen counter, a washing machine that just washed (I even had to run water into it through the sink via the hose, and drain the water into a hole in the floor via the same hose), and a fan. Later the people next door who moved out, left me their ceiling fans – one of the greatest gifts I could have received in that desert land! Another one gave me a smaller plastic table. Another offered me a TV and I said, "NO thank you." I was there to learn from Abba, not be entertained by uselessness. Another one gave me their stainless steel pots and pans when they left.

There were always people exiting, either angry, disgusted, or in despair. The leader-lady often riled people up by being controlling, and by making rules that were not from Abba, to say the least. There was also friction because of how she treated our Sudanese refugees (about 15) that we were sheltering, and her involvement with the local government, and other big wigs in town.

After moving into my apartment, I rarely had a visitor. The people were very cliquish. I've never been a part of a clique--I find that silly. After signing the lease for the apartment, my friends told me it would take at least two weeks to get my bank account set up, my phone hooked up, my P.O. Box key, the electricity in my name, and the water put in my name. It took me less than two hours to get everything either done, or set in motion. To get my bank account and my P.O. Box, took me a few minutes in each place. They said no one had ever done that before! I walked into the Post Office, asked for a box, they signed me up, I paid them 5 JD for the year, and they gave me my key. In Arab culture, confusion is the norm, but, not that day!

In 2000, in getting my residency with the same abundant favor, without a lawyer, and with 44 cents in the bank, made them upset. Some mocked me. But by 2001, I had 56 cents in the bank, and didn't even need a second blood test. I have never been proud, haughty, or arrogant, about the favor He gives me! I fear Him! It is a gift that is only to be used for His purposes! It makes me very humbled and contrite. It is His doing. I do nothing, absolutely nothing, to manipulate favor in my direction. Like in China, the Open Doors people were amazed that the ticket people always gave me the Chinese rate.

All my life I have been highly favored. Even in my sin, He never removed this gift – for "the gifts and callings of Yahuweh are without repentance." Once He chooses someone based on his foreknowledge, He bestows gifts that continue on through their life. **Romans 11:20**: This is why He never cast off the whole of the House of Ya'cob. He has always had a remnant that He foreknew from the foundation of the world. I never used His favor as a manipulation tool for personal advantage over others. Those things are not my nature. So, when they got so disgruntled at me because of the favor, even later mocking my Torah-guarding, I just kept quiet. Those who have no hidden agendas or personal ambitions for themselves, but are humble and contrite, have no problem with me!

I met several of the Condote Roma personnel who lived in the apartment building. Some had families, but most (all men) had left their families in Rome. The head of the road-repair project was a Jordanian engineer. He and his family lived just two roads up the hill, just below the King's Highway. (**Numbers 20:17; 21:22**). He was an engineer in a Jordanian company that built the Dead Sea Highway--the "straight highway"--from Aqaba to Amman, that goes along by the Dead Sea, using 400 Chinese workers. He said he gave gospel tracts to each of the Chinese workers. He and his family are believers. They went to the Evangelical Free church in Aqaba.

In 2,000 he was given a computer by his company and a disc of their engineering specs that they wanted updated, and gave him a deadline to update them. He did not know how to use the computer, let alone use the disc. So, he asked the leader-lady if she knew anyone who could do typing for him. For some reason, she recommended me. That was nice of her! As I was typing in the new specs for him, using the old ones and adding and changing things, I was so overwhelmed that the wording was close to the wording in the Scriptures regarding the rebuilding of "the King's Highway" in the last days. I realized that instructions were given to the Condote Roma workers in the book of Isaiah. I wrote the article "There Shall Be A Highway" as my first article after getting my computer from Michael and Theresa in 2000. I later jokingly told one of the consultants on the project that their road building methods sure had changed drastically. When the Romans built the King's Highway over 2,000 years ago, they laid down huge stones. But, in Isaiah it talks about re-building the highway--removing the stones, mounding up the dirt, leveling it, and making it smooth.

Before I signed the lease for that wonderful apartment with the balcony that overlooked; the Israel border crossing with Eilat, the Eliat airport, the Red Sea, and Egypt, a woman who was visiting the leader-lady wanted to share rent and live with me. I thought she had been a good friend of the leader-lady, but later found out that she was just an acquaintance. I did not have a good feeling about her. She was extremely controlling--a little bleached blond spit-fire. I didn't need that. But, I needed to save the money. So, before she left to the U.S., I told her that I would accept her offer to pay $175.00 a month. We went out to lunch at Ali Baba's – the best place in town to eat – and we talked. She began telling me which room she wanted in the apartment, what she was going to do to decorate the entire apartment, and telling me all of her plans for it. I just sat there in amazement – she was taking over the whole apartment. She said the second bedroom was for her sewing room. I told her I had to have the big area for my office and bedroom – the second living room or dining room area. She didn't like that. Where did she want me to sleep – on the couch? In essence she was totally taking over my power to make any decisions on my own. She had even bought some material to make curtains, which she showed me--telling me her color scheme.

Before going to the U.S., she gave me a check for her part of a year's rent. I was sick inside. But, I deposited her check. For an overseas bank to release funds for an American check, it takes about 27 days. During that time, I wrote her and told her that I couldn't do it – that I would send all of her money back, which I did. It would have been a disaster! Abba had plans for me to be isolated, so that He could begin teaching me, and start my writing ministry.

I signed a lease for my own apartment within about a month after arriving. After returning from Africa, the group began honoring me since I was going to Russia with Ebenezer (Operation Exodus). This organization helps Jews return to Israel from Russia, and the former Soviet Union countries.

During 1999, the group leader rented a large compound in Aqaba for our meetings. We had been meeting in the Anglican church on Saturday. This new compound had a large attached courtyard, which we used for our new moon offerings, and other celebrations. The Sudanese men lived in the bedrooms and were caretakers for our compound. These Christian men had fled from Sudan, several had seen their families massacred in the Christian area of the south. The government of Sudan is Muslim, of course. The atrocities done to the Christians in the south were horrible. I worked with them via the Voice of the Martyrs for some time, taking goods and Bibles for them to send to the needy, and especially helping those in Uganda, since Sudan is on the northern border with Uganda. These men were precious!

The family, whose father had worked with Ebenezer, had come from Colorado to live in Aqaba. They saw that the Sudanese were not included with what we did. They petitioned the leaders for some changes, but they were met with opposition. They, and their friends from Colorado, who had also moved there at the time, came against the rule of the leader-couple. Because they hit a brick wall in the protests, their friends left Aqaba very angry. They had sold everything in the U.S. to come there, but the family stayed. The leaders came and went to the U.S. In 2000, when they left, they left an older couple (retired Methodist pastors) in charge of our meetings. We had prayer meetings each morning in their apartment, which was just to the right of my apartment.

In fact, each time they left, the unity and peace among all the people, Sudanese included, was awesome. The retired pastors were loving and kind. They counseled me several times when I needed someone to talk to. Everyone had a chance to minister, not just the leaders. They included the Sudanese. The Sudanese would sing and testify. We prayed for them, and they prayed too. It was a loving, united family.

We met at my Texas friend's apartment for fellowship and sharing on Friday nights. It was there one evening, that we all did "brainstorming" about the ways that Abba speaks to us. I listed 40 ways that we came up with, and checked them out with Scripture. This later turned into my article: "Forty Ways Elohim Speaks To His People"/August 2003/revised January 2008.

I got to teach too. I even had a Sudanese interpreter who interpreted my messages for his people during one Saturday service. Miracles happened there. Like I said, when the leaders left, we had a family. People came to visit me, and there was love among us all. As soon as the leader-couple returned, they stopped the retired pastors from being our pastors. They said that only they, our Hebrew scholar, who was their close friend, and a Pentecostal pastor whose church we attended on Sunday, could preach. The Sudanese were not allowed to sing in our services. Finally we helped all the Sudanese to get visas to Egypt, or to Damascus. There are long stories I won't go into, but when the leaders left, we went back to being a united family. Everyone was treated equally!

The family who had come in 1999, had spoken up for the Sudanese. The leader-couple informed them that they were blackballed from our group--they could not come to our meetings for two years. They had four children at that time, a fifth one came along while they were in Jordan. They were in Jordan for 9 years, because Abba sent them there. But, the whole group was told that we could not talk to this family for they were ostracized. My friend on the third floor and I thought that was ridiculous. So, sometimes we would walk up to their road, which faced the King's Highway. If any of the family were outside, we'd talk to them. Finally we just went to visit them and became friends.

We went on trips to different parts of southern Jordan and to the beach on the Red Sea many times. During these two years, the family made friends with local Arabs--both Muslim, Palestinian, and Christian Arabs. They learned many things from their Arab friends who confided in them. Then this family, feeling the loneliness after two years, apologized to the leaders for their insubordination. They were invited back for a few of the meetings, but they really didn't go back like before.

Most there never did embrace the Torah, not really. Most of those who came there to live, did "Jewish things," but it was a loose-goose kind of thing--depending on what they wanted to do. So, as I became more Torah-guarding, not going out to dinner with them on Friday evenings to restaurants, they labeled me "Jewish," and some bitterly mocked me. One evening, I told them that I could not go out for pizza if I had to pay after sunset. They came to get me at sunset. I told them I could not go. I had no food in the house but a cucumber and a few crackers. I sat on my couch, took up my Bible, and all of a sudden I felt the Presence of Yahushua in the room. For two hours I asked Him questions, and He answered me. I later told the pizza eaters that I had made the right choice. They could not answer back.

Slowly, as 1999 went on, I got more friends, including the pastor and his wife of a little church that was within walking distance. They were of the Pentecostal Holiness denomination, both children of pastors from Louisiana. I loved them! They were good to me. It was the wife, Karen, who took me to the Russian Embassy in Amman to get my visa for Russia. Though I was coming into guarding Torah, they were my pastors for about five years.

While the leaders were away, we had Torah-midrash on Thursday night, and Shabbat dinner on Friday night at their house. I loved that. Betty, who led the midrash, did such a good job. We had such unity. I loved sitting around after Shabbat dinner, talking about the end-times. But, when the leaders came back, it ended.

When I returned from Russia, I found out about the major upheaval and that some of my friends had left angry. Two families later converted to Judaism. I was also told that the group had begun to guard the Rosh Chodesh--New Moon Festivals. My heart sunk. What next? I was just understanding Shabbat, the Festivals, and His Names and Titles. But, I respected our Hebrew scholar, who had begun the new moon celebrations.

So, I studied, using my Strong's Exhaustive Concordance, with Hebrew and Greek Dictionaries. I found that Shabbat, the celebration of the seven Festivals, and Rosh Chodesh--the sighting of the first sliver of the New Moon—were intertwined. The verses that convinced me of the unity of the three, eternally, was **Isaiah 66:22-23**.

They were going to have a new moon celebration; dinner, Hebrew dancing, and Scripture reading. Then we would have a ceremony in the courtyard by our rented compound. My attitude was: OK—if Abba likes it, I will accept it, but I have to know if He likes it. That night, we went outside after the other festivities in the community building. Our Hebrew scholar lit the fire pit. We had been asked to bring an unleavened cake of flour, water, and oil, or a bunch of fresh grain, one for each family, or each individual. The recipes are in **Leviticus 2; Numbers 28:11-15**.

We sat around in folding-chairs. I looked at each one there, and a strange thing happened. I felt His Spirit bonding us together. Here we were celebrating Rosh Chodesh in a Muslim land. Tall apartment buildings surrounded our courtyard, so we had to be very discrete. Our Hebrew scholar, took the meal cakes one at a time, salted each, and called out our names and then threw them into the fire. He ended with the "drink offering." We all stood up by the fire for this. I felt His Presence so strong. All I could think was: "He likes it; He likes it." Finally, we all packed into the storage barn and the shofars were blown. But, after the Muslims complained to the police years later, all of this wonderful celebration stopped.

I celebrated Rosh Chodesh in America, by speaking several times in East Texas, though without the grain cakes and drink offering. Again, the unity among the people was incredible. I think it was because we joined in unity around the celebration from the ancient ways of His calendar, in preparation for the great YOM TERUAH – ROSH CHODESH – when Messiah will descend amidst the blowing of trumpets.

Our Hebrew scholar started teaching Hebrew language lessons at the compound. I was doing so well. It was exciting. But, the police found out, because they were constantly watching us, and listening to our conversations. They put electronic devices in cars that they parked outside our buildings. So, we had to stop it.

I was lonely for my family, and for anyone who would befriend me. I thought that if I bought living room furniture people would come visit me. My apartment was empty, except for my bed, a plastic table and plastic chairs someone had given me. So I went to the furniture store that they all went to, and bought a brand new living room suit. I bought a large plastic white table and four chairs. Later people gave me things, and I also used wooden boxes for small tables. I decorated with seashells and rocks. I put maps on the wall, of course.

I thought my apartment would then attract friends. NO! They had no desire to come see my new furniture. Even my Texas friend was angry because I asked her to come see it. She actually said to someone in my hearing: 'Why should I waste my time coming to see her furniture?" My isolation paid off, but it was painful at the start.

When the ministry was incorporated in 1990, I had no computer. I got a word processor, but I gave that away when I moved to Jordan. So, when I moved to Jordan, I got out and walked a lot. I remember my first Christmas in Aqaba. I was so lonely. It was a horrible day. I looked out my window and saw my friends walking together, but they did not invite me. I spent the day writing letters to my children. I had stopped celebrating Christmas by this time, but still, when you grow up with Thanksgiving and Christmas--both family times--it is lonely when you're not with your family. I got over it. In editing this, it will be Thanksgiving 2012 tomorrow. I am in Israel. My whole family is together at my oldest daughter's house in Tennessee. But, ya know what? I am not lonely anymore! Beginning in 2002, when I started writing and getting so much response via the computer, I had no time to be lonely. I am very happy to be by myself, for I am never alone--Abba has become my constant Companion and Friend!

There was a wonderful couple in the apartment to my left, but they left angry, while I was in Russia. However, while they were there, we had some good social times, playing domino train. Each morning after our early-morning prayer meetings in the apartment to my right, many of us would go to the apartment on the left of me to listen to Michael Rood's CDs on "The Feasts of the Lord." It was Michael's teaching that excited me about guarding the Festivals. How was I to know that later I would become friends with Michael and Judith in Israel? In addition, their Israeli editor became one of my closest friends. It was this couple on the left who left me their ceiling fans, when they left Aqaba. Our early-morning prayer meetings had to stop because the Jordanians had technology that aided them to listen in on our prayer meetings. They would park a car near where we met, turn on the listening device, and record what we said in our apartments.

I was in a fetal position a lot at first, because of the cliquishness of the people. I hated Shabbat. People were busy all week and had no time to talk to me. Some would sleep in until afternoon each day then stay up almost all night. On Shabbat, everyone would take their phone off the hook, and even then, I still couldn't talk to anyone. When Abba began my 12-14 hour-a-day research and writing routine, from 2001 on, I really came to love Shabbat. I learned that He speaks more on Shabbat than at any other time in the week, if we spend time listening to Him.

In 2001, I was still an ordained minister with my own corporation. I was a mover and shaker. I could get more done in a day than most people did in a week. After I stopped working secular jobs, I kept business hours to do the work of the Kingdom--I still do. I know how important it is to be very disciplined. It upset me so much to see the laziness of the Americans who were in our group. One family slept in until 1:00

or 2:00 in the afternoon, because they didn't get to bed until almost dawn. I dubbed them "The Dracula Society." But, that's pretty typical for Americans in third world nations, across board. Because they don't have the routines of American society to discipline them, being naturally undisciplined, they get little done of any value. So, they bring the attitudes and lifestyle of America into the foreign country, and are no good to anyone, not even to themselves.

One thing I learned about this region--whether on the Muslim side or the Jewish side of the border--what one really is inside will eventually manifest on the outside. The masks drop off, and the real face is exposed. It is shocking! Someone can look really nice and spiritual in America, but when they move to a non-western country, what was hidden surfaces--the masks come off! But, remember, Aqaba is a U.S. zone. Drug dealing, prostitution, pornography, violent movies, violent music, gambling, excessive alcohol drinking, and every other vice is there. Wherever American money goes, so go their "industries." Around 2002-2003, America gave the Aqaba zone two billion dollars. The game goes: Take our money, take our package deal. America destroys every country it touches! I learned this first hand so many times.

Around 2003, the largest U.S. pension fund – the California Workers Pension Fund – invested millions into the Aqaba zone. I found out that America is expecting about 300,000 Americans to move into this previously exclusive European resort town in the next few years. They are building like they expect the influx, especially of the very rich. The area of Petra is a center for the U.N. All around Petra is an underground American military base, even taxi drivers know that!

In February of 2002, the U.N. announced that the Aqaba area would be the only world port-center for refugees. Since 1963 the World Food Bank has been storing grains and other goods in underground and top ground facilities, making that region the only center for famine and disaster relief in the world. With all the disasters, not one kernel of stored wheat has left the zone. These plans go back over 100 years! But, also remember this about that region--Chedorlaomer was there. (**Genesis 14**) The Midian mountain area at Aqaba, and down into Saudi Arabia to Mt. Sinai, was home to warring tribes for thousands of years. It is a place that has seen much war, strife, division, controversy, and inhumane cruelty. I found the same spirits on the Navajo Indian reservation that caused divisions and strife in our missionary groups that went there.

Unless a person is walking in the nature of Messiah (**Galatians 5:22-24**), in the Spirit of Yahuweh, being led by the Spirit, and taught by the Spirit (Spirit of Yahuweh) while living in America, they will go there and be the same old worldly bums they were in their own country. The "jezebel spirits" are horrendous there. Remember the original Jezebel worshipped Ba'al (the "Lord"), and Astaroth, his consort (the Queen of Heaven). In Catholic terms that's Jesus and Mary. So the pagan spirits of Christianity, whose roots are in Nimrod, are there. Islam was created by the Roman Catholic Vatican to be their sword – to conquer for them, to give them Jerusalem and the Temple Mount, and to destroy their enemies – the children of Ya'cob. Islam has worked well for the Vatican!

In February 2010 I wrote an article that I particularly meant for Americans living in Aqaba: "By This Shall All Men Know – The Paramount Distinguishing Sign of the True Remnant of Yahuweh"/February 8, 2010. I gathered so much information while living there, which matched the prophecies of the Tenach (mis-called the "Old Testament"). So, I was actually watching prophecy being fulfilled right before my eyes. I tried teaching this to our people, to compel them to do prophetic-action intercession over the Red Sea for the coming of "the fleeing remnant" from all over the world. Here they were, just 1 mile from the Red Sea, and except for myself, and periodically a few others, most made no effort all those years to put their foot in the water and declare the return of Ephraim. The Red Sea crossing point, of **Exodus 14**, was just about an hour's ride by fast-boat to Nuweiba, Egypt.

In 2005, I was sitting at my computer, working on an article, when all of a sudden Yahuweh's Presence came into the room and He began to give me a prophecy. My lips went numb and felt fuzzy. He gave me a prophecy for all of those living in Aqaba, and to all those who would move there. It was so powerful that I was shaking. I typed up what He said, printed it out, and made copies for everyone there. It was rejected 100%. I also wrote an admonition that went with it. Here is what I wrote. You in America, take note:

PROPHETIC WORD from Yahuweh, spoken in Aqaba, Jordan: January 2, 2005 AM --To all those who have moved, or are moving, to Israel or Aqaba, Jordan, from America, the UK, and other Greco/Roman cultural nations

"*My people are coming into Israel and Jordan, bringing with them the elements of Babylon. Instead of leaving Babylon, they are putting Babylon into containers and shipping Babel to Israel and to Jordan. They are bringing Babylon in their hearts and minds. They are bringing Babel--in the same way that Lot's wife did not want to leave Sodom. They are holding onto the things of Babel, packing up Babel and moving it to Israel and Jordan--even as Rachael brought out her father's household gods, and sat on them. Because they are bringing Babylon here, they are bringing with them the destruction of Babel and My wrath on Babylon. Let go of your ties to Babel!*

Lot's daughters brought Sodom with them into the cave with their father. The results were the Moabites and the Ammonites-- foreign sun god worshippers of Baal, who destroyed My people Israel. They are bringing sun god worship with them without realizing it, trying to offer it to others, and perpetuating it in this place. Learn My ways! The ones coming from Diaspora are bringing the Babylonian religion into Israel and Jordan--to bringing Babylon's end-time religion to the Edomites, the Moabites, the Ammonites, the Canaanites, the Philistines, the Egyptians, the Israelites and the House of Judah. They are perpetuating the abominations of Baal.

They are bringing abominations into My worship calling them `fun' and `American.' They are stubbornly still calling on the Names of the Baals though they know better, instead of using My Name, which I gave to Moses. They are mixing the false sun god religion of Baal with My true worship, as the Israelites did with the golden calf in this wilderness, saying `tomorrow is a festival to Yahuweh.'

Tell them `stop the American culture and enter into My culture--My Torah--My Shabbat, My Feasts, My ways, My thoughts, My lifestyle, My purposes', and totally come out of the ways of Babel. I require purity in the inwards parts.

I have brought all of you here to stand in the gap for the House of Joseph and for the House of Judah--to prepare the way for My remnant, whom I will preserve in this place--not to bring Babylon and its ways into this place. `Be set apart as I am set apart.' Holding onto Babel in the days ahead will exact a great price.

The time is short! Change, Change, Change! Drop the ways of Babel that are in your heart, unless you want to receive the judgment that is coming--that is due to Babel (Revelation 18:4)

This attachment to the ways of Babylon will be a yoke upon your neck, a stumbling block to your feet, and a deceptive hook in your jaw, to keep you tied to what is of Baal and Babylon--through your possessions, your mind-reasoning, your lifestyle and your beliefs.

*Repent! Drop all that is of Babylonian idolatry and thinking-- FREE YOURSELF! Learn My Word! Know Me! Learn total dependency on Me! Stop running to man and depending on man for your security and help! Remember **Jeremiah 17:5-10**. For what will you do in the days ahead, if man is your arm on which you lean for your security? Man cannot do what I can do! Don't continue to curse yourself by holding onto what is of man and the ways of Babel. Enter into what I am doing in this place. Let go of your own ideas. Find out what I am doing through My Word, and by My Spirit. Know My voice! Stop listening to the voices that are not of Me! Be led by My Spirit. Be taught by My Spirit. Do not depend on your own reasoning. And, please, love one another, without restrictions, as I have loved you!"*

Aqaba helped me lose all the moving and shaking early on. I dissolved my corporation and ordination in 2001. I calmed down, and Abba began teaching me His Torah, His ways, His nature, and His thinking. He began bringing me into what He had ordained for me from the foundation of the world! All of my past training/schooling was to quickly embrace what I would learn in Aqaba in that apartment. He poured out His opinions, His teaching of the Word, into the portal of my eternal re-born spirit, and filled me so full that I had to overflow. That's when He began my writing. As He began pouring into me, I cried out to Him over and over: **"You are giving me such a huge message! It needs to get out to the world. I only have 15 on my address list. How are You going to get Your message to the world?"**

I began the normal lifestyle of a servant/disciple. Day after day I obeyed Him, and He did it all! I am, above all, His servant! Notice: In **Romans 1:1** the Apostle Sha'ul declared he was a servant first, and an Apostle second. I still work for Him about 8 to 12 hours a day. He has brought the increasing. In 2013, because of my work for Him, His message is going out to six continents, reaching about 100,000 a year, in about 60 countries. His work keeps expanding, but that's the way He runs His universe!

As you might remember, 1999 was the panic year of the Y2K hoax. Everyone feared January 1, 2000. I knew it was a hoax. Nothing happened, except those that panicked were registered by the "powers that be." [Refer to: "Quiet Wars and Silent Weapons"/October 29, 2007 to find out what the Illuminati has done to YOU]

Tony Blair arrived right after Christmas and was staying at the King's Palace. He stayed a total of ten days. I watched his golden helicopter flying past my kitchen window. The group was going to the family's house for a big party to see in the New Year, and the new millennium. They had quite a spread of food!

There were Christian Palestinians, Arab friends of the family, and Muslim friends of the family at the party. The party went well past midnight. This family lived on the top floor of a four story apartment building. They had rented the two top-floor apartments because they had so much stuff. They had a balcony that wrapped around most of the top floor, so you imagine the awesome view. In their view was all of Aqaba, the Red Sea, Israel, Egypt, Saudi Arabia, the King's Highway, and the King's Palace. So, just before midnight we watched the King's fireworks display for Tony Blair. Then at midnight, we watched the King's fireworks for everyone, and also the fireworks in Eilat, and in Taba, Egypt. That was so great!

PART VI - The Middle East & Travels Beyond

For those six years, the sun set each night out my kitchen window over the hills of Egypt, the Red Sea, Eliat and the border with Egypt. I saw things that few get to see. Just to walk along the beach of the Red Sea was awesome enough.

JORDAN
(2000)

2000 was a year of transition. It was also a year of great mixture of the very joyful and the very emotionally painful.

I went back to the U.S. in the summer of this year. I never thought I'd return to see my family, so it was like a dream. My Aqaba friend from Texas called me at my son's house not long after we both got back to America. The pope had come to dedicate the real baptism site on the Jordan River, south of Amman. (**John 1:28**)

During 1999, we had seen a big two-page spread in *The Jerusalem Post* about Avi Ben Abraham, head of world cloning, and the freezing of the dead. He had made an announcement to all of Israel that he was the resurrection and the life, and the Creator. He proposed taking DNA off the Shroud of Turin to clone Jesus, and bring him back. The man was a genius, literally worshipped by the world's elite. My friend had seen Avi Ben Abraham on T.V. at the White House with his ten doctors and President Bush. Avi had said he would give all the secrets of DNA to these ten doctors. So, my friend and I had much to talk about. No one was in my house, and no one was in hers. So we talked about very hush-hush things. We talked about an hour. When we got ready to hang up, we both heard clicks on our phones. She said: "Is anyone in your house listening?" I said "NO." She said: "There's no one here either." She said, someone had been listening to our conversation and we needed to be more discrete from then on. Our phones were tapped. Every time I got on the phone someone was listening. One day a friend called, and, as usual started talking about the one world government, and other hush-hush things. All of a sudden we heard music on our phones. She asked: "What's that?" I said: "They're listening to our conversation, so we have to hang up." Immediately we heard clicks, as someone hung up their phone.

Every time I returned to the U.S., the custom's officials treated me like a criminal. I was pulled out of line, my things gone through, and I was interrogated. They asked: "What are you doing in Jordan?" At first I replied: "I went there to visit friends." That was the wrong answer. They would very meanly ask: "Who are your friends in Jordan?" I'd answer something like: "Some Americans on vacation." It was true ... I never lied. I learned in China how to tell the truth without saying anything incriminating. This kept up. Then one day in 2005, when I was checking in at the Dallas/Fort Worth airport to fly back to Jordan, the lady asked me: "They want to know why you do not have a return ticket." I said: "Because I have residency in Jordan." She said: "That's what they wanted to know." After that, no more phone taps, no nasty greetings at U.S. Immigration and Customs, just "Welcome home." Maybe they checked with the ASEZA and found I was OK with the USA.

A new friend, who rented an apartment upstairs from me in Aqaba, was from Switzerland. She had an apartment in Montreux also, right on Lake Geneva. She lived within a very short walking distance of the lovely Castle of Chillon. When I went on that tour of Switzerland in October 1996, our tour bus flew past the castle, and I got a few quick pictures. We proceeded on into town, where I sat at an outdoor pastry shop eating Swiss chocolates and drinking coffee. We had about 1½ hours in Montreux before meeting back at the bus. I really liked that little town. I went to a stationary shop and got the famous poem by Lord Byron about that castle. I also learned that the Dukes of Savoy burned the Jews in that castle, and about how Christians were tortured and burned who stood up for the Jews. Little did I know that I would be back twice to stay there right near the castle. She invited me to come visit her in Switzerland, which I did in 2001, and then again in 2003. She spent part of the year in Switzerland, and part of the year in Aqaba.

That year the leader-lady created an import company for a line of vitamins and other health-products. She filed with the port authority to be able to dock their ship in the Port for unloading. She was told it would ensure hers and her husband's residency, and the residency of all who were in her company. She put down the names of those with them in Aqaba whom she deemed worthy of being in her company, even the name of her Filipino maid who stole her jewelry. She left out the family, one of the main supporting couples of the group, two single women who were the most loyal to her, and me. The chosen ones got special residency cards.

Just as it was with Ruth Potter, she had no company, no ships, no nothing. She was always going to do something spectacular, but nothing she or her husband ever tried to do there ever came to pass. I later understood more fully the terms "visions of grandeur," "megalomania," and "manipulation." Her husband was given a large expanse of land north of the airport, by the authorities in Aqaba. He said he had a water project he was going to put there for the good of the city. He was a geologist. He went to America to get support. He even stayed with a couple for a year, until they told him he had to leave. He could not drum up support for this project. He even went to Muslims in Saudi Arabia to get support. After about five years, he still had no support, so they took the land back. She was going to put in a bed and breakfast in Taybet Zaman. They bought an old goat pen from a local family and began cleaning out that wretched building. Then they poured much money into it to have it renovated. But, of course, the Muslim cheaters wanted more and more money, so the project had to be abandoned. The owners of the facility were very angry. She even had attempts on her life. Nothing that was ever tried ever worked. One day in 2007, as she sat in my apartment accusing me of something I didn't do, I asked her if anything she or her husband ever tried to do in Aqaba worked, or even got off the ground, and she honestly said: "No."

She had a man trying to buy an island for her off the coast of Scotland, but it came out during the sale of that island that he was a crook. Yet, she told all her rich friends in Dallas that she was buying this island for the remnant to flee too. Another time, she said she was going to save all the orphaned Sudanese children and bring them into Israel. But, she couldn't even get a visa to get into Sudan. Yet, all the while, her rich friends in Dallas sent her money.

She even got in with multi-millionaires to support her supposed projects in Israel. She was going to put a clinic in Israel, a school, and a farm. That didn't work either. She got into the high inner circles of the Israeli government, even being invited to their special January planning meetings. But, finally Israel got tired of them, and so did Jordan. I'm NOT saying all this to slander her. If I wanted to slander her, I'd use her name. But, as the years went on, quite a few people who had heard her appeals came to me in private to ask what I thought of it, some were very concerned about their wealthy friends who were selling everything to follow her. They knew something was wrong, but they did not know what. I saw it all up close. I just answered questions. I never initiated conversations about her. But, when they asked questions with deep concerns, I felt I had to tell them the truth.

At one point, I was working with a well-known man who was working on a project for Sephardic Jews in the Negev. He, and his wife, and his congregation near Austin, Texas, were good friends of mine. I had taught in his home in Austin, and been with him in conferences. He called me "Ms. Negev", because I lived in the Negev Desert.

At this time, the leader-lady was working with the multi-millionaires in Israel. They were giving her money to fund her project to build an agricultural school and clinic in the Negev. But, they wanted to remain totally anonymous. They gave her a Cadillac to drive, also. However, being naïve, I told my friend about the leader-lady's project in the same area of the Negev where he was working to build a compound for the returning

Sephardim. I said that he should meet her. So, also being naïve, this man discovered, quite innocently, her backers, by asking a lot of questions about a place to build.

So, he asked them if they could help him. Talk about "the__ hitting the fan!" The multi-millionaires were very angry. Their cover had been blown. They threatened the leader-lady, saying they were considering backing off from the project. I sure got in trouble with the leader-lady! Just before it hit the fan, after a Friday night dinner, I was sitting on the couch at my friend's house, and I told her that I was working with this man who was putting a project near hers in the Negev. She looked right at me and said: "I'm on his Board of Directors." I was shocked. The next day I e-mailed him and asked him about it. He said he never heard of her before. She was a pathological liar, and used this ability to cause all sorts of havoc, which hurt many people. I was hurt by many of her lies against me. Lying is a sure sign that a person is controlled by The Liar--Satan. (**John 8:44**)

The desire to be worshipped, "narcissism," is also a Satanic/Luciferic characteristic. I talked to a Messianic Jewish lady who attended one of her meetings in Fort Worth, thinking it was me who would be the speaker. She told me about all the adoration and worship that was given to this lady. It is the spirit of anti-messiah/Apollyon. The gods of Greece and Rome, ancient Nephillim, were called "gods" and "demigods." These type of people wield a lot of control over the minds of their loyal subjects who were afraid to cross them. These people so often hide in religion or politics. Leader-lady had run for a seat in the U.S. Senate also. She was wealthy, and well known in Dallas. I won't go into any more details, but her scams began to catch up with her. I do not say these things to malign her, just to warn you, as do the Scriptures, to only trust Abba in these evil days!

For some reason, being left out of her company in 2000 was a devastating blow to me. I laid in bed in a fetal position. My mind shut down. I just stared at the white cement block walls and the brown dirt and rocks outside, and could not move. I had no challenge to even move. I do NOT have a rejection complex! It was just that it was such a dirty deal, not just hurting me, but hurting my friends.

I was sinking into despair. I knew I had to talk to someone. So, I got up and got dressed to go up the hill to meet with the father of the family. I needed counsel. He had been an associate pastor in a church in Colorado, and he had wisdom. So, I forced myself to go to talk to him. I sat at his kitchen table and poured out my heart. He just listened. Then he very quietly asked me a question: "Do you really want to be a part of that company?" I thought for a few seconds and said: "NO." He said he was happy he was not a part of it either. I laughed, and the stronghold that the enemy had on my mind was broken. I was filled with joy and peace. No, I didn't want to be a part of that mess.

Before returning from America, Abba impressed me to get the Yellow Fever vaccine at a local clinic. It's like playing Russian roulette at the border crossings in Africa. If you don't get the vaccine, which is an international requirement, countries like Uganda can legally pull you over at Immigration and stick you with the vaccine right there – usually with a needle they use for everyone. I did not want to get the vaccine, but He told me to. Before going to the clinic, he added an addendum: Get the vaccine for typhoid fever. OK, but why? But, again, I obeyed. I got a yellow international shot record card.

When I returned from America, I went to visit my Swiss friend in her new apartment up the hill. I ate her food. I drank the water. She got deathly ill. She went to the hospital where they treated her for a common illness. But, later, they found she had typhoid fever. The older couple in our group who lived above her also got it, and two or three in the family got it. Unlike malaria, which can stay in the bloodstream up to three years, typhoid never goes away – it stays in a latent form, and can infect all who have contact with food or drink from the one infected. One of the first symptoms of typhoid is diarrhea. I had a bad case of diarrhea, however I did not feel sick. I was lying in bed one day, and remembered reading that overdoses of Magnesium cause diarrhea, because it is a laxative. I was taking Magnesium in three different vitamin/mineral compounds. I looked in my *Return to Eden* resource book, and there it was: Too much Magnesium taken each day causes diarrhea. I went off the Magnesium for two days, and no more diarrhea.

I found out that the water that had sat dormant during the construction of the apartment building had typhoid in it. Then I learned that Muslims sometimes put typhoid germs in the water of those they considered enemies. They thought we were Jewish, even though the local Greek Orthodox priest had come and made a big production of anointing our houses with holy water. He was a great guy--Father Shemeah. He helped us a lot.

By my obedience to Abba, I was spared the typhoid fever. But, my friend got worse and worse. Two of her three children came to be with her. The hospital sent her home to die. While she was in the hospital not one person from the group came to pray with her, or even just to check on her. That says a lot doesn't it! She had given a lot of money to the leader-lady too. In fact, at one point, the leader-lady borrowed thousands of dollars from her, but felt no responsibility to pay her back. Sounds like a carbon copy of Ruth Potter. But, that's also the spirit of Jezebel!

My friend got to where she had not eaten for days. Her breathing was very shallow. She had not slept for about three days either. Her daughter called me. She asked me to please come up and pray for her mother--no one else had come. I got so angry. Those miserable selfish people; they would have cared less if she had died, probably would have been angry because they would have had to arrange a funeral.

I got dressed and stormed out of that apartment to go up the hill to her apartment. I got to the outside door and couldn't open it. Just then, one of the Roman men came and opened it. They had changed the locks and given new keys to everyone--except to me. I walked up there so full of His anointing and in the anger of my Abba.

I walked into that room where she lay. I laid hands on her chest and commanded that the demons get their hands off of her. I commanded that she sleep. She took one great big breath and fell asleep. The next morning she was fine. But, she kept the typhoid to this day. Tragically, after my second trip to Switzerland, she turned against me, and began slandering me. I had spent time praying also for her children, and thought her to be a dear friend. Why she turned against me, I have no idea. But, after so much of this through the years, I am no longer shocked or disappointed! I just pick up and go on. I don't analyze what happened, because there is never any sane reason why it happened.

During this year, my son called me from America to tell me that my husband had prepared divorce papers for me to sign, for a "no-fault divorce." I never got child support, or support for myself. My son told me that he wanted the divorce so he could marry another woman. So, when I went back for the first time to America, I signed the papers and that was it. I came back to Aqaba totally devastated, but I knew I had to be there.

My youngest daughter got married while I was in Jordan. I missed her terribly. I could not go back for the wedding. I needed someone to befriend me at that time. I never wanted the divorce. I wanted to be at my daughter's wedding. But, no one would talk to me about it. They had gossiped among themselves. It began two years of totally imploding. Abba brought me out of it by giving me my assignment to study and write, to reach out to the world with His message.

The day of my daughter's wedding, the leaders were hosting a big-name minister and his wife. I was talking to the minister's wife about my daughter getting married that night. She looked at me and said: "Is anyone going to be with you to pray with you?" She was so surprised at their coldness. But, that coldness drove me to Yahuweh, and He began to teach me. I am not writing these things to get pity – oh no! I am just reporting what I fought through to get into the perfect will of Abba. And, it wasn't that I did not have some really good times. I sure did. I was like most westerners--raised on fantasy. I had to face reality, and it was painful.

Before going to Aqaba, I learned of a lady there named Betty. She had worked in Kaifeng, China, with a Chinese Jewish man. I was so excited to meet her and talk to her about China. This man was helping to smuggle Jews out of China. For in Kaifeng the Chinese authorities were taking their Jewish identity cards and changing them to read "Chinese." This lady had an apartment in Aqaba, and a second apartment in Taybet Zaman. I went to stay with her a few days in Taybet Zaman, along with my Texas friend, and a couple of others who were close to her, like Rita, who became a friend. Her apartment in Taybet Zaman, was on the second floor and had a balcony. I stood on the balcony, overlooking those awesome hills, looking towards Petra. Petra is Greek for "rock." It's original name was Mount Seir, named after Mr. Seir, leader of the Horites (cave dwellers that Esau ousted).

While standing on that balcony Abba gave me a prophetic song to sing: "**Rejoice O Seir for those who will come to you, rejoice O Seir for those who will come to you, rejoice O Seir for those who will come to you, the outcasts of Israel**." I couldn't stop singing this song for a long time.

The next day, we went out where we could look into the valley around Petra. Later Betty and her friend Rita, rented half a duplex that was high on a hill above Wadi Musa (the springs of Moses), where we could actually see down into the Siq (the gorge) going into Petra and into Petra itself, along a ridge by the house. My Texas friend rented the duplex next to it. It was in Betty and Rita's house, in 2000, that I slept through the night for the first time in many years – it was so peaceful!

In Aqaba, our little group went to the beach a lot. We also took a boat, from a hotel to Pharaoh's Island, off the coast of Egypt. There we did intercession. The tiny island had a huge Crusader castle on it. From off the boat, I got to swim in the Red Sea. Before we got into the water, our Egyptian sailors fed bread to the barracuda. Of course, they might have been the benign "trumpet fish", that is long and skinny like the barracuda, but still they sure looked like barracuda. The water was filled with little brightly colored tropical fish. I just went into the water in my long dress. To be in that beautiful clear water, with Egypt on the west and

Saudi Arabia on my right, was so mind bogglingly awesome! Then we had the most wonderful buffet of cooked lamb, beef, and chicken shish kabobs for us right there off the side of the boat on a grill, with fresh vegetables, and all kinds of accompanying goodies.

What an awesome outing! I was so happy. What an awesome outing! I was so happy. Even though the roar of the boat motor drowned me out, I found myself singing loudly the Israeli National Anthem, the *HaTikvah* ("The Hope") in tongues.

In June, Valerie, from Dallas, came to Aqaba to join me. We went to Africa together. As previously reported, I returned from Africa in early August, in obedience to Abba's request, at a time when terrorists had invaded Aqaba. I came back weak from the second bout of malaria.

GREECE/PATMOS-ATHENS-CORINTH
(2000)

Before going to Africa, Abba gave me instructions to be on Patmos on September 29th. He always gives me exact timing for my assignments. I had no idea what that date was about nor the importance of it, but in 2007, I learned just how extremely important it was. Because I was so weak from the malaria, I asked Him if I could do the intercession in Jordan. I finally said to Him: "I cannot go," even though I knew intercession had to be done on site. Telling Him "no" is just NOT smart! I know now how awful that was and how much mercy He had on me! You just don't tell Yahuweh "NO!" When He makes a command, He expects it to be obeyed. He's not cold and calloused, but He really is not interested in our feelings. By going, He always heals, strengthens, and provides. I did not know the extreme importance of that mo'edim on Patmos. But, Abba's assignments are never ho-hum--they are always very important. He never gives options either!

He had told me to be on Patmos on September 29, 2000, to proclaim the release of the seal judgments and to represent the Bridal remnant. He emphasized that I was to proclaim Revelation 5:1 through 6:1. If it was now, with the wisdom I've gained, I would have gone if I had to be carried on a stretcher!

How important was **September 29, 2000/2001** – Yom Teruah, a shmittah year? Please read "The Shmittah Year Prophecy" and "The Forty-Eight Hour Transition"/2007. It was an eternal mo'ed. That date was prophesied hundreds of years ago, that on it something would happen that would shoot the history of the world forward into eternity. It was the end of the Oslo 7-year Accord. On that day, Ariel Sharon went up on the Temple Mount, read **Ezekiel 37**, and the Muslims started throwing stones--the second Intifada began.

Four hundred years before, it was prophesied by Jewish sages, going back to the time that Joshua entered the land with the children of Ya'cob at Passover time, that on that date, a war would begin in Jerusalem that would not end until Messiah came. It was the second of the final three seven-year cycles before the coming of Messiah. But, also, it was the very day, from Creation, that we entered the 7th millennium. He had let me know, in June Joyner's class back at Grace Temple, that my main ministry would be inside the 7th millennium. He began me writing in 2001.

On September 29th 2000/2001, a man named Richard Honorf from Jerusalem walked with a group of Messianic Jews from the Mt. Zion Hotel in the Hinnom Valley to the Gihon Springs. The men were dressed in Levite clothes, carrying shofars and a horn of anointing oil. I talked with one lady who was with that group, and with Richard in Jerusalem. Richard believed that on that day, not knowing what was happening on the Temple Mount, they were to anoint the shofars, blow them, and proclaim the beginning of Messiah's end-time ministry. He sure heard from Abba because surely that was the opening of the 7th millennium, and the second of the last three 7-year cycles before Messiah comes. So I regret leaving myself out of this awesome day. Do you see how important it was that I went to Patmos to release the seals on that day? On Yom Teruah--the next shmittah year, September 12, 2007--He asked me to release 18 things that He gave me, including the time of the trumpet judgments. We entered the last 7-year cycle before Messiah comes on that day.

In mid-October, my youngest was in her ninth month of carrying my first granddaughter. I had two fine grandsons already. Baby Desiree was due in mid-November. But because of complications, the doctor said she would have to be taken by C-section. Her doctor told her that if she had any signs of contractions to come to the hospital immediately. I told my daughter that Desiree could not come until I got there, and to tell Desiree to wait because grama was coming. I got there November 13th. As soon as I got to her house, I laid my hands on her belly. I spoke authoritatively: "Desiree, this is your grama. I am here, so you can come out now." Later that evening, my daughter began feeling labor pains. On the 14th, Desiree was born. She was just a little over 5 pounds. I would sit with her asleep on my left shoulder, supporting her with my left hand. Desi just had her 12th birthday a few days ago (2012).

That December, I played the Christmas game so that my children wouldn't feel bad towards me. My son was concerned because his wife wanted me there for Christmas gift-opening. If I was not there, she would have thrown a fit. So, I bowed to pressure. But, oh I paid for that! I had bought a hand-carved soap stone chess set in Kisumu for my son. The chess pieces were in the shape of animals. I think the king was a lion, for example. It was beautiful. I paid $12.00 for it. Kisumu was the headquarters for the soap stone mining. That stone is gorgeous, beige with pink streaks, some different colors mixed ... but that area is the only place you can get real carved soap stone that is not commercialized.

When my ex-husband saw what I gave my son for Christmas, he was very angry. He got up without saying anything, took his new wife by the hand, and left, leaving a depressed family. And who did most there blame for ruining their Christmas? ME! It was the last time I tried to appease my family at Christmas. [Refer to:

"Joyful Abominations"/November 2003/revised November 2007] This article got me into more trouble than any other article. Christmas, being the pagan celebration of the birth of the sun gods, carries powerful demonic spirits with it.

JORDAN
(2001)

This was one of the busiest years of my life. It was this year that He began my writing, and sent me to many places. He gave me visitations, dreams, visions, words of knowledge and wisdom, and fulfilled prophecies to me. He began sending me to bring His Name into places on earth, even remote areas where His Name has either never been spoken by His people, or not spoken for thousands of years.

From the time I was baptized into the Spirit, I received all of the nine gifts of the Spirit (**I Corinthians 12:4-11**) But, added to that was the gift of interpreting dreams and visions. He gave me a sure word of prophecy, both "word of knowledge," and "word of wisdom," through which He spoke into people's lives to confirm what He had showed them. He also gave me prophetic words to His people, and to the nations. He gave me the authority over the weather elements, for His purposes, and over wild beasts, and anything that might harm me.

He gave me the authority of proclamation and declaration of His Word so that what was written would come to pass as it was timed to come to pass. Thus, in releasing such things as John wrote in the Revelation, like the seals, I was simply bringing into our realm the Word that He spoke from eternity past, so that He might have entrance to fulfill it in the present. I fear Yahuweh! I never make up what to say in intercession, or work hocus pocus formulas that are often so prevalent in Christian intercession. Man used his will to shut out Elohim. Elohim respects our will, and will not override it. Therefore, throughout human history, as it has been recorded, He had to call men like Noah, Moses, and the Prophets, to declare His will into the earth, and invite Him to do as He wills. For, unless His remnant calls for His return, He will not come. He is no bully! He is no tyrant. The Elohim of Israel is respectful of the will that He gave us.

So, He began increasing my authority, my relationship with Him, my prophetic boldness, and then set me to writing what He was showing me. I became Spirit taught. Yahuweh is the Spirit; the Spirit is Yahuweh. So I became Yahuweh taught. So many so-called "believers," don't want Messiah to return. They are too busy with their own agendas in this present world--"foolish virgins" to be sure! But, in my calling for His return, and others calling for His return, He listens to us! He is coming on schedule--His schedule!

I returned to the U.S. in March. As I reported earlier, on March 31, 2001, my wonderful second daughter got married to my wonderful son-in-law. She went on to finish college, paying for most of it herself. He had graduated the previous December with two engineering degrees. He was a Magna Cum Laude student. He immediately got a job with Lockheed. They offered for me to live with them. He grew up with a grandmother in the house--his mother's mother--until she died. So, he felt good about having me there. What a blessing! It has been my U.S. home base since. I believe in home bases! We all need a "tent." But, beyond that, I live as a nomad in His service, going and coming as He directs. My children have gotten used to my lifestyle! They are very supportive.

I thought Abba had released me from my Patmos assignment. NO! I missed my mo'ed ("divine appointment") on September 29, 2000, to proclaim the seals from there. But, I did proclaim it from Jordan. I don't think that was really valid--intercession must be done on site. Scriptural intercession opens portals for Yahuweh to be able to enter our realm and do His will. Scriptural intercession uses His words to proclaim, and His words ONLY. He has to trust His true intercessors. To be able to trust one of His creation, He has to test and test each one over and over! We cannot say one word out of line when speaking for Him. We must fear Him!

Before returning to Aqaba in the third week of April, He instructed me to go to Bookstop on Hulen, and get the *Lonely Planet Travel Kit --the Greek Isles*. I saw that they had just issued the first edition of the Kit on the Greek Isles. It was $16.98. With tax, it was over $17.00. I didn't have that kind of money to spend on a book! But, He said: "Buy it." I was mad. I bought it. I took it out and threw it as hard as I could in the backseat of my car, saying: "That was a waste of $17.00!" I took it back to Jordan with me.

Not long after returning, I was asked to teach the Torah portion for the week. In studying for it, I forget what made such an impression on me – but He used it to tell me: "I have not let you out of your assignment." He let me know that releasing the seals was already done. I guess He got someone else to do it. But, He said explicitly: "**I want you on Patmos on May 11th.**" What did I use to plan my trip? -- the *Lonely Planet* book! It gave me every detail I needed. I used my phone to call Greece to set up the details of hotels, boats, and planes. Phoning from Jordan internationally was inexpensive.

On May 10th, I flew to Athens, then to the Isle of Samos to spend the night in the lovely resort area of Pythagorio, at the Blue Dolphin Inn. From my third-story balcony I could look right at the coast of Turkey, 3 km away. I walked to various archeological sites near there, and along the waterfront. It was a wonderful time. I got a ticket for Patmos, leaving the next morning. I arrived on Patmos May 11th, as He told me. On May 12th, I went up to the cave where John received the Revelation. I took with me my papa's handwritten letters and notes on the book of Revelation. I read them out loud there. The cave was almost empty. I sat on the front bench for two hours writing what He showed me in **Revelation 5:1 – 6:1**. That was what I was to prophesy the previous September 29th.

He gave me overwhelming revelation on why John wept. He took me to **John 11:32-44**. Even now this revelation gives me chills. He let me know that Yochanan (John) was symbolic of the Bride of Messiah, but also, Miriam of Bethany. Yahushua said to me: "**When I see the Bride weeping, and the Jews weeping together for My coming, THEN I will return and raise the dead**!" He was speaking of the resurrection of the righteous.

John wept because no one would open the seals. **If the seals are not opened, the Bride will forever be waiting at the altar!** She cannot marry Yahushua until the judgment on the wicked is finished. John knew this, and so He wept. But, "the Lion of the Tribe of Judah" has prevailed, and opened the seals. September 29, 2000/2001 Yom Teruah, a shmittah year, opened the second of the last three cycles before Messiah's return.

May 13th was the 50th anniversary of my being born again. I celebrated by going once again into the cave where John received the Revelation. This time I sat in the back, just reading papa's notes and praying. Tour groups were coming in, staying a few minutes and then leaving. But, one group came and sat down on the front benches. The young Greek Orthodox priest who oversaw the place, spoke to a group of English-speakers, and another man interpreted into English. The priest told the history of the cave, and how they knew it was where John received the Revelation. It was not one of those Roman Catholic sites, chosen by Constantine's mother, Helena, that was fake. This history came from oral tradition through the centuries. John, it was said, would walk down to the main town by the sea and preach. He would baptize believers, and many were also healed.

There sure was an anointing in that cave! That priest never once mentioned anything about Mary, or the saints, nor gave spurious tradition. He used the Scriptures, and history, to give his speech. I celebrated that night by having a fine Greek dinner near the lovely villa where I was staying. Talk about Abba setting everything up! The father of the owner of the villa I stayed in, had a villa next door--the Australian. He served breakfast on a high rooftop overlooking the island. The view was spectacular. I could see clear to the top of Patmos, where the Monastery of St. John was, with its huge museum, and also to Chora – a little town where most of the people of Patmos lived.

After going to the cave, I walked up to the Monastery, and went through the museum. They had a fourth century copy of the Gospel of John there. Then I went on up to Chora and walked around. It was a tourist center. I had so much fun shopping.

On May 15th, I started my trip back to Athens, via Samos, to prepare to return to Amman, then to Aqaba. Leaving the island, I tripped and fell near the boat dock. Being double jointed, I landed on my left hand, but the fingers bent backwards all the way to my wrist. I got on the boat. The Aegean Sea was very choppy. It was not long before I was vomiting terribly. I had forgotten to take a Dramamine tablet. Upon disembarking, I went with a nice young man who helped me. We got a taxi together. I kept vomiting all the way into Vathy – capital of Samos. I found the big ship that I had booked passage on, and they assigned me a room. No one else was in it. I took the bottom berth. I was still very sick, and the knuckles of my left hand were very sore. It was an all-night ride to Piraeus, the port of Athens. I slept some, and then a lady came. She was grossly overweight. She wanted the bottom bunk. I told her I was very sick and had to have the bottom bunk. She got another cabin.

We docked about 4:00 AM. I got a taxi to my hotel—the Niki Hotel in downtown Athens. I was within walking distance of the Parthenon. I slept a short time. Then I thought: "I cannot lose this day." So, I found how to take a bus to the modern town of Corinth. I got there, and had to ask a lot of people, but found out how to get a bus to the ancient city of Corinth. While I was there, I was the only visitor to the ruins of Corinth. I had the place to myself. I saw the Bema (judgment seat) where Sha'ul preached, and was later arrested. I saw the Temple of Apollo, just across from the Bema. I sat on the Bema and looked at the Temple, and remembered so many words that Sha'ul wrote to the Corinthians that were reflected in what he was seeing, exhorting them that their bodies were the temple of the Set-Apart Spirit of Yahuweh.

As I left to go across the street to the bus stop, my left knee turned out of place, and I fell in the street. But, I got right up-- that dirty enemy! I got back to the hotel in time for a fine dinner, and then slept. The next morning, I went down for breakfast and asked the waiter where to get the bus for the airport. He said that Greece was having a national strike and no transportation was running. I looked out the window, and across the street sat a man in a travel agency. I went over, and he checked my flight. He said because there were only three flights a week from Athens to Amman, my flight was due to go out that afternoon. If I had waited until the strike ended, I would have had to change my ticket and not leave out for another 3 days. He said he had a friend in a travel agency around the corner, who had a friend who took people to the airport. Maybe he could help me. I went to that agency, and he set up for me to go with his friend to the airport at 3:00 PM. But, the man wanted $20.00. All I had was Jordanian Dinar. I learned that all the banks and exchange places were closed. But, I set off to find one that was not closed. I walked up the street past the hotel about two blocks, and to my left I saw an exchange place OPEN. I thought: "No one is going to change Jordanian Dinar for dollars in Greece." On their list of countries that they exchange currency with, first was the U.S., second was the U.K., third was Jordan. What are the odds of that!! I got $20.00 in U.S., just what the man wanted. These were the days before the Euro.

I did not want to waste the day, so I went exploring. I walked to the Parthenon. But, it was closed. I did see it from below, however. I went for lunch on a little walk-only street, and just enjoyed Athens. At 3:00, I walked to meet my escort, and he was there. He was very handsome. He had black wavy hair. He was about 35 years old. He drove a black Mercedes. He got me there after a wild ride in traffic. He was leaning out the window yelling and gesturing with his hands, just like the other Athenians.

I got to the seat of my plane. As I was waiting for others to board, Abba interrupted my train of thought about His goodness and said: **"WELL DONE, GOOD AND FAITHFUL SERVANT."** I was very surprised, but I rested in His words.

SWITZERLAND--ITALY--FRANCE
(2001)

In early June, my Swiss friend returned to Switzerland. She invited me to come visit her. Montreux is so beautiful. It is in the French-speaking part of Switzerland, on Lake Geneva. I flew into Geneva, and she picked me up, and we returned by way of Evian. We stopped for a brief time and looked around Evian (France). That place has so much history, which I studied in detail for my assignment there in 2003. Then we re-entered Switzerland and drove to her apartment. Boats were abundant on Lake Geneva. The train ran just past her apartment building too. Montreux was covered in flowers and exotic trees--such a gorgeous place!

For 700 years it was a center of world trade, since the Rhine River flows out of Lake Geneva to the Mediterranean Sea. It was also a center of rule by the Savoy (Sahv-wah) Dukes. It is also the place where President Franklin D. Roosevelt, and the leaders of major European nations, met in 1938 to decide the fate of the Jews trying to flee out of Germany. The result of this meeting forced the Jews back to their death. So, in reality, because of the decision made by the U.S., which the other nations followed, America fed the Jews to the ovens and gas chambers of the Holocaust. America backed Hitler, as did big American corporations, like Ford and GM who funded him. Elite families, like the Bush family, funded him too. Prescott Bush, father of George Bush, Sr. used Jewish prisoners at Auschwitz to work in his factories. Today, Evian is most famous now as a Spa center and for its Evian water. I would go back in 2003 to do intercession, for Evian would be the meeting place of the G-8.

Every week they had a huge "flea-market" in Montreux. I loved that. I visited the castle of Chillon several times. It was also the time of the Narcissus Festival. The hills were covered with these lovely white, beautifully-scented flowers. Not long after I got there, the family of five from Aqaba wanted to visit her too. They put their van on a ship out of Haifa and sailed to Athens. They drove across Greece. Then they put their van on another ship that sailed into Venice. They gave us the day and time when their ship would be docking in the Port of Venice. My friend, and I, drove to Venice, through Milan, and stayed in a lovely little hotel on one of the canals. The hotel gave us a free trip out to Fire Island, where they gave us a tour of the famous Venetian glass-blowing facility. Yesterday, in going through boxes of souvenirs, I found the small delicate wine glass--Venetian glass--that I had bought there. We went on to an island that was exclusively dedicated to their renowned hand-made lace industry, then on to Lido Island. We went on one of the large canals in a gondola. We went to the

PART VI - The Middle East & Travels Beyond

famous San Marco Square and had dinner. I never saw so many pigeons!

The next morning we were supposed to be at the Port at 10:00 to meet the family. We had a leisurely breakfast out in a garden connected to our hotel. Then we went to check when the ship would dock, so we could check out of the hotel and drive over there. Well... the ship had come in an hour before. They called us a taxi who took us quite fast to the Port. We saw their van parked by the entrance area. So we got out and ran in two different directions trying to find them. I remember their teenage daughter coming out of the bathroom, seeing us and yelling with joy, then hugging us. They had spoken the most sad message on my friend's message unit at her home in Switzerland, saying they were there, but they guessed we had forgotten them. What a grand reunion. They went on a gondola down a canal, and we went back and packed, then met them by her car.

They followed us way back to Montreux, this time over the San Bernard Pass, which had just opened. The family had two girls and two boys. The boys were in our car. Everyone was so hungry. Yet everywhere we stopped, there was a bar in the restaurant, and the family wouldn't allow their children to eat in a place with a bar. So we starved. We got up high onto the pass, and their youngest son was hanging out the window grabbing piles of snow. Their parents kept stopping to take pictures. Finally, by the time we were within just a few yards of the Italian/Swiss border, it was dark already. We saw the lights of a hotel set way back on the left. The parking lot was full of melting ice. It would be our last chance to get anything to eat before getting to Montreux, for by then all restaurants would be closed. So we pulled into the parking lot and walked through the slush of ice and snow, and went into the hotel. To our left was a family playing cards. They were shocked at our entrance. We asked if they had anything we could eat. The owner of the place told us that he would go to the freezer and see what was there. He came back with a downcast expression and said: "I'm sorry, all we have is spaghetti." We all looked at each other and all eight of us said boisterously in unison: "WE LOVE SPAGHETTI!" We had a feast! Then we went to the border. This is the famous place where the Monastery of St. Bernard is, and where the famous St. Bernard dogs are kept. We saw the dogs. We went in at the close of a Mass in the church, and then we headed out to Montreux.

Our Swiss friend took us to so many places of interest in different parts of Switzerland. Just to name a few: We went to Bern, the Capitol, and saw the famous Bern bears. We went high up into the Alps to villages where she taught music. She taught the children of the British Royal family there, as well as the child of Bernice Weston, founder of Weight Watchers. She taught music in Francis Shaffer's Bible College. She was a professional flutist who performed in Switzerland with Stravinsky. She was also a super race car driver, so we had some exciting times on those small mountain roads. We met some of her friends in villages in different places.

We went to Evian where we spent the day wandering around there. The next day we went to the Nestle Chocolate Factory. Talk about Willy Wonka! I never saw so many delicious chocolates in my life. Because we took the tour of the factory, we were allowed to take all the chocolates we could eat, but everyone also stuffed their pockets. They had 40 different varieties of chocolates on a conveyer belt, and all we had to do was grab. We bought chocolates in boxes too. Another day we went to the Gruyere Cheese factory where we took a tour and bought cheese. In the same town there was an old castle, which we also went through. Another day we went to a salt mine. I couldn't believe there was a salt mine in Switzerland. They filled the caves with water, the salt in the rocks comes out into the water, and then they extracted the salt from the water. We went deep into the earth – it was a magnificent tour. We also spent a day touring through the Castle of Chillon. Then she took us up high into the Alps. In short, we had a marvelous time together. I went back to Aqaba, and within a couple of weeks, I was in Africa for my final trip. I returned to Switzerland in 2003 to do intercession over the G-8 Summit in Evian.

During this year, He had me doing about three months of research on the roots of Christianity. He provided the resource material. When I was in the U.S., I did quite a bit of teaching in home groups about the Torah, and about Israel. I was solid in the Torah by this time. Back in the states in July, I taught in home groups in the Fort Worth area, in home Messianic congregations and in other facilities, and even traveled to teach in different places in Texas. I kept quite busy with many meetings in various situations. I went to the weekly meetings at Dee Ann's in Flower Mound.

I attended Messianic home meetings in different parts of Fort Worth, and in the "Mid-Cities." I attended one regularly in North Fort Worth. The rabbi and his wife were friends. I fit in, until the night I taught what Abba taught me from the whole Word on the reuniting of the Two Houses of the tribes of Ya'cob. The hostess actually screamed at me, telling me that I was wrong and she'd found a rabbi on the internet that agreed with her. Her parents were sitting across the room, but they said nothing to her. I never went back. My rabbi friend ended up hating "Paul," denouncing Messiah, and converting to Judaism. It was a great heartbreak because our group was so close-knit. The rabbi encouraged their sons to join him in his defection. His wife left him. But, this type of violent rejection of His Word became frequent. In some meetings, I would give out so many Scriptures from the whole Word, and some would be angry because I crossed the teachings of their pastor, a favorite rabbi, or someone whose writings they had read in a book, or read on the Internet. They cared little what the Word said.

I was invited to have meetings all over the area – even in the "Mid-Cities" of Arlington, Bedford, Hurst, Flower Mound, Lewisville, and other cities of the north between Dallas and Fort Worth. I met a couple who lived in a mid-city area between Fort Worth and Dallas. She and I became good friends. She and her husband had a rather large congregation that they pastored. I ministered there several times. They rented a building. It was she that taught me about how Elohim builds authority in us for the tasks He wants us to do.

In 2000, one whom I met at Dee Anne's prayer meeting, Christie, invited me to teach at her home in North Fort Worth. She had quite a group of aristocratic and sophisticated people, some knowing the Bush family, some knowing people in the CIA, and some having their own Christian ministries. But, I did not know of these connections until later. I was put in danger several times without knowing it. Her husband was a well-known plastic surgeon at Baylor Medical Center in Dallas. He was a kind man. He was not a part of the deviousness.

I went on my first trip to Houston, Texas, during December. I had spoken in several homes. I remember a young man to my right who told me I might be interested in a book coming out in April, entitled *Constantine's Sword*, by James Carroll. Because of the research I was doing on the roots of Christianity, I made a mental note to find the book. In April of 2002, I went to Bookstop and saw the book. But, when I looked at it and saw that James Carroll was a Catholic, I was disgusted. I thought that he would probably defend Constantine, so I put it back on the book shelf. About a week later, Christie came to visit me at my daughter's house. She had something in a sack with her. She said that she was in Barnes and Noble and asked Father what she should get for me. I looked in the sack and my heart sunk – it was *Constantine's Sword*. After she left, I threw the book on my desk and laid down on my bed. I looked at that book and said: "Father, why?"

I picked it up and looked at the middle of it, as I usually do--and it's a large book. I read the center paragraph and it was exactly what I needed to know. I began reading forwards and backwards from that point. It became the central reference book for the massive study: "The Foundation of Deception." But, I got my answers. Christianity is a compilation of the worship of many sun gods – from Egypt, Greece, Rome, and Persia. I expose the system. I do not attack those deceived by it. Sha'ul and the Apostles were fighting the early beginnings of this Greek-created religion, and the early stages of rabbinic Judaism. [For more information on this, please read the documented article: "Exposing Rabbinic Judaism and Its Link to Rome"]

I purchased a radio in the U.S. Back in Jordan, I began listening to Israel's Kol-Israel station four times a day--in English. I learned that the U.S. was getting almost no news that was important, related to the U.S. especially. For example, when the space shuttle blew up, I heard all the joy before it happened, and all the grief afterwards, from Israeli radio, about Ilan Ramon (the first Israeli astronaut). I went to the family's apartment up the street and watched the CNN reporting on their giant TV. I heard things from CNN Europe that I never would hear on U.S. news. Both CNN and BBC Europe report much differently than the CNN and BBC that is broadcast in the U.S.

While U.S. news was talking for a year about the O.J. Simpson trial-- headline news every night--millions of our brothers and sisters were being slaughtered for their faith in Muslim Indonesia and Muslim Sudan. I found out later that the slaughtering of the Christians in southern Sudan was supported by America to acquire the oil that is so abundant there. America has worked with Saudi Arabia since the 1930s to do with the oil, making pacts with them, and other Muslim nations, when America has enough oil to support itself without any foreign input.

The more I studied the Torah, and wrote, the more my mind became clear. I was "accused" of having a photographic memory. I knew I didn't. I blamed it on my eating so much tuna--a supposed brain-food. Read my article: "Living From the Eternal Mind – The Secret of Never Being Deceived." In it I tell how the mind of the re-born spirit takes in knowledge from Yahuweh's realm, so there is no end to the capacity to receive it and retain it. I knew from my experiences in Africa, that the mind of the spirit operates just like the natural mind, but it has no end to its abilities, and the memory-level is eternal.

I saw things out my kitchen window in Jordan that few saw. During the week-long Summit, when President Bill Clinton, Yasir Arafat, Yitzak Rabin, and Ehud Barak, met at Taba, Egypt, Israel was willing to give over 90% of their land to the Palestinians. The whole week, I watched the lightning flash sideways, almost continually day, and night, over Taba -- not over Aqaba, just over Taba and the Israeli border.

I learned things from the taxi drivers that few would ever hear. For example, how George Bush, Sr. told the Saudi sheiks he partnered with in the oil business, "when my son is elected, you will get your Palestinian state." Of course George Bush, Jr. was elected, but they did not get their state. I heard of George Bush's statement to King Abdullah not long before he was elected: "I can't wait to fool those stupid Christians." I learned that the Arab news media was saying things in Arabic that were totally not translated into English correctly. In other words, the Arabs were telling the truth from their viewpoint, but the translation into English was deceptive.

I learned the tactics of the Arabs in getting world sympathy. I learned how they use women and children as human shields, even putting their children in the line of fire, and blaming it on Israel. But all that is approved by the Koran. So, my education was extensive.

In March (2001) the ASEZA (Aqaba Special Economic Zone Authority) had lowered the money requirements for us to get residency. My friend from Fort Worth said that Father had them lower it for me. The $100,000.00 required, went down to $10,000.00. But, my U.S. bank balance hovered around a few cents. By faith, before going to America, I went and got an application for residency. I got my two pictures required, my initial blood test, a copy of my bank statement, and went to talk to the director ASEZA. Privately, the director told me I had the "golden passport," because the whole system was set up by the U.S.

I had gotten a blood test at a local clinic. This is funny: I shock friends by telling them I was stabbed seven times by a Palestinian, then I laugh. A young Arab man was to take my blood. My veins are very deep. He stabbed me in the left arm with a needle at least seven times, but no blood. He called for a helper. A young Muslim girl, covered totally except for her eyes, came in. She tried the right arm, and immediately got blood, to his amazement. I asked them to check to see if malaria was still in my blood. It had just been a year since the last time I had malaria. I waited for the results.

The young man was looking in a microscope. I asked him if he was born in Aqaba. He said: "No, I am a Palestinian." Then the Muslim girl came in. She handed me the papers. She said they found no malaria in my blood. Then she said: "Your blood is so good that you never have to have another blood test." I asked her to put that in writing, which she did. I took all requirements to the Director of the ASEZA. All was well until he saw 44 cents as my U.S. bank balance. I don't think there was much more in my Jordan bank. But, he issued the residency card for a year. I walked out of there as one in a dream. I was so stunned, and praising Abba. I was so excited to show it to my friends, but they just looked at it astounded, and began mocking me in disgust-- "44 cents!" "How could you get this?" The next year they looked at my bank balance in the U.S., and it was 56 cents. The young man handling the re-issue of the residency said ever so kindly: "It would be good if you had a few thousand dollars in your account." I explained how the money came into my account in the U.S., and then I transferred it to the Jordan bank, and then paid my bills. He said: "OH, you are independently financed." I didn't know what that meant, but I said: "Yes." Someone else asked me where my blood test was. I said: "Last year at the clinic they told me my blood was so good that I never had to have another blood test." They said: "OK." This is how it went the rest of my time in the ASEZA.

The rest of Jordan was different. It was under Muslim/Hashemite rule. But, this Zone was ruled by the U.S., the E.U., and the U.N. I met the ambassador from the U.S. I met the official who lived in Aqaba from the E.U. Then I learned in 2003, after the initial stages of the war in Iraq, that the U.N. had moved into Aqaba with their equipment. I went to meet the Director. He was from Sweden. They had rented the top floor of a hotel in Aqaba. I asked if I could get a job with them. I saw they were unloading about 50 computers. I told him I was good on the computer. I didn't really want a job with them--but it was a good cover. He explained that all of their personnel were coming from U.N. headquarters in New York. I asked Him if after the war in Iraq they would leave. He said: "No, we are here to stay."

As I began sending out what Abba was teaching me to my tiny little address list people, they began sharing what I was writing with others. I got e-mails from people asking theological questions, questions on the coming of Messiah, questions about what was really going on in our region, and questions related to their personal lives. I began spending 12-14 hours a day researching and answering e-mails. Most of the question e-mails took about 2 hours to answer. I did so much research throughout the Word to answer correctly. I went from Genesis to Revelation, through every verse on every subject, to bring a correct picture from Abba to the people. I had, maybe, 5% say "thank you" for my work, but it was my learning experience as well.

It was here that I realized that in religion, man takes a few verses to prove his opinion, but that is cheating. It is "dishonest research." I wanted to do "honest research!" I had my pre-1995 *Strong's Exhaustive Concordance* with me, with its Hebrew and Greek dictionary. As you can read in "Shabbat is Eternal", I include all the Scriptures on that subject. In 2001, Michael Lavarda bought me a Franklin electronic Bible. Oh what an awesome help that was/is to this day. I bought a large desk to start with, then later I bought a computer desk.

One Shabbat I thought: "What shall I study on Shabbat?" I reasoned that it might be good to study about Shabbat. So I began at 9:00 AM, in Genesis. I had a tiny breakfast. At 1:00 PM I took a 10 minute break to go to the bathroom and eat a banana. I finished at midnight. It took me fifteen hours to go through every verse on Shabbat in the Bible. Yet Torah-hating Greece and Rome and their religion says that we don't have to guard the Torah of Yahuweh. Christians celebrate Sun-day as their day of worship, by edict of Emperor Constantine, 4th century Rome. Sun-day is the day of the worship of the sun gods—the "Ba'als" -- the "lord's day."

That is how He taught me to study. If I left out any passages on a subject, I would be cheating. So, this is why it took me about two hours or more answering questions about the Bible. He had taken out of me all the falsehood of my church-teaching. He taught me His nature, ways and thinking. Thus I was hearing Him on each subject. His Spirit directed my studying and my research. He was giving me dreams, and visions, and prophecies often! I began compiling them, and others, from the past. It is quite a thick book now.

I find that those in the west almost have zero concept of living out of the eternal mind of the spirit. It is like I am talking mysticism or occult philosophy. NO, NO, NO! It is the norm for life with Yahuweh. I would often begin writing by 7:30 AM, because I wanted to keep "office hours." Then at times, I would look at the clock and it would be 1:00 PM, or even 3:00 PM, and I had not even had breakfast. Then I would have to read what I wrote.

In winter, in Aqaba, oftentimes it would be so cold that my hands could hardly move over the computer keys. This brought me out of my eternal state one time, and I saw I had lost five hours of time. I had no memory of what I had written, but I had written an entire article.

But, then I began to notice that people were asking the same questions on certain subjects. So why spend two hours repeating what I had already written to another? I got smart and began saving my answers, and turning them into studies, articles, or updates. The problem was, once I really began writing a lot I was spending at least 12 hours a day studying, researching, and writing, and not taking care of myself, or the apartment. I would take a bath maybe once a week, and because it was hot I went barefoot and my feet were black from the dirt, dried out and crusted. My house was collecting enough dust to grow vegetables, the balcony too. I had little time to eat, so I was very thin.

So from the early years in Aqaba, I would sometimes be caught up into His realm for days, even weeks at a time. Once I lock into something and am focused on it, I don't break focus. It is a major shock to my whole body to have my focus broken. In fact, the shock is so great that it could produce a heart attack, or I could go into a shut-down shock-mode. This is because once He begins speaking to me, I am in His dimension. My spirit is in His throne room. My mind is turned off, and my body is at total rest. Almost every time I pick up a Bible, He begins to teach. If that link between my spirit and His throne room is broken by someone's loud noise, or interruption, it is dangerous for me.

Most people think nothing of interrupting me, even if they see me reading the Bible, writing, or studying. They have no idea that I am not totally in this world. So I have often been forced to use ear plugs! But, then, if they are not acknowledged, they often touch me, which does the same thing as the noise. This is because so few understand what it is like to be "in the secret place of the Most High," or "sit in heavenly places with Yahushua Messiah." This is not figuratively – this is reality! This is why the prophets so longed to go into the wilderness to be alone with Him. This is why I appreciated the wilderness of the Negev for eight years.

I was lonely for fellowship with other humans. In 2003, people started coming to visit me. In the U.S., I love being with my children and my grandchildren. But, still, when I need to hear from Him and be closed in with Him, I must draw my boundaries. I worked so many long hours sitting at the computer, in so much pain daily from pinched nerves in my back, that I had knots all over my back where the muscle had knotted up from the vertebrae being out of place. If the pain got so bad I could not think, I still kept writing until I almost collapsed from the pain. Then I would get Ibuprofen, but keep writing. That has been a habit over the last 14 years.

When I was eleven years old, I jumped over a wall and somehow lost my balance. I fell backwards across a low-hanging tree limb, landing on the middle vertebrae of my back. It ruptured the vertebrae. I went home in great pain, but being medical people, my parents let me lie on the couch and paid no attention to me. That vertebrae has given me trouble all my life. It slips easily and causes my arms to go numb, especially while sleeping. My hips also stay in pain if I sit too long. So you can imagine the pain I have gone through, sitting at the computer so many hours a day for so many years. You can imagine the pain on long flights overseas. Most trips total between 30 and 40 hours, including layovers.

In 2003, two friends, Laura and Kim from Fort Worth, came to visit me after they had been in Israel. When they saw me in such a horrible condition, my African-American friend, Kim, had me lie on the floor, face down, with pillow under me. She worked on my back for over an hour, working out each knot until the muscle relaxed. The other lady, Laura, introduced me to Dead Sea lotion products and the foot cream by the Sea of Life company in Arad. She left some with me. That changed my not so good pattern! I learned to pace myself. I loved those lotions! My daughters are spoiled because I bring them the lotions when I return to the U.S., either Sea of Life or Sea of Spa – both made in Arad.

While I lived in Aqaba, in going to Jerusalem, the #444 Egged bus from Eilat always stopped along the Dead Sea where there was a Sea of Life outlet. I always stocked up. Then the bus changed routes. But, I found Sea of Spa products on Ben Yehuda Street in Jerusalem. Now they are in the Jewish Quarter in Jerusalem, and in Tiberias. I began writing studies, like the one on Shabbat. So, eventually my writings became: 1) articles 2) studies and 3) updates. Some home groups have used my articles for study along with the Torah portion each week, and on Shabbat. The articles became door openers for me to teach in many countries, as well as the U.S

Meeting my angel with the funny hair

I returned to Aqaba in August of 2001. It was around 120F daily. Abba asked me to stay in Aqaba for six weeks and just set aside the time to hear from Him. I believe now, that the six weeks were from Elul 1 to Tishre 15--Sukkot. That is significant to me now, but it was not then. I had not been to Israel for a Festival at this point. All the other Americans had gone home, as they usually did in the summer. It was so hot that I put my mattress on the floor under the ceiling fan. I used a squirt bottle filled with water to squirt on the sheets at night. The fan air hitting the watered sheets made it cool.

One afternoon, during this six weeks time of staying inside, except for getting groceries once or twice a week, I was sleeping on my mattress on the floor, underneath the ceiling fans. I was in a deep sleep. I awoke suddenly and there in front of me, between the end of my mattress and my big desk, stood a man about 5' 10" tall. He was leaning his left hand on the desk, looking down. I saw his profile. He had very chiseled features, very white skin, and was dressed in baggy white pants with a long white tunic over them, tied with a wide sash. But, his hair was what amazed me. It was combed from the center of the head straight down. Then it was curled under towards the head, all the way around. As soon as he saw that I was awake and saw him, he flew over my head about twelve inches, and disappeared. As he went over my head, I looked at this hair. It was funny. So, I named him "my angel with the funny hair." I knew, when he passed over me, that one day I would be in extreme danger, and I would see him, recognize him, and feel safe in letting him help me. On Yom Teruah, 2010, in an airport hotel in Panama City, I had a long detailed vision, and he played a big part in my protection.

During the six weeks, Abba spoke to me in so many ways, revealing things in myself that had to be removed if I was going to go forward with His work. One day during my 6-week alone time, I sat on the couch to rest, and Abba began speaking: "**I have given you the rod of Moses and the mantle of Elijah.**" I was so stunned. I said: "NO Lord." Those are two words you never put together when dealing with Yahuweh! I thought: That is too big, too high. I am just a woman who has messed up her life. Later on He explained that the authority that was vested in those symbols was the authority He wanted to put into me, so that I would proclaim His will and go as He directed fearlessly, not to "minister" to please man, but for Him. That only served to make me more humble, contrite, and totally non-religious.

During this time, with no one I knew there, I had spells of loneliness--but not like before when it possessed my life. One afternoon after about a month had passed, I was walking past the back of the couch in the living room, and I stopped and asked Abba: "Please, if it is possible, I would love to hear the human voice of a believer in English, and I would love to have some chocolate pie." About thirty minutes later, I heard a knock at the door. I opened it, and there stood Pastor Chip, who had returned from Louisiana. I did not know he was back yet. He told me that our Hebrew scholar had also returned the day before. Chip held something in his hands. He said that he had made a pie (he loved to cook) and took half to the Hebrew scholar, and wanted to bring me the other half. I bet you know what kind of pie it was! Yip! Chocolate! That was sure a fast answer to my desires – thank you Abba!

ISRAEL
(2001)

In 1999, I went on my first trip to Israel. You can read about that in Part V (Israel 1999 -- The Maiden Voyage). It was early September and still very hot. I was taking a nap in the living room on my mattress under the ceiling fan. I was not far from the entry hall of the front door. I woke up and saw an object hanging in the air, turned towards the northwest. It was not large. It looked to be pure gold. It was a menorah. It just hung there, turning a little to the right and left, but facing in the direction of Jerusalem. My great desire was to go to my first Sukkot in Jerusalem, but I thought that there was no way that the leader-lady would ask me to go with her. She was taking my Swiss friend, and the Pentecostal Pastor, Chip.

In about two weeks, all the Americans in our group arrived back to Aqaba. To my great surprise, she invited me to go to Jerusalem with Chip and my Swiss friend. The menorah was a sign from Abba, I suppose. We were going to stay with the man who runs a bookstore in the Old City, and his wife. I really liked this couple. The man was from Finland, from Lapland. He was a real student of the Word. He had led quite a few Jews to salvation, also. If a Jewish man wanted to know about Messiah, they would come secretly, like Nicodemus did in **John 3**. This man had worked with Ya'ir Davidy, doing research for Ya'ir's book *The Tribes.* The book traces the history, language, symbols, legends, and archeology of the individual ten tribes after they were finally all scattered out of the Land in 722 BCE by Assyria. We had wonderful fellowship. His wife was a New York Jew – a Christian who did some Jewish traditions. She never tapped into the depths of Yahuweh that he did.

The leader-lady, pastor Chip, and others from the group who had arrived in Jerusalem, all registered with the International Christian Embassy for their week-long Sukkot. Another lady, whom I really liked, a real estate lady from the Negev area, joined us too. At that time, because we were known to the ICEJ and their financial director, we were allowed to register as locals, and so only paid 30 shekels for the whole week of meetings, whereas Americans coming from America paid $200.00 a week.

The International Christian Embassy Jerusalem attracts Christians from all over the world who want to touch their Hebrew roots without leaving Christianity. But, it was a start for many Ephraimites who would go on to embrace Torah.

At the Jordan border at Aqaba, they would not give us Israeli plates for the car, so we went into Israel with Jordanian plates. Chip drove. He parked his car outside the apartment, where we were going to stay, which was in a very Orthodox Jewish neighborhood. The next morning was Shabbat. It was so quiet in that neighborhood. I began playing my recorder/flute, and the lady of the house quickly told me to stop. As Chip was drinking his coffee looking out the front window, he saw that police had surrounded his car. The lady of the house, ran out yelling for them to stop. They were going to blow up the car. They had found Chip's passport in the door of the car. They had found Jordanian money in the leader-lady's coat she left in the car. And then there was the bag of trash that I left in the back seat, as well as our Jordanian license plate. The police made us put signs all over the car windows saying that police had checked the car and it was all right. What a close call!

I had lunch one day with Esther Dorflinger – known well through her book *Come Away My Beloved*. In fact, it was my reading a borrowed copy of this book in early 1999, that my desire to go to Patmos grew. During this week, we went with a former IDF soldier, Steve, to the settlement area of Gilo near Jerusalem. It sits on a hill not far from the Arab town of Beit Jalla. Beit Jalla was between Gilo and Bethlehem. The Arabs had been sending rockets from Beit Jalla into Gilo, and some of the rubble from that was still present. We saw Israeli tanks along the hill slope from Gilo. Steve was a believer in Messiah. He was a friend of David Stern, and his wife Margaret. David translated the Messianic Bible, which so many use today. Steve had been invited that afternoon to go to his Sukkot party at David and Margaret's home, situated in a lovely hilly area of Jerusalem.

As we walked along in Gilo, Steve told us not to stand still more than 3 seconds because it took a sniper 3 seconds to zero in on a person and fire. Thanks Steve! We kept moving. But, then, he saw an Arab house on a little plateau, sticking out in the area of fire. Steve got the brilliant idea of knocking on their door and asking questions about how it was to live in that volatile place. The Arab man who opened the door was named Iesous/"Jesus." He said that he was delivered by a Christian Arab doctor on Christmas, and she named him that. They served us tea. This was a three-generation family. The children were at school. But he told us, in good English, what it was like living there and the dangers of it. They were so nice! They even let us pray for them. We left with blessings. So, when we got ready to leave, Steve said: "Why don't you join me at David Stern's party?" So we all came into David and Margaret's party. It was very nice. They are a very nice couple. That was a special day!

I began going to the ICEJ (International Christian Embassy Jerusalem) week of Sukkot meetings in 2000. I continued to attend their week of meetings for five years. In 2003, I began going on the tours that they offered with Christian Friends of Israeli Communities, with Sondra Oster Baras--the Israeli Director. When they stopped having tours with the ICEJ, I continued going even up to this last October, 2012. I will tell about the most powerful of the trips in 2004--to Gaza.

To finish up this year (2001), I felt strongly that Abba wanted me to go back to Samos, and from there to the seven assemblies of Asia, to bring His Name into those places, and to proclaim and prophesy. (**Revelation 2 and 3**) The original itinerary Abba gave me read: Amman to Athens, Athens to Samos (Vathy), Vathy to Kusadasi, Turkey, Kusadasi to Ephesus, then north to Smyrna, to Pergamum, then turning south to Thyatira, Sardis, Philadelphia, and finally Laodicea. The next day after going to Laodicea, I went to the hot springs at Pamukkale and to the ruins of Hieraopolis (**Colossians 4:13-16**). These places were close to the ruins of Colossae, but I did not go there. Then to return via Kusadasi to Samos by boat, from Samos to Athens, Athens to Amman, and Amman to Aqaba by plane. As He put this trip into my spirit, He gave me the characteristics of those whom He wanted to go on this assignment. I listed eighteen.

I asked two ladies from Aqaba to go, Betty and Rita. They had become good friends. When I asked Betty, she said that Abba had instructed her to go to Patmos, so our trip could be just after Patmos. She said that she knew she was to go, because Abba had told her we were going to close down the "church age." These cities of the seven assemblies of Asia are characteristic of church history through the centuries, but combined were a symbol of the church in the last days, each one representing a different group of believers in the last days.

In those days, I had not yet learned to be protective of Abba's plans. I blabbed what He wanted me to do because I was like a little child in a candy store. I loved going on His assignments. I did not brag, but I was very exuberant – too exuberant! I told one lady I should never have told. I met her in Aqaba in 2000. She lived in Jerusalem. I had stayed with her for a week in June of 2000, over the time of Shavu'ot. She was house-sitting for a lady who had rented a house in Beit Shemesh, which she used as a House of Prayer. But, it was just this lady and I the whole time. The lady who ran the ministry was called back to the U.S. to deal with a tragic family problem, and left this lady in charge.

It was during this time that I attended the congregation that had been pastored by Ruth Heflin in Jerusalem. After Ruth's death, it got out of hand spiritually. People were receiving gold dust on their skin and saying it was because Messiah was sending gold to His Bride before He came. Give me a Scripture on that! There isn't one! I also met a lady there who had a large walking stick that she said God gave her. She said that the walking stick would turn into a serpent and move by itself. I should have known! Dumb me! I invited her to come to Aqaba because she needed to renew her visa in Israel. She came. The next thing I knew, the leader-lady called to tell me that the Jordanian police had kept her and her husband up much of the night interrogating them, asking why one of their people (me) was hosting a known terrorist from Israel. Ohmagosh...

She had been with some Messianic people when the Israeli police had raided a house to arrest suspected terrorists. So she was also arrested. Though she was not a terrorist, they stamped her passport "terrorist" anyway. So, why did Israel let her out, and why did Jordan let her in? Anyway, the Jordanian police told us to get her across the border immediately, which we were happy to do!

But, back to my staying at Beit Shemesh: During that week, while at the Ruth Heflin's assembly, I found out that Paul Wilbur was going to do a concert at the Convention Center and I could get free tickets from the woman who took over after Ruth Heflin's death. Nancy gave me two tickets, one for me and one for the lady I was staying with. We went to be a part of the singing audience when Paul Wilbur recorded the *Lion of Judah* CD. After recording, Paul said it was the first time he had ever done a live recording that he did not have to repeat any songs, or make any corrections. It was so wonderful to be a part of that recording!

After the recording, my hostess-friend from Beit Shemesh, whom I have dubbed "large lady," rather than using her name, introduced me to her friend who would become "thorn in the flesh #2." I don't mean to be condemning, but this lady who was taking care of the facilities in Beit Shemesh spent most of her day eating, lying on the couch in the downstairs living room watching TV. I went into Jerusalem every day. She never moved much off the couch unless it was to eat. Her verbiage was shallow. She did not talk about Abba, so our fellowship was nil. I took walks each day too. But on Shavu'ot I had a wonderful experience. I was on the second floor. Just below my window was a synagogue under construction. The Orthodox Jews were meeting there regardless. They were singing, and I was listening. They read the Torah portion about the giving of the Torah at Sinai. As they did, I stood in the window and read **Acts 2** from my Bible, about the outpouring of the Spirit at Shavu'ot on those Torah-guarders who believed in Messiah Yahushua. I prayed that there would be those of that congregation who would receive Yahushua as Savior and

Messiah. That week, I also read the bluntly awesome book *How Saved Are We?*, by Rabbi Michael Brown.

WESTERN TURKEY
(2001)

Continuing with the 2001 report: I knew Abba wanted me to go to the seven assemblies of **Revelation 2 and 3**. I bought the *Lonely Planet Travel Kit Turkey*. I carefully planned the itinerary, for myself and the two ladies who also qualified on those eighteen points. It would take seven days start to finish. Betty was coming from Patmos, so Rita and I met her on Samos. From Samos, Greece we would take the boat from Vathy (the capitol city of the Isle of Samos) to Kusadasi, Turkey.

Abba appreciates those who do their homework and are disciplined and organized within His perimeters and boundaries of His plans. By this time I had organized many trips. So, we three were very excited. I was e-mailing the large lady whom I stayed with at Beit Shemesh. In our correspondence, she mocked Eliyahu as being a sissy. I was very angry about that. But, jezebel goes after Eliyahu to tear him down one way, or the other! And, I made the horrible mistake of telling her about the trip to Turkey. What would that trip have been like without her, and her friend I met at Paul Wilbur's concert? Oh Abba, you know...

But, like most Americans, I loved to talk about what was exciting to me, not thinking about jezebel spirits that might try to ruin the trip. Well, she asked if she could go with us. Now, I would have told her "no", but then, I was still afraid of aggressive personalities. I was still unsure of myself as an individual. She was very aggressive. So, I told her to come. She invited her friend too. That made five of us. I have to confess: I had been complaining to Abba about being tired of going alone on my trips, and I wanted people with me. I have had people with me that were a tremendous blessing, like Sharon in 2010, Maureen from Wales, Cheryl in Egypt, dear African pastors, and my son in Israel. But, this time, I was punished for complaining.

She said she was going by herself to Patmos, then she and her friend were going a day early to Turkey. I should have remembered Darlene in 1999 in Africa. Large lady e-mailed me from Patmos as to how awful it was because the men were so mean to her. She had rented a motorcycle and didn't know how to drive it. She wrecked it, and the owners yelled at her.

Anyway, it was Friday. Betty arrived from Patmos, and the three of us had a nice lunch. Then we went and bought candles, bread, and wine, for our Shabbat celebration that evening. We got an upstairs room, where I was before, at the Blue Dolphin Inn. The balcony opened into a grape arbor, and grapes were hanging everywhere. We helped ourselves. We sat there in the cool of the evening and directly in front of us, 3 km away, was the outline of the coast of Turkey.

Early the next morning was Shabbat. Not being astute Torah-guarders at that point, we went to Vathy by taxi. The Aegean Sea was roaring, and our boat was not going to Turkey until the sea stopped roaring. So we waited all day. It was Betty who figured that Abba wanted us to guard Shabbat, since it was His assignment. Late in the day, we boarded the boat and headed towards Kusadasi. We saw dolphins jumping. It was a super boat ride that took about an hour.

When we arrived, the sun had just set. The other two ladies were there waiting for us with a rented car. They took us to their hotel so we could get a room, and then we had dinner. I was finally realizing that large lady was taking over to run the whole trip. She had rented the car, and she was the driver, so she was in charge! I thought of Darlene from Connecticut, arriving early in Kenya to make sure she got the meetings she wanted for herself. I told her I had the whole trip planned out, but she said: "We'll just be led by the Spirit." I'm sorry to say, but most "flaming Charismatic" women, with pride, haughtiness, and loud mouths, do NOT have the nature of Yahuweh! To them, being led by the Spirit means they are in control!

The next morning, we left late. I am an early-bird. I believe that wasting time is a sin against the Creator. The Scriptures teach that too. I should have remembered that the life of the large lady consisted primarily of eating, drinking alcoholic beverages with her meals, sleeping in until noon, and doing as little as possible the rest of the time.

Ephesus

We got to Ephesus about noon. The Roman ruins of Ephesus are huge. It is the largest and best preserved Roman city in the world. The Library of Celsius is there, and two large amphitheatres. I took all day to go through it. Ephesus used to be on the coast, but the land became extended into the sea, and it became landlocked through the years. Large lady wanted us to climb to the top of the largest amphitheatre. It was there that Sha'ul preached. She put on her tallit, and took out a long shofar and began blowing it. She led everyone in prayer. I had a very hard time climbing up there, but I figured if I didn't, she would be upset. I wanted to go exploring to see what Abba wanted me to see. It was obvious that this "team" consisted of those who obeyed the large lady, and me--"the fifth wheel." Her loudness was interpreted by the others as boldness and authority from God.

I was feeling the jezebel spirits, and I could not stay up on the amphitheatre any longer. She belonged to a prestigious Christian cult-group in America. Most all of its members, that I have met, are very "spiritual"--religious, proud, and haughty, with strong controlling jezebel spirits. So, I went down to the lower road on my own. Bad move! In her eyes, I was rebellious. They came down and went in the area of the Roman baths. They huddled together near a secluded column to pray. I joined them. The prayers were so boring, so self-centered. I was there to do Abba's business. So I got up again and began walking in the Agora--market area. From then on I was considered a rebellious woman that crossed the leadership of the ruling large lady. Of course her friend sided with her, and the other two kept quiet. That night large lady wouldn't speak to me.

The next morning, we met in her room to find out her plans for us to go to Smyrna. I sat down, and immediately, she began screaming at the top of her lungs at me. Remember I had three nervous breakdowns, and for someone to scream like that was very traumatic. She had a voice as low and powerful as a man's voice. She accused me of coming against her authority. I burst into tears. Then Rita told how she was put in charge of a prayer-outing with five people in Aqaba, and how I went off on my own to do intercession. I couldn't believe this. I told her that Abba wanted me to go stand on a rock by the sea and turn in all directions, singing praises to Him and calling forth His remnant. I also let her know that I was trying to escape a man in our little group, who was aggressively flirting with me. I was not trying to rebel. But, women who are put in authority, whether in the secular world or the religious world, especially women in ministry who do not submit to Yahuweh, are generally controlled by jezebel spirits.

I had thought of going on this trip by myself, and letting Abba lead me. I even had a dream about going by myself and letting Him lead. I should have gone on by myself, because it cost me not only mental, emotional and physical pain, but also about $500.00 extra dollars, because this woman was so lazy. We never got started before noon, so the trip was extended another three days. We missed our flight from Samos to Athens, and Athens to Amman. So, we had to return through Istanbul. I am sorry to say, but this slothful attitude is common for charismatic "intercessors." I teach Scriptural intercession—in which one works personally with Yahuweh's Spirit, which is a totally different type of intercession!

Before founding the group that large-lady was a member of, the cult leader was mentored by the teachings of occultist Annalee

Skarin, as well as by a form of mystic Catholicism. I read all of Annalee Skarin's seven books, during my rebellious stage. She is a New Age mystic/occultist. But, when, in her seventh book, she said that Jesus was not God, I threw out her books. So, you can imagine the "spirits" I was dealing with on this trip.

As we headed towards Smyrna, we passed a hotel that I had recommended from the *Lonely Planet* book. She and her friend mocked me and laughed. They said that God was going to get them far better than anything I had planned. It went from bad to worse. It was a wonder I survived the ten days. However, when all the smoked cleared, I did what Abba told me to do. In doing what He tells me to do, I've had so much opposition from jezebels, and other spirits of the enemy, that have tried to slander me, ruin my reputation (character assassination), and even take over the ministry Abba has given to me. They know they can't stop me, so they try to ruin my reputation with deceptions and lies.

Smyrna

What a blessing to be in this place! The ruins are small in comparison to Ephesus. In **Revelation 2**, Messiah had nothing but good things to say about the assemblies of Smyrna and Philadelphia – Smyrna represents the faithful martyrs, and Philadelphia represents the Bridal remnant of Messiah. The next day we drove to Izmit and stayed overnight. We spent the early afternoon in a strange type of intercession over the sea. We got salt from a local restaurant to throw into the sea. The cult leader of the group large lady was in had created all sorts of strange props that are used in intercession. Some of them were highly dangerous because they attracted demons. So we lost a day there. We went on to Pergamum the next day. The large lady slept in until nearly noon. Then we went to get something to eat at a restaurant, and she gorged herself, and drank a couple of beers. I have nothing against beer, but not before intercession.

Pergamum

We got to Pergamum, an expansive area of ruins, with so much to see, at about 2:00 PM. We should have been there at 9:00 AM. I tried to tell them that, but they all defended large lady. Then we went to one small area of Pergamum by a pagan temple. We did a minimum of intercession, and then it was 4:00 PM, and the ruins closed. Before we left, I saw where the Pergamum Altar sat before being removed to Berlin, and I got a picture of it. I wanted so bad to spend the day there, just praising Abba and bringing His Name there. I did play my recorder and prophesied over the area.

Thyatira

Large lady began to lead us in pseudo-intercession, which she learned from her cult-leader. I did not participate in the hocus pocus. She prayed over a bottle of wine and a communion wafer. Then she poured the wine on the wafer, which she had put on a stone of one of the buildings. I understood **Haggai 2:11-14. With all my training in the realm of the demonic and Satanism, I understand that you do NOT consecrate something to Yahuweh--setting it apart as undefiled—and then pour what is undefiled onto the defiled, mixing the two**. The undefiled (the set-apart to Yahuweh) touching what is defiled does not make the defiled undefiled. But, quite the opposite! You place what is undefiled on what is defiled, and the defiled makes the undefiled defiled. Read the Scripture in Haggai!

The practice of finding "ley lines," and going to demonic strongholds, and doing charismatic witchcraft in the name of "Jesus", only draws demonic spirits. In Steve Lightle's awesome book, *Operation Exodus II*, he talks about taking a team to the ancient ruins of Babylon (Iraq). He was the leader of the team. But, upon going to where the Ishtar gates of Babylon once stood (they are now in the Pergamum Museum in Berlin along with the altar of Zeus from Pergamum), one of the pastors in his group asked if he could do a symbolic act over where the gates of Babylon stood. Steve, being a laid-back type of man, told him to go ahead. The pastor did the same hocus pocus, which Steve knew was not from the God of the Bible. Later when the team got back to the U.S., all sorts of awful things began to happen to the families of the team members. One man's young son even died.

This is why so many in the charismatic movement, and in cults like this one, experience so many awful things after they return from "intercession" trips. Large lady even told me about all the things that happened to her in a previous trip to another part of Turkey with the leader of the cult. It is because this pseudo-spirituality is rooted in paganism that deceptive spirits are free to work, making the person extremely arrogant and proud, while deceiving them into embracing others who are deceived also. Thus, those involved are all walking in true spiritual blindness.

Yes, this cult teaches love for Israel. To show their solidarity with the Jews, they usually guard Shabbat and the Festivals. But, they consider themselves "gentiles", so they guard the Torah very loosely. Of course, religious spirits thrive on this mixture greatly. They idolize the Messianic Jews, especially those big names in ministry in Israel. Mixture-religions are always a horrible mess. Messiah says in **Revelation 3:14-16** that He will spew the mixtures out of His mouth.

The next day we went through the western countryside of Turkey, where the peasant people were picking lots of cotton. It was lovely. We stayed in a hotel before proceeding to Sardis. The food was great and the hotel staff was pleasant. But, the large lady's friend, not having lived in a Muslim world so that she had wisdom, wore a lot of make-up and dressed in the usual American immodesty, and was very friendly to the Muslim men. A woman must not act friendly to Muslim men. Most think all America women are whores, anyway. But, she was pretty and flirty. And because we were five women on our own, the phones rang all night to our rooms, because they thought we were prostitutes.

We were back on the road, and for some reason I was given the map. Large lady kept getting lost. But, every time I told her to turn somewhere, going by the map, she would scream (I mean scream) at me "SHUT UP," calling my name interspersed with more "shut ups." By this time my nerves were shattered, and I was crying out to Abba to give me grace and mercy so that I didn't crack up.

This is one example of how the anti-messiah/Beast/son of Lucifer—Apollyon will be able to control people. They will worship the Beast because of his commanding control! No one seemed to think she was doing anything wrong. But, Betty was always kind to me. I really appreciated her! It really was hers and my assignment, so we kept peace between us. It is so extremely important to know the nature, ways, and thinking of the Elohim of Israel to be able to discern different spirits, and their source!

Laura, my friend from Fort Worth who introduced me to the Dead Sea lotions, attended one of this cult's big conferences. She told me what the founder, guru-lady, said. Laura heard this for herself. The lady said that God had told her that John F. Kennedy and Jacqueline would get out of "purgatory" in 300 years. So, can you see more of what I was dealing with on this trip? Guru-lady is like a god to her loyal subjects. The loyalty to her is overwhelming.

Sardis

For some strange reason we got to Sardis at a fairly decent time. We stayed longer at Sardis than any other place, which I am grateful for. Sardis has the ruins of the largest synagogue in Asia Minor, built in the 5th century AD. We stood in the ruins of that huge synagogue. They wanted to stand where the "seat of Moses" sat to pray and proclaim Scripture. I did not want to do that.

Before I left America, my youngest daughter had phoned me saying that she had read **Revelation 2 and 3**, and she knew she had the characteristics of Sardis, but she desired to be like those in Philadelphia. So, while they were doing their deal over in the middle of the synagogue, I picked up a white smooth stone and wrote her name on it, and the names of my other three children and grandchildren. I took that stone to the ruins of Philadelphia and threw the stone down at the base of the great pillars at the gates of the city, symbolically to agree with her that she would be a part of the end-time remnant that would be pure and set-apart to the coming of Messiah!

Also, I felt to read **Deuteronomy 6** from behind the large table where the Torah scrolls were opened and read. This table is called "the bema" –the judgment seat--because we will be judged by the Torah, when our High Priest, Yahushua, comes. (**Zechariah 6:12-15**) The power of Yahuweh was on me so strong, I could hardly read. But, I projected my voice out through torrents of tears. Rita took a picture of me. That is a priceless picture to me.

As I read all of **Deuteronomy 6**, I felt that it had not been read there for centuries, and that Abba wanted His Name used. Messianics probably had been there, and many Jewish tour groups go there, but neither use His correct Name. Most use pagan title-substitutes. So, I felt as if I were saying His Name for the first time in that place.

We spent the night in a hotel near Sardis. The next day we proceeded on towards Philadelphia. Like Thyatira, Philadelphia had been given a Turkish name, so we really got lost trying to find it. I had the map, but it was "shut up" time again.

Philadelphia

We did not get to Philadelphia until just after sunset. It is the smallest of the ruins. Philadelphia pictures the "precious few" Bridal remnant of 144,000 from all the tribes of Ya'cob. No one in Messiah is a "gentile." "Gentile" means "a heathen, barbarian, pagan, a stranger, alien, or foreigner," to the covenant of Yahuweh. He made absolutely no covenants with gentiles. He says He will destroy all gentiles. Messiah came to renew His Father's Kingdom-Covenant with those He had to scatter into all nations because of our sin--the House of Israel (Ya'cob)/Joseph/Ephraim. (**Matthew 15:24; 10:5-6** as examples) In doing so, He also redeemed the House of Judah. No one in Messiah is left out of the family of Ya'cob. This is throughout Scripture. The wicked ones of religion have twisted His Word to support their own secret ambitions and hidden agendas to control the minds of others. [Refer to: "Are You A Gentile?"/2007 revised and "Who Are the Ten?"/2005]

We stayed there until about 8:00 PM, and then got a hotel for the night. The next day we went towards Laodicea. Due to the many delays caused by getting started too late in the day, our schedule was thrown off by days. We would have already seen

Laodicea and be finished with the trip had we gone by the itinerary I set up. Not only did we miss our scheduled plane flight that afternoon to Samos, but also our scheduled plane that evening going back to Amman through Athens. It would be three more days before we got back. I was just sick about that. Therefore, we had to find another way of returning to Amman and that meant at least $500.00 extra on my credit card that I could not afford. I am very disciplined, so being forced to be with such a lack of discipline was very hard, and costly.

Laodicea

Upon arriving near Laodicea, we first went to Pamukkale. It was where the hot springs were at the top of the mountain. The white sediment from the water running out of the ground down the mountain was thick and hard, and looked like snow-peaks. The water was hot bubbling out of the ground, and there were many places where we could sit in the water. The water also deposited a green mud at its hottest source. It was here that the hot water flowed down the mountain to Colossae. When it got to Colossae it was cold. In between the water went from hot to lukewarm. This is the example that was given of Laodicea in **Revelation 3:14-16**. "So because you are lukewarm, and neither hot or cold, I am going to I spew you out of My mouth."

The large lady pulled up in front of Hotel Pam. I took one look at it and said: "I cannot stay here, it is too expensive." The hotel had a fountain of their own hot water, and in the basin was the green mud. It was a spa hotel, with buffet dinner, etc. The large lady said, "You're going to stay here whether you like it or not." I shut up. I have to admit, large lady made a good choice! How wonderful to find out that it was not expensive at all. Upon finding how inexpensive it was, she puffed up with pride like a "puff adder." I saw a puff adder below my balcony in North Carolina. I threw something down on it. It is a large snake. I watched as it puffed out into a larger snake. That's what Jezebel does. If someone challenges her control, she puffs out into a very large snake, in fact, she puffs into a python/anaconda – the largest of the snakes. The spirit of python/anaconda is what rules America. The headquarters of python worship is at Arlington, Virginia, near Washington D.C. The python is a symbol of Apollo – Apollyon--the son of Lucifer/anti-messiah!

I did enjoy the hot water and the green mud--I really did! The next afternoon, we finally got on the road about 3:30, and went to Laodicea. There were ruins scattered all over the low hills for about two miles, but we finally got to the amphitheatre. I could not believe the sea shells embedded in the rocks. Laodicea was 300 miles from the sea. Yet at one time it was on the coast.

We did some intercession there. The large lady's idea of intercession was about 20 minutes of prayer, with shofar blowing. But, this was the grand finale. Remember, I said that Betty, the one I had actually invited, felt we were going to close the church age? She really did hear from Abba. She remained my one source of comfort on the whole trip. As the sun set on an almost cloudless sky, I looked up and saw one cloud only, right in front of us. It was almost in a circular ring. The ring was thin. But, the shape of the ring was exactly the shape of the placement of the seven assemblies. The ring was closed. Right now I am getting chills remembering it. I ran to get my camera out of my backpack. I took a picture of it as it began to fade into gray.

Betty was standing next to me. I turned to her and said: "Look at the cloud." She saw it and burst into tears. I said: "We did it. Our obedience closed the church age." No wonder the enemy fought so hard! Recently, watchmen have been saying that the church age is closed. The great apostasy has begun. Recently I read in an article in the *Prophecy in the News* magazine by Gary Stearman, where he said that he felt the church age was closing. It has closed Gary. The final "restoration of all things" (**Acts 3:19-21**) began about 1995, with the restoration of the Torah to the House of Israel/Ephraim--the not lost anymore 10 tribes of Ya'cob.

From that evening forward, October 19, 2001, as far as Yahuweh is concerned, the counterfeit "church" that He allowed to invade western culture, had so turned towards its pagan base in Nimrod that He considered it finished! Look at the deterioration of "the church system" since that time. We were inside the 7th millennium, and His judgment on the church had begun!

The next morning was October 20th. It was the birthday of the daughter I stay with. Strange--on October 20th 1999, I was with Russian war veterans, enjoying the day with the Russian Social Service, and Susan. Both those October 20ths were days of completion of a phase of an assignment.

We went to breakfast. Large lady had set aside the day to soak in the hot water, and so had the others. I looked up at the reception desk. I thought to myself: "I am not going to spend my daughter's birthday sitting around doing nothing." So I got up without saying anything to them, went to the reception desk, and asked for a taxi to take me to the ruins of Hieraopolis. Hieraopolis is mentioned in **Colossians 4:13**. I came back to our table and told them of my plans. They where shocked that I was doing something on my own--again. But, the trip was ending so they didn't care what I did. It was mid-morning.

The ruins of Hieraopolis were very extensive. I love archeology. I love just walking around old ruins. I had a chance to pray, sing, and relax. I then went to the river where people were swimming in the warm water, and had lunch at the resort's restaurant. It was a glorious day! I had made a right decision! I really believe that if I had gone on my own, as I know to do now, the whole trip would have been glorious. But, then, I would not have seen the ring in the sky, and neither would Betty have seen it, for she was looking in another direction. I suppose the trip was redeemed.

That night we had one final meeting in the large lady's room. She asked me if there was anything I wanted to say regarding her leading the group. That wasn't laughable, that was tragic. I very gently, with no emotion, told her what I thought. She immediately broke down in tears and cried out loudly: "I'm being persecuted; I'm being persecuted." The other three ran over to comfort her, and left me with my mouth open in shock. But, back in our shared room, my Betty, Rita, and I, had good closure. Betty went over those 18 qualifications, and then told them to Rita. I know Betty understood. Yet, when large lady wanted to go on another assignment, Betty was her sidekick. The next day we split the cost, and paid a taxi man $100.00 to take us all the way to Istanbul to the airport. That was a long journey. That evening we flew back into Amman. Large lady and her friend flew into Tel Aviv. Then large lady had the nerve, two years later, to ask me if she could come stay with me in Aqaba because she needed to renew her visa with Israel. I said "no."

I didn't go into such detail in this story to condemn, judge, criticize, or take revenge on large lady. But, we must discern the spirits of the enemy, for when they operate, they bypass any decency, and any sanity, yet the religious bow to them. This is a picture of the world's people, who will bow to the same spirits in the false prophet (**Revelation 13**). We must not be naïve, or make excuses for demonic wickedness. This naivety, a false tolerance, will cause many to submit to the anti-messiah.

Messiah's words in **Matthew 24, Mark 13**, and **Luke 21**, warn us of the coming betrayal by supposed friends, family members, and those of our religious community. The betrayal will be so bad that even children will turn in their parents to their death.

JORDAN
(2002)

I went to Jerusalem for Passover week, then I went back for Sukkot. I stayed at the Jaffa Gate Hostel, and became a regular customer there during Festivals. Like those in our group, I made friends with the pastor and his wife of the Anglican Church in Aqaba. They were from England. For a while we used their facilities for our Saturday night services. Later this year, I would go with them on a wonderful trip to the new baptism site. We attended their services on Sunday mornings.

This year also, is when Abba turned up the fire in my spirit. He began teaching me in depth. I was spending 10-12 hours a day writing, warning, explaining theology, counseling, answering questions, and teaching in meetings in many places, as well as in America. Upon returning to America, I stayed busy with meetings--in homes, school rooms, community buildings, libraries, and wherever people could find room for me to teach.

In May, I wanted to do something special for my 51st spiritual birthday. I wanted to go to Gedera (Umm Qays) in the north of Jordan, overlooking the south end of the Sea of Galilee (Lake Kinneret). It was in the Gilead area of Jordan, north of Amman. So, I took the Trust Bus all the way to Irbid. Irbid is a center for pressing olives, and bottling some of the best olive oil in the world, but also a Muslim stronghold with terrorist organizations. For some reason, the bus did not go to the bus station, but stopped at a hotel area. I got a taxi for a good rate to take me to Gadara.

There was the modern village, and then the extensive ruins (**Mark 4:35-5:10**). I found that there was one hotel run by a family--and I was the only guest. They had an Egyptian man sleep on the floor at the end of the hall from my room for the two nights I was there to protect me. The bathroom was, of course, down the hall. It was May 12th, 2002. The next morning, May 13th, my 51st spiritual birthday, after breakfast with the family who owned the hotel, I walked to the ruins of Gadara nearby. There were groves of olive trees there that were over 2,000 years old. Jews from Israel used to come over and buy olive oil there, because it was so rich and pure, until the Intifada in Jerusalem happened in 2000. I took my time walking among the ruins. There were tombs all down the slope of the hill towards the base of Lake Kinneret. From Gadara one could see a boat coming on the Lake below.

The wild flowers were gorgeous, growing up alongside the ancient basalt buildings. I was there about six hours. It was almost sunset when I walked back and got a falafel to take with me to my room. I intended to spend the evening in the Word. But, I had been out in the heat all too long without a hat, and I had a horrible headache from the heat. I was so sick I was afraid I'd throw up the falafel if I ate it. I lay there in the dark and said to Abba: "This is a fine birthday present." Within a few seconds, the headache was gone – He healed me! Now that was a fine birthday present! But, the best was yet to come...

He then began to teach me about the man at Gadara. He told me about the man's family, his being a businessman, his being wealthy and well-known throughout the Greek Decapolis--the "ten cities." He told me how he had become demon possessed. He told me how he lived in the tombs on the side of the hill going down towards the south side of Lake Kinneret, and how he cut himself with the rocks, and was violent. Then He told me how he was delivered and born again, and sent back to his family and to all who knew him in the Decapolis to give his testimony of his deliverance through the Jewish Messiah, Yahushua. His teaching went on until about midnight.

The next day, I went by mini-bus to the bus station in Irbid. What a mass of chaos. I finally got to the right ticket window and bought a ticket for Amman. In Amman, I stayed overnight at my usual hotel-- the Geneva Hotel at the 7th circle. The next day I went to Aqaba on the trusty Trust Bus.

I also went to Petra with my Swiss friend and others in our group. My friend from Fort Worth rented a little duplex in Wadi Musa. Betty and Rita had rented another duplex next to it. They sat on a ridge above Petra. Walking along the road by the duplexes, we could look right into the Siq and into Petra. There were fig and olive trees by the duplex, and grapes. The best pomegranates I've ever tasted are grown in Wadi Musa. I stayed with Betty and Rita. We visited Muslim families in the area, with whom they had made friends, and went into Petra. It was a wonderful trip! There were such good times to offset the bad ones!

My Fort Worth friend and I went to stay in the famous hotel in Taybet Zaman. It was made famous by an article written for British Airlines, posted in their travel magazine. This hotel was made from using rooms that were built of stone thousands of years old. On various trips to Petra, we often ate there for dinner, because their buffet dinner was so awesome. It is impossible to describe. They also had shops there where you could even buy big natural chunks of real Frankincense and Myrrh. I bought my first Bedouin dress in a tiny shop in Taybet. It was so beautiful, all covered with dust from the street.

Betty still had her apartment in Taybet. She was friends with her landlord, Mahmoud. We visited Mahmoud and his family, and were invited to the birthday party of his little 1-year old. He put on quite a feast. We went in the women's entrance into the house and sat on the floor with the women, and the babies and little girls. In Muslim homes there is a women's entrance and a men's entrance. Even in the large apartment building where the typhoid was originally in the water, the builder and owner was a staunch Muslim, so each apartment had two entrances. For some reason, which I can't figure out, every night I spent in Taybet, or in Wadi Musa, I slept better than I ever slept anywhere else in the world. I would sleep all night without waking up. The peace there was amazing.

I began to learn how the U.N. had taken over the Petra area. Queen Noor was the overseer. She put an electric grid around it, so at night no one entered Petra. She had a young American couple arrested and taken to the airport and deported. They had moved into Wadi Musa. Their young son went to school and told the children that they were there to help the Jews flee to Petra. Queen Noor said that no Christians were allowed to live in that area.

Back in the 1940s, as Noah Hutchings told, Christians put New Testaments into crevices in many of the caves, for they knew it was the one protection zone for His people in the last days, and yes it is. [Refer to: "Petra, Edom, and the Re-gathering and Preservation of All the Tribes of Israel in the Last Days"/Revised January 15, 2008] If you read this article, make sure you read the Appendix, and be sure to look in Collection XII for the amazing story of how I got this information for the Appendix.

During my second or third trip to Petra, I was sitting below the steps that go up to a high level where many caves wrap around a high hill. My friends had gone up. As I sat there, a little Bedouin girl named Honey, maybe age 7, came up to sell me one of the colored rocks that the children find so abundantly in that area. She wanted 1 JD for each rock, but I gave her ½ JD for one and she was happy with that. Later she sold me two rocks for ½ JD. Lots of little Bedouin children sell rocks, or donkey rides, or jewelry and other Bedouin-made things. Their mothers watch close-by to make sure their children are doing their work of making money. Every time I went, Honey found me and I bought more rocks. The last I saw of her, she looked to be in her early teens. One time, it was during Ramadan. I was sitting on the amphitheatre steps eating a sandwich. I offered her food and water. Her mother saw that, and her father later yelled at me. They fast from sundown to sundown during Ramadan.

As people came to visit me, I took them to Petra. It was getting more and more expensive by the year. After the first three years, my friends stopped renting their homes in Wadi Musa. So, in 2003, I started staying at the Crown Plaza at the entrance to tourist-Petra, because I got a nice sized breakfast for free along with a discount on the big buffet dinner. They also gave me a good rate because I was from Aqaba. Cute story: I became known among the Bedouin as "Miss Aqaba" because of all the times I was there bringing friends. One boy, about six or seven years old, was selling jewelry. He wanted to sell me a lovely hand-made necklace for 6 JD. His brother was sitting on a ledge on a rock and said to him, "she's one of us." He then said: "2 JD." I bought it.

I felt at home in Wadi Musa and Petra. I felt at home in Aqaba. I did not make friends of the Muslims during those eight years, but I had my favorites in certain places – the phone company, the Post Office, the bank, the green-grocery store which "Mr. White Hat" ran. He was a friendly man--a devoted Muslim, but he was good to give me discounts. He only spoke Arabic and a little English, so I thought.

The country of Hungry had a special flight for their citizens into Aqaba. With their gypsy mentality, they tried to get Mr. White Hat to lower his already low prices. One day after a group of them had left, I entered his store to buy vegetables and fruit. He was so angry. He began telling me in perfectly clear English with a California accent how angry he was at those people. I commented on his good English. He said he had studied Engineering in the United States, and had gone to the Hebrew University in Jerusalem. So, we developed an unusual relationship of trust – he confided in me at times. One day he said to me with tears: "I love my God."

In June of 2002, I took Trisha, a young lady I had met in Fort Worth, to the Baptism site on the Jordan River. She had been teaching in Thailand and had recently come to Aqaba. It was 130 degrees F that day. The site was not officially open yet, for they still had land mines along the river. It was a border area between Jordan and Israel's "west bank." She drove a rental car. It was so hot that we were the only ones there. We were supposed to meet a young man who was a friend of a friend of hers, who was going to give us a good deal on a tour. But, by the time we found him, the water in my water bottle was hot and there was not much left. So, he said he would take us to meet his boss in the new air conditioned tourist center building. His boss had a fine office on the second floor. He served us cold Coke and then cold water, and gave me some tourist books that had just been published. In those books, there is factual information about Yahweh the God of

PART VI - The Middle East & Travels Beyond

Israel. I used those books later to teach His Name to local born again believers in Aqaba, opening doors for them to hunger to learn the Hebrew roots of the Scriptures.

This "boss" knew people I knew in Aqaba. During our discussion of the area, three Hashemite Jordanian archeologists who were the original archeologists on this dig came into the room. One had found a second-century map in a tile floor in an old church in Madaba – the Byzantine area of Jordan. From this map, they saw that the real baptism site of John the baptizer was just above the headwaters of the Dead Sea, along the east bank of the Jordan River. The site faced directly into Jericho and East Jerusalem, with Mount Nebo behind, in the plains of Moab. Fifteen Scriptural events happened right there, including; the burial place of Moses, the place where Joshua and the children of Israel crossed the Jordan, where Elijah sat by the brook Cherith, where Elijah went up to heaven in a whirlwind, where John baptized "beyond the Jordan at Bethabara--**John 1:28**--where Messiah was baptized, where Messiah spent 40 days and 40 nights in the wilderness, and more.

Did you know that where Messiah was baptized and pronounced "the Lamb of Elohim who takes away the sin of the world" is today in modern Jordan? Just about 50 miles straight north of this site is Tishbe, where Elijah grew up (**I Kings 17:1**). I was just above the ruins of Tishbe in 2006 on that mountain. Do you know that there are 120 Biblical excavated sites in modern Jordan? There are...

As these archeologists came in, they sat down and we "fellowshipped" for about two hours in the Scriptures. How does a non-Muslim believer in the Elohim of the Scriptures fellowship with Muslims? Well, let's just say that we "touched base" in the Scriptures. They use the Bible to do their finding of things, and they are amazingly accurate! They work with the Israeli archeologists and have meetings with them in Aqaba twice a year at the big Swiss Movenpick Hotel. When I met a key Israeli archeologist in Glen Rose, Texas -- Moshe Bronstein -- he said he had just come from a meeting in Aqaba with Jordanian archeologists.

The "boss" wanted for us to be taken by van down to the Jordan River. We set off for the river in their official van, but we were stopped by the Jordanian military and could go no further because all the land mines had not been completely cleared from the area. I was greatly disappointed.

The leader-lady had quite a few American visitors. Of course we met them at weekly gatherings. It was this year, more than ever, that I began seeing the masked Americans without their masks.

One lady who came to visit, got to the border from Eilat, and asked the Jordanian immigration officer where she could find the people who were protecting the Jews in Petra. Another lady, a holocaust survivor, had brought a team to meet us. They were wearing Israeli jewelry, Israeli t-shirts, and had brought lots of food and water with them. The customs people confiscated all the food and the water, and interrogated the leader for two hours. You just don't provoke a rattle snake and expect it not to coil and strike.

It was the stupid things that caused so much trouble for us. The leader-lady got Messianic magazines sent to her in Aqaba without anything to hide what was on the outside cover. Oftentimes, the Star of David and other Jewish symbols was on the cover, with anti-Muslim propaganda clearly shown for anyone to see. These were totally open to all Post Office personnel. Whenever we got a package from home, we had to go into a little room with the Custom's official and they had to open the package and check the contents before it would be released to us.

I will never forget getting a manila envelope with my mail in it, that I had my son send me. I did not know the manila envelope was full of "Jewish things." I opened one package in front of the Custom's lady. But, since she was on the telephone she didn't see it right away. Out fell all those magazines with clearly Jewish symbols on them. I hid them quickly, and she never saw them. It reminded me of taking those Bibles into Beijing at midnight. I stuffed everything back into the envelope, and when she turned her head back to me, I opened it and showed her quickly that it was only printed material.

The leader-lady had given money to Angus and Batya Wooten's organization of Ephraimite Torah-guarders, and her name was printed in one of her magazines, along with many other names. But, Al Qaeda had spies, and they saw her name and knew she was in Aqaba. They sent 13 terrorists into Amman to kill her and all of us. The Jordanian police got wind of it, and they put us on the third-floor roof of the leader-lady's house. All of us had to stay there the whole week of Sukkot, sleeping out on the roof under the stars in our sleeping bags. We actually had a good time!

However, at first I fought joining the group on the roof. The American "Warden" in Aqaba, spokesperson for the U.S. Embassy in Amman, had warned us to stay inside every Friday, and we were wise to do it. But, this one day, there was a demonstration against Americans. I lived right down the street from a major mosque. I was so tired of being told what to do. Then the leader-lady called telling us that we were in danger and we had to stay at her house, and for me to pack a bag and I'd be picked up in an hour. I was so mad at all the fear stuff. I told them I was not coming, but they said I had to because the Jordanian police said so. So, I went. I got to their house and the leader-lady's husband, right in front of everyone, began shouting at me that I was rebellious and I only wanted attention. I suppose it was because I balked at coming.

Like I said before, that is not in my nature to try to get attention. Years later, when I was accused of wrong doing against the leader-lady, she kept mocking me that all I wanted was attention. I just accepted my fate and stayed the week with them. We slept on their roof top. It was a nice time together after all. We learned that the Jordanian police had caught the 13, executed the two leaders, and imprisoned the other 11. There were other times when we were told that Hamas was coming for us, and we had to have Jordanian military protection.

I grew closer to the family who lived up the hill, and we did have some marvelous adventures together. My Swiss friend took the mother in the family, and I, and a couple of other ladies, in her old van to Petra. Then we went to Little Petra where the Bedouins live out in the desert, where Esau had his residency, and Job too. She liked to do humanitarian projects. She, and her friends in Switzerland, were always collecting things to give to the poor. She had quite a few boxes of clothes and other things, like blankets, given to her in Switzerland. We took some of these to Bedouin families in the Little Petra (north of Petra) area, called Uz in ancient times. (**Job 1:1**)

We also went between Petra and Bozrah – a fertile valley of about 40 miles that is pristine farm land, with many sheep, goats, and camels. We came back and stayed at the Dana Reserve at their Guest House. The Dana Reserve is a wildlife refuge in Jordan near the Dead Sea. It has all types of wildlife, water, and wild foods in it – a perfect refuge for those fleeing out of Israel, out of Damascus, out of Lebanon, or out of Amman. I loved going to this place. I went there about three times during the eight years.

Later, on a trip with the leader-lady, Chip, and a couple of others, we went to the Dana Reserve. We then went to the ancient mountain where Herod had his palace on top, where he beheaded John the baptizer. Did you know that he was beheaded in what is now modern Jordan? One could walk up the side of that mountain to see the ruins of the palace. At the top of the mountain a person could see the Dead Sea to the east.

It was during this excursion with Chip and the leader-lady, that I heard the leader-lady's conversations with the man who was supposed to be buying her an Island off the coast of Scotland. While in Jerusalem, I had heard her telling some rich Texas friends that she already had the Island, but of course we heard it on the news--I heard it for myself on CNN news--that this man's bid for the Island was cancelled, and he was called into question for he was a known crook.

While still attending the church of my pastor Robert, from Zimbabwe, I met a couple from Fort Worth, Homer and Ruby, who were friends of my pastor. They had moved to Ariel, Israel, to work with Mayor Ron Nachman, and Ariel's spokesperson, Dina Shalit. My pastor hosted Mayor Nachman several times in Fort Worth, and promoted projects he had in Ariel to help the people. Mayor Nachman had/has a wonderful program for the elderly, and for the youth – as his family originally started Ariel as a center for new immigrants. One time, Pastor Robert hosted a large dinner to collect money for the new immigrant project. That was the time I went up to Mayor Nachman's wife, Deliet, and told her I was praying for a close friend of theirs who was very ill. She grabbed me, hugged me, and thanked me. Pastor Robert also became friends with Benjamin Netanyahu and other Israeli dignitaries at that time. Homer and Ruby invited me to come visit them in Ariel. They had built a "Texas Mini Golf." It quickly became popular. Then they put in a hamburger stand and sold ice cream and sodas too.

In early September, I took Trisha to Israel with me. She knew several in Aqaba from Emanuel Christian Fellowship, so she was staying in Aqaba for a while. We went to Jerusalem first. We had such a good time seeing the sights around the Old City. I remember our visit to the Garden of Gethsemane especially. A priest let her into the area where the 2,000-year old trees were, so that she could pray. She gave me a rock from inside the enclosure, which I put in my backpack. That was the rock that I pulled out that day when I was preparing to go to one of Robert's Sunday morning meetings, when Abba said: "You will never, ever, go into another church again." That was my "Gethsemane rock." After Jerusalem, we went to Ariel. Homer and Ruby hosted us. We met David and Leah Ortiz and their family, including Ami who suffered so terribly when a Purim package blew up in his face a few years ago. Homer and Ruby, and David and Leah, Grant and Barbara Lovingood and a few others too, had wonderful prayer meetings together. I was privileged to be a part of some of them.

I had come to Israel this time specifically to do intercession over the side of Mt. Ga'ash, where Joshua is buried. Ariel is built on this mountain. Ariel has the University of Judea and Samaria, with about 7,000 students. Ruby took me to a private and lovely site to do the intercession. I had bought one of Homer's hand-carved olivewood walking sticks, and used that in the intercession too. I did not understand why Trisha did not get out of bed in the mornings for our prayer meetings. In fact, she stayed in her room a lot. She had just come from Thailand and was quite upset at having to leave. So in the afternoons she would talk to Ruby at length about Thailand.

While there, we went with Homer and Ruby to Tel Aviv to the flea market, then to the beach area for lunch. We also went to the old town of Jaffa – and to the port where Jonah left from to go to Tarshish. She took a picture of Simon the Tanner's house near the port of Jaffa and gave it to me later. We went by the art district on the way to the Port. It was a lovely day! Because Trisha and I kept Shabbat, Ruby was quite annoyed at us. Homer kept trying to tell us that the Torah was obsolete, and that Jesus had made a new covenant, and cancelled the old one. We tried to avoid those discussions.

One evening, they had a big dinner and invited the Ortiz family and a friend of theirs who was visiting from New York. That was pleasant. It was during this time that Homer and David embarked on a very dangerous mission. There was a Palestinian evangelist and his family who lived in an Arab village below Ariel. They were getting death threats from the muftis because of their faith. One night, it became critical. If they did not escape to freedom, they would all be killed. Ruby, Leah Ortiz, and I, were the prayer backers. Homer and David were the rescuers. They had official papers from the Israeli government to go into the village, with the IDF backing, and rescue this family. Tickets had already been bought to get them into Canada, out of Tel Aviv. That night we stayed up in prayer. Trisha never came down to join us. The operation was a success! I was so proud of Homer and David, and the IDF who assisted them.

Trisha began to distance herself from me more and more. I did not know why, and she gave me no indication as to why. I did not know then, that she considered herself a jezebel, like her mother, and that she was jealous of me because of my relationship with Abba and with others. I get so tired of that – it is so ridiculous! But, after 29 years of marriage, I found out that was the root of all my suffering--jealousy.

This year, I continued on with and increased my researching and writing. I was getting bolder and bolder in my proclamation of His Truth. I had been in the Word so much that my mind was crystal clear. The enemy continued attacks on me physically while I was alone in my apartment, as well as at my daughter's in America. Oftentimes, I'd wake up with my spirit leaving my body, and severe chest pains. It was not my heart--my heart is very strong. It was pressure from witchcraft on my chest that could have stopped my heart, as happened in 2008 and 2011. One time, I was dreaming that I was with Messiah, walking up a steep mountain. I looked much younger. Perhaps at times, I have gone to the "other side." But, each time, I would plead with Yahushua to let me live to finish my course.

I asked one of my "friends" in the group, that because no one came to see me, what would happen if I died--no one would know it. He laughed, and said: "No, we'd just figure you went back to the U.S." Later I confided in his wife that I was very lonely. Her answer: "Why don't you visit Muslim women; they like company." It is hard to believe that people who say they are "believers" can be so cold. All I could think of when she said that was Marie Antionette's statement to the poor starving masses in France: "Let them eat cake."

To show you a little of how the enemy fought me in my writing: My old computer had Windows 98 programmed on it, but it had neither the emotions represented by smiley or frowny faces, nor any Greek fonts. One night I was furiously coming against the spirit of Greece. All of a sudden, I started typing in Greek. I could not change the font. I kept typing in Greek. I did spiritual warfare, and finally the Greek stopped. I wish I had saved that page with the Greek writing to find out what I had typed. Another night I was coming against Satan and all of a sudden frowny faces appeared on the page. I did spiritual warfare and that stopped. But, over and over, whole paragraphs and whole pages just disappear into cyberspace. Oftentimes, even after deleting the script "Times New Roman," it would take over while I was writing. Because of the name of the script, it is repulsive to me.

While in the U.S., I met with the well-known Christian Colonel Jim Ammerman for the first time. Laura knew him well and considered him her spiritual father. So, we went out to lunch with he and his wife. I told him about Aqaba being set up by the U.N., E.U. and U.S. as a refuge base as per **Revelation 6:12-17, Daniel 11:41**, etc. He just had his arms folded, listening. I told him some top secret things that only we knew in Aqaba. He never showed any reaction. I had heard that he knew all the secret underground bases in the U.S., where the concentration camps were being set up, the truth about the Waco Super Collider being turned into a giant oven for the cremation of millions, etc. He was the Army Colonel who got the baptismal tarps into Iraq during the 1991 war, when so many soldiers were being born again through born again chaplains whom he stationed there. At this time, he was a strong, healthy, and an active 71 year old. After we got up and were walking outside the restaurant, he told me that he understood everything I told him about Aqaba and it was all true. I met with him one more time a year later.

On the morning of the day I was to return to Jordan, in early September, I got a phone call from a lady named Carol, from Knoxville, Tennessee. A lady who was on my e-mail list, named Darlene, attended a Messianic congregation in Knoxville. She told Carol and her husband, Gene, about me. She and her husband felt they were to come to Aqaba and go to Petra. She wanted to know if they could stay with me and if I would take them to Petra. Her lovely spirit made me say "Yes."

So, in October they came. We went to Petra. We had such a marvelous time. Their daughter Gina, and a friend who lived on their lovely mountain property, came to Israel also to dance in a Sukkot conference in Jerusalem. They became very good friends to me. I visited them several times in their lovely country home outside of Knoxville, and taught in some meetings there where I met more special friends.

In September, Christie, who had opened her home so many times for me to teach, wanted to come to Aqaba and Israel for her birthday later in October after Carol and Gene had left. I had some strange experiences with Christie, but we did have a good time together. I had met her at a prayer meeting in Flower Mound, Texas. Her husband was a noted plastic surgeon who had an office at Baylor Medical Center in Dallas. They were quite well-to-do. She had been a stewardess for Southwest Air Lines. She later gave me one of her free flights to go to Houston to minister there a second time.

After meetings, no matter how late, and some went very late, she would take me out to dinner at some expensive restaurant and tell me to get anything I wanted. I had developed a life-pattern in my poverty. I would only look at the prices on a menu at a restaurant and find the cheapest thing on the menu. Then I would see what it was, and if it was OK, I'd order it. Ordering what I wanted was foreign to me. It still is, if what I want is expensive.

For entertainment in our early marriage, my husband and I went to posh restaurants in Beverly Hills and Century City, where the waiters bring your napkins hanging over their extended arms. But, for the two of us, for the most expensive food cost us about $25.00 total, including tip. Nowadays, that same meal would be over $100.00. But, that was our rare outing. We'd walk around the expensive shops in the area, see movie stars' homes, and not spend a dime.

Anyway, what bothered me was that Christie delighted in telling me after the meeting who had been at the meeting. I was speaking freely against the Bush family, and exposing things that few knew about. She had invited people in the oil business in Texas who knew George Bush Sr., and George W. Bush personally. She had also invited members of FEMA, the FBI, the CIA, reporters, and other dignitaries. She was incredibly astute in pampering me on the one hand, and sadistically undermining me on the other.

At that time, I had yucky yellow bumps appear under my eyes with a disgusting name--"cholesterol plaque." If you look closely by the right eye of the Mona Lisa, you see the same little bumps, painted into her picture. Christie asked her plastic surgeon husband to cut the bumps out. For about three years I looked decent, until the bumps returned. I really appreciated her help, but the hooks were in my jaw. Her husband was just an easy-going guy who was likeable. She was very devious, as I found out later. They had two little boys who were also quite rebellious.

My training with these kinds of people now reminds me of **Daniel 11:35: "Some of those that have insight shall stumble, to refine them, and to cleanse them, and to make them white, until the time of the end—for it is still for an appointed time."** We are at "the end," -- inside the tribulation period now, and all my stumbling has done a good work, but oh the suffering in the process!

Christie wanted to come to Aqaba and Israel for her birthday in late October. I should have said NO! But, she had done so much for me. I did not know it was all manipulation. Thinking I owed someone for being nice to me has been a stumbling block for me most of my life. I understand now what "false responsibility" is all about.

If I allow someone who is masked--a jezebel, usurper, or devious manipulator, to do something nice for me, like let me stay at their house, give me money, give me gifts, invite me to speak at their group or congregation, flatter me, etc., sooner or later I find that I am ensnared. Then it takes a bomb blast to get free of their entanglements. It is a black widow spider spirit. It is also the python spirit, which slowly devours its victim--the victim being held fast by its powerful muscles. In getting free, I am slandered, and treated as a crazy or wicked person. I end up being blackballed to their whole group of friends. I can't tell you how many times I've fallen into that trap by someone being "nice."

Well Christie came. Within 15 minutes of being in my apartment she began freaking out. She had told me that her husband was going for counseling, because he was a narcissist. That didn't seem right. But, then she asked where my mirrors were. I had one about 5" X 5" mirror in the bathroom. I told her that was my only mirror. She really got hysterical. She said she wanted to go right then into town to buy a mirror. So, who was the narcissist?

Then we had to meet the family for dinner at downtown Aqaba. She took so long fixing her hair that we were an hour late. I was angry. If there is anything that disgusts me, it is women's pride attitudes, especially those who come to a third world country and have to blow-dry their hair, curl it, or straighten it, put on makeup, etc., or they can't face anyone. My attitude is "put on a ball cap and get on with life!" The pride thing makes me ill. But, then **Isaiah 2:10-22**... it makes Abba very angry!

After dinner, we went to a petting zoo area that was put in along with fountains, parkways, palm trees, grass, and flowers, using America's two billion we gave Aqaba. She began acting "manic," chasing the family's 8-year old boy around the petting zoo, running into Muslim families, laughing hysterically. I don't think she was bi-polar. We went to Petra. Then we went to Jerusalem. Here is the story of leaving Jerusalem, from my article "Betrayal – A Major Plague of the Last Days", pages 1 and 2:

I have always loved hosting people in my home. I had seen signs here and there of something not quite right, but I dismissed my concerns over and over... Christie displayed other strange characteristics, showing out in a manic way in front of the Arabs in town. My friends who lived in Aqaba questioned her behavior. We went to the Red Sea to do snorkeling, and again she showed unusual behavior that made my friends not like her. As we were getting ready to leave Jerusalem, we packed carefully, for I told her about the dangers at the border crossing into Jordan. I showed this lady how to pack all the Israeli things—CD's with Israel pictures on them, Bibles with Hebrew letters on them, and other things with Hebrew letters and pictures—putting all in the bottom of backpacks and suitcases, wrapping them in clothes. I was satisfied that all was OK. We were to leave on the 10:00AM bus for Eilat. I went to the bathroom—being in there less than a minute.

I came out and we proceeded to go to Eilat and the border crossing with Jordan. When we got to the customs on the Jordan side, there was a man there who openly appeared hostile and angry. I had not seen him before. Even though I presented my Jordanian residency card, he motioned for us to open all the suitcases. There on top of her suitcase were all her Israeli things open to view. When the man saw the CD with the Orthodox Jews at the Wailing Wall and the things with Hebrew writing, he went crazy with rage. He started screaming. She smiled. I went cold, but inside I was also in a rage. I told him it was just music and souvenirs, but this did not calm him down. I could not believe her sadistic betrayal. She smiled and said: "Father told me it would be all right." I knew it was not Yahuweh who told her it would be all right.

All I could think of was that precious new baby that the family had. One phone call from this hostile man to his terrorist buddies and we all could have been killed. I was so furious with her, but she was so flippant about it, as if it was a joke. She went back to Texas and proceeded to slander me and try to ruin my reputation with all her friends. She said that while the man was opening our luggage, I had to go to the bathroom, and never saw anything like I said I saw. I have made hundreds of border crossings. It is impossible to go to the bathroom while a Custom's officer is going through your luggage, but that was her first visit overseas and she was ignorant of reality. I was there the whole time!

In December, I went back to the U.S. once again to be with my family until March, 2003. During my time in the U.S., I taught in more meetings, and got more contacts that led to more meetings and new relationships that brought much joy. Abba was increasing my work for Him, and all I did was hear daily and obey. "My yoke is easy, and My burden is light," He said – and so it is!

JORDAN
(2003)

I returned to Aqaba in early March. On March 18th, Abba asked me to read **Daniel 8**. I thought that was strange, because in teaching the Tenach for so many years in Bible Colleges and churches, that was one chapter I wanted to throw out – Daniel 8. No matter how hard I tried to understand it, it was a blank to me. But, I obeyed. I read it, and to my shock, I understood every word. He explained it all to me; it was like reading the newspaper. On March 20th, Gulf War II broke out. Since November, we had been seeing convoys of U.S. troops going from the Port of Aqaba by night to the Iraqi border, taking supplies and tents for refugees.

On March 19th, Chip came to bring me some pie from his wife. While there, he said that the day before, Father had directed him to read Daniel 8. I asked him what Abba taught him from Daniel 8. You guessed it--because the Spirit taught me, and the Spirit taught Chip-- it was the same thing, all about Gulf War II to the rise of anti-messiah to rule the world. The turmoil in Iraq and Afghanistan was purposely started by "false flags" to initiate chaos in the Middle East. It would be radically accelerated to bring the chaos necessary to bring in the new world order. The Illuminati motto is: "Out of chaos, order."

EVIAN, FRANCE

I returned to Switzerland in May. I stayed with my Swiss friend near the Castle of Chillon in Montreux. I had an assignment from Abba to intercede on site in Evian, over the G-8 Summit, which would take place June 1-3. I took several trips to Evian, taking the train from Montreux to Lausanne, and then the ferryboat across to Evian (France). I walked around and prayed. I took the little train up the side of the mountain above Evian and saw the hotel, where in 1938 the world's leaders, led by the United States, decided not to receive any Jewish refugees into their countries. [Refer to: "Chilling Parallels"]

Evian is famous for its water, but was once a very strategic historic town. It was the center for world commerce for 700 years, and for atrocities against the Jews, led by the Savoy Dukes. I took many walks into Montreux to pray, and also to the Castle of Chillon. It was here, by the order of the Savoy Dukes, that Jews were tortured and murdered, including the Christians who helped them. It was during the time of the Bubonic Plague, which was blamed on the Jews.

On this visit, I went with my Swiss friend to many locations around Montreux. I went up into the mountains and picked Narcissus, for this was the time of the Narcissus Festival. I had asked my friend before staying with her, if she wanted to join me in the intercession. She agreed, yet, once I was at her house, she said "no." This was a deep hurt to me. She mocked my intercession. Yet the more I learned about Evian, the more I knew why I was there, and about the assignment I was to do for Abba. My ticket was set for me to return to Aqaba on June 4th. I wanted to stay during the time of the Summit to pray. I told my Swiss friend that I felt it important to stay and intercede during that time. At the very end of May, security forces in France stopped all transportation coming into Evian that was not screened by the G-8. So the boat was stopped from Lausanne.

Then, my Swiss friend told me that we could get passes for almost no money to take the train 24 hours to anywhere in Switzerland. I reinforced that we must not go between June 1-3. But, she got the passes for June 2nd. At that point in my life, I was still afraid of displeasing people, especially people who hosted me, so as upset as I was, I agreed to go. She said for me to tell her the train stops that I wanted, so she could get our individual train tickets. I picked out my favorite places. But, on the first stop of our trip, instead of transferring trains, she said we had to stay on the train. That train was returning to Montreux. To make this long story short, everything I really wanted to see on that trip was changed. It became clear that cruelty and sadism were at work.

At the end of May, I learned that President George W. Bush was meeting with King Abdullah on June 4th, in Aqaba, at the King's residency, not far from my apartment. From al-bab.com: *A summit meeting to begin implementing the road map was held in Aqaba, Jordan, on 4 June 2003. Hosted by King Abdullah of Jordan, it was attended by President George Bush, Ariel Sharon (the Israeli prime minister) and Mahmoud Abbas (the Palestinian prime minister).*

I felt strongly I should be there. I was just sick about my plane ticket being for June 4th. So, I was going to change the ticket for me to fly out June 3rd. But, in the meantime, the train trip came up, so I did not change my ticket. This made me doubly upset.

In June, after returning from Switzerland to Aqaba, I went immediately to Shavu'ot in Jerusalem. I stayed in Christ Church. In climbing the steps to my room, I saw two ladies going in the same direction as me. I asked where they were from, and they said "America." They asked where I was from. I said I lived in Aqaba. They stopped, had surprised looks on their faces, and told me this amazing story: They were intercessors, and in January of that year, both of them, separately, were instructed by Abba that they had to be in Aqaba on June 4th. They had no idea why. But, they were obedient, and got their tickets. Then they learned of President Bush's visit with King Abdullah. They said they got as close as they could to the King's residency where the meeting was taking place. They stood in the sand on the beach, and did intercession over that meeting. Even now I am crying. Abba knew of my flubbing up in Switzerland, and made provision early with two of His trusted servants. Those two did what I would have done if I had been there. I was so grateful to Abba. The three of us rejoiced greatly. We kept in touch for a long time.

That week in Jerusalem, the eve of Shavu'ot, I met Don Esposito's wife, Petra, in the old church there. She was decorating for a Shavu'ot service. Don came in, and I told him I had done intercession over the G-8 Summit in Evian. He told me that in March, Abba had explained Daniel 8 to him, and then he proceeded to tell me what the Spirit had told Chip and I. Yahuweh always confirms what He teaches!

Everyone had left Aqaba by early March except for the local people. The Ambassador from the U.S. had told us that the Embassy staff was going to Cypress until the danger to Jordan was over. The family, my Swiss friend, and I, decided to stay. The family had built a bomb shelter for themselves – and did not want the my Swiss friend or I to come to their apartment anymore. Even though Chip had an elaborate bomb shelter built into his house, he and his family left for the U.S.

The landlord in the building where the family and the my Swiss friend stayed, told us that he and his family would take care of us. People in town asked us why we were still there. I told them that it was my home, and I didn't want to leave. I had asked Abba if I needed to get extra food and water. He said "NO." I had no money for even duct tape, let alone making a bomb shelter in my apartment. I asked Abba if I needed duct tape. He said "NO." I had collected a lot of plastic water bottles, and I filled them with water and put them on my sink counter. I called that my "war effort." He had told me I didn't need to do that. Everyone was scared because Saddam Hussein had threated to "dust" Aqaba with chemicals. But, nothing happened!

In fact, the U.S. military, using the "Sound of Silence" technology, the same technology that is in all digital TVs, went into Iraq, faced Saddam's finest troops, and they all cried like babies and put down their weapons. Some put their heads on our soldier's shoulders and cried. The whole Arab world was in shock. How could Saddam's finest troops be overcome without any of them firing a shot? But, that technology will be used on the American people when our takeover begins. The "Sound of Silence" technology is in all TVs worldwide.

In April, I went to Jerusalem for Passover. Trisha had followed me to every meeting I had in Fort Worth. At church, or wherever I taught, she would lie on her face on the floor and cry during meetings. I trusted her so much that I confided in her what was on my heart, and she confided her innermost secrets to me. I thought she and I were very much alike. I was horribly wrong. I learned, through much suffering, never to share any personal data with anyone. No one is to be trusted. Is that paranoia? Is that fear? It may be in some people, but NOT in me! To me, it is Scriptural wisdom. Here are warnings from the Word: **Micah 7:5-6; Jeremiah 9:2-9; Amos 5:13; Matthew 10:34-39; Mark 13:9-13**. The wise keep their mouth shut. But, that truth didn't sink in until 2005, when a friend from Wales applied it to our intercession trip to the Golan. We have to trust a few, but maybe the few is one or two, as allowed by the Spirit of Yahuweh, because He knows who has hidden motives, and who doesn't. The prophet Micah and Messiah, both warn us not even to trust spouse, children, or close friends. Never trust the religious, who appear to be "spiritual," but who hide ambitions and secret agendas!

The mind programming is so fine-tuned, that when the time is right, the mind-altering technology that is already being used on American citizens will turn people against people in the most vicious ways. Right now, some of our U.S. soldiers are being chipped and sent out to do heinous crimes, which are against their very nature. Beware of any piercing of the skin for any reason.

To go back to 1999 at Christmas, Abba revealed a warning to me that I could not believe, but it proved 100% true. He took me to **Jeremiah 9:2-9**. I said: "No, not my neighbors. They are my friends." Then the next day, I opened the Bible right to **Jeremiah 9**, and the next day too--three times in all. I later saw it happen.

Trisha and I went together to Jerusalem for Passover. We stayed with the couple who hosted leader-lady, Chip, my Swiss friend, and I, in 2001. We went on an 18-hour tour together with Don Esposito and Micah Ashkanazi into the back area of Judea; to where David killed Goliath, down to the ruins of Tel Be'ersheva, to the very rare Ramon Crater, to the ruins of Avdat, up the Dead Sea coast to Gomorrah, where we found sulfur balls (some people lit them and they glowed), and then after dark we got back into Jerusalem. It was a magnificent trip.

Trisha kept talking so much to the people on the bus that they were disgusted, and one told me so. From the very first of the tour, she kept her distance from me, even acting like she didn't know me. It was strange. She actually acted hostile to me. She later lied to the Aqaba leader-lady about me, and to my Swiss friend, and then to four Messianic congregations in Fort Worth. I did not know what was wrong until later in the week. But my Swiss "friend" believed her, and turned against me to become her friend. There were obvious problems with my Swiss "friend" before that, but I overlooked them. She had a sadistic streak. I remember her trying to kick Father Sameach in the rear. While up on Mount Paran, unloading goods for missionaries we had met there, she turned to me and began mocking me, saying how weak I was and how strong she was. Petty things like that. She'd use me to set up a meeting with someone in town that she wanted to meet, then she would spoil it for me. She was a horrendous gossip as well. Others noticed the inconsistencies too, but everyone was loyal to themselves.

After the tour, we stayed with the same couple. It was the day of Passover. The woman of the house was very up-tight. It is common for a Jewish woman to fix an elaborate feast for Passover. She was going to put on a traditional Passover meal. Everything had to be perfect. So, I ironed the table cloth, napkins, and other things. She brought out all of her expensive china, etc. I don't do "Jewish" stuff if it takes away from the real meaning of what Abba is saying, but I went along with what she wanted and tried to help. But, my Swiss "friend" liked to impress people with her hard work and helpfulness, so she insisted on doing all the dish washing, cleaning of the kitchen and the house.

That morning we went to hear our hostess' husband speak about Passover. I loved his teachings. After the teaching, I asked Trisha why she was so distant during the tour. I asked her if I had done anything wrong to offend her. She became hostile and self-defensive. She gave me some excuse that didn't make sense, but her anger was what surprised me. I did not yet have the jezebel spirit so clearly identified. But, she had previously admitted that her mother was a jezebel and that she was just like her mother. That night at the Passover meal, she was very rude to me. After the dinner she went out walking. That afternoon she had taken my Swiss friend aside to emotionally tell her what she did not like about me. She always used emotions to manipulate, and people felt so sorry for her.

We had reserved a double room at Christ Church. The day after the Passover meal, we moved over to our reserved room. It was here that things got worse, but they led to something awesome from Abba. On Friday I had bought a book by an Israeli archeologist--Dan Bahat. I was studying it all day on Shabbat, looking up Scriptures--totally delighted. Trisha said she'd be back so that we could have Shabbat dinner before sunset. She did not come back. I cried. I had no food to eat, and I was very hungry.

All of a sudden, about 6:30 PM, Abba said very sternly: "Get on your shoes, and get down stairs to the dining room immediately." I got my shoes on, but I was wearing old jeans and a t-shirt, and my hair was a mess. But, I obeyed. When I got to the dining room I saw that the leader-couple were lighting the Shabbat candles and saying the blessing. I opened the door, and someone came running to me. They asked if I had a reservation. I didn't. Since it was a buffet, they went to ask the cook if it were all right for me to eat with them. The cook came and saw me, and said "Yes." That morning the cook and I had been fellowshipping at breakfast. I went in and got some food, and then looked around and I didn't see any seats available. I saw a table over in the corner. It looked like there was one seat left. I went over there, and the ladies from Wales and England offered me the seat. They asked where I was from, and I said "Aqaba." The ladies from Wales began asking me about Aqaba, and I began telling them. That was about 7:00 PM. We talked until 10:00 PM. They were so excited at what I was telling them.

Their leader, and her associate, were from Bournemouth, England. They had organized the tour for the Welsh ladies. I later found out that the leader was the chief intercessor for Ebenezer, and she was the one who had told me to come out of Russia when I hurt my knee, and then again when I got arrested. She was the one who was so furious at me for not obeying her. She, and her friend, got tired of me about 8:30, so they returned to their hotel. I stayed with the six Welsh ladies until about 10:00. Three of them were named Maureen. About every 30 minutes, the one to my left kept asking me the same question: "Why would the Father be telling me to go to Jerash?" Each time I would turn to her and say: "I don't know."

I knew Jerash was the second largest Roman ruins, after Ephesus, and very famous in Jordan. Finally, just before they had to leave, she turned to me again with the same question. Preparing to say again "I don't know", Abba blocked it with a vision of a map of Jordan. I turned to her and said: "I KNOW! You must come to visit me in Aqaba and we must go together to Jerash."

She later told me that she couldn't sleep all night for joy. I did not know that she and blond Maureen had been talking that day about Jerash. Father had been impressing dear Elaine for 10 years about doing intercession in Jerash, but no one could help her. She was close friends with Christine Darg who worked among Muslims in Jordan, but Christine did not know what to tell her at that point--now Christine understands. So that very day, Elaine had been asking blond Maureen why she couldn't get Jerash out of her mind. And there I was offering to go with her to Jerash.

I found out that Elaine had been a nurse, was a specialist in massage and other therapy. She traveled a lot, and had a ministry of her own. She later told me that the English lady at the head of the table, the chief intercessor for Ebenezer, had asked her to plan out their trip to Israel, which she did. But, then, exactly as "large lady" did to me in Turkey, she usurped Elaine's authority and shut her down. So, when I met her, she was as meek as a mouse, which is quite different from her personality. She's a bold lady!

That night Trisha stayed out past midnight. The Christ Church compound gate is locked at 11:00, so she must have been on the grounds somewhere. But, I can't sleep if someone who sleeps in the same room as me is out somewhere, because they usually come in, turn on lights, and make noise when they come in. But, besides that, I was a mother who would not sleep if my children were out on a date, or with friends, until they came home. I laid awake. This went on for three nights. But, that Shabbat night she came in about 1:00. I asked her why she came in so late. She said she was talking to friends. Then she opened up as to why she literally hated me. She had come in and seen me studying that afternoon. She said that it was because I journaled 20 pages, and she couldn't journal one page, because God wasn't talking to her. She said I heard from God, and she didn't. She was angry at her dad because he heard from God. Sounded like Darlene in 1996 in Kisumu. Jealousy! Jealousy, jezebel, witchcraft--It projects demonic activity onto their victim. I woke up the next morning, Shabbat, and I could hardly walk--my knees hurt so bad.

She was going for a walk around the gates to do intercession. Before going to Jerusalem, we had been sharing Scripture and planning on doing an intercession walk around the gates. But, this morning she was very agitated at me. Yet, she said "OK." We walked down the long stairs towards the outside of the Western Wall Plaza. Then we proceeded out of the Dung Gate, around the corner to the left, and up the steps to the Eastern Gate. Then we proceeded on to the Lion's Gate, the Muslim Quarter gate going onto the north Temple Mount.

I asked her if I could go into the Arab Quarter just a short distance and go to the grounds of St. Anne's Church, where the ruins of Bethesda were. I wanted to take pictures for my son who was attending Bethesda Community Church in Fort Worth. She said "OK." But, she was really seething inside. We walked to the garden by the church and I began sobbing. Yahushua had spoken to me in His lovely baritone voice: "**After 38 years**." I did some quick math, and understood. Thirty-eight years before was 1965. That was the year my life fell apart, and I met my husband. I knew that He wanted to remove the pain of what happened in 1965.

I walked towards the entrance of the ruins, where in **John 5**, the man was healed after 38 years of waiting and hoping. Notice, the man was healed after 38 years on a Shabbat! As soon as the Pharisees saw that he had been healed on Shabbat, they were furious and tried to take Messiah down because He broke their rules for Shabbat! He chose this Shabbat to heal me of the pain of my past.

I got to the entrance of the ruins, just past the church, and she went on a few paces. But, I froze in my tracks. There He stood right in front of me – Yahushua Messiah. He bent over slightly with a big smile and made the sweeping motion for "**Welcome**." I was looking right in His face, and all I could think of was "He looks the same age as my son." Then He disappeared. I was sobbing so hard. She was more furious than ever when I told her I saw Him. She knew I did. She never doubted my teaching, or my experiences with Abba! We went around the ruins, and when we came to go out, He spoke to me, as He had done to the man in **John 5**: "Go and sin no more." I understood! After that day, the enemy could not depress me with regrets. We continued on around the gates. My knees hurt badly, but I was so joyful. It was strange, when I told her my knees were so sore I could hardly walk, she acted as if she knew it had to do with her hate.

The next morning was Ishtar (Easter) Sunday. She had become friends with a couple who lived in a little rented house right in the City of David, Area G – the Royal Acropolis. I asked her if she would take me to the City of David, because I did not know how to get there. It would be the first of many, many trips there--it is "the apple of His eye."

Psalm 132:13-14: "**For Yahuweh has chosen Zion. He has desired it for His dwelling. `This is My place of rest forever; Here I dwell, for I have desired it**." This is where King David had his palace. This is the very place where Messiah Yahushua will live when He comes in His Kingdom.

She was very disgusted, but agreed to show me where it was. We walked down the long stairs towards the HaKotel (Western Wall) so that we could go out the Dung Gate. But, about 2/3 of the way down, where the steps make a turn to the left, I saw thousands of people standing very quietly. I walked over to the ledge, and saw that the whole Western Wall Plaza was packed with thousands of people. No one was saying a word. I saw what looked like an American with a video camera. I whispered, "What's going on?" He whispered: "The waving of the barley sheaves and the High Priestly Blessing." I was in awe. Then I remembered: IT WAS FIRST FRUITS! On this day Messiah rose from the dead. I was so filled with joy.

After the blessing, we went out the Dung Gate and proceeded along the southeast wall of the Old City. Joy was filling me so much that I began singing praises out loud. She walked on ahead. As we came to the Ophel, which King Solomon built to connect the City of David, the real Zion, with the Temple Mount, we crossed the street and then went south, down the street to the City of David. I was so full of joy, I was crying for joy, as I had the day before. I said to her: "Isn't this incredibly awesome that we are standing right where Messiah will build His Palace when He comes to reign?" She blurted out: "NO!" We went to the house just up a few steps where we visited the couple. John leaned over his patio wall and pointed out the Water Gate, rebuilt by Nehemiah, where Ezra read the Torah to all Israel after the Babylonian captivity (**Nehemiah 8**).

We then went down a lot of stairs to the Kidron Valley floor, and to the Gihon Springs. On the way I slipped, and almost fell. We walked down to the Siloam Springs. I dipped my face in the water and drank a handful of the delicious water. She did not want to come down there. Later she wrote me a letter, in which she talked very ugly to me. I wrote her a letter back. I told her she had to "get off her high horse", and stop being so arrogant. That provoked her to slandering me, and to try to ruin my reputation. She even told lies about me to four Messianic congregations in Texas. I saw her three times after that. The next Sukkot, Don Esposito asked me to join his tour as they went to a spice market in the Arab Quarter. She was on that tour. I came up next to her and said "shalom." She did not respond, except to say that she had paid for that tour, and I had not, so I didn't belong there. I saw my former Swiss friend and Trisha again at Don's meetings a few years later. I put my arm around my Swiss "friend". They were so shocked that I greeted them with love and joy. It was genuine. I hold no grudges!

Trisha had joined the dance team of my friends from Knoxville, who were to perform at a Sukkot meeting in Jerusalem. They thought she was the most precious spiritual woman alive, and told me so. It's OK. The more friends I lost by the works of the enemy, the more friends Abba gave me who were genuine friends. Several friends I lost ended up believing damnable heresies, like denying the deity of Messiah, or totally denying Him to covert to Judaism. But, they went their way and I went mine.

After leaving the City of David that morning, Trisha and I began the steep ascent towards the Dung Gate. I saw about 50 Nigerians. The ladies were dressed in full cultural regalia, with beautiful dresses and head wraps. The men also were dressed in traditional Nigerian clothes. This year (2003), as I was in a prayer meeting with friends in Aqaba, He gave me my **Ezekiel 3** calling to America, to be a watchman. It was this year that He began opening many doors for me to have meetings in Texas, and especially in East Texas.

Back in the U.S., I met Tony, and her group in Flower Mound. They asked me to speak many times. I became a regular. I loved the people. Her husband, Gary, was reading the Word for himself, and finding so much that contradicted what the church taught, and even what the Messianics taught. Their two teenage children were precious. People were coming from long distances to hear me speak there. It was Gary who loaned me his truck to drive down to New Braunfels to meet with Constance and her group.

But, when I began using my gift of prophecy, and having visions of things Abba showed me in her home that were not of Him, she told all of her closest friends--the ones in her inner circle who had become dear friends of mine--that they were never to talk to me again, or e-mail me. She told Gary and the two children the same. I learned later it was jealousy, as well as the fact that what Abba was saying to her through me, cut against her power of control and manipulation of her family and her friends. But, it was at one of my meetings in their house that I met Johnny and his family, and some from his congregation in Frisco.

They, as with thousands of others nation-wide, had come out of the World Wide Church of God when its new leaders told them they didn't have to observe Torah anymore. Johnny's family is Swiss and his wife is from Colombia. Their little son looked like a Swiss doll. What a precious family! He and others from his congregation came twice to Flower Mound. Then he asked me to speak at his congregation. That started it – talk about a mo'ed!

Some came to hear me from congregations all through East Texas. This opened up the wonderful family that I became a part of. I've made so many close friends from those united congregations. That one meeting at Johnny's opened up meetings in almost every one of those congregations, beginning with Big Sandy, Marshall, Longview, etc.-- from Dallas to the Louisiana border.

I remember my first meeting at his congregation. I had just gotten up to speak, and Johnny raised his hand and asked me: "What do you think of the trinity?" I was surprised. I answered by what Abba had taught me. Later at his house he said: "Did you know that you gave World Wide Church of God doctrine on the trinity?" I told him I just said what Abba had taught me.

I had met Don Esposito, an ex-World Wide Church of God teacher, in Jerusalem about 2001, and we became friends. He was married about 2003. I attended all of his meetings when he was in Jerusalem. The only thing I starkly disagreed on, and wrote a study to refute it, was the doctrine of "soul sleep." I researched for months to write a complete study on the topic of what happens to us at death. I went through every verse in the Bible about it. I even read theology books (smile). I saw that Lew White also believed in "soul sleep", so I sent Don and Lew a copy of my research. "Soul sleep" is not in accordance with the nature of Yahuweh. So many doctrines appear correct to the intellectual mind, but they cross the nature of Yahuweh. Therefore, unless a person knows Yahuweh they will be deceived.

In Don's first book, *The Great Falling Away* (an excellent book), he describes what he thinks of the pagan "trinity doctrine" that began with Nimrod. When I read his description of the trinity in his book, it was the first time I ever heard anyone speak or write what Abba had shown me. I know in my BIOLA years, Herbert Armstrong, and his son Garner Ted Armstrong, and their World Wide Church of God, were considered a cult. I liked Herbert's teaching on the end-times. I never understood why it was a cult. Then I found out that they taught and practiced the guarding of Torah. Yes, it was a personality cult, but Herbert had a lot of things right on many Scripture-subjects!

I just knew what Abba taught me about Himself and about His Son, Yahushua Yahuweh—TWO--"echad": two in unity as one, a family word. Yahuweh is the Spirit; the Spirit is Yahuweh (**II Corinthians 3:17-18**). Herbert did not understand the Spirit, relegating Him to an "it"--a force. Abba used me to clarify some of that to the ex-World Wide people in later years. But, because of our mutual love for Abba, I fit in just fine with all of those ex-World Wide Church of God precious people in East Texas. Herbert taught them to study the Word, and they did. Abba led them.

One of Johnny's best friends in their congregation told his mother about me. Cathy came to hear me. She, and I, and her son and daughter-in-law became good friends. She opened the door for me to teach in Big Sandy. It was after this meeting with several groups of ex-World Wide Church of God assemblies, from Johnny's across to the Louisiana border, that they opened up to me. They were meeting in small groups--in homes and rented buildings. They asked me what to do because they had no leadership structure. I told them to keep meeting in homes, studying the Word for themselves, and to appoint an elder, or elders, over each assembly.

The year before (2002), at one of Pastor Robert's weekly meetings in a restaurant in Fort Worth, I met Laura, and her husband Gil. Their heart was for Israel. Laura offered to be my transportation to East Texas. I kept her busy. She also took me to Boo Summer's house for meetings, and to other meetings around the Fort Worth area. She had a good friend in Pine Hills, who lived out in the country. I met Mary and Larry. I spoke in their home several times. We became friends. Mary had good friends, a couple, in another town close by. The man was a pastor. So, he invited me to speak several times at his little church. I really feel privileged to have met so many really awesome people in all of my travels!

About 2007, Johnny e-mailed me to ask if I would like for him to post all of my articles on his blog site--we're talking 450 at least. I had been spending hours every day sending out articles to those who asked. What a blessing! He is the man who has the **laydownlife.net** site! He is still a great blessing!

I went to East Texas. Laura and I stayed with Larry and Mary in Pine Hills. A lady named Jamia in Tyler, Texas, invited me to come speak at her house. As with Larry and Mary, Jamia and Mark and their family attended a congregation near Tyler. As Mary and Laura were taking me to Tyler for that meeting, the enemy really came strongly to me that we were to turn around, because something was not right with this Jamia lady. But, I kept quiet. By the time I got to their BIG house near the center of town, I was emotionally upset. Wow did the enemy mess with my thoughts! I was supposed to teach a few ladies that morning, and then that evening at a big celebration with many congregations coming together--most of them were ex-World Wide Church of God congregations, but also from Messianic congregations in the area. It was a "new moon festival." I sure am glad I did my homework on that! **Isaiah 66:22-24**: An eternal monthly celebration.

Mary and Laura were born again, Spirit-filled "charismatics," so were Jamia and her husband Mark, and their close friends. But, they all guarded Torah. In that area almost no one guarded Torah, so they started going to Tim and Angie's congregation. I had not met Tim and Angie yet, only heard about them – all good. After arriving at Jamia's house, she asked me if I wanted water or herb tea. I suppose this "broke the ice." I said, as delicately as possible, "Do you have any of that teeth-rotting black fizzy stuff they call Coke?" She looked at me so blankly. She's a real health-food observer. I got ready to teach the ladies, and here came her

PART VI - The Middle East & Travels Beyond

husband, who set a can of Coke in front of me. I was endeared to them for life.

The meeting that night was a life-changing experience for me. That Devil! He knew that Jamia would become one of my dearest friends, and we'd be together many times in Tyler, then in Panama for over a year, and also in Israel. Jamia and Mark had been missionaries with YWAM (Youth With a Mission) in Albania, Fiji, and Germany, and I don't know where else. They even had to flee out of Albania for their life, with two children. They have five children now.

There was so much food that night--all delicious. People were snacking. Then the new moon was spotted. Men, women, and children went running outside. Several blew their shofars to announce the new moon, new month (Rosh Chodesh). I was amazed. Here we were in the center of Tyler and all these shofars blowing. I got used to it. We had meetings in the center of a lot of places, and when that new moon was sighted, out we went to blow shofars.

Then it was time for the meeting, and for me to speak. Their very large living room was packed with people. They were all around me. But, right in my front view, a few seats back, was a couple who stared at me the whole time. The man folded his arms and neither made any expression the whole meeting. I learned they were Tim and Angie. I went up to talk to the man after the meeting, when we were all eating again. He was a friend of Steven Collins – one of the best writers ever on finding the "lost tribes" of Ya'cob. He had worked with Ya'ir Davidy and Rabbi Abraham Fels. We had several things in common, so the ice totally melted quickly. I later found out that they were there to find out if they could accept me, or not. Angie told Jamia that if I said something specific, which she had turned into a test, then she'd accept me. I said it, not knowing I'd passed my test. Then the dancing began. Angie was a Messianic dance leader. While that was going on, people came to ask me questions.

Well that started a wonderful relationship with Tim and Angie, members of their congregation, and others throughout East Texas! They opened up so many doors for me to have many meetings in East Texas. They became family to me. In my first combined meeting with Tim and Angie, and the whole East Texas group, I became accepted into their inner circle, into their heart, and they said they loved me and blessed me. At the close of this combined meeting in 2004, in Big Sandy, Tim and elders from the different congregations came up and surrounded me. Then they laid hands on my shoulders, and Tim prayed. He prayed the most awesome prayer. I remember one thing he said very clearly, "We trust Yedidah." I was so stunned by that. They loved me and trusted me, and I was able to teach them things that they longed to know, with no one offended. A miracle!

Johnny's mother, Helen, was in her 80s at that time. I remember that precious lady telling me that the last time she had taken an aspirin, for a headache, was in 1941. Her mind was so sharp. She was of the "old school" in the World Wide Church of God. But, as far as I know, she did not disagree with what I brought from Abba. When I spoke of hearing from Him, she was one of the first to ask for further information.

One Shavu'ot, they gathered from all over East Texas to a place I'd never gone to. Again, they had loads of food. Tim was the first to teach. He taught on the giving of the Torah. Like I said, their former church did not teach them about the ministry of the Holy Spirit. They knew there were TWO, but the "Holy Spirit" was regarded as a force, not the Person of Yahuweh. After Tim taught, I got up to teach on **Acts 2**. I taught about the Spirit from Genesis to Revelation, crossing their former church's doctrine by saying that the Spirit is Yahuweh Himself. Helen was there, as were others who had been in that church all their lives. I know I said things they may not have heard before. I said that an "it," or "force," has no personality, but the Spirit has a definite personality, for He is Yahuweh Himself. The Spirit within us communicates the emotions of Yahuweh – love, compassion, joy, grief, and anger. There were two things that HE told me not to mention: 1) the gift of tongues and 2) demons. They had relegated those things to Charismatic and Pentecostal people. I did speak of the gifts of the Spirit, but didn't zoom in on tongues.

Laura had taken me to stay with Mary and Larry, so she was at that meeting. Please don't think I am criticizing Laura--she was very good to me. But, Laura wasn't just being kind to me in taking me all those places. She tried to use me to get into my ministry inner circle, and take advantage of my favor with people. I call that "riding piggy-back."

One evening after I spoke at Bob and Boo's house, I saw her gathering people around her for her to teach them. I noticed that everywhere we went, no matter where, I introduced her to all my friends who hosted me, and then after I would teach, she would gather groups of people around her to teach them. But, her teaching was all about what she thought. I have no problems with people sharing after my meetings. But, her conversations, while going to East Texas, particularly--a four hour drive from Fort Worth--was typically so negative that I got physically ill. I got so nervous. She would criticize even her friends bitterly, and a couple of her daughters. Laura had a fascinating life and her story is amazing. But, she'd take me to her friend's houses because they wanted to talk to me, and then usurp my time by telling them stories of her life--the same very long stories, over and over.

Yet, she was loyal to me in many ways. She finally got to Israel. Gil was ill, so he didn't come. It was here that I learned more about her. I asked her if she'd like for me to show her the City of David. Her response was, "I don't have time to see those tourist places – I want to go shopping on Ben Yehuda Street." TOURIST PLACE! I told her the City of David was the core of the whole Word. When she came to Aqaba, she kept talking about "them Jews." I finally realized that, like a lot of people who are so pro-Israel in America, when they are among Jews in Jerusalem, they end up despising them. I took her to Mea Shearim, a main entrance street to the Jewish housing area in East Jerusalem. She had nothing but negative things to say about the way the Orthodox Jews lived, in their "ghetto." She was shocked, however, when she bought a hand-made lace tablecloth for 30 shekels, and the lady shop-keeper gave her a big hug.

One of my friends in Aqaba was a man who was retired Air Force. He and his wife were very good to me. They were kind and gentle. I chuckle when I remember his taking Laura and Kim to the border. Laura leaned over the backseat and began talking in his ear about "them Jews" in a derogatory way. He was shocked. He said: "Well, maybe we should pray for them." I loved that!

So at this Shavu'ot meeting, after I finished speaking, Laura raised her hand to say something. I acknowledged her. She, then, launched into her "testimony" which was about 20 minutes, telling how she was baptized in the Holy Spirit, and spoke in tongues. I imploded...Then after the meeting, Larry drove us back to Tim and Angie's house for fellowship. We sat out on their big porch, and enjoyed desert treats and coffee. Laura again usurped the conversation, and began talking about demons. She would not shut up. Tim tried to shut her up, but she kept on. I was again horrified. It was like everything I had said was cancelled.

I had met Boo Summers through Women's Aglow. She had been ordained by the same group that ordained me. She invited me to speak at her house. I worked with Women's Aglow Night Chapter in Fort Worth for five years, and Boo worked with them too. I had some good meetings in their home. What a fantastic home!

One particular evening, they invited Moshe Bronstein from Israel to one of the regular monthly meetings in their home. Carl Baugh, of the Creation Science Museum in Glen Rose, picked Moshe up at the airport, and brought him right to the Summer's home. I told Moshe that I lived in Aqaba. He said that he had just been in Aqaba a few days before with other archeologists for a meeting with the Jordanian archeologists. Moshe was a commander of IDF troops that were part of taking the Western Wall Plaza in the 1967 war with Jordan. As he was about to lead his troops towards the Western Wall, a hand grenade hit near him, blew up, and blinded him for 2 years. After recovering his sight, he began working as an archeologist-assistant with Kathleen Kenyon in Jerusalem. When I met him, he had become one of the directors over the excavations at the City of David.

A well-known intercessor with Christine Darg's ministry, whom we called Sister Florence, lived in an apartment in St. Stephen's Monastery for 18 years, which was at the north head of the Kidron Valley. Laura knew of her, and her intercession friends from many years before. Laura told me the most amazing stories about these pioneer intercessors. Florence's daughter was in a meeting at Boo and Bob's house. While talking before Moshe began his talk, she asked Moshe: "What is going on in the Arab parking lot across from the City of David?" I was on the front row, as usual, and I saw his expression. The color drained out of his face. He said: "How did you know about that?" She told about her mother who lived at St. Stephens. The "Givat parking lot" dig has become famous. Later Bob Summers and a man from Argentina worked with Moshe on this. I became good friends with the couple from Argentina, and visited in their home and had several meetings there. He showed me pictures down in the tunnels they had tapped into from the Givat parking lot.

On July 4th, Carl had his traditional cookout on the Puluxy River. Carl had finished a week of a Dinosaur dig on the Puluxy. While staying with Boo and Bob, I was also invited to attended the cookout. Boo cooked hamburgers. I got to give my testimony of seeing the Pterodactyl in Tanzania. It was at this cookout, during our eating time, that I met Claudia. I had previously left some books for her with Boo, and she returned them to me that night. While eating my kosher hot dog--I did have a choice--Claudia introduced herself, and we talked a little. Still being a big mouth with little brain, I said: "Why don't you come to Aqaba?" She said something that I thought to be quite presumptuous: "I was looking for someone to travel WITH ME." I was staying in Keller at that time with my son and his wife, and she was close by, so we went a lot of places together.

I met quite a few people in that area who became friends. From north Texas, to East Texas, and to south Texas--all over Texas--I had my best meetings in those areas, going to many places. I even spoke in Dallas! There were so many meetings in Texas, I can't begin to remember them all. Texans are fine people! Most of them that is...

As Abba instructed, I returned to Aqaba in early September in time for the Fall Festivals. Others began to return also as summer was ending. In mid-September, I went to Jerusalem. For about a month, I had been getting e-mail from different Messianic groups, saying the real Sukkot would be in October. I became so disgusted. I went in September, as Abba had instructed me, to be with the people at the Wall on the eve of the Festival. While there, standing behind the men's section, I saw a young man standing at the Wall, wearing a long tallit. He turned sideways so that I saw his profile. He looked to be in his early 30s. He had a nicely trimmed beard. Abba asked me: "Where would My Son be tonight?" I burst out crying. I said: "Right there where that young man is standing." Later, upon returning to Aqaba, I learned that the true time of the real Sukkot was September. After all that waste of time in arguing, Abba had the right answer all along! Why don't His people ask Him?

At the invitation of Homer and Ruby, I returned to Ariel. I did more intercession over Mount Ga'ash. There was a lady there from England, who was a friend of Grant and Barbara's. I had met her the last time I was in Ariel. She stayed in an apartment that the Ortiz family had rented for visitors. We decided to travel together to Jerusalem to attend the International Christian Embassy Sukkot. Every morning she'd come, and we would get the bus to Jerusalem. We did not know that Homer and Ruby were upset at our going to Jerusalem to celebrate Sukkot, and our observance of Shabbat.

During our attending the week of celebration at the International Christian Embassy, which they hold at the Convention Center in downtown Jerusalem, we had lunch almost every day at the Crown Plaza behind the Convention Center. It was here that I had my restoration with Pam Brinke from North Carolina.

One morning, I came down for breakfast and Ruby greeted me with a question: "Do you still believe in Jesus?" I was shocked. I told her that He was my reason for living, and that without Him I would have no salvation, or eternal life. She seemed OK with my answer. But, wow that hurt. Then that evening when I returned, before dinner, Homer called me into the living room to tell me that I talked too much about Father. He said that there was an order to reaching God. We had to go through the Holy Spirit to Jesus, then through Jesus to the Father. His basic argument was that we did not have to guard Torah because Jesus gave us a New Covenant, which deleted the Old Covenant.

One evening, coming back from Jerusalem, I had the local bus bring me to the Texas Mini Golf. When I got off the bus, I saw several people sitting around a table. There I met Ephraim and Ramona Frank. I was #12 in the group that sat around the big table. Barbara and Grant Lovingood were there too. Ramona said that she was wondering who would be #12, because that would be special. There was a lady who sat to my left. She had on a bright red dress with a big red wide-brimmed hat. She said with a very southern drawl: "I just love your articles." How did she know me? She said she was a good friend of one of my best friends, named Ann. Ann, who lived in the Fort Worth area, had driven me up to visit her friends in Arkansas, where I got to speak in a couple of home meetings. Small world! I was also with Ann in Israel in 2007. As we sat there, Ephraim began to talk to Homer about guarding the Torah. I tried hard not to smile. He left one of his booklets with Homer.

After Sukkot, I took a day-trip to Haifa from Ariel by bus. After seeing Haifa and Mount Carmel, I intended to get a bus to the ruins of ancient Megiddo, so that I could see "Har Megiddo," or Greek: "Armageddon." Megiddo is a little hill that rises off the Jezre'el Valley floor. It is nothing more than layers of civilizations of the past, making it a small hill. The day before, I had tried to get information from the Jewish locals who met at Homer and Ruby's Mini Golf for hamburgers, ice cream, cokes, and chitchat, about how to get to the ruins of ancient Dothan. They told me it would be too dangerous to go to Dothan because of terrorists. So, I took the bus straight to Haifa.

During my intercession in 2001 in Ariel, I was facing Dothan from the top of Mount Ga'ash, doing intercession for the House of Joseph. Remember Joseph was sold into slavery from Dothan. But, they all told me that I could not go--it was dangerous. It was near Tulkarem, a Palestinian terrorist stronghold.

As I was on the bus to Haifa, via Petah Tikvah, leaning my head against the bus window, I began to envision how it would have been for Joseph, a boy of about 17, to be betrayed by his brothers, sold into slavery, and having to leave his precious father and mother. I literally felt his spirit – his confusion, and his grief. His young mind did not comprehend the reality of what was happening to him. Then, out the bus window, I saw a city-sign for Hadera. It was the closest I could get to Dothan.

Once in Haifa, I got a local bus supposedly heading towards Mount Carmel. But, the driver let me off by a park along the Sea. I had no idea where I was. A group of Jewish ladies told me about the Eschol Towers at the Haifa University. I got a taxi driver to take me there. I went up in the Eschol Tower to the top floor--

PART VI - The Middle East & Travels Beyond

about 33 stories up. I could see all of Haifa, the Port, and clear to Rosh HaNikra. I could even see the beginning of the Jezre'el Valley. It was awesome.

Then I tried to get a taxi driver to take me to the top of Mount Carmel to where Elijah had the contest with the prophets of Ba'al. I could not find one that spoke English. Finally, when I said "Eliyahu", he figured out what I wanted. "Eliyahu" is the real Hebrew name of "Elijah." He took me up a high hill, to the Carmelite Monastery. He charged me more than he said he would, and then he said he'd be back for the same amount of money. But, I barely had enough to pay him, and still get my bus back to Ariel. I had not eaten either. So, I told him not to come back. I was up there, far from civilization, without any way down. I saw tour groups.

One tour bus driver said he would take me to the Druze village below, but no further. I went to look over the side at the Jezre'el Valley below. Little did I know that just inside the gate, and up a few steps, was most likely the real place where Eliyahu prayed for rain, and the servant saw the cloud like a man's hand over the Mediterranean, and from where Eliyahu ran down the hill into the Jezre'el Valley all the way to Jezre'el, near Jenin. On one side of the rooftop you can look west and see the Mediterranean, and on the other side see the Jezre'el valley clear to Mt. Tabor. The brook Qishon, where he slew the prophets of Ba'al is just below this hill. I went back another time and saw this place with two friends from Tiberias.

Then I saw a taxi, who had let some people off there. He was on his way home, but he said he'd take me to the Druze village. He took me, and let me off, not charging me anything for the ride down the mountain. I walked a little ways, praying. I did not know where I was. I asked Abba why that happened. He let me know that because I had an Elijah anointing, the spirits of jezebel were at work. Then I saw a Druze man putting out some clothes to sell on the sidewalk. His sister spoke English. She said they had no bus service to Haifa from there, but her brother was going into town in a few minutes, and would take me to a sherut (a shared taxi van). Oh what good news! The sherut was there waiting for me. He took me into Haifa and let me off on a street corner. I needed to get to the bus station. No one spoke English. I went from one shop to another, trying to find someone who spoke English, but I found no one. Finally I saw a bus pull up. I asked: "Where is the new bus station?" How was I to know there were two, and the one I wanted was the old one? He told me what bus to take. So I took a local bus to the new bus station, which was way out of town. They told me that there were no buses to Ariel until the next morning. I got a bus to the old bus station. When I got there, the last bus to Ariel was just about to leave. Talk about mo'ed (to-the-second timing)! My life is full of mo'edim (plural for mo'ed)!

I did not know what to tell the bus driver. I said to take me to the Texas Mini Golf in Ariel. He did not understand "Texas Mini Golf," but a lot of people on the bus did, and told him where to take me. He let me off right at the Mini Golf. It was almost 7:00 PM. Ruby was there, and she took me back to the house. When we got into the car, she turned on the car radio to hear the 7:00 PM news. The top story was about the bombing of bus #19 at the Megiddo Junction. Everyone on board had been killed. It was the bus that I probably would have taken from Haifa. Abba ordered my day, so that I didn't get killed!

I attended a Friday night prayer meeting at the Ortiz' home, and then we went to join Homer and Ruby at the Mini Golf. We got free hamburgers, fried vegetables, and drinks. I sat with some Argentina Jews. They asked Homer why he sold hamburgers on Friday night, as it was Shabbat. They were seculars so they didn't care, but this is what he said: "We observe Sunday as our day of worship."

The Argentine family took me back to the house. On the way they were talking about "the Ancient Book," which secular Jews call the Bible. I was still shy--afraid of offending anyone. Looking back on it, I would not have offended them if I had told them that the "Ancient Book" had prophecy about today, and was not ancient. But, I kept my mouth shut. I have been in so many situations where I did not speak because I felt I dare not speak because my hosts would be angry and kick me out. This happened several times when I did not speak at all-- they just "hated me without a cause."

Anyway, that night I was so sick--I vomited all night. I figured it was because I ate food cooked on Shabbat in rebellion against Yahuweh. I also got pressure from Homer and Ruby because I didn't eat pork. The day before I was to return to Aqaba, Ruby took me to the home of some Russian Jewish friends, seculars, whose son was taking cooking classes to be a chef. He had made a special soup for us. It was so delicious. Just as I was finishing my second bowl, I stopped eating, and just sat there numb. What if this bowl of soup with all those different meats in it, contained pork? I quite casually asked the young man for the ingredients, because it was so delicious. He named off all the meats, the last one being pork. I was so upset at Ruby, and at me. But, what if I had asked the ingredients before we ate? I could not have eaten it, and I would have gotten blasted from Ruby and Homer later on. That night, you guessed it, I was horribly sick, and couldn't sleep.

The next morning, I took Ruby's sister and her husband with me to Eilat on the Egged Bus 444. I was still very sick from that soup. I had nothing to eat since eating it. Of course, no one else got sick. After four and a half hours on the bus, still sick, we approached Eilat. I looked over and saw Aqaba across the border. All of a sudden, for some reason, I was instantly healed of the nausea and felt good.

We had a good week, of a sort. The husband was totally ignorant of life in a Muslim nation. So he kept accusing me of making wrong decisions, until finally I proved him wrong. Because of my regular taxi driver putting Elaine and I in so many perilous situations on the way to Petra, I never called him again. They wanted to go to the Red Sea. I told them we had to walk down the street towards town and get a taxi from there. The man was so mad at me: "Why can't you call us a taxi," he said; "Why do you make us walk?" I knew no taxi driver to call, but the walk was so short. We had no sooner gotten to the street below the apartment, when a taxi pulled up. He said he'd charge 2 JD to the south beach (quite a long ways), and 2 JD back, and he'd wait for us for 2 JD.

This was my meeting with my wonderful taxi man who would be my helper and friend the rest of my time in Jordan. When he let us off in front of my apartment, we paid him and I said good bye. Then I thought, this man is so honest and kind, a fatherly type of man about 60 years old, I should have taken his name and number to call him for future taxi rides. But, there are probably 100 taxi drivers just in Aqaba, and most of them looked alike to me, so I was really upset at myself. But, you'll read about the miracle that came later in 2004.

Then October arrived. Elaine came for us to go to Jerash. Because I knew the vast difference between charismatic intercession and true Scriptural intercession, I wrote down some things to ask her. She had learned Christian intercession from Christine Darg. I sure did not want us mismatched if we were going to intercede together. But, within a few minutes, I relaxed because Abba had taught her. So we immediately bonded in the Spirit. She had much wisdom!

We went to Amman, stayed the night at the Geneva Hotel, and then got a wonderful taxi driver to take us to Jerash. It was a marvelous day! We heard from the Spirit exactly the same time about everything we were to say and do. We were in that awesome unity that only He can bring. We did intercession over the Red Sea also. She invited me to come teach at her house in Wales.

After she left, I got back to my studying, research, writing, counseling and communicating. Again, spending 10 or more hours a day to make sure that everything I wrote, taught, counseled and lived, came from One Teacher and One only!

In November, while in Aqaba, like the rest of the group, I had been attending the Anglican Church on Sunday mornings. The pastor and his wife from England had become friends. They planned an outing to the baptism site that was finally open, and I joined them. We had a fine tour of the baptism site. I saw where Elijah went up to heaven, where the "thickets of Jordan" were, where the caves were where John the baptizer stayed, and all the wonderful things that the Jordanian archeologists had discovered under the sand of that barren wilderness – the "plains of Moab." Then we went on to the top of Mt. Nebo, the Catholic version anyway, which was made famous by the Franciscans.

Then we went on to Madaba – Jordan's Byzantine Christian center. There the pastor's wife bought lots of Christmas decorations and presents, things she could not buy in other parts of Jordan. We saw the ancient tile map in the floor of the Madaba church, which showed that John baptized just above the Dead Sea, as the Scriptures tell. It was this tile mosaic map that the Jordanian archeologists used to find this barren sandy landscape and begin their "dig." A huge Byzantine church with a large mosaic floor was found also, facing Jericho and the backside of the north side of the Temple Mount in East Jerusalem.

In December, the daughter I stayed with had gotten down to decorating their Christmas tree with only five large bows on it, and her teddy bears underneath it. She was fazing out Christmas a little at a time. We had just moved into a house in Benbrook, Texas. The electric outlet in my bedroom was not operational, so I brought the computer out, sat down on the floor, and plugged it in behind the couch. I was just a few feet away from the tree. I was going to send "Joyful Abominations." My address list was still very small. So it didn't take me long to send out this article. The next morning I went shopping for groceries. When I got back, I saw that the tree was by the street curb, put out for the trash collector. I walked in and saw pine needles strewn between where the tree sat and the door. I asked: "What happened?" She said: "It died." I had to keep from laughing. I thought to myself: "I killed it." This was four days before Christmas. I think that was their last tree. On December 25th, they went to his parent's house for Christmas Day.

I stayed at the house. I studied **Revelation 9**. Abba showed me what that was all about, and that in March 2003, with the start of the Gulf War, the pit for the rising of Apollyon/Abaddon was opened. I found out later about the finding of the grave of Gilgamesh/Nimrod at the ancient gates of Babylon, by German archeologists, which were secured and taken by the U.S. The U.S. was dedicated long before the year 1600, to resurrecting and reincarnating Nimrod to rule the world. The restoration of Atlantis was the express reason for the founding of America. Atlantis, was the fabled city ruled by Nephillim.

JORDAN
(2004)

I went back to America from December to March. In early March, Claudia came to visit me in Aqaba for three weeks. She had little money, so I hosted her in Petra. I had nothing but my over-worked credit card, but I wanted her to have a good time. I did that with other Americans, too. Some left money to help me, some didn't. Then we went to Jerusalem, where we stayed at Christ Church. I showed her around Jerusalem. Then we went to Migdal, which is four miles north of Tiberias. We stayed at the Davis' B&B. Mr. Davis loved showing his guests the local places. He took us to Capernaum, and Tagba, and other sites around the Lake. His wife cooked us marvelous meals, which we ate family style around a big table with he and his wife, and other guests.

Afterwards, Claudia and I went to a Kibbutz at the south end of the lake, and stayed there for a few days with friends. Since she was from the Glen Rose area, and friends with Bob and Boo, Claudia also knew the daughter whose mother, Florence, stayed at St. Stevens. Florence was an intercessor with Christine Darg. I met Christine one night at last year's Sukkot celebration in Jerusalem. I was with Florence. Christine hugged me. She was so happy that Elaine and I were doing intercession over Jerash because she had Jerash on her heart too. I like Christine.

Claudia and I went and saw Florence and her daughter at St. Stevens, when we were returning through Jerusalem. Upon leaving Aqaba, Claudia would be coming back across to Jerusalem, before going on up to Tel Aviv to the airport. So, they said for her to come stay with them. They also said that they were happy to host me when I came for Sukkot later that year. That would help me a lot since I was poor. Claudia bought so many expensive souvenirs that when she got ready to cross the border, she did not even have enough money to pay the 5 JD exit fee, or the bus fee to get to Jerusalem. So, I gave it to her out of my food money. When she first arrived she told me she had brought money as an offering to me, but she spent it all on souvenirs. I did not know what she had done to me until I e-mailed Florence's daughter to tell her when I was coming to stay with them during Sukkot.

She wrote back the coldest blunt note, saying that plans had changed, and they did not want me to come. I was so shocked, and hurt. I e-mailed them to find out why. They never e-mailed back. But, I found out from Rabbi John, who was over the home congregation that I attended, and later from Tony, whose group I was also teaching, that Claudia had told them I was crazy, and to have nothing to do with me. She said I had taught them wrong about the name of Father, and that she should be their teacher. They shut her down. But, she teamed up with Laura, who eventually turned against me. "Birds of a feather flock together." Laura tried to get me to apologize to Claudia for hurting her. I was dumbfounded. I had to apologize to Claudia? Is there no practice of **Matthew 18:15-17**? I did not hold a grudge against Claudia, but her lack of "I'm sorry" put her in the **Jeremiah 3:3b** category.

Later, I went by Florence's apartment to talk to her, but when she opened the door and saw me, she had noticeable fear in her eyes. She said she could not see me, and closed the door. The only thing I could think of that set Claudia against me was when we were leaving Jerusalem to return to Aqaba, she pulled something weird at the bus port, where we were waiting for Egged 444. I had terrible pain in my back and head. I just needed for her to massage the upper shoulder and neck muscles a little to relieve the tension. I asked her to do that, but she put her head down and stared at the floor. She wouldn't touch me. I asked her why she wouldn't help me. She said she was praying. I was flabbergasted. I was also angry, but I tried not to show it. I did not act crazy. I kept my "cool." People who hide their true nature, are often shut down when asked to do something genuine. I had to dismiss it as just another bump in my road. I do not hold a grudge. Since, Claudia has tried to get back into my good graces, but to this day she has not said "I'm sorry" for anything, even though because of her I lost two very good friends in Jerusalem.

Remember this about those with a jezebel spirit in Christian ministry, and Messianic ministry: They are after the destruction of the genuine. They attempt to usurp the favor and hard work of the genuine, and if not successful, they slander, lie, and take revenge any way they can, but they never repent. They can't stand for another to have what they don't have. They are eaten up by jealousy if someone is honored or favored above them! Remember what Jezebel did to Naboth at Jezre'el! **Jeremiah 3:3**: "...you have a whore's forehead; you refuse to be ashamed." Mindboggling to watch, but this spirit is taking over the church, the Messianic movement, and the whole earth. It is the spirit of the great whore of Babylon--**Revelation 17**.

In April, I returned to Jerusalem for Passover. I stayed at the Jaffa Gate Hostel. I met so many nice people there! I met a couple in Jerusalem--Greg and Sylvia. He worked for Bridges for Peace and she was a vocalist and worship leader at King of Kings assembly. They worked later with The Covenant production as actors. I invited them to come to Petra. She was also a photographer for the ICEJ. I remember her awesome pictures.

Once back in Aqaba, in preparation for their coming to Petra, I decided to go to the little bus station to get the bus schedule for Petra. Upon arrival at the bus station, I was met by a swarm of taxi drivers. They told me it was Ramadan month, and the buses had all been used to take people to the Hadj in Mecca. That was true. I asked what they'd charge to take my friends, and I, to Petra, to stay for 5 hours, then bring us back? That was a usual tour-deal. They were yelling different prices. Then one soft-spoken well-dressed older man gave his fee. It was the normal fee. I said: "Let me tell you how to get to my apartment." I walked with him to his nice clean taxi. He and I both had on sunglasses. I gave him the address, and he took off his glasses and looked at me and said: "Didn't I pick you and your two friends up to take you to South Beach." IT WAS HIM! I exclaimed: "Praise God." He exclaimed: "Praise God." We just stood there and kept saying "Praise God." I know we were praising two different Gods, but WHAT A MIRACLE! He became my loyal driver. If he could not drive my friends and I to Petra, or my friends by themselves, he always sent a friend of his who was also loyal, faithful, and pleasant to take us.

Well, the couple from Bridges for Peace, and another lady I had met, planned on a date to come. I was to meet them at Ali Baba's restaurant in Aqaba about 11:00 AM. That morning, I took a walk along the King's Highway. I had just gotten back to my apartment when the phone rang. It was a man at Bridges for Peace calling for Greg and Sylvia. He said that they had gotten to Eilat, but that an "incident" had just happened at the Jordan/Israel border crossing, and they would not be able to come over until it was settled. That was about 10:30 AM.

Later they told me how some terrorists on the Aqaba side, had opened fire on a group of Egyptian tourists who were crossing from the Israeli side to the Jordan side through the short "no-man's-land" crossing. They were all killed. There was blood everywhere. I finally got hold of Greg in Eilat. They were told that if they joined the 400 Palestinians who crossed from Aqaba to Eilat each day to work in Eilat, that they would be able to get across. So at 5:00 PM, they joined the Palestinians, who put them in front of the line because they were all scared. When they got to the immigration/money change place, they said there were still bloody hand prints and foot prints everywhere. But, they got across. We had a nice dinner at Ali Baba's.

The next morning we went to Petra. Then we went to "Little Petra," where Esau and Job lived (in the land of Uz), and where Bedouin live now. It was a wonderful trip. We came back that night, and they spent about three more days with me before returning to Jerusalem.

If I told all the stories of my life in Jordan alone, just those eight years would take about 1,000 pages to cover the details, let alone the meetings and experiences, and "mo'edim" (divine appointments) in the U.S. If I wrote about all the dreams, visions, revelations of Scripture, His personal dealings with me, the "mo'edim" that He set up for me, the inner working of so many intricate things that produced His will, I would be writing for another 7 years or more, writing thousands of pages. So, when I say this is a "mini" autobiography, I mean it!

Almost every day, from 1999 to this very day in January of 2013, He did something that was important, for me, and for others. Mixed with all the tremendous blessings and miracles, the enemy never stopped. The jezebel attacks continued. Other spirits tormented/vexed me. Yet, I had no one to talk to about it. I understand how the Israeli Jews feel: The Palestinians shoot 1,000 rockets into towns in the southern Negev, along the Gaza strip, and the world says nothing. If Israel tries to defend its people, the world screams that they are killing Arab children, and to "use restraint." Israeli children are targeted by Hamas, the PA's Fatah, and Hezbollah, and yet the world says nothing. Most of the Arab children and adults are purposely killed by their own people, so that they can blame Israel.

WALES
(2004)

In June I arrived in Cardiff Wales. Elaine and her husband were there to pick me up. We went back to their lovely home in the country near Carmarthen. I was to speak at Elaine's that Shabbat. In the meantime, we went on tours of the area, and I fell in love with Wales. When I arrived at Elaine's house, I also met their two sons.

Just after arriving, she told me a fascinating story. The famous 1904 revival under Evan Roberts, was centered in the coal mining area of Wales, in what is known as the Rhondda. It was the 100th anniversary of the outbreak of that revival. That revival was so powerful that it influenced Rees Howells in Swansea, Wales, and spread to America as the great Pentecostal movement, which was best known as the "Azusa Street" revival. Shortly after, as this spread to Germany, the German government officially banned it, and all teaching about the in-filling of the Holy Spirit, which we know is Yahuweh Himself. They literally officially banned the Holy Spirit from Germany. The protective covering of Yahuweh was thrown off, darkness covered Germany--the result-- WWI, WWII, and Hitler.

So in this little town in the Rhondda, in 2004, on the hundredth anniversary of the revival, people from a local church began meeting at 6:00 AM for a restoration of the Great Welsh Revival. But, they were a "replacement theology" church and believed that the church replaced Israel. One morning at their prayer meeting, they all stopped praying at once, for the Spirit of Yahuweh had spoken to all of them the same thing. One spoke up and said: "He has told me to turn my heart towards Israel." They all said the same thing. Then one said: "But, we know no one to tell us about Israel." Another said: "I know of a lady in Carmarthen who goes to Israel, maybe she can help us." This lady phoned Elaine. Elaine told them that in two weeks, a lady was coming from Jordan to teach on Israel--ME. I had my first meeting in Elaine's living room. Quite a number of ladies came, some from long distances. A delegation from the Rhondda drove at least 2 hours to come. It was almost Shavu'ot.

They checked with their pastor and he said for me to come and speak. It was on Shavu'ot when I spoke there. I spoke on the Torah given at Sinai and the Holy Spirit falling on the disciples at Pentecost. This was a shocking comparison they had never heard of before. But, I saw them taking notes. Afterwards, one lady in her 80s came up to me and said that in all her life she had never read the Old Testament, but she was going to. Another one came crying. She said that she had relatives in the Holocaust, and she wanted to learn her Hebrew roots. That opened a door for Elaine to be able to return and teach. Within a year, things sure were different in that congregation--more on that in 2005. [Refer to: "Replacement Theology"/2005]

As Elaine and I left that evening to return to her house, it was so dark, it was hard for Elaine to see the road. We had a long ways to go before we got to the main highway. We came to the top of a ridge, and it appeared that the sky was on fire. It remained "on fire" for about 45 minutes, helping us to see the road as we left. Talk about a miracle! Sunset does not take 45 minutes. For more on this meeting and miracle, refer to "Fire in the Sky"/2004.

Elaine introduced me to a lot of her friends. I felt at home, as if with family. But, like with Tony in Flower Mound, and Constance in New Braunfels, and Laura, and Claudia, in 2008, the enemy moved with lies, and jealousy, jezebel manipulation, and downright evil, to divide me from these families. Finally, the enemy even divided Elaine and I, because of lying slander. Some lied to remove me from friendships that I had with their group members that were precious to me.

But, not one time did anyone in East Texas who were a part of the ex-World Wide Church of God assemblies ever pull any jezebel stuff on me! They loved me, they included me, they prayed for me, and opened their homes for me without any hidden agendas. They are family-oriented people. When we got together, the food, the dancing, the blowing of shofars, the midrash, and the friendship, were all awesome! Abba was teaching them. The last I heard, there were some who wanted to hear Him for themselves and learn about the in-filling of Abba's Spirit.

Back in Wales, Elaine had a friend in Swansea named Maureen--this was another one of the Welsh ladies named Maureen. But, this one did not attend the fellowship in her home. This Maureen had been attending prayer meetings for Israel at Rees Howell's Bible College, the Bible College of Wales, in Swansea, as well as at her Christian church. Elaine contacted her, and we had a day of marvelous touring. Maureen took us to tour the grounds of the Bible college. She took us to where Rees Howells and his prayer warriors prayed through World War II, right in site of Swansea Bay, where Hitler's forces were trying to bomb. [Refer to the inspiring book: *Rees Howells Intercessor*]

There were people at that prayer meeting who had prayed with Rees Howells in the 1930s. The two that conducted the meetings each week, Nolly and Norman Brand, had prayed with Rees Howells during WW II. Also, two ladies who attended the prayer meetings were in their 90s. They had been attending the college and prayed with Rees during the war. Maureen arranged for me to speak at the prayer meeting, in the very wing of the building where Rees Howells had lived. I met so many wonderful people there!

I spoke there two more times in 2005. Their hearts were turned towards Israel, as was Rees Howell's heart. In fact, he built that Bible College to also house Jews fleeing out of Europe, especially Jewish orphans. But, no Jewish people came. It was built for our day! This revelation on why it was built, and about "our day," is one of the most fascinating set of circumstances I've ever heard, and the conclusion won't come until Messiah does!

I learned that seculars from Scotland had bought the college. One of the first things they wanted to do was to tear down the old buildings that Rees Howells used. This meant that Norman and Nolly had to be removed, and the prayer meetings stopped. The new owners were very anti-Semitic. While there in 2004, Father gave me a prophecy to these secular owners. I sent it to the owner, and to all on his Board of Directors, and to those in the prayer meeting. In 2006, the secular owners tore down the old building where Rees had lived, and stopped the prayer meetings. So, Norman and Nolly, who had been living there, went into a rest home. They were in their 90s, but they continue on with the prayer meetings to this day.

Each one of the dormitories had Hebrew names over their entrances. The grounds are gorgeous. I did much intercession over that place! We saw another room where they prayed also. One of the students in the college gave us a tour. During the tour, we went into the dining room, formerly called "the blue room." We were told that the table by the window that overlooked Swansea Bay, was where Rees and staff prayed against the bombs of Hitler's military, and the bombing ceased. To the right of the table was a gigantic portrait of Rees Howells, and to the right of that was a gigantic portrait of his wife. As I laid my hands on that table, I felt like electricity going all up and down my arms. Yahuweh spoke to me: "**Restore the vision. Restore the vision!**" I knew that the vision was to help fleeing Jews and Jewish orphans in a time of turbulence and war. That's for the very near future. But, I found out in 2011, that a young man from South Korea was working to buy the college to "restore the vision." I had the privilege of meeting him, and talking with him about it. In 2004, Maureen had taken us to Moriah Chapel in Swansea, where the revival broke out in 1904. But, the doors were locked and we could not go in. In late 2005, Abba gave me a prophecy for those in the prayer meeting to encourage them.

Blond Maureen, whom I met in 2003 with the Welsh ladies at Christ Church, had been working in Israel as a house keeper for a prayer ministry. She came back to Wales while I was there. I went with her to her mother's house where she also lived, in Pembroke, just south of Milford Haven, near where the Irish Sea empties into the Celtic Sea. We went down to the port to see the ferries that were leaving for Ireland. We sat on the dock and she shared about going to Morningstar Assembly in Tiberias. She met a young man there who had come from Russia, actually from Birobidzhan, where I had worked with the Jewish Agency. He was quite a bit younger than she, but she thought he showed signs of liking her. This was June. I told her to take it slow. But, she had never been married, and was enamored with this young man. I went to their wedding in Tiberias in September.

I met the woman named Leslie at Elaine's house in 2004 at my first meeting there. Leslie was one of Elaine's best friends. She came with us to the Rhondda. I have an incredibly strong gift of the discernment of spirits, and when I met her at Elaine's after the first meeting, I knew something was not right with her. So I avoided her offers to get together in Israel, from then on. More on this in 2008...

Abba kept me busy with meetings and touring southern Wales during those three weeks at Elaine's, from late May to mid-June. I told her that I felt Abba wanted me to go to Milford Haven, but it did not work out in 2004.

Back in Aqaba, Abba shocked me by saying that He wanted me to stay in Jerusalem from the end of June to the end of July--five weeks. I listed fifteen things that might be the reason. I was so looking forward to July with my family--the July 4th cookout, and my birthday week of fun. But, I am an obedient servant.

I asked the couple from Bridges for Peace, whom I hosted in Aqaba and Petra, if I could stay with them. They said "yes." They had an apartment in my very favorite area of Jerusalem--Rehavia. Right down the street was the Prime Minister's house, a market, and Rambam Street. Not far away on King George Street was Hekal Shlomo--the Great Synagogue. I loved going there. The Cantor had a deep baritone voice, and sounded like an opera star. His male choir was incredible. The acoustics are incredible for sure. The women sat in the balcony. On my first visit, I sat next to what appeared to be a very wealthy woman. She helped me understand the order of service. Then there was a Bar Mitzvah. That was fascinating. Ladies were throwing wrapped candy down from the balcony after it was finished. I spent about three weeks walking the streets of Jerusalem, praying, seeing what He wanted me to see, and hearing what He wanted me to hear.

On July 4th, I walked all the way to the Jaffa Gate, out through the Dung Gate, and down the Kidron Valley to the apartment where Florence and her daughter stayed in the north Kidron Valley. Claudia's damage had not been done yet, for they were happy to see me. Out their window I could see the Eastern Gate up on the right, the Mount of Olives on the left, and could look straight down the Kidron Valley. The north Kidron, which used to be a river but which is now full of olive trees, is the "Valley of Jehoshaphat"--**Joel 3:2**--where Messiah will gather all nations for their judgment (**Matthew 25:31-46**). Right in front of that Eastern Gate in that valley is where King Josiah brought the priests from the Temple Mount who had been involved in paganism, and burned them alive.

After talking a while, Florence fixed us a nice lunch. The daughter said: "Why would we want to be in the U.S. when we can be in this awesome place in Jerusalem." On my birthday, I decided to treat myself, so I stayed for one night at Christ Church, and asked for room 3--the only guest room with a balcony. The new cook had become my friend, and one of the workers, so I was not alone. I spent the day walking to the City of David, down to the Siloam Springs, and up through the Kidron Valley. It was a precious day to me! Later, when I returned at the very end of July to the U.S., my children had a wonderful birthday celebration for me.

Certain things stand out during those 5 weeks, like going into a small Judaica shop on King George Street, to buy a small silver cup. The owner was an old Orthodox Jewish man. As I was purchasing the cup, he began making gestures towards heaven and patting his heart. I said the Hebrew blessing to him that is given on Shabbat evening over the cup. He was so thrilled. He began praying and praising, in Hebrew of course. He walked out with me and stood waving, like Brother Lamb had done in China.

I went to the big Israeli Museum. I went into the Shrine of the Book, to view the Dead Sea scrolls on exhibit. I did not want to leave there. In 2009, 2010, and 2011, I went to Qumran, and the revelation that Abba gave me in Qumran changed my life.

I also was privileged to be at the Convention Center to see the musical production *The Covenant*. Greg and Sylvia were two of the stars. I went to several sessions of the Knesset, and had the grand tour of that place too. I was there so much that they stopped asking me to check my backpack, and let me take it with me. I sat in the gallery and watched the proceedings below. What a circus! I saw Prime Minister Sharon, Shimon Peres, and Netanyahu, who was the Finance Minister at the time. Netanyahu gave a speech, which no one seemed to listen to. People were walking around drinking coffee and talking. Then when it came time to vote on something, many were out of the room in the hall talking. There were two large "score boards," one on the right of the room and one on the left – just like at football games in America. When the buzzer sounded for them to vote on something, they'd all run to their buzzers and push their choices, and then the scores would appear on the score boards. Then they'd go back to talking. It was funny.

But, going my first time held a special blessing. I was in the Christ Church Heritage Center, and was asking the man serving beverages how I could get to the Knesset. He didn't know. But, a lady sitting at a table nearby heard our conversation, came up to me, and said that she went to the Knesset often to do intercession. She said she could point out all the main people in the cabinet, as well as the speakers of the different parties (about 12 different parties), and she would love to go to help me. So she did. She explained everything to me. What a blessing--another mo'ed.

After being in that one apartment for three weeks, the lady grew agitated at having me there, even though I bought my own food and tried to help her. She said she didn't want me there during the day. She was working on music for her performances at King of Kings. So for several days, I stayed out until evening. That was hard.

One day I sat in the park down from the Knesset for several hours. I watched Orthodox youth, with peyots (side curls) flying, wearing shorts, playing soccer. That was cute. I got back to the apartment and she was doing housework. She stopped, and then told me she was still working through deep emotional problems from her past. She shared some things with me. She said she didn't want me there anymore, even thought I offered to pay them. Her husband wanted me to stay, since we had enjoyed discussing the end times together.

I've met so many twisted people mentally, and emotionally, who act like good Christians, or Messianic people, yet hide their real self behind a mask of fake spirituality. Yes, I was hurt over being kicked out. I packed up, not knowing where to go. I called the Finnish Guest House, where I had stayed before, and they had a dorm room for me for a few days. The Guest House is next to where the Christian Friends of Israel offices were--about a ½ mile from the Jaffa Gate. I met people from Finland, and we walked to different places together. I even went to the American Consulate to get more pages in my passport. But, by staying at the Finnish Guest House, as reasonable as it was, I was running out of money.

The family in Aqaba had friends who ran the organization for Jonathan Miles in Jerusalem. They stayed in the ministry headquarters house just around the corner from the Finnish Guest House, and up the hill on "Prophet's Street," Ha Navi'im. I called them, and they had an extra bedroom, so they asked me to stay with them. I was with them about 2 weeks; they made me feel like part of their family. This place was close to Ben Yehuda Street, and so I walked down there a lot. Abba engrafted into me a love for HIS CITY and the House of Judah! I was in Jerusalem until the day after the 9th of Av, making my total stay about 5 ½ weeks.

Jonathan Miles started an organization called *Save the Heart of a Child*. He is a Jewish surgeon who does heart surgery on children whose parents could not afford the operation. Most of these were Arab children. The family from Aqaba, after 8 years of living in Aqaba, went to Jerusalem to work with them. The family-dad's job was to go into very dangerous Palestinian areas to get the children and bring them to where they would have heart surgery – like Gaza, Tulkarem, and even meeting a child coming in from Iraq.

I was perplexed as to why I had to stay in Jerusalem all that time, when nothing bad was happening. I had figured maybe He didn't want me back in the U.S. because maybe something bad was going to happen in the U.S.

I was on my way to the Knesset the last time, and was on bus #9. I had my head leaning on the bus window, thinking about my time there and what a blessing it was. As we rounded the big corner at a big intersection, going down to the Knesset, He spoke softly to me: "**If I do not love Jerusalem above my chief joy.**" (**Psalm 137**)

I burst into tears. I was astounded. I said quietly: "It was a test wasn't it? You wanted to know if I would love your city more than being with my own children. And I passed didn't I?" "Yes" was His answer. It was "yes" on three counts! None of my 15 reasons even came close to this surprise. I just cried, because He had done a work in me so deep in those few weeks that would have eternal value! I returned to the U.S.

HOW I GOT THE NAME "YEDIDAH"

I returned to Aqaba in early September. He began teaching me further. One morning, I was reading II Kings. In 2000, I bought my first copy of *The Scriptures*, and have used this translation ever since to this day. C.J. Koster, in his translation, removed the 25 pagan words that form the basic "christianese" language, and put in the real Hebraic meaning. He worked 20 years on this, and it is a standard translation in many Messianic assemblies. So many Christian words are Greek abstracts that take our understanding away from the reality that is rooted in the Hebrew language.

As I read **II Kings 22:1**, I read: **"Yoshiyahu (*Josiah*) was eight years old when he began to reign, and he reigned thirty-one years in Yerushalayim (*Jerusalem*). And his mother's name was Yedidah..."**

I went no further. A baptism of love for that mother's name went all over me and through me. I put down the Bible in shock. I was stunned. I said out loud: "What is happening to me?" He spoke so clearly: **"THAT'S WHAT I CALL YOU."** I didn't know what "Yedidah" meant. I ran into my office/bedroom and grabbed the Strong's Concordance and looked up the meaning. Then I was really stunned. "Yedidah" is the feminine of "yedid", which means **"BELOVED."** It referenced the nickname of King David, "doo-deh," or "doo-doo," which also means "Beloved." Actually, in Scripture, both words are used for "Beloved." The prophet Nathan referred to Solomon as "yedidahyah"--"the beloved of Yahuweh."

In His grief over the sins of the northern ten tribes, whom He had to scatter into all nations AMONG the gentiles, He refers to them as His "yedidah nephish"--"the beloved of My soul." As I've said, a great part of my life paralleled the history of the ten tribes of Israel. They will have a glorious finish! I pray I do too!

After learning what He called me, I was so overwhelmed. I went and sat down. I thought back to in 1986, after arriving in Fort Worth and renting our first house, how angry I was at Him for so many things. I stayed up so late crying so hard that I could hardly stand up, or hardly see. I remember throwing the Bible into a chair and saying bitterly at Him: "Is there anything you want to say to me before I go to bed?" I went over to the Bible that had opened, and was lying flat on the chair. I looked through my blurry eyes. Only one thing had been underlined on both pages. I picked up the Bible and put it close to my eyes to read what the one phrase was. I read: **"You are greatly beloved."** That was what HE called me. In all of my rebellion, and sin, and hate of Him, He called me "Beloved." Then I really cried even harder. How can one understand such love? In 2004, there in my apartment in Aqaba, I pondered these things.

The next day, I received an e-mail from Elaine about the plans of several of my Welsh friends to come to Maureen's wedding in Tiberias just before Sukkot. They said they would meet me in the Christ Church garden area, and then we'd all pitch in and rent a van to take us to Tiberias. I wrote them back. I wanted to tell them what happened about His giving me my new name, but I was scared. What if the Israelis think it is a weird name? What if the Messianic Jews would make fun of me if I used that name? I got ready to send a reply to Elaine's e-mail without mentioning my new name, and HE came into the room in anger. I stopped cold. I said: "Yes Sir." He said, "**I gave you that Name – USE IT**!" So, I told them about my new name, and I asked them to call me "Yedidah" from then on.

I went to Jerusalem for Yom Teruah, Yom Kippur, and Sukkot. I stayed at the Finnish Guest House again. Nice place, nice area! It was right next to the headquarters of Christian Friends of Israel. I had met several of the workers, and I loved going there. I walked up to Hekal (also spelled "Heichal") Shlomo to find out when the service times were for Yom Kippur. There were several friends I had met who also wanted to go.

That night, upon getting there, I first went to the bathroom before ascending to the women's balcony. I took off my glasses, and brushed my hair. But, I forgot to put on my glasses again. I got half way up the stairs and realized I'd left them in the bathroom. I ran down to the bathroom, but they were not there. I hurried up to the balcony because the seats would all be taken quickly. I sat at the very top of the balcony for the Yom Kippur service. Afterwards, I left my friends, and headed down to find a security man. I told him I had lost my glasses. He brought me about four pair of glasses that others had left, but none of them were mine. Finally they called in the head of Security, a Canadian Jew by the name of Yude (pronounced "You-dah"/Jude). He said no one had turned in any glasses like what I described. But, he said it was probably a woman who had come for Yom Kippur, and would most likely come back the next morning. I gave him the number at the Finnish Guest House.

In Israel, on Yom Kippur, the whole nation shuts down. Even the traffic lights are off. The only ones allowed on the street are the police and ambulances. People were standing in the street outside of Hekal Shlomo--Temple of Solomon (also known as "The Great Synagogue"). I walked down the center of a major street towards Ben Yehuda to cut through and go to the Finnish Guest House. As I walked up past Independence Park, I was singing very loudly in tongues. No one even paid attention to me. It was dark, but I had no fear. I got back and began praying for the one who had my glasses. Oh I prayed hard for them.

The next morning was Yom Kippur day. I first walked clear up to Hekal Shlomo, but no one had turned in the glasses. So, I walked back to Christ Church. When I entered the Christ Church garden, the Welsh delegation all turned towards me, and in unison called out: "Hi Yedidah." That was cheery! Before that, I had asked a Messianic lady at a hotel in Jerusalem what she thought of the name "Yedidah." She went into an "ooooh so beautiful" discourse. I asked a Messianic man at Christ Church what he thought of the name. He said, "Oh, that is so beautiful." Later, back in Texas, I asked a secular Hebrew language teacher what she thought, and she said: "Oh that is so beautiful." I later told a local grocer in Tiberias my name, because he asked, and he said: "Oh that is so beautiful." He said that in modern Hebrew, if it is said like this: "Yeh-dee-DAH", raising the voice on the "dah," it meant "friend." If it was just pronounced "Yeh-deed-ah", with no raising of voice inflection, it was a name. That was good information.

Later, my good friend Miri took me to a restaurant for lunch, and we had to give our name so that when the order was ready, they'd call our name over the loud speaker. I gave the lady "Yedidah." I brought back my food to the table. I was so happy. I had heard my name spoken by an Israeli over a loud speaker. Then my friend, Ann, from England, and I, went on a boat cruise on the Sea of Galilee (Lake Kinneret). She introduced me to the young boat captain as "Yedidah." He exclaimed: "Oh, you are the friend of God." I said: "Yes, I am."

I told the Welsh group about my glasses situation. Christine Darg was there, and she prayed for me. I even went to an eye doctor in the Arab Quarter to see about getting another pair of glasses, but Christine advised me to wait, that Abba would help me. Yom Kippur services are very hectic for that large synagogue's personnel. I spent the rest of the day walking down the middle of major boulevards, and praying. After the evening service, which closed Yom Kippur, unbeknownst to me, Yude had tried to call me. He told me later that he had tried to call me after the service that night, but the switchboard at the Guest House was shut off. Then he tried to come to the gate on his way home, but it was locked. The whole security team got involved in this. It is laughable now, but oh I prayed. I prayed more for the person who took the glasses than for finding the glasses.

The day after Yom Kippur, I was to meet my friends about 10:30 AM at Christ Church, and we would all go together to

Tiberias. I had to give it one more chance concerning my glasses, so I walked clear up to Hekal Shlomo again. The security man remembered me. He called Yude. In about 15 minutes, here came this wonderful man holding up a pair of glasses – MY GLASSES! Oh did I ever thank them! He said a woman had come for the day Yom Kippur services and given them to him. So, two lovely Orthodox Jewish people had my glasses in their homes!

I walked back up to Christ Church and met with the Welsh people. We went to Tiberias for the wedding. Maureen and Dennis had a wonderful wedding at Morningstar! At the time they were renting facilities at the Scottish Guest House. It was at this wedding that I met people I would later be with in Tiberias.

We stayed in a large house that faced the Lake. I opted to sleep on a mat on the big wide balcony. The weather couldn't have been more perfect. We ate out there too. The joy of being by the Sea of Galilee – Lake Kinneret – under the stars is such a great privilege. In going to Tiberias, Elaine gave me a great compliment. She said that I was not like an American; I was like the Welsh Celts, and I was one of them. The lovely Irish lady who, with her husband John, lived in that wonderful house in the City of David, was also there with us.

On the way back to Jerusalem, I was on a bus that was packed with IDF soldiers. It was a 2½ hour trip. For about an hour, one soldier from the Ukraine stood by me and poured out his heart to me – in good English. He had been serving in a special service unit in Gaza. He told me about an IDF inside the IDF, and how they were killing people to bring about a hidden agenda. It broke his heart. I knew everything he said was true. He told about the reality of Arabs there. He kept quoting the Bible. Finally, he apologized for talking about the Bible. I told him not to apologize. He was precious. He did not know that I understood everything he said, down to the last detail. I wish so much I had recorded what he said. I told some of what he said to Barry Chamish, and he also wished I had recorded it. I learned so much truth about the reality of deception inside Israel.

I got back to Jerusalem just before Sukkot began, so I registered with the ICEJ for their meetings. But, I had no place to stay because of what Claudia had done to me. I e-mailed Ramona Frank and asked if she knew anyone. She said that their friend, John, had begun a bed and breakfast out at Maoz Zion, about 12 miles outside Jerusalem, and I could possibly stay there. John had a Dutch lady to help him. He lived in a big house that overlooked Ein Karem. I did stay with him most of that week. Two men also came to stay with him. I went into the ICEJ meetings every day from there. It was a lovely time. He had worked with Ya'ir Davidy on *The Tribes*, and so did Ephraim Frank. It was through John that I met some lovely ladies from Scotland, whom I visited in 2005 at his house. His Bed and Breakfast did not last long because of Israeli laws, but it was a good place to be. We discussed his new book while I was there. I also stayed part of this week at the Finnish Guest House before returning to Aqaba.

During the week with the ICEJ, I found out that the Christian Friends of Israeli Communities was hosting a tour of Gaza. I knew I had to go. So, I went to get a ticket. They said there was one ticket left. I didn't have money with me, but they reserved it for me, and let me buy it the next day. I wouldn't have missed that trip for anything!

In the Gaza Strip, we visited five of the more than 20 different settlements named "Gush Katif." We met with the people. For example, we listened as a grandmother from New York told of founding her beautiful community. We saw the beautiful green houses, whose fruit and vegetable produce, and flowers, were sold in Europe. We visited a new settlement on the Mediterranean, where we had a Sukkah party. I will write more later about the 2005 pullout of 8,000 people from Gaza.

In December, 2004, I had invited Betty from Glen Rose to come visit me. She had hosted me several times when I came to speak in Glen Rose, or when I came to hear speakers at Bob and Boo's monthly meetings. Betty was/is still a retired school teacher, a researcher, a fine musician, and one very knowledgably on the end times. I had been working months doing research and writing a study entitled: "The Hebrew Names and Titles of the Creator of the Universe--The Father and Messiah of Israel." I finally finished it. Betty was coming the next day. So, I started to prepare to send it out to all on my address list. As I did, Abba firmly said: "**DO NOT SEND IT**." I was shocked. I thought: "But, it's finished. I want to get it out before Betty comes." I obeyed Abba.

She came to Aqaba about December 20th. Before we went over to Jerusalem, I had been studying the armor in **Ephesians 6:10-18** and comparing it to the garments of the High Priest in **Exodus 28**. Of course, Sha'ul would not compare the armor of Elohim with that of a defiled Roman soldier! The two matched perfectly and I wrote: "Correct Intercession and Spiritual Warfare in the Garments of the High Priest." Betty was/is an intercessor. One thing that stood out was how these "garments" matched Yahushua's garments when He comes in judgment – i.e. **Isaiah 59:17**. Of course, He is of the rightly biological lineage of the Zadok High Priest, as well as being of the lineage of King David. Messiah is both Judah and Levi.

But, what really stood out was the golden crown that went over the head wrap of the High Priest. Upon the crown was written "Set-Apart to Yahuweh." Unless the High Priest was wearing this crown, he COULD NOT intercede for the people. So, I was more than fascinated with it. That's why Moses told Aaron not to take off his head wrap in his grief, because he would have had to remove the crown to do it. (**Leviticus 10**) I taught this to Betty.

Then we went to Jerusalem. On December 25th, a Shabbat that year, we went to Hekal Shlomo, walking in the rain. It was so cold! She loved it. There was a Bar Mitzvah afterwards. She stood at the railing of the balcony watching. Being a musician too, she loved the Cantor and the choir. Then we walked all the way back, and went to the City of David. I took her also to see the Eastern Gate, the Garden of Gethsemane, and the Kidron Valley. My knees were hurting so bad from the cold. But, she's small and wiry, and she did fine.

The next day was so much better. It was sunny. We went through the Arab Quarter from the Jaffa Gate. Then we turned right and went through an Israeli check point, coming out into the Western Wall Plaza. She had bought some souvenirs in the Arab Quarter, and had them in a small sack. Going through the check point, she accidently left her sack. So, when we got to the plaza, she realized her sack was gone. She hurried back to the check point to get it.

As soon as she left, a nice-looking older man with white hair and very blue eyes came up to me and asked: "Do you know Yahweh?" Being Jerusalem, I didn't answer right away, for there are so many strange religious people running around. Then I cautiously said "yes." He smiled, sat down next to me, and said his name was Roy. He said that he had seen me coming down the stairs, and the Holy Spirit had said that he had something I needed. He said he was working with a Messianic Rabbi, Reuben, who was up in his 80s had spent many years of his life researching the Names of the Father and the Son. Roy was in his early 70s, half Welsh and half Jewish. He lived in French Hill with his 90-year old mother who was having dreams of the destruction of America.

Immediately, the Spirit in Roy, and the Spirit in me, bonded together. For about 15 minutes we had rapid-paced awesome fellowship. It was like the fellowship we'll have when we get into the Kingdom. He and Rabbi Reuben had been coming down to the Plaza every day for a long time, from early morning to night, to speak to the Orthodox about using His Name. I told him my friend had left a sack at the check point and had gone off to get it. He smiled and said, "I know, Father sent her away--I was to talk to

PART VI - The Middle East & Travels Beyond

you." Just before Betty returned, he opened his briefcase and took out a stack of printed material. It was research notes – conclusions of Rabbi Reuben on the Names of the Father and the Son. He said "this is what the Holy Spirit told me to give you."

Then she returned. I told Roy that I was going to take her up on the Temple Mount. He said: "Oh no, don't do that – you must take her to the Temple Institute." I thought, "OK, Roy is so Spirit-led that I will take her to the Temple Institute." We went to the Temple Institute, where there are items on display that have been made for the Third Temple (**Ezekiel 40-46**) to be used when Messiah comes. I am tearing up again at this because as we walked into the room, where the big glass case displayed large objects for the Third Temple, I saw the altar of incense, covered in pure gold of course, but right at its base, sitting on a little platform, was the gold crown. On it was engraved in gold "Kodesh YHWH," in Hebrew of course. I sat there stunned, just staring at it. Messiah will wear that over His head wrap, as He intercedes for His people as High Priest.

We went back to Aqaba, and Betty returned home. I got out my study on the Names, and went through it, incorporating almost everything Rabbi Reuben said--for his notes that Roy gave me confirmed everything that He has shown me about the Names and titles. This is what I mean by HIS confirming His Word, in His own way. I never have to go looking for confirmation. He brings it! I sent it out in January 2005. Throughout, you will see references to Rabbi Reuben.

JORDAN
(2005)

I returned to Jordan in early March. Before I left for Passover, I got a chance to teach in the home of the family in Aqaba. The father had started a Bible study, which attracted people from many different countries. This group consisted of a mixture of born again Filipino people, who were servants of King Abdullah at his palace in Aqaba, people from India who were managers in a major factory in Aqaba, people from America, and people from other different countries, like Europeans, and Jordanian believers. Being just before Passover, I taught on Passover from **Exodus 12**. One of the Jordanian believers was a medical doctor in Aqaba, but he also doctored Bedouin in the region as a free service. During my collecting of Jordanian tourist books, I found the Name "Yahweh" used several times. I found out that the ancients put "Yahweh" on the steles if they defeated Judah, saying that their god defeated Yahweh. So, when I taught, I brought the books and taught on His Name.

The next meeting after Passover, the doctor told this story: He was so excited about using the Name. He was so excited to learn about the Festivals, especially Passover. His simple testimony of being born again is precious! He said that he had gone to doctor some Bedouin. They asked him why, every year at that time, they found a perfect lamb, laid hands on it, transferred their sins onto the lamb, killed it, and put its blood on the outside door of their tents. Wow! He was so excited because of what I had taught that he ran to his truck, got his Bible, and read to them from **Exodus 12**. He said they were thrilled, after all these years, to learn why they did that, at that time of year. Awesome!

I went to Jerusalem for Passover in March. I had gotten used to staying at the Jaffa Gate Hostel, so I stayed there. Right after Passover, I returned to Aqaba. By late March, it became more and more obvious that my time with the group was over. I could not even attend a home prayer meeting with three others, without two of them starting a conversation about my Torah-guarding, bringing up the typical three statements of "Paul" that Christians use to refute the Torah, and questioning me about them. I answered all three.

On the anniversary of my mother's death, which was March 30, 1995, my friend from Emanuel Christian Fellowship in Texas called to tell me that the leader-lady had been told by Trisha that I had betrayed her. I had not! It was a pure lie. My friend told me that, for that reason, the leader-lady had told the members of the group not to speak to me until she returned from America, then she would deal with me. After I hung up the phone, within 15 minutes I got very sick with diarrhea, and stayed horribly weak for days. Then I got sick with the flu. I knew I had to get out of there, and get an apartment away from the others. But, I did not have strength to even get groceries, and I was hungry. That older loving couple from up the hill, who believed that we should love our neighbor as ourselves, came and got me and took me to get food. I never exposed their kindness to the leader-lady. She put fear in the hearts of so many to obey her, or else.

In mid-April the leader-lady came to talk things out. I confronted her with many things, even her "projects" that never got off the ground – and she admitted to everything I said. She knew what I had been accused of was a lie. But, her decision was that I was on probation and could attend their Torah studies on Thursday, but nothing else. I went to one of the studies after that, and felt the presence of death so strongly that I never went back. I was treated like an outcast.

The man to whom I had taken my film to be developed all those years, had told me about a house he was building in the 10th district – the most northerly district of Aqaba. He said the lower part was a house for his family, but that he had put two apartments up above for people to rent until his two children got married and wanted to live there. The children were about 7 and 9. He said the apartment would be ready by May. This man, and his family, were Armenian Catholics. His wife was related to the family that ran the Armenian Tavern in the Old City of Jerusalem.

As weak as I was, after the March 30th phone call, I went to talk to this man about renting one of his apartments. He took me to see it, and I loved it. In that area all the houses were painted bright colors. His was bright hot-pink. The windows looked right out at the Israeli border check point coming into Eliat. But, I told him that I wanted a place with a balcony. He took me up one flight of stairs to the roof. He had tiled the entire flat roof! He said: "This is your balcony." He told me he would give me a key to the roof, and I could even sleep up there in the summer. AWESOME!

I had been paying the equivalent of $350.00 a month in JD, but he charged me the equivalent of $213.00 a month in JD. It was a two bedroom apartment, with a big living room, kitchen, and one bath. One bedroom was big enough for an office. But, I put the computer desk in the living room. After meeting with the leader-lady in April, I went to him to see how soon the apartment would be ready. He said by the first of May. I had to be in Wales in June. But in May, the apartment was ready for me.

I hired four men and a truck for 40 JD – 10 JD each. They carried out everything, put it on the truck, and then hauled it up the second floor of my new apartment. I was given a nice-sized plastic table and four chairs, which I took up to the roof-balcony. I sat there in peace, looking at the Red Sea towards Eliat, right at the Israeli border, and could even see the King's Highway behind me near the mountains. I loved the brightly colored houses. It reminded me of Saltillo, Mexico. The Aqaba airport was just 2 miles down the road, just after the exit road to the Israeli border. As the planes came in from Saudi Arabia to land in Aqaba, they came right over my roof-balcony. The planes were so low that I could see the people inside. I loved that so much! It was especially wonderful at night, when the lights were on the plane. It was from that roof top that I saw "smart-missiles" being fired over Eliat towards Iraq, from the U.S. base behind Eilat. Others watched it too – huge missiles that turned towards Iraq once they got up about five miles over Saudi Arabia.

The story of my previous landlord is quite amazing. It was rumored that he was the head of the Jordanian mafia, and that is why he was asked to build the building for the Condonte Roma employees. For most of the six years I lived there, I saw almost daily "drug drops" from my kitchen window. I had become friends with the cook at the Chinese restaurant in town, and Egyptians who worked there. It was my favorite place, after Ali Baba's. Even King Abdullah liked going there to eat. But, in 2005, I was sad to see that the cook was also involved with the drug smuggling. It was so obvious. But, Aqaba is primarily an American zone! And, where America goes, so goes the drug "industry," prostitution, liquor, violent movies, and violent music, gambling, and the enslavement of the people.

This first landlord tried to seduce me one night. I was terrified. I pulled a whiny stunt, and he left. He made it hard on me in his final inspection of the apartment, trying to say I had damaged this and that – pointing out a few marks on the wall of the apartment. I burst into tears. He let me go. I had paid all my bills. But, I found out from my new landlord that he had tracked me down, and called him about the water bill – which I had paid. His second wife lived on the top floor with their four children. She was from Lebanon. We had become good friends. His first wife was somewhere else in Aqaba. He wanted another wife, but I was not interested.

I went to Jerusalem for Shavu'ot. It is my favorite time of year to be in Jerusalem. Then, since Elaine had invited me back to Wales in June, after returning from Jerusalem, I left right away for Wales. One of the first things I said upon arriving at her home was: "Is there any way to get to Milford Haven? I must go and do intercession over the Irish Sea." The next morning the phone rang. Elaine talked to someone. Then she came to me with a big smile on her face and said: "I was talking to some people who have a Messianic fellowship in Milford Haven. They want you to come speak."

Before going to their home, we found a little road going down towards the sea that was private. I put my feet in the water and began to call out the names of all the tribes of Ya'cob. As I did, the anointing of the Spirit came on me so strongly that I was doubled up in "travailing Intercession." This had not happened to me in many years. We drove around and found a private place for Elaine to blow the shofar over the sea. I got her picture. In taking it, I tried to avoid taking a picture of the big pile of rubbish behind her, but it was the only angle in which I could get her blowing the shofar and the sea. As we were leaving, I went to see what the rubbish was that got into the picture. It was a huge pile of tangled and rusted barbed wire. Here she was blowing the shofar for the deliverance of the House of Ephraim, and next to her is a prophetic picture of that deliverance. Awesome!

Then we went on to the meeting. There was a fine group there. But there was also a Messianic Jew and his Jewish wife there. I had spoken with them at Elaine's house the year before. We had touched base on the "safe houses" that are all over the U.K. for fleeing people. I let him know that they had to go outside the Straits of Gibraltar and around the horn of Africa, into the Red Sea, because the Jews would not be able to get into Israel at the time of fleeing--they'd have to go into the port of Aqaba, and then to Petra.

The Orthodox Jews in Jerusalem know where to flee when Jerusalem becomes "a cup of trembling." They know that they must flee out of Judea across the "eagle" in the topography of the Dead Sea onto the Jordan side and proceed to Petra, or come up through the Red Sea out of the nations. (**Zechariah 12:1-4; Revelation 12:14**) I talked to Noah Hutchings about this – about the House of Israel coming up the Red Sea – as per **Micah 2:12-13**. Noah was so excited that he interviewed me via phone for his next Southwest Radio Church radio broadcast.

I found out later, that the dad in the family up the two hills in Aqaba, and his oldest son, had gone to Colorado to be with his dad who was dying. While there, someone gave him a cassette tape of someone talking about Petra. On the way back, they got a ship out of Greece into Haifa. He was bored, so he got the tape and went down into the ship's hole to his van and listened to the tape. It was ME! It was the interview I did with Noah Hutchings. I established a phone and e-mail relationship with Noah, a grand old man who has been reporting on the end times since the 40s.

He was coming into Aqaba the following year and wanted to meet me, but I sadly told him I was leaving for the U.S. just before he would arrive. That was his last tour of Petra, but through the interview he understood that His people would be fleeing into Petra via Aqaba also, up the King's Highway.

Back to Milford Haven: That night, Abba wanted me to talk about the restoration of all the tribes of Ya'cob back to the land-- there are 224 passages of Scripture about it. The people were so excited. I told them about their ancestry as Welsh people, in the tribes of Simeon and Levi, and others. The Messianic Jew folded his arms across his fat belly and glared at me. His wife sat to my right. I didn't know why he was glaring, until I stopped teaching. The people were so full of joy to know that they were the sons of Ya'cob, NOT GENTILES! I showed them how no one in Messiah is called a "gentile", how Elohim never made any covenant with gentiles, how He says He will destroy all gentiles. I spoke on the House of Israel – the not-lost-anymore ten tribes. I was exhausted by the time I finished.

After I spoke, the people were so happy. Then the Messianic Jew motioned to his wife to read a verse in Ephesians 2--ONE VERSE, taken out of context! He twisted the meaning, to "prove" that everything I said was false. My mind went blank. The people sighed and became silent. Because this man was a friend of our host and hostess, he was respected. One man said in despair: "I guess we're gentiles, then, so what do we do?" He destroyed their joy and their hope. Then he proceeded to sneer at me in mockery. I asked him if he had ever been to Israel. He grunted a disgusted grunt, and said "NO! I have no interest in going to Israel." I lost those friends because they thought he, a friend of theirs, was telling the truth and I wasn't.

This has happened to me so many times. The pride of Judah believes that there are only Jews and Gentiles in the world, and the Jews are exalted above the gentiles, even if the gentiles guard Torah. The Orthodox Jews go as far as to say that gentiles cannot guard Torah. So, I left both angry, and totally exhausted.

But, during that second time to Wales, I met so many more wonderful people. I spoke in Maureen's home in Swansea, and in the Bible College of Wales too. I was told upon arrival at that meeting that a lady had come who was with Operation Exodus. She was to lead the singing and then tell about her role as the head of the intercessors with Operation Exodus/Ebenezer before I spoke. I did not recognize her. But, on the way back to Elaine's house, she told me it was the lady who had usurped her plans for their Israel trip in 2003, and the very lady who was the head of intercession of Ebenezer who was so angry at me. I was shocked.

I wondered why she seemed so cold towards me. I had made a point of telling her how lovely her music was for our worship, but still she was cold towards me. Is this the nature of one who is born of the Spirit of Yahuweh? I think NOT!

Then I was invited to go back to the Rhondda to speak. Abba had given me the message "The Gospel of the Apostles." I argued with Him all the way to the meeting. This was a "replacement theology" church. On the way, we picked up a young man with long curly hair, who had been a rock star in Wales. Elaine had led him to salvation. He came with such a joyful smile. That was precious Howie, whom I would mentor in the Torah, and who would, to this day, be a very special friend.

At the church I sat down in the second row, waiting for the meeting to start. I was still arguing with Abba. I told Him I could not get up there and tell about the "Gospel of the Apostles," for their gospel including guarding the Torah. Elaine hid a surprise from me. I had met the new pastor. Then the meeting started.

This is so funny: He went behind the podium and asked everyone to stand for the singing of the Sha'ma. Someone blew a long shofar (which I found out later Elaine had given them), and they all sang "Sha'ma Israel." Then they started playing recorded Hebrew music for us to sing to, and several ladies came up and got flags with Hebrew words and symbols on them, and began twirling them. Elaine gave me a sideways grin. Surprise! Elaine had returned since I had spoken there the first time, and mentored them in the Torah.

The new pastor was making it a Messianic congregation, teaching them Hebrew roots. He had gone to Israel already twice. I apologized to Abba and then gave the message. Everyone took notes, and were very excited about it. I had even brought gifts from Israel to those whom I had met before. Along with Howie, Elaine had brought her close friend Leslie – the one whom I felt uneasy about the year before at her house. Leslie went to many places that Elaine and I went to. She and her husband went to Israel a lot, and she, like Elaine, had met many in the Christian-Messianic community. This is very common in America, the UK, Australia, and other westernized nations, to ADD OR MIX Jewish religious ways with their Christianity in their "love for Israel." After my initial week at the ICEJ festivities for Sukkot in 2000, I continued to go every year from 2001-2006. I went on all of Sondra Baras' Sukkot day-tours, through the ICEJ, and then on my own from 2002-2012. I met so many awesome people, and heard so many awesome speakers, and enjoyed the wonderful musical productions by Chuck King, of the King of Kings congregation.

But, as Abba began teaching me, I realized the phoniness of this mixture. This mixture had so many big-named teachers, prophets, and gurus, that the people could pick and choose what they wanted to do – how much Jewish stuff they wanted, and how much Christian stuff they wanted. I saw that several of the Orthodox Jewish rabbis who spoke there, talked just like Christians. Of course, that gave them invitations to America, where there was a lot of money to be had. Yes, I do think it is good that Christians are learning their Hebrew roots, but they are also getting false "Jewish" doctrine, causing some to deny Messiah and convert to Judaism!

My good friend Darlene, from Tennessee, belonged to a dance group that often went to perform at Sukkot in Israel. I remember watching them dance outside the Jaffa Gate. Then they went with Barry Seigal to dance around the walls of the old city. I was critical. Abba interrupted my criticism and said: "Ephraim is simply beginning to return home the best way they know how." I repented! Ephraim has to start somewhere. Darlene had a pure heart. She was one of the Ephraimites who was returning with praises to Yahuweh and Yahushua.

After returning from Wales, I enjoyed my roof top balcony. While sitting up there one morning, Abba flashed my birthday in New York with the India people in front of me. I had been asking Him for a long time why my husband was allowed to usurp my speaking time, when Abba had given me the message of salvation to bring. In a flash, He gave me the answer. He said that the authority to give His Word had been given to me, and it was my responsibility to make sure that it was given. I allowed my husband to usurp my chance to give the message of salvation to those wealthy people, members of the India Methodist Church, who were not born again. That was a shock. He had given me authority, and I had not used it to do as He wanted me to do. From then on, that kind of thing didn't happen again.

It was also on this roof that He said to me: "I want you to go to the Golan, to Katzrin, in November, and tell Lars and his wife (who were from Sweden and had a prayer ministry in Israel) about the fleeing out of the north of Israel." I was fine with that. I had been teaching about the fleeing out of the north of Israel, and about the worldwide fleeing to come. I knew that my good friend and leader of the group in New Braunfels, Texas, Constance, considered Lars to be her mentor. She also said she considered me to be her mentor, too.

Then a little later, Abba instructed me to go to Jerusalem before Sukkot in October. That was when I had a problem with His instructions. I had no money to go once, let alone twice. I was upset. WHY should I go in October, and why before Sukkot? But, I knew His voice.

Elaine was coming in November to meet with her Tiberias friends, and to join with her English friend Clare, and to go to Katzrin/the Golan for intercession. We were to go to visit Lars at the same time. Elaine and Constance had worked with Lars during a large prayer conference. After visiting Lars, Elaine wanted to go back to Jerash, and to Petra, and then come visit me in Aqaba. So, as it went, Elaine and I decided to go the whole trip together.

I was again a lollypop sucking Shirley Temple. I suppose I had not learned my lesson to keep my mouth shut. But, Constance was my friend. So, I told Constance about our trip in November to meet with HER mentor. Of course she knew Elaine too. So, she kept pestering me, and Elaine, to join us. I loved the lady, it's just that this was a special intercession trip, and it took a lot of understanding before making such a trip, besides needing a "word" from Father about going. Constance was very aggressive and controlling, and Elaine and I flowed together in the Spirit and did not need someone aggressive with us. Elaine agreed with me. I knew I had hurt Constance's feelings, but I have to be obedient to Abba. I can't allow tagalongs. I've suffered too much from tagalongs.

One week BEFORE Sukkot, I went to the Jaffa Gate Hostel to stay. I met with Maureen and Dennis, who were still happy love bugs. I met another lady from Wales who was their friend. It was a week of seemingly nothing but waiting on Abba. Maureen took me to meet Rebecca on Abraham Lincoln Street. She lived next door to the apartment of a lady who had a prayer ministry that they worked for. I stayed with Rebecca at times after that.

Just before Sukkot, a Jewish lady called Yehodit, whom I had met at Constance's fellowship in New Braunfels, invited me to stay with her. She had a lovely home in Maoz Ziyon. After staying with her, we kept in e-mail contact. She had told me, at Constance's house, that because no one listened to her talk about Israel, no one would listen to me either. She said her son in Texas had written a book about Israel, and she hoped people would listen to him. At one of our meetings, she openly mocked me in front of everyone, which caused some raised eyebrows. She steadily grew more angry when she found out that people were listening to me. She e-mailed me in Aqaba, asking how I could write so many articles. I told her that journalists, news reporters, scientists, educators, etc., wrote articles everyday, and no one asks them that question.

When I went to stay with her in October, she told me that none of what I was saying about the end times was true. Then she invited a good friend of hers over for dinner, who worked for Bridges for Peace, who also had his own blog site. She highly respected him. She told him some of the things I had said about the end times. To her shock, he agreed on every point. This upset her more. She was going to introduce me to another well-known Jewish couple in Israel, whom I had wanted to meet. They invited me to dinner. But, this lady e-mailed me that I would cause too much controversy at their home, so she didn't want me to meet them. She cancelled the dinner-meeting. Why did I stay with her? I don't know. One time she took me out walking in the woods, but she walked so fast, and I couldn't keep up with her. I fell and twisted my knee. I could hardly walk.

Enter Abba! This lady had invited a friend from Tiberias to join her for the opening of the ICEJ week of Sukkot at the newly excavated Siloam Springs. Natalie came, and we all had soup for dinner. While we were eating, I told Natalie that I lived in Aqaba. She asked me questions about Edom in general. Then she put down her spoon, and said: "I'm not going to the ICEJ; I'm staying here to talk to you."

So Yehodit went on to the ICEJ and Natalie and I began talking. She said that her Bible study leader in Tiberias had been teaching on Edom and Petra, but none of them had been there. She picked up her phone and dialed Miri's number. I heard her say my name, and then I heard Miri scream "Yedidah!" Natalie gave me the phone. I had never talked to her before. I didn't know her. I didn't know that she and Elaine were good friends, or that Natalie and Elaine were good friends. Miri told me that the Holy Spirit had told her that day to get hold of Yedidah in Jerusalem. She had heard my name, and knew I lived in Aqaba, but that's all. She had called blond Maureen to find out if she knew where I was. Maureen didn't know, but knew I was still in Jerusalem. So Abba had orchestrated the whole week to set me up to meet Miri. Miri invited me to teach her combined Bible studies in November. This was early October.

Constance, and a friend in her group, Judy, came to stay at Yehodit's house, during Sukkot. I was to leave the next day and return to Aqaba. After Sukkot, they were coming to my apartment in Aqaba, and I was going to host them, and take them to Petra. In the meantime, Constance invited three other ladies to come join them. I did not know these ladies. And, it was Ramadan.

There were hardly any taxis on the streets at night, and they wanted to meet me at Ali Baba's for dinner. I told them it would take two taxis for the seven of us. I knew it would be hard to find any transportation. We could walk it, but they would have their luggage with them. I told her to tell the ladies that I also didn't

PART VI - The Middle East & Travels Beyond

have enough room for them. They'd be on the floor with no bedding. But, instead of saying "I'm sorry," Constance was very angry at me. But, she told the ladies what I said, and they said they'd come over at another time. I was most upset at her presuming on me, inviting people to come without asking me. I didn't have enough money for food for all of them either. But, these were affluent ladies, so what did they care? Constance and Judy came earlier in the day, got a taxi to my apartment, and by sunset we were sitting on the roof-balcony enjoying the cool air, and the awesome sights. I fixed them dinner.

When the sun begins to set over the Midian Mountains, they turn pink, then purple. There is such a beauty about that wilderness area up by the King's Highway. The mountains of the Sinai Peninsula also turn a gorgeous color at sunset, just beyond Eilat. Then the planes started coming over, and they just loved it.

How was I to know that Constance had begun seething against me because I had crossed her will in not letting those lady's come over with them? How was I to know that Constance was really seething because she was not invited to go with Elaine and I to Lars' ministry at Katzrin? We made a trip to Petra and stayed the night at the Edom Hotel. The next morning after breakfast, my faithful taxi man came back to pick us up and take us to Aqaba. He took them to the Israeli border.

In November, I went to Tiberias and joined Elaine, Miri, Natalie, and their combined groups and taught them about Edom, Aqaba, and Petra.

Miri had told me about her daughter's profound dream she had about Petra. None of them had been there. These people were from Morningstar congregation in Tiberias. The pastor's wife came. I asked Miri's daughter to tell her dream. It was about her being in a cave with all necessities provided. She said that she saw planes coming over, trying to bomb them, but when the bombs dropped out of the plane, they went shooting to the east and west and could not fall down on them. She described Petra well, especially Little Petra. Then she turned to me and said: "Why couldn't the bombs drop on us?" I had all the answers about Petra except that one. I turned to her to tell her "I don't know", and out of my mouth came "**Job 1**." I was surprised, but proceeded to give her what He was showing me: Satan had to ask permission of Yahuweh to touch Job (Iyob), who just so happened to live around Little Petra – land of "Uz." In other words, Satan can do nothing unless Yahuweh allows him to. Satan has told his human agents that they can bomb the world, but they cannot touch Petra. This is why the world's elite will hide out in Petra

(**Revelation 6:12-17**). I've seen their preparations--quite elaborate.

Then others began raising their hands, including the pastor's wife, to tell their dreams. All the dreams were about the same, describing Petra as I knew it. So everyone was very excited. A few years before, I had gone to meet the lady who ordained me in Burleson, Texas, so that we could go to a conference together. As she hugged me, she said that she had a dream 18 years before that she was in Petra, and then the resurrection occurred and she saw herself rising to go be with Jesus. I bought her the video by Noah Hutchings that showed Petra. I sat with her as she watched it. She kept crying and pointing to the Siq and to the caves, saying that she saw those things in her dream. She was perhaps in her early to mid-60s then.

The people in the meeting were poor like me. But, after the meeting Miri brought me an envelope with offering money in it. She looked overwhelmed. She said that she had never seen them give so much. It was exactly the amount I needed to pay for my stay in Katzrin and go with Elaine and Clare on our journey through north Jordan, back to Aqaba. ABBA KNEW!

He tells us to do the most mind-blowing things some times, but when we do them, he opens up hidden doors of provision and of mo'edim, leading to more assignments.

The next day, Miri and Natalie fixed a nice lunch for Elaine and I. Miri asked me if the church was the "Bride of Messiah." I answered: "No, the Bride is a special remnant within the assembly of Messiah." I saw her look in shock at Natalie. She had never heard anyone say that, but she knew it was true. In Israel, May 2013, Miri and I were having dinner together, and she reminded me of that, as we discussed what Abba was showing us about the Bride of Messiah.

Before Elaine, and I, went across by bus to Katzrin, Miri, and a couple of others, laid hands on us to commission us as going for them to prepare the way for them in the days of fleeing ahead. That was so humbling to me. I really took that as a sign that Judah, in blessing Ephraim, was a small picture of His uniting of the two Houses of Ya'cob back together in His hand – a strong sign of these last days!

Miri has visited me in Florida a couple of times since. But, I always see her when I return to Israel. Our relationship grew from that point upward. Miri remained a loyal friend.

We met with Lars and his wife. Then Clare joined us in Katzrin. Lars, and a man who was a guest at his facility, took us to Banias, to Mount Hermon, and along the East Golan. It was my first trip there. I did intercession over the borders with Lebanon and Syria, for the first time. I had been doing intercession over the Red Sea, and the border of Jordan and Israel, but not there.

Then the three of us crossed into Israel at Bet She'an. We got a taxi to take us to Irbid, where we stayed at the Al Joude Hotel. It was a good decent place. Through the hotel, we hired an awesome taxi driver. We split the very reasonable fare, and for three days he took us to the most amazing places where we did intercession. He took us first to the ruins of Pela, where it is said that the believers fled from Titus in 70 CE.

The next day he took us to Gadara, where I had gone for my 51st spiritual birthday. We did much intercession around the town, and were there about six hours. As we came back out towards the town, several armored cars full of Jordanian military men drove up to the front of the museum, right where we were standing. With them was a limousine. One opened the door of the limousine, and a handsome young man got out. Jordanian officials warmly gave him the "holy kiss" of the Middle Eastern men. We just stood there and watched. They were within a few feet of us, but acted like we were not there. How did we know we were front row spectators of a secret meeting?

The next day, while in Irbid, our driver took us to the border of Jordan and Israel by the Yarmuk River, across from the Golan Heights. There is just a fence separating Jordan from Israel there. Later I would do intercession with Miri, and Maureen and Dennis, on the Israeli side, at the base of the Golan. Only a small area separates Gilead (north Jordan) from the Golan Heights of Israel. After we finished our intercession there, the taxi man was noticing we liked to go to borders. Even Pela was on the border of Jordan and the "west bank" of Israel. He said: "There is one more border I want to take you to." He drove us out into a deserted area. He pulled up at an iron cattle-crossing, on a dirt road. To our right was a small guard-shack.

Standing next to it were two Jordanian soldiers, with big guns. They were smiling. We got out to take pictures of the shepherd and his flock of sheep on the other side of the iron barrier. The soldiers said we could take pictures, but not of them. It was the border of Jordan with Syria. On the Israeli side there are "Danger! Danger!" signs approaching that border, telling people to turn back. But, on the Jordanian side, it was quite different. Then, our driver took us back to our hotel in Irbid.

I had told Elaine and Clare that I had to get to Tishbe, where Elijah grew up. (**II Kings 17:1**) The next day we were to go to Amman. On the way, this same driver took us along the Jordan border with Israel to the top of a mountain. The road was very steep. Up there was Tishbe--Listib in Arabic. He took us to the church just above Listib where tourists go. It was on that mountain, that I loudly called out "Yahweh" three times, facing the valley running deep below the mountain, and each time His Name left my lips, thunder crashed and rolled down the valley. That really shocked Elaine and Clare! Then our driver took us to Amman, and to the Geneva Hotel.

At the hotel, I saw a newspaper in Arabic with the picture of the young man we had seen in Gadara. I took it to the front desk to find out who he was. I learned he was the Crown Prince of Abu Dhabi. The man who told me this acted so proud that he would visit Jordan.

The next morning, I got a bus back to Aqaba. They stayed at the Geneva Hotel. Then, they went to Jerash and on to Petra. After Petra, they came to Aqaba, to stay with me for the night before crossing back over to Israel. We sat on my roof top balcony sharing adventures. I liked Clare. She was a dancer, and a friend of some of my friends in Israel. But, she made the trip very uncomfortable for me because she kept singling out Elaine and only talking to her, not looking at me at all during a conversation. It got so bad, that at Gadara, I just left them and went walking on my own. At least neither were offended by me going off on my own. It's good that I don't have a rejection complex!

After they left, I opened the computer to catch up on e-mails. I got an e-mail from Constance. She had previously invited me to come to a lady's "Tea" at her house when I got back to the states. So, I figured she was going to tell me when to come. Was I ever shocked! Her e-mail said that I was no longer welcome in her house, and that I am not invited to her "Tea." Talk about childish! She said that I had told her about aliens on the moon, and other crazy stuff, so she thought I was unfit to teach her group anymore. She told her group that they were to have nothing more to do with me because I was teaching crazy things. I tried to communicate with her after that, until finally her husband told me politely, and gently, to stop.

The thing about the aliens on the moon: I had told her about my daughter and I in 2004, going to Jason's Deli for lunch, about how President George W. Bush came on the T.V. at noon, and made a 20-minute speech that American youth should prepare to colonize the moon and Mars. Everyone in the Deli heard the speech. Later, I was reading a book by Steve Quayle, and he talked about that speech in 2004. I was just reporting information. She knew that. She never questioned me until I rejected the situation with Lars. At the bottom of the e-mail, she added a P.S.: "Just so you'll know, I AM NOT JEALOUS!"

But, what grieved me most was that there were wonderful people in her group who were so hungry for truth. They loved me so much. A few days later, I got an e-mail from Judy, saying "take me off your address list." That broke my heart because I loved that lady.

In 2011, during my stay in Black Mountain, N.C., at the home of a friend, a lady came to visit who looked familiar. It was Judy. My friend in Black Mountain had told her I was coming, and she wanted to see me. We were re-united. In 2011 during Sukkot, Judy and her husband came, and joined us on a tour with Sondra Baras. That was Abba!

Sitting on my roof top balcony, after Elaine and Clare left, He spoke to me: **"You are a gatekeeper."** I, then, did endless hours of research on the gatekeeper, listing every Scripture in the Bible on the words "gate," "portal," "door," and "border." I research everything I can to learn what He is saying to me. I found over 100 Scriptures on the subject.

The year before, He gave me **Isaiah 28:5-6**, which I shared with the group. Even the husband of the leader-lady was interested, for it, and other Scriptures I gave, showed our purpose for being in Aqaba – to be gatekeepers. **"In that day, Yahuweh of hosts is a crown of splendor and a head-dress of comeliness to the remnant of His people, and a spirit of right-ruling to him who sits in right-ruling, and strength to those who turn back the battle at the gate."**

Beginning in 1999, I have been doing intercession over gates (ports, borders, doors of entrance and exit) in many places around the world. It took me three years (2006-2009) to do intercession all around the Gulf, up the rivers of Texas, over rivers within the U.S., and clear up into Alaska, to prepare the way for the great world fleeing to come. He has taken me to many countries to do intercession, as well as many places in Israel. In 2010, He sent me to bring the end-time message of Yahuweh, via Enoch, to seven strategic places of the enemy's strongholds from ancient times.

In June 2011, He took me to the Outer Hebrides--a place where the House of Ephraim amassed to sail to the "new world" after their dispersion in 722 BCE. In August 2011, He took me to Iceland. [Please refer to: The Iceland Report for that exciting adventure in timing.] In 2012, during the time of the Olympics in London, He sent me to Rome, back to Patmos, and to Delphi, Greece. [Refer to: "The Declaration Assignment"]

JORDAN
(2006)

I returned to the U.S. for a couple of months, before returning to Jordan. Then I crossed the border to go to Jerusalem for Passover, and Shavu'ot. I stayed both times with a lady whom I had come to know. She had been an actress, so I will refer to her as "Actress Lady." She was so happy to have me stay with her. She thought I'd be her buddy, and we'd do everything together. She had daily cared for her mother until she died. She told a dear friend of mine that it was like having her mother back with her, even though she and I are the same age. She did not understand my calling, and so was upset at me because I couldn't submit my life to her whims. She went shopping for hours, almost daily. She expected me to go with her. She was redecorating her apartment, and said I was her inspiration to do so. Only a few days passed before I realized I was a prisoner of her will. This led to friction later on in 2007 that was devastating.

During Shavu'ot, Abba gave me a special assignment for my summer in America. He said: "**I want you to go on three trips to the four main river mouths of the Gulf of Mexico, to do intercession for the House of Ya'cob. You must finish by the end of June**."

I returned to America in early June. But, before going, I began my preparations for the first of the three trips, to the mouth of the Trinity River at Anahuac, (alligator capital of Texas), then to Galveston Island, and a trip down the Houston shipping canal. I knew that Mary in Pine Hills knew that area well. She had lived in Galveston. I asked her to go with me. She was very excited about the trip. I also asked Laura to go too. In doing intercession, I only allow 1-2 to go with me, and I have very strict rules. With Laura's very verbal disdain of Jews, not only in Israel, but Jews in Florida, I probably should not have asked her to come, but she was my transportation. Our task was to prepare the way for the fleeing of His remnant, through proclamation of His will for all the House of Ya'cob from America, as per **Micah 2:12-13, Jeremiah 16:14-16, Jeremiah 31**, and **Zechariah 8:20-23**.

Abba gave me a list of Scriptures to declare, which I wrote out on one page. I gave both Mary and Laura a copy. I have used these same Scriptures during many intercession trips. In all my intercession assignments, He has given me the background, and the Scriptures, so that I went into the assignments with full knowledge of what I was to do--why, where, when, and how.

We went to many areas where there were fishermen, but I noticed there were few fishermen--symbolic of the time of the fishermen coming to an end, for we are now inside the time of "the hunters." (**Jeremiah 16:14-16**) I cannot go into detail about all my intercession trips from this point on, because each trip would take many pages. So, I will be as brief as possible.

FIRST TRIP

We went directly to the area of Anahuac, pronounced "ANA WHACK." At Anahuac, I remember walking along the wooden planks out to the sea, and seeing lots of alligators rise to the surface upon hearing our footsteps. Anahuac was called "the alligator capitol of Texas." How did I know that by the end of the year, I would be living in alligator land--Florida? In 2012, my son and his new wife moved to Florida. The house backs up to a lake. Not long after moving in, they saw their own lake alligator taking a sun bath on their lawn. They named him "Fred."

Mary, Laura, and I, went to several places from Anahuac to do intercession along the Trinity River. Those river mouths are gigantic! Then we went all the way down to the tip of the Mainland peninsula across from Galveston Island. We took the ferry across the bay. On Galveston Island we went to several beach areas to do intercession. Then we went into Houston. I wanted to do intercession down the Houston shipping channel. We found that we could take a free tour, so we did. As we were on the boat, we did a lot of intercession along that channel. For I knew, and it was confirmed later, the Houston shipping channel is the main area of escape out of America for His people, especially for the Jews. This had been planned since the 1960s. I tell about that a little further down.

I had a world map that I used as I taught on these things in East Texas. He showed me the path of escape for the Jews, all the way from the north of America to the Gulf of Mexico. The main path from the Northeast to the Gulf is right through East Texas. All during this trip, Angie kept calling Mary. Angie's daughter-in-law was about to have a baby, but there were complications, and the baby was turned sideways. She kept calling Mary for advice, and prayer. Mary told her that her son had the authority to lay his hands on his wife's belly, and command the baby to turn. Angie told this to her son, and he did that. The baby turned downward. Through all of it, Angie saw the hand of Abba, and hungered to know more about His power and love.

SECOND TRIP

I asked my dear friend Lori, from Fort Worth, to go with me. She, and her husband, Norman, were good friends who attended Emmanuel Christian Fellowship. She was going to drive Norman's truck. But, in the meantime, Houston was flooded and the rains did not appear to be stopping. The day before we were to leave, the weather channel said that there would be more flooding in

Houston. So, Norman questioned the sanity of our going. But, Abba had told me when to go. It was mid-June. I told Lori to tell Norman that Abba said to go. Abba had said that we would have sunshine, and blue skies with white fluffy clouds. That became a customary confession on other trips too. He never failed! The next morning, the morning we were to leave, I turned on weather news at 6:00 AM, and the weather lady said something like this: "WE DON'T KNOW WHAT HAPPENED BUT, the rain has stopped, and the flooding had stopped, and the streets of Houston are clear." So we went. We went first to Galveston Island to do more intercession, since it is through that shipping channel that Jewish-owned ships, and others, will be taking many of Abba's people out of America.

The next morning we went on to Freeport to the mouth of the Brazos River. That mouth is gigantic too! Lori had never been on an intercession trip before. We found remote beaches to go to. Lori would stand out in the water to do the intercession. Abba gave her visions. She saw little ships and boats taking people out to the ocean liners. That started me praying over little boat and yacht areas. Then I found out that there are fishermen with boats off of Bradenton, Tampa, and St. Pete, Florida, who are ready to take people out when disaster comes—people who know about the great fleeing to come.

I had prayed our way through all the rain and flooding, and Abba had cleared our way. But, the next day, when we went to leave through Houston, the heavens opened up. We were in rush-hour evening traffic coming out of Houston. We could hardly see the cars around us--we were in a giant traffic jam. It took us two hours to get out of there, but amazingly no one honked at anyone – everyone was patient.

THIRD TRIP

I had asked my friend Ladell from Fort Worth to go with me. She had one daughter who was in her 30s, who had been brain damaged from birth and had to be carried and fed like a baby. But, she was a very sweet girl. Ladell had to take her. Her husband had a job that kept him traveling a lot. I did not mind the girl at all--she was so quiet and good. Ladell pushed her around in a wheelchair. We put 1,000 miles on her van. We went all the way to Matagorda Bay at the mouth of the Colorado River. Gigantic mouth!

At Matagorda there is a peninsula that comes off the mainland, so we went down there to do the intercession, then to the mouth of the Colorado River. We had to drive around a ways to find the mouth of it, but finally down a little street of a fishing village, we found it. Ladell could blow three long shofars at the same time. She had brought two that she blew at the same time.

We went to fishing piers in different places. Upon getting out of the van at one pier, I looked down and there was a piece of a palm branch – split into two parts at the top. I still have it – showing that the two Houses of Ya'cob (Jacob) will be one in His Hand (**Ezekiel 37:15-28**). As I said, almost all of the intercession He has given me has had to do with the restoring of a humble, repentant remnant of the House of Israel from the nations – a major theme in the Word. [Refer to the Scripture list in "Aliyah Scriptures"/February 9, 2007]

We then tried to find the mouth of the Guadalupe River. But, we finally realized that the mouth did not flow into the Gulf at a place where we could get to. It was concealed in thick underbrush. Ladell drove down a long dirt road to find the river mouth, but we came upon wild hogs and stray cattle. It was eerie.

Finally, after lots of driving, we found that we could get close to the Guadalupe River. But, the road we were on ended at a couple's house. Ladell pulled up in their front yard and honked the horn. The man was outside, so he came over to see what we wanted. We told him that we wanted to blow our horns towards the Guadalupe River and pray. He said that was fine. So, standing on some grass near their house, Ladell blew two shofars at one time--our "horns." The river was in view, but a ways away through much underbrush. As she blew the "horn," the wife came out of the house. We did our proclamations, thanked them, and left. They acted like they liked us, and didn't think we were strange – at least they did not act like they thought we were strange. They were Texans, and for people to pray is natural in Texas. That was June 28th. We had two days before my time-limit was up. We got back to Fort Worth on the 29th. **MISSION ACCOMPLISHED**!

From July 27th to 30th I went to Mississippi and Alabama. I had been invited by a Messianic Rabbi to hold three meetings over that weekend at his congregation in Grand Bay, Alabama. I flew into the Gulfport/Biloxi airport. Barry and Donna picked me up and we went on a sight-seeing intercession trip, beginning with the Port at Gulfport. I saw the devastation of the area from Hurricane Katrina. Several in their congregation were still living in FEMA trailers. Barry blew the shofar over many places along the way. Then he took me to meet the lady who was to host me, who lived on Dauphin Island. We went to Fort Gaines, where we did more intercession.

Dauphin Island is at the mouth of Mobile Bay. I could see several oil rigs from there. We went down to the tip of Dauphin

Island. Then Barry and Donna took my hostess and I to meet with Rabbi James at a restaurant near his home. Almost immediately the rabbi and I clashed over what to do on Yom Kippur. He was very religiously Jewish, and I certainly was not. I went back to the home of the lady on Dauphin Island. She had just recently come into the Messianic movement. She and I had such a wonderful time. She took me to the meetings.

The rabbi had contacted a couple in New Orleans, to come hear me. They were going to a convention to hear Monte Judah. But, Abba instructed both Susan and Bob to come hear me instead. They came all the way from north of New Orleans to hear me. After the meeting, without conferring with each other, they both came to me at different times to invite me to speak at the opening of their Sukkot at a campground above New Orleans. I knew I was to go to their Sukkot. The rabbi invited me back as the main speaker for his week of Sukkot, after I went to Louisiana. So, I accepted both invitations. I went back one more time to stay with the lady on Dauphin Island. We returned to Fort Gaines to do more intercession.

Then on July 30th, I flew to the Dallas/Fort Worth Airport (DFW). (Read about my losing my wallet in the Dallas airport, and the absolute miracle Abba did for me, in the Collections).

Before I went to Mississippi/Alabama, back in Texas, Tim had previously invited me to speak twice at their big Sukkot at Murray Lake, Oklahoma. I would be a speaker along with Brad Scott and Bill Cloud. I was flattered. But, when I told him I had accepted an invitation to speak in Louisiana and could not go to Murray Lake, he was hurt. I tried to explain, but he did not understand. I felt so bad. He had brought me into his inner circle, which was an important one. They had trusted me and loved me, and here I was turning down this prestigious invitation to go to Oklahoma. How could I have known what was ahead? I should have spoken in Louisiana, and then gone right up to Murray Lake. All Abba had told me was that I was to accept the invitation to join Susan and Bob at their Sukkot. (More on this story later)

I returned to East Texas several times. The congregations always came together when I came to speak. I stayed with Mary and Larry but also with Tim and Angie, Jamia and Mark. I had more new moon meetings with Jamia and Mark, who lived in Tyler. I also had more meetings in the Fort Worth/Mid-Cities area.

In traveling along rivers in different states, I noticed that along all of these rivers was much undergrowth where people could hide from helicopters. In 1978, I had a dream of hiding in the forest area of North Carolina, with helicopters flying everywhere trying to find people. Today, helicopters are equipped with heat-sensor

PART VI - The Middle East & Travels Beyond

technology, so it would be hard to hide anywhere. That is why Abba warns over and over for His people to flee out of America. He's been warning us in the Scriptures for 2,500 years. But, He will protect those who fear Him and who guard His Torah, as He says throughout the Word.

In one meeting at this time, I began showing the groups in East Texas a map of the world. From this map, it is easy to see the main exit ports out of each nation that borders a sea or exiting river that flowed into a sea. It is easy to see how all nations could send ships into the Red Sea into the Port of Aqaba. In 2002, the U.N. named Aqaba as the only open international port for refugees, and for disaster and famine relief. It has been prepared by The World Food Bank since 1963.

I had a large combined meeting in East Texas, in which I talked about this. About 20 minutes after the meeting started, a man came and sat down among the Texas-dressed Texans, wearing a suit and tie. His wife was also nicely dressed. He sat there chomping on his gum, with arms folded. After the meeting, I asked if anyone had questions. If so, they were to come up and use my microphone. I had a severe deafness in my left ear. I later found out that an earplug had become lodged in my ear. One day while praying for it to come out, it just popped to the surface of my ear and I took it out.

This man came up, took the microphone and said: "I have Jewish friends in Wisconsin. I am going to tell them what you said. They have been looking for an exit route out of America, because they know that the Jews will have to flee out." He went on to say that his Jewish friends had checked the Atlantic as an escape route, and it was way too rough. (Yet, the leader-lady in Aqaba had been telling everyone to flee over the Atlantic to her island off of Scotland. I knew that was very wrong.) He said they checked going into Canada, and there were problems with that. They checked going down a river, but they were in a land-locked area.

During that next week, a precious congregation elder, Jim Rector, died. He had suffered a long time from cancer. When I met him he could hardly talk. Cathy, who first invited me to East Texas, told me that Jim had died. He was a dear friend of hers. She said he was to be buried in Arkansas. I thought my meeting that was scheduled for the next weekend would be cancelled. But, she said: "No." She said that Jim was so excited about my coming to his congregation, and he would have wanted me to come. How precious! He was a great man, who had so much insight into these end times. He wrote profound articles on the end-times.

So, the whole of the East Texas assemblies gathered for this memorial service for Jim. Abba had given me Scripture and what to say in opening the memorial service. Then they danced to his favorite songs, like "It is Shabbat." We also had a wonderful feast, as usual. I had never done back-to-back meetings in East Texas because it took so long to drive there--four hours one way. But, I had to go. The couple from Wisconsin, Ken and his wife, were there too. Before the meeting started, Ken called me over. He was very excited. He told me that he had called his Jewish friends in Wisconsin, who were so perplexed about an escape route. He said he told them what I said. They told him they had not thought about the Houston shipping channel, but that they had Jewish friends who owned ships in the channel. So, they called one of their ship-owner friends, who gave them a message for me. Ken said that they said: "**Tell that lady she is right-on, we are ready to take our people out**." That thrilled me so much! More of Abba's confirmation!

From the late 1960s Jewish ship owners have been on stand-by, prepared to help Jews escape out of America. In the late 1960s, when President Johnson was in office, some Jews were fleeing Cuba, trying to get into the U.S. by boat, and he had turned them away. His wife, "Ladybird", Claudia Taylor, who was ½ Jewish, said: "NO! Those are my people." So Johnson let them in. The word went throughout Houston, and the prophecies flowed: "**As the Jews came into Houston, so they will go out of Houston.**"

While I was in the U.S., war broke out in Israel in June, 2006. A lady, Zeporah, whom I had met in Aqaba, who lived in Poriya, Israel, had given my articles to a lady at the Golani Junction. This lady, whom I would meet later in the winter, was the editor for Michael Rood's ministry. Connie read my articles in her bomb shelter. She had so many questions for me. I became like a mentor to her. We became good friends.

Also during this time, Miri, who was in the U.S. with her ministry, e-mailed me about what was happening in Tiberias. Her daughter and son-in-law were in her apartment. They said they hardly had time to eat a sandwich because the air raid sirens kept going off. I was in contact with Natalie, too. Natalie said that she was walking past her windows that faced the lake, and a rocket went past and shattered her windows. She had run to the bedroom. Zeporah told me about being in downtown Tiberias and ministering to the traumatized Jews between the air raid sirens going off. I heard from other ministries who were trying to help the soldiers. Tiberias was really attacked.

That summer, at another meeting at Jamia and Mark's house for Rosh Chodesh, Jamia gave me a bookmark with the picture of two Jewish people whom she had met--Glen and Bella. He was from South Africa, and she was from Russia. She was a psychologist who was helping traumatized children who were suffering from the attacks of the Arabs. They also had a ministry that helped Ukrainian Jews back to Israel – "The Ships of Tarshish." Jamia told me that they had come to the U.S. to find boats and ships to take the people out when the time of fleeing came. I was so excited. I took the bookmark and told her that when I reached Jordan, I would try to meet with them.

I knew I had to get to Alaska. But, at this time, I was still man-bound for security to a small degree. I felt I had to have a contact to stay with. Also, hotels were expensive. So I checked to see if there was a Messianic Congregation near Anchorage. There was not. But, about 1½ hour's drive from Anchorage, there was a congregation in the country home of Rabbi James and Mary McIntosh, near Wasilla. They were associated with the assemblies started by Angus and Batya Wooten--the MIA.

On September 13, 2006, I arrived a little after noon at Ted Stevens International Airport. This airport is the 4th largest cargo airport in the world. It is called "the air crossroads of the world." They were there to pick me up and took me to their home. Wasilla was near Houston, Alaska. I kept interlocking with "Houston." Fascinating that in the 1970s there were people in Nome, Alaska, who were preparing for the Jews who would flee out of Russia across the Bering Strait and come through Nome on their way south. I found out that they had prepared buses all along the way to HOUSTON, Texas.

When I was doing intercession over the mouth of the Trinity River with Mary and Laura, we were just north of NOME, Texas. Texas names got so interlocked with Alaska names it took 15 pages for me to journal it. I stayed with the rabbi and his wife. Their son, Jim, lived nearby. They told me there were only three Messianic congregations in Alaska and one had converted to Judaism. I asked them if they knew about the fleeing of Jews across the Bering Strait. They said: "No." I asked them if there were Jews in Alaska, and he said: "About 4,000." I asked them if they prayed for the salvation of the Jews and did anything about reaching them for Messiah. He said: "No." I told them why I was there: To do intercession for both Houses, but primarily for the Jews who would be fleeing across the Bering Strait from Kamchatka, Russia, through Nome and down. They thought I was crazy--wasting my time on such foolishness. But, they had offered to take me to Anchorage, and they did.

Because of my fear of not having a place to stay, and thinking the hotels were too expensive in Anchorage, after checking rates online, I did not obey Abba. He told me to go in August. I went in September, because this couple would not be returning to their home until September. I learned later that Anchorage had nice hotels for low fees. Because I did not go when Abba told me to go, the day we went to Anchorage it was cold and rainy. They let me off at the tourist bureau and from there I walked for 2 hours around the port area, praying, watching, learning, and taking pictures. Then they picked me up and took me to a place along the Knik River just above where it emptied into the Cook Inlet and the Gompertz Channel that eventually flowed to the Pacific Ocean. From the point that reached out into the River, I could see four different types of cargo and private transportation--car/truck, train, plane, and ship/boat. Just north of the point was Elmendorf Air Force Base.

I had them stop along a point south of Elmendorf Airforce Base. (In 2010 it became Elmendorf-Richardson Airforce Base). Further south was Ted Stevens Airport. At one time, a person could fly to Israel quickly over the North Pole from that airport. I prayed that those flights would resume as needed. Just behind me, as I faced the Knik River, was the train depot. In front of me were ships and boats of all types that carried cargo from the Pacific Ocean up-river to Anchorage. Near there, also, was one of the few highways that ran from Alaska down into the main U.S. It was a major truck route. While I did the intercession, the rabbi read a newspaper. His wife just sat there staring out the window.

This might seem insignificant to you, but it was not insignificant to me. In Petra, I saw a stone that was broken open. In the middle of it, naturally as part of the stone, was the Hebrew letter "ayin", representing the eyes of Elohim over His people. Later along the Red Sea, I found coral shaped exactly like the ayin. I had collected six samples of rocks and coral that had the ayin shape naturally. As I turned to go back to the car, seeing all the very unusual stones on that point, I thought to myself, "I wonder if I will see my seventh ayin?" I looked down and saw a stone that had unusual markings on it, so I put it in my pocket. I got back to the car and looked at it. On the stone was etched a perfect ayin, as part of the rock.

I got back to their home, and asked Abba: "Did I do any good coming here?" He gave me a vision. I saw a door that had formerly been closed, open just a little. He said: "**You have opened the door. Now, I can go through it**." True, Scriptural intercession is about opening a door/portal for Yahuweh to be able to come into our realm to accomplish His will.

Tim and Angie had good friends, family too, I think, who lived at the tip of a peninsula that jetted out into the Pacific. I called them, and we had a nice talk. They invited me to come visit them. The next day, being a beautiful Shabbat morning, I walked along the path by their home in the country and prayed. Later, I attended their Shabbat meeting. Wow was it boring--very formal and ritualistic. During the week the rabbi played Sudoku, and she played Bridge on the computer. I had no fellowship.

We did spend a day having lunch and shopping in Wasilla. That was great. We stopped for lunch and did a little shopping in the nearest town to them. The next day they took me back to Anchorage to the airport. But, as we neared Anchorage, since we were early, I asked if we could park north of the airport along the river, so that I could do some last intercession closer to the Pacific. So, they found a spot for me. But, they read the newspaper while I did the intercession.

I had stayed with them a week. I thanked them at the airport, and that was that. I know now that if I had gone as Abba said, by myself in August, I could have gotten a room near the river for about $59.00 a night, and done the intercession, and been gone about 4 days sooner. But, the job was done.

In early October I returned to Gulfport/Biloxi. Barry and Donna picked me up, and I stayed with them a few days. Then they took me to Dauphin Island to be with my friend again, the hostess lady. On October 5th, she and I took a car ferry across to the other side of Mobile Bay to Fort Morgan. We saw a lot of oil rigs on our way to Fort Morgan. Once there, we took a ride around the area. We went to a bay known as "Safe Harbor." There we did more intercession for the fleeing remnant.

On October 6th, she took me to Louisiana to meet with Susan and Bob. I spoke at the opening of their Sukkot that night. After the meeting, I met a lady named Tina and her friend Linda. By this time I knew we were moving to Florida in November. So, Tina said she would get some groups together for me to teach.

The next morning, October 7th, day one of Sukkot, the rabbi from Alabama came to get me to take me to their campground out in a remote area of Alabama. But before we left, he spoke at the morning session. It was so dry and boring, and so religious. I sat in another room and waited it out. On the way to the campground, about two hours drive, he stopped along the way to buy something. It was Shabbat. I reminded him that it was Shabbat, and he said: "Oh, I forgot." I began noticing things were not right. So often, outward religious practices are used to mask a person's true nature.

At the campground I was put in a tent that leaked, and the mattress deflated in the night. The rabbi and his wife, and Barry (his assistant rabbi) and Donna (his secretary), slept in a nice apartment overlooking the campground. I actually had to ask for food in the mornings. I went once to the apartment, and the rabbi's wife was watching TV. If they could not even observe Sukkot without wallowing in the world, they sure did not know Abba! Barry re-inflated my mattress. I stayed out where my friend from Dauphin Island had her tent--"outside the camp."

Then I taught the first meeting, and as Abba had instructed me for years, to begin each meeting, I had to drop a plumb line from a string, and read **Amos 7:7-8**. Well, that's all it took for hell to break out. I did not know that in my meeting was a practicing warlock, and women who were living in sin with their boyfriends. I did not know the sins of the rabbi and his sons. He had been skimming tithe money to give to his sons for gambling at the dog races. He had allowed one son to bring his pregnant girl friend to live at their house. In fact, his sons and their girlfriends were sleeping together in one of the front tents near the meeting area. He did all types of unscrupulous things for himself and his sons. He was a RAT. I confronted him in a private and righteous manner. He was very religious before his people, but his life was rebellious against purity and set-apartness to Yahuweh. I have found this to be so typical of many Messianic rabbis. What hurt so much was that Barry sided with his friend, the rabbi.

I often wonder about that check they gave me after speaking three times in that first weekend. They took collections every night. It was a large congregation. They said they would give me the money in one check at the end of my stay. They gave me a check for $500.00. I bet they took in a lot more money, and the rabbi kept some for himself.

After dropping that plumb line, which is typical about everywhere I drop it, things started happening. One woman came to me for council. She was going to marry a man who beat her up all the time. I told her not to do it. She went back to the camp and started screaming--telling everyone I had contradicted the counsel of the rabbi.

By the third day, walking back to my tent, Abba spoke to me about the rabbi: "**This is an Eli situation**." That evening, I called the rabbi aside and told him what Abba had said. He quickly moved his sons to the back of the camp. Barry called me to tell me how angry the rabbi was at me, and went on to say that I was wrong. I thought he and Donna were my good friends. I had so much fun staying at their home with them earlier. But, he sided with his rabbi buddy.

The next morning, one of the elders came to tell me that he and his wife had to take me to the airport, about 2 hours away, because the rabbi had paid $100.00 to change my flight, which went out at 4:00 PM. On the way to the airport, I found out that these two pure-of-heart people who had gotten mixed up with this rabbi, were ex-World Wide Church of God people. Ladell picked me up at the airport in Dallas. I should have gone to Murray Lake! But, I was so devastated inside, that I had her take me right to East Texas to a Sukkot that was organized by my friends Jamia and Mark. That whole situation was so humiliating! Kind Ladell said she would take me to East Texas any time I wanted to go. So, she became my new driver. She fit in very well with them. They blew their shofars, and she joined right in.

My son-in-law had taken a job in Florida. My daughter and I were sick about having to leave Texas. Now we know it was a blessing from Abba. But, it was traumatic for us at first. On the morning of the move, in November, my daughter went to grab the cat out of some shrubbery and ten yellow jackets stung her hand and arm. She was in agony, and we had to drive over 1,000 miles. The movers came. Then we left. I was with her in the front seat of her Jeep Cherokee, with my baby grandson in his car seat in the back. My son-in-law drove his truck with some of our things in the truck bed. We formed a caravan. The baby screamed a lot. I sat with him to feed him part of the time. How my daughter even drove in that much pain, I have no idea.

The movers would arrive with our things in 10-12 days. By the time we got into Louisiana, we realized we had entered a tropical storm. The rain was so intense that we could hardly see. I remember crossing Mobile Bay at Mobile, Alabama, and trying to take pictures, do intercession, and talk to my oldest daughter who had called at that moment. The storm went on all day. We stopped for the night, and tried to find a clinic for her. We finally found one that gave her a shot to stop the pain and itching.

The next day was sunny and lovely. We entered Florida, and began driving down I75. As we passed west of Ocala, where Linda lived, I thought I'd call Tina. She told me that in five days she had arranged for me to speak in three combined meetings and she'd pick me up. I was leaving for Dallas in 10 days, to return to Jordan. Just hearing of meetings arranged for me made me happy. Our furniture did not arrive until a couple of days before I was to return to Jordan.

I had not been to Florida since the 1970s, and did not know one person in Florida except Tina and Linda. But, by the time I left, I knew about 100. The meetings were excellent. I met so many who are friends. There was one lady whom they introduced who had just returned from Israel. She had worked in a soup kitchen on Jaffa Road. I bonded with her quickly – it was Launa. We had so many adventures doing intercession together, traveling to several states for my meetings, and then in Israel, traveling the Land. Because she took 15 of my articles to her missionary-friends in North Carolina, I gained good contacts, and later I found out that her missionary friends began guarding the Torah. It was through these missionaries that I got in contact with a family in Colombia, whom they had led to salvation. They began guarding Torah. This opened the door for me to go twice to Colombia.

This is what I mean by "daily flowing in His perfect timing." One thing leads to another, but telling Abba "no," even once, breaks the flow.

While in Florida, He told me to do two things. I obeyed, and two good things happened. First, as I was making my bed, He told me strongly, "Call the airlines right now!" I stopped what I was doing and called the airlines. They said they were so glad that I called. I had not given them a number to contact me in Florida. They said that my flight had been changed to several hours earlier. If I had not called, I would have missed my flight to Jordan. Oh the joys of obeying Yahuweh!

The second thing was that He spoke strongly to me, "Write Glen Haines" – the man of the couple on the bookmark Jamia had given me. I thought to myself: "He's going to think I'm crazy." But, I e-mailed him, telling him about the intercession that I had done for the exiting of the two Houses of Ya'cob. The next day, he e-mailed me back and said we had to talk in Jerusalem.

We had moved to Ellenton, not far from Bradenton. I noticed on a map of Florida that Ellenton was on the Manatee River. I thought: "Oh good, another river to do intercession over." In going to Walmart in Bradenton the first time, we crossed the Manatee River. I saw in the distance large container rigs. I blurted out: "It's a container port!" After living near the Port of Aqaba, which is a container port, and being at so many other container ports, I was still elated. I did not know at the time that this port was special. It is the closest U.S. port to the port of Panama, and the Panama Canal. They are actually considered "sister ports." This port also is the only port in the U.S. that is the teaching center for port safety. In 2009, I did intercession over the Panama Canal. In November of 2008, Launa and I took a tour of the Port of Manatee and did intercession.

I told my daughter I had to go to Anna Maria Island to do intercession before I left. I took her Jeep and spent about 5 hours there. Another day, I walked along the Manatee River in Bradenton and did more intercession.

I flew to Dallas, and stayed the night with Ladell. My daughter called from Florida, and asked me if I knew a lady named Barbara Brown. I said "no." She said: "Well she sure knows you--she wants to buy you a new computer." Dear Barbara! When I got back the next time from Jordan, she bought me a new computer, and later on she bought me a device that holds two teeth, to replace two teeth that were falling out of my mouth. How wonderful when others are led by the Spirit. I was not going to get new teeth until Abba told me what to do about it, and they were so far fallen out, that one was resting on my upper lip. Barbara called and told me that the Spirit had told her that she couldn't get her dental work done until she took care of me. That's an awesome story.

After returning to Jordan, in a few days I went to Jerusalem. I met with Glen and Bella on Ben Yehuda Street. The first thing I asked Glen was: "Where was the first place Abba sent you two, to find ships and boats to take the people out?" He said: "THE PORT OF MANATEE." I was stunned. I blurted out: "WE JUST MOVED THERE!" I found out that they had gone to many of the places I had gone to for intercession, including just below the river that flows from Anchorage! They had found boats, yachts, and ships, in St. Petersburg and Tampa. They had gone all around the Gulf of Mexico. Talk about a mo'ed! Abba always confirms!

I went to Tiberias in early December and stayed with Actress Lady through early January, 2007. Just after arriving, I called Connie. Her reaction was: "You don't sound like the lady who writes the articles." I assured her that I was just a normal human. On December 5th, my dear friend, Actress Lady and I took a trip from Tiberias to Jezre'el to the top of Mount Carmel. While up at the Carmelite Monastery, at the top of Mount Carmel, my dear friend took this picture of me facing the Jezre'el Valley. Off in the distance is Mount Tabor. The ancient ruins of Jezre'el, where Jezebel and Ahab, and Naboth lived, is south of Afula a few miles. It is very possible that Elijah was here (**I Kings 18:42-46**), because in front of me, directly across from where I am standing, I could clearly see the Mediterranean Sea. Read this passage of Scripture carefully for locations. After Elijah's servant saw the cloud the size of a man's hand, Elijah ran down to the Qishon River, which is just below this mountain, and all the way to Jezre'el - a straight shot east, then a tiny bit south to Jezre'el. I really believe this is the place!

I went to the Hanukkah party of my dear friend in 2006. It was so much fun! I was friends with many at Morningstar congregation. They had parties during Hanukkah, too.

On Christmas day, Actress Lady invited me to join her with a friend to watch old black and white Christmas movies from the 40s and 50s. I literally became sick inside. In fact, I panicked. I told her "No," which upset her. I told her I could not enter into paganism after Abba had delivered me. I didn't know what to do. I was emotionally failing. So, I called my new friend Connie and asked if she could come to Tiberias, because I needed to talk to someone that honored Torah.

Of course in Israel, December 25th is just another day. Connie stopped her editing work, got on the bus, and met me in town about an hour later. We sat on the steps of the Tiberias Archeological Park, and talked. She gave me courage that someone had listened and learned. She had to get back to her work, but it saved my day. Why I reacted like that I have no idea. Today, if that happened, I would have been grieved at my hostess had said, but not panicked. However, on December 31st, I was used to watching fireworks. She told me that no one shot off fireworks except perhaps some drunken Russians. I got up at midnight and looked over the lake. The moon was high in the sky. It was so peaceful. Then from down into Tiberias town came one big burst of fireworks. That was all. That was enough for me. I smiled and went back to bed.

I had asked Abba to see Mt. Hermon, but I was told that it was hidden until about January, then it could be seen. But, in December, I got up early to pray out on the balcony. It was about sunrise. I looked up, and saw the Hermon ridge clearly. Then, later in the day, I had come back from town to the apartment, and I saw that it was covered in snow. He softly said to me: "**It's the Bride's mountain**." "She" had her snow-white wedding dress on!

I later learned that it was on that ridge that the Covenant was cut between Yahuweh and Abraham. It was on that ridge that Messiah was transfigured with Elijah and Moses – the Groom's attendant, and the Bride's attendant. It was staying with Actress Lady during this time that I wrote the studies, "Mount Tabor and Mount Hermon," "Why Megiddo?" and "The Galilee and the Galileans." I returned to Aqaba shortly after January 1st.

JORDAN--ISRAEL--AMERICA
(2007)

This year, as had become the "usual" for my life, there was heartbreak that led to freedom! I had been in Aqaba almost eight years--eight years on April 18th.

Abba was opening up so many places for me to teach in the U.S., in Central and South America, and in the UK. So, I knew I would not be back to my apartment for at least a year and a half. I could not pay rent for all that time of being gone, even though it was only $213.00 a month. Utilities added up to about $12.00 a month, but for a year and a half, with me not being there, would cost me way too much money. I tried to get someone I knew from America to sublet the apartment, but few were interested. I even tried to get two or three families to join together to have a time-share apartment in Aqaba, but no one was interested in that. I was getting desperate. I wanted to keep the apartment! But, as time went on, Abba made it more and more clear that He wanted me out of Jordan until He willed me to return, if He ever willed me to return.

I met a couple who had three children. He was from the U.S. She was from Brazil. They had come to Aqaba and were living in a dumpy apartment about a mile from me. I went to visit them, and we got acquainted. I thought Fannie's stories were a little odd-- about their marriage, and about fleeing out of the U.S. because he had not gotten permission from his ex-wife to take the children out of the country. She talked so much, and told the same stories to everyone she met. I got so tired of it. They were interested, but only for a while. I thought that if Fannie and her family rented it, I could keep it. But, something was not right about that family, and I couldn't quite figure out what was wrong, and still can't even to this day. But, they agreed to rent my apartment. Then they moved south of the town into a nice roof apartment overlooking the sea. So I proceeded to pack up as if they were coming. My landlord had agreed to their staying there, because he and his wife did not want me to leave. I met with this family many times, and for the most part, we had a good time together. I even thought they were my friends. But, as it turned out, they did not rent the apartment, and left me in a bad situation that was very traumatic.

Also in early March, the group-family in Aqaba, who was still talking to me, said they had seen strange red stars above the border with Israel – right in front of where the U.S. military base was. They stayed in the sky a few seconds, then faded, then reappeared. Because this family stayed up almost all night, like the Muslims, they walked downtown a lot until at least 2:00 AM.

They saw all kinds of fascinating things. A few days later, while folding clothes, I looked out my bedroom window, which faced the Israeli border, and there they were – the fire stars. So, I went running up to the roof and stood there for 45 minutes watching the fire-stars, about 7 or 8 of them across the sky, becoming bright, remaining for about a minute, then fading, then another one appearing.

The air was unusually warm and still. I could see the lights of the U.S. base behind the hill. I don't know what it was. It was similar to the "Phoenix Lights". The next morning began a week of heavy storms. That was as rare for southern Jordan in the Negev Desert, as snow over the Red Sea – a new event. The lights could have been created by HAARP, because of the storms that followed their appearance. But, they were exactly like what hundreds have described in viewing UFOs. A top military man, at the same time, said it was a UFO, and went public with it. But, he was shut up quickly by the military, saying they were only military-operation flares. That month there was a full eclipse of the moon that could clearly be seen all over the region, which happened around 1:00 AM.

In 2006, while in Texas, my former Pastor Harold at Grace Temple, gave me two cassette tapes by Billie Brim, saying that the Holy Spirit had impressed him to do so. Yes, truly, the Spirit had impressed him to give it to me! Back in Aqaba, I listened to it, took a few notes, then put it with all my cassettes by Don Esposito. It talked about "The Shmittah Year Prophecy." But, in early March of 2007, Abba instructed me to get out that two-tape set and listen to it again. Then it really meant something to me. It was talking about the last three 7-year cycles before Messiah came. I asked Abba to confirm to me, if indeed, 2007 Sukkot began the final cycle before Messiah comes.

Around March 23rd, my dear friend Karen, who had been a missionary to the Igbo in Nigeria, came from Texas to be with me, and to help me get back to the states. I took her to Jerusalem before Passover. We stayed for a couple of days at the Christ Church Guest House. I put my feelers out. I heard one after another make this statement: "We don't understand it, but we have to get to Jerusalem for Passover." I heard that all spring and summer, in Israel and the U.S. But, there, I heard it from Europeans too. I figured on that Yom Teruah (Tishre 1), as we passed into 2008 on His Creation calendar--a Shmittah year (**Leviticus 25**)--going into the final cycle before Messiah returned, that Sukkot would be the biggest Sukkot since the time of Solomon. I also knew from Scripture that is was the end of Ephraim's punishment--using the math of **Ezekiel 4 with**

Leviticus 26, which was confirmed by the Orthodox Jews too. Even Chaim Richman, of the Temple Institute, told Billie Brim that it would begin that final cycle before Messiah came, and the judgment on the nations. I learned from Orthodox articles on the Internet that they knew that this Yom Teruah would begin the final 7-year cycle before Messiah would come.

I had set aside several large suitcases to take to Israel. I would not have been able to make the move later on if Karen had not been there to help me. On our trip to Jerusalem, we took about five suitcases. Once at the Central Bus Station in Jerusalem, Karen helped me get one large suitcase to the Christian Friends of Israel warehouse, just one block from the bus station. Then she helped me get everything into a taxi to the Jaffa Gate Hostel. We were in the dorm. It only cost us $11.00 a night to stay there. I showed her around Jerusalem for a few days. Then she helped me get the suitcases into another taxi to the Central Bus Station, and onto the bus to Tiberias. It was awful! There were so many people pressing each other to get on the bus. Then we had to wait for another bus, then another bus. One bus driver took off with my personal suitcase still under the bus. I retrieved it in Tiberias.

That was probably the most devastating Passover I've ever had in my life, outside the one with Trisha in 2003. Actress Lady said Karen and I could stay with her during Passover week. But, when we arrived she said she was too sick for us to use her stove and dirty her kitchen, even though we would have kept it clean. She said that she had made a deal with a new lady from Canada, Moriel, who had moved in next door, to cook on her stove. Actress Lady had a grudge against me. During a previous visit, I learned that she had abandoned friendship with my dear friend, because she thought I would be her new best friend. At first, she was so happy to have me stay with her. She thought I'd be her buddy and we'd do everything together. She had daily cared for her mother until she died. She told my dear friend that it was like having her mother back with her, even though she and I are the same age. She did not have respect for my calling from Abba, so she was very upset at me because I wouldn't submit my life to her whims. She went shopping for hours, almost daily. She expected me to go with her. She had wanted to redecorate her apartment and said I was her inspiration to do so. Only a few days passed before I realized I was a prisoner of her will. Also, shortly after moving in with her, I crossed her will and she set out to pay me back.

During one of our prayer meetings in her home, I told Actress Lady I needed to go walking, and pray by the lake. She wanted me to wait for her to go with me. The day before, I told her I needed to get out to walk and pray, but she insisted on going with me. She talked the whole time, and I had no time to hear from Abba. But, on this morning, I just went out while the prayer meeting was going on. When I got back, she was furious with me. I was not the controlled companion she had hoped for. Earlier in 2006, my dear friend and I were doing intercession together in many places across the north. Sometimes we invited Actress Lady to go, but it was obvious that she was only going for the fun.

We went to Rosh Hahira on the Lebanese border, and interceded for those who would flee out of Lebanon in the pending war. We did not know that by June, war would break out and the Lebanese believers would flee across the border into Israel – a closed border – and be rescued by Messianic ministries in Haifa. My dear friend and I needed to do serious intercession across the northeast of Israel without Actress Lady, but getting around her control was not easy. Finally, Actress Lady found out that my dear friend and I were going places without her, and that was it for me. I was not only not her friend anymore, I was treated like an enemy from then on. So, why I asked Actress Lady to let Karen and I stay with her during Passover week, I don't know.

After Karen and I got settled, we went and got a few groceries. My dear friend had invited several guests, including Karen and I, to attend Passover Seder at her house. Everyone invited was to bring something. All we could afford was deviled eggs, so we bought lots of eggs. But, when we went to Moriel's apartment that afternoon to ask her if we could fix lunch and boil the eggs for the Passover Seder, she acted annoyed. She yelled at us because she thought we were harming her new pan. It was nerve-wracking. At this time, a lovely lady from England named Ann had come stay with Moriel. I liked Ann. She became a good friend. After the Passover Seder, Karen and I went over each day to cook our food at Moriel's apartment. Moriel grew more and more angry at us. She finally told us that we could not come any longer, because she wanted to "bond with Ann" and she didn't want us bothering her, so Karen and I spent most of Passover week eating boiled eggs. I ate lots of rice cakes too.

Actress Lady had two balconies off of her living room. Karen and I used the left balcony to eat our meals. During Passover week, Actress Lady pretended to be seriously ill. My dear compassionate friend did not see the fakery and went to herald. But, Karen told me: "She's not ill; she's faking it." I also knew Actress Lady was faking it. She had been a professional on-stage actress! Also during that week, a journalist-friend of hers from Jerusalem came to visit. She was also shunned by Actress Lady who stayed in her room languishing--literally pretending to be on

PART VI - The Middle East & Travels Beyond

her death bed. Her friend also thought it strange, and didn't appear to be very concerned about her. Actress Lady sent me to buy wine and food for her to prepare for my dear friend, whom she had been invited to share dinner with her. Actress Lady said she had no cash to give me for the wine. She never paid me back. When I told her the amount I paid--I had bought very good wine--she said that was part of what I owed her for the room-rent, even though she had told me the room was free. So, while Karen and I ate hard-boiled eggs on the left balcony, we watched Actress Lady and my dear friend eating fine food and drinking fine wine on the right balcony. I learned later that my dear friend thought Karen and I just wanted to be alone that night, or at least that is what Actress Lady had implied.

Later, thank Abba, my dear friend saw the truth. We were able to talk it out and get understanding. She's still a dear friend. I was so ashamed that this happened on Karen's first. and only, visit to Israel. What I found out later was that Actress Lady had NOT told Moriel about our cooking in her apartment, and that Moriel had thought we were crazy. Later, I talked it out with Moriel, and she was nice about it. In 2009, when Moriel returned to Canada, she let me stay in her apartment for three months for free.

One awesome thing happened this week. I wanted to take Karen on one of the wooden boats that sail across Lake Kinneret (the Sea of Galilee). I knew we had to get to the boats at the marina in Tiberias by 8:30 if we wanted to join a tour group. When we got there, I saw about 10 white people on a boat, and I asked if we could join them. They said: "no." That really angered me. Then I saw another boat docked down further, so I ran to it. Now Karen was dressed, as usual, with her Nigerian headdress. As we got to the boat, around the corner came 95 Nigerians. There was one white man among them – their tour guide. I asked him if we could join them. He asked the Bishop, and the Bishop said: "Yes." They started singing and dancing as they got on the boat. Karen started doing the Nigerian "shuffle" dance, and I did the Kenya "shuffle", and we all shuffled onto the boat together singing. The whole trip across, the Nigerians wanted to take our picture and hug us. Abba was smiling!

Karen had low blood sugar and took medicine for it. If she did not take her medicine she'd go into a coma. She ran out of medicine shortly after we returned to Jordan. I gave her three ½-glass doses of colloidal silver three times a day. Her blood sugar went to normal, and while she was with me she needed no medicine. She'd walk into town almost every day, 5 miles, and walk back.

All this time, I'm packing, and leaving nice things, because I thought Fannie and family were moving in. Just before I was to leave, they said they were not moving in. I could have sold my furniture, and given to a lot of people. I was so grieved and hurt. My landlord was upset. Of course, he wanted my things out of there so that he could rent the apartment. So, the group-family, and the kind elderly couple who helped me earlier, packed up my things and got them distributed to needy people in Jordan, and with the Jonathan Miles' group in Jerusalem. I was in the U.S. while they did this for me. But, during their packing, Abba gave me this verse, **Revelation 3:7**: "**And to the angel of the assembly of Philadelphia write: `He who is set-apart, He who is true, He who has the key of David, He who opens and no one shuts, and shuts and no one opens**…' "

Number one: The first name of both my landlord, and the father of the family who helped me so much, was David. Group-family David went to landlord David and got the key to the apartment to go pack up my things. The key to my apartment was held, then, by two named David. Number two: Abba shut that door, and no one could open it! Number three: Abba opened a door for me in a good place in Tiberias, and no one can close that door until He wants it closed! Number four: The verse is **Revelation 3:7**. The numbers 3 and 7 are numbers representing "conclusion, end of cycle." I was there exactly 8 years – leaving on the exact day I arrived 8 years before, April 18th. The number 8 is the number of new beginnings! Truly! Abba's fingerprints were all over this! -- Praise His Name!

I had bought a ticket to join Karen on her flight back to the U.S. I didn't think about the date on the ticket until later. **The ticket was for April 18, 2007, eight years to the day that I arrived--April 18, 1999**. My three boxes were so heavy, that the morning of our departure from Aqaba, Karen had to put each one on my ironing board to pull them down the stairs. My faithful taxi driver and one of his friends came, and helped us get the boxes into the taxi and out of the taxi at the Aqaba airport. Because each one of my three "dish-pack" boxes was over 100 pounds, Royal Jordanian charged me $150.00 in overweight fees. That was a standard rate for most airlines.

The lady checking us in at the Aqaba airport, told me that I could not check my boxes all the way to Tampa. She said I had to get them in Chicago, and re-check them to Tampa onto American Airlines, a co-share partner with Royal Jordanian. So, she only booked my boxes through to Chicago. When we got to Chicago, after clearing Immigration, getting the boxes off the conveyer belt, then going to the re-check-in, American Airlines would not put the boxes on the plane, for they were way beyond their weight allowance. I asked them what I should do, since everything I owned was in those boxes. They just shrugged their shoulders and said "sorry." Karen stayed with me. Just then, two other people, a man and a woman, came to the desk. They were entirely different. They said they'd help me. The lady called U-Haul. I talked to U-Haul. They said they'd come get the boxes and deliver them in about 2 weeks to our new home in Florida.

When I got to Tampa, I called my daughter. She said she'd been on the phone with U-Haul and the airport for 45 minutes, but all was OK. In two weeks, here came the boxes, unopened, all intact. That was a huge miracle! It's kind of interesting that when U-Haul arrived, my ex-husband and his new wife were there visiting. I wonder what they thought. The U-Haul driver commented on how heavy my boxes were!

Back in the U.S., I began teaching and doing more intercession right away. I was invited to meetings in East Texas. In late April, in East Texas, I stayed with a friend named Kathy. I taught in their home, and then went to visit one of her friends. During this time, her husband told me he had something for me out in his tool shed. A friend of his had given him a copy of an unpublished work. The friend had been in Intelligence in the U.S. government. He wrote about things he learned that were TOP SECRET. So Kathy's husband took me out to the tool shed, and from behind some tools, he pulled out this book to give me. How I get information that Abba thinks I need to have, is constantly amazing! While staying with her, she and I went on a most awesome intercession trip. Intercession was new to her, so she backed me as I proclaimed His Word.

Near Jefferson, we went down a river on a small boat and learned that the river was once a major port at the Gulf of Mexico. Now it was covered in undergrowth and looked like a giant swamp. Then we went to Cado Lake and did more intercession. This was a real swampy backwoods area, though there was a nice museum there for us to go through. We then proceeded on and went to Bossier City, Louisiana, to do intercession over the Red River, which flows into the Mississippi River on the other side of Louisiana. We went to the river by a large mall. I noticed that the decorations on all the light posts were white cards with only a spiral on each of them, very unusual. The spiral and the circumpunct (a circle with a dot in the middle) are the two most common Luciferic symbols in America. For examples, they are put on clothes, on toys, on baby diapers, high chairs, product covers, and used as logos for many companies. After this intercession,

Kathy and I returned to her house totally exhausted--it was about a 16-hour day.

Back in Florida, Barbara Brown brought my new computer over to Tina's house, where I was staying. I had several meetings around Tina's house north of Tampa. Launa, the lady who worked with the soup kitchen in Jerusalem, and I, went on several intercession trips. One of my favorite trips was to Tarpon Springs. It is on the Anclote River. Tarpon Springs is a Greek center, also world famous for its sponge industry. We took a boat down the river on a "sponge boat." We did intercession all the way down the river. At the point where it flowed into the Gulf, there were many dolphin families swimming around the boat. We had a fine Greek meal. Launa also took me to beaches along Clearwater, and other places to do intercession, even to an old historic Fort. I spoke in different places in Florida. I continued to do research on things He was teaching me, writing, counseling, and teaching. But, everywhere I went I heard people saying, with a perplexed look on their face, "we don't understand it, but we have to get to Jerusalem for Sukkot."

In May, a lady, whom I met via e-mail contact with my California friend Ann, wanted me to come visit she and her husband in Kentucky. I felt in my spirit to go. I also found out that they were ex-World Wide Church of God people. I keep finding them everywhere. This is how I met Jamie and Bob--two of my best loyal friends and supporters. By sending my articles to many people around the world, this couple has probably opened more doors for me than any one else. We've been together twice now in Israel, so far.

On my route to Lexington, Kentucky, my plane flew to Cincinnati, Ohio first. Then I got another airplane to Lexington, a 30 minute hop. Flying into Cincinnati, I was sitting in a window seat. I looked down and saw a massive river below. I had to find out what that river was. Once inside the airport, I went to the information desk and asked what that river was. The lady said: "The Ohio River." I always ask a lot of questions-- to get directions and to find out information--of people, and of Abba. But, I get a lot of answers that way, too!

Jamie and Bob had arranged for a small meeting in their home. A Messianic family came, as well as three people, who came all the way from the Nashville area of Tennessee to hear me. The three from Tennessee became good friends: Gayle, Paula, and Yochanan. Gayle invited me to come to her home, which I did. Later I spoke at Gayle's congregation, visiting with her at least twice. I spoke in Paula's home, at least twice, and in her congregation later on. I was with Paula two different times in

Israel. Yochanan sang at various places I taught at. Through them, I had many open doors in Tennessee, some were friends of theirs, some came as Abba opened unusual doors. But, Tennessee became one of my main places to teach--in many different areas--especially the Murfreesboro area, the Nashville area, then later in southern Tennessee.

Once at Jamie and Bob's, I told her I had to do intercession over that river. She said she felt led to take me to the National Underground Railroad Freedom Museum on the Ohio River. I thought: "Oh no!"

During one of the East Texas meetings, I think the memorial service for Jim Rector, an African-America lady on the front row turned to Laura and said: "That woman reminds me of Harriet Tubman." I didn't know who Harriet Tubman was. Karen, who became a precious friend of mine, told Laura that Harriet was a leader in the underground railroad. I thought she was comparing me to someone who worked on a train. I was not impressed. After that, I kept hearing about the underground railroad and Harriet. I had no desire to learn about anyone who worked on a train. So, when Jamie said she felt led to take me to the National Underground Railroad Freedom Museum, I was disgusted. I thought: "OH NO! I did not come all the way to Kentucky to go to a train museum." I asked Jamie why she felt led to take me to a train museum. Jamie kindly corrected my faulty thinking. The "underground railroad" was a network of people from the south to the north, who helped slaves get to freedom. Then she told me about Harriet Tubman, a freed slave who dedicated her life to rescuing other slaves and taking them to freedom!

Harriet Tubman was nicknamed "Moses." Remember what Abba said to me in the prophecy He gave me in February of 2003? – "You are Moses, deliver My people…." Abba must have been smiling. I did not know what a compliment Karen had given me! She and her mother, Dorothy, became good friends, and still are to this day. They are precious born again, Spirit-filled, guarders of Torah, and lovers of Yahuweh and Yahushua. I love them!

Bob drove us to the museum. It is right next to the Cincinnati Reds Ball Park. They had not been there before, so we each took our time and went our own way through the museum. We got headsets with the information for each display. I noticed that on the second floor of the museum they had a Schindler Exhibit about the Holocaust. The first display was a huge quilt hung on the wall, showing the history of the slaves. The first square of the quilt was about Solomon and Sheba, and how so many of the slaves were their offspring. I later learned that, factually, the major groups of slaves were either from the House of Judah or the House of Israel, like the Igbo of Nigeria from the tribe of Gad. Like I reported under "Africa," I met so many of the House of Judah from the Bantu people of historic Ethiopia.

I sat there crying. I cried through the whole first floor, and second floor, of the exhibit. It had a profound impact on my life. I wrote the articles: "The Return of the Underground Railroad," and "Raising up Moses," in 2007. In 2012, I learned that many slaves fled south into Florida for safety, and blended in with the local Indian tribes, like the Creek Indians.

While we were there, we did intercession over the Ohio River, just below the museum. It was at that place where so many slaves crossed. So, we prayed for the slaves to escape out of the prison house of end-time Babylon/America, which is a place of slavery and illusion, a matrix of the imagination.

True freedom is moving daily in the will of Yahuweh to reach out to a lost and dying world with the Good News of Messiah's Redemption, to teach the Word, to help people know Yahuweh!

Jamie and Bob had not done intercession before, so I taught them. I told them to just say: "Oh Yahuweh, save Your remnant," from **Jeremiah 31:7**, over all the rivers they came to. They got so good at it that when she went to New York for a College Career Counselor's convention, being in a high-rise hotel that overlooked Manhattan, she called out "save Your remnant" over all those Jews and Ephraimites below. She said it as she walked the streets of New York too. She and Bob began doing intercession over certain areas along the Kentucky river, blowing the shofar and proclaiming deliverance for His remnant. Now they are going other places doing intercession in western North Carolina. They understand that intercession opens portals for Abba's entrance into the earth to do His will.

For Mother's Day that May, they took me to a Shaker Village. At this village, they worked as people did in the 1700s-1800s-- weaving, and candle making, etc. We even saw a sheep-shearing demonstration. It was a most beautiful lovely day! From there, we went to do intercession over the Kentucky River. We actually went to two places along that river, but this day we took a special ferry boat from the Shaker Village. The Kentucky River flows into the Ohio River, which flows into the Mississippi River, which flows into the Gulf of Mexico. All along the shorelines of these rivers, is undergrowth – places for hiding. Also, there are fish in the rivers and natural food along the way.

In late spring, I also had a wonderful Shavu'ot meeting at a friend's house in Florida. There were many from several congregations there. One meeting always led to another one. In June I told Launa about the intercession that I needed to do down the "Keys"—small islands off the Gulf Coast of Florida. She said she'd drive me to wherever I needed to go. In July we set off to go down the coast from Sarasota. We started with Anna Maria Island. Then we stopped on almost every main island all the way down to Naples, where we spent the night. Laura was horribly sick, and I took over the driving. I was really afraid for her. It took us hours to find out hotel, because we got lost. The hotel staff gave us terrible directions. Finally she called her husband who gave us directions from what he saw on the Internet.

By the next morning, Launa was well enough to drive. We drove past Naples to the head of the "10,000-Keys"--until we couldn't go any further. Then we turned east across the Everglades, and went to Key Largo, then on to Key West. I loved it in Key West! We had such a wonderful lunch at a fish restaurant. Just before sunset, we headed out to drive back to Key Largo, where we spent the night. Just after crossing the "Seven-Mile Bride," I looked back and saw the most awesome sunset. We stopped to take pictures.

The next morning, we headed back across the Everglades. We stopped at Everglades Safari and took an airboat into the Everglades. The Everglades is actually the world's slowest running river. It is junked up with lots of undergrowth, and lots of alligators. Now, it has python, and 7' Nile lizards in it. Our airboat trip was awesome. Included in the price of our ticket was a visit to the alligator shelter. An official wildlife ranger was feeding the alligators. What huge mouths they have! Then he came out of the cage and picked up a small alligator that had its mouth taped shut. He asked our group who would like to hold SNAPPY. Launa was the first to volunteer. Actually, she was the only to volunteer, as I remember. She said Snappy was cold. I got her picture.

Also this summer, because I had met Paula, Gayle, and Yochanan, at Jamie and Bob's house, I had an invitation to come to Tennessee to speak. Gayle picked me up at the airport. I stayed with her. We became like sisters right away. Pastor Norman, who was teaching his church Hebrew roots, invited me to come speak at his church. It was here that I met David and Emily and their seven children. Their eighth child was born on the roof of the Petra Hostel at the Jaffa Gate in Jerusalem, in 2008. Norman went on to make his church a Messianic church. Wonderful people! She took me to Paula's house, some distance away, where I had a meeting and also spoke at her congregation. I met more pastors there, and had more meetings.

In early August, I was invited to teach in an assembly in Georgia. Gayle had told elder Harold about me, and he contacted me to come. We talked a lot on the phone, and really bonded in the spirit. The others elders were happy for me to come. I stayed with a couple, the man being another of the elders of the congregation. I went with Harold, and his lovely wife, Dotty, to Jekyll Island to do intercession over that area. It was on this island that America's debt system was created in the early 1900s, which took us from almost no debt at all, to the multi-trillions of dollars of debt that we are in now. We had such a lovely time together. I knew that I had to be back in Jerusalem for the most historic Yom Teruah before Messiah's return. I knew that this would be the largest gathering of all the tribes in Jerusalem since the time of Solomon. I went back to the U.S. for a wonderful summer. I stayed excited about returning to Israel for the historic Yom Teruah, Yom Kippur, and Sukkot!

September 12, 2007: This day began the 2008 Shmittah Year (**Leviticus 25**), which opened the last seven-year cycle before the return of Messiah Yahushua! I stayed at Christ Church Guest House. On the eve of September 12th, eve of Yom Teruah (Feast of Trumpets) I was excited to get down to the Wall. I had listed eight things that He had told me to prophesy/proclaim. The major one was the opening of the last 7-year cycle, but equal to it was to proclaim the end of Ephraim's punishment. After 2,730 years, the House of Ephraim/Joseph/Israel was released from their captivity in the nations. [Refer to: "Who Are the Ten?"] The Orthodox Jews certainly knew it. [Refer to: "The Shmittah Year Prophecy," "The Forty-Eight Hour Transition," and "The September 12, 2007 Report from Jerusalem"]

As was on my way to the HaKotel (Western Wall of the Temple Mount) to do the proclamation of the eight things He had given me on that Yom Teruah. Just as I was leaving my room at Christ Church, He gave me a ninth thing to proclaim. He said: "**I will give you a second chance.**" I stopped and quietly exclaimed: "Oh no! Are You saying that you want me to proclaim the opening of the trumpet judgments?" I understood what He meant. I had failed to go on the previous shmittah year to Patmos, as He had instructed, to release the opening of the seals. I reached the Wall area and sat down. He then kept adding things for me to proclaim. When He was finished, He had given me a total of 18 things. After I finished writing them all down, I began the proclamations.

Earlier this year, I learned from physicists, astronomers, and others, who were interviewed later on the History Channel in the U.S., that they believe that the first four "trumpet judgments" -- **Revelation 8:6-12** -- were coming between **2008 and 2015**. Take note of that! The next shmittah year begins on Tishre 1,

Yom Teruah, 2014/2015 and ends the day before Tishre 1, Yom Teruah 2015/2016, by the Creator's Calendar!

I went back the next evening to close the day. I had been wearing a knee brace with the knee part cut out, like runners use. The next morning, as I was getting ready to go down to breakfast and send the report, my knee popped forward and I fell into the bed. It pulled many ligaments. I could hardly walk down the steps. I was in a lot of pain. I was glad I had written the report the night before, so all I had to do was send it: "The September 12, 2007 Report From Jerusalem."

I took the computer to a table, paid for 30 minutes of their wireless time, and began writing my report. All the while, I am praying: "Abba, how am I going to get to Tiberias?" I had two suitcases and a carry on bag. I would have to get a taxi, check all that in at the bus station through security, then up to the third floor, then to Tiberias on the bus, then get another taxi to Actress Lady's building.

As I began to write, a man came up to me and softly said: "Yedidah." I looked at him but did not recognize him. He said "It's John, from the meeting at Grace's house." I said: "What are you doing here?" He was staying at the Imperial Hotel. He was just there because Abba told him to come. He did not know I was at Christ Church. He had just come there to meet someone. He asked if I had time to talk. I told him I had to get the report sent, and asked if he could come back in 30 minutes. He came back, and we talked for a while. He asked me if there was anything He could do to help me. That was a question I wanted to hear! I asked him if he would help me to the bus. He said he would be glad to, and even ride with me to Tiberias if I needed him to.

The next morning, the time had fallen back, and he got there an hour early, but that's OK--he got me onto the bus through all that usual pushing and shoving. When I got to Tiberias, my dear friend picked me up. I had met John at my first meeting at Grace's house. She said he'd probably disturb the meeting with his questions, but he didn't. In fact, he liked what I taught and we became friends.

Talk about "poetic justice!" Moriel had gone back to Canada, and she needed someone to stay in her apartment while she was gone, so she let me stay there, free of charge. I got the other suitcases from Actress Lady and moved into this lovely apartment all to myself!

I went back to Jerusalem for Sukkot. I stayed with Launa, and three other friends--Paula from Nashville, Christine and Gloria from Florida--in a large upstairs room at the Petra Hostel at the Jaffa gate. We had a little balcony that overlooked the main street, across from the Citadel, at the entrance to the Arab Quarter. That area is the thoroughfare for, and the mingling pot of, the three monotheistic religions – Christianity, Judaism, and Islam. So being up that high on the 3rd floor, it was like looking down on a sampling of the entire world. Just above us was the roof. It was considered one of the three best views of all Jerusalem.

There was a huge living room area outside our room. You could sit on a couch, look over the Temple Mount, and see the sunrise over the Mount of Olives. Many strange people came up there to use that living room area to give teachings on their favorite topic of the Bible--and there were some strange people there! What was sad is that the three ladies with Launa and I listened to one very demonic teacher and were so swayed by him that they had all types of emotional problems from what he said.

Then there was Gabriel--one of the main employees at the hotel. He was dedicated to tearing down the person of Messiah, demoting Him to a created being. His teachings affected these three more than anyone else. Christine was so confused after listening to his intellectual arguments, that she said she'd have to find someone to convince her of Messiah's Deity. I gathered the whole group, by this time we numbered about 15, in our room to lay it all out to them. I was the catalyst for the group. Jamie and Bob were there, and my friend Ann who had taken me to Arkansas to have meetings with her friends, and a few others I do not remember. I met Esther from Hungry, a precious lady.

I had met Paula at Jamie and Bob's house, as I mentioned above. I met Christine and her daughter at a home gathering the previous Shavu'ot. She and her family lived down the street from us in Ellenton. I spoke at her home twice. I met Gloria in a big combined meeting that I had in Florida. After the meeting, she came up to me and said God had told her to move to Aqaba. She actually went there and stayed for five months in the apartment that I had left. I thought that was wonderful. Then she met a man, moved to Colorado, and married him. In fact, as I will tell later, I was part of their wedding. But, oh the turmoil at that "intersection of the world" below the Petra Hostel! That week we went as a group to Yad Vashem – the Holocaust Memorial Museum in Jerusalem. I was angry all the way through it, knowing that if it were not for America, there would have been NO holocaust. [Refer to: "Chilling Parallels"]

In that same week something happened that would set me up for devastating cruelty the following year. The Welsh woman, Leslie, that I met in Wales at Elaine's home in 2004, had come to Jerusalem. I was trying to avoid her in Israel. From the time I first met her, I felt there was something strange about her, even though she was outwardly nice to me. Ever since I met her, each time she came to Israel, she tried to get me to join her, and one of her friends, on a pleasure trip--like to a spa in Israel, to the beach in Eilat, or to Petra, Jordan. Jamie and Bob were staying at Christ Church, along with Ann from California. Launa, and I, and the other ladies, went to breakfast at Christ Church every morning, and we sat outside in the sukkah/garden and talked. One morning, Jamie told me that Leslie, who was staying at another place, but who came to eat lunch at Christ Church, had come over to their table, got her face almost down on the table, moved herself up into their faces, and whispered: "Witchcraft has begun." Leslie was theatrically dramatic. But, I later found out what she meant. She said she had a prayer partner in Cardiff named Lisa. I had put Lisa on my e-mail list. Lisa was well known in Messianic circles in the UK, as was Leslie. Lisa was a puzzler. She seemed nice, but every once in a while she'd send me an e-mail saying something like: "You will burn in hell; you are of the Devil; you are evil." I was so lollypop-brained at that time. I thought she was speaking of someone else, even though that was her e-mail to me. I did not know she was speaking of me.

Leslie, and her husband, had been to Israel many times. She was in Jerusalem, but I had not talked to her yet that Sukkot. One afternoon, I was sitting in the sukkah/garden at Christ Church, talking to Ann, when all of a sudden Leslie walked up the table. I greeted her, and she sat down. After we talked about a minute, she exclaimed: "Look who is here!" She pointed at the window that looked down into the dining room. There was only one table that I could see, but sitting at it was Pastor Darryl from the Rhondda, the one who had changed the church from a replacement theology church to a Messianic Church. He came out with someone he had brought with him from Wales. They sat down to talk. He told me that it was I who had turned them all around, and that they were very grateful to me. He loved Israel. I "thought" it was Abba who had arranged that meeting. The pastor asked me to return to Wales and speak at his church again. I was delighted. Then Leslie proceeded to invite me to stay with her at her home in Cardiff, Wales. She said we'd have meetings in her home, and she'd arrange one in Newport.

Wow! I was really set up! Because the pastor had invited me, I thought all was well. She also said that she and her husband, and Ann, the Ann I had met with Elaine in 2003 at Christ Church, were going to France, and I was invited to join them. In addition to her home in Cardiff, Leslie and her husband owned a 2nd home in the country, near Toulouse. I had relatives from France, and I thought it would be a good chance to do some intercession in case some of my relatives were still there--from the Fox family (Fuches in France--a Jewish name. I forgot my funny feeling about her. Jamie told me later about her "witchcraft has begun" weirdness. My knee was still very sore, and the climb up the steps of the Petra Hostel, first to the lobby area, then up to our room area, was very hard on me. So, I didn't over-do my walking. Jamie, Bob, and Launa, went to work in the soup kitchen on Jaffa Road-- Ichlu Re'im--run by a Sephardic rabbi and his wife. Really sweet people!

During that week, I went with Launa, Paula, and David, the man from Mexico who married Emily and moved to Tennessee. We cut up vegetables for the evening meal at the soup kitchen. I specialized in onions and garlic (smile). That evening, Jamie, Bob, Launa, and Christine, went to serve dinner at the kitchen. Bob wore his tzitzit. A rabbi came in and saw Bob serving. He went up to him and began talking in Hebrew. In the course of his dialogue, he kept saying "Yosef." Someone interpreted, and told Bob that he was asking if he was from the House of Ephraim/Joseph. When Bob said, "Yes." The rabbi hugged him and kissed him on both cheeks. That same evening, Paula was stopped near the Petra Hostel by an Orthodox Jewish man who asked her why she wore tzitzit. She said she guarded Torah. He asked her if she was one of the "Joes"--a term they call the ten tribes/Ephraimites. She said "yes" and he started jumping up and down for joy.

Yes, it was the greatest Sukkot since the time of Solomon – and they knew that it was the end of Ephraim's punishment and that a remnant of Ephraim was coming "home." This is the story in **Luke 15** of the prodigal (Ephraim) and the elder brother (Judah), and the joy of the Father at the return of the prodigal son. They knew that seeing Ephraim coming to Jerusalem for that Sukkot was their sign that Messiah is coming, and indeed we are in the last 7-year cycle.

All those people who said: "I don't understand why, but I have to get to Jerusalem for Sukkot", had come, so the Old City was filled with Torah-guarding Ephraimites, and Christians who couldn't figure out why they were drawn there at that time.

After Sukkot, I went back to Moriel's apartment and worked on healing my knee. It was at this time, that I sat overlooking the lake, and wrote some of my most profound articles and studies. The apartment had a large balcony, and every morning for six weeks I got up to see the sunrise. I wrote "The Sunrise Lessons" from what He taught me those six weeks. I took about 150 pictures, for every sunrise was different. The sun always comes up, but in its own time, not ours. He is faithful, in His own time,

PART VI - The Middle East & Travels Beyond

not ours. It was here that He took me into the future, as I wrote: "The Two Witnesses, the Bride of Messiah, the Forerunning Company, and the Fleeing Remnant." It was here that He taught me so much about my future. I was in Israel from September until early December – a full three months. It was a wonderful three months!

I returned to the U.S. in late November. For Hanukkah, Launa invited me to visit her group where she was teaching Torah to Christians who asked her to teach them Hebrew roots. But, when she talked about having a Hanukkah party with no Christmas decorations, the man at whose house the party was to be held, threw a toddler-style temper tantrum. He wanted Christmas decorations and presents. He wanted a tree. But, Launa stood her ground. That afternoon I was staying with Grace. She and her husband were going to the party too, so I was riding with them. While taking a nap before the meeting, I had a dream in which a small blue snake bit me on the leg. The wound bled, but I was all right. When I got there, my spirit became very heavy. I was the principal speaker of the evening. There was lots of food there. How did I know that one lady had brought beans and ham hocks? How did I know that the man was going to be drunk, and the booze would flow, and it would be a Christmas-style bash? It grieved Launa to the max.

I sat away from the group until it was my time to speak. As I sat there, I could feel the rebellion. So, when I got up to speak, I spoke as a prophet, and shocked most of the people. Then there were the games, and the presents. The host-man was drunk. He was in charge of the games, but he turned sadistic. He had invited some of his "good ol' boy" friends, who were also drinking and rebellious. It turned out to be a horrible fiasco.

The next day Launa was taking me on a seven-state trip for teaching and intercession. Our last stop was a return to the congregation in Georgia, with Harold, and Dottie, and other friends I had met. They were excited I was going to come back. But, that very same night of Launa's Hanukkah party, little did I know that this congregation was having an elder's meeting. And the enemy had begun to work! The elders were all excited for me to come again. But, during the meeting, three of the wives of the elders showed up. They had read two of my articles and were protesting my coming, saying I was too "harsh." Harold called me and told me that I was being blackballed. One of the wives was his daughter-in-law. We talked about the jezebel spirit that had invaded his congregation. He said the elders talked about it, and they still wanted me to come. The protestors did not have to come. This was the snake that bit me on the leg--it hurt, but it did not stop me.

I had been staying with Grace and her husband. Launa came to get me, and we took off the next day on our trip. We drove up through Georgia, then into South Carolina. We were headed for Beckley, West Virginia (December 7-10) to speak at Carolyn and John's congregation. We stopped for the night in Charlotte, South Carolina. That night, the enemy tried to get me to turn back. I had a dream that was so vivid that it almost ruined the trip. I dreamed that the daughter I was staying with had vanished. My other children would not tell me where she went. I found out she had committed suicide. In the dream, I felt every speck of it, as if it were real. I woke up and felt as if it were real. I was in such fear that she needed me. I asked Abba if He wanted me to go on. Then, I began comparing the dream with Abba's nature. Would He have given me the dream? I concluded that the dream was of the devil, and we went on.

The meetings in West Virginia were awesome. The time we had with Jamie and Bob was awesome. We not only went back to the National Underground Railroad Freedom Museum in Cincinnati, but we went to Ken Ham's Creation Science Museum in Hebron, Kentucky. Now that was one awesome adventure. I wanted to stay in the Noah exhibit room for hours. If you get a chance to go there, do so! It is a multi-million dollar complex, with displays from Genesis, dinosaurs, and other things, showing that the present re-creation of the earth is not that old. It is a rebuttal to the teachings of Evolution!

We visited Tom and Audrey in North Carolina, stayed there nearly a week, and had fine fellowship. They had been missionaries in Colombia, and ministered for many years in many places. Audry had worked in Israel also, years before she met Tom. After Tom died, in 2011, Audry went to Israel with Launa. As Audry and I were sitting inside the ruins of ancient Shiloh, Audry told me how they came to guard Torah.

Launa had taken 15 of my articles to them to read. They had sent the articles to many friends. I became friends with several of them, which led to meetings in several new places. Audrey told me that one day after reading, that they should keep Torah. She asked Tom if he thought what I said was right or wrong. Tom said I was right. From that time on, they began to guard Torah together. She said I changed their lives for good. That was so humbling to me. And she told me this right where Samuel grew up as a child in the tabernacle at Shiloh. Then, because of family problems, Launa told me she'd have to let me off in Georgia, but she had to go on to Florida. On December 22nd, I flew back to Florida from Georgia after my meetings there.

It was December 21st, my son's birthday. I had asked Grace and Dennis to do me a big favor. I asked to stay at their house until the 26th of December, since they did not celebrate Christmas. My daughter and her family still celebrated Christmas, and from December 23rd until December 26th, if I was around "Christmas" celebrations, I was always attacked viciously by the enemy. So, I wanted to escape that. They said they'd pick me up at the airport on December 22nd, and take me to my daughter's on December 26th.

But, on the morning of the 21st, I got an e-mail from Grace. She told me that she and her husband had been reading my articles about the end times, and gotten afraid. It caused them to argue. She said that I could not come, because my articles upset them. I was traumatized. They said they'd pick me up at the airport and take me to my daughter's house. I was numb. The enemy tried to stop the trip, then proceeded to attack me on my way home. It was a very traumatic time those three days, from the time they picked me up and took me to my daughter's house until December 26th. It was the end of a very rough, but also a very productive year. Abba Yahuweh makes all the difference!

AMERICA--ISRAEL--WALES
FRANCE--IRELAND--COLOMBIA--ENGLAND
(2008)

I flew to southern California, January 17th through the 20th, to stay with a family who lived near Yucaipa. Joanne and Phil had invited me to come and teach. They have four lovely homeschooled children. Our fellowship was awesome! I got up very early, I thought. But, upon entering the kitchen, Phil would be sitting at the kitchen table studying the Word. Even before I got my coffee, he would begin asking me questions. They had a beautiful home. Phil had a very prestigious job. But, in following the Lamb, they left it all and went overseas to be apart of what Abba is doing in these last days. I appreciate them very much. They've stayed straight with the Word, even in the midst of persecution from fellow Americans for it!

In late January, Launa and I did more intercession in new areas over the Gulf. In February, I went to Tennessee for an extensive set of meetings. I did not know it would be below freezing, and I had dressed Florida style. At first, I stayed with Gayle. Then she took me to north Tennessee to stay with David and Emily, whom I had met at Norman's congregation the year before. I had a good meeting and good fellowship with them. They became wonderful friends. One couple who came to the meeting was Joseph and Deborah. Deborah and a couple of other ladies had found a "Yedidah" on the Internet – the one who is a Kabbalist. I was supposed to stay with this couple, but they were leery of me. I told them I was not that woman! Then they traced me through some of my articles, in which I had left my legal name, and I was approached by the snaky words: "I know who you are." It upset me tremendously that people could be so low-class and shallow.

I was also asked to have a combined meeting in a restaurant on Friday night in Murfreesboro. Norman came with his group, and others who had heard me before. I was looking forward to meeting the couple who was coming from Alabama. I had talked to her on the phone. It seemed like we were really on the same page about everything. I was still so naïve. Because I am an optimist, I don't think negatively about people until they expose themselves to be on the dark side.

The night of the meeting, the restaurant put us in a room that opened onto the buffet bar outside. There was no door we could close. A waitress even seated two customers at a back table inside our area. I had made it explicit, since it was a Friday evening, that we would not eat after sunset, or pay the bill after sunset. If anyone wanted to eat at the restaurant, they would have to go there ahead of sunset.

PART VI - The Middle East & Travels Beyond

The couple from Alabama got there after sunset because of their sick dog. I knew right away by the wife's conversation with Gayle that something was wrong. Her chit chat was very petty and shallow. Her husband said he was going to get something to eat. I couldn't believe that. Why didn't they stop to eat before they got there? He and his son sat in a booth to the right of my chair, from where I would be speaking. I had asked Yochanan and his brother to sing before the meeting. It was so beautiful. But, the waitress kept coming in to bring this man and his son food and drink. He was slobbering over his food noisily during the singing. I saw the waitress serving the couple at the back of the room. I did not know they were not with our group. Then four "ladies" came in past me, and sat at the opposite end of the area. I did not know they were infamous jezebels who would later do all they could to slander me--even all the way to England.

It was time for me to speak. The spirit in me was highly disturbed by all this confusion, and blatant rebellion against Abba's Torah. I was numb. I couldn't speak, but I tried to overlook it and just proceed on with my message. The waitress had again come to serve the couple at the back of the room. I turned to ask the waitress to please leave the room, since we were beginning the meeting. But, when I turned to call out to the waitress, I was shocked. Out of my mouth I heard myself begin a prophecy at full volume. I was listening to Him speak through my mouth--my mind was blank. It was a scathing prophecy that blistered all the "lily whites" in the room, and greatly upset the jezebels. To this day I do not remember what I said, but it sure caused the roof to fall in on my head the next day. After He was through with His "word," I began to give my message. I knew that I had "offended" the crooked, but I proceeded on because there were those there who were not crooked to Abba's plumb line.

Earlier that evening, I had gone to the home of Joseph and Deborah, where I would spend the night and have a meeting in their home the next day. By this time, I really liked them, and they liked me. They wanted to go to Israel, but were total naive greenhorns. I tried to bring reality into play. Then I took a nap. When I got up, they told me they had bought tickets to Israel to stay for 3 months. I just gave them to Abba. They went to Israel, stayed 3 months, then stayed another 3 months. Abba led them, and they did great!

As I came down the stairs into their living room the next morning before the meeting, Abba said: "**The rising of the tares has begun.**" How did I know that the jezebels would come in mass to her house? Gayle and I talked about what happened the night before. She was kind, and tried to understand, but it was on her shoulders to explain, since she had arranged the meeting.

After this meeting, I stayed a couple more days and then went with Paula to her apartment. It was a time of peace. She took me to her congregation for a meeting, which afterwards spilled over into hours of teaching at her house. That was a good day!

Through Gayle, I learned about a pastor in Murfreesboro. I forget how, but somehow he had heard of me too. He contacted me to come speak at his congregation. His name was Dan. He was a friend of Norman's. But, because he had problems with Yochanan, his ex-wife being a part of his congregation, Gayle and Paula advised me not to go speak at his congregation. I asked Abba. Abba said for me to go speak at his congregation. I was to speak Friday night in his home, then in a large gathering on Shabbat. The large gathering drew people from Dan's congregation, Norman's church, another pastor's group, and some people who even came from different states. They rented a large auditorium.

From our first meeting in his home on Friday, Dan and his wife, Kathy, and her brother and his wife, and I, bonded in the Spirit. I consider them good friends to this day. I met most of those on my Tennessee e-mail list at that Shabbat meeting. Dan was friends with a ministry in Israel, and was preparing his congregation to go to Israel. He and Kathy were so precious to me. I did not like being in the middle of a controversy between my friends Gayle, Paula, Yochanan, and Dan. But, because I see from Father's viewpoint, I saw both sides. So, as you can see, my time in Tennessee was very productive! Abba blessed it! I returned there for another set of meetings in 2009.

In early spring, I got an e-mail from a couple in western Tennessee who wanted to invite me to their home for Passover. They had read my articles. I accepted their invitation. Oh, I wish I had not! Our time at Passover in their home was very good. We had good fellowship. They were so excited about coming to Israel. I told them I'd help them any way I could. Passover Seder night, the couple also invited friends of theirs who lived down the road. During our after-dinner talking, I found out they had denied the deity of Messiah. I had dealt with this before, and was most agitated by their flippancy about it. It was like it didn't matter what they thought of Yahushua. The couple took my side. How was I to know this couple was just using me to get into Israel, and cared nothing about what Abba was saying? They came to Israel at Sukkot 2008. Their story is found in 2009.

During my week with them, the lady took me to meet my daughter from North Carolina in Cleveland (Tennessee). I stayed with her for three days. She brought me back, and the lady picked me up in Cleveland. Also that week, they took me to Sequoya's birthplace. (Notice the "yah" sound at the end of his name?) Being part Cherokee, it was a wonderful learning experience. I learned more of their Hebrew past, and mine.

In June, I went to Texas with my Florida daughter for my son's wedding. He had planned a rehearsal dinner for Saturday night. They were getting married the next morning. But, the dinner was early, and I could not break Shabbat. So, I told him I could not come, which he understood. I was supposed to meet the bride's family that night, but I couldn't help that. I had to obey Yahuweh. Knowing the dinner would violate Shabbat, about two weeks earlier, I e-mailed my friend Gezelle. I asked her if I could come over and have Shabbat with her. She turned it into a meeting for me. She invited all sorts of people from Texas to come hear me in her home. It was so big that her whole house was filled with people. It was a glorious meeting. That night I met people who would become solid friends, and some who would turn from faith in Messiah Yahushua. Gezelle was also a friend of Ladell's. We had some good times in East Texas together.

In 2007, Sukkot, I mentioned how Leslie had used the pastor of the church in Rhondda (Wales) to lure me to accept her invitation to her house for "meetings," and then to go with her, and her husband, to France. I really fell for that one. Leslie told me that the evening I would arrive, I would have a meeting at 7:00 in Newport. I had planned for many meetings in many places, since I was going to be in Wales, France, and England, almost a month.

After leaving France, I had planned to go to Wales. My friend, Maureen (from Swansea), and I, were going to the Wicklow Mountains, south of Dublin, Ireland for four days. Her son had found a trip-package for us. I was to have a meeting in her home when we returned, and then to go two places in the north of England to speak. Then I was to return to Wales and have a big meeting at Elaine's house.

While in Florida, one of the ladies who was to host me in North England sent me an e-mail saying that a lady she had met on Facebook, from Tennessee, had told her how vicious I was and not to have me come to her house. It was the chief jezebel from the "restaurant meeting" in Murfreesboro. But, my friend Jamie from Kentucky had told her about me, and given me a good report. So, I told her what happened, and she decided to have me come.

I will try to tell this story as simply as possible, because it has many entanglements and much mind-boggling betrayal attached to it. I flew from the U.S. on Friday, June 13th to Paris. From Paris,

I was to take a local commuter plane into Cardiff, Wales. Because of a delay getting out of Dallas/Fort Worth, the plane landed in Paris about 10 minutes after my flight to Cardiff. I had to buy a whole new ticket. For me the $270.00 ticket was devastating. I was still living on my credit card. My offerings were next to nothing. The flight would go out in six hours. I was exhausted. But, that would ruin the meeting in Newport. I tried to get hold of Leslie but I couldn't. Finally in Cardiff she picked me up. I was so distraught. Friday the 13th for sure – a nightmare! Leslie told me right away that something was wrong with her prayer-partner Lisa, and I would not meet her. Remember Lisa – the one who sent me those weird e-mails saying "you are evil," that I thought was a mistake? Leslie then told me that the people in Newport had cancelled the meeting anyway. Of course! There was no meeting in Newport to start with. She had not set up any meetings in her home either, as she had promised me. I should have known something was wrong.

I was supposed to visit the pastor, Darryl, and his congregation in the Rhondda. In May, I e-mailed Darryl and told him I'd need lodging to spend the night, then I'd speak the next day. But, instead of being his usual friendly self, he did everything to discourage me from coming. I thought that very strange. Of course Leslie had told him evil lies about me. The first night I was with her, she went to buy Ann and I "fish and chips" for dinner. She came back and said someone had frightened her while using her credit card in the ATM and she left her credit card in the ATM. She turned to me and said that she lost it because I had brought bad spirits from the airport in Paris. I told her I brought no bad spirits into her house. To show her play-acting deceit, in about five minutes, she found her credit card on the table near where she was standing, but she did not apologize for her outbreak at me.

Ann was a lady I met in 2007 at the dinner at Christ Church. I liked her very much. She was going to come with us to France. I had prayed for Ann's daughter, and there was a time we had good fellowship via e-mails. During those first few days, the three of us had a lovely day touring around Cardiff, and visiting old ruins by the Sea. On our way to France, going towards the English coast, we stopped at Winchester Cathedral. Leslie's husband was our driver. Then we went to where we'd get the ferry across the English channel from Portsmouth to Calais. All was well, it seemed. But, I was uneasy. Leslie kept isolating Ann, and shutting me out. I loved the ferry ride--an all night ride. I slept all night. I took lots of pictures of the sunrise over France.

It was at least a 10-hour drive down to Toulouse. Leslie sat in the front seat, and Ann and I sat in the backseat. All the way, Leslie kept turning around to Ann, expressly calling her name to tell her things, and ignored me. I tried to rest. Once at their lovely home in the country things got really bad. I was given a bedroom on the second floor, with windows opening onto the patio below. The second night, upon lying down to sleep, I felt as if heavy stones were on my chest. I couldn't breathe. I got horribly nauseous. I had diarrhea on top of vomiting. But, I began gasping for air because of the weight of the pressure on my chest. I was doing serious spiritual warfare. When I cast out the spirit of witchcraft, the pressure instantly lifted and I could breathe. But, I was very sick.

The next morning, Ann came to get me for breakfast. I told her I was very sick. But, I got down to breakfast and ate a little. Except for going to breakfast, and dinner, I mostly stayed in my room and studied the book of *Enoch*. I went with them into town the next day. I took short walks among the fields, too.

Leslie was obsessed with taking me on Saturday to the market. I told her I couldn't go because it was Shabbat. Ann said she had no problem buying things on Shabbat. Leslie said it was OK to buy on Shabbat. They both say they are "Messianic," but they are Christians who play games with obedience to Yahuweh. I asked them if they had ever read **Nehemiah 13**. They stared at me blankly. Then Leslie shook her head no, and said she had never read **Nehemiah 13**.

Another one of Leslie's friends came to stay two days. She was a nice young lady. But, all the while, Leslie kept pressuring me to go on Shabbat to the market with them. I wouldn't go. She even pressed me into the side of a building in town and got right in my face with a pained expression and asked me why I could not go. Later I realized that I tormented her. But, I also think that she was trying to get me to break Shabbat so that she could slander me as a phony and a fake. She and her friend Lisa were out to destroy my ministry, and my reputation – that's for sure. But why? I still can't figure that out.

We went to a famous castle nearby to do intercession, but she totally cut me out and only talked to Ann. I kept talking to Abba wherever I walked. Leslie later asked me if I was speaking in tongues, because she saw my lips moving. I said I was praying. Her husband was a nice man, but very passive--a former well-known physicist in Wales, who spent his time watching Rugby. They were quite wealthy. After retiring as a physicist, he did not keep up with the newest findings in physics. So, he was quite ignorant of many things that I had studied, which were current news.

The day I was to leave, I was very exhausted. I took down the top sheet she had given me for my bed to give to her for the laundry. She acted very disturbed that she had not given me a bottom sheet. I didn't care, but she sure did. It was 6:00 AM. She said we had to get to Toulouse to the airport because of morning traffic. It was 45 minutes to the airport, and my plane did not go out until 11:00. We got to the airport by a little after 7:00. There was hardly any traffic. I had four hours to wait in that tiny airport, and I was sick. Upon saying "goodbye," I hugged Ann. Then Leslie said: "I will pray for your salvation." I thought that strange. I said "thank you for letting me stay with you", and then went into the airport. I was looking so forward to seeing Maureen from Swansea. She was so sweet to me. I was looking forward so much to our trip to Ireland. That whole 10 days in France was so traumatic. Later I found out that yes, she had been planning to ruin me, for a long time.

IRELAND
(2008)

I flew into Cardiff, and Maureen picked me up. I had a meeting in her home. The next day we began our glorious trip to Ireland, across from Fishguard, Wales to Rosslare, Ireland. She took her car, as it was a car-ferry. She drove up the coast to our lovely hotel in the Wicklow mountains. We went to many ports. I love marinas and ports! But, our special trip into the Wicklow mountains was incredibly wonderful. I saw several Irishmen who looked like papa. We went back to Swansea, and I spoke at a meeting in her home. Sadly, after I spoke, a lady asked a question. In my answer, without knowing it, I said something that spoke contrary to a very important doctrine in their church, and almost all of them walked out furious at me.

Then I took the train 7 hours to Leeds, England. I was met by a lovely lady, Marian, whom I stayed with. She took me to her house. It was a lovely English house. I found out that she was also a former member of the World Wide Church of God. I had a wonderful visit with Marian. Then she took me to the train station and I went by train to Durham, a small town near Newark. I stayed there with a young American woman and her two daughters. I had two meetings there. It was this young lady that the jezebel from Tennessee had tried to block. We did have wonderful fellowship. She was glad that she listened to Jamie, and didn't cancel our times together.

During one of the meetings, there came a Jewish Messianic rabbi and his wife. I was told that his wife did not talk to anyone. She was a nice lady, she was just very quiet. But, before the meeting, she came and sat at the kitchen table, where I was having dinner. She asked me: "Where I was from." I love that question. It always makes me laugh. And I laughed this time. I said: "I'm from wherever I was last, but I am staying in Tiberias, Israel, as much as possible." She was so amazed. She said: "I love Tiberias." She opened up to me, and when they left, she hugged me, to everyone's surprise. We had good e-mail dialogue for some time. I had such good fellowship while I was there with this lady.

While I was there, I was told about a man in Newcastle to whom I had been sending my articles. He was a good friend of Simon Altaf--the Muslim convert to Christianity who became a Messianic rabbi, who has a synagogue in the main city of Pakistan with a big menorah on it. This man has become a big name in America and in the UK. He wrote books on the end times saying that the Bible was loaded with things about Islam in the last days. I learned that this man was sending my articles to Altaf, who was using them to mock me, and tear me down, in order to "prove" his teachings.

Now, think about this sanely: Pakistan is under the most strict Muslim law. They publically execute any Muslim who converts to Christianity. And here is Altaf with a big synagogue, with a menorah on the front of it, in the capital city, untouched by anyone. I smell a "mole." I leafed briefly through Altaf's book on the end-times. His conclusions are ludicrous to anyone who has understanding of the Bible, and the nature of Yahuweh. But, ignorant westerners buy into lies and deceptions easily, if they are promoted by someone who is "new and different."

I was scheduled to take the train to Elaine's in two days. I was to have a meeting there at her house, then she was going to take me to Cardiff to get the plane to Edinburgh, then I was to fly to the U.S. Elaine had been on a missionary trip, and was coming in two days before me. I had bought my train ticket. I was so excited. We were such good friends! I loved it at her house. But, when it came time to leave for Elaine's meeting, I found out some of the devastation that Leslie caused.

The day before I was to leave, Elaine called the lady who was hosting me and told her to tell me not to come. She said she was tired from her trip, and could not host me. She called Elaine back to ask more questions, finally telling Elaine to talk to me. A short while later, I talked to Elaine. She sounded very strange, as she made excuses as to why I could not come. I pleaded with her, saying I didn't have to have a meeting, I just wanted to see her. I could not get her to tell me the truth. Finally, I told her I would not come, but this left me with a broken heart.

That night, Abba hovered over me with His Presence to comfort me. He told me to read **I Kings 17-19**. I had read that so many times, but I obeyed. The next morning, I went downstairs to get coffee. My hostess was already at her computer. She said she wanted to read me an e-mail sent to her by a lady named Valerie, which had come from Don Esposito's ministry. The letter from Don was about someone who had seen Eliyahu (Elijah) in person in Jerusalem. First of all, Valerie was on my e-mail list, and I knew her. Small world! But, the description of Eliyahu was identical to what I had seen in a vision of Eliyahu in March of 2008, along with Moshe, Enoch, Dani'el, and Yochanan (John) the Apostle. The man who saw Eliyahu in Jerusalem was one of Don's friends. He spoke fluent Hebrew, and ancient Aramaic. Eliyahu spoke to him in Aramaic. Abba was using this to encourage me. I cancelled my flight out of Cardiff. I bought a 1-way train ticket to Edinburgh. When I got to the train station, I saw that I had bought a first class ticket. I smiled. Abba wanted me to leave in style. I enjoyed my bus ride from the train station to the airport too. It was kind of a tour of downtown Edinburgh.

When I got back to the U.S., I got an e-mail from a loyal friend in Tiberias. Leslie had sent e-mails to all my friends in Israel, and to the heads of Messianic ministries, whom she was affiliated with, saying that I was a witch, and that I put spells on people. She said I took hair out of their hairbrushes to put curses on she and Ann. She said I was writing notes and hiding them in the curtains, then throwing them out of my window, and when she came to see what I was doing, I told her that the spirits of my ancestors would curse everyone. There were no curtains on her windows! It was all a horrible lie!

Everything she said was 100% against my nature. I said nothing, nor did nothing, to even bring such a thought to their minds. I just wanted to talk about Abba the whole time. I even had a special talk with Ann about Abba, which she attentively listened to. As soon as Leslie got back from the airport, she began slandering me to many of my dear friends. Lisa also chimed in to slander me to people in the UK. A loyal friend on my e-mail list in England got this report from Lisa and told her to stop her lies. Leslie convinced blond Maureen, in Israel, that I was a witch, and tried to convince another friend also. My loyal friend, Connie, went to war for me, and shut up the slander quickly. But, it spread to Actress Lady too. Because blond Maureen liked me, she figured I had a mental breakdown, and she spread that message. She could not believe that Leslie had lied. But, much damage was done to my reputation.

The next time I saw blond Maureen, a year later, was at one of Michael Rood's home meetings. She came up to me and commented on how good I looked. I knew what she was saying--I looked good after my mental breakdown. What was so tragic to me was that Elaine believed Leslie, and was terrified for me to come to her house. To this day, Elaine still believes Leslie, even though Swansea-Maureen told her it was not true. Elaine did reimburse me for the train ticket that I did not use, and for the train ticket I had to buy. That was kind.

It was mid-July. I went back to the U.S. devastated, but I was soon on the road again with Abba's business. I had been invited by Gloria and Gene to come to their wedding in Colorado, and be a part of it. Her fiancé, Gene, had written me to ask me what date in July I thought was good for the wedding. I told him July 25th was my birthday. So, they set the date for July 25th.

About a week before, a couple offered to let me stay in their house while they were on vacation. I flew into Denver. I stayed at the home of Nita and Ross. From there I took wonderful walks, and people came for visits and counseling.

My first afternoon there, I went to lie down, read the Word, and pray in the bedroom they had assigned me. But, I noticed that the Presence of Abba, which I am so used to, was not there. I didn't know what to do. I tried reading the Word, but it was dull. He was not teaching me like usual. I rose up, threw my feet onto the floor, and looked straight at a large framed copy of a print/drawing/painting, that hung by my bed. Then I noticed three more of these large framed drawings. I also saw some small ones, leaning up against the wall, not yet hung. I am not a detail person. I did not notice them upon entering the room. I gasped. I was looking at a picture of a Southwest Indian chief, who looked to be Sioux or Cheyenne. Around him was a drawing of the desert, and included were symbols of their ability to change themselves into hawks and wolves. Their religion is very demonic, and opens portals for them to be used by demons. I saw that the other pictures were similar. So, I gently took down the pictures, and put them all, facing the wall, at the end of the hallway. Upon returning, within a few minutes, they asked me why the pictures were at the end of the hall. I told them the story. During that week, they put them all in their van and took them to a dumpster. They were nicely framed. I am sure, since they are popular prints of the Southwest, that they represented a lot of money.

After the lovely Messianic wedding, which I also participated in, I was invited to speak at a meeting on a ranch with some people who were on my e-mail list. Several congregations came together for this meeting, hosted by the Murphy family. It was a very special meeting! I still have people on my address list from that meeting.

After the meeting, everyone ate and ate. I sat in the living room talking to two couples. I can still see it. The ones in front of me were W. and S. The ones sitting to my left on the couch were T. and R. The men were brothers. T. and R. were not yet married, but soon to be married. R. said she worked for Michael Rood in Israel for a year and a half. I about fell off the couch when I heard that. I asked her if she knew my loyal friend who fought for me that early July--Connie. She said that she and Connie worked together for a year and a half. Small world!

T. said that once they got married and moved to Panama, where W. and S. already lived, I was welcome to come stay with them. I said I would come. Gloria's husband had lived in Panama. I had gotten interested in Panama from contact with the "May His Teachings Fall Like Rain" group in Texas and Colorado. I learned later, most shockingly, that it was T. and W. who started the

PART VI - The Middle East & Travels Beyond

group. Because of this meeting, I would spend a year and a half in Panama.

To give you a little more background on this, it was earlier in the year, a friend from Florida, Carol, had taken a couple of my articles to her daughter. The daughter gave articles to a couple, friends of hers, in Gainesville, Texas. I did not know until later that this couple had come to Gezell's meeting earlier in the year-- the night before my son got married. This couple was a member of the "May His Teachings Fall Like Rain group." So, they sent the articles to Colorado, to the headquarters there. I got a deluge of e-mails from this group. I didn't know who they were so I was very skeptical of them, but they were precious. How was I to know that T and W started this group? So, you see, this is just one example of the incredible networking power of Yahuweh!

In late July, I had received a very large check from a woman who lived near Tampa. I did not know her. I asked a few people, and they did not know her. Why was she sending me this big check? I thanked her. Then she, Yvette, invited me to speak at her house on Shabbat, and to stay Friday and Saturday night with her family. I agreed.

In early August she came to get me. I learned her family were Sephardic Jews from Spain. I went to speak at her house. I was to have one big meeting. Friday night was for meeting her friends and relaxing. She and her husband have five lovely homeschooled children. They have a gorgeous home on an inlet of the Gulf. The living room is big. While sitting in her kitchen, a couple walked in. I just froze. I thought to myself: I am in Florida, is that right? It was T. and R. whom I had met in Colorado. How does this lady know them? Long story... They were friends of dear Yvette, and she had invited them. How they teamed up is a monumental story in itself.

The meeting on Shabbat was large--she had invited a lot of people. Some of them I knew from my first meeting in Florida, and some were on my e-mail list, but I had never met them in person. This meeting began a very special friendship with Yvette, Jon, and their family. She has been a blessing to me, and to my entire family!

In September, I went to Colombia for the first time. I met with Rocio and her Torah-guarding home group. They followed her out of the church system when Rocio resigned from her evangelical church position as pastor and started guarding Torah. It was a wonderful visit. They treated me so well. She told me how Tom and Audry had led them all to salvation. I met her mother and two sisters. Rocio lived in a small village high in the mountains above Medellin. During my stay there, we went to an ancient

Indian village, Pueblito Paisa. Then we went into the city. We also visited at Magnolia's home and had dinner. What a wonderful day! I taught at meetings in Rocio's home. On my way out of Colombia, since they did not have an x-ray machine, the security guards had to hand check all my luggage. I will never forget one man picking up my Bible, putting it to his nose, and thumbing the pages to check for drugs. So funny!

AMERICA--ISRAEL--PANAMA
(2009)

I went back to Israel in March for Passover. The couple, whom I had met the year before in Cleveland, Tennessee, had come to Israel. I helped them get Moriel's former apartment. They became friends of the landlord. But, before they left Tennessee, they called the landlord to make sure the apartment had been reserved for them. In the course of their telephone conversation, he asked her if she was Jewish. She said, "yes." She was full-blooded Italian. He might have been Jewish. He was from Poland. But, basically, she lied.

They got to Tiberias shortly before I returned. They asked me to stay with them, which I did. Launa met these two in Jerusalem. They realized they had met before, so it was grand reunion. Yvette, and her sister Michelle, came to join Launa and I during Passover week. We all attended a private Seder on Passover eve, put on by the Sephardic rabbi who ran the soup kitchen that Launa worked with. Launa was also hosting an Australian lady, whom she had previously met. The Seder very special, and we all felt welcome by the rabbi and his wife. We thanked Launa for allowing us to attend.

On Tuesday, April 8th, the day of the spring equinox, an every-28-year event happened--Birkat Hahamah. From *The Jerusalem Post*, April 7th: "Jews around the world will greet the sun with a once-in-28-year prayer on the eve of Passover: Hundreds of thousands of Jews around the world will awake before dawn on Tuesday, climb to high advantage points and wait for the sun as they recite a prayer said only once every 28 years." The whole Western Wall area was packed with thousands of people, also standing on higher elevations above the Wall.

Launa, the Australian lady, and I, were staying at the Petra Hostel. We got up about 3:00 AM to join the throngs of Orthodox Jews at the Wall to watch the rising of the sun. I wrote an article entitled "Birkat Hahamah," with pictures, to show what happened on that day. I was dressed in all white, with a bridal-type head covering. Yvette gave me a rose bud, which I still have. I was pressed in with so many people, but they almost all wore black, so I really stood out. But, as I stood there, all I could think of was **Ezekiel 8:15-18** – and how they "put the branch to His nose" while venerating the sun rising over the Mount of Olives. It was/is an abomination to Yahuweh. In ancient times, they would put palm branches over their eyes to shield them from the rays of the rising sun. In other words, they wanted Yahuweh to be included in their worship of the sun god. This is the origin of the Easter Sunrise services – pagan sun god worship. It was quite an education, as you can read from the article, "Birkat Hahamah – The Blessing of the Sun/May 2009.

Launa was playing "tour guide" for the Australian lady. I went with them on some of their touring. Yvette and Michelle, were staying at the House of Prayer. They had rented a car, and tried to follow us around, but we were too speedy. We rented a car and escaped from Jerusalem about 8:00 AM on "Easter/Ishtar/Astarte/Diana/Isis" day to have a peaceful day outside the chaos of the Old City. The first place that we went to was Qumran. I had wanted to go there for a long time. She and her Australian friend went off on their own, and I began wandering among the ruins. I could not stop crying for some reason. I felt at home. They left the ruins before I did, but they didn't rush me. That experience changed my life. I felt the presence of Yochanan the Immerser, who was there, and the spirit of the Essenes who lived there, enveloped me. The Essenes were Zadok priests, rightful priests, who fled Jerusalem, when the Romans came in.

When I went back to the U.S., I wrote: "A Radical View of Set-Apartness." I had a dream about the "sons of Belial" being there, and the people not letting them into their enclosure. It was in the present-day setting. I would return three more years to visit Qumran.

We went on to Ein Gedi. As they went up the side of the mountain to the high upper waterfall, I walked to the first waterfall. Yvette and Michelle got there after we did. Then they came with us to the Dead Sea beach area, where tourists can float on the heavy salt water. I did not participate in that.

In the north, Launa and her friend went to key tourist places. I went with them. I have been to Banias so many times, but this time, they also decided to go to the Banias Falls, then to Tel Dan. I did not walk down to Banias Falls, but I did go along the path in "Ancient Tel Dan." Because Launa and her friend were hikers, they went on ahead of me. I was using my cane to support every step. The huge rocks going up to the area of the golden calf altar were very steep. I had to walk very slowly. Once up through the ancient Gate of the City, I had to cross several streams. The Dan River, which supplies the "Yardan"/Jordan River, comes down from the melted snows off Mount Hermon. The river rushes incredibly fast. From above the river, streams of water flow down towards the huge river. They cross the stony paths. The rocks are slick and unstable. One wrong move and my ankles and knees could go out of place, and I'd be washed away. I was by myself.

But, every time I came to a scary place, Abba arranged for some Israeli tourists to come to help me. I'd heard some say:

"She is so brave," or "she is such an adventurer" – things like that. I'd smile and thank them profusely. But, it hurt, that I was not only left to myself, but Launa often made fun of me because I am slow, and use a cane. She called me "Gimpy." The Australian lady went back to Australia and soon let Launa know that she rejected the Torah and all that Launa had told her about it. Launa wore herself out to show this lady Israel, and that was the response.

After returning to the U.S., I went on my 2nd trip to Colombia (May 27-June 1), and stayed with Rocio and her momma in Itagui, above Medellin. Again, my time with them was wonderful! I conducted a meeting with her group in her home. Many were baptized in the Spirit. I had prophecy for almost all of them too. This was Shavu'ot, 2009.

T. and R. had gotten married and moved to Panama. They invited me to come. I flew into Panama City in early June, and took Panama Air to David (pronounced Dah-veed in Hebrew). At that time, T. and R. were staying in a rented house with W. and S. close to David. I had a meeting in their home, and several people they had met attended. But, each couple needed their own house. So, I went with T and R to look for housing. They went towards Boquete, and found a very large house with 5 bedrooms, two very large living areas, two bathrooms, an open-style kitchen, big front porch, and lots of land around it. The landlady, Anna, was from Chile. She lived in the big house next door. T. and R. were balking at the rent price, so she lowered the rent price because she liked us.

She had married a wealthy man from Switzerland. But, he had died. She was lonely, and wanted neighbors. She and I were about the same age. I said I'd split the rent with them. I said it would be a good center for Shabbat get-togethers and fellowships, and having people come stay with us. The landlady said she'd hold it for them until the first of August. They picked out the best bedroom in the house for me. So, in August they moved down there, and I moved down there before leaving for Israel for the Fall Festivals.

While there, they took me on some "field trips" of the area. We went to the Pacific Ocean, to Puerto Armuelles on the Golfo de Chiriqui. We lived in the Chiriqui (pronounced Cherokee) region of north Panama. There we visited a lady who was on my e-mail list. We visited a Hydroponics Center in Boquete. We went down to the huge river also, which fed a huge hydroelectric plant.

I wanted to buy one of the Indian dresses that the local Indians wore. R. told me that there was an Indian store up above Boquete. I thought she meant a "real" store. They drove up into the lush rain forest, along a River. Then they pulled up at a 3-sided hut. There were about 15 Indian dresses in different colors, all my size--I bought two.

By this time, R.'s sister, Cheri, had come to join us. T., R., Cheri, Anna, and I, made a trip to Volcan Baru (the volcano name is "Baruch" in Hebrew – "the volcano of blessings.") We had some huge rocks in our yard from those "blessings." They took me up to the ruins of Sitas Barias, an ancient site where Luciferics came to worship during the year. It is such a magnetic site that the river flows backwards. It was an ancient area where a huge city had been built by Chinese and Africans who settled there.

While climbing the mountain to the Volcano area, I told T. about how I met them, about how Carol took the article to her daughter, etc. and how this group—"May His Teachings Fall Like Rain" e-mailed me, and I got invited to Colorado. T quietly said: "W. and I started that group." I was so shocked. Abba really knows how to put puzzle pieces together to create His pre-planned outcome! So, I went back to the U.S. to prepare to move to Panama in August. In the meantime, I kept busy for Abba.

In July, I had been in contact with a young couple in Whitefish, Montana, and a lady named Viola, in Libby, Montana, both on my e-mail list. Both needed fellowship, so I hooked them up together. I've always been a good "networker." They invited me to come. I would first go visit the young couple, then go visit with Viola. In the meantime, I got an invitation from a family in another part of north Montana. I flew into Kalispell, and Jason picked me up. I went to their home in Whitefish. I was in Montana August 11th – 19th. Elizabeth and I walked to Whitefish Lake several times. It was so peaceful and lovely. They had a 1-year old named Ani.

One day she took me to Glacier National Park--to Logan Pass--the Continental Divide, 6,648 feet up. It was so gorgeous. The Rocky Mountains are higher in some places than the Swiss Alps. During that trip we also made a fast 30-minute trip into British Colombia, Canada. It was at the border of Roosville, in the Yak Region. We couldn't stay long because I was to meet another family who would take me into the real northwest, where they lived. We met them, and they took me to their house just 3 miles from the Canadian border along the Yaak River. They had built a very large wooden house in a clearing in the woods. I slept downstairs. It was at their house, going down the stairs that He spoke to me: "**Return to the ancient paths**." I now understand more fully! (**Jeremiah 6:16**)

The fellowship there was awesome, people came from many miles around. I did not have to teach – our fellowship was one continual teaching session. He had an ancient Torah scroll, which

I got to hold. Then Viola came to get me, and took me to her house in Libby. The next day she took me back to Jason and Elizabeth's house, since it was near the airport where I would fly out.

I had learned that a Messianic website had posted some of my articles, and given me credit for them, as well as **laydownlife.net**. While riding with Viola, I told her about that, and she told me that it was she who sent them my articles. I bless those that use my articles without changing anything, giving me, and the website they get it from, credit. That is the only honorable way to function. But, some Messianic sites that use my articles are not honorable – they give no credit to me or to the two websites who post for me now, and often they change the way I spell Yahuweh and Yahushua – to the way they spell it. That is blasphemous to me, and to Him--He is the One who told me how to say His Name.

Montana is gorgeous. I learned however, that like Nevada, Utah, and many other states, all of the national parks are U.N. International Biospheres. In other words, all of America's National Parks and wilderness areas belong to the United Nations. For example, approximately 87% of Nevada belongs to the U.N. Viola told me land in Montana, what land was left for private ownership, was very expensive.

While sitting in a parking area, waiting to reconnect with Jason and Elizabeth, I got a phone call from the Florida daughter. She said the Tampa airport was closed because of a hurricane coming in, and Delta had rescheduled me into Atlanta and put me in first class. Jason and Elizabeth were happy to host me an extra day. So, I actually flew back on August 20th. While waiting at the airport, I asked Delta if they had an earlier flight to Tampa, and they put me on a direct flight, bypassing Atlanta. So, it worked out fine. Later Jason and Viola both began posting my articles on their blog sites for a while.

In late August, I planned a "Texas tour." I would go first to Corpus Christi and finish the intercession along the Gulf there, at Port Aransas. Then I would visit my son in Fort Worth. I was invited to have a meeting in the home of a couple who were in the "May His Teachings Fall Like Rain" group, who lived in Gainesville, Texas. Then, I would fly to Fort Smith to visit my Aunt Ahnie and my cousins. Last, I would fly to Tyler, Texas, and visit my good Jamia, Mark, and their family, and have a meeting in their home. Jamia also set up for me to have personal one-on-one meetings at her house with three of my closest friends in the area. But, before I went to Corpus Christi, something awful happened to me.

One day, with no warning, I got knife-stab pains in my lower right side, to the right of the appendix area, just above the hip. The first attack of these pains, which was worse than natural child birth, lasted 9 hours until I passed out literally from exhaustion due to the pain. I had a couple more attacks like this before I got to Texas. When I got to Corpus Christi, I was met by two ladies. One, with her husband, was visiting from Dallas, and the other one and her husband were my hosts. I was to have two meetings--Friday night, and Shabbat. We went to do the intercession over Corpus Christi and Post Aransas. But, against my pattern that Abba gave me, the two ladies had invited two others to join us, besides the two husbands, so there were 7 of us in all. We went out to eat after our intercession.

That night, as I laid down to go to sleep, I felt demonic spirits in the room. Then I saw a "skinhead" young man walking back and forth under some dried roses that were hanging from the ceiling at the foot of the bed. I was staying in the room of the couple's college-student daughter. All night, the demonic spirits were manifesting at the end of my bed. They won't come near me--I've learned that. The next morning, I told the couple about that, and they threw away the roses. They said that their daughter had been dating a skinhead who had given her the roses. I am not a mystic, or a spooky person. I just know the world of Yahuweh, and the world of Satan.

I got a severe pain in my left eye just before the meeting Friday evening, which continued during the meeting. One lady's husband was a chiropractor from Dallas. He helped alleviate the headache. On Shabbat, one of the ladies who had gone on the intercession trip with us the day before, came to the meeting. She was from Jamaica, or Puerto Rico (?). She had three daughters who were unruly, so her husband was given a place to take them in the back of the house. The girls kept screaming, and running around outside too. I knew they were demonized, which was confirmed later.

After the meeting, I went back to the bedroom. Earlier, I had put all the money I had, which I had taken out of the bank, in a money belt that I kept at the bottom of my backpack. I had my computer too, and all of my belongings out in the room. Not thinking anyone would be in the room but me, I put the computer on the floor. But, when I entered the room, I was horrified to the point of near hysteria. The husband and those girls were given that room to stay in. I saw that my backpack had obviously been gone through. I checked to see if my money was still there, and it was. That night, I realized that my earplug box was gone. It could

PART VI - The Middle East & Travels Beyond

not be found. I can't sleep without the earplugs - throwback to traumatic days with my husband.

I could not believe they would do that. I am a very private person, and such a violation of my privacy was beyond belief to me. I did not sleep well that night because the earplugs were gone. The next morning after breakfast, as I was repacking, there, near the top of the backpack, was the earplug box. It was not there the night before, but no one claimed to have put it back.

In returning to Florida, one night trying to go to sleep, Abba's Presence came into the room, and He let me know that both women were highly dangerous; they were into deep witchcraft. This was confirmed by others later. Later these two couples moved to Jordan. I had friends who knew them and reported on demonic spirits that emanated from them. The pains, in that one place on my body, began as soon as I accepted their invitation to come to Corpus Christi.

The next time, upon returning from Panama, via Houston, when I got off the airplane, I went to the bathroom. All of a sudden the pains came hard and fast. I had to go through Houston Immigration, and customs, and go through security again, and then get to my gate – all in that condition. Once at the gate, I laid down on the floor of the airport to await my flight to Tampa. The pains lasted for many hours. The pains, at first, were all centered around times I was in Texas. I am sure that witchcraft was done against me, and it continued. This type of witchcraft is called "voodoo." My ex-husband was powerful in witchcraft. He was raised by a black "nanny" from Haiti. He might have learned voodoo from her. But, I don't think he was involved with these attacks. It could also have come from Lisa and Leslie in Wales. However, from what I learned later, the origin was from Corpus Christi. As time went on, I learned of the rising of witchcraft/jezebel/**Revelation 17** all over the earth.

I began checking the internet for symptoms of appendicitis, kidney stones, intestinal blockage, and the like, and also learning what to do for such things. I began studying different types of water, and about taking herbs and other products to cleanse my system. But, the pains kept up. They continued in Florida. Each time they could be associated with a pattern. So many times they were connected to an event related to witchcraft. Finally, you'll read about how this terrible 2½ years of pain ended in 2011, and about what lessons I learned.

After going to Fort Worth to visit my son, he took me to the Dallas airport for me to fly 45 minutes to Fort Smith, Arkansas. Then he went on to church. As soon as I got to the gate, the knife-stab pain came quickly. There was no warning to them--the attacks just came like a knife stab and then the pain would increase quickly to where it was like having a baby naturally, but worse. The pain took its time, sometimes lasting from 5 hours to 10 hours. To make matters worse, my fight was cancelled because American Airlines is infamous for cancelling short commuter flights due to not having enough passengers to give them the money that want. They always say it is a mechanical problem, but if that's so, they have more mechanical problems than any other airline in the world.

They announced that the flight was cancelled. I was in so much pain that by the time I got to the re-schedule line, I was re-scheduled on the last plane--at 9:00 PM. I noticed that there were only 10 on that flight, so that is why they cancelled, not for mechanical problems. It was about 11:00 AM by this time. I would have a 10-hour layover to go 45 minutes. They put me on standby for the other flights too. I tried to call my son to come get me, but he had his phone turned off. I longed for a place to lie down other than the floor. I walked to the next section, and there was a real lounge with recliner chairs. I laid down in one of those. The pain kept up until early evening. I went to get something to eat. While in line at a buffet, a man came up next to me and asked me something. I turned to face him, and it was my son. He had gotten my message. They let him in to help me. It was so wonderful to see him. We had a good time of fellowship. Then I got to Fort Smith and all was well. I had a good time with my aunt and cousin Larry. It would be the last time I'd see Ahnie alive.

I then flew to Tyler, via Dallas. Jamia picked me up and we went shopping. A couple from the Austin area had driven all that way to meet with me. Jamia took me to their hotel. The lady was a Young Living essential oils distributer. Young Living oils are real steam-extracted essential oils that work. She gave me about $400.00 worth of oils that day. That started me on getting the oils, and wow have they been a blessing! The couple stayed to hear me in about three meetings.

When I got to Jamia's house, she and Mark wanted to talk to me about direction for their lives. They had been YWAM missionaries in Albania, Fiji, and Germany, and wanted to get back into action. They had met a lady from Aqaba who offered opportunities in Scotland. They had gone to Scotland to meet her. But, they felt something was not right. She was being called "the anointed lady." They wanted to know what I knew about her. They had met the Aqaba leader-lady. Evidently, she is still deceiving, still has megalomania, is still raking in money from rich fools, and is still exalting herself as a goddess. When I finished

PART VI - The Middle East & Travels Beyond

my short distortion on why they should run the other way, Mark asked where I thought they should go. I said: "Panama." Mark went to the computer, and by the next morning they knew from Abba that they were to move to Panama. Abba really worked everything out for them. They moved to Panama less than a year after I did. It was so wonderful having my good friends with me in Panama. They stayed with T., R., and I, until they got a place of their own. What a reunion! They brought the two youngest of their five children, the girl about 11 and the boy about 15, and they were such an asset too.

Before my first meeting in Tyler, I met with three friends, and answered questions. That was a blessing! The meetings were wonderful, and it was a good trip. I was reunited with my African-American friends from East Texas also. They're a blessing to me! On the way out, there was a delay--American Airlines again--and by the time I got to Dallas, my flight had gone. So, I got to stay with my son for another night. The next morning American Airlines put me in First Class and flew me to Tampa. They had shut down their whole wing of the airport the night before, put the people in hotels, and would not let them take their luggage off the plane. It was weird.

In August, I flew to Panama, bringing some belongings to move in. By this time, others had also come, and we were bonding together like a family. Three weeks later, I was at the airport in Panama City, and I had a five hour layover before my plane went back to Florida. I had wanted to visit the Panama Canal. I hired a taxi man with a nice van to take me there. He was so super! He told me all kinds of inside things about the U.S. presence there, and the Chinese who controlled the Canal. He waited for me to go up to the visitor's area, see the Canal, intercede in prayer, take lots of pictures, and do souvenir shopping. While overlooking the Canal, I also did intercession for Abba's people who may need to escape through this route. He took me back another way so that I would see the Atlantic Ocean and the Port area. What a wonderful tour!

In flying back from Panama into Miami, a couple sat across the aisle from me, but one row back. It was late at night and most people were trying to sleep. They had their light on above their seats, and were playing Backgammon. They kept throwing dice, which was very nerve-wracking. I noticed that she had a large diamond ring. It was so big that there had to be two bands on which to rest it. I couldn't take my eyes off that diamond. I've never seen one so big, except for the Hope Diamond at the Smithsonian in Washington D.C..

In September, I flew to Miami to get the plane to Paris, then on to Tel Aviv. I sat at the gate in Miami, waiting to board the plane for Paris. As soon as I sat down, a young couple came and sat beside me. Their accent sounded Swedish. They immediately got out a Backgammon set and began to play the game. I looked over at them, and then I saw her ring. It was the same couple who was on the plane from Panama. My mind went blank. I stood up, looked down at them, staring at her ring. The man noticed and made a frown on his face, so I walked away. On the flight to Paris, he kept coming down the opposite aisle and staring at me. Was that a coincidence? Or were they tracking me? To this day I can still remember that ring and that Backgammon set.

Back in Tiberias, I again stayed with the couple who had invited me to Passover in 2008, in Tennessee. Because I helped them get the apartment, they let me stay in one of the bedrooms. But, I paid ½ the rent each month. I do not take advantage of anyone's kindness. I have integrity. I am NO MOOCHER! I also share my end of the work when I stay with people, and my share of the food that we all use. At first all was well. We even went on an intercession trip across the north of Israel together. They were Catholics who had converted to Protestantism.

As I said previously, she is full-blooded Italian. He is Polish, and may be Jewish. But, because Israel only takes the lineage of the mother for someone to make aliyah, they desperately tried to find her Jewish side to her family, to no avail. They told me that if they had to deny Messiah, they would, because they had to stay in Israel. They started going to an Orthodox synagogue up the road, and began identifying with the Orthodox Jews. I've heard of other American Messianics who thought that God wouldn't mind if they denied Messiah, just to get aliyah (citizenship). Some said they would lie about denying Messiah, because it would be all right with God, since God wanted them to stay in Israel. Do you see the insane thinking that has brought so much grief to Yahuweh and Yahushua, and to His servants, like me?

When this couple's three-month visa was almost ended, they went on a ship to Turkey for a few days. Upon returning, they still had a week left on their visa. At Israeli Immigration, the lady went on and on about how they loved Israel and wanted to live there. She was so scared that Immigration would not let them back in. That annoyed the lady at Immigration, and she told them they had to be out in one week because then their visa would expire. In a panic they went to the landlord and pleaded for help. Their landlord, the one who was also Moriel's landlord, liked them. His wife worked for the Ministry of the Interior that handled aliyah. Also, remember, before coming to Israel they had told the landlord they were Jewish?

As time went on, the landlord had a hard time convincing the Ministry of the Interior to keep renewing their visa. But, they eventually converted to Judaism, denied Messiah, and are still in Israel. While I was staying with them, they slowly became paranoid about my being there. They kept the lamp on all night on Friday night, because the Jews were watching them. If they turned off the lamp after sunset, of course they would be breaking Jewish law. They were motivated by so much fear. They were afraid for me to have Messianic guests.

During that time, Actress Lady, after eating a nice Shabbat dinner with the couple and I, invited us to her apartment next door to watch a YouTube production in which her daughter was performing. She kept us there quite a while, but she could never find the right YouTube video. I know now that it was a diversionary tactic to keep me away, while the man left to do some dirty work in the apartment. He changed the electric outlet so I could not use the computer on Shabbat, or make a phone call. When I discovered what he had done, I was both sick inside and angry. I was going to Michael Rood's meetings at 4:00 PM on Shabbat. Abigail was taking me. And, at times I needed to confirm the timing of her picking me up, or to cancel her picking me up, but I had no way of reaching her. I stayed with them four times in Israel, but it got worse and worse each time. I stayed with them approximately 3 months each time beginning with Passover 2008 into June, Yom Teruah through Sukkot 2008, Passover 2009 into the early summer, and late summer to Sukkot 2009.

Before Sukkot 2009, Howie from Wales and his wife from Nashville, Tennessee, stayed in Actress Lady's apartment, house-sitting, while she was in England. I had felt that Abba wanted me to do intercession over the north area again. But, I knew I could not ask this ex-Catholic couple to go with me. They were getting so devious and strange. Every time I would go into the kitchen to fix something to eat, she would run and turn on the fan, and face it out the window, as if my cooking would stink up the house.

I talked to Howie and his wife about going across the north. They were very excited and wanted to go too. So, we planned a trip and went--it was marvelous. Howie had only been a believer for four years, yet his maturity level in the Word in knowing Abba was amazing. They had been playing instruments and singing at Hippy Festivals and New Age Festivals in Israel; sharing the Good News of Messiah. They even ministered on the Lake and in Hippie camps.

When I returned from our trip, the couple was sitting on the couch in the living room, waiting for me. They quickly asked me where I had been, and what I was doing. Like Actress Lady, they thought I would include them in all of my intercession trips. But, how could I? Their hearts were far from the Elohim of the Bible, the true Elohim of Israel. So this added to the tension. I found out they were jealous of me being able to go and come as I willed, and also that I had many friends. Jealousy is such a stupid thing! But, it is the basic motivating force of Lucifer against Yahuweh and His set-apart ones who love Him.

The couple isolated themselves among the Orthodox, so of course they had few friends that were not Hebrew-speaking Israelis. Besides being friends with Launa, and an American family who had denied Messiah and converted to Judaism, they stayed alone most of the time. They had also been given a huge TV. I commented that I did not watch TV. The paranoia over that increased the tension too. I even brought them DVDs to watch on it, but they borrowed the same DVDs from a lady downstairs. Then I noticed that when I came out of my room, they started retreating into their room. The tension was building more. I could do nothing right. I got scolded by the lady several times a day. Before going to Jerusalem for Sukkot with Launa, who had become close friends of theirs by this time, they asked for my key to the apartment. I thought that strange.

For several weeks, because of my discovering their treachery to do with blocking my ability to use my computer or make a phone call on Shabbat, I began spending weekends with my new friend, Devorah, in her shared apartment with Cheryl, in north Tiberias. She became a very special and dear friend. So, by this time, my stress level of being with this paranoid couple had reached its maximum.

During Sukkot week, Launa and I stayed at the Petra Hostel. Devorah and her soon-to-be-husband, Malachel, came to visit me there. While they were there, Actress Lady, who had returned from England, was staying at Christ Church. She came to visit me too, at the same time. I was pouring out my heart to Devorah about this couple, how I feared their taking my key, etc. Actress Lady heard it all. I did not know she would go back to Tiberias and tell them what I said, but she did.

That week Launa took me to Shiloh. While in Shiloh, Launa got a phone call from the man of the couple I was staying with, asking for me. I got on the phone, and he said they were packing up all my things, and I was not allowed back in the apartment. I told them to put my things at Actress Lady's. I was soon to leave for the U.S. They told me that she was too upset and sick to keep my things. I knew she had told them what I said. Yet, I think they probably had this all planned before I left for Jerusalem. So, I told them to put everything in Zeporah's house in Poriya. I stayed with Zeporah a few days before I left for the US. But, it was very traumatic for me, since I had very personal irreplaceable papers I had hidden in my room at the apartment, and I had to tell them where they were.

Launa is friends with them to this day. I cannot see how anyone can be friends of such traitors. But, that's the thinking of most Americans--if someone is nice to them they don't care how they treat someone else, even those they call "friend." After that, Abba taught me that friendship was a covenant-- and true friends are loyal to each other. So, the one I thought was a friend, was not a friend at all. I found this out later, to my hurt. In the selfish American mind-set, all things are "relative" to the situation at hand, including truth and loyalty. The belief-system is adjusted to fit a person's desires at any given moment.

I returned to the U.S., but by July, I began planning my trip back to Israel for the Fall Festivals (2009). Because the couple had kicked me out, I had no where to stay. Cheryl, with whom Devorah was sharing an apartment, was a Christian. Cheryl didn't want me staying with her because of my outspokenness about the Torah. But, after returning to the U.S., I got an e-mail from Abigail who had taken me to Michael Rood's meetings, saying that Cheryl could not get her visa renewed, even though she was trying to make aliyah, and she had to return to Canada. She was told that she could not return to Israel for at least a year. So, Abigail and her husband had rented Cheryl's apartment. She asked if I would like to rent a room in the apartment. Of course I did! So, that began about two years of staying in that apartment.

Even though I knew about the Creator's calendar, I also knew that Abba wanted me at the Western Wall with the people for the beginning of all the Festivals, especially Yom Teruah and Sukkot. During November, after Sukkot, I joined other friends of Michael Rood's and we had a wonderful Thanksgiving dinner at his house. Afterwards, we all laid down in his living room, ate popcorn, and watched the 1956 version of *The Ten Commandments,* starring Charlton Heston as Moses. After the movie, Michael said he wanted to get the 1959 movie, *Ben Hur,* also starring Charlton Heston. After returning to the U.S., I found that movie quite by accident, at a Target store. So, I bought it for Michael. He was so happy. He told Connie to give me any one of his DVD sets free.

After a Michael Rood meeting, in which I got the DVD, *The Creator's Calendar*, I knew I had to begin studying it. At this time, Abba told me that I did not have to be with the people on rabbinic dates, unless I want to be, but that He wanted me to keep His calendar. I studied about it, and began doing it. I still like being with the people to pray with them – but I also guard His calendar on which He has been revealing timing.

This year, the daughter and her family that I stay with in the U.S., bought a house in a subdivision that is in the country, about five miles from where we lived before. They moved while I was in Israel. I got the special room that I have now.

In December, my dear friend set up an intercession trip to Anatot – the birthplace of Jeremiah. It was very cold. I dressed in five layers of clothing. I looked so fat! There were four of us who did the intercession. I did a lot of research about Anatot, and what happened with Jeremiah there, especially from Jeremiah chapter 32. I found that whenever the Bible talks about the Euphrates River, it is always talking about the headwaters, 83 miles east of Damascus. Only once, is it talking about the Euphrates near Jeremiah's home.

Jeremiah 32 tells about Jeremiah burying a signed and notarized deed of his purchase of a field outside of Anatot, so that one day Levites would again live in this Levite town. So, we went to a little Arab pottery shop, and bought little jars to put our requests in. We went to Anatot, and saw that there were homes there already with the names of Levites in the yards, written in different languages. What Jeremiah did by faith had begun to come to pass. We also went just below Anatot to Ein Prat – a tributary of the Euphrates River that runs into the Jordan River above Jerusalem. This is **Jeremiah 13**--where he buried the girdle.

There were other things we did – prophetic action and verbal intercession. We buried our little jars in the same field outside the town. We went to the home of one of the ladies for lunch. It was a precious day with much being accomplished.

Then I returned from Israel, but this time to Panama. It was on this flight that I had a big realistic scare, along with the miraculous intervention from Abba that I wrote about in "Training Mission – A Day in the Life of Yedidah." Panama would be my new home until Messiah came – so I thought. He had led me there.

PANAMA--AMERICA (THE GEORGIA GUIDESTONES/ WASHINGTON, D.C.)--BOLIVIA--STONEHENGE--GERMANY ISRAEL--EGYPT--PANAMA--BACK TO AMERICA (2010)

In February of 2009, I was at my youngest daughter's house in North Carolina. She and her husband had gone to work, and their two children were in school. I had invited people on my e-mail list, who lived in the N.C./North Georgia area, to come visit me. I was expecting two ladies and a young man that morning, so I got up early. I had been reading a novel about the crystal skulls that put in story-form what I had read in a documented book on the subject. I was near the end of the book, and it talked about the calling of the world's people for the return of the Dragon, and how the skulls played a part in it. While engrossed in the story line, all of a sudden, as is His usual modus operandi, Abba interrupted, saying: "**You will walk into the face of the Dragon and come away unscathed**." I put the book down and pondered that. What did "unscathed" mean? He used a big word on me. I did not know that *The Jerusalem Bible*, 1966 edition, used that word in **Psalm 91:7**, and that years later I would listen to Kent Henry read Psalm 91 on his "Sword of the Spirit" CD, in which he quoted from *The Jerusalem Bible* (1966 edition).

Verse 7 from Kent's CD: "**A thousand shall fall at your side, and ten thousand at your right side, but it will not come near you--you shall remain unscathed. Hear it again: A thousand may fall at your side, and ten thousand at your right side, but it will not come near you – you shall remain unscathed.**"

The three people came, and we had good fellowship. One woman, Sharon, was to become, not only a good friend, but a travel buddy. It was Sharon who would go with me on three strategic intercession trips in 2010. She invited me to stay with her in North Georgia, which I did. I met some of her friends, who had come from Texas to talk to me. I had been wanting the book by David Flynn *Cydonia-The Secret Chronicles of Mars*, but it was out of print, and even on Amazon.com it was over $100.00. I don't know why I mentioned this book in our conversation, but I did. And one of the ladies said she had it, and would give it to me. I took that book to Panama.

In preparing my trip to go to Tiahuanaco (Bolivia) in 2010, I had studied about Tiahuanaco for so long, in so many ways, that I needed a break. I went to my library, and saw the book *Cydonia*, which I had not yet read. I thought that it would be a nice break from all my studying on my next intercession assignment in Bolivia. I laid down on my bed to read it. I got just a few pages into it, and Flynn began writing about Tiahuanaco. A great portion of the book was about Tiahuanaco. This is how Abba brings me research that I need to know. I do not have to go looking for it!

In early January, I was in Panama. I had taken several of my resource books to Panama. Abba asked me to go get the book of *Enoch I* off the shelf, and look at the message that Enoch gave to the fallen angels regarding their eternal doom in these last days. I knew the message was near the front of *Enoch I*. The book of *Enoch I* was considered Scripture in the first century. Almost all New Testament writers quote from it. It is very Messianic, and filled with information about these last days. One famous quote from *Enoch I* is **Jude 1:14-15**.

Abba had let me know that I was to go on seven intercession assignments in a row. He gave me certain Scriptures to proclaim. But, for Tiahuanaco, He also gave me the message of Enoch to the fallen angels, Lucifer's angels, to proclaim from then on at key sites He would direct me to. The final assignment was to be at the Great Pyramid of Giza, Egypt. But, He made it very clear that I was NOT to give Enoch's message there, but only to speak to the gods of Egypt. I was NOT to speak to the stones of the Great Pyramid. Demonic spirits often dwelt in symbols, idols, pyramids, and religious objects, in places like Tiahuanaco, in the statues on Easter Island, in Angor Wat, and in average homes of average people. He did not tell me why, and I didn't ask – but I know to only obey what He tells me. So, at the Great Pyramid, I did not speak to the stones! I only delivered a message to the gods of Egypt, who are returning in full force in these last days.

Enoch took the message of Yahuweh to the fallen ones before the Flood, at a time when the Nephillim were starting to increase on the earth. The fallen ones who bred with human women to produce the Nephillim and the Repha'im (giants) came down on Mt. Hermon in the "days of Jered." Jered was the father of Enoch. Enoch's message from Yahuweh that he gave to the fallen ones, came in response to a plea by the fallen ones who requested mercy from Yahuweh, and even a chance to return to His favor. Yahuweh, through Enoch, responded to them that their request was denied, that they would have no peace forever, they would see their offspring scattered as dung on the earth, and they would spend their eternity in the lake of fire with their chosen leader, Lucifer.

Abba gave me explicit instructions about each of the seven points/places. I was to be gone from February 25th to May 25th. As I obeyed, His manner of confirmation linked each point together in the most fascinating way. Only He could have orchestrated them. It is so fascinating to serve Him, for He manifests in the most unique ways!

PART VI - The Middle East & Travels Beyond

Point 1
The Georgia Guidestones

I flew back to the U.S. to begin the intercession trip in February. Sharon drove us to the first assignment--the "Georgia Guidestones", in southeast Georgia. The Guidestones are known as "the American Stonehenge,". Carved into stone, in several major languages, are the rules for the "new world order." We used the Scriptures that Abba had given to me to do intercession. It was an icy cold day. I walked around it seven times. Sharon was right with me! Then, we went into town to the Museum and saw more about it. The more I learned about it, the more I knew that it was a portal for the enemy into America.

Point 2
Washington, D.C.

The second of the seven-point assignment was Washington, D.C. In the second week of March, Sharon and I flew into Ronald Reagan Airport. We got a taxi to our hotel. Then we got a taxi to the Washington Monument. Wow was it cold. But, we did intercession there. Then we walked by the Smithsonian, and into the heart of Washington D.C. to see and hear what Abba had for us. Then, we found a nice restaurant for dinner. Abba had outlined a tight itinerary for us. I had done my homework. I had read David Overson's *The Secret Architecture of Our Nation's Capitol*. I had a map of the Masonic and occult layout of the city. I learned a lot from Tom Horn's *Nephilim Stargates 2012* and *Apollyon Rising 2012*, as well as from the DVDs on the real history of America--"The New Atlantis," "Riddles in Stone," and "The Eye of the Phoenix." I had studied the writings of Manly P. Hall, and the Masons for years, also Dave Bay's Cutting Edge reporting on the Masons. I was prepared.

In doing intercession, one must do research on everything that they are to do, so that there is clear understanding. The Spirit will use the knowledge as He wills, so that our Yahuweh-directed words hit their target. We must never say one word on our own. He has to trust a servant to only say what He wants said, no more, no less. To have such a mutual-trust relationship with the Creator, He has to put us through many tests for a long time. For the Creator to trust us, we must fear Yahuweh. If we do, say, or think, one thing out of line, we are eligible for disqualification. (**Psalm 111:9-10**; **Matthew 10:24-28**)

The next day, we were signed up for the earliest tour of the Capitol building. I had studied about the "Apotheosis of Washington" painted into the dome of the building, and the painting by Brumidi around the dome, and the history behind it--incredible information. After going there, He wanted us to walk the face of Baphomet (the goat-head pentagram) that is laid out in the streets of Washington D.C.

I took breakfast bars and pretzels. We would not be eating until after going to the House of the Temple. But, there were signs everywhere outside the entrance to the Capitol, that all food items would be confiscated. So, I ate the breakfast bars. But NO one was going to take my pretzels from me. I would need them to sustain me for the next part of the assignment. I went over to the dumpster, across from the entrance for the tour, and put my pretzels, which were in a plastic bag, in the right lower corner of the dumpster.

That tour was awesome. It told me so many things that I had previously studied concerning the history of it. Of course, the dome represents the womb of Isis, and the Washington Monument the phallus of Osiris. It is patterned exactly like the obelisk and dome in St. Peter's Square and the Vatican Basilica dome. The whole layout has to do with the reincarnation of Nimrod/Osiris/Apollo (Apollyon).

After the tour, I dug deep in the dumpster, and fetched my pretzels. There was a little ice cream on the plastic bag, but I wiped it off (smile). Sharon, and I, laughed about this for a long time afterwards. Then we took a taxi to the park across from the White House. Crossing the street, we went beside the White house, and there began our walk up the face of Baphomet, in the layout of the streets.

It was March 16th. As we began walking up 16th street –we literally were walking the face of Baphomet, the goat head pentagram representing Satan, from the White House to the House of the Temple – headquarters of the Scottish Rite 33rd Degree Freemasons, the headquarters of the Grand Master who controls Washington D.C. The form of Baphomet is laid out in the streets, and it is well known by the Washington elite hierarchy that he is represented there. In this layout, the beard of Baphomet actually touches the White House. On his head, between his horns, sits a lighted candle, which reaches to the House of the Temple. Scott circle is at the head of Baphomet. We walked around the circle until we got to the top of his head at 16th street, and began walking up the candle that sits on his head to the lighted top at the House of the Temple. Of course, Lucifer is known as the "illumined light-bearer."

While walking 16th street, I planned to do spiritual warfare over my family. The male leaders of my mother's family were 33rd degree Masons, and very powerful in politics in North Carolina. I knew from Tom Horn's *Apollyon Rising 2012*, the power that this "Temple" has over everything done in Washington. I had also read

PART VI - The Middle East & Travels Beyond

Dan Brown's *The Lost Symbol*. The story line centers in the Capitol building, as well as the House of the Temple.

As I stepped off the curb to begin the journey up 16th street, instead of doing my usual spiritual warfare against the enemy, a different kind of warfare welled up from my spirit, and came out of my mouth. I began singing praises to Yahuweh in tongues with great joy--the spirit of victory hit me. His anointing, bringing His joy, began to flow through me. As Abba instructed me, we walked up 16th street, on March 16th, 2010. That date in math: 3 + 1 + 6 + 2 + 1 = 13. The number 16 is also a very occult number, as are 3, 6, 9, 11, 33, 36, and 72. I walked the face of the Dragon. I not only came away "unscathed", but with victory!

When we got into the House of the Temple, there was a man who said he would take us on a tour for $3.33 each – equaling $6.66. In this Temple, with every President, they enact the Egyptian (Osiris) "ceremony of the rising." (Google: "Apotheosis of George Washington.") Our tour guide asked why we were there. I told him my family had many 33rd degree Scottish Rite Masons in it, and I wanted to visit the headquarters of the Scottish Rite in the U.S. I could tell, however, that he was suspicious of me. He said that so many had come for the tour after reading Dan Brown's book, *The Lost Symbol*. He may have been suspicious because I asked too many questions for an average person--questions pertaining to things only Masons know. The whole place was covered in occult symbolism. I understood it all. He gave us the grand tour, however. We went into the room where they do the "ceremony of the rising."

Since earliest times in America, our illustrious "fathers" have been preparing for the rising of Nimrod/Osiris/Apollo, to come and rule the world. The plans and intents of that House are 100% Luciferic. Their grandmaster, Albert Pike, whose remains are in a column in the Temple, wrote of the god of Freemasonry: "Our god is Lucifer." He wrote that Yahuweh was the dark God who kept illumination from Eve, and that Lucifer, the light bearer, came to give illumination to mankind through Eve. There are quotes from Presidents that they can make no decisions unless they first consult the Grand Master of the House of the Temple.

Point 3
Bolivia

I flew back to Panama in late March. I worked and worked on an itinerary for   , Bolivia. There were so many details to this trip of only 3 days, that I was literally sick from brain-strain. Also, a woman had moved into the house who was demonized--a jezebel who manifested demonic spirits. It was constant spiritual warfare. We had so many manifestations of demonic spirits in that house, even demons walking around that could be seen by all. The spirits also from Volcan Baru were beginning to manifest greatly. Yet, I wrote a lot of articles during my stay in Panama, so Yahuweh's work did not cease.

During this time, I was supposed to meet a couple, and their son, who were on my e-mail list. They were coming from Costa Rica to stay in Panama a few days, to renew their visa. They wanted to meet me. They said after crossing into Panama, they would go up to a village on Volcan Baru and meet me at a guest lodge there. I thought that would be good. T. and R. said they would drive me there. They would have to leave early enough to be able to return to Boquete before dark. But, the closer it got time for me to go, I began feeling serious dread, as in "danger, danger!" The night before I was to go, I had a dream.

In the dream, I went to the guest lodge, and then T. and R. left. I got my room. But, it was night by then, and the couple and their son had not come. Then I heard someone breaking into the room. I had turned off the light to try to rest. After a short while, several men broke in, and violently killed me. When I woke up, Abba strongly said in my spirit: "DO NOT GO!" He was not just warning me, He was commanding me. He was letting me know that what I saw in the dream was true.

The next morning, I was still going to meet them up there, even though severe dread was taking over me. I didn't want to disappoint the couple who wanted to see me. But, I was overcome with foreboding. I went into the kitchen, to talk to R. about it. She told me that she also had a dream that I must not go. Before very long, five other people said they had warnings from Abba that I was not to go. So, I cancelled my trip.

Later, I found out that the couple had crossed the border after dark, and it was late before they got to the guest house. I also learned that many of the Indian locals were calling for their sky gods to return, and doing all sorts of rituals to open portals for them. It is very possible that they were offering human sacrifice, from what I learned. I carry a heavy anointing from Yahuweh, and just my presence in certain places produces danger for me.

Abba has only come to me about five times like that, but each time, He saved my life. If I did not know His voice, His nature, and ways, I would have pressed on with my human reasoning many times. But, I know His voice. I know Him. Thus, He has protected me.

In working to go to La Paz, then to Tiahuanaco, Bolivia, I researched the requirements to obtain a visa. Of course, I learned all about altitude sickness. I researched hotels, flights, distances, etc. I also wanted to go to Lake Titicaca, which was only 10 miles from Tiahuanaco. I found, in order to get a decent price for my flight, I would have to go on seven flights. American Airlines was the only Airlines that flew into La Paz that had a decent flight schedule too. The itineraries of the other airlines, and their prices, were horrible.

I knew I could not do this trip by myself, so I asked Jamia to go with me. Her and Mark were living in Panama with the two youngest children, and were doing very well. Jamia was excited. But, Mark decided not to let her go. I was devastated. So, I e-mailed Sharon to ask if she could possibly go with me. I told her what flight I was going on out of Miami, and what hotel I had booked in La Paz. She would have to fly from Atlanta to Miami to meet me, to start our journey.

About an hour later, I got an e-mail back from her. She had already booked her tickets and gotten her hotel reservation. She said she knew she was supposed to go with me, and was just waiting for me to ask her. What a trooper! I was so happy she was going with me! Abba did the most incredible job of linking trips--back and forward. With each trip, He linked the one before it and the one coming.

Just one example, in doing the logistics for Bolivia, I had to get my picture taken for the visa. We went to a small print shop in Boquete. While there, I noticed the wallpaper on a computer screen, and there was a picture of Stonehenge--the place I would go after Tiahuanaco. Tiahuanaco is the oldest known city on earth, estimated between 12,000-14,000 years old, 13,000+ feet up in the Andes Mountains. It was built by Nephillim. Its 600-ton stones were moved from a quarry 200 miles away through the oxygen-starved air to be fitted into massive temples with massive gates. Most likely they used "anti-gravity" technology, which we now have today.

A few days before we were to leave, Sharon got a notice from the hotel in La Paz. They said that while we were there (for 2 days) the weather would be icy, with snow. The roads would be impassible. We had to go to Tiahuanaco, about 2 hours drive up higher in the mountains. I told Sharon that since Abba was sending us, the weather would be gorgeous. I prayed that the weather would be at least above 40 degrees. I did not tell Him either Fahrenheit or Celsius. What a sense of humor He has!

I flew from north Panama, to Panama City, then to Miami. I met Sharon in Miami. We then flew overnight into La Paz, Bolivia. La Paz is built on the side of a mountain. It is 13,000 feet at the airport, but 9,000 feet where our hotel was. Even though I was exhausted because I did not sleep on the plane, the landing was spectacular. Because of the thinness of the air, the plane came in at top speed for the landing. The pilot did it perfect. It was amazing watching the plane going so fast just before we touched down on the airstrip.

I had studied about altitude sickness. Tourists were warned to allow themselves seven days to adjust to the extreme difference in oxygen pressure. We had come from sea level. I knew that when the plane door opened, my body would begin starving for oxygen, and it did. It is an awful feeling. I took with me three genuine essential oils with sesquiterpenes. These correctly processed natural essential oils from Young Living were Cedarwood, Sandalwood, and Frankincense. The oil had the life of the wood and resin in them. The sesquiterpenes go beyond the blood-brain barrier to bring life, but also into all the cells of the body to bring oxygen into the blood stream, and I needed oxygen. As soon as that plane door opened, I began taking deep breaths of these oils. I went through immigration, customs, and stood in line for the money exchange. I was weak, but my body was satisfied with the additional oxygen from the oils. I saw big tanks of oxygen that they had ready for tourists who might pass out.

We got a taxi to our hotel. It was about 5:00 AM. They checked us in, and gave us a room. We went to breakfast. I drank lots of coco tea. Even the locals drink it to stop altitude sickness. We slept a little. I kept sniffing the oils every time I woke up because of oxygen-need. Like I said, I asked Him to make sure the temperature was above 40. I meant Fahrenheit, but He must have thought I meant Celsius. The skies were totally clear, but up that high, the sun rays are HOT. It was in the low 90s. When we got ready to leave, we had to sit on the tarmac for an hour because the pilot said the weather was so bad. Sharon and I laughed. For two days Abba had postponed the bad, freezing stormy weather for us! That first early afternoon, we got a fine lunch in the hotel restaurant. Then we hired a taxi from the hotel, and he took us into La Paz to do shopping at an outdoor market. Many shops sold local handiwork. I got a t-shirt, and a handmade magnet for my daughter. I always bring her magnets from different countries, which she puts on the refrigerator. Then he took us to a museum of local history, because the big archeological museum was closed. That was disappointing to me. The people of Bolivia dress like, and look like, the travel brochure people. The women wore derbies of different types, and long cotton skirts like the Navajo women.

We had NO altitude problems after about 5 hours, and what we experienced of it was miniscule. We felt great! We had a super dinner. The next morning, we hired the same wonderful taxi driver to take us to Tiahuanaco. What a prince of a fellow! We drove up higher into the Andes, where the mountain tops were covered in snow. It was so gorgeous! The sky was clear, and the sun was very warm. Abba had created perfect weather conditions for us!

We spent about 2 ½ hours doing thorough intercession over the ruins at Tiahuanaco, using the specific Scriptures Abba had given us. Oh the things we learned! Then our driver took us to the ruins of Puma Punta – about ½ mile away. They were not nearly as extensive as Tiahuanaco. The Scriptures for Tiahuanaco were very pointed – addressing the gods. Of course, I was to bring the message of Enoch, which I did. The demonic spirits of these gods were still there, expressed in symbols on the stones. The famous gate of the sun god stood by itself. We saw the "Great Idol"--a huge idol with symbols on it that are very prevalent today on so many American products. Those Nephillim, from so many thousands of years ago, are still roaming the earth as demons-- seeking a body. They often hide in stones, crystals, and other material objects. At times, Sharon and I worked together, and at times, we went our separate ways. But, we met up with the taxi driver, who had friends there and was having his own good time.

After Puma Punta, he asked if he could take us anywhere else. I told him I wanted to go to Lake Titicaca. This lake is so huge that it borders both on Bolivia, and Peru. He took us all around the whole lake on the Bolivia side. I have such gorgeous pictures. While doing Abba's work, He also allows us to enjoy our trip. We were gone about 18 hours. We got back in time for dinner. I had trout from Lake Titicaca. What a great dinner! That little restaurant was super. I had so much energy, and so did she.

As I related earlier, the next morning we sat on the tarmac for an hour because of bad weather. Then we flew to Santa Fe, Bolivia, with a short layover. Then we flew to Miami. She had a flight to Atlanta. I had two more flights. In all, I had seven flights.

Upon landing in Miami, we sat on the tarmac again. The captain came on the intercom and said that we would be there 30 minutes because "there were dignitaries in the area." I began praying in tongues, and so did she. In English I prayed: "Abba we are Your dignitaries. Move the other ones out of the way so that we can get on with Your business." About 5 minutes later, the captain came on the intercom and said: "We have clearance to pull into our gate...If you look out the right side of the airplane, off the tip of our plane, you will see Air Force One." The wing tip of our plane went right by the wing tip of Air Force One. President Obama was the dignitary we prayed out of there! Serving Abba is so much fun!

Obama had arrived 15 minutes before we did for a meeting with the Governor. The Air Force One plane looked dirty and old-- it was unimpressive. We got through customs in time to have dinner. I got to my gate, and flew to Panama City. I stayed the night at the airport hotel. The next morning I had a taxi take me to the regional airport, where I got an Air Panama flight to David.

Point 4
Stonehenge

Onward to the next trip! From the travel agent in Boquete, who was an absolutely amazing help to me, I got a ticket to England for a good price. In doing the logistics for this trip, my credit card company cancelled my card right in the middle of making reservations for hotels and flights. After paying cash for my flight out of Panama to England, I then made reservations using my credit card for hotels in the UK and Germany, and flights within Europe, and to Tel Aviv--all one-way flights. The credit card company had no record of the purchase of the flight to England-- so they cancelled my card. My daughter e-mailed me saying that my credit card's "Fraud Department" had called her, and said for me to call them. One lady had Skype on her computer, so I used it to call America and get my card cleared up. Then while in the process of making another hotel reservation, they cancelled it again. I had to get on Skype to get that cleared up. It happened three times. I was angry! But, what are the odds that while out in the country of Panama, the people I stayed with just so happened to have Skype? Later, Skype came in handy when Turkish Air lost my luggage. R. helped me so much to get it back!

For the Stonehenge visit, I was going to stay with Maureen in Swansea. Her grandson was going to drive us to Stonehenge (England), about a three-hour car ride. I got to London. Then I took the National Coach Express bus to Swansea. The next morning, her grandson took us to Stonehenge. We did intercession there. Then we returned to Swansea. I was only there a few days, for I had three more places to go on this assignment.

On the day before I was to leave for London, Maureen asked me if I wanted to go anywhere else to do intercession. I said "yes." I wanted to see King Arthur's stone – the very one that legend says he pulled the sword out of. It was in the Gower area, below Swansea. Maureen had been a care-nurse in that region, so knew it well. We first went to Worms Head at Rhossili Bay, where we had gone another time. It is so gorgeous there. I walked along the path along the sea. On our return we had lunch at the King Arthur Hotel. Then we went to where the stone is. I walked down a grassy path to it, and did intercession all around it for some time. It is a very occult/demonic symbol--binding the people to the demonic in that region. That was an awesome day!

Point 5
Germany

The next day I took the National Coach Express back to London, and got a plane to Berlin, Tegel Airport. I took a shuttle bus from the airport to the train station and got a ticket for my next place to stay, which was in Bavaria near the border with the Czech Republic. I was going to see a family I had corresponded with online, who wanted to build Mongolian gers in Israel for the people to have shelter in the time of fleeing. That project was greatly on my heart, and I had been involved with several people in Israel to do with it. I did not know at the time that Howie knew how to build gers. But, the project was being launched, and I wanted to talk with the head of the project. He had invited me to go to Mongolia, which I wanted to do. But, that never worked out. The enemy got in and put that project into oblivion.

It was the fifth of May. I had a taxi driver take me to the Pergamum Museum. I did not realize at the time, that the museum was in what used to be East Berlin. I had plenty of time to see the Pergamum Altar, the Ishtar Gate, and other artifacts from Sumar, Assyria, and Babylon. Then I got a taxi to take me to the train station. I took the train to this tiny village in Bavaria, and stayed for five days with this family. They lived in a house where Jews had lived. Because the Jews refused to put out the Nazi flag on their house, they were killed. The oppression in that village was so horrendous that I could hardly walk or lift my head because of it. My strength was drained out of me.

During the week, a couple and their children came to visit me. They wanted to talk about Israel. I could hardly get out of bed to go talk to them. But, I sure am glad I did. At Passover (2012), I met friends in the big Hurva Square in Jerusalem. A young man came and knelt in front of me, and told me how good it was to see me again. I did not recognize him. But, it was the young man of the family that had come to visit me in Bavaria. He and his family had been to Israel two times already. What a glorious reunion. My host and hostess in Bavaria were distributers of very fine essential oils. I enjoyed seeing his workplace where he bottled them.

Just before leaving for the airport in Munich, I got an e-mail from a young lady who lived in Panama. I had given her all my Israel contact information. But, because she was so naïve about crossing a border, she had made the Israeli immigration suspicious of her. They pulled her aside and questioned her for five hours, finally calling in the head of the terrorist bureau. She had told them she got all of her contact information from me, which was true. But, in the process, because of fear, she gave them all my personal information. In other words, she exposed everything I had worked so hard to keep private. She exposed my children also to incredible danger. I was horrified. Through the information she gave, others were exposed, besides leaving my bank account information, my credit card information, my address, phone number, etc., open for tracing. They wanted to know who I was. They thought she was a terrorist.

My host and hostess took me to the train station, where I got the train to the Munich airport. I had to press forward, not knowing what kind of reception I would get in Tel Aviv. At midnight, my plane flew out to Tel Aviv. I had not slept. I fell into a deep sleep and felt better. All went well at Immigration. I thought maybe they had investigated me, and found me to be of no problem.

Point 6
Israel

Upon landing in Tel Aviv, that mysterious energy that flows up from the earth of Israel took me over, and I felt terrific. It was 4:00 AM when we landed. I took the train to the closest stop near the Central Bus Station. I walked about four blocks to the bus station. The first bus to Tiberias would leave at 6:30 AM. I had a hard time finding the bus platform where the bus was waiting, however I finally managed to find it. I got to Tiberias about 9:00 AM, and took a taxi to the apartment where I would be staying with Abigail again.

About 10:00 AM, I began feeling horrible danger, like I felt about going up on Volcan Baru. I wondered if I had been followed. My hostess had gone to the market. I should never have done it, since the authorities knew my e-mail address, but I took my computer and went right to my e-mails. During answering the first few e-mails, I felt a force come off of the computer screen and hit me to the right of my heart, in my upper stomach area. It was a tangibly-felt blow. I thought I was just hungry. Instantly, I felt nauseous. But, like me, I kept going with the e-mails. Then I opened an e-mail from someone whom I had been writing for some time, someone on my e-mail list. I thought he was a pure-of-heart man, zealous for Torah. I did not know he was mentally ill--insanely religious. I had written an article entitled "The Blood of Messiah." He wrote me often about how he and his family kept Torah. I was always encouraging him. He seemed so kind and sweet. But, when I wrote about Messiah, he attacked me viciously. It was the most evil demonic e-mail I've ever read. I could not finish the e-mail, because, once again, a tangible force came from the center of his e-mail right into me. I felt the blow of its impact. All of a sudden the room started spinning. I went into full blown "Vertigo." I had heard of such a thing, but it had never happened to me. I ran to the bed and laid down. I kept my eyes closed because the room was spinning so fast, and the ceiling fan was whirling around. I got up and tried to unpack. But, I was getting sicker. Finally, the nausea took its toll and I threw up. I went back to my room, grabbed the Myrrh and Frankincense oils, and took deep breaths of them. That stopped the Vertigo. But, it had gone on for about an hour.

That night I had a dream. In it, I was in an apartment with a young blond blue-eyed lady, who was a friend. There was a knock at the door. She told me to hide in the bedroom because it was her boyfriend. She opened the door, he burst into the room, and began beating her. He beat her to death. I heard the whole thing, blow by blow. I knew that if he found my door locked, he'd know someone was there. I prayed! He started going into different rooms, but I woke up. It was a warning from Abba that my life was in danger. Abba let me know that for seven days I was not to go out of that apartment into town. I went twice to the little market, just down a block on our residential street, but not into town. After a week, He let me know it was all right to go into town, or wherever I wanted to go.

I later confronted the girl who betrayed me in Tiberias, and she really repented. She did not know anything about me, and so did not know the extent of what she did in exposing me, and my children, and others with me. I had previously promised her I would take her on a tour of the north, which I did the next day. Abba rules!

I went to Jerusalem for Shavu'ot. I was to be there for three days. As always, I stayed at the Jaffa Gate. I was going to Egypt after that. I had completed five of my seven points. One of them was in Israel, but Abba had not told me where in Israel. I figured He'd let me know. It was Thursday. Shavu'ot had ended on Wednesday. I was leaving for Eilat on Friday. I didn't want to waste a day, so I went early to the Central Bus Station. I didn't know where I was going to go, but I just wanted to go somewhere new. So, I looked at the bus schedules, and saw the town Ashkelon. I had not been there. I had heard they had an archeological park. So, I went to the platform for the bus, and the bus was there waiting. I got on, sat down, and thought: "I'm on my way to Ashkelon and I don't know what I'm doing." I got there, and got a taxi driver who spoke no English. But, he did understand "beach." So, he took me to a nice beach. I put my feet in the Mediterranean and did intercession for the restoration of the remnant of the House of Israel.

But, that's not why I came to Ashkelon. I wanted to see the archeological park. I did not know it was just above that beach. I walked out to the main street to find another taxi driver. I found a really nice man who spoke a little English. I asked him to take me to the tourist bureau. I figured maybe they had one. He had to call his headquarters to find out where it was. He waited while I went in. It was a very tiny place. No one there spoke English. But, one man went over to a shelf and pulled out every brochure they had on Ashkelon. When he pulled out the one from the Park's Association, I knew that was it. I showed it to my taxi driver, and he took me right there. He even took me to the first exhibit on the printed tour. It was the oldest arched Canaanite gate ever found! They had found statues of Ba'al there, and had a picture of one on display.

I walked down to the gate. No one was there but me. I sat down by the gate and pulled my worn copy of the Scriptures He had given me for this seven-point tour from my beltpack. I began speaking them toward the stones of that gate. All of a sudden, I was very aware that real beings were coming out of the stones. A group of them hovered in the air in front of me, and I spoke to them directly. Then I walked through this expansive archeological park. Back at the entrance, I had them call a taxi for me. He took me to the bus station, where I got a bus back to Jerusalem.

While riding back, I realized that this gate was the 6th point that Abba wanted me to touch for Him. I had been bringing messages to the fallen ones about their final demise, speaking to the stones in which their presence still resided. I felt peace.

Point 7
Egypt

The next morning I went to the Central Bus Station and got the 444 Egged bus to Eilat. This bus ride was very familiar to me, having taken it so many times when I lived in Aqaba. It was Friday morning early. The Muslim day of worship is Friday. I thought that, being a Consulate, surely they'd be open in the morning for me to get my visa for Egypt. I asked Abba about it, and He was silent. Whenever He is silent when I ask a question, it means "wait and see." Once at the bus station in Eilat, I took a taxi to the Egyptian Consulate before I went to my hotel. But, the Consulate was closed. I was sick about it. I did not want to get my visa on Shabbat. But, the timing of this trip was His. So, I went to the Prima Musica Hotel, just one block north of the Red Sea, very near the Egyptian border. I got into my room, and looked out the window. What I saw made me numb. I started crying. It had been three years since I had seen that sight. I was directly across from the port of Aqaba where the Red Sea narrows at the top--straight across from that giant "Hashemite Rebellion Flag" that the King put up in his rebellion against Saudi Arabia taking Hashemite land. It is the tallest flag pole in the world. I could see where I used to walk along the water. I could see where both my apartments were. I did not want to see those things. I was homesick for the life I had there. I got out and walked down to the Sea. There, just in front of the hotel was a round-about. In it was a Masonic stone and memorial for the Eilat Masonic Lodge. How awful! But, the sea was lovely, and I enjoyed walking.

Shabbat morning: Abba had wanted me to have a back-up to go with me to Egypt. A lady named Cheryl, whom I had met in the north of Israel, came to my mind. She had transferred from staying in Merhavia to staying in Jerusalem with a friend. She had gone to Jordan because she felt led to move there. She only had two more weeks left on her visa before she had to return to North Carolina. So, I asked her to come to Eilat so that we could go to Egypt together. She prayed about it and agreed to come because Abba had said for her to go with me. We were leaving for Egypt Sunday morning. She had already gotten her visa for Egypt while in Jordan. I went to the Consulate early and got my visa.

I spent the rest of the day with Abba. I told Abba that this linking thing between trips was fascinating, HOWEVER – there was no way He was going to link Ashkelon with the Pergamum Altar in Germany--points 5 and 6. I was lying on the bed waiting for Cheryl. I looked at my Israel *Lonely Planet Travel Kit* book. I learned that Ashkelon had belonged to Egypt at one time, and that they had worshipped the goddess Hathor, who was in the form of a bull – the horns representing power. I wanted so much to go to Timna Park nearby, but didn't have the time. There is evidence at Timna that the Israelites worshipped Hathor there. We would spend three days in Egypt, then return to Israel. After I returned to Tiberias, I would have four days to prepare to leave to fly back to the U.S. While lying there, I went through the brochures from the Tourist Bureau in Ashkelon. One brochure said that there was a discovery in Ashkelon of two coffins, both hand sculptured in marble. The rest of the brochure told how they believed that they were carved by the same one who carved the Pergamum Altar. I was so shocked. I am laughing now. Abba DID IT! He actually linked Ashkelon with the Pergamum Altar.

While in Turkey, 2001, I actually stood in front of where the altar of Zeus stood in ancient Pergamum. It was from there that German archeologists took the altar to East Germany, and later the Ishtar Gate from Babylon. I saw the Pergamum Altar in East Germany!

Cheryl came, we discussed our trip, and we had dinner. We went early to the Egyptian border crossing. There was hardly anyone there. No sooner had we gotten over to the Egyptian side, that the knife-like pain I had since July, 2009 hit me, and it got worse and worse. We saw sheruts, and hired one just for us, to take us to Cairo-- a 5-hour ride across the Sinai Peninsula. I needed to lie down, which I did on the seats. The man who drove the van was a very kind man. But, about thirty minutes into the trip, he stopped to pick up five Egyptian men whom he said were policemen. Cheryl was scared. I had been around so many Egyptians, that I perceived they really were policemen. They were polite. They never even turned around once to look at us. They were neatly dressed in civilian clothes, but nice haircuts. I had no fear. I reassured her that they were policemen. The driver was taking them to their station near the Nile. So they would be with us for 4 hours. We had one stop out in the middle of no-where in the barren Sinai Peninsula--our bathroom break.

When we got into Cairo, we paid this man a little more to take us to our hotel. I had booked the Le Meridian Pyramids. It was a 5-star plus hotel. I have never seen a hotel that awesome. It had five restaurants, a shopping area, and a main dining hall on the second floor that overlooked the pyramids. They served gourmet food--even for breakfast. I went through Expedia hotels to find it. Cheryl and I paid only $147.00 each for the two nights in this expensive hotel! The first night, we sat at table #3. Dinner was extraordinary.

Abba made it clear that I had to be in front of the Great Pyramid of Giza at 8:00 AM on May 25th. I did not sleep well that night. I laid awake for hours. After falling asleep at 4:00 AM, I awoke with a headache. I didn't want to turn on the light and wake Cheryl up. But, I got my pill box out of my purse and took what I thought was Ibuprofen. It was not Ibuprofen--it was Melatonin, a sleep inducer. We got up at 6:00. Can you imagine how drugged I felt. We sat at table #3 for breakfast. Then we went looking for a taxi. We got another really nice taxi driver. I always pray beforehand, that I will get a kind, fair, taxi driver.

Now before I go any further, I must tell you about Abba's little joke. I had watched the trilogy on the Pyramids three times, which I had bought from *Prophecy in the News*. It told how Enoch and the angels of Yahuweh built the Great Pyramid. The pyramid has no capstone. **Isaiah 19:19-20** tells about this Great Pyramid being an altar to Yahuweh. **Zechariah 4** tells about the capping of this Great Pyramid. But, I was a know-it-all. I thought the

PART VI - The Middle East & Travels Beyond

Nephillim built it. Of course, it was built before the Flood of Noah's day, as was the Sphinx. About two weeks before the trip, I kept asking Abba who built the Great Pyramid of Giza. I knew that it had been covered with 144,000 white limestone casing stones that glistened so brightly in the sun that it could be seen in Jerusalem.

While in Panama, T. had brought out a stack of W.'s old books and put them on the table by me. (By this time, W. and S. had moved back to the U.S.) He pulled out one little tiny white paperback book, and told me that Abba wanted me to read it. It was about Iceland. T. told me that I would be going to Iceland. He did not know that on my way back from Israel to London, I would fly to Iceland, spend the night, and then to the U.S. on Iceland Air. But, in that booklet, it said that twice a year, the white limestone casing blocks would glisten so that they could be seen from Iceland. If you draw a line from the capital Reykjavik to the Great Pyramid, the line crosses the top of the pyramid, and goes around the Delta, and shoots off directly to Bethlehem, Israel. The number 144,000 is the number of the Bridal remnant (**Revelation 7:1**).

For several days, after I went to Ashkelon, Abba had told me something regarding this pyramid. He said in a firm voice: "DO NOT SPEAK TO THE STONES – Only speak to the gods of Egypt." The morning of May 25th, in getting ready to leave for the pyramid, He said that again, very harshly. I said: "Yes, Sir! I will not speak to the stones. But, who built it?" He was silent.

We got out of the taxi, got our tickets, and walked up to the base of the Great Pyramid. I looked up at that huge monument, which looked like it had been built the day before, and felt a familiar power coming off of it. Scientists had tried to x-ray it from outer space, but said they couldn't because some mysterious force was in it that jammed their instruments. As I stood there, I knew what that force was - the anointing of Yahuweh! I weakly said to Abba: "You built it. You had Enoch and Your angels build it." It was like it was alive with His Presence. It is a monument to the translation of the Bridal remnant, the "first fruits" of the resurrection (**Revelation 14:1-5**).

We walked all around it, and to other pyramids near it. We were there about 2 hours. While walking towards the three small pyramids built by a Pharaoh, an Egyptian man came up to me and reached out to take off my white scarf from my head. I jerked back and yelled at him, and he backed off. He said he wanted to show me how to tie the scarf. It was tied the way the Arab man in Petra tied it--the one who sold the scarf to me. So, I wonder what prompted that!

We got back to the taxi. I didn't want to leave. I just wanted to stay and babysit the pyramid. He showed me that it was built by Enoch and His angels as a witness to the Bride of Messiah. The burial chamber was sealed so that nobody could be laid in the stone coffin within it. It had no capstone. Messiah is the STONE which the builders refused to lay. The day Zerubbabel places the capstone on it, is the day Messiah sits as King on His throne in Jerusalem. [Refer to: "This is the Day"] This is the day of rejoicing!

It is amazing that all of the latitude lines of Satan's monuments from his angels, like Tiahuanaco, go right across the Great Pyramid... and so did the BP oil rig that blew up. If that line is continued to China, it comes out just about where a second great oil spill occurred not long after the BP oil rig blew up. I wrote so much about this during 2010. I did extensive study on the BP oil rig explosion. BP had produced a board game in the 1970s that showed a rig blowing up in the Gulf. The ramifications of what happened because of that explosion are huge. Even to this day, the oil is still seeping out under the sea. It stopped the Gulf Stream and thus Europe and the eastern U.S. went into a mini-ice age in the winter.

Our wonderful taxi driver took us to the Sphinx. I really enjoyed seeing it up close. Behind it rises the Great Pyramid, and two other big pyramids. The Sphinx is a woman and lion hybrid. It is a time clock. It begins with the constellation Virgo (the woman) and ends with Leo (the lion), giving the time period of the rotation of the zodiac around the earth of nearly 26,000 years. This is the significance of December 21, 2012. While nothing outwardly manifested on that day, still, by the calendar of our solar system, a 26,000-year Era ended, and the fifth of the corresponding Ages within the Era ended. Each Age is 5,125 years within the Era. This rotation of the zodiac around the earth is not just a Mayan observation calendar, but is repeated in the calendars found in Tiahuanaco, among the Cherokee, Chinese, and other ancient people groups.

Our driver then took us through the most incredible traffic I have ever been in, worse even than in Mexico and Kampala, Uganda. We were ½ inch from other cars at times. There are no stop lights in downtown Cairo. He was an awesome driver. Every time another car got a ½ inch from us, he'd say "Welcome to Egypt!" He took us to the famous Cairo Museum of Egyptology. He said he'd meet us in the car parking area across from the Museum in about 4 hours. That museum is huge. We saw the entire King Tut exhibit up close. We came to the area where the mummified remains of the most famous Pharaohs were laid in glass cases. I knew I had to go see them. I paid a little more money, and went downstairs to see them. There, right under my nose, I saw Ramses II. I saw the Pharaoh whose daughter adopted Moses-- the daughter who became a Pharaoh. There were several Biblical Pharaohs in there. I was very upset to hear that during the 2011 riots in downtown Cairo, the museum suffered much vandalism, including the desecration of some of the Pharaoh's remains. I wish I could have stayed longer in that place.

We went to meet our taxi driver at the car park. A man came up wanting to sell us things. He was so persistent that I had to run him off--literally. I was wondering what Cheryl thought of me. But, I had lived among these people, so I had no fear. He took us back to the hotel where we had a wonderful dinner in one of the other five restaurants.

The next morning, we went to breakfast. It was in the upstairs restaurant where we had sat at table #3 twice. I wondered what table our waiter would put us at. Of course – table #25. I should never be surprised at Abba's confirmations, but I was once again surprised. He had told me to be there on May 25th at 8:00 AM at the Great Pyramid, and we were. Then, I found out that the pyramid was built according to the measurements of the "sacred Egyptian cubit", which was, of course, 25" long. The cubit is the distance from a man's elbow to the tip of his third finger.

We called the driver who brought us to Cairo. He was back in Taba. He drove all the way across the Sinai Peninsula to get us at our hotel. He drove us all the way back – without picking anyone up. We crossed the border and took a bus to Jerusalem. I stayed one night with Cheryl, who was staying with a lady in French Hill-- a community in East Jerusalem. Then I returned to Tiberias. Four days later, I boarded the plane for London. That night I flew from London to Iceland. Then the next morning, I flew from Iceland to America. It was the end of May.

I spent some relaxed time with my family. Then I returned to Panama for June and July. Upon arriving in Panama, I stayed at the airport hotel, I usually stay at. Before going to sleep that night, I had a visitation from the principality/power over Volcan Baru. He came into the room, and stood between the outside window and my bed. He told me everything he was going to do to me on that mountain, IF I had gone up on Vulcan Baru to meet my friends. Local Indians were going to most brutally sacrifice me to him. I raised both hands into the air and began praising Yahuweh, and Yahushua Yahuweh, and he quickly left. I slept well. Abba once again saved my life! I spent time in Panama, and enjoyed life there once again.

In early August, I felt I needed to get out and do some teaching. I put a bulletin out to all on my e-mail list that if anyone wanted me to come and teach, to write me. I got quite a few requests. Requests came from people in Oregon and Pennsylvania, and all in between. I had quite a few requests from Tennessee. A lady named LaDonna said I could stay with her, and have a meeting in her house. I also contacted my friends Dan and Kathy and they said they'd work with LaDonna to have another combined meeting too. Paula wanted me to come. Gayle did too. Even though I had multiple requests across the country, I had no desire to go anywhere else but Tennessee. But, one man named Andrew kept insisting that I come to Pennsylvania. I told him I could not come. I had little money. He said that he was going to Ohio, but that he'd wait for me. I started to hit "delete" and Abba strongly said: "NO!"

About the same time, Johnny, with **laydownlife.net**, had sent me some e-mails from people who had contacted him about my articles. In it was an e-mail from a man in Canada, named John. I had been hitting "delete" on a lot of what Johnny sent me, after reading them, because they were just nice well-wishes. When I went to hit "delete" on this man, Abba firmly said: "NO!" Sometimes I think: "What if I had deleted those two?"

The whole scenario of this interwoven miracle is in the Collection that includes "miracles of timing." If I had deleted these two and not gone to Pennsylvania, my life from then on would have been lacking. Then Andrew wrote me that some woman had told him who I stayed with in Panama. He also knew my friends in Treasure Island. That did it – I panicked. I went to delete again, and Abba said firmly: "NO! DO NOT DELETE!" I wrote my friends in Panama and my friends in Treasure Island. I thought to myself--this man is tracking me down, maybe he works for the CIA. But, I was reassured that Andrew and his wife and children were OK. I learned that he was going to pick garlic at W. and T's parent's house in Ohio, and that he was a friend of W's. Their parents have a huge garlic farm.

So, I decided to go to Pennsylvania and Andrew met me at the airport. He drove about 2½ hours into Amish country. I stayed in the home of Joe and Judy--a Mennonite family who were now guarding Torah. Two families had driven down from Canada to meet me. People stayed in trailers around the home. Andrew and his family lived in one of the trailers. While doing introductions after I arrived, Andrew looked at one family and said: "I think you know them." I didn't know them from appearance. But, it was the John Davies family of six, from Canada. What a blessing they have been in my life! How they got my articles is another miracle

PART VI - The Middle East & Travels Beyond

that I write about in the Collections. It was a fabulous non-stop three days of teaching and fellowshipping.

One man in the group took me on a tour of the local Amish community. We went to a buggy-building shop. It was awesome. They also made sleds. It was so amazing to me to see the Amish men in particular, who dressed identical to the Orthodox Jews in Israel. We were out in the country near Lewisburg. Andrew drove me back to the airport. I flew into Nashville for another three days of extensive teaching. LaDonna picked me up at the airport. I was so tired that I fell asleep. It was about a 2 hour drive to her house. I woke up as the car stopped at an intersection. In front of me was a sign with a town name--Lewisburg. I thought, "Am I back in Pennsylvania?" What are the odds of that!

We had three days of extensive teaching and fellowship. She took me to meet Dan, and I stayed at their house. He took me to Jessica's house for a third meeting. Jessica has been on my list a long time. We had a good time together. Then she took me to the airport in Nashville, and I flew to Tampa.

In late August, I flew to Panama. T. met me at the bus station in Panama City, and we took the bus to David. On the bus, he told me something that rattled me to the core. He said that he and his wife were going to work with a ministry in Israel, and that they would not be returning. I was hoping to stay in that house with them until Messiah came. I was devastated. I had taken almost all of my clothes and other things down there, thinking I'd work out of Panama in the years to come.

I loved it there, despite the fact that it had been hard because of a jezebel who kept an abundance of demons in the house. I sure wasn't going to stay with the jezebel. I had friends there, including Jamia and Mark, but they didn't want to move there either; a very wise decision on their part. I didn't have enough money to pay that rent by myself. So, bottom line was I either had to leave or fend for myself alone. We had a "garage sale." I sold many of my things. I had three weeks to pack up all the things I could take out in one time, and leave. I left quite a few things with Jamia and Mark to keep or sell for me. It was heartbreaking to me. We had such a large group of people that were fellowshipping with us. Twice a week we had the most awesome prayer meetings each morning, beginning at 6:00 AM. We grew to love our times of praise and worship, the reading of Scripture, and prayer so much that our very early-morning prayer meetings often ended at 10:00 or 11:00 AM. Then we'd have breakfast together. We were a family. I believe it was the enemy that broke up our family. There were about 40 there at that time in different areas, but we were united in Abba's Spirit! Now most are back in the U.S.

I did not know what to do. I had invitations from two families to stay with them. I really should have taken them up on it, and stayed longer. I previously had Yvette and her husband take about four large suitcases of mine down there with things for winter trips. I felt I was to go back to Mongolia, and also back to China. Later, in early 2011, Jamia sold things I didn't want anymore, and then shipped the rest back to the U.S. I appreciated that so very much!

Instead of taking the local commuter plane to Panama City, I rented a car, one way, for $200.00, for us to drive down to the airport. We left about 4:00 AM. T. and R's flight was later that night.

That night began Yom Teruah. I did not want to violate the Festival day, so I stayed at the hotel two days before flying to the U.S. All day on Yom Teruah, I spent worshipping Abba, reading Scripture, and praying. After dark, I ate at the hotel restaurant. I went back to my room to go to sleep. But, as I was waiting to fall asleep, all of a sudden I began watching a vision.

In the vision I was walking towards the City of David. As I approached the Dung Gate, gunfire broke out. Terrorists were attacking. I jumped over the low wall to my right, onto the ground below, and hid in a rock outcropping. A man jumped over with a rifle. I hid further into the rocks. I turned to see that there was an opening behind me. I saw a ladder going down into an abyss. I got my little flashlight out of my beltpack, and began descending. As I did, a soft light filled the tunnel below. I saw the same angel I had seen flying over me in Aqaba in 2001. He helped me down into the tunnel. At this time, I knew nothing about what the tunnels under Zion, the Ophel and the Temple Mount looked like, but later saw a picture of tunnels that looked just like what I saw. The vision was very detailed. He asked me if I was hungry. I said "yes," He went through an opening in the tunnel to the left, and soon brought me a large fruit about the size of a baseball. As I bit into it, I can still feel the juice as it ran down my left hand. It tasted like a combination of a peach and other fruits, even a papaya, which is my favorite fruit. I sensed it came from the Garden of Eden, which is underneath that whole area. The Gihon is just down from the City of David. Then, in walked the five "brothers" I had met with, and talked with in a vision in 2008.

But, I met more. I asked detailed questions of these men. I asked Enoch if his book was written by him or by someone in the 2nd century BCE as scholars say. He said that he left it with Methuselah, who gave it to Noah, and Noah brought it through the Flood. Years later I read in the book of *Jasher* that Noah brought it through the Flood. I also met Iyob (Job). To this day I remember their faces, especially Iyob's. In January of 2011, Iyob's "test" would become mine. The only thing that baffled me was that Moses, as in 2008, would not look at me. I got my answer also in January of 2011. The angel then said that the Master was calling him, and he had to go. The vision lasted about 45 minutes.

One thing stands out more than anything else. After eating the fruit that the angel gave me, I felt a state of purity come over me that I did not think possible. I could not have imagined it, nor can I try to imagine it now, or describe it. I was asked if I wanted to stay there. I thought of my daughter and grandchildren that I live with in America. Only for a split second did I think about it with sadness, then I said: "Yes." This vision interlocks with a dream I had about my future in 2006 at Mary and Larry's house in Texas. I then fell asleep.

The next morning I got on the plane for Miami. During takeoff, I remembered the vision. I got out a pad and pen and began writing it down. I even wrote the details of my conversations with several of the "brothers." It was soon after this that I wrote the article "East Jerusalem." Abba taught me all about it--past, present and future.

I went back to Tiberias. I was still staying with Abigail in Tiberias, except for visits to Jerusalem for Festivals. Launa had come with our mutual friend Carol. They stayed at the Petra Hostel. They were planning on going to Qumran. I had so longed to go back. I had been there in 2009 with Launa and the Australian lady, and it was life-changing. But, I did not invite myself. Carol told Launa that Abba had told her that they had to take Yedidah to Qumran. So we went.

It was another life-changing day. I asked Abba what His message to me was from that place. He said: "I want you to be more set-apart." I went over to look over the canyon below cave four and I lifted my hands in praise, to declare praises. When I finished, I looked down at my feet and there was a grinding stone. I had taken archeology classes at Cerritos College in California. I had found a grinding stone in Arizona. I knew it was a grinding stone – but what was it doing at my feet? There were no such rocks of its type anywhere around. I knew it was a message from Abba. I have that stone to this day. Launa also had a man make a representative tribulum board, with holes for me to put stones in. I have that to this day. I got stones from many places in Israel. Along with my plumb line, I use the tribulum and grinding stone in intercession.

That week, on the second floor of the Petra Hostel where they were staying, Nehemia Gordon and Keith Johnson came. Nehemia spoke on the "Our Father" prayer. I bought the book. Later, when Launa and Carol came to Tiberias, we went to the Horns of Hattin to see where the Sermon of the Mount was most likely spoken. We took the north tour again, and had some lovely times together.

During this time in Israel, several couples, families, and individuals, came on tours or by themselves, and I met them in Tiberias. If they had time, I took them on a tour of the north of Israel. That is my great delight, to share that area where so much prophecy will soon be fulfilled.

Upon returning to the U.S. in December, I prepared for intercession during the December 21st lunar eclipse. You can read my report on this in "The Rare Lunar Eclipse" and "The Mystery of the Lunar Eclipse." I stayed up all night doing intercession and taking pictures of the different phases of the eclipse, from just outside our back door. The sky was so clear. I also took pictures of Venus behind me. The pictures of Venus were very clear and you could see the planet without any glow around it. It was very exciting to me. The eclipse began about 1:30 AM and ended at 5:00 AM. I was calling on Yahuweh's Name, and proclaiming Psalms and victory over the enemy during the eclipse.

Three days later, on the 24th, I began to feel very strange. I had pains in my heart. This happened once in Panama--my left shoulder collapsed down, pushing a rib out of place, giving me severe pains in my heart and left arm. On top of that, the sharp pain in my lower right side began in its severity. I have never had more pain in my life, than I did that day. I let out one "silent scream" after another. It went on for about six hours.

The night of the 25th, because of the dropped position of my left shoulder pushing out a rib, the pressure on the left side of my body pushed against the heart. I woke up having heart spasms, knowing I was near death. I had been lying on my left side too. If I had not awakened, the pressure probably would have stopped my heart. I have a good strong heart. My son-in-law went to the market and bought me some cayenne pepper, which I put in hot water and drank as a tea. It opens the heart valves immediately, and brings calming to the whole body. Afterwards, for about a week or more, I was as feeble as a 120-year old woman. My mind was in an infantile stage. I was very joyful, and was babbling all the time about everything, like a toddler. My mind was not working well. Yet, I continued to write updates and study about what was happening to me, even with the pain still attacking my lower right side, as it willed. My spirit was not feeble! During this time I wrote: "From Death to Life." The "mind of the Spirit" in my spirit was functioning well, just like when I had the malaria, and couldn't remember my own name.

One's true nature is seen openly by their outer actions, either of one living in their "carnal flesh"/soul, self-centered with negative emotions, or one who lives from their eternal spirit who stays in Yahuweh's realm, is centered on His will, and has His nature.

A little later Yvette took me to her therapist/chiropractor in Tampa, who spent an hour with me explaining what happened to me. Yes, it was a heart attack, but not from heart disease, or stress. He confirmed what I thought had happened. He showed me what was pressing on my heart. He was very concerned about me because his father had a heart attack not long before.

So, I entered 2011 very weak. But, His joy was like a well-spring of life coming out of my spirit. His "joy" is His might. "The joy of Yahuweh is your strength." (**Nehemiah 8:10**) I knew His Presence so strongly, yet I was feeble and weak. (**II Corinthians 12:9-10**)

I stopped drinking coffee, and switched to green tea, and fine-tuned my already good diet even more. Because I did not know what was happening with the pain in my lower right side, I took kidney support herbs, did colon cleanses, and everything naturally that I could do. I had done research on what possibly could be wrong with me, but nothing matched my symptoms. I refused to go to a doctor. The last time I had been to a doctor or hospital had been in 1981, when I had my last baby. I was strong-willed against going to a doctor. Besides, I had no money for a doctor or hospital. 2011 became a year of revelation and deliverance.

AMERICA--ISRAEL--WALES
SCOTLAND (HEBRIDES)--ICELAND
(2011)

Though weak and feeble, I sat up in bed and kept researching on what was happening in the U.S., and around the world that showed end-time prophecy to be right on course, as Abba had showed me. In January, Abba instructed me to go to Israel in March on the exact day as the vision in 2008 in March. I don't ask questions anymore. But, I knew He had to do something to help me physically so I could go. I used to ask "why" to everything, but no more. So, I got my ticket.

On January 4th, about 10:00 AM, the knife-pain in the lower right side of my body hit quickly and the pain became intolerable. I did not tell my daughter what was happening. I just went into my bedroom and laid down. The pain was so severe that later on I thought my appendix had burst. I laid there in that condition for 10 hours, but neither my daughter, or grandson, came to check on me. That was very strange. My son-in-law was at work. He came back about 6:00 PM.

I wrestled with Abba about it. I felt His Presence hovering over me as I did when I was dying of malaria, but He would not speak. Finally, feeling that I was dying, but having such peace, **I said to Him: "OK: You are El and I am not. Whatever you want is alright with me. Even if I have to go to the hospital, it is all right. I will not stand against Your will."** That's what He was waiting for. He said to me: "You will not die." Then I felt warmth going through my body, and the pain disappeared. I did not know at the time, but I had passed "the Iyob test." Refer to the article: "The Iyob Test"/January 30, 2013. Abba asked Iyob (Job) sixty questions, showing He was the Creator, the Almighty, and Iyob was not. He finally said also: "You are El and I am not!" Abba had to bring him to the place where he knew that Abba was the Creator and ruler, not him. Iyob was a good man. But, like him, so many of us have our own ideas ABOUT a God we really don't know. It is through suffering that we learn His true nature, and finally know Him.

After 10 hours of severe pain, I was very weak. I got up, and went to sit in the living room. I told my daughter what had happened. She was shocked. I did not know what to eat. My son-in-law had fixed some beef patties. First Abba said for me to eat some yogurt. I ate a few spoonful's of that. Then He said to take 2-3 tablespoons of apple cider vinegar and honey. Then He said to eat a beef patty. After I did that, my strength returned.

The morning of January 7th, my daughter went to visit the 20-year old son of one of her best friends, who was dying of cancer.

PART VI - The Middle East & Travels Beyond

They had moved him from the hospital to a care center. His mother was there with him. When my daughter got to the care center, she found that he had just died. So, she stayed with his mother to comfort her. While she was comforting her friend, she got a call from the hospital in Bradenton saying that Lauren was about to give birth to the baby they were adopting.

My daughter and son-in-law had wanted a second child for a long time. They had been checking adoption agencies in other countries, as well as in the U.S. The fees were about $26,000.00 for adopting in America. They were praying so much that Abba would give them the right little girl. My son-in-law had named her years ago – Abigail Joy. Then one Sunday morning in church, Lauren's sister came up to my daughter and said that her sister was having a baby girl and wanted to put her up for adoption. The family was so afraid that the State would take the baby. My daughter and my son-in-law felt this was from Abba. So, they got a lawyer. The mother was a drug addict. She had been in prison. The State Social Service/Child Protection Agency came several times to check them out to see if they'd be good parents for this baby.

That morning, my daughter came back to the house to tell me what was happening. The young man had just died, and the baby was being born. My daughter was already an emotional wreck and crying, as you can imagine. So, I hugged her and told her I'd pray. She got to the hospital just after the baby was born. Lauren had taken a Valium tablet before birth, so Abigail just slid out. She was not breathing at birth. The nurses attending the birth, told my daughter that it was a good thing she was not there. It would have panicked her. Of course they put Abigail on oxygen immediately. Lauren did not want the baby. She wanted to leave the hospital the next day. The birth-father was there, so my daughter and son-in-law got to meet him. "Abby" was born with hard drug addiction to five major illegal drugs, including cocaine and heroin. She had to breathe through a tube. She could not digest formula. She had other complications, and was in intensive care.

The next morning Lauren said she was leaving. So, my daughter called their lawyer, who came immediately. The State people were there too – to take the baby if the papers were not signed for the adoption. So, the lawyer filled out the papers, they were signed, and the Child Protection Agency left. My daughter and son-in-law were left with a damaged child, not knowing if she would live, go through withdrawals from the drugs, or what would happen to her. The hospital staff kept a close watch for any signs of drug withdrawal. They took turns, staying with her night and day. They held her, prayed over her, spoke Scripture over her, and cuddled her. She was breathing through the tube fine, but she was not digesting her formula. It was just staying in her stomach.

On January 10th, I knew things were critical with Abby. I put my tallit (prayer shawl) around my shoulders, and went into the living room to pray. They both were at the hospital with her. As I was praying, I looked up to see a man kneeling on his left knee, a few feet in front of me. He had a distinctive-shaped face and clear blue eyes. He was smiling. I knew immediately it was Moshe (Moses). How did Peter know that Eliyahu and Moshe were the two standing by Yahushua in **Matthew 17:1-4**? -- By the Spirit of Yahuweh, of course.

To my right stood Iyob, smiling. I knew I had passed my test. Therefore, Moses, attendant of the Bride, could now come. I had been concerned because in the 2008 vision and the 2010 vision, he would not look at me. He would stare straight ahead as if I was not there. I also knew that I had to pass that test, or I could go no further with Abba's plans for me! I had to take my hands off of the reins of my life, or else He would not be able to use me in the days to come. Iyob was there to confirm that he passed his test too. I looked up at the clock. It was 11:00 AM exactly. Abba spoke to me: "She's all right now"--meaning Abigail.

When my daughter came home, I told her that Moses had come for a visit and knelt down in her living room. She was happy about that. She knows her mother. I once told her about some of my other visitations, and asked her if she thought her mom was crazy. She said: "NO mom! You are not crazy. That is just part of your life."

I asked her what happened at 11:00 AM. She said: "At 11:00 AM, a new neonatal doctor came in to check Abigail, and said they would put her on a super sensitive formula for 24 hours. Her little tummy could not digest the milk from the regular formula. They put her on the super sensitive formula, and within a few hours she began digesting the food. From that point on, she gained strength. They had told my daughter that she would be in the hospital for at least six weeks. But, after a few days, she began breathing fine on her own. She kept digesting food normally. She got jaundice, but that was treated, and she was fine. Her other difficulties disappeared quickly. And to the shock of the doctors: THEY FOUND NO TRACES OF DRUGS IN HER BODY! Abba had intervened!

They checked her blood when she was born, and found residue of all the drugs her mother had taken. In other words, she was born a drug addict to cocaine, heroin, and other powerful drugs.

But, within about five days, Abba had cleaned out her blood, and she went home in seven days, a normal, healthy little baby. Praise Yahuweh! They kept her swaddled, cuddled, and kissed. I called her the princess. We still call her "the princess." Now Abby is 2. She is one of the happiest, most adorable children I have ever seen. She has a personality that is exciting. She is very smart. She is bold, and very loving. She loves to snuggle. She is our miracle baby!

January 22nd: We were celebrating my grandson's 5th birthday a few days early. They had arranged a party at a local farm and invited all of his school and church friends. He went to a Christian school for pre-school and kindergarten. Now he is home schooled! All four of my children had come to participate in this birthday party weekend, from Texas, Georgia, and Tennessee. Yvette and my children are friends, so she came to take me to the party. But, as we rode to the party, the knife-pain hit me very hard, and began to increase. By the time I got to the farm, I was in terrible pain. I stayed a few minutes, then told Yvette to take me back home. I laid down on my bed. My children came back in about 1½ hours. They gathered around my bed. They had never seen their mother in that much pain. Like I said, those pains were worse than natural child birth. My last two were born naturally, so I know.

They said they'd put me in my daughters van, and drive me to the local hospital. My son-in-law kept the children, and four grandchildren, in another room so that they did not know what was happening to grama. But, when I went to sit up, I had pain that was so strong that I winced. I could not hide it. They all panicked. My oldest daughter who has had medical training said to call an ambulance. I protested a little, but remembered what I had told Abba on January 4th – that if I had to go to the hospital, it was all right. I had not been to a hospital since 1981, when my youngest daughter was born. But, I had peace. I just let it happen. I knew that without insurance, my bills would be horrendous. One daughter kept saying: "Don't worry about the money mom." I knew that none of them could help me with the bill.

The ambulance drivers came, lifted me off the bed, and put me in the back of the ambulance. One drove, and one began poking around my veins to find blood from my arm. Of course, the pain, which I later found out was voodoo/witchcraft, left while I was in the ambulance. My children followed the ambulance. They were so scared for me. Once in the emergency room, the nurse started her routine. My oldest daughter told them what tests to give me. She kept ordering tests and telling the doctor what to do. They found a small cist on my right ovary, but it was too small to bring such pain. My intestines looked a little funny on the right side, the doctor said, but there was nothing they could find that would produce that type of pain.

The doctor was an old guy. He asked why I had let this go for over two years. I didn't want to tell him I was trusting Abba to heal me. He would have thought me "mentally ill." So, I said I was a stubborn old lady. Of course that was true too! He just shook his head. He could not figure me out. But, the bottom line was, after all the tests, they could find nothing wrong that would produce that intensity of pain. At one point, the pain started returning, and the nurse was going to give me a full dose of pain killer into my blood stream. My oldest daughter told her that I took no medicine except over the counter things occasionally, so to only give me a baby dose. Even the baby dose was strong for me. But, it sure felt good to relax painlessly.

My children were allowed in to see me two at a time. My future daughter-in-law was there too, and I got to know her better. I was there six hours. During that time, when it was just my oldest daughter and I, something happened that made it all worthwhile. I realized how desperately I needed this daughter. I told her that I didn't know what I'd do without her help. I burst out crying. During the crying, I don't remember the whole of what I said, but I said something like: "I am so sorry for anything I have ever done to hurt you." Like papa had said to me, with tears.

She later told me she had waited for that apology for 30 years. I did not do anything intentionally to hurt her. I never knew I had hurt her. But, she had been lied to by her father about things I had done to her, and also she held things against me I didn't know that I had done wrong. At any rate, what I said dissolved the bitterness and hurt of all those years. They dismissed me from the hospital, and my children brought me home. Upon entering the house, I saw seven boxes by the door. Jamia had sent my things from Panama. It was like two finalities in one afternoon.

The next morning, I had a chance to talk to my oldest daughter, who had been staying with us for a few days, and she began crying about how good Abba was to restore us. I put my arm around her and held her. She said it was the first time she ever remembered me holding her when she cried. I had held her so many times when she cried. But, children forget. I forget the affection my parents gave to me. I know it was there, for they were kind people. I just don't remember. The enemy so often erases memory of good things, but continually reminds us of what was wrong, hurtful, painful, and damaging, to us.

I worked very hard after that to prepare to go to Israel in March. In the meantime, I started getting bills. The hospital took off 20% because I had no insurance. But, the doctor, the ambulance, and the radiation department had no mercy. In finding out what it would take to get Medicare and Social Security, I had to decline. I would have had to expose my meager finances, exposing those who gave me offerings, and the finances of my daughter and son-in-law.

I asked Abba what I should do--should I make payments, should I put it on my credit card, should I join Medicare? He said this: "**BE MY SECRETARY. TELL THE HOSPITAL YOU'LL MAKE PAYMENTS. THIS IS MY BILL. I WILL PAY IT.**"

So, I was His secretary and set up payments with the hospital. They wanted a $900.00 deposit before the payments. Sharon had sent me $600.00, and someone else had sent me $300.00 a few days before my hospital experience. So, I had the deposit already. Then the other bills arrived. I asked Yvette if I should make this need known to those on my e-mail address list. She said it would be a good idea, and that if I needed confirmation of what happened, she'd write a letter that I could send to all on my list. She's so good to me!

So, I wrote a letter telling what happened, saying that if anyone felt led by the Spirit to help me, please do. That was all I said in my behalf. I made no pleas. I didn't ask for money directly. I just said that if anyone sent me anything, they should make it plain it was for the medical bills, not for my travel expenses. I also told them that when the bills were paid, I'd alert everyone to stop sending for medical bills. I went to my P.O. Box about a week later, and there was a fist-full of letters. Everyone told me to use the money as I saw fit. Some even thanked me for alerting them of this need. What a great bunch of people I have on my list!

Yes, I have needs. I work on the computer, yes, but I travel extensively to do Abba's will. I buy my own food wherever I stay, and share with my host. I have integrity with money. I've been poor most all of my life, so I know how to be frugal. I respect the money that people give me, for I know it is given out of love, in Abba's Name. I have been with ministers who receive money for their ministry work, and watched them spend money for expensive clothes and jewelry, and for eating out at expensive restaurants, staying in expensive hotels, etc. I can't do that! Abba has supplied things from thrift stores, from gifts from others, and even from garbage cans. And, I shop at Walmart too (smile).

I also spend hours a day to prepare the articles, studies, and updates for His people. I spend much time each day counseling

His people too. But, in the nearly fourteen years of writing and teaching, less than 5% of the people on my list have given me any offering at all. Yet, Abba has supplied in different ways. Now, I can pay off my one bill each month--a credit card. Praise Abba!

Because of the generosity of those on my e-mail list, within 5 weeks, my bills of over $6,000.00 were totally paid! But, in going to the P.O. to pay my last bill to the hospital, the knife-like pain hit me again, and I had to drive back quickly and lie down. It was as if the enemy was letting me know he was not finished with me. It also confirmed more than ever, that it was witchcraft.

Abba reminded me of the 2008 dream. In that dream, I was sitting on a hillside at night. I was sitting in a large black marble gate that was just sitting by itself, deep in the ground on the side of the mountain. To my right was like a guard shack, which I knew was where everything I owned was kept. Below me was a deep valley. I saw a gate going up into the hill above. I saw the shape of the hill. I saw twinkling lights across part of the hill. I knew it was Zion at the time of King David, before his palace was built. I knew I was the watchman over Zion. I was in an olive grove – on the Mount of Olives. It was a peaceful scene. I wondered why I was a watchman over Zion when there were no enemies around.

So, Abba instructed me to be in Jerusalem, on the Mount of Olives, on the same day as I had that dream in March of 2008. I figured what that day would be in 2011, and got my ticket. The enemy threw serious problems in my path during the time of preparing. An example: I was out walking on our residential street one morning, having walked around the big lake. I was returning towards our house, and the cartilage behind my right knee shifted, causing the left knee to turn out of place (I had a bandage on it, but it was a flimsy bandage). I fell along the curbside. I rolled onto my back to check to see if my left knee had gone back into place. It had. I was staring up at the sky. My cane was no help. It lay on the curbside grass. Nobody saw it happen. No cars passed by. I just laid there, laughing. Here I was lying in the street, staring up at the sky, and I was relaxed. But, I forced myself to get up and walk two blocks to the house. I told my daughter what happened, making it sound humorous. But, she didn't see the humor. I went and laid down. It took a few weeks for my left knee to heal. In the meantime, as always, the research went on, the article-writing, the e-mails, and life in general.

On the day of my flight, March 25th, I flew to JFK in New York. I had an 8-hour layover. The flight was to go out at 11:30 PM. About 8:00 PM, while just sitting at the gate, the knife-pain came again. The doctor had prescribed some strong pain killer medicine, and an anti-spasmodic. As the pain increased, I took some of the medicine. I thought I'd be able to sleep on the plane, but a young man sat next to me who was so nervous that he was always moving around, hitting my arm, and getting out of his seat. I had the aisle seat. I got no sleep. When we got to London, there was a layover. Then I boarded my first flight on an El Al plane. We got out on the tarmac and sat there. Then the captain said: "They are calling us back to the gate." Everyone thought it was for some mechanical problem, but the captain gave no excuse. We returned to the gate and sat waiting for an hour. Finally, we had clearance to leave.

Upon arriving in Tel Aviv and clearing Immigration and Customs, I got a taxi to my hotel in central Jerusalem. It was nearly midnight. It was rainy and cold. Because of no sleep, and exhaustion, I was sick. I had a head cold and bronchitis, and I was aching all over. My immune system had broken down. The next morning at breakfast, I sat at a table that seated four. The restaurant was full. Two ladies needed a seat, so I invited them to sit with me. They asked me if I had heard what happened yesterday. I had not. They had come on the El Al plane after mine. They said that their flight was held up too because there had been a terrorist bombing at a bus stop near the Central Bus Station, and they had closed the airport for a while. Welcome to Israel! It was the first bombing in a long time.

I transferred to Christ Church for two days. Then on the third day, I went up to the Panorama Hotel on the Mount of Olives, in the area of the Ras Al Amoud neighborhood of Silwan – an Arab town on a hill overlooking the City of David/Zion. It was on this hill that Solomon kept all of his wives and concubines.

From the hotel's fifth-floor restaurant, I could see the whole area. The hotel was just off the road that went by the Church of All Nations, which is the caretaker for the Garden of Gethsemane. Abba had given me the Scriptures to proclaim from the top of the Mount of Olives.

The next morning, He had instructed me to do the intercession. I was to walk to the Garden of Gethsemane and continue up a very steep road that curved around to the right, passed the Garden. I continued on up that steep path to the Dominus Flevit Church, whose dome is shaped like a tear drop and where Messiah supposedly had stopped on His descent of the Mount of Olives, and wept over Jerusalem. I had done my homework in all the Gospels, and this tear-drop-shaped church was about where that would have happened.

There were proclamations I had to make from the courtyard of that church, which overlooked the whole Temple Mount, and

Kidron Valley. After breakfast, I went to get my things for the walk down the hill and up the very, very steep hill. I was still very weak and sick. My head hurt, and I was aching all over. I took two Ibuprofen tablets, and went out the door. As I walked along the road to the Garden of Gethsemane, the knife-pains hit me very hard. I was in excruciating pain. But, I kept walking. I walked up that incredibly steep hill to where I was to do the declarations. It took everything in me to keep going. But, by this time, coping with such things was part of my life.

There were tourists, body-to-body up there. I found a little place where I could overlook the Temple Mount, and I began to read the declarations of His Word that He had given to me. I wanted to stay longer, but I was driven by the pain to go back down the hill and to my room up the hill. I'm telling you the absolute truth, as I have in every detail of this autobiography, the second I entered my hotel room, the pain instantly left, and I began getting stronger from that time on. Again, the enemy tried to stop me from doing Abba's will, but he failed! I had a fabulous dinner that night. Their food was excellent.

The next morning after breakfast, I was to check out. But, before checking out and relocating to Christ Church for a night, I had more declarations to do, as Abba instructed me. He did not specify where I was to do the declarations, so I walked down again towards the Garden of Gethsemane. I was very tired. I saw there was an open gate to the tombs that are all over the side of the Mount of Olives. I went in and sat down on a ledge among the tombs. I faced the Temple Mount, and proclaimed **Psalm 83**. It was peaceful there. Abba gave me more insight. I was sitting surrounded by the two conspirators that united against Israel--a Muslim stronghold right in East Jerusalem, and the Roman Catholic Church. The intercession was finished.

I went back to the hotel and checked out. I got a hotel taxi driver to take me to Christ Church. He told me he could not take me into the Jaffa Gate. I'd heard that before from Arabs who just didn't want to go up into the gate. I told him to go. He did. But, he had told me the truth--he really was not supposed to go into the gate. An Israeli police officer stopped him and charged him 200 shekels for being there. I gave the taxi driver 200 shekels (about $50.00), plus his taxi fee, which made him very happy. I thought it only fair.

During my stay in Jerusalem, Abba confirmed my dream of where I sat on the Mount of Olives, with three paintings. The first one was at Christ Church. On a wall in their dining room hangs an old oil painting of East Jerusalem in the days of King David that had been painted in England. It shows the hill of Zion as it rises above the Kidron Valley on the East, above the Hinnom Valley on the South, and the Tyropean Valley on the West. It showed the little gate that I saw in the dream – an ancient Canaanite gate that archeologists uncovered not long ago. The second painting was on a laminated place mat that I bought in the Jewish Quarter. It was a scene of life in the Kingdom, when we will return to ancient Zion through the Eastern Gate for the Festivals. The third was found while I was in the City of David Park bookstore. It was in their official book: *Discovering the City of David--A Journey to the Source*. In the book was a painting by Lloyd Townsend. It was a picture as it would have looked at the time of King David. It looked just like what I saw in the dream! Since I was walking, I did not buy the book. The distance from the bookstore to Christ Church was just too great and I couldn't carry such a heavy book that far, especially up all those flights of stairs. But, later during my stay, I went to a bookstore below the Jaffa Gate and bought it. It is a treasured possession.

Also, standing in Area G in the City of David/Zion and looking towards Silwan at the Panorama Hotel on the top of Silwan, I saw that between the Panorama Hotel and the Kidron floor was exactly where I had sat in that gate in the dream. It was right there in the Kidron Valley in 2010, that Arab children had thrown rocks at me, just below the ascent to Area G. [Refer to: "The Rocks That Nearly Hit Me"] In the dream, it was a peaceful place, but now it was a place surrounded by enemies. Today, where I sat in the dream, would be right in the heart of the north part of Silwan, right where the bullets flew when I was in Jerusalem in May, on the Arab's "Nakba Day." I now knew the symbolic nature of the dream--a dream set long ago in the time of King David but also a dream that gave me instructions for being a watchman now.

I stayed one more night at Christ Church, then the next day I took the bus to Tiberias. Abigail and Jamia picked me up at the bus station. It was so awesome to see Jamia there. It was hers, Mark's, and the two children's first trip to Israel. She had been taking Hebrew lessons online for several years, and speaks fluent Hebrew. I got my old room back at Abigail's apartment. Jamia and family were staying there too. I sat down on the couch to talk to Jamia, and she said: "I saw the tree." I knew what she meant, but I asked her "what tree?" She said: "THE TREE."

She said she was on the Mount of Olives. She was looking at the Temple Mount from the area of the Dominus Flevit Church, when all of a sudden from the southeast corner rose a huge tree, rising about 100' into the sky. She said it was gorgeous, and had lots of fruit on it. I had to smile; of course it was in the southeast corner. That is where the angel got the fruit for me in my 2010 vision in Panama City.

SCOTLAND (OUTER HEBRIDES ISLANDS)
ICELAND
(2011)

After being there one more day, they left. The next day, upon returning from town to the apartment, I found two new couples there. One couple said they knew me, and even mentioned several mutual friends, including T. and R. I did not know they were the ones who started and led the ministry that T. and R. had volunteered for. Yvette also had come to be with that ministry, but she lasted less than a month. They are a Christian religious group, and Yvette, like me, is definitely NOT religious! I thought they were going to stay too, but they left. Daniel and Carol, who had come with them, stayed. Daniel and Carol were Spirit-taught. We were together a week and on the same page all the time. He began talking about the return of Ephraim, and where they had left from in the UK. Daniel mentioned the Northern Hebrides Islands of Scotland. It was like a spiritual sock in the stomach when he mentioned the Hebrides.

Since 1992, my first overseas visit, I had the Outer Hebrides Islands in my heart. I did not know why. As the week progressed, Abba instructed me to go to the Hebrides. I was still a little sick, and weak! I would be flying over the Hebrides to Iceland on my way back to the U.S. in June. I thought I would do intercession over them from the air. But, Daniel said: "You know you have to go there." I knew that! I had to be on site. Abba gave me **Jeremiah 31:10**.

That next Shabbat, Ephraim and Ramona Frank came to Abigail's apartment to minister to us. I had started out that morning listening to Abba's instructions about my trip to the Hebrides, and when they came I was still going over the Scriptures He was giving me to declare off of the most northern tip of the Hebrides--the Isle of Lewis. I heard Ephraim teaching in the living room. My bedroom was just off the living room. But, Abba kept teaching. He kept teaching while they ate lunch too. So, I missed the whole Shabbat teaching and fellowship with Ephraim and Ramona, and others there. Abba stopped talking about the time they left. Oh well, I'm sure Abba was more enlightening!

In the course of my talking with Daniel and Carol that week, I learned their connection to the Davies family, and to Andrew. It was Daniel who had sent one of my articles to John Davies. Small world when Abba is at work! The complete story is in the Collections – and WOW what a story! No one can orchestrate events like Abba can! He is a MASTER STRATEGIST!!!

While I was still in America, Zeporah was looking for me for an apartment in Tiberias. I knew that unless she found a place for me to stay, I would have to leave Abigail's before Passover week and return to the U.S. after only being in Israel for three weeks. Abigail had others coming to stay with her Passover week and onward, so she could not have me stay with her that week too. My friend Zeporah had been looking for me for weeks. She could find no place for me, especially during Passover week. I was going to write Zeporah and tell her to stop looking, and that I would come back to the U.S. after leaving Abigail's. When I pulled up my e-mails, I saw that she had sent me an e-mail. "Good News" was in the subject line. She had found an apartment in Tiberias for me to rent. The owners lived in Jerusalem and worked with an old established mission. They were given the apartment and had never used it. Friends of Zeporah's were staying there, but they were leaving. Talk about timing! So, I stayed with Abigail up until Passover started and then moved into my apartment.

I went to Jerusalem in April, met Liz, paid for two months, and rented the apartment. Zeporah helped me move in. Not only were there suitcases from my present trip, but boxes and suitcases from back in 2007 when I had moved up to Tiberias. Abigail had been keeping them for me for over a year. I had been able to rent a room in her apartment up until she started her Bed and Breakfast, then I had to work around others being there.

I met some good people through Abigail. One lady, from Corpus Christi, Texas, had been with Abigail for a week. She was friends with Constance in New Braunfels. The day she was to leave, we had a chance to talk. It was an anointed session. I told her a little of my 2010 Panama vision on the night of Yom Teruah. She said that she and her intercession friends knew that on that very night, there was a shift in the spirit realm over this world, and that from that night on, things would move swiftly towards the end events before Messiah came. What confirmation! She also took a message from me to give to Constance--my attempt to try to reconcile with her. I even wrote Constance an e-mail, but she never contacted me back, but I tried.

The very day I got to that apartment, and Zeporah helped me move in all my things, the enemy started attacking. Before Zeporah even left, the knife-like pain hit me again. She prayed, and the pain instantly left. I became not only suspicious, but dogmatic, that the pain was witchcraft. That apartment is in a secular Russian area, where there is a lot of witchcraft. I didn't need more witchcraft! Zeporah invited me to have Passover Seder with her family and those who had rented the apartment before me. I accepted the invitation.

But, within a day after being there, deep depression and oppression came on me so that I could hardly function. It was so heavy that I could hardly walk. I just wanted to lie in bed. It began because of my deep sorrow over one of my children. Even though the oppression continued, I went with Zeporah's son to her house. I could not even enjoy the Seder. The next day was a high Shabbat, so I stayed in. I was wondering how in the world I would be able to do all those logistics necessary for the Outer Hebrides trip in that condition.

The apartment was on the third floor overlooking a large soccer field, basketball court, Lake Kinneret/the "Sea of Galilee", and the Golan Heights. But, the wireless service in that apartment was almost non-existent. Even hanging almost out the window, I could not get a wireless signal to last me more than a few minutes at best. It was so discouraging, which added to my deepening depression.

The next morning, I knew I had to get groceries. So, I took the bus into town. Thank goodness the bus stop is close to a small market. I also knew I had to get a cell phone. I could not be alone in that apartment on the third floor, with a lock that was frighteningly unpredictable, without having access to call friends if I needed help. Before getting groceries, I started down the steps to the marina to the Internet store to get the phone. Thank goodness I was holding the hand rail. I had been down those steps so many times. But, I had a poor knee brace on – the elastic was gone on it.

As I descended the first step, my left knee went out of place, and stayed out of place. That had not happened for many, many years. A restaurant owner saw I needed help and came to help. But, he could not get the knee back in place either. I held onto the railing until I finally got it back into place, but the ligaments and tendons were very torn. After all of that, I still went and got the phone. I think the man sold me an old, used phone, but it worked. It still works. I went to the bus stop, took the bus back, walked up the steep hill to my apartment, and then up three flights of steps. I got ice on the knee. I sat in my living room chair stunned. I knew that the depression had opened a portal for the enemy to be able to do this to me. All of a sudden, I felt Abba's Presence. In an instant, He lifted the depression and oppression, and joy filled me. I was free of the depression!

However, the knife-like pain kept coming on and off, and my knee was in much pain. I called my friends, and, one by one, they brought me food from town, and came to just visit. About ten days later, Abigail asked me to come for a Shabbat dinner. Daniel and Carol were still there and would be present at the dinner along with another couple she had invited. I had met this couple through my e-mail list, and they wanted to visit with me. So, they came to pick me up at my apartment to go to the dinner. I did not know how I would get down and back up those 3 flights of stairs. But, I did.

It was early May. I had so wanted to celebrate my spiritual birthday in Jerusalem. But, I thought myself crazy for even thinking of it, because my knee was still not healed, and if I went to Jerusalem, it may keep me from being able to do all that walking in Wales and the Outer Hebrides. I told the couple at the dinner about wanting to go to Jerusalem over that time, and they said they were going. The man had told me about a place that had opened in the Jewish Quarter that had rooms in a refurbished 1,000-year old Yeshiva. By faith, I reserved a room there. But, I knew I could not go on the bus alone. I am no fool. So Connie offered to go with me.

So, we went. Connie helped me greatly. Then she went back to Tiberias. I did not walk much. The room I was staying in was down a steep set of steps. I did get down where the big menorah is along the steps going to the Western Wall to do intercession. It was peaceful. I had a good celebration. During the time we were in the Jewish Quarter, on my spiritual birthday, the Arabs had "Nakba Day"--their day of rage for Israel becoming a nation. The Arabs had hoped to get one million people to march against Israel that day, but their plan was not fulfilled. However, there was rioting in the Ras al Amoud neighborhood where I had stayed, with gun fire, burning tires, and the usual rock throwing. One man was shot and killed. We heard the gun shots. Also, Syrians had broken through the fence along the border below Majdal Shams, along the eastern Golan Heights. There was rioting all over the country. But, the most protected area by the IDF, in Israel, was the Jewish Quarter in Jerusalem. I was so glad I went. Why stay away from danger if Abba says it is all right to go? Then I went back with these two to Tiberias. They had rented a car. Then, I seriously began planning my trip to the Outer Hebrides north Isle of Lewis.

Daniel had told me that when the Ephraimites got ready to cross the Atlantic, the northern tip of the Isle of Lewis was a major place where they left from. It would be a major place to go to call a repentant humble remnant of Ephraim home. [Refer to the study of Hosea: "How Could I Give You Up Ephraim"/2011 **(Hosea 11:8-10**)

I was to fly into London, take the National Coach Express the five hours to Swansea, and stay with Maureen. Then a few days later, go to the Outer Hebrides via Glasgow by train, then fly to

Stornoway, the capitol of the Isle of Lewis. Yes, the wireless service in my apartment was next to zero, but every time I needed to get a hotel, in Glasgow, or on the Isle of Lewis, book the trains, or arrange the planes to and from Stornoway, the wireless service stayed on for hours. ABBA AGAIN! I booked such nice places and good transportation! He really led me! I had such joy in doing it too!

During this time, the Davies felt they were to join me. John said that Abba had given him **Jeremiah 31:10**, just as Abba had given me the same verse. They had finished their across Canada intercession, sold their van and travel trailer (which Daniel and Carol had given them to use in their across Canada trek), and wanted to meet me in Stornoway. What a blessing! By the time they went to book hotels on Lewis, they were all full. It was tourist season--we were going in early June. They had purchased heavy tents and camping gear. They knew they were to fly into England, trace their family roots, and join me to do intercession. They were going to take a ferry across the sea from Ullapool to Stornoway and meet me there. Then the Davies six were going to backpack across Europe, and end up in Israel. I would meet them again in Jerusalem for the Fall Festivals.

June 1st, I flew to London and got the bus to Swansea. It was good to see Maureen again. It was a little more than a week before Shavu'ot. I took the train to Glasgow via Crewe. When I got on the train at Crewe, the knife-like pain hit me, always in the same area. When I got off the train in Glasgow, the pain instantly left. The reverse happened on the way back. NO coincidence!

I spent the night in a nice hotel in Glasgow just across the street from the entrance to the airport. The next morning, I took the 1-hour flight to Stornoway. One hour later, the Davies arrived via ferry. We got the local bus. I got off at the Dooney Brae Guest House where I was staying. They went on to their campground, and set up camp. The next morning, it was cold and rainy. But, we got a bus part way to the Port of Ness, at the northern tip of Lewis, then we got another bus into Ness. But, the bus let us off about 1½ miles below the lighthouse. I had not prepared for such cold weather. My knee was aching. But, I set off with them.

It was drizzly and foggy. Rain was blowing in our face, for the wind was blowing rather strongly. I went as far as I could go. My hands were numb from the cold. I saw the sea ahead, and to my left, over a hill, I saw the top of the lighthouse. Then I had to turn around and go back towards the little village of Ness. We agreed to meet back at a little restaurant we had seen. I did not know how I would get back, for I had walked about a mile, but I set off. They went on to the lighthouse. Just below the lighthouse area was a natural stone arched gate in the sea, symbolic of the gate of Ephraim – leaving for America. America has the largest concentration of the 10 northern tribes of Israel, more than any other nation on earth, as well as first in number of population of Jews outside Israel.

It was heartbreaking for me not to make it to the lighthouse. But, I continued to do intercession as I walked down the hill. Just then, a car pulled up and asked if they could take me into town. I was so relieved. They took me to the restaurant. I found out the Davies sent them. I also knew right away they were Jews, by the way they dressed, the way they looked, and by their ways of expression. Bless them Abba!

About an hour later, the Davies returned and we had lunch. Then we got the bus back to the crossing where we'd get another bus. By that time, it was raining hard, even hailing a little, and the wind was very strong. But, we each made it to our own destinations. After this intercession, we planned to have a holiday. The next morning the weather was gorgeous! We got a bus out of Stornoway to the Isle of Harris--the next isle south. It was a glorious day, one of many good memories!

The following day, again the weather was lovely. We went to the Callanish Stones, which were much like Stonehenge. There were no barriers, like at Stonehenge, but we kept our distance. Of course these stones were laid out in a circumpunct also, with the large stone in the middle where human sacrifice took place, and orgies, and rites of worship of Satan. We prayed for the release of the people bound by the demons in that place.

The next day, we spent the day looking around the town. Then I went to a lovely bed and breakfast about 3 miles from the airport, on the sea. The next morning, I flew to Glasgow. I got a commuter bus to the train station. I got on the train to Swansea via Crewe, and immediately the knife-like pain came. When I changed trains in Crewe, it left me. After that, I began recording patterns of the pain's appearing and leaving, and there were definitely patterns. In Israel, the pain came always before I would meet someone in Tiberias town, having to do with my work for Abba, or while I was going to do intercession in Jerusalem.

I had a good Shavu'ot with Maureen. I returned by bus to London, and flew to Iceland. It was mid-June. We landed at the airport about 1:00 AM, and yet the sun was still high in the sky. A hotel owner was there to pick me up. I slept well. Iceland Air got me to New York, and Delta Airlines to Tampa.

In August, I knew I had to get back to Iceland. You can read my detailed report on that trip in Part XII. But, here is a brief summary: I was to do intercession in two places: 1) Out onto the sea in the Bay of Reykjavik, and 2) in the interior of the island at Gullfoss Falls, Geyser, and Pingvellir National Park. Under Iceland, particularly under the Pingvellir National Park area, three tectonic plates come together – the Asian Plate, the European Plate, and the North American Plate. These three are separating. We could see the results of the separation. I studied much on it, and prepared well. I was to be gone five days. I got my hotel and booked my whale watching tour, and the all-day tour of the main places in the interior.

But then, hurricane Irene happened. My flights were cancelled. I was to fly Jet Blue to and from Boston, and Iceland Air to and from Iceland. Jet Blue routed me to Toronto on Canada Air. Canada Air had mechanical problems, and the delay was just long enough for me to miss the Iceland Air flight out of Toronto by five minutes. I had to wait two days before Iceland Air had another flight out of Toronto. I thought I had rebooked with Iceland Air while in the Tampa Airport, but after waiting two days, when I got to the airport in Toronto, they had no record of my rebooking. A manager was called. I explained the situation, and she put me on that flight anyway. I had only two days to do the two things I needed to do. I arrived in Iceland about 6:00 AM, and took the long bus ride to Reykjavik. My hotel had not cancelled me, nor did they charge me a cancellation fee. They put me in a room overlooking the bay. As exhausted as I was, for I had not slept all night, I went on the whale watching tour for four hours out into the bay. It was so cold! I slept very well that night. The next morning, I went on the all-day tour of the interior. Early the next morning, I was at the Airport to fly out. There were so many miracles on this trip! Besides other details in Part XII, I wrote "My Iceland Report," which you can read.

Next came one of the greatest joys of my life! My son was coming with me to Israel for Yom Teruah, Yom Kippur, and Sukkot for three weeks. I was staying 2½ months. We met in JFK, but we actually went on the same plane together. He came from Dallas, and I from Tampa. It was just before Yom Teruah. The plane was filled with Orthodox Jews all concentrated in one area-- the area we sat in. When it came time for morning prayers, we were surrounded on all sides. There was an area behind our seats where they stood davoning and praying--all wearing long tallit's, phylacteries, and tefillim. It was glorious! What a special blessing for my son!

My son told me he was coming to Israel to find out Abba's will for his life. He had a friend he was thinking of marrying too. I told him: "No, do not come to Israel to find direction for your life. Find the passion of His heart and align to that." That changed everything for him. He found the passion of Abba's heart--for the restoration of the House of Israel, the reason why Messiah died and rose again. Abba's passion became his passion. We stayed at that lovely 1,000-year-old Yeshiva, where I had stayed in May. It was such a joy to him.

The Davies were in Jerusalem. We had such a fine time together. Derek learned his way around quickly. He loved going to the City of David, and so did the Davies. It was the day of the eve of Yom Teruah. My son had ordered a very special tallit from Yavne. It was too late to have them mail it to Texas before we left, so he told them he'd give them an address in Israel. I asked Liz, whom I rent the Tiberias apartment from, if I could use her P.O. Box for the company in Yavne to send his tallit to. That morning, I had to pay Liz for my rent. He and the Davies went on to the City of David, while I met Liz at Christ Church. I had prayed that he would receive his tallit in time for Yom Teruah. That morning, she came and gave me the package containing the tallit, and I gave her the rent.

I went to the City of David. He did not see me come up. He was standing overlooking the Kidron and Silwan. I called to him, and he came down to where the Davies and I were, just next to the palace area of King David. It was there that he opened his King David, specially designed, hand woven, tallit. He got tears in his eyes. It was such a special moment.

That night he wanted to wear it, but was afraid to. He did not know how the men wore their tallit's, and didn't want to appear to be a "gentile." But, he watched them. The next night, he went to the wall. Then he just stood back to observe. He saw John dancing with some of the Breslov Orthodox men, with his Aussie hat bouncing up and down. One man grabbed my son's hand, and they all went dancing. I let him go on his own as much as possible, so that he could have communion with Abba. He and the Davies also went through Warren's Shaft, through Hezekiah's Tunnel, and down to the Siloam Springs. They came up through the Givat parking-lot dig. What a thrill for him!

After Yom Teruah, we took the bus to Tiberias. He stayed with me through Yom Kippur. On Yom Kippur eve, and day, he walked clear to Tiberias town--a long ways from where I stay. The next day, we rented a car and went through Kiryat Shmona to Dado Point above Metula, then to Banias and Mount Hermon, then down the east side of the Golan Heights where we stopped and ate at an outdoor Druze restaurant. We crossed the Golan, and went to Katzrin and the Golan Heights Winery. We ended up at the Galilee Boat exhibit on Lake Kinneret.

The next day we got to the Yardinet, the traditional place of Christian baptism on the Jordan River south of Tiberias, when they opened. We were the first ones in there. My son wanted to do a mikvah. It was a very special mikvah! After that, we headed around the lake towards Capernaum. Then we went to Korazim. Then we headed towards Megiddo. Before going to Megiddo, we stopped at McDonald's in Afula and he got a "Texas Burger." It was an amazing time in Megiddo. I saw things I had not seen before.

The next day, we headed to Akko, then to Rosh HaNikra. We took the cable car down below the Lebanese border, and went through the sea caverns there. Then we went through Haifa to Caesarea. We got to Caesarea before sunset. The sunset over the Mediterranean was spectacular. His driving was spectacular! Coming out of Haifa, the left lane disappeared all of a sudden, and a truck was closing in to crush us, but he maneuvered correctly, and saved us from disaster.

We went back to Jerusalem for Sukkot. This time we stayed at the Imperial Hotel at the Jaffa Gate, so that we could easily get in and out for our traveling plans. One day we went to Qumran, then to Ein Gedi where he climbed up to the highest falls. We also stopped at the Dead Sea where he picked up salt crystals as souvenirs to take back home. It was a glorious day.

The next day, we went through Be'er Sheva to Tel Be'er Sheva, then to Ashkelon, where we had lunch at the marina, then to Ashdod. We really had directional problems getting out of Ashdod. I thought the port area might be like it is in Haifa, but it sure was not! This is funny: As we were trying to find our way out of what seemed to be a container/shipping port, we kept getting lost. My son was driving and was using the GPS on his phone. The directions it was giving kept us going around and around in circles around the port. We would get on a little road that the GPS told us to go on, and we would end up going back towards the sea and port area. Finally, after this routine had gone on for about 20 minutes, I spoke up and said, "GO <u>AWAY</u> FROM THE SEA--GO <u>AWAY</u> FROM THE SEA." He turned around once again but this time we found the same road we had come in on--going away from the sea. We still laugh about it to this day.

Another humorous event (but not so humorous at the time), was the day we walked down to the City of David. We had walked to an area that overlooked the Hinnom Valley. I wanted to show him this valley because of the significance it has to the fulfillment of future prophecy. As we left that area, we began the walk down to the City of David. I kept walking down the hill and had almost reached the ramp to the parking lot at the Zion Gate when I stopped and realized my son wasn't with me. I turned around and there he was, still up near the top of the hill. He had been stopped by the Jerusalem Police and was being questioned. My son said he was probably stopped because of his appearance and what he was carrying. He had his bandana on, sunglasses, full beard, carried a backpack and was walking alone. In Jerusalem, that list of things definitely spells trouble. The policeman had stopped him but I didn't hear or see it, so I had kept on walking down the hill. I turned around and went back up the hill to "bail" him out. By this time, he had emptied everything in his backpack including his passport, driver's license, and a pocket knife. The policeman was quite interested in the knife. My son tried to explain to the policeman, who by the way didn't speak English, what the knife was for and why he was carrying it.

My son carried the knife for protection, but thank goodness, the only time he used it was to open a ketchup packet at the Armenian Tavern. By this time, I had reached my son and the policeman at the top of the hill. I tried to vouch for him, but the policeman didn't understand me. He asked (in broken English), "Are you American?" I said "Yes." With that, the policeman gave my son all of his possessions back and sent us on our way. My son had tried to explain where he was from and even showed him his driver's license and passport. Nothing seemed to convince the officer until mom came to the rescue. Per mom's "orders", the knife stayed in the hotel room the rest of the time in Israel.

After our going to the City of David, we got separated. So, I returned to have lunch with the Davies. He went off somewhere else. Later I found out that he had gone through the Ophel Archeological Park. He wanted to take me. With my wobbly legs, knees and ankles, I would never have been able to see it well without his help.

While in the area below Robinson's Arch, below the southwest wall of the Temple Mount, we heard lots of gun fire from Silwan. It went on and on. Then we realized that terrorists who had been released from Israeli prisons had gone home. It was the day that IDF solider Gilad Shalit had been released after being held in captivity by Hamas for five years. They were celebrating in Silwan.

It was a sad parting. My son left at night for the airport. The Davies and I stayed on to finish out Sukkot. Then I returned to Tiberias. The Davies came up to Tiberias about 3 weeks later. They camped out on the beach by the lake. We knew we had to do intercession together for Ephraim and for the nation of Israel. So, we rented a large van for the seven of us, and took three days to go where my son and I had gone. Later, we rented the van one more time to return to the trek across the north, this time going to Tel Dan also. On our way to Megiddo, we decided to stop at the ancient ruins of Jezre'el. They really enjoyed being there. It was here that I proclaimed Psalm 9 over the cliff, right in the area of where Jezebel fell and was eaten by the dogs.

Abba gave me so much to research and things to write about. It was hard getting it all done. But, it sure was good to have the Davies family so close. Later in November, we met at the ancient Hamat Synagogue south of Tiberias town, did intercession there, and learned a lot. Then we rented a van for the day and went to Tzippori – an extensive ruins and synagogue in the mid-north region of Israel. After that, we went to the Beit Alfa synagogue on the way to Beit Shean. That was quite a day of education and intercession.

Later in November, the knife-like pain hit me very hard, and I laid down in bed. Abba's Presence was hovering over me. After enduring it for a while, I began moaning my usual: "WHY?" He would not answer. It was as if He had His arms folded. I said: "Why is it that whenever I need You the most, You act like You are on vacation?" He was silent. I was so disgusted. I was so tired of my reaching my pain threshold, then breaking down in despair. I remembered that He could not help me if I was in a negative mode, because negative emotions open portals for demonic activity. I said to Him: "What if I keep praising you no matter how I feel, pain or no pain?" It was as if a huge burden lifted. He unfolded His hands. So, I started praising Him. The pain left. He taught me that if I would keep praising every time the pain came, it would leave. If it was witchcraft, I was not dealing with something that had to be healed! I was dealing with demonic spirits, spells, curses, and human channels for demons.

King David wrote **Psalm 57**. In it, he tells how he is surrounded by enemies, hurts, pains, and confusion, but that he had learned to keep praising Abba no matter what he saw, heard, or felt. That is a prominent faith principle! Negative emotions draw demons like a magnet to harm us. Faith draws Yahuweh like a magnet, to help us!

One day, I met Connie in town for lunch. We went to the Marina. On the way back up, the knife-pain hit me so hard I doubled over. I said this: "OK Devil, just go ahead. If you want to give me pain, go ahead, but I will just use the time to praise Abba more and more." The pain instantly left. I had learned the secret! I broke into praises of Abba every time that witchcraft/those devils tried to put the pain on me, and finally those demons got the idea and left me alone. I have not had the pain for about 1½ years now, and I know it will NOT return! I also applied this lesson to other things. I intellectually knew the "secret", but He had to let me find out how to use it in real life, even in such intense pain. He is constantly testing us, and educating us. He is a Father! Out of it all, I grew stronger. Out of it, I was restored to my daughter. He wanted me to learn this most-important lesson, that no matter what happens, if I will keep a positive heart with peace and joy, He can work to set me free.

Habakkuk 3:17-19: "**Though the fig tree does not blossom, and there is no fruit on the vine, the yield of the olive has failed, and the fields brought forth no food, the flock has been cut off from the fold, and there is no herd in the stalls, YET I exult in Yahuweh. I rejoice in the Elohim of my deliverance! Yahuweh, my Master, is my strength! He makes my feet like those of a deer, and makes me walk on high places**."

I was in Tiberias until December 15th. I hated leaving the Davies, but they were going to Australia to be with his parents for three months. We knew we'd meet up again in March. At the end of 2012, right there below Mount Hermon, down from Majdal Shams, and along that east Golan border, Syrian troops were firing into Israel. Damascus is just 40 miles away. Talk about prophetic fulfillment! Now, 2013, Syrian troops are firing into Israel's ski-lift area of Mount Hermon, as well as into the Golan itself.

December 15th I flew to Amsterdam. From there I was to get a plane to London. But, the plane was very late getting out of Amsterdam – about an hour late. I had booked the National Coach Express for the 4:05 PM trip to Swansea. If I missed the bus, I could get another one – but the tickets would be much more than what I paid online.

This is my miraculous "He backed up time" story. There is no way to figure it out. How can a plane leave an hour late, arrive at the destination 30 minutes early, and still fly the same distance in the same time-allotment? Of course, I took into account the hour time difference between Amsterdam and London too. I checked the watch of the man sitting next to me. It was still on Amsterdam time, as was mine. It said 2:40 PM--1:40 PM in London. We still had 40 minutes of flight time left. How could we land at 1:30 PM in London? But, we did.

In my despair, after we took off from Amsterdam, I asked Abba to help me not miss the bus. I added: "even if you have to back up time to do it." I had to get off the plane, get my luggage, go to another terminal by the airport train, then get off and walk a long way to the National Coach Express on a lower level. It would take at least an hour and a half to do it, as slowly as I walk. I had so many people helping me. I got to the National Coach Bus station earlier than I thought--10 minutes before the 3:05 PM bus would leave. So, I waited an hour there before I got my bus to Swansea. To change my ticket would have cost a lot. So I relaxed, and re-organized my things. In all that cold, my knee was still giving me trouble, but I could walk!

I got to Swansea and Maureen picked me up. Maureen had invited a lady from a Christian intercession ministry in Jerusalem to stay with her. They were friends. Since Messiah Yahushua was born on Yom Teruah in 3 BCE, I had long ago forsaken celebrating the birth of the sun gods on December 25th. I tried to keep from any involvement in it, but it was hard. I knew I'd have a hard time avoiding it.

Abba had told me to birth my new website. This would consume my time in Wales to a great extent. My son and I had been e-mailing about it for about a month. I knew from Abba that it was time to get my own website. I wanted a name for it that included "Watchman." But, my son wanted to use the word "mikvah" in the name, since he said my message was all about set-apartness and purity. I didn't want a site that said "mikvah" (smile). I thought: "Who would go to a site with that name?" We had taken pictures of so many mikvahs in the archeological park, in Qumran, and in Korazim. Abba spoke clearly to me: "Listen to your son." OK! Let's go with mikvah.

I listed about 10 different names that included mikvah. None seemed right. Then I thought, my site is supposed to be an invitation. So, I wrote down: **"Come, Enter the Mikvah"** – and that was it. Abba said to get the site operational by the end of December. I was staying with Maureen until January 2nd. So, I had from December 15th to January 2nd, for my son and I to get the site online. Thank goodness she had wireless service throughout her house!

Maureen and her Christian friend did all sorts of Christmas things, like shopping for presents and buying special foods for our table. I couldn't go. I was under a mandate from Abba. Maureen was miffed at me. She thought wrong of me. She actually became angry at me, and let me know it several times. However, I did meet with some of her friends. I tried to be social, but I stayed in my room most of the time, because of the work to get the mikvah site operational as Abba had mandated.

Early on, Maureen and her friend were going to a meeting at Moriah Chapel, the very place where the great Welsh Revival started--at Evan Roberts' church. But, the speaker was what fascinated me. In my spirit, I knew I had to go hear him. I told previously how I had become very personally involved with the restoration of the vision of Rees Howells and the Bible College of Wales. Here was a man from South Korea, to whom Abba had given the job of restoring the vision. The man's name was Qday. I found out later he was a friend of Howie's too. Small world! That meeting was extraordinary. I even had a prophecy for Qday, and those working with him. I was supposed to attend that meeting. It gave closure to what Abba had told me to do in prayer.

I went with Maureen on one shopping day, and bought her a lot of groceries. I made sure I showed her that I was appreciative of her hospitality. The other lady, an intercessor in Israel, was steeped in what I know to be false teaching and paganism. She also thought well-known false prophets were good. I kept friendly to all. They had a Shabbat dinner for friends, which I participated in, but it turned into a Christmas party. I was polite. I was not there to criticize or judge. I did not mean to be aloof, it was just that, as always, doing work for Him takes many hours a day, and in the case of birthing the website, I had to take the time necessary to do it right.

By the end of December, the site was ready to go. We put certain articles into ten collections and listed them as "mikvahs." During that time, I wrote several articles just for this site. For the first three collections, I wrote one introducing myself, one explaining the mikvah, and other introductory articles that were from my personal testimony. With a name like, "**Come, Enter the Mikvah**", I knew Abba had to promote it. By the end of January we had about 5,000 people from 19 countries visit the site.

I left January 2nd for London on the National Coach Express into Heathrow Airport. I left that night for America.

AMERICA--ISRAEL--ROME--GREECE
(2012-2013)

On March 22nd, I got an e-mail from Nehemia Gordon's Karaite Korner saying that because of the snow in Jerusalem in winter and the cold afterwards, there was no barley found in the Aviv stage in or around Jerusalem. He said it would be rare if they had a second Adar Bet in a row (leap year-13th month).

After reading that, I went walking around one of our residential area lakes. I was pondering what Nehemia said, since I had studied the ancient ways of the Creator's Calendar. Abba spoke to me: "**Indeed we have another Adar Bet**." I stopped to listen to what He was saying. He said it had to do with the timing of the Fall Festivals. He said that the anti-messiah did not want to usurp Passover. He wanted to usurp Sukkot--the Feast that speaks of His dream to tabernacle with His people on earth, forever. (**Revelation 21:1-7**) It is the dream of Yahuweh that Lucifer/Satan wants to destroy. Then I thought ahead: If we have an Adar Bet, when would Sukkot come? I stood there shocked. It would come during the time of the presidential elections in America. It would be a time of the unleashing of the darkness of the evil ones over the earth.

The next morning, I read that Nehemia and his team were asking for prayer because they were going near Gaza to find ripe barley in a warmer climate. They found it there and in along the Jordan Valley – where it is warmer. Of course they would! But, according to the ancient ways, it had to be found around Jerusalem, not in ancient Philistine territory.

Jeremiah 6:16-18: "Thus says Yahuweh, stand in the way and see, and ask for the ancient paths where the good way is, and walk in it, and find rest for yourselves. But, they say, `we do not walk in it.' "

I studied the ancient ways again and learned more. The true Passover would be May 5th eve. [Refer to: "Aviv 1-Barley-New Moon and Prophetic Fulfillment in 2012"/March 23, 2012]

I returned to Israel in March just before the pre-set rabbinic Passover. The Davies had returned too, so we had a good reunion. There were quite a few people to see this time – and if ever there was a season of several mo'edim for me and others, it was at this time. [Refer to: "Your Only Chance of Survival: The Mo'edim Lifestyle"/June 2012 for details] It was one mo'ed-- "divine appointment"--after another.

Back in Tiberias, I prepared for the real Passover. The eve of the 4th there was a "Super Moon" that was astounding. It was Abba's sign of His Passover. I was so excited about this one. I would spend it by myself, but His Presence was so strong in the apartment that I knew I was not alone. I had bought a very hard avocado. I was raised in an avocado grove. I loved them. It sat on my table by the big windows. It could not possibly ripen by the eve of May 5th. But, on the afternoon of May 5th, I checked it, and it was perfectly ripe. I call this "my sign of the ripe avocado" (smile). Abba sent many signs to me, and to others who also felt the same as I did. As I ate my matzo during the week, Abba took away any desire for bread, or deserts with leaven, or anything with leaven. He spoke to me that I was to maintain the "unleavened lifestyle," until He said differently. It is now June 2013, and He has not said differently. On November 15th of 2012, I wrote: "My Unleavened Lifestyle, Why? -- Abba Finally Explains - and His Message is for All of His People."

He finally told me why I had to maintain it. As I was walking out of the kitchen to sit down in my chair, He said: "**It has to do with Exodus 12**." He let me know that I was doing prophetic action--a symbol of those who prepared, as they were in Egypt, to flee from the world Beast/Pharaoh as the Master directs. So the real Passover week for me was a wonderful time, actually, the best Passover I ever had!

He had me doing a lot of research on His ways of calculating time. He revealed His secrets of His timing to me over and over, and I shared them in articles. (**Amos 3:7**) Abba had filled my plate with work, studying and writing and communicating, so my days were very full.

On April 25th, Israel's Independence Day in 2012, two couples who were studying at the University in Ariel came to meet me at the Marina in Tiberias for lunch. Then they came back to my apartment and we had good fellowship. One couple was from New Zealand, and one couple was from Iowa. About a month later, the couple from Iowa returned home. They wanted to see me when I came to teach in Iowa that summer, and I wanted to see them too. There were also several people on my e-mail list in Iowa and surrounding states that I wanted to meet.

In May, I felt strongly I needed to go on a teaching assignment. I had been e-mailing a lady in Iowa who was also keeping Festivals by Abba's ancient calendar. We talked about the real Shavu'ot being July 1st. I returned to America on June 5th, after rabbinic Shavu'ot. I kept the rabbinic festival to be with the people, but in doing so, both Passover and Shavu'ot 2012 was like watching a movie in a movie theater. Nothing seemed real. It was like people were going through the motions, but there was no life of His Spirit there. It was dead and dull, except for my being with friends. He works with individuals. He does not work with the majority - people as a group - just people as individuals. But, on His real days, His Spirit is mighty!

During my return flight on June 5th, upon leaving JFK, the plane was late, so I didn't know if I'd make the flight to Detroit or not to get my flight to Tampa. Again I prayed. The plane left JFK 30 minutes late, and we arrived in Detroit 15 minutes early. Once again, Abba ruled!

I was invited to speak on Abba's Shavu'ot, which would be Sunday July 1st. I flew into Cedar Rapids. My hostess came to stay with me in a large house, while the owners, her friends, were out of town. That Friday night, June 29th, I attended a home group for their Torah midrash. I spoke on Shabbat, then on Shavu'ot/Sunday. On Friday morning, Abba instructed me to buy a plumb line and drop it at the Shabbat meeting, and read **Amos 7:7-8**. I had not done that since 2008. The plumb line prophetic action would be for the people present, yes, but more than that-- it was for the nation. Iowa is in the breadbasket of the nation. I was among corn growing farmers. After I returned, He gave me clarity on why I had to go to Iowa. I wrote two articles: "Dropping the Plumb Line – Separation: The Grief and the Joy/July 13, 2012, and The Release of Judgment on the Nation – Shavu'ot 2012 and Current Events/July 14th, 2012. The details to this story are in these articles.

My son had married his good friend, and they moved the day after their wedding to Florida, to live about 5 miles from me. I had the privilege on July 8th, of giving them a special Hebrew blessing on the beach on Anna Maria Island. Abba gave me just what I was to say in a short 6-7 minute blessing. We went down right by the water. It was a gloriously gorgeous day! We then ate at our favorite restaurant on the Gulf – The Beach House.

The next day, the heavy grieving heart of Abba returned again. I feel His grief at times so strongly. So few understood the urgency of preparation for disaster. I wrote more warning articles, until one day back in Israel, November 2012, as I was writing an Update, He came and stood to my left with sadness. I said to Him: "I'm wasting my time aren't I?" I knew that now almost no one is listening anymore to any watchman's cry, except perhaps to enjoy the suspense and excitement of being scared for a while, then back to life as usual. They are not prepared, and we would enter "night" soon – the night of the tribulation. Because of my many years of studying end-times, yet not understanding the nature, ways, and thinking of the Elohim of Israel – the Elohim of the Hebrews - I wrestled with the Greco/Roman obsession with the "42 months", (3½ years) in **Revelation 11, 12 and 13**. There is no mention of "42-months" in the Tenach. I knew the

Roman Catholic Church, loved the 3½ year scenario for their own twisted eschatology timing-agenda.

Passover 2012 should have been the mid-point of the last seven-year cycle, as per Hal Lindsey, Jack Van Impe, and all the Evangelical end-time teachers. But, neither during rabbinic Passover, or the real Passover, did anything happen out of the ordinary. According to Christian eschatology, Elijah was also supposed to come at Passover, with another "witness", and minister for 3½ years. But, Abba showed me **Malachi 4:5-6** once again. Elijah would come "**before the great and awesome day of Yahuweh**." There was no timing set for the coming of this principle witness of **Revelation 11**.

I talked these things over with the Davies. John asked how long John the Baptist's ministry was. I said less than a year. John reminded me that John the Baptizer was a shadow picture of the return of Elijah. We knew Messiah's ministry was only one year, from Passover 27 CE to Passover 28 CE. From His mikvah in the Jordan to His pouring out of the Spirit was a total of 490 days. We talked about His people being in a U.N. refugee camp in Petra for 3½ years. It would be crazy for His servants, especially for His Bridal remnant to twiddle their thumbs for 3½ years. We talked about the anti-messiah reigning for 3½ years--the son of Lucifer/Satan/Devil/Dragon--and how crazy that is, since he starts out with WWIII and the destruction of the earth.

We talked about how the Roman Catholic Church added two extra Passovers to the book of John, making Messiah's ministry 3 ½ years, when it was only 1 year. We talked about how Constantine ordered a re-write of the Messianic Writings, because at that time they only had fragments. We spoke of how Bishop Eusebius admitted that the book of Revelation had holes in it, and he filled in the holes – thus we have the "pearly gates" (the pearl is from an oyster – a defiled creature). He also left out the Tribe of Dan from the list in Revelation 7. We talked about Abba operating within seasons, not Roman absolute date-calculations of the Gregorian Calendar.

So, when we got through talking, knowing why the Roman Catholic Church was obsessed with 3½, we saw that Abba's reckoning of time did not match Hal Lindsey's reckoning of time. I must hear from Abba. I can't go by Hal, Jack, or anybody else. The Spirit is my teacher. If you will study with me through my study "The Foundation of Deception", a thoroughly documented study, you will see the foundational roots of the church which are pure paganism, from Nimrod. For those who study the Word with the Spirit, it is easy to see where the church messed with the Messianic Writings, by removing some things, and adding to some things, and putting words in some places that are definitely not Hebrew understanding.

Abba spoke to me years ago: "**If the root is defiled** ("*to be foul, contaminated, polluted, utterly unclean, filthy, vile*") **the tree is defiled, the branches and leaves are defiled, and the fruit is defiled. And anyone eating of it is defiled.**" (Italics mine)

I came to the conclusion a long time ago that unless something is clearly taught in the Tenach, it must be set on the shelf for the Spirit to explain it. Taking two to three verses out of the Messianic Writings, which were re-written in the 4th and 5th centuries by the church, to prove something that is not in the Hebrew Tenach, is very dangerous. Yet, many base their faith on what some pastor or rabbi has said about a few verses of Scripture that are taken out of context. So few know how to hear from the Spirit, yet the Spirit of Yahuweh is our only valid Teacher of Truth. Yes, we must read the Messianic Writings, for most of it contains truth that we must know to give us a clear understanding of the Messiah of Israel. But, even Kepha (Peter) said of the Greek Christian's, who messed with Sha'ul's writings, that they twisted what he said to make him non-Torah guarding. (**II Peter 3:14-17**) Yet right there in the Book of Acts, over and over, Sha'ul's Torah-guarding is confirmed.

Going back a ways to go forward, in late 2011, Abba began calling me to return to Patmos for more declarations and proclamations. But, I put the assignment on the shelf because Abba said nothing specific about it. In returning in March, 2012, I felt like I had let Him down. I thought of flying to Athens and back during my stay in Israel, but then, I didn't think Israeli Immigration would be too happy with me about that. I had thought of going to Athens before going to Israel, but I would have all that luggage with me to lug.

Also, I did not have enough mileage on my Delta mileage chart to get a free flight into Tel Aviv. It would take 80,000 miles and I only had about 68,000 miles to my credit. So, I paid full price for my trip to Israel in early 2012. I felt like I'd really let Him down. But then, He had not told me when to go to Athens and Patmos. He had not told me what to declare or proclaim, or even details of where to go. I had no desire to plan a trip from Israel. I wanted to keep Israel happy with me, but also, the logistics for getting to Patmos are horrendous, and the apartment wireless service was worse than before.

Then about May, 2012, while in Israel, in looking at a map of Greece, I looked over and saw Italy, and a big star over Rome. It leaped off the page, and I said to Abba: "OH NO! YOU WANT ME

TO GO TO ROME TOO?" I never wanted to go to Rome. I was leery of going anywhere near the Vatican. I had spent so many years studying the Vatican, and it was "no, no, no!" But, I know the way He deals with me, and I knew He wanted me to go to Rome first, then to Patmos. He began clarifying from then on. In my study, I was also drawn to go to Delphi, where the ancient Cumaean Sibyl prophesied the resurrection of Apollo in our day. I did not know how important this was at the time, nor how it would tie into the London Olympics and their calling for Zeus and Apollo to come rule the world. I began doing more logistics. I felt peace. Abba could not give me full instructions until I learned about the London Olympics, going to Rome, and to Delphi.

While still in Israel, I began to learn about the plans for the London Olympics. A good researcher in England sent me a lot of material too. I learned much from Joseph Herrin's reporting. From the beginning, I saw the underlying purpose of these occult Olympics. This was to be the kick-off of a plan that would bring down the wrath of Yahuweh on the nations.

The bottom line: Everything that was done in physical preparation, in ceremonies, in occult magic, and witchcraft, was to bring together millions of people who would cry for the return of Zeus and his son Apollo (Apollyon/**Revelation 9:11**) to rule the world. Along with them were multi-millions of New Age people, ancient people groups in Mexico, Central and South America, the United States, and around the world, who were also calling for the return of their gods to rule the world. It was a multi-billion member choir of Satan, calling for the overthrow of Yahuweh and His Torah, and Yahushua as coming Messiah, and for Their creation to be replaced by the gods of ancient times, Nephillim. (**Genesis 6:2-4**)

We are indeed "in the days of Noah!" This hybrid mixture, making "fit extensions" for Lucifer's fallen angels into the earth, became the gods of Egypt, of Greece and Rome, and the gods of every culture on earth. My assignment was to go to the headquarters of Satan worship on earth--the Vatican--then to Patmos, where John received the Revelation (**Revelation 1:9**), then by bus to Delphi, about 3 hours ride west from Athens.

Until I started making plans, He did not even tell me what I was to proclaim/declare, to open portals for Him. This is a top faith principle – He will not lead until we are in motion, moving in the direction He has told us to move in! He told me I was to address the Luciferic hierarchy face to face, with a message from Him to them. I knew that He would flank me with His powerful angels, and He did. I would walk into the face of the Dragon once again, and come away "unscathed." He set up the scenarios everywhere. He gave me just what to say. He opened doors for me, even showing His humor at the Vatican Museum.

I would leave on July 20th--two days after the Olympics began, and return August 7th, two days before it would end. For a condensed report on the reality of this Olympics, read "The Unleashing – London Olympics – On July 27th the Gate/Portal Will Be Opened/July 22, 2012, and "The Unleashing II – The Rise of the Dark Kingdom/July 23, 2012. My complete report on the trip to Rome and Greece is in: "The Declaration Assignment – In Praise of My Abba/August 8, 2012.

In September, I returned to Israel by a free ticket from Delta. I went directly to Tiberias from the airport. Because this Yom Teruah was a rabbinic pre-set day, and not by Abba's calendar, I cancelled my reservation in the Jewish Quarter and stayed in Tiberias for rabbinic Yom Teruah and Yom Kippur. Abba gave me so much revelation about His timing, and all was confirmed over and over. I did a lot of writing.

A few days later my son and his new wife came to Israel and went to Jerusalem. My son said he knew where to take her, as if he had been there the day before. He remembered that whole Old City area, and how to get to Ben Yehuda Street. They stayed at the Imperial Hotel. I joined them at the Imperial on the eve of rabbinic Sukkot. We went to the Wall that evening. The next day, a rabbinic High Shabbat, we walked together to the City of David. The next day, Tuesday, they went their way and I went mine. I asked Abba where He wanted me to go. I felt strongly to return to the Temple Institute. I had not been there since Betty and I went in 2005. I was the first one to enter that day. In the main display case was the altar of incense, the crown, and a full-sized manikin that was wearing the garments of the High Priest. To the right was a manikin of a Levite in his special clothing. The Temple Institute is preparing the clothing to be used by the true Levitical Priesthood, in the service of Messiah, when He comes to restore the final Temple.

One tour after another came, but I did not want to leave--so I joined different tours. One tour packed the little movie theater. They began playing a DVD of the history of the Temple and the Ark of the Covenant that was produced by Doko and shown on the History Channel in the U.S. About 5 minutes into the DVD, which was actually in English, they showed how a golden cord was attached to the waist of the High Priest on Yom Kippur. While wearing the cord, he would enter the Holy of Holies to stand before Yahuweh on behalf of the nation, for the salvation of the nation. In 1992, Abba had given me a dream of myself teaching the Word. I was standing in mid-air teaching an unseen audience.

I had the same golden cord around my waist as I saw in the DVD. The Spirit in my spirit was taking over my whole being – that's called "the anointing." I did not want to leave the Temple Institute for some reason. I bought that DVD for myself.

Later that evening, we had a wonderful dinner with the Davies. The next day my son and his wife, and I, got a taxi to the front of the Convention Center, across from the three-story Central Bus Station. It was the day that Christian Friends of Israeli Communities was having a tour of Samaria. I have been going on their tours for about nine years – but each one is different and unique. Because this organization works to supply the needs of the settlements, and of the displaced Gaza refugees within their own country, they go to settlements that few people get to see, and learn about their lives there from the actual people who live there. Sondra Baras is the Israeli director. We first went to her house. Her village/settlement has been targeted by terrorists several times. Their security operation is intense. Karnei Shomron is a lovely town, peaceful, and serene, yet surrounded by Arab towns as are most of the "West Bank" settlements. We went to Itamar, which overlooks Mount Gerizim and Mount Ebal, as well as other lovely settlements. Then last went to the Psagot winery. After the all-day tour, we had a good dinner back in the mall below the Jaffa Gate.

The next morning early, we rented a car and my son drove us to Tiberias. We had three full days of touring the major tourist sites, as well as my special tour of the north, from Kiryat Shmona to Metula and Dado Point, which overlooks Lebanon, to Banias, to the top of the Israeli portion of Mount Hermon, down the east side of the Golan. This day I had a very special treat. We got out at the ski lift area on Mount Hermon. It was cold. I had on a thin short-sleeved top from Walmart. I told them I would stay in the car while they went to see the ski lift area. Israel has 7% of the mountain, and they put in a ski lift. I had never seen the ski lift operational. I was on Hermon once when there was snow, but still not enough for skiing. But, they came back to the car, and my son said: "Mom, the ski lift is working, and they're giving rides up to the top of the mountain." There was a bicycle competition in progress, bicyclists riding down the paths from the top of the mountain. I thought to myself, "NO way!" With my bone feebleness, it would not be smart! But, I told them I'd go to the lift and watch them. A heavy cloud had settled over the top of the mountain, hiding the top of it. It was cold. They went to get their tickets. My son asked if someone would help me onto the lift and off at the top, and onto the lift at the top, and off the lift at the bottom. They said "sure." So my son came to tell me. How could I pass up this opportunity! If I had passed it up, I would regret it until eternity. I didn't care if I froze. The trip up was a lot longer than I thought--about 20-25 minutes. I ascended into the cloud. My son was in the lift behind me, taking pictures, even a video of me. I got out at the top, and they helped me to the next lift down. On the way down, an icy wind began blowing. But, I did not care! I loved it! My son got pictures of me descending too. They stayed behind me to make sure I got off OK. At the bottom, I saw that no one was flying to help me off. But, when I called for help, they went into action quick. Those helpers were super!

The next day, they both had a mikvah at the Yardinet. I was their photographer. Once again, we were the first ones there, so we had privacy. It was very special! While back in my apartment, my son showed me how to tap into a public wireless network that was 5 bars in strength. The server wanted me to sign up with them, but they also gave me the option of not signing up, which was in the fine print. I had not read the fine print, however my son saw it and pointed it out to me. I could register or not register - both are legal. After seeing the fine print, I chose not to sign up. Because of this, I had wireless service through most of the apartment, almost as good as in the U.S. What a relief not to have all that frustration and having to use the Internet Café. I hated to see them go. They left at 4:00 AM for the airport. I waved to them from my window. It was then time for me to get working hard on this autobiography.

In November of 2012, Abba told me: "**When the recorded history of your life is finished, everything will change**." That's His wording, not mine. I never thought of my autobiography as "recorded history." After returning to the U.S., He added this: "**When you are finished recording the history of your life, your life will then consist of things that cannot be recorded**."

He impressed on me some of the changes. They are well embedded in my mind, as I am close to finishing "my recorded history." I welcome the changes that will shift me into another level of service for Him! It will set me in position for my final work as His servant before Yahushua comes!

I returned to Jerusalem a third time for the first two days of the real Sukkot. I stayed in the Jewish Quarter. The Davies were there, and we had a good time of fellowship. I returned to Tiberias to finish Sukkot week. After the real Sukkot, which took place the first week of November, during the time of Hurricane Sandy and the elections in the U.S., I felt the darkness descending. He let me know that the season of tribulation before Messiah's return, had begun. Soon, things really started deteriorating world wide.

I kept hearing jet planes flying low over the lake to the Golan, day and night. Syria began firing into Israel. Hamas provoked Israel, and there was war brewing on the Gaza border. Israel was firing in, and taking out many Hamas leaders. Hamas was putting their children out every time an Israeli missile came in, so that their children would be killed, and all blame would go on Israel. The world community turned on Israel. The Vatican said the Jews were baby killers.

Abba had shown me in March, as I walked around the lake, that after Sukkot, after the elections, the season of the tribulum would begin. Other watchmen, also, began speaking of the descending darkness over the world.

Before leaving for the U.S., I contemplated all the electronics that I had to carry because of Abba's work, the two heavy suitcases and plane-needs bag, besides my heavy belt-pack around my waist. Everything I carry is for His work. I longed to be able to travel with a backpack or small suitcase. However, to be alone, not really able to carry much more than 5 pounds, carrying nearly 100 pounds of luggage, forces me to be totally dependent on Abba, as always.

Just before returning to the U.S. in early December, Abba gave me what I call: "The sign in the green grocery bag." Abba's message was clear: "**You will lose nothing- not the smallest thing**."

The story: In early November, I took the bus into town to do some shopping and meet Connie for lunch. I took a green-fabric grocery bag with me from what I nicknamed the "Tiberias Publix." I also took three small plastic jars to put my vitamins in, 2 green and one blue. Before meeting Connie I did my grocery shopping. At lunch, I took my vitamins, then carefully put all three jars back into the grocery bag with my groceries. When I got home, I emptied out the groceries, and found only a blue and a green little jar. I went through everything thoroughly, but the second green jar was not there. Like so many little things I carry, I needed it. I am a "creature of habit," so I always fold up the green bags and put them on a pile of junk across from the washer. That was something I had always done--a habit. Never, had I ever once, put the green bags under the table across from the sink in the kitchen - never! I am very disciplined, organized, and highly methodical. The same things go in the same place all the time. So, I thought the little green jar must have fallen out. But, as I was doing final packing to return to the U.S., I rounded the corner from the bedroom into the kitchen, looked down, and saw a green grocery bag under the table. That stunned me. It was not there before. I picked it up, and <u>off the top of it</u> fell out the little green jar. I am used to angels and visits from the set-apart ones of the past – so I figured one of them put the bag and jar there. I went and sat down in my chair and He gave me the message that I typed above. He was letting me know that not one thing, of all that I had, would be lost, so do not worry about anything. I received the message well!

Then on December 4th, when I returned to Tampa and went to my son's house to spend the night because it was so late, I had another sign of like type. In the middle of the night, I needed my peppermint oil because I was getting a headache. I had placed the little green bottle of peppermint, and the little blue box containing two pairs of earplugs, with my backscratcher on the bed to the left of me. But, when I turned on the light to get the peppermint, neither it nor the earplug box was on the bed. I figured they fell on the floor. I turned on the overhead light. When I wake up, I am never groggy – I am always very alert. I went around to the other side of the bed, and there was nothing on the floor. I looked under the bed, behind the bed, and in the covers – and did not find these two items. I thought that in the morning I'd ask my son to look. The next morning, I got up and went around the bed to look again. There, sitting side by side, were the two items right in the middle of the floor--both upright, as if placed there by someone with organization-intelligence. Once again, He was saying that not one thing, no matter how small, would be lost if it was something I needed, and wanted. I remembered losing my lip protector gel in Africa, when I was with Godfrey. It had disappeared, and then all of sudden it started rolling across the floor about a day to two days later.

Abba reminded me of **Psalm 32:8** from the Tehillim: "**I will guide you by what I have seen**." I had held onto that, and to **Psalm 121:8**, "**I will guard your departure and your arrival from this time forth and forever**," since He gave them to me in 2008 for my travels. "Departure," "arrival": Both airport terms. I have learned to hold onto the phrase "**I will guide you by what I have seen**" with all my heart, as if it was a tangible thing I could grasp.

I returned to the U.S. on December 4th, because my visa was running out. I wanted to stay. As I was getting on the plane in Tel Aviv, a lady next to me, speaking to her friend, said: "We'd better spend all our money, (speaking of their trip to Paris) because the world money is coming soon and our money will be no good." Soon after the plane took off, they ran what I thought was a movie. It looked like a new disaster movie. I wondered what the name of it was. They showed storms worldwide and a huge council room where they were discussing what to do regarding

Greece and Spain and their economic problems. Then they showed the weather and sports. It was euronews. I was shocked – I thought it was a disaster movie.

The flight from Tel Aviv to Paris was supposed to take 5 hours. That's long enough, but we were in the air 5 1/2 hours already. I went back to talk to a flight attendant, and he said that the flight would be another 45 minutes because they had to drop several tons of fuel before landing. On my schedule, I had one hour and thirty minutes from the time the plane landed in Paris, until my flight to America took off. I needed the whole time. But, when we landed, I had 40 minutes left to get through security again, and to my gate. Thank goodness for wheelchair assistance! The lady I had pushing me was awesome. I got to the gate five minutes before it closed. I had peace the whole time because of that one phrase-promise that He gave me. He has guided me by what HE HAS SEEN OF THE FUTURE. If I walk perfectly in His path in obedience, I never have to be in anxiety or fear, for He is in control, not me!

My flights were good, long, but good. From Paris to Atlanta, on Air France, they put me in a bulk-head seat behind Business Class, with one lady next to me who was tiny. How awesome! I got on the plane in Atlanta for Tampa. I was so exhausted. I can't sleep on planes--on trains, buses, ships, and in cars, yes, but not on planes. I was the first on. I said something to the flight attendant helping me with my luggage like, "I am so tired. I have been traveling for nearly 30 hours." She asked: "Where did you come from?" I said: "Tel Aviv, Israel." Her eyes got big, and she said: "OH tell me how it is in Tel Aviv? Have they stopped the rockets yet?" We talked a brief moment because other passengers were boarding, but she really had her heart with Israel. I sure wish I had a chance to talk to her further.

In America, I spent much time working to finish this autobiography. I also had fun playing with my grandchildren, fellowshipping with my son and his wife, and watching events in Israel very closely.

To date I've been on nearly 400 individual flights. I've been on 47 different airlines, in 37 different countries, to Israel about 40 times, and to Jerusalem over 50 times.

In late January, I began doing much reporting on the Super Bowl, and other things that were happening that pointed to signs of the tribulation. On the day of the Super Bowl, February 3rd, while preparing to walk around the lake here in Florida, I stepped down into the back patio, and my right ankle twisted so badly that my legs went up underneath me, and I had the worst injury I have ever had in my life. Earlier that morning, I had mumbled to

PART VI - The Middle East & Travels Beyond

myself: "I must get my tickets to return to Israel." I pulled myself up, called my daughter-in-law, and she came immediately to help me. That was Sunday. I had already booked tickets to fly to Chattanooga to see the two other daughters and their families on Thursday. I could barely walk at all. I used two canes to stabilize me. Yet, I was determined to go to visit my children and grandchildren, and my great grandson.

I learned that President Obama was going to be in Jerusalem March 20-22. I had to go. So, only two days after the injury, I bought a ticket to Israel. I was so full of joy. Abba gave me peace. I asked a lady to go with me to help me. I should not have done that. It turned sour on me, even though I did get to places I needed to go after Obama left, to do intercession outside Jerusalem, and in Tiberias. I found out, once in Jerusalem, that my leg muscles were as strong as before, so I could climb steps, even the three flights of steps to my apartment and back. Abba did well!

On Thursday, four days after the ankle injury, I flew to Chattanooga. Allegiant Airlines treated me so well. I had a wonderful week in Georgia. But, the ankle was not healing very fast. I got back to Florida, knowing that it would take at least six weeks before I would be able to walk much at all, let alone go to Israel. But, by Abba's mercy, on March 19th I flew to Israel from JFK, with help from the airlines, the Israeli airport crew, and the lady I had asked to help me. We went to Jerusalem. You can read my report of Obama's visit in, "He Will Have Arrived – My Brief Report on Obama's vs. Yahushua's visit to Israel"/April 2, 2013.

Syria had been firing into the Golan Heights right below Mount Hermon. The lady, the friend she had invited to go with her, and I, went to Jerusalem for a few days of rabbinic Passover. Afterwards, we returned to Tiberias, where, by faith, we took a trek across the north, including down the Golan Heights, and to many other places. I was the tour guide. After the lady and her friend left in early April, I worked hard to finish the autobiography, and I did. Then would come the long professional editing process.

In June, I returned to America. By this time, Abba had given me another assignment in Rome. I invited my son and daughter-in-law to come with me. We formed a team. From June 7-12 we were there. This was the most serious assignment, next to the one in July-August of 2012, that I have ever done. He sent us to the root of all that Nimrod, Semaramis, and Tammuz started, which is alive and increasing in power within the Roman Catholic Church. This time it was to the tap-root itself in the Basilica of St. John Lateran, which is tied to **Revelation 16:13-16**. The

Lateran--the Cathedral of the Bishop of Rome (Pope)--was the first church ever built in Italy, built by Constantine. He drew from all the pagan religions of the Pantheon to produce a composite religion that united Constantine's empire. The Lateran pre-dates the Vatican by over 1,000 years, and its name, "Lateran," means "the hidden frog." Even with all the research on the Vatican that I have done for years, and all of the concentrated research we did to prepare for this trip, still, it was a tremendous education to be there, and go to the very places where the Great Whore of Babylon has her headquarters (**Revelation 17**).

Today is July 29, 2013, and this autobiography is finished. All professional editing is finished. It will soon be published on electronic media. My prayer is that it will help others know our precious Creator, our Father, and love, worship, and obey only Him! I have already bought tickets for my return to Israel. Praise Yahuweh! The Great Adventure has just begun!

Even though I have already told a lot of amazing accounts of Abba's goodness, here in the next section, Parts VII – XII, which I call "**The Collections**," I begin my itemized sections of personal accounts of His help in poverty, healings and miracles, protection, guidance, "mo'edim," miracles for my children, and of His intervention in the daily things of life. I repeat a few stories that are very significant.

BE ENCOURAGED! What He has done for me, He will do for you, if you let Him! I encourage you to joyfully humble yourself as a little child, and let Him be the Most High, the Almighty in your life. Love Him, fear Him, obey Him, know Him! "This is the life like no other – this is the GREAT ADVENTURE!"

THE GREATEST MIRACLE OF ALL IS ABBA'S LOVE AND MERCY!

SHARING GOOD MEMORIES
A PHOTO JOURNEY THROUGH THE YEARS

**Momma and I
(18 Months)**

Papa and I
(Age 2 - November, 1946)

**Papa, Momma and I
in Flagstaff, Arizona after my
3-month Practical Missionary Training**

**Graduation from Biola
(June, 1966)**

On the Great Wall of China
(March 21, 1994)

**With Pastor Samuel Lamb
in Gong Zhao, China
(March 18, 1994)**

**With Hans on the Island
of Hainan, China city of Haikou
Dining in a restaurant in a lilypond
(1994)**

**Outside Ulaanbaatar, Mongolia
after having chased a yak
and fallen in the mud**

**My birthday surprise by my students
Left to Right (Jargel, Yedidah, Tsengelmaa, Khasbaatar)
(1996)**

**At the Mongolian Circus
Yedidah in her "del" hugging Sarnai**

My Mongolian students from different colleges in Ulaanbaatar

By the Amur River in Blagoveshchensk, Russia After visit with the Russian Social Service (China is across the river)

**Visiting Jewish homes
around Constantenovka
(November, 1999)**

**Permission given by the militia
in Blagoveshchensk for me to go
anywhere I need to go - Jeremiah 40:4
(November, 1999)**

My orphanage run by Pastor John and Margaret Aloss Kisumu, Kenya

Preaching in Pastor John's new church by the orphanage

**Preaching in Bugobero Spiritual Church
in Uganda
(December 13, 1997)**

**Week long conference at Pastor Elijah's
Namungo, Uganda
(1999)**

Hugs from ladies in Musoma, Tanzania (1998)

**Peres and I at Vincent's house
in Bungoma, Kenya
(June, 1999)**

Vincent Wanyonyi Wabuke
My African Director

**Dr. Stephen, Mary and I at Edward Buey's
Church near Lwakhakha, Uganda
(1997)**

**Standing on Ben Yehuda Street, Jerusalem
(October 4, 2001)**

**At Christ Church Guest House
Old City, Jerusalem
On my 60th birthday
(2004)**

**Overlooking the Jezre'el Valley
from the top of Mt. Carmel
(December 5, 2006)**

With Pam Brinke in Jerusalem
(2003)

Gathering seashells on the Red Sea, Aqaba, Jordan
(1999)

"Indiana Mom" at Petra
(2000)

The ancient Roman ruins at Jerash, Jordan (October, 2003)

With Honey, my Bedouin friend in Petra

**Breakfast on the Isle of Patmos, Greece
(Revelation 1:9)
On my 50th spiritual birthday
(May 13, 2001)**

**Eating cherries by a canal
in Venezia, Italy
(June 16, 2001)**

Teaching in Carmarthen, Wales
(June 5, 2004)

**Picking Narcissus near
Montreux, Switzerland
(2003)**

**Assignment Finished!
Standing by Reykjavik Bay, Iceland**

**Overlooking Lake Titicaca, Bolivia @13,000'
"Notice the clear skies?"
(March, 2010)**

In front of the Great Pyramid of Giza, Egypt
(May 25, 2010)

**Ruins of ancient Sardis, Turkey
Yedidah reading Deuteronomy 6
from the 5th century Bema
in the Synagogue**

**Sunrise over the Golan Heights
and the Sea of Galilee**

Long Salt

Six-year old Moses

Julius's Letter

Julius Osilo
P. O. Box 2074
MBALE - UGANDA

12th February 1997

Happy New Year!

Greetings in Jesus name. I write to thank you for yours which I got some time in December 1996. We apologise for the delay to reply.

We appreciated your visit to Uganda and especially to our family. Sorry for what happened to you on your way back to Kenya. We learnt of your sickness.

We are well and my wife greets you and she is looking forward to seeing you again. You were a blessing to us all. Though the time was so short but you managed to minister something. Brethren were so blessed and they are asking when you are coming again. My prayer is that you come soon seeing that the days are evil and the Lord is coming soon. This time I am requesting you to come direct to Uganda from U.S.A.

We now have a telephone in the house the No. is   you can ring during early morning and evening hours. i.e. 7.00 p.m. onwards when we are at home. We have a Fax machine in the house the number is the same. Whenever we do God's service, God meets our needs. Come with more brethren but do not miss to come along with   has not written and I wonder why?

Send me your Fax number so as to communicate easily. Write and inform me the programme as to when you are arriving in Uganda.

Yours in Christ's Service

(JULIUS & GRACE OSILO)

The miracle book
--The Inn of the Sixth Happiness--
and my airplane ticket to China

"Pretty curls Mr. Pat"

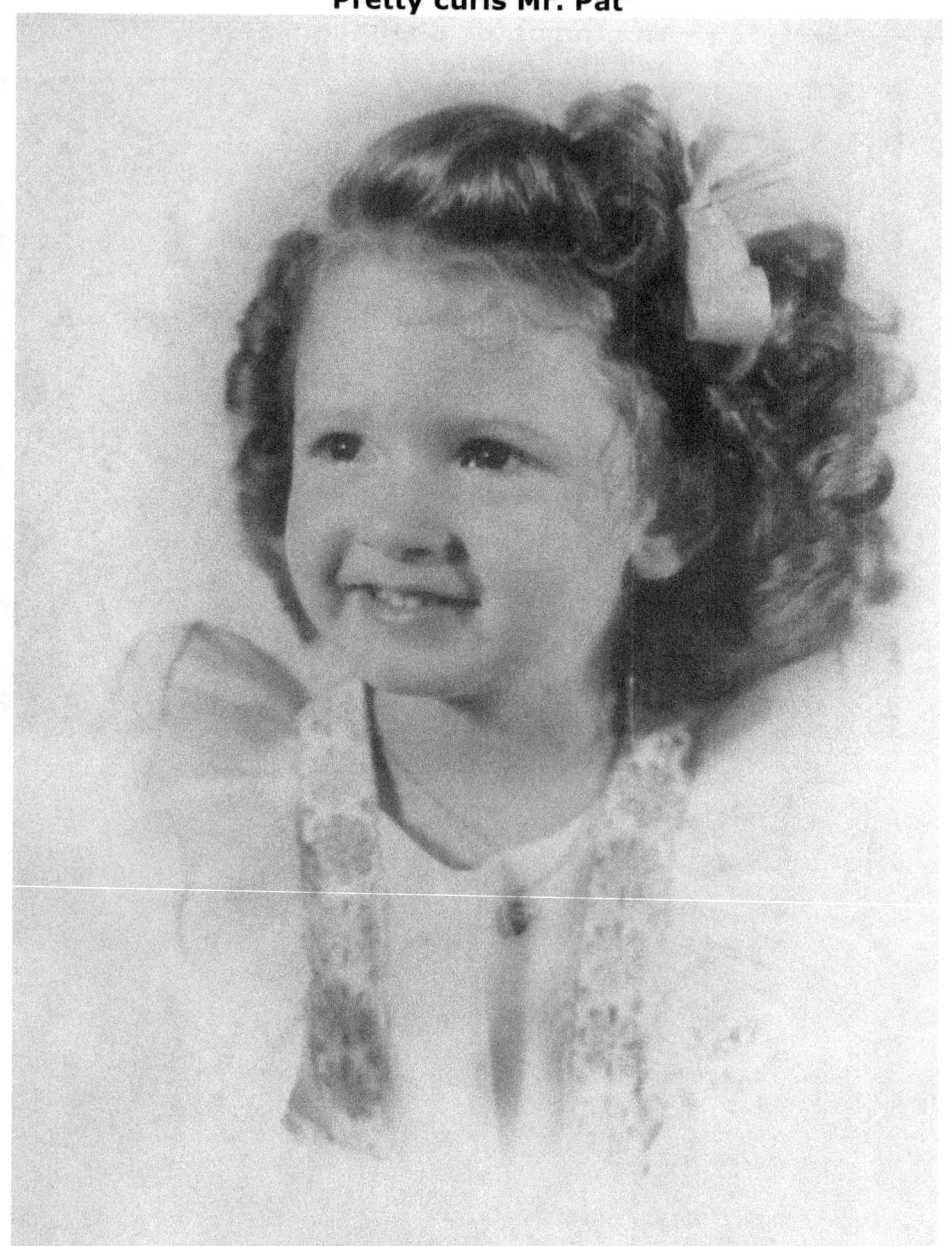

**All clothes pins were grouped in
2's or more so that none were lonely**

Sharing the adventure with my buddy!

Africa
(1996-2001)

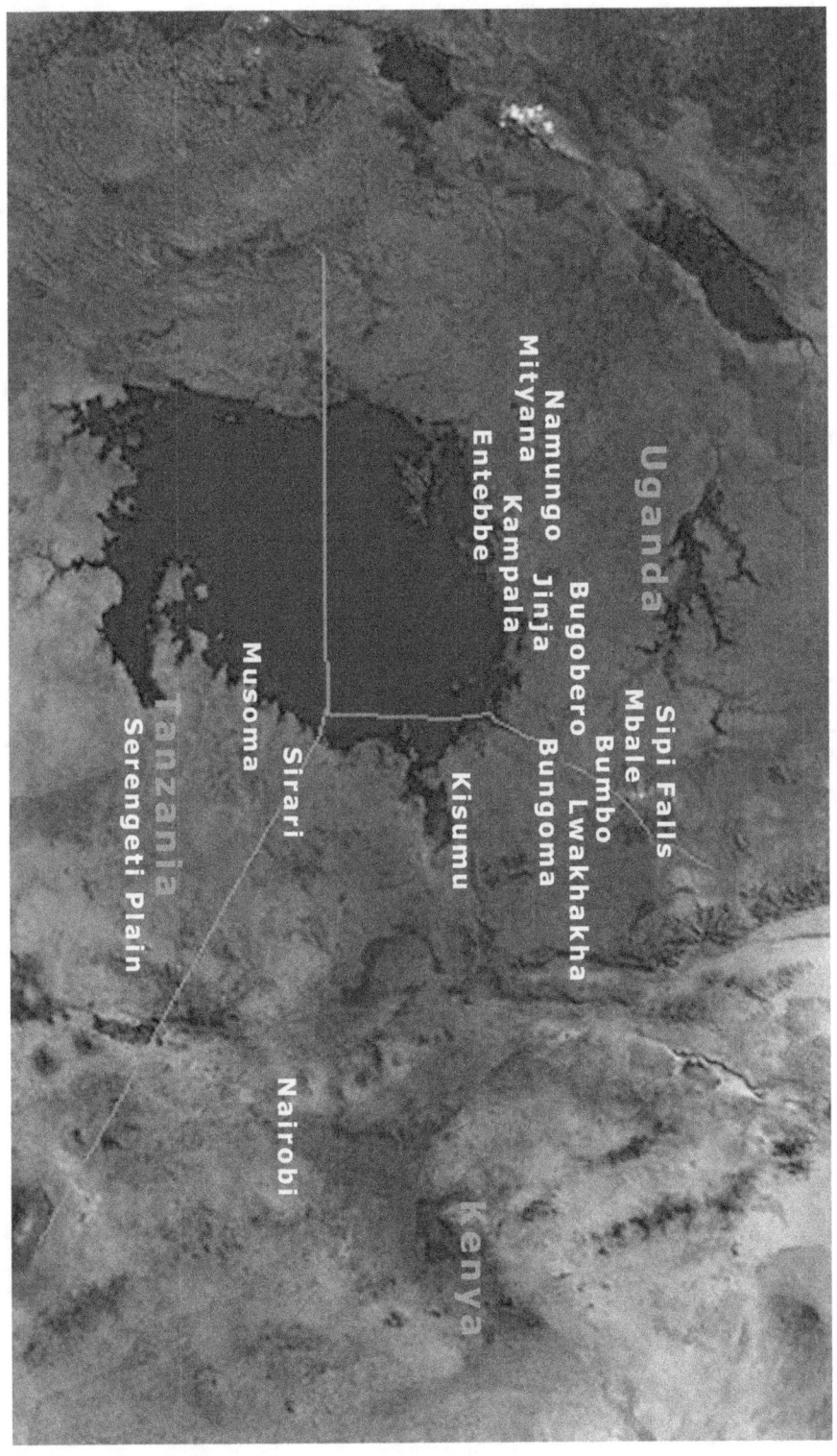

The Seven Assemblies
(2001)

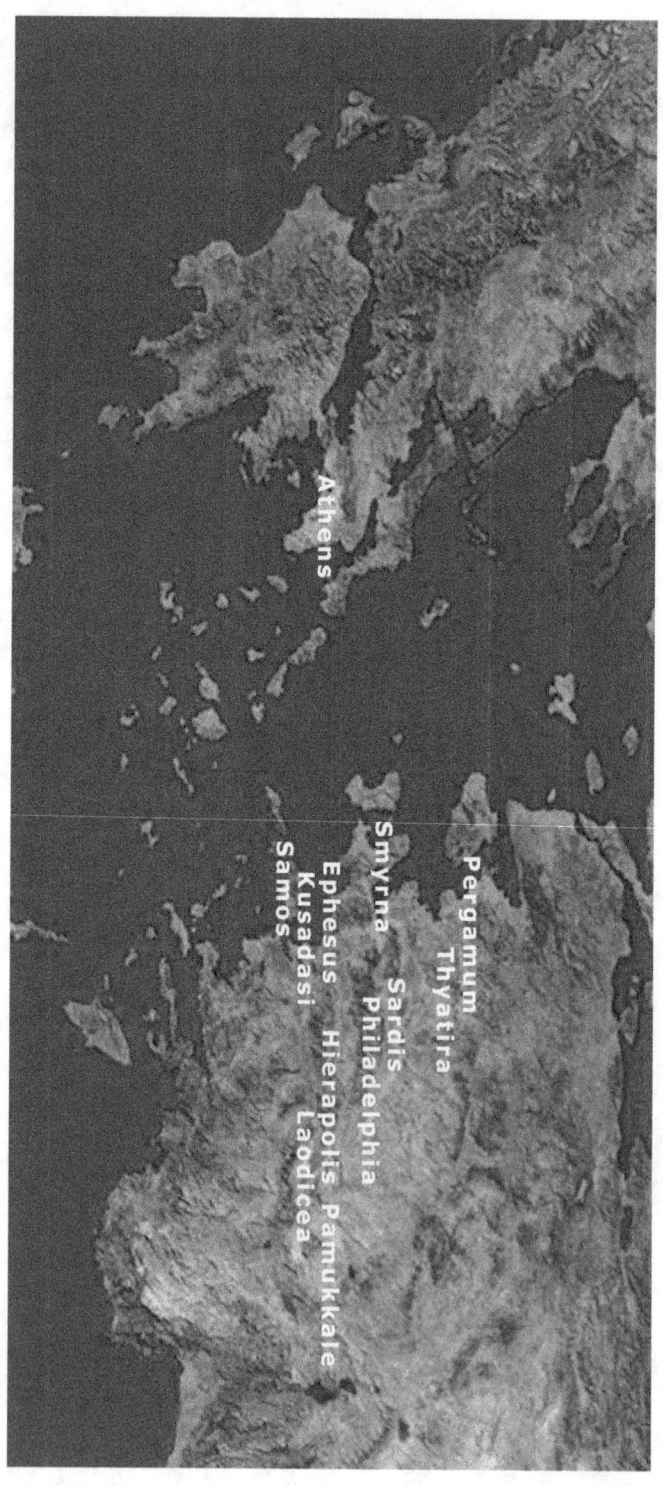

The Seven Point Assignment
(2010)

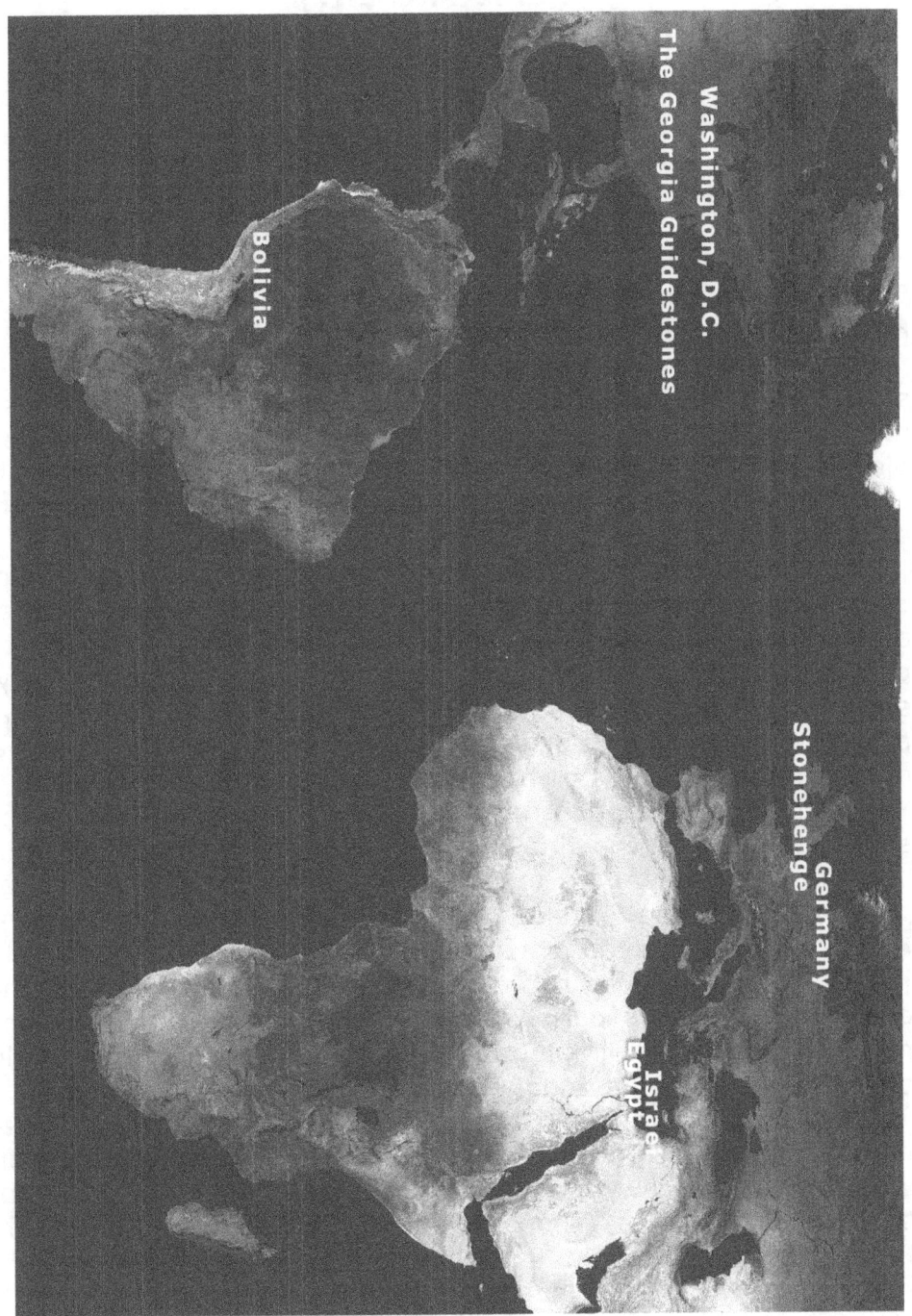

A COLLECTION OF MIRACLE STORIES
(1946-PRESENT)

PART VII
MIRACLES OF PROVISION
HE NEVER FAILS OR FORSAKES US!

Ya'cob (James) 2:5: "Hearken, my beloved brethren, has not Elohim chosen the poor of this world, rich in faith, and heirs of the Kingdom, which He has promised to all them that love Him?"

For most of my life I have lived below the poverty level by U.S. standards, but I have chosen to be rich in faith. Faith acquires all that we need from our Father. "Without faith it is impossible to please Him." (**Hebrews 11:6**) Fear acquires nothing but suffering. I have often written that we need about 2% of what we think we need. I now have lowered that percentage to 1%.

Faith has nothing to do with a "belief system" or a religious dogma. In Scriptural understanding, "faith" means obedience and action based on what the Master has said. Faith means letting people see what you believe by your actions. For example: If you say you believe Messiah died and arose to save us, and you have prayed to received Him as your personal Savior, then as a servant of a new Master who bought you (redeemed you back to Yahuweh), in preparation for eternity, it is your prime mandate to share the Good News with others. If you believe He is returning, then it is your mandate to act like it, share it with others, and prepare. Otherwise, you don't believe it! It is as simple as that. He has to see what you believe in action.

Life within man-controlled structures, or life based on one's own reasoning, is a boring life. Life with Father and Messiah is more exciting than climbing Mt. Everest or walking across Africa, or Tibet, like some have done, and a lot safer. He is calling out an "exploit people" - those of **Daniel 11:32**, who do things that have not been done before in obedience to His commands, at a time when most are cowering in their closets. I have been through tribal wars in Africa, almost died of malaria, been arrested in Russia, almost arrested in China for Bible smuggling and had many harrowing experiences in the service of the Master--I'd rather have those kinds of adventures than ones orchestrated by men. His ways are always an adventure!

The test of mammon (*a pagan god of money, materialism and personal wealth*) is one of the hardest of all. Messiah said: "No man can serve two masters...you cannot serve Elohim and mammon." (**Matthew 6:24**) From the story of the "rich, young ruler" in **Luke 18:18-30**, we see that the test of money is a huge one. The man kept the commandments, but when Messiah said that to follow Him he would have to forsake his wealth, he turned back saddened. The two greatest sin-traps of ministers are money and pornography/illicit sex. I was in the Christian ministry for many years, so I report just facts - pride, arrogance, greed, lust to control others, promiscuity, lust for power, competition and jealousy are driving forces in Christian and Messianic religion. Humility, contriteness, living the nature of Messiah, under His control, dying daily to self-will, submission to Him - these are the characteristics of the true servants of Yahuweh. Even though poverty has been a problem most of my life, I never considered myself "poor." I just considered myself frugal. He has taught me to be totally dependent on Him for everything.

THE MAILBOX STORY

When I was pregnant with our first child, we had so little money! Oftentimes we had little to nothing to eat. It was then that we began "playing the game" with Father. Someone would give us groceries, and we'd share. Someone would put $10.00 in our mailbox, and we'd give $5.00 in an offering at church. When I was in "hard labor" with our first child--seventeen hours--a nurse came in to give me a message from my husband. She said that he wanted me to know that "God had been to the mailbox." I understood that to mean someone had given us money.

OBEDIENCE KEEPS THE LIGHTS ON

I don't mind telling on myself. I have nothing to hide. One night we went to hear an evangelist at our church--Davey Joe Hissom. The next day, we had a $400.00 electric bill due by 5:00PM, or they would turn off the electricity. We only had $35.00 to pay on it. That night my husband said we should put the $35.00 into the offering. I suppose it was because Davey Joe had given him a prophecy, but my husband was often generous to a fault. I didn't want to give the $35.00 to the evangelist. I said "no." We got in the car and I sat in the back seat with the children. Then His Spirit said: "Give it." I told my husband to turn back and we'd give the money. We had a hard time finding Davey because he'd gone with the pastor, but we found him, and gave him the money. You might as well do as Yahuweh says the first time, because fighting with Yahuweh is a losing deal. The next morning I remembered that the local Social Service often paid the electric bills of the poor. I went into town to register for payment of our bill. At 4:00 PM that afternoon, I got a phone call: The

Social Service paid all $400.00 of that bill. Talk about "egg on my face."

If we make a habit of dependency on man, we will be stranded, betrayed, and eventually cast out. Most people have no loyalty to you, even though you think they do. When life and death survival situations come in the days ahead, most likely even members of your family, your friends, your pastor or rabbi, won't help you. They will be too busy helping themselves to care about you. Trusting Father for everything has made me love Him more than ever. He has NEVER failed me!

NEEDS MET IN UNIQUE WAYS

We lived on food stamps a long time. But, we also tithed the groceries to a poor family out of what we bought with food stamps. Food stamps gave us access to government food aid also. While living in North Carolina, I would go once a month, holding onto the hand of my youngest child, and stand in government food lines to get monthly rations of government cheese, flour, sugar and other commodities. Father provided in many ways. I learned to find edible plants in the forest for us to eat as well.

TRUST AND PRAISE KEEPS THE DOCTORS AWAY

In the late 1970's, we began terminating our medical and life insurance policies. We had to depend on the Father for healing. He never failed! The last time I went to a doctor, of my own will, was to have my fourth baby in 1981. January 22, 2011, my four children, in unison, panicked and called an ambulance because they saw me in such severe pain from a mysterious affliction. Abba finally cured that affliction as I learned to praise Him.

THE CREATOR'S REMEDY - A GUIDE TO STAYING HEALTHY

I worked in a retail store in our town in North Carolina. One day, when my children were young, in the early 1980's, I was shopping there and saw a display for a sale on all sorts of cold/flu medications. My children always got a cold in the spring and autumn. My pragmatic reasoning said to stock up on these medications on sale. But, as I reached out to take a bottle of Nyquil, the Spirit said to me bluntly: "**You buy it, you get it**." I jerked back my hand. I understood--if I depended on the medicine, my children would keep getting sick. However, if I depended on Yahuweh, my children would stay well. I didn't buy any and my children never got any more spring or autumn colds. Many times He taught me how to use herbs and other natural remedies to heal my children. In North Carolina, I grew 50 different types of herbs, some wild, mostly domestic. I made teas and medicines, kind of like Granny Clampett in the "Beverly Hillbillies."

HE IS FAITHFUL - DAY BY DAY

We were always praying for bills to be paid. I guess Abba got tired of it. One day, I was driving down our two-land road onto the Blairsville Highway, asking Abba when the money was coming for an electric bill. He said this: **"Is it due today**?" I said: "NO." He said: "So what's your problem?" That's the way He works--on a need basis--day by day. This takes all control out of our hands and places all control in His hands! The money always came somehow, just when we needed it! **Lamentations 3:21-26: "This I recall to my mind, therefore I wait: The loving kindness of Yahuweh! For we have not been consumed. His mercies have not failed. They are new every morning! Great is Your faithfulness! `Yahuweh is my Portion', says my soul, 'therefore I wait for Him'. He is good to those waiting for Him--to the soul who seeks Him. It is good both to wait and to be silent for the deliverance of Yahuweh."**

PEACE BE STILL - HIS WAYS ARE BEST

One of my daughters had occurrences of severe PMS. One night she came to get me about 3:00 AM, because the pain was so bad. I gave her a cup of Dong Qui tea, and then had her lie down on the floor of the living room with a pillow under her head. I covered her up. I laid my hand on her forehead and prayed for the peace of Yahuweh to come down on her, and within a minute she was fast asleep. He teaches those who look for other ways of doing things besides the usual man-made ways. I studied nutrition for many years. If you want to save money, learn natural ways. My children learned to come to me for prayer for healing, and to also pray for healing for others.

THE SALTY RICE MIRACLE
A SURPRISE IN THE MIDST OF UNCERTAINTY

I was in Aqaba, Jordan, preparing to leave for America in a few days, but I was out of money except for a few pennies, and the electric bill was not paid. I didn't even have bus money to get to the airport. I had no food in the house except a little rice. I cooked it. I had a little butter left and about a tablespoon of soy sauce. I sat eating the rice with butter and soy sauce, and the spirit of thanksgiving came so strongly to me that I began crying from such gratitude, that in the midst of such uncertainty, I had soy sauce to flavor my rice. My tears were falling into the rice. As I was crying and praising the Father, He spoke to me in my spirit: **"You will leave America with all of your bills paid."** That included the big one --a credit card debt of over $6,000.00. I was curious as to how He would pull it off.

I had been asking Him for almost seven years to help me sell a piece of land that was part of my inheritance from my mother. My mother had bought it with her brother. Her brother had died, his wife died, and two of his daughters had died. If the land was ever sold and the price divided, it would take the signatures of a lot of people. So, in seven years, even though we had a buyer, a cousin of ours, it was not sold because people kept dying on my uncle's side. Being an only child, I alone held the deed for the other half. When I got to the States, I went to Tennessee to visit my youngest daughter. While there, I thought I'd write a note to my lawyer in North Carolina and ask about the land sale. I enclosed the phone number of my daughter in Texas. Out of desperation, in the letter I suggested that someone buy out my half of the deed for $5,000.00 if possible. When I got back to where I was staying in Texas, my daughter told me that the lawyer in North Carolina wanted me to call immediately. His secretary told me jokingly, "Do you want us to buy you out for $5,000 or do you want $10,000 when the sale closes?" They had sent papers clear to Jordan to try to find me, for they didn't have my Texas address. If I had not written that letter in North Carolina, it would have been months more, after I returned to Jordan, before I got the money. The land sold and I paid off the bill. I returned to Jordan with rent money and living expense money for about a year

North Carolina law had said that if a woman owned property, and wanted to sell it, her husband had to sign the papers too. That law hung over my head, and my husband, whom I was separated from, was more than anxious to get his ½ of the money. But, by the time it was sold, that law had been erased, and I could sell it without his signature. That was Abba's kindness. Never try to second-guess how He's going to pull something off. He has a whole eternity of surprises. Just trust Him!

My African-American pastor from Zimbabwe once said: "**If you are filled with anxiety, then you know you are trying to control your life. If you are at peace, then you know you have turned all over to Him!**" Living with anxiety, stress, and worry, is no more than living with fear of the unknown. He knows the unknown, and if you know Him, He has a way of making the unknown all right. He usually gives us a hint of what is coming, so that we know the outcome, and therefore, can walk boldly with our head lifted high.

UPON SEEING THEIR FAITH
TAKE UP THY BED AND "MOVE"

In 1985, we were living in our beautiful home in the woods, in the Blue Ridge Mountains of western North Carolina. Yet, we felt strongly that Abba wanted us to move to Texas. We put our house up for sale with a realtor, but houses at that time were not selling. I had a little job that paid for the gas to get to work and back. My husband had taken a job in Chattanooga, Tennessee with a Christian radio station, but he had to quit it because we couldn't afford for him to drive 1½ hours one way, each day to work. So, to put "beans on the table" he got a job working in a local supermarket as a bagboy. I was so proud of him for that! We had no money to even move across the street. Yet, we knew that He was calling us to Ft. Worth, Texas.

We had been attending a prayer meeting in town with believers from all different churches. Occasionally, one would put an envelope in our hands with money in it, to help us. We had some good friends in that prayer meeting! We told our friends our predicament. One man suggested that we write all the major Christian ministries in the U.S. seeking a position with their ministry. We did. We wrote all the big names, and we got back personal letters from each of them thanking us for our inquiry, but saying they had no position open for us in their ministry.

I have found in walking by faith that if He has told you to go to New York and you get to the end of your driveway, turn the wrong direction and head towards California, before long, He will tell you to turn around and direct you back to the right road. But, one thing's for sure: "**He cannot direct a parked car**!" Unless you get your life moving in obedience to Him, He cannot and will not direct you! He has to SEE YOUR FAITH IN ACTION! Only one ministry did not answer our letter--Kenneth Copeland, in Ft. Worth, Texas.

Abba does not lead by circumstances – He leads daily as we flow in His perfect timing, hearing and obeying, hearing and obeying – like good servants of the Master. Then circumstances line up. One day shortly after that I was sitting in my favorite chair, just resting, and the Spirit spoke to me very clearly: "**Write Gloria Copeland**." I whispered to myself: "I don't want to write Gloria Copeland." He said slowly and loudly, with intensity: "**WRITE GLORIA COPELAND!**" It shocked me; I said "Yes, Sir!" I wrote under His direction. About two weeks later, I got a personal letter from Gloria Copeland giving about an inch opening in an otherwise closed doorway. So, we began praying about moving to Fort Worth.

On one of Kenneth's broadcasts, he introduced his pastor, Harold Nichols. We called him. Brother Harold encouraged us to come on, come to his church and they'd welcome us. To this day, Brother Nichols and Sister Lou are like parents to me. I love them dearly! But, we had no money, and no one was buying houses at that time in the late 1980's. To make matters worse, it was 1986 and the Texas oil market had bottomed out. There were few jobs in Texas and everyone was hurting because the government had ordered the capping of the wells so that we could be dependent on Saudi Arabia oil.

We were told it was stupid to move to Texas. We had no jobs to go to, either. We had no place to go to--no family or friends there. But, I kept telling people from faith in my spirit: "**If we have to stand in the middle of Highway 64 with our thumbs up, we're going to Texas because God said so.**" My faith grew greatly. No, Abba did not quantum leap me into guarding the Torah (His instructions and teachings of the Kingdom of heaven). He lead me one step at a time. We, as individuals determine how fast we move forward! A person can balk at any point and stop His leading. However, **Romans 8:14**: "**Those that are led by the Spirit, they are the sons of Elohim**." Only those flowing daily, being led by the Spirit, taught by the Spirit, counseled and convicted by the Spirit, allowing the Spirit to transform them into the image of Messiah, with Elohim's nature, ways and thinking, will ever reach the goal that Yahuweh has planned for them! I never balked at His leading – so yes, I was quantum leaped at one point.

During this time, our marriage was at its best. We were united in purpose. It was not free of demonic activity, but it was a time of relative peace in a marriage sea, where peace was extremely rare. No one wanted to buy our house. We had a realtor, but she was hurting for business too. We wanted to sell the house without realtor fees. We told our real estate agent about our decision, and she understood.

Because we could not afford to pay for the house, even though our mortgage payment was only $350.00 a month, our house was going into foreclosure, and we had one month to get out. To show our faith, we started packing--based on **Mark 2:2-12**, especially verse 5: "**And seeing their faith**, He said unto the one sick of the palsy, `Your sins be forgiven you'..." "Seeing their faith": Well we wanted Him to see our faith, so we started packing up everything and storing it downstairs.

My husband had left a wonderful job in advertising sales, working also as a sportscaster, newsman and anchor for the most popular local radio station. He also was the sportscaster for teams in Chattanooga. He had tried to find another good job, but jobs were scarce, so he worked for a Christian radio station in Chattanooga. He worked there until one day, on his way home from work, he had a horrible car accident. People who saw the crash thought he was dead.

After this, we could not afford for him to drive that far to work. So, to help with food, he got a job as a bagboy in a local supermarket in Murphy. I must say that he always was a responsible and hard worker. As a bagboy at the supermarket, my husband found favor with the Christian Manager. I was so proud of my husband for being willing to work at a menial job, when he had been such a celebrity in our small area. People had even asked for his autograph. The store owner told my husband that he could take home all of the bent things, dented cans, crushed boxes, etc. that are either thrown away or sold at reduced prices. We had our cupboards so full! At a time when coffee was $13.00 a pound, we had 15 cans of Folgers and Maxwell House coffee in our freezer, all free. For seven years, I had made noodles every day for the family. I made my own sauces, my own bread, and did a lot of canning and freezing. Abba blessed us with health to a high degree.

One day in 1986, I was lying on the bed praising Abba. My son came in with the mail – and in the mail was the foreclosure notice. I just kept praising. Abba showed me a vision of a sheet rising off of the earth. He said two words that sounded like: "ramah" and "see." I thought the words sounded Hebrew. He told me to look in the Strong's Concordance. When I did, I found that both words meant "to lift off." He was going to lift off what was holding us down! I rejoiced greatly!

Every day, after getting the foreclosure notice, I walked around and around our beautiful house in the country by a stream, in the forest, on a little more than an acre, praying that it would sell without a realtor. I kept telling Abba: "You are not going to get any glory if this house goes into foreclosure." He gave **Psalm 46:10a:** "Be still and know that I am God."

We had a short time left, then the bank would take our property and Abba (Father) would be shamed, and so would we. All of our faith was in Him. It was a II Chronicles 20 situation. A couple of days later, we got a phone call from our pastor. He and his wife had gone to South Carolina with church funds to buy a van for church purposes. While there, our pastor had a dream. In the dream Father told him to go home--not to use the money for a van. He and his wife obeyed. They got home and his wife was looking in the newspaper. They had been hoping to buy their own house. She saw our advertisement to sell our house. This is why our pastor called. He did not notice it was our phone number. He and his wife came over to see the house. They loved it. They applied to the bank for a loan to buy it. We had less than a week before the foreclosure was final. Father kept giving me "Be still, and know that I am God." The bank approved the loan and we closed on the house two days before the foreclosure was final. We hired a moving van, and we left for Texas.

We had been trying to sell our furniture, my piano, and other goods, all along. We had sold all but a few large things, which we could not fit on the moving van. Two days before we left, a lady who had been obnoxious and a problem to us, called and asked if she could come look at our things for sale. Of course we said "Yes." She came and bought everything at a good price. Never pre-judge anyone!

When we got to Texas, we got a realtor to take us to look at houses. Abba led us to the perfect neighborhood. We rented a house. My husband got a job with a large T.V./radio ministry. The local schools were touted to be the best in all of Ft. Worth, and yes, they were excellent. My son was in his sophomore year of High School, one daughter was a 10-year old, the other a 5-year old.

Before the moving van got there, we stayed in a hotel. Sitting out by the pool, I felt like I had come home. Years before, during one of my parent's summer trips across country, I had been sleeping in the backseat and woke up just to look out the window at a sign that said "Fort Worth." I felt then, as a teenager, that it was some place special. It was His will for us to go there. We lived there for 23 years.

No, the job at Kenneth Copeland's didn't work out. It was strange, but my husband got the job at the Christian T.V. radio station that used to belong to the man who took the job my husband wanted at Kenneth Copeland Ministries. Abba playing chess, I suppose.

Years later, I was able to personally thank Gloria for her note. During those years, I became friends with Jerry and Carolyn Savelle, and Kenneth and Gloria. I came to know men like Meadowlark Lemon of the Globetrotters, and many well-known ministers of the day. I taught end-times at the church, was in the choir, taught adult Sunday School, and prophesied. I was close to Brother Harold and Lou. Abba sometimes uses a series of events to bring us to the place He wants us. Each event may look separate, but they all tie together. I have had so many of these "series" of events throughout my life, especially in the last 18 years.

But, I warn you: If you fail to obey and do not stand in faith with Him in one of these events, then the whole chain of events breaks, and the wonderful conclusion that He has for you won't happen. If we take control away from Him, He will let us and He will back off. He won't interfere with our free will! He cannot help those who leave Him for what looks natural and logical. "Without faith, it is IMPOSSIBLE to please Him." And faith is shown by obedience!

PART VII - Miracles of Provision

PACKING UP AND WALKING ON WATER

I stayed with my third child in Texas whenever I returned from Jordan. She and her husband had been trying to find a house to buy for two years, but either their credit wasn't good enough, or the house that the realtor showed them was not "the right one." So, following our example in North Carolina, she and her husband began packing up their things in their rented house. They gave the landlord a month's notice that they'd be leaving. About twelve days before they had to be out, their realtor called. It was my birthday. We were getting ready to go to dinner. She said she had a house for them to look at in Benbrook. Someone else had put a bid on it, but they said they'd pay the whole asking price, which was low anyway. The next day, I got the call from the realtor saying it was a "go." They moved into their new place, less than a week before they had to be out of the rented place. The owners of the house they were buying made them a deal to be able to live there until the closure on the sale. It wasn't until they packed up and gave the notice to the landlord that Abba opened the door for them to have their own house in a very expensive neighborhood, but at a really low price. It was wonderful.

Basic faith principle #1: He does nothing until He sees that we are doing something to prove our seriousness of what we are asking for. Faith is not based on what we see, hear, reason, think, feel, taste, or smell. Faith is based solely on what He has said, either in the Word or to us personally. The greatest enemy we have is our own reasoning apart from His nature, thinking and ways!

My daughter and her husband had learned the major principle of faith: Step out in faith, and THEN, AND ONLY THEN, in seeing your faith in action, will Father move to do His part. As long as you stay in the boat, He cannot help you walk on water. You have to get out of the boat. A Catholic nun once said: **"Faith is like standing on the edge of a cliff, with one foot in the air and a queasy feeling in your stomach, and God saying: `Jump!'"**

THE BUTTER FOR MARGARINE STORY

While in a state of dire poverty, waiting to move to Texas, we had several wonderful provisions of food. One day our church was asking people to give to the poor. We didn't think we were poor. I went to the store and had so much fun buying as much as I could for $10.00 to take to church to give to the poor. I bought margarine on sale, cans of vegetables, flour, sugar, and other staples—all on sale. We took two grocery sacks full to the church that Sunday. That afternoon a truck pulled up in our driveway. Some of our brothers from the church brought us about $100.00

worth of food. They brought us steak. And they brought us butter. **After that we praised Him who gives "BUTTER FOR MARGARINE."** Praise and worship our Father for the little things--give to the poor when you are poor, and reach out to the needy when you are needy.

GIVING AND RECEIVING - ABBA'S WAY

When we were, by faith, preparing to move from North Carolina to Texas, we were on food stamps. I took 10% (tithe) of the food stamps and bought food for needy families. I gave food to a pastor and his family. It was illegal to give away the food stamps, but not the food. I LOVE TO GIVE. When you love to give, He loves to give back to you. The principles of Proverbs 19:17 and 28:27 are real.

CONSIDER THE LILIES OF THE FIELD
CLOTHING FROM ABBA

When I was in my 9th month of pregnancy with our youngest child, we had no money to buy her clothes. We did not know what to do, except to buy one or two things and keep them washed. One day, my oldest daughter was walking with her friend by a trash dumpster that was near her friend's house. There, by the dumpster, were several bags of baby clothes—sizes from newborn to age 4. There were nice clothes--name brands, and some nearly new. They took the bags back to the friend's house, and her mother washed them for me. Thus Abba gave me more than I could have asked or thought. Today, my youngest has two daughters of her own, and her family is wonderfully dressed in nice clothes.

In 1985, our son was in need of jeans, shorts and shirts. We had no money for them, and he said he wanted Levis jeans. They were very expensive. Yet, while working as a secretary at the local Catholic Church, some Floridians brought in a box of clothes and told me I could have what I wanted. In the box were Levis, Nike shorts, and real Polo shirts—all in my son's size. Proverbs 11:24: "There is he that scatters and yet increases, and there is he that withholds more than is right, but it tends to poverty." When we are generous to share with others, Abba takes notice. Giving to the poor, to widows, to orphans, and to strangers, opens doors for blessings for us.

BLESSING BEYOND IMAGINATION
A THANKSGIVING STORY

After about a year in Texas, we moved to a rental house about two miles away on Wind Chime Drive. It was the Wednesday before Thanksgiving, and we went to church. We had almost no food in the house and only $5.00. On the way home the children asked: "Are we going to have a turkey and Thanksgiving dinner?"

PART VII - Miracles of Provision

By faith, I said: "Yes." I had planned to buy a very small turkey with that $5.00.

On Thanksgiving morning, to show Him my faith in His provision, I made cornbread to start the recipe for stuffing. I had no idea about the rest of the meal. We didn't even have the other ingredients for the stuffing. About 10:00 AM the phone rang. It was the secretary of our church asking if we would be home and wished us Happy Thanksgiving. I thought it was a strange phone call. About 11:00 AM, a truck pulled up in our driveway. Glen was from our church. He brought us not only a big turkey, but everything imaginable to make our Thanksgiving wonderful--even treats that only Abba knew would please us, like Eggnog. He brought so much fruit that it filled a big bowl. To me, a bowl full of fruit meant we were rich. We invited a man from my husband's work who had nowhere to go on Thanksgiving. Glen had even brought us a table to use, because we had no dining room table. Abba blessed us, and we were able to bless someone else.

A WHISPER HEARD AND THE FEAR THAT "SLIPPED" AWAY MIRACLE IN AN ICE STORM

How I met Herb and Karen: Abba led us to rent a house in the southwest side of Ft. Worth. We had been to Grace Temple and gotten a bumper sticker with the church name on it. Herb and Karen lived down the street. As they drove passed our house and saw the bumper sticker, they stopped to welcome us and invited us to their house. They became such wonderful friends!

Shortly after moving to the Wind Chime duplex in Ft. Worth, the same house as in the previous story, we had completely run out of food. I had some wheat in a quart jar in the freezer in the garage, but that was it. An ice storm was already pelting Fort Worth, and the roads were getting iced over and very slick. We were washing dishes from our meager evening meal, and I barely whispered to Father, "I'm a miracle worker when it comes to feeding my family on next to nothing, but this time I need help." About twenty minutes later, the phone rang. It was Karen. She said that she and her husband had been praying and the Holy Spirit spoke to them both, so she was calling me to ask a question. She was reluctant to ask the question since she thought it might embarrass me. She meekly asked: "Do you have any food?" I quietly said "NO." This lady didn't go out if there was a little rain. By this time, the streets were solid ice, and it was expected to get worse in the night--with possibly power outages. This woman got in her car, slid down to get me (about 2 miles), slid down to the supermarket, bought us $100.00 worth of good food, slid back to my house, then slid home. The fact that she did that was a miracle in itself. But, how precious! Herb has died. She has been very ill and homebound for years. Yet, she called me that day full of faith and joy in the goodness of our heavenly Father. What a wonderful friend! **FAITH CANCELS FEAR!**

HIS WAYS ARE ALWAYS "ONE-UP"

In 1993, Father called me to go to China with Open Doors to take Bibles to the persecuted underground church. My first thought: Money! Where do I get the $1,800.00 necessary for plane fare, living expenses and travel expenses for three weeks? I thought of a friend who had a housecleaning business. Linda said I could work for her. For months I worked cleaning houses, hurt my foot, hurt my back, and generally wore myself out. I had two envelopes. In one, I kept my money I earned from cleaning houses. In the other I kept offerings that were given to me for the trip by believers who wanted to be a part of my work for Him. Just before going, when getting my plane ticket, I got out the two envelopes to see how much money I had. I knew that I had saved $1,800.00 in the envelope from housecleaning. But, I had not counted the money and checks in the other envelope. When I did, I was shocked numb. I had received from others: $1801.00. I'm not kidding! Abba was letting me know that if I had consulted Him, I would not have had to work cleaning houses. He always has a better way. [Refer to: "Walk the Hard Road" – in it I talk about following the Spirit and not letting head reasoning get in the way of walking by simple, child-like faith]

THE MARK 6:41 STORY - HE'S STILL IN THE BUSINESS

I told this story earlier, but it bears repeating. Yahushua still multiplies food: In 1997, in Kisumu, Kenya, the missionary I was staying with had instructed our cook to make us a dinner of four pieces of tilapia, vegetables, and salad. So, Nicholas cooked four pieces of tilapia, a can of corn, some mashed potatoes, and made a small salad. In the afternoon, the missionary invited fifteen people to come to dinner that night, including Pastor Kegohi and his wife Joyce. She called to tell the cook to increase the food to feed fifteen. But, the cook had already bicycled home--a long distance from Kisumu. When the guests came, we got out the fish, the corn, the mashed potatoes, the salad and bread, and put it all on the table. I wonder what the guests thought, but they didn't say a word. The missionary asked me to pray over it. I had no anointing to pray in faith, but I asked the Father to multiply the food to feed us all well. How did I know He had practice in multiplying tilapia? (smile) We all got our food, we had seconds and some had thirds, and we had food left over. I later learned that the fish that was most likely multiplied by Yahushua was tilapia, from the Sea of Galilee. It's now called St. Peter's fish.

In looking at the famine to come, I asked Abba how He would preserve His people in the wilderness. He reminded me that He had not changed. Messiah multiplied food, healed the sick, and provided for Peter's, and His, taxes in a fish's mouth, and He would do the same for us. **Psalm 33:18-19**: "**See, His eye is on those fearing Him, on those waiting for His kindness, to deliver their soul from death, and to keep them alive during scarcity of food**." The secret is "fearing Him," and "waiting for His kindness." **If you fear Him, you won't fear man!** If you wait for Him, you won't make stupid mistakes.

UNTO THE LEAST OF THESE

Father blessed my parents. As I wrote about earlier, I watched my mother feeding beggars who came to the door asking for food. Torah puts an emphasis on blessing the poor, the widow, the orphan and the stranger. Volunteer to work in a "soup kitchen." Organize projects to collect clothes and goods to give to the poor! **DO SOMETHING TO ACT IN OBEDIENCE!** Find out what the needs are of widows and orphans and collect things to give to them.

I have always been project-minded. In working with the Voice of the Martyrs I collected Bibles from churches, Christian schools, and individuals to send to Nigeria. Churches had been burned and Bibles burned. I collected coats, blankets, and other goods to send to Russia. I visited the Voice of the Martyrs headquarters in Bartlesville, Oklahoma, and met some of the volunteers there.

Do something daily to help those around you--physically, mentally, emotionally and spiritual. In the days to come, you will either reach out to help, or turn inward and take from others for your own survival, depending on what you do not do to prepare yourself mentally. "Blessed are the merciful, for they shall obtain mercy!" (Matthew 5:7 KJV) Matthew 5:7 from *The Scriptures*: "Blessed are the compassionate, for they shall obtain compassion."

The Word says that when you come to Jerusalem for the festivals, not to come empty handed, but bring offerings. I had so little in Jordan, but I always managed to bring something to Jerusalem--clothes, shoes, school supplies. I made sure it was in good condition and clean. I took the things to Christian Friends of Israel to give to poor Jews in Israel. Many of the people who come to get goods from them are new immigrants. The Jewish people are Messiah's "brethren." As Matthew 25:31-46 says, in giving to them, we give to Him. But caution: Be careful to whom you give. When you give to the poor--know the individuals or organization--for there are some shysters out there using poor Jews and Christians as bait to get money.

THE FAMOUS NICKEL STORY

My dad died in 1982, and my mother died in 1995. I, being the only child, took care of her burial and the estate. After the funeral, the bill came due. But, I had no money to pay for the funeral. Years earlier (1974-1986), after moving from California to North Carolina, I was going almost daily, for many months, to early-morning prayer meetings (6:00 AM) with born again, Spirit-filled Catholic nuns, who were nurses at the Catholic hospital in Murphy. Before work, they would meet at their convent for prayer--and because they were filled with the Spirit of Elohim, they knew how to pray unreligious prayers. So, I enjoyed praying with these ladies. I was the secretary, music director, social director, and children's Catechism teacher (though I taught the basics of the Word without Catholic interpretation, geared towards salvation) at the town Catholic Church.

One morning, I drove in the dark, the ten miles into town, on snowy roads, for it had snowed heavily the night before. I had only a few pennies to buy a stamp to send an important bill in the mail. But, I lacked one nickel to being able to buy the stamp. As I got out of the car at the convent, there next to my car door was a high snow bank. On the top of the snow bank was one nickel--I tell you the truth! I bought the stamp and sent the bill, praising the Savior greatly.

In 1995, after my mother's death, I took several trips back to North Carolina to take care of her business. As a home base, I stayed with my oldest daughter in Tennessee, near the North Carolina line. One morning, I was on my way to try to get a temporary loan from the bank to pay for my mother's funeral. I walked out on the porch. They had painted the wooden porch dark brown. I looked down to see a round raised place on the porch. I leaned over to pick up the round object. As I did, the Spirit spoke to me: "**Remember the nickel in the snow.**" The round object was a nickel, which I still have to this day as a reminder. He was saying to me the message of the nickel in the snow: "**I will take care of you. What you don't have, I will make up the difference.**"

I went to the bank, and of course got no loan. Our credit rating was horrible. My mother had taken out a life insurance policy for her burial in 1964 with the California Teacher's Association. When I got back to Texas I called them to get the $400.00, which was the amount listed on the policy. I needed a little over $4,000.00 for all the funeral expenses. I gave my mother's name and the policy number and the lady on the other end of the phone said, "Wait a minute." She came back and said they would be sending a check for approximately $5,500.00. The policy had earned interest! Abba knew that! **The nickel told the whole story: What I did not have, Abba had provided.**

LOST AND FOUND - A STORY OF VICTORY!

In July of 2006, I had come home from teaching a series of meetings and doing intercession in Alabama. I was at the Dallas/Fort Worth airport, waiting for my children to pick me up. I tried to make a phone call. None of the phones were working. And, because I was so tired, I left my wallet by one of the phones and walked away. In the wallet was my offering (check and cash of $500.00) from the meetings I'd had in Alabama, my credit card, my debit card, my house key, and other valuables, including the nickel that I kept--the story is above. About an hour later, as we stopped for something to eat, I found that the wallet was missing. Immediately, the peace of Yahuweh came all over me, and I knew that Abba was working to bring about good. The peace grew and grew. I cancelled the cards and told the people in Mississippi to stop payment on the check. But, all the time, Abba kept giving me joy, and I proclaimed Psalms of praise to Him. I called "Lost and Found", but they had not found it.

The next afternoon, about 4:00 PM, I opened my Bible, looked down, and read **Psalm 116:7: "Return to your rest oh my soul, for Yahuweh has treated you well."** I began to rejoice-- Abba was "up to something good." At 4:05 the phone rang. The call was a Manager at the airport. He was working at the check-in counter across from the phone booth. He saw the wallet lying there and took it. He locked it up in the safe rather than sending it to "Lost and Found." He said that they'd steal the wallet at "Lost and Found." I drove to the airport to meet with him and get the wallet. Everything was still in the wallet--what a nice man! I rejoiced, of course, as one who awakes from a dream. Yet, the real victory was won during the 24 hours before the phone call. I had victory, rejoicing, faith, trust, and peace, BEFORE the wallet was found. My Pastor Jim preached: **"If you don't get the victory before you get the victory, you do not have the victory." SO TRUE!**

HIS TIMING - A TEST OF PATIENCE--A LESSON OF TRUST

In late 1997, I had plans to return to Africa. I had reserved my ticket at a travel agency. They told me that on the Tuesday before I was to fly out, I had to have the ticket paid for. I had no money. I went to church that Sunday morning, and a man I did not know stopped me and asked me what I needed for Africa. I told him that I was taking Bibles and clothes to pastors. I made it my policy never to "hint" about needs. Hinting or looking poor is not faith--that is manipulation to control. He turned around, and I saw that he was writing a check. I put it into my purse, for I don't look right away at my offerings. When I got out to the car, I saw he'd written a check for $770.00. One hour before I had to have all the money to purchase my ticket, I had it. I called the agent and said to hold the ticket. Abba is not early (usually) and He's not late (by His standards), but He sure does make us hold out in faith a lot of the time so that we test ourselves as to how far we can go without panic. Life with Yahuweh is not easy, but it is the best! Each time, we get to know our Father's modus operandi a little better, so that we hold out longer. Finally, we stop panicking, because we know He'll show up--in His time.

LIVING VICTORIOUSLY IN EDOM

He takes care of those who are astute to guard His Covenant. In Jordan, in eight years, I changed two lamp light bulbs. I never had plumbing problems, electrical problems, and almost no computer problems. I remained healthy, and He protected me, a single woman in an Arab world, without any harmful incidents. And, I had favor with the Aqaba Special Economic Zone authorities.

THE LUKE 14:11 THEME - FAVOR IN THE WILDERNESS

This is a repeat, but it bears repeating: Initially, from 1999, when I came, to get a year-at-a time residency in the Zone, one had to have two passport-size pictures of themselves, a blood test every year, at least a $100,000.00 dollars in the bank, or an equivalent investment in a Zone industry, besides personal references and a rent contract. All my friends were getting residency by using a lawyer and transferring money back and forth into their banks to make it look like they all had the required amount. But, in March of 2001, the rules changed. All you had to have was approximately $10,000 in the bank, plus the other requirements. I had 44 cents in the bank that year. I had 56 cents in the bank the next year, when I went for my residency. I was the behind-my-back joke of our Messianic community.

As I reported earlier in the autobiography, the clinic personnel told me, after I got my first blood test, that I didn't ever need another one because my blood was so good. But, at the ASEZA (Aqaba Special Economic Zone Authority) office, they looked at my 44 cents and said, "It would be better if you had a few thousand in the bank." I told them that money came into my bank in America and I drew it out and put it into my bank in Jordan, and then paid my bills. The man handling my case said, "Oh, you must be independently financed." He got that right. They gave me my residency that first year and each year afterwards. When I went to give my praise report to my friends, all were shocked and some were angry. But, Father gives favor to who He wants to give it to.

I didn't have furniture for the first few months, except a bed someone had given to me. No one came to visit me because I was considered poor. One lady I considered a friend got very mad at me for staying with a friend from Texas who had moved there, because, she said, I should not be mooching off of her. It was 120 degree heat, and she had invited me to stay with her, since she had air conditioning. But, that is the way I was looked at by my rich "friends." They told me I'd have to pay $4,000 for appliances alone. Abba led me and I paid $400.00 for a counter-top three burner hot plate, and a small Japanese refrigerator, my washer that washed and nothing else, and my fan. My furniture was around $700.00 total, and people gave me other things. My next door neighbors blessed me greatly with ceiling fans when they left in late 1999.

Before buying the living room suit for $700.00, I asked Abba if it were all right to buy furniture and make it a home. He asked me: "Can you walk away from it at any time?" I quickly answered Him: "Oh yes, no problem." But, eight years later when I had to walk away from it, He finally had to sever me from it drastically. It was a problem. I didn't want to leave. That was the last "home" of my own that I've had. But, as Hebrews 13:14 says, I look for the "one to come."

JUSTICE FOR THE NEEDY - "THE YA'COB 1:27 MISSION"

I had an orphanage in Kenya. I met John and Margaret when I first visited Kenya and taught in the Charis Bible College founded by Andrew Womack in Kisumu. They had taken in about 15 boys and 15 girls. The children slept on mats in a very small area. The kitchen was the size of a tiny closet. Abba laid it on my heart to help them. In 1997, I brought clothes, shoes, children's school materials, Bibles, kitchen needs, and toys for the children. At that time I began working with John to get a place where he could have his church, his orphanage and his day school. At that time he was renting a building for his church, and renting a separate place for the orphans.

I went back a second time in 1997, and helped John rent buildings that housed the orphans, had room for his school, and for the church, as well as for his family. The school was named after my last name. The children had little patches on their clothes with the logo. We retained the name of the orphanage that John gave it--"**Soon Children's Home**"—which he named for the soon return of Messiah.

John and Margaret had two children of their own. Because of my help with getting a good place for the orphans, the school, the church, and for John's family, it became my orphanage and elementary school. I invited a team from my church to come.

They came and ministered to the children with the Good News, entertainment, presents, and medicines. The school grew to nearly 100 children from little ones to teenagers. I had to totally depend on Abba for provision for the rent and other needs for the orphanage.

I ministered with John in his church also. In one year, John's father died, his two children died, and then John died. John was 31 years old. I will never forget calling my son when I was in the frozen north of Far East Russia, in Svobodny, and my son told me that John had died of cerebral meningitis. In 2000, I had lost my African Director, Vincent Wanyonyi Wabuki to tuberculosis. I had traveled with him for five years. It was Abba's provision that kept me going to Africa and being able to help.

But, finally, the day came when I could no longer support the orphanage. On that day, I contacted the Missionary Department Head at my church--Bethesda Community Church in Fort Worth. He said that they would be happy to support the orphanage. Later, I learned of a pastor in Murray Bridge, Australia, who wanted to get the orphanage registered with the government so that they could get support. I worked with him for a few years. Then the orphanage became independent, registered with the government, and self-supporting.

NO RISK - NO REWARD
MIRACLES FOLLOW OBEDIENCE

In 1998, I had sent many things to pastors and their families in Africa. One day, I had collected a room full of things. My bedroom was filled with things. I made a small path to my bed. But, I sat on the edge of the bed and cried, because I had no money to send the things. As I was crying, Father spoke to my spirit: "**Call your friends. Pack everything, label the boxes, and put them by the front door ready to go.**"

REMEMBER faith principle # 1--show Him your faith! Do all you can do and He'll take up the slack. So, I called two friends over, we got boxes and boxed up everything. We labeled everything. I figured it would cost about $600.00 to ship, by ship (taking 6 months to get to the destination). We put everything by the front door. In about 3 days I got a check for $600.00. It came in miraculous timing from someone who said Father inspired them to send it. I shipped all the boxes for just about $600.00, like I had figured.

If you try to operate by having your "ducks in a row" before you step out to obey Him--forget it! You and your ducks stay home. He wants those who are willing to step out in risk – even risk of your life – to obey Him.

Those that know Him well, know that He doesn't let us sink. Messiah was standing by Peter's side. He didn't need to fear. He realized that on the way back to the boat. **One thing you do not want, especially now, is to be taken back to the boat!** The world's boat is sinking. Now, to fail in your faith-test could cost you loss of great reward as well as your relationship with the coming King. **Luke 9:61-62**: "And another said to Him `**Master, I shall follow You but let me first say good-bye to those in my house. But Yahushua said to him, `No one, having put his hand to the plough and looking back is fit for the Kingdom of Elohim.'** " **Luke 17:32**: "Remember Lot's wife." (**Genesis 19**) She put too many obstacles in her path as to why she could not abandon her life to take up His. What is stopping you from stepping out of the boat?

THE STORY OF THE MISSING GLASSES

I've also told this before, but it is a marvelous story that bears repeating: I was in the Great Synagogue, Hekal Shlomo, in Jerusalem. It was the eve of Yom Kippur, 2004. I went into the bathroom to fix my hair, and left my glasses on the counter. I got partway up the stairs, and realized my glasses were gone. I ran back to the bathroom, but they were not there. I contacted security, but no one had turned them in. I walked back to the Guest House where I was staying. In Jerusalem and throughout Israel on Yom Kippur, no cars are allowed on the streets except ambulances and police cars. So, I walked down the middle of the street. I sang at the top of my lungs in one of my heavenly prayer languages. No one cared. Everyone else was out meandering through the streets too. I prayed for the person who took my glasses. The security guard told me to check back the next morning, but no one had found the glasses. The main security man, a Canadian Jew named Yuda, took my phone number.

In the late afternoon of Yom Kippur, I got a phone call from Yuda. He said a lady had picked them up and taken them home, and then brought them back to the synagogue the next morning. He said he would bring the glasses to me that evening. But by the time Yuda got to the Finnish Guest House they had closed the gate, and wouldn't open it for him. The next morning, I went to the synagogue again. The security guard called Yuda. Not much later, here came Yuda with my glasses. Those glasses were in the homes of two Orthodox Jews. I feel they were blessed. I walked immediately to meet my friends at the Jaffa Gate, and we went on to Tiberias together for a wedding. Talk about perfect timing!

'YES SIR' - MAKING THE IMPOSSIBLE POSSIBLE

In September of 2005, I was preparing to go to the Golan Heights in Israel to a ministry, to tell them about the fleeing from the north of Israel. I was invited to come in November. I had just enough money set aside to go. Sitting on my roof-balcony in Aqaba, looking at the Israeli border, Abba spoke and said: "I want you to go to Israel also in October." I said, "You don't understand, I have no money to go in October." He said: "GO!" So I said: "Yes Sir!" I went the week before Sukkot. The whole week, as I was spending money, I was upset because nothing was happening. The last day I was staying with a Jewish lady. She had invited a friend from Tiberias to come to Jerusalem to go with her to the International Christian Embassy's opening night for Sukkot at the Pool of Siloam. This lady and I were having soup. I said I was from Aqaba. She began asking questions. Then she put down her spoon and said: "I am not going to the opening of Sukkot tonight; I am staying and talking to you." She said her Bible study leader had been teaching on Edom, and should talk to me. So, she phoned the lady, and in a minute, I heard screaming on the other end of the phone. Natalie handed me the phone. On the other end of the line was the very lady that Elaine (with whom I had done intercession in Jerash, Jordan, and who had hosted me in 2004 and 2005 in Wales) had wanted me to meet. She said very excited: "Yedidah!" I said, "Yes." She said that very day the Spirit had told her to get in touch with me and invite me to come to Tiberias to teach. She had learned about me from both Elaine and Maureen, a mutual friend in Jerusalem. But, when Miri called Maureen, she didn't know where I was. Elaine was still in Wales. Miri was perplexed because the Spirit was so emphatic that she get in touch with me that day.

Here again, as is common for me, the Spirit had orchestrated a "mo'ed" (a "divine" appointment). I told her I was coming in November to go to the Golan and would be happy to teach in their combined Bible study on Edom and Petra. I was going to do intercession with Elaine, who would be coming in from Wales the next day. We were going to the Golan together and then cross down into Jordan with her and a lady from England, to do intercession for the fleeing remnant out of north Israel. First we were going to the ministry on the Golan, whom they all knew.

After I spoke on Petra in Edom, Miri's daughter said she had a dream of being in Petra. She described it perfectly. The pastor's wife was there. She said she also had a similar dream, and described it perfectly. Then about four others described similar dreams, each describing the cave areas perfectly. None of them had been to Petra or seen pictures of it. None had told their dreams to anyone before. After the meeting, they took up an offering for me. They were all poor people, so I didn't expect much. But, I was wondering how He was going to get me money to make the trip in November to the Golan. Miri brought me the offering, and was very shocked. She said it was the largest offering she had ever seen them give. It was enough to pay for my time on the Golan, and in north Jordan. HalleluYah! I made friends in Tiberias, and from 2006 onward, it has been like home for me.

NEVER EARLY - NEVER LATE--ALL IN HIS TIMING

As I related above, so many times when we lived in North Carolina we were out of money before the next paycheck. On Friday, we'd race to the bank before it closed to deposit our pay checks, praying we'd have enough gas to get there. Many times, I'd be out in the car praying about a certain bill. Always, Abba would ask me: "**Is the bill due today**?" I would have to sigh and say "NO." Then He would always say: "**Then what's your problem**?" It was not my problem, it was His! **I remember Corrie Ten Boom telling about what her father said, as she was anxious about something. He asked her: "When do you have to give the ticket to the conductor to get on the train?" She had to reply: When it is time to get on the train."** That's faith!

THE LITTLE HOUSE IN LONG BEACH STORY

In 1970, my husband and I felt we should move to Long Beach. We had been living in Glendale. We had been attending an Assembly of God church in Sun Valley, near where I taught school. I was the choir director and my husband was the assistant pastor. But, friends of ours had found a church in Long Beach called Community Chapel, which was really moving in the Spirit and reaching out in evangelism to the rough elements of society. So we began driving twice a week to attend meetings there, in an old car we bought for $200.00. We met a lot of people who would be good friends.

In faith we drove to Long Beach week after week trying to find a place to live, but found nothing in our meager price range that was decent. Most people didn't want to rent to couples with children. We were so very discouraged. Our new friends at the church did all they could to encourage us and help. We had given our landlady a notice that we would be out at a certain time. It was getting very close to Sunday, when we had to be out. It was Thursday. We drove to Long Beach that night with heavy hearts. People had been praying for us. Near the end of the service, a lady named Betty came up to us and said that the Lord had led her to tell us about a house they owned that was for rent. We were so shocked. She was very quiet. She always sat a few rows behind us. We had never talked before. She said her husband was an atheist and hated Christians because they had cheated him so much that he refused to rent the house to Christians. But, she said she'd talk to him about us. She called Friday morning and told us that he agreed to rent to us, which was a miracle. On Sunday we moved into our little house in Long Beach, with the huge backyard, where we stayed many years until we moved to North Carolina. In Long Beach we paid $125.00 a month in rent.

Like the Apostle Sha'ul, I can say: "**Not that I speak in respect of want: for I have learned, in whatsoever state I am, therewith to be content. I know both how to be abased, and I know how to abound: everywhere, and in all things, I am instructed both to be full and to be hungry, both to abound and to suffer need. I can do all things through Messiah who strengthens me.**" (**Philippians 4:11-13** KJV)

He has NEVER failed me! He has taught me to depend on Him for everything! To the frustration of my friends, I have waited on Him to tell me what to do, even about simple things. But, in waiting for Him, I got great blessings. I have no pride. Without Him pulling me out of a deep pit, I would have lost my salvation.

I owe Him everything!

PART VIII

STORIES OF HEALINGS AND MIRACLES OF DELIVERANCE

THE DOLL THAT SAVED ME ALL PRAISE TO ABBA

When I was two, my mother and I were visiting a friend, and I got off the floor where I had been playing with my doll, and walked over towards a wood-burning stove to get warm. But, I tripped, and fell onto the stove which was about my height. I landed with my right hand right on the grate of the stove, and my left hand, still holding my hard-headed doll, landed on the stove too, but Dolly Dimples saved my left hand. Of course the adults ran quickly to grab my hands off the stove, but my right hand had been badly burned. They immediately called a doctor, who came and put salve on my hand and wrapped it in bandages. He told my mother that my right hand was not repairable--that it would be drawn up and unusable. But, my hand healed, and I spent most of my life playing the piano and typing. There are no scars either. All praise to Abba Yahuweh!

HE SAVED ME - IN MY MOTHER'S ARMS

Also, when I was two, I was lying on my mother's bed. She saw something was wrong with me. She picked me up. I kept passing out. She ran outside quickly into the fresh air, where I could breathe. Once in the fresh air I revived. But, I could have died, if my mother was not so aware that something was wrong with me. The gas stove was leaking. I've heard that a smell was added to the gas later on, so that people could smell gas leaking and get help.

ABBA'S HEALING TARGET AND THE ARROWS OF COMPASSION

When I was in High School, I took archery for P.E. (Physical Education). I was good at archery. One day we were out shooting arrows at targets, and it was very hot. We were out in direct sunlight, near noontime. All of a sudden I got deathly ill. I went temporarily blind. It looked like a white film covered my eyes and I could not see anything. The teacher helped me to the Nurse's Office. I had experienced sun stroke. I remember lying on that bed, unable to see, and being so nauseous that I kept throwing up. Yet, there was a girl next to me in another bed who had PMS pains. I had so much compassion on her I cried. I found through the years that if I was in great pain, then I would burst into tears in overwhelming compassion if someone else was in pain near me. It was something that came from my spirit that I could not control. In a few hours, I regained my eyesight. Abba healed me of what could have been deadly. I have met so many who have lived in luxury and ease who have no feeling for anyone else's pain. Suffering is something they run from.

WARFARE AND CLAWS
THE MIGRAINE DELIVERANCE STORY

For many years I had migraine headaches so severe that I had to go to the emergency room at the hospital. They would pump the drug Demerol into me, and then Morphine, but I would get up and walk out of the hospital after hours of drug pumping, still with the headache. One day, I promised my son that I would take him to buy a computer monitor, which someone in downtown Fort Worth was selling for $35.00. But, when it came time to go get it, I had a terrible migraine and was vomiting. Yet, I drove to the man's house and my son got the monitor. My son was about 14 at the time. He had been born again, and filled with the Spirit of Yahuweh. One night, I was experiencing a vicious migraine. I went into my dark bedroom to lie down. My son was so tired of seeing his mother sick and in so much pain. He was mad at the Devil. He was in the living room. He began coming against the Devil and his agents who were putting these headaches on his mom. He commanded them to leave me. I heard him, for he began yelling at the Devil. All of a sudden I felt about six long slender needle-like claws sliding straight up out of the top of my head, as if someone were pulling them out all at once. A strong heat hit the top of my head and went straight through my body to my feet. I was instantly healed, and I have never had another migraine headache.

PANIC ATTACKS AND THE WARFARE THAT CRUSHED THEM

When living in Fort Worth at our Wind Chime Drive house, I used to have panic attacks that were severe. They would come on me with no warning. My legs and body would turn to "jelly" and my heart would beat so hard that it would push out my shirt. I did spiritual warfare, and finally they left.

In 1992, we went to Germany to see our new grandson. My son was in the Air Force. He took us to Trier, which predates Rome by 1600 years. We visited the dreary catacombs where prisoners and lions were chained before being released into the arena. It was in Trier that Constantine built his first Cathedral to house "the robe of Christ" that his mother, Helena, had brought back from her trek to Israel. It was to this Cathedral that Hitler went to declare his war against the Jews, noting in that place that they were "Christ killers." There were also, as in Rome's Coliseum, believers that were killed for their faith. As I went through that damp place, damp because it had been raining, I came out mumbling a question to myself: "I wonder if the spirits that were here in the days of Rome are still here?" As soon as those words left my mouth, I went into the most horrible panic attack. My legs felt like they had turned to jelly and my heart pounded so hard my shirt was going up and down. I grabbed onto the railing and tried to call my son, but he was well up the hill. He turned around, however, and saw me in such a state, and came running down to help me. He commanded the Devil off of me and instantly I was all right. I never had another panic attack since.

FAST PAIN RELIEF WITH ABBA

When I was eleven, I tried to jump over a wall and ended up falling across a large tree branch onto my back. The pain was terrible, and it loosened a vertebrae that never quite set back into place after that. This vertebra often goes out of place still, and stays out of place. At times, it pinches a nerve that runs to my left eye and to my stomach. This brings violent headaches, with vomiting. One day around 1988, my son was desperately trying to get the vertebra back into place, but it wouldn't move. (I had taught my son basic chiropractic adjustment procedures, and he was/is good at it.) I was sitting in my chair, with my head in my hands. I had not been to the doctor since 1981, for the birth of my youngest child. But, that day I said: "Holy Spirit, if You don't do something, I'm going to have to go to the emergency room of the hospital, because I can't stand this pain anymore." Instantly, I saw an opaque man's hand coming towards my head. As this hand passed through my left eye, the pain was instantly gone, and I was healed. I was in such shock that I went to lie down to sleep. I arose feeling wonderful. Praise Abba Yahuweh! I have no doubt that the hand was Yahushua's hand!

WHEN I FALL, I WILL RISE - A SERVANT NEVER STAYS DOWN!

As I told earlier in this autobiography, when I was 10 years old, my left knee turned out of place for the first time and I fell on the sidewalk. Later I also had similar problems with my right knee and right ankle. I have very flexible vertebrae, joints and ligaments. They move all the time in and out, and pinch nerves and/or cause me to fall. This began a lifetime of all too often falling from my knees turning out of place, or my ankles collapsing. The sciatic nerves on my left side were often pinched. The condition has been labeled "Sciatica": "pain in the region of the hips or along the course of the nerve at the back of the thigh." The pain I had ran from my left hip, down the side of my left leg to the knee, making the whole side and front of the left leg numb. I tried to live a normal life. I loved "jump rope." Later I played basketball, tennis, field hockey, baseball, badminton, volleyball, and even some football. I was the High School champ in badminton. I also enjoyed swimming. I loved to dance, from the bebop to the Twist, from jiving to the polka, and Hebrew dance later on. I fell many times, but I got back up and kept going. It was part of life. I have fallen physically since age 10 until recently at age 68. But, I have fallen in all ways – in mind and emotions more. Today, I can boldly proclaim to all of my enemies, both human and demon: **Micah 7:8: "Rejoice not over me, O my enemy! For when I fall, I will rise! When I sit in darkness, Yahuweh is a light to me."**

I WILL WALK!

I dreamed of being an ice skater, but my ankles were too weak for that. I couldn't take ballet because my legs were turned inward at the hip. When I would lie on my stomach, my feet would overlap each other. I could not turn my feet outward in a ballet position. I've lived with varying degrees of pain since childhood. I also have had headaches from pinched nerves, as well as from sinus problems and migraines. My vertebrae in my back are very unstable. The muscles holding them in place are weak. So, the pain of pinched nerves has been with me since age ten. Because of vertebrae being out of place, and my hips out of place, it caused deformity in my knees and lower back. My respiratory system was affected, and I would gasp for air under the shower. My circulatory system was affected, and it would take at least an hour after I arose from sleep to be able to bend over to pick up anything from the floor. I praise Abba for every step I take. Here in Israel everything is up and down, down and up, steep hills. My leg muscles are strong. I was a hiker in my youth also.

But, in the last few years, my lower back has become so caved in that my inner organs are making my body protrude in the front. This causes a lot of pain in my hips. But, still, I CAN WALK. My walking is getting slower, and I use a cane, but I CAN WALK! I have to have wheelchair assistance through large airports too, and I am thankful for that! But, I know that if I keep praising Him and doing what He asks me to do, He will keep me going.

I Corinthians 1:27-31: "But Elohim has chosen the weak things of this world to confound the wise, and has chosen the weak things of this world to confound the things that are mighty. And the base things of the world, and things which are despised, has Elohim chosen, yes, and things which are nothing, to bring to nothing the things that are, that no flesh should glory in His Presence...that, as it has been written, `He who boasts, let him boast in Yahuweh.'"

PART VIII - Healings and Miracles of Deliverance

In 1986, a chiropractor showed me my back x-rays and told me I'd be in a wheelchair shortly. I saw the x-rays. My spine and hips looked terrible. But, I said to myself: "I will NOT be in a wheelchair--I WILL WALK!" We can either agree with facts, OR we can listen to our eternal spirit and get the mind of Yahuweh on the subject and then believe Him! **Faith principle: First we get the mind of Yahuweh on a subject, and stand with Him in uncompromising faith, and THEN we get to see His results. If we waver in our faith—we get nothing! (Mark 11:22-24)**

For years, I stood in "healing lines" to be prayed for. I would feel the power of Elohim tangibly. One time I felt it like electricity shoot between the visiting evangelist and me, but not through me. I would always go back to my seat and touch my left leg, which had been numb from the hip to the knee from the sciatic nerve being pinched from childhood. Upon feeling that it was still numb, I would go into deep depression. I would say: "I am not healed." I was basing my healing on what I felt. I was going by circumstances, rather than the Word of Yahuweh! Faith principle: **DO NOT BASE THE ANSWER TO YOUR PRAYER ON VISIBLE CIRCUMSTANCES OR FEELINGS!** Yahuweh deals in the realm of faith and the spirit, not with fleshly feelings. He expects us to trust what He has said to us, not go by what we "feel" or think. **Faith bypasses what the five senses tell us**, and goes strictly by what He says, by His nature, ways and thinking. And in these things that I have suffered, I have learned endurance.

TYLENOL VS ABBA - LET THE SHOWDOWN BEGIN

From around 1980 I went to my chiropractor in North Carolina about three times a week. While carrying my last child, I was in so much pain that I could only crawl around the house on my hands and knees. Here's where it gets good! In early 1986, I was working for a Catholic Priest as his secretary--the office was in his home. Following one of my chiropractic "adjustments," I went back to the office. The priest was gone, and I needed help. The pain was so bad I was gasping for air. I got up intending to get some Tylenol. I went into the living room, and made this speech out loud to God: **"I am going to get some Tylenol in the bathroom. In about 20 minutes the pain will subside. I would love to trust You, but frankly, I'm sorry--YOU'RE TOO SLOW**!" I meant it in all sincerity. I really didn't mean to be rude to Him. I did want to trust Him, but I was hurting too bad in my body and in my mind. I was like a wounded animal that wants help but is afraid to trust the Veterinarian, so growls and snaps at the doctor. As I picked up my right foot to turn towards the bathroom to get the Tylenol, a very hot heat hit my lower back-- like someone stuck a heat lamp an inch from me. I froze in place.

The heat traveled slowly up my spine to my neck, and as it did, the pain was gone. I was totally numb. I kept saying to Father: "I'm sorry Sir; I'm sorry Sir." That began my hope that I could trust Him for healing.

THE GAS STATION HEALING

Beginning our move from North Carolina to Texas, I started the trip with my right hip out of place. It hurt so bad that I knew I couldn't ride 900 miles like that. I got out at a gas station to get a map. I prayed that He would heal me of the pain. When I got back into the car, His heat hit my hip intensely and for 900 miles I had no pain.

THE FAITH OF A CHILD

When miracles were needed or healings, my children learned to come to me for prayer. But, they also developed a faith of their own, and many times they prayed for me. Once a big dresser fell on my left foot--the pain was awful. My third child dropped immediately to her knees and began rebuking the pain, which left immediately.

FAITH IS: JUMPING OFF THE HIGH DIVE

One day around 1993, a lady Evangelist, Joyce Still, came to our church. For three days she prayed for people and there were many miracles. In the meantime, I had filled my mind with faith Scripture. I had learned never to go by what I felt, saw, heard, or reasoned. I learned never to go by circumstances. So, on the last night she was there, she simply said, "If you have not been prayed for this week and would like healing, come forward." I had not gone to be prayed for to be healed in years. But, I went. She simply put her hand on my forehead and said "Be healed in the name of Jesus." I went back and sat down and I DID NOT TOUCH MY LEFT LEG. I was depending on His Word to heal me, not what I felt.

At that time, my circulatory system was so bad that each morning upon arising, it took at least an hour for me to be able to bend over at all. During the night, after Joyce prayed for me, I felt vibrations moving all over my back. I pondered the vibrations that felt like someone massaging my back. The next morning, I sat on the edge of the bed and saw something on the rug - a piece of lint probably. I reached over to pick it up and realized that I had no pain. He not only healed my circulatory system but also my respiratory system. I then could jump off the high dive at the local swimming pool. My youngest child's friends applauded, because I went under water and turned backward flips. HalleluYah!

In telling my story of this healing in a village church in Saltillo, Mexico, I emphasized that my healing was not based on touching my numb leg, but on pure faith. People were being healed all over the church of different ailments. Incidentally, He left my leg numb so that I would remember the lesson. Their faith had been activated by hearing my testimony, and they received what they needed. Share your testimonies!

THE LEGS THAT STRAIGHTENED - A CREATIVE MIRACLE

In one of the Tuesday prayer classes at Grace Temple, my mentor in practical spiritual ministry, "Momma June," told me she wanted to pray for me. She had authority. We saw so many miracles, even creative miracles, in that class! So many were saved, baptized in the Spirit, delivered from demons, and healed--it was amazing! That day, she sat me in a chair and prayed that my legs would straighten out. My left hip was turning inward so badly that I dragged my left leg. When we left North Carolina, it was so bad that my friends were concerned about me. After she prayed, for about thirty minutes I felt heat and vibration going all up and down my left leg. I went home and laid on my stomach on the bed and my legs were straight. My husband came home and saw me lying on my stomach. He said, "Your legs are straight, what happened?" People who had known me previously would ask me to just walk, so they could marvel at the miracle. I could then do ballet positions very easily. I bought a pair of ballet slippers to celebrate my healing. It was a CREATIVE MIRACLE. He literally turned my hips outward.

Our answers sometimes come in part I, part II, part III, etc. Father wants us to trust Him totally, and not look at what we see or feel or think, so that He might get all the glory. Oftentimes He makes us wait for answers so that we learn to tough it out in faith--but He is faithful and always answers those who do not waver in their faith in Him. **Mark 11:22-23**: "**Yahushua...said to them, `Have faith in Elohim. For truly, I say to you, whoever shall say to this mountain, "Be removed and be thrown into the sea, and does not doubt in his heart but believes that what he says shall be done, he shall have whatsoever he says. Because of this I say to you, whatever you ask when you pray, believe that you receive them, and you shall have them.**" This passage has been twisted into a "blab it and grab it" mentality in the so-called "Word of Faith" movement, yet the words of Messiah are valid!

THE HEALING AT CANA

The bones in my mouth were vanishing and I lost many good teeth because the bone was not substantial to hold the teeth in place. In 2006, two of my front teeth were falling out. It had gone on a year like that because I had no money for dental work. I still traveled and taught. If I had any pride, it was crushed, because I was not a pretty sight. One day, I was with my dear friend and Actress Lady on our way to Nazareth. Actress Lady had been trying to get me to go to her dentist. I'm sure he was a fine dentist, but Abba had not told me what to do about my teeth YET. We were passing through the Kafar Cana – the village of Cana. (**John 2**) This is where Messiah performed His first miracle in public. I began having pain in my mouth. The pain went throughout my upper and lower jaws so badly that I was about to tell them to take me home. My dear friend asked me if I had any anointing oil. I just so happened to have some. She pulled the car over in an empty lot. She anointed my gums with the anointing oil, and commanded the pain to cease. The pain stopped. She went on towards Nazareth. The pain never returned.

MOVED TO THE FRONT OF THE LINE - ABBA 'SMILED'

Two years later, I was still teaching with those two front teeth barely hanging in place, and sticking out. A lady in Florida e-mailed me and said, "Father has told me that I cannot have my needed dental work done, until I pay for yours to be done." My daughter had just found a good dentist and I went to him. Because I had no insurance, they gave me a 20% discount on everything. My surrounding teeth were so loose that they couldn't fit in a bridge, or do a bone graft, so they put in a temporary fixer. Barbara thought it might cost as much as $3,500.00. But, with the "fixer" and the discount, everything only cost $700.00. She paid it joyfully.

GREATER WORKS AND THE "NOT-LAZY" ABBA

My husband had what is called "a lazy eye." The pupil of his right eye would not stay in the center, even though he had surgery as a child to correct it. One day I got mad seeing him like that, and I grabbed his head between my hands and said: "In the name of Jesus, eye, you go move to the center and don't you ever cross again." I watched his eye move to the center and it never crossed again. I know, I know – He healed, and still heals in the name of Jesus. But, unless someone has heard otherwise, Yahuweh has mercy on ignorance. Once we learn truth, we're responsible for it! Then we have to repent of our participation in falsehood, and embrace truth without compromise.

Jeremiah 16:19: "**Oh Yahuweh, my strength, my stronghold and my refuge! In the days of distress the nations shall come to You from the ends of the earth and say: `Our fathers have inherited only falsehood and futility, and there is no value in them.'** " Yahushua said in **John 14:12-13**: "**Truly, truly I say to you, he that believes on Me, the works that I do shall he do, and greater works because I go to the Father. And whatsoever you shall ask in My**

PART VIII - Healings and Miracles of Deliverance

Name, that will I do, that the Father may be glorified in the Son."

The "greater works" does not mean doing flamboyant signs and wonders that show off the greatness of the "performer." It simply means that as we go forth in His power and anointing, in humility as a servant of His, we will experience and perform the works that He did while on earth, and even greater amounts of works, more extensive works, so that the Father will get praise and glory. He raises our authority level as we die to self and submit totally to Him! The Apostles went on to raise the dead, perform miracles and healings, prophesy, deliver people from demonic possession, and bring salvation to multitudes. We are left with the same ability, if we humble ourselves outside of religion, and obey Him. Once His anointing goes forth, healing is on a "whosoever will" basis.

HEALINGS THAT RUN AND JUMP

Three of my children learned to move in healing, deliverance, and miracles by His Spirit. Two went with me on mission trips to Mexico and the Navajo Indian reservation. The youngest went with me to Africa. Three went on a mission trip together to Haiti in 2012.

I took my youngest daughter with me to Saltillo, Mexico. She was eleven years old. From age five she was leading others to salvation, was filled with the Spirit and powerful in deliverance and healing. I had taken her several times to minister on the Navajo Reservation in New Mexico. At this particular meeting in Saltillo, Mexico, after I taught, many came forward for salvation and for healing. I ministered to individual adults of all ages for healing. She ministered healing and salvation to parents who brought their children for help.

She led several to salvation. Carl Lupnitz, the host-missionary, was translating for her. At one point Carl came up to me, eyes wide with wonder, and told me that she had prayed for a little boy who had been in a car accident, who had a hole in his lung and a damaged hip. He could not walk well or run. After she prayed, he took the boy out into the parking lot, and the boy ran around perfectly healed, breathing normally.

The next oldest daughter also has prayed for people to be healed and seen them healed. We were on the side of a mountain in a church one night in the Guadalupe Mountains. She was praying for people. I asked her how it was going. She said she prayed for a man and all of sudden he started jumping for joy. She figured he got healed because he became very joyful, but she didn't know because he only spoke Spanish. (smile)

Teach your children how to minister in faith, in power, and in the anointing of the Spirit of Yahuweh. The faith of a child is great. Teach them before the evil one destroys their faith! Teach them to stand strong and not deny Him in the face of death--for once a child gets older, even before being a teenager, the enemy throws many doubts into their heart. "Train up a child in the way he should go, and when he is old, he will not depart from it." (Proverbs 22:6) "Old"? -- In Hebrew thought, that is when a boy reaches 13 and he can shave and his voice drops, and when a girl is old enough to have a baby.

THOUGH I FALL, I WILL "DELIVER"

My third child also has moved in miracles and healings. She also hears from Father, and is a teacher of the Word. Two weeks before she was born, I fell in a dark bank parking lot. The toes on my left foot bent backwards towards my ankle and I cracked three bones across the top of my foot. The other foot came up between my legs and I thought I'd give birth right there in the dark on the ground. She was 10 days overdue already. She was down in the birth canal for at least 20 days before she was born. Someone found me and I was taken in an ambulance to the hospital. I got a cast on my foot. She hung in there another 10 days.

NUNS, PRAYER AND AN X-RAY TO 'GRIN' ABOUT

October 21, 1976: The day after I gave birth to her, my doctor told me that her bones had grown together in the front of her head, and she would have to be taken immediately to Emory University Hospital in Atlanta to have a metal plate put in between the bones so that her skull could grow normally. Those precious born again Spirit-filled nuns came to visit me in the Blairsville, Georgia, hospital. They were nurses in the Catholic hospital in Murphy, North Carolina. These were the same sisters I prayed with so early in the morning. I told them about my baby's situation. One took my hand and smiled. She said that they would pray, and all would be fine. They said to bring my daughter for further x-rays at their hospital before having her rushed to Emory.

The next day, papa helped me take my daughter to the Catholic hospital were they re-x-rayed her. My papa went to find out the results of the x-ray in the lab. I'll never forget that grin on his face as he came out. They had found a hairline crack between the front head-bones. She had been in the birth canal for so long that I suppose the bones had pushed together. She never had to have a plate put into her head. Abba is so good!

Yahushua gave credit to the one being healed for their faith, often saying things like: "According to your faith, so be it," or "Go, your faith has healed you." It is faith, not hope, that brings the answer. Faith Expects! It is not based on wishing. Be sure that your own sins don't keep Him from working in your life. His view of what is sin, and man's view of sin, is often very different. Man has new words to brush off "sin" like; "Issues," "mistakes," and "problems." But, Yahuweh's eye penetrates to the heart – to examine our intentions. He goes to the source of what produces the sin. We need to pray Psalm 139:23-24: "Search me O El, and know my heart. Try me and know my thoughts. And see if there be any wicked way in me, and lead me in the way everlasting." When He does convict us of sin, we must repent immediately. Repent means to get rid of the sin, not coddle it, or make excuses for it.

LENNY'S STORY

About 1992, after moving to our Wind Chime Drive house in Fort Worth, I learned of an Avon saleslady who lived about 2 miles away. I liked Avon, so I called her. She came to the house, and this is how I met Lenny. Lenny told me that she had an unusual disease in the tips of her fingers. The doctors had set a date for the tips of several of her fingers to be cut off. I loaned her Gloria Copeland's little booklet on healing, which had many Scriptures in it. Lenny said she'd read it. I told Lenny that I would pray for her. In about 10 days, Lenny brought me my Avon order, and gave me the book back saying, "I'm Jewish." I was stunned, but blurted out that God healed Jews too. I reemphasized that I would pray for her.

The next time Lenny came, she told me that the disease had disappeared to the amazement of the doctors, and she did not have to have any surgery. I learned that Lenny was originally from New York, and had married Ed, an Episcopalian. Ed was a kind man. Lenny had attended the big synagogue on Hulen Street in Fort Worth, but when their oldest daughter lost her battle against cancer, she lost all faith in God and in Judaism. But, because my prayer had been answered about her fingers, she told me that one of her daughters was getting a divorce and had to sell her house right away, but that there had been no buyers. I told her I would pray that she sell the house quickly for a good price. Less than a week later, I felt to stop by Lenny's house. We had become friends. She opened the door, grabbed me, and hugged me. Then she proceeded to give me gifts from her garden. She said that the night before, at midnight, a buyer had come to purchase her house, and paid cash.

She was growing in faith. So, she told me about the other daughter who wanted a baby, but something was wrong with her and she couldn't conceive a baby. She told me that her daughter lived with a man. They wanted to get married, but felt they could not because of financial burdens. I told her I could not pray that her daughter get pregnant until she got married. Lenny was mad at me, and let me know it. I told her I had to go by the Bible. She understood, but still was upset. She let me know that it was impossible that they'd ever get married. Within a week, she let me know that her daughter and boyfriend had decided to get married. I told her I was very happy about that, and now I would pray for her to get pregnant. Within two months, she got pregnant. I came home from shopping, and saw a note attached to the front door knob. It was from Lenny. In big letters, she wrote: "I believe!" She wrote that her faith had returned in God, and that she wanted to go back to the synagogue.

I went with her to a bar mitzvah. She very proudly introduced me to all her friends. I heard the rabbi speaking in Hebrew. I leaned over to Lenny and said, "I speak in tongues, and my prayer language has words in it that the rabbi is saying." She said: "Well then, you probably know more Hebrew than I do." Lenny was not ready to believe in Jesus, but she began attending the synagogue. When the baby, a boy, was born, I prayed for him for a long time that he come to know the Jewish Messiah-Savior Yahushua. One day Lenny said she wanted faith like I had. I prayed for that. Her little granddaughter, Fiona, became a friend of my third child. I sometimes think of Lenny, and pray that she has found eternal peace with Elohim.

--GOING THROUGH--
HIS PRESENCE CONQUERS DEATH

I know! I told this before, but I must tell it here again: In 1997, I was up in the mountains of Uganda above Mbale, and got a mosquito bite on the index finger of my right hand. That is the finger that is referenced in Hebrew regarding the Torah, which means, "to shoot out the finger to teach." After that bite, I began having what I thought were flu symptoms. I took painkillers, but still the symptoms wouldn't go away. I was going with my African Director, Vincent, to a new location to minister--in Tanzania. It was an eight-hour bus trip from Kisumu, Kenya to the border town of Sirari, Tanzania. By the time we got to the border I was so weak I could hardly stand up. I began having a fever. I was not going to admit I had malaria. The trip from the border town to Musoma was a long way. At one point, though I could hardly walk, I had to go to the bathroom. There was one horrible concrete structure in the middle of town, open to all, with holes in the concrete. I had to go there. I was so humiliated. We reached the pastor's house in Musoma and I knew I had malaria, but I just laid down on the couch.

PART VIII - Healings and Miracles of Deliverance

The pastors were in the next room talking. I went in there and simply said to them: "I have malaria." You'd think they were shot. They jumped up and ran immediately to get me some "Metakelfin"—a drug made in Italy, used to stop malaria before the fever can break out. It makes one profusely sweat out the disease. But, my case was too far along for the Metakelfin. I was manifesting thirteen of the fifteen symptoms of malaria. They were so scared. The church folk were fasting and praying for me. It wasn't long before I was totally dehydrated, and couldn't keep enough water down. Then I lost my ability to remember my own name. I had a keen sense of Father's presence over me, but I could not think. I was so weak I could not sit up, and it had gone into the final stage of the "black water disease"--blood in the urine. I could eat very little. I craved soda crackers and grape juice, but they had neither in Musoma.

Witchdoctors were walking around the house chanting. I heard the voice of the enemy, which I knew well, saying: "You will never leave Tanzania alive." I asked Father to let me see the face of my youngest daughter one more time. She was living with me in Fort Worth at the time. I could quote Scripture and talk to Him, for those things came from the spirit, not the mind. Finally, my spirit was agitated. Vincent had preached 25 of my 27 meetings. I asked Pastor Joshua to take me to the church and let me preach. I still didn't know my own name, even though I tried to remember. They took me to the church, and propped me up in a chair with pillows. I preached two hours. They took me back and laid me down. That night they took me to the church and I preached another two hours. They took me back and I laid down.

The next morning, I preached two hours. I preached non-stop, with fire and passion. How did I do that? I heard the voice of Yahuweh's Spirit in my spirit (in the belly area, behind my belly button, where the eternal spirit is positioned). It is from the spirit that we hear from Him, receive His impressions, and interact with Him. Our re-born spirit has a mind of its own. I heard His voice, and I repeated what He said, and Joshua translated.

The next day, they set me up in the front seat of a public bus and I was transported back to Kisumu, an eight-hour trip. I didn't want my missionary friends to be astonished at me, or know I was in the final stages of malaria. But, when they opened the door at my knock, they stared at me in fright, and said: "You almost died didn't you?" I had a relapse, but Abba healed me totally. Within two years, I had no sign of malaria in my blood! Later I asked Him why He didn't heal me since I was so used to His healing me for so many things. He said this: **"I wanted you to know what it was like to go through that with just My**

Presence, so that you can go through the tribulation with just My Presence, to the coming of My Son."

THE AFRICAN "CURSE"

Later on, after returning to the U.S., I had reoccurring symptoms of malaria, every night at exactly 6:00 PM. I went to visit a brother in the faith, Mike, and his wife Pat. Mike was powerful in healing and spiritual warfare--a big-sized Indian from Canada. I told him about the reoccurrence of the malaria symptoms. His response was: "Oh great! I've never had the chance to get rid of an African curse before." He commanded that curse off of me, and that night at 6:00 PM, I did not have symptoms of that near-death malaria again.

In 2000, I got another bout of malaria, but this time it wasn't nearly as severe as it was in 1997. I knew to take the medicine before the fever broke out, and it passed quickly. It left me weakened, however, which I allowed to block my assignment to Patmos. I know now that if I had gone on the very day He told me to be on Patmos, that He would have healed me. I regret that. That whole story is in the section "Jordan (2000)."

FATHER KNEW!

There are many ways Abba Yahuweh prevents disease. I had been in and out of Africa, and one thing they suggested was that everyone who came into Uganda should get a yellow fever shot. International shot records were recorded on a yellow "International Vaccination Record" that could be shown at borders. In Uganda, sometimes they asked to see the yellow fever vaccination record. If there were no record, they'd pull out a needle and give the vaccination right there. There was no way of telling if the needle was sterile or not. So, I thought I'd get a vaccination record just in case. On my way to the health clinic, Father spoke to me to get a typhoid fever vaccination. I thought: "What? Father is telling me to get what?" But, I knew His voice. So, I got the vaccine. It was six tablets, two to be taken at a time, two days apart. The vaccine was good for ten years.

I thought it had to do with my next trip to Africa, since typhoid fever is a killer there. It wasn't long before I got to Jordan, when my Swiss friend upstairs decided to move to a newly built apartment building up the hill. I helped her move. My upstairs friend became very ill shortly after she moved. She was put in the hospital and treated for amoebae. She almost died before they found that she had a severe case of typhoid fever. It seems that there was typhoid in the drinking water in the new building. They sent her home to die. The elderly couple that moved in shortly after her were also sick, but not as sick as my friend. I had been in her apartment and drunk the same water, but because of the typhoid vaccine, I did not get typhoid. Father knew! The full story is above in Part VI.

ABBA - HE'S SO PRACTICAL!

One time in Africa, I was in a village that only had a bored well-only 6" deep. The water was therefore polluted greatly. I got terrible diarrhea. I came back to the U.S. at Thanksgiving time, still sick with the diarrhea. I was going with my son to Ft. Smith to my aunt's house for Thanksgiving. All my immediate family was going to be there. But the idea of eating made me feel sick. My son was to pick me up at 9:00 so we could drive up there. I knew to go to the health food store and get some Acidophilus tablets, but they were closed. I was driving back towards my apartment, and Abba spoke to me: **"Go to Braums and get two 8 oz. cups of yogurt."** Brilliant! Why didn't I think of that! I went to Braums and got the vanilla yogurt with live cultures, which had Acidophilus in it. I took them back to my apartment and ate them. Immediately the pains stopped in my stomach, the diarrhea stopped, and I felt terrific. I went to Ft. Smith and ate and ate and ate. How Abba is very practical!

THE MYSTERIOUS ATTACKS

After suffering from knife-like pains in my lower left side, and even being taken in an ambulance to the hospital, thanks to the panic of my four children, no one could find anything that would cause the pain. I knew in my spirit that from July of 2009, it was witchcraft/voodoo. Before going on this trip, which began July 7, 2009, I had a dream. Abba was warning me. I was standing on a balcony of a house that had no railing. I overlooked a large living room below. All of a sudden a man, dressed in a dark suit, wearing a dark hat, burst into the room and fired a machine gun straight up at me, hitting me in the area where the knife-like pain would come in actuality. I felt the bullets hit lightly, as if pushing on my skin. I fell to the ground pretending to be dead. He came up the stairs. I was paralyzed with fear, because there was no blood and I was still breathing. He stood over me, but didn't do anything to me. I woke up. I knew who the man was, a warlock who moved powerfully in demonic projection. But, the network of worldwide witchcraft has made a tight web over the earth, and it is increasing against the set-apart ones of Yahuweh more and more.

While in Texas, after having the meetings in Corpus Christi, I stayed with my son in Fort Worth. I invited my dear friend Karen to come and visit me. We went to the huge Grapevine Mills Mall. After lunch, we went into a store. Coming out of the store, the knife-pain hit me again. She took me to my son's house, where it slowly let up.

Then I had another meeting in the north of Texas. The next morning my hostess took me to the Dallas/Ft. Worth airport about 10:00 AM. I got into the airport, and through security, and then the pain hit again. It was so strong I could hardly breathe. I had to look "normal" or else they wouldn't let me on the airplane. Then they cancelled my 45 minute flight to Arkansas. They put me on a flight 10 hours later. I didn't know what I was going to do. I tried to call my son, but no one answered. I asked Father for help. I walked to the next gate, and there was a lounge chair area. I lay down in the chair, and slowly the pain subsided. I missed the 1:00 PM stand-by. After I missed the second stand-by at 5:00 PM, I decided to get something to eat. I was in line at a barbeque restaurant and heard a voice to my right. I turned and there was my son. He had heard my phone message. He had gotten a pass to come into the airport to see me. We had dinner together, and about 3 hours of fellowship before I got on the 8:30 PM flight to Arkansas. These attacks continued for over two years.

In flying back from Panama into Houston, before going through Immigration, the pains came again so strong that I had to lie down on the floor by my gate. I knew if they thought I was ill, they'd not let me on the plane, so I pretended to be tired. After my children panicked and called an ambulance on January 22, 2011, and the hospital tests found nothing that could cause such a pain, I was sure it was witchcraft, possibly voodoo. Though the attacks were related to witchcraft in Texas, they also manifested in Florida, in Panama, and in Israel. The pains kept coming more frequently and the length longer. Through it all, I have learned absolute dependency on Abba to tell me what to do, how to do it, and how to take care of myself. The complete hospital story, and the story of the heart attack, December 25, 2010, is in **Part VI**. Because of the January 22nd incident, I was restored to peace with my oldest daughter after 30 years of her being hurt towards me. HalleluYah!

ON-THE-JOB TRAINING
SCRIPTURAL SPIRITUAL WARFARE

Throughout my life, I've had many types of healing, and protection from Abba. From age 26, I had three nervous breakdowns because of severe ritualistic satanic abuse, and severe abuse of all types--mentally, emotionally, and physically. I have faced witchcraft multiple times, jezebel/python/anaconda spirits, demons of all ranks, and even Lucifer himself, multitudes of times throughout my life. I have quite an education in spiritual warfare, as you can imagine. The enemy has tried to kill me over and over. His attempts to depress, to slander, to betray, and to kill me are even increasing. The enemy often traps me with people I think are friends, and in situations where I am locked into staying with them and can't get away. Then I find out, by my reaction to their spirits, that they are jezebels and out for my harm. Whenever I am around Jezebel spirits, python/anaconda spirits, I become extremely nervous. So often, because these spirits hide themselves well in nice talk and spirituality, I have had to do much spiritual warfare just to survive and keep breathing. The witchcraft spirits sit hard on the lungs, and choke off breathing, and it feels like my chest is crushing in.

But, my thorough education will really pay off in the dark days to come! I have the equivalent of many PhDs in demonology, Satanism, the plans of Lucifer, and his nature, ways and thinking. I also know well my Master's nature, ways and thinking, so that I can easily tell the difference between the two. Oftentimes, the counterfeit of the real is very subtle, and the two are hard to distinguish apart. That's why people think evil is actually good at times – for the deception of the evil world is incredibly well-hidden. As the powers of darkness try to take over the earth, the targets are those who refuse to bow to the prince of darkness. Few in America – the western world in general – have seen me minister in the power and anointing of the Spirit. If you saw the authority He has given to me in action, you'd know why the enemy is so powerful to try to stop me! I say that in all humility, because it is Yahuweh's authority, and the enemy hates any vessel in which HE flows through!

One of my strongest gifts, because of my training, is discernment of spirits. One time I was going to teach in a meeting, and my host put me up in a house near them. They were house-sitting for a couple who had gone on vacation, and I was allowed to stay there. I found out that the wife was from Jamaica, which says a lot. I got ready for bed, and upon turning out the lights, I felt the presence of demonic spirits at the foot of the bed. They could not come around the bed, but stayed at its foot. I got up to see what gave them the right to be there. Over the door of the bedroom hung a large crystal, and other occult symbols. I took it down and put it in the kitchen, ordered the spirits out, and went to sleep.

If you are a threat to the enemy, the enemy will attack. But, they can't do anything but try to scare you or make life miserable for a while, unless you have left a portal open to them to allow them to stay! The enemy does not attack those who are already under his control. He only attacks if someone is a threat. So many think "the devil's after them", but it is just a matter of reaping what they sowed. Usually, it is Abba trying to teach and discipline lazy people.

THE ONE WHO STOOD BESIDE ME

You've read about my adopted granddaughter, Abby, and her amazing story (2011). One morning, after Abby came home from the hospital, I was sitting in my chair thinking of the troubles to come, and myself in the tunnels under East Jerusalem, as Abba had shown me in a vision in 2010 in Panama. I stopped complaining as I sensed Messiah's Presence coming into our living room near my chair. He softly said: "Yes! But there IS the Garden." I remembered my life-changing vision on Yom Teruah night 2010 in Panama City. I wrote regarding this: "Back Beyond the Garden Gate." My hope is His promises to me of my future, and the future of my family.

Friends came to visit me while I was at my daughter's house in Florida. Yvette had come to join us. We were preparing to go to lunch. I was waiting for my daughter to decide if she wanted to come with us, or not. After they left for the restaurant, that knife-pain in my lower right side came again. My daughter called the others to come back. Tom came in to pray for me, and all the others stayed outside my room. After he finished praying, he asked me who was standing by him praying with him. He said he heard someone praying along side of him. I said "no one" came in.

I had my eyes open. He went out and asked who had come in. No one had come in. I know it was the same One who spoke to me earlier in the morning--my Beloved! I rose off the bed still weak, but went to the restaurant, and was immediately healed after my first sip of raspberry tea, the pain stopped. Don't ask me what raspberry tea had to do with anything (smile), but Ruby Tuesdays raspberry tea is SUPER!

HIS HEALINGS ARE "ON THE LEVEL"

September 2011: The excruciating pain I had for over two years, was continuing, and I was about to leave for Israel again. I was teaching in a meeting in a home in Florida. The lady hosting it knew how to pray for healing. I told her that for a long time, my shirts, blouses, and t-shirts, would fall over my right shoulder, and my bra strap too, because my body was lopsided. Looking at myself in the mirror, I saw that my body leaned to the right. My inner organs were also were falling to the right. I had learned the spring before in Israel, that when I got the pain to begin to praise Abba. Thus the pains were getting less and less frequent, but I had two severe attacks in early September. It was the patterns of the pain that let me know witchcraft/voodoo was involved.

Before the meeting, this lady called me into the bedroom to pray for me. She has the same methodology as June Joyner. She quietly put her hand on my lower back between my hips. She simply and quietly, but firmly, commanded the spine to line up straight. The lady whose house we were meeting in was also in the room, and she can testify to this too: I felt my whole back, from the hips to the neck, rotating to the left. It was a slow moving process. It could be seen by the other ladies. Then she commanded any spirits of Kundalini, which I may have picked up, to leave my spine. I may have come in contact with them when I attended "revival" meetings in Texas. Oh the things we suffer from ignorance! After this, I was standing so much straighter than before. I looked in the mirror and my shoulders were level. HalleluYah! The healing has remained, because it was from Abba!

TESTIFY!

If Abba has healed you, write an article about it and share it with everyone you know – at your church, your congregation, your social club – wherever people will gain faith by your testimony!

I KNOW "WHO THIS IS"

NOTE: In my writings, and in face-to-face teaching, I sometimes say "Abba said"…, or "He led me to" … There are forty different ways at least, with precedent in the Word, that He speaks to His people! He taught me to hear Him since age 4. Yahuweh is a Person. Yahushua is a Person. They talk! They have voices. They talked to people all through the Scriptures. But, of course, They never say anything outside of Their nature, ways, and thinking, but only in line with Their whole Word--start to finish. So, what's so weird about hearing Him if one knows Him? He mostly speaks to us through the Word, as He teaches, or by impression to the spirit. He speaks into the spirit – not to the head. People do not hear Elohim so often, because they only go by what their head, or emotions, dictate. They do not live by the mind of their eternal re-born spirit (in the loins area of our body). They want to control their own lives, and only include Him when it suits their agenda. Yahuweh is Spirit. He speaks from within our re-born spirit that is a portal to the eternal realm – if we keep it open.

Our reasoning mind and our emotions are so unstable that they are always in flux. So, He speaks to the re-born spirit. He only speaks based on His written Word. That's how you know it is Elohim speaking. But, also we must know Them by knowing Their nature, ways and thinking, as well as the nature, ways, and thinking of the enemy (Lucifer/Satan) because he's a counterfeiter. So, once you know someone's voice – what's so weird about trusting and knowing them? Is it weird if your wife or husband or friend calls you on the phone? Do you ask: "Who is this?" I don't have to ask "who is this" when Yahuweh or Yahushua speak, either!

PART IX
PERSONAL STORIES OF HELP ALONG THE ROADSIDE
THE 40 MILES PER GALLON MIRACLE

I told you about the miracle between Amboy and San Bernardino in our 1949 Hudson of His stretching gas, but it bears repeating here with a speck more detail. It was my first experience in seeing Abba work miracles. I was about six at the time. My parents and I had been on a very long trip across America. Our Hudson had broken down in Alabama, but Abba had someone right there to help us get the car to a mechanic who fixed it. Yahuweh says, and Yahushua says: "I will never leave you or forsake you." The word "forsake", in Hebrew picture language, means to "strand along the roadside with no help." He will never leave us without help, IF we call on Him to help us! (Hebrews 13:5)

In returning to California, we entered the California desert at night. My parents saw that the gas tank was sitting on empty when we reached a little town called Amboy. The town consisted of a gas station, a store, and a few houses, out in the middle of the California desert. My parents had no cash for the 15-cent, or 19-cent-a-gallon, gas. They wouldn't take a check. So, my parents asked me if I had any money. I had about 20 cents. We bought 20 cents worth of gas and headed out 40 miles across the desert towards San Bernardino, on a very lonely two-lane road. I stood in the backseat and kept my eyes on the gas gauge. It never moved. A 1949 Hudson, at that time, only averaged 12 miles per gallon. When we got into San Bernardino, they found a gas station that took checks.

STORIES OF OLD CAR BREAKDOWNS
ABBA SAYS: "I JUST LOVE HELPIN' FOLKS"

Back in my college days, I went with my friend David to San Diego to visit his brother. He and I went to college at BIOLA--about two hours drive from San Diego. It was late when we left San Diego to return to school. We chose to take the faster new freeway. It had few lights on it, but saw no traffic at all. It was one lonely stretch of road. And it was night. We were out in the middle of no-where with no cars in sight, and all of a sudden we heard an awful noise as the car blew two rods and shut down totally. David had forgotten to put oil in his old car--and it was ruined. He jerked the car to the side of the road, as it stopped. We looked up and just a few feet away we saw a wrecker. I'm not kidding! I do not make up or exaggerate any stories! The wrecker had come to help another car that was stranded. I had to push my friend out of the car to go talk to the wrecker-driver, because he was in shock. He came back and said that the wrecker-driver would tow us in into Santa Ana, ahead of the other car. We got to Santa Ana and left the car to be sold for parts. We got the last bus going to La Mirada. I have a history of old car breakdowns, running out of gas, and having to pull along side of roads. Never has He left me stranded with no help!

One morning, in North Carolina, I was heading to work. It was 3 degrees F outside, and I ran out of gas. I had my youngest baby in the car. I saw no life on the road but a red fox. All of a sudden, a car came on the other side of the meridian. The driver saw me and pulled around next to me. An old farmer got out and asked if he could help. I told him I needed gas. He said, "I just love helpin' folks." He took me to get gas, and then I went on to work.

In all the years of having old cars, breakdowns, and being left on the side of the road--never have I been left more than a few minutes before help came. Sometimes, I'd run out of gas because we didn't have money to get any until payday, and someone would come and give me enough gas to get home.

In 1974, when we moved from California to North Carolina, we had an old car, and we were pulling a medium-sized U-Haul. We got as far as Arizona, when, out in the middle of nowhere in the desert, we had a flat tire. We pulled to the side of the road. There, right in front of us, was a house-trailer. We went to see if anyone was there, and a friendly man came out. He had the right tool--a heavy-duty "jack"--and helped us put on a new tire. Now tell me, what are the odds of us pulling right next to a guy out in the middle of nowhere, who just so happened to have the right tool?

Later on that trip, we were in Tennessee on a lonely stretch of road and a tire blew on the U-Haul we were pulling. All around us was forest. It was a lonely stretch of freeway. But, just ahead of us was an off-ramp leading into what looked like more forest. We prayed over our U-Haul, which contained all we owned, and detached it from the car, and went up the hill to see if there was a sign of anyone who could help. When we got to the top of the hill, we looked down in shock. The only thing in sight was a large U-Haul dealership. Yes, I'm telling you the truth! I told you my life was full of miracles! Not one tiny detail is exaggerated! They came out and fixed the tire, and we were on our way to our little cabin in North Carolina.

THE LITTLE CABIN TO THE BIG FARMHOUSE

But, when we got to the little cabin we'd reserved, all of our things didn't fit. So we took them to a relative's house and put most of our few belongings out in an open space, exposed to rain and theft. The next morning, we explained our predicament to our new landlady. She said that she had a friend who was renting their house. She directed us to this house. We were told that several people had already put in their bids to rent the house. But, when I mentioned my Aunt Fairy--who had grown up in Andrews (the next town north of Murphy) to this "friend", who was the sister of the owner of the house-- she was shocked with happiness. Aunt Fairy was one of her best friends. She said, "You're family--the house is yours." He not only doesn't leave us stranded along the roadside, He makes sure we have safe and decent lodging on our journey. Oh how nice to get our belongings and take them into a large farm house with a huge front yard, a field for a huge garden, and a driveway up to what became my precious friend's house.

MOVE THAT CAR! - A "WORD OF KNOWLEDGE" STORY

Shortly after being baptized into the Holy Spirit, in late 1966, my husband and I were going to meet some friends and go hand out Gospel tracts and witness about Jesus in Los Angeles' Chinese district. One of the "gifts" of the Spirit that I've had since childhood is the "word of knowledge." It has saved my life, my children's lives, and saved me a multitude of grief, anxiety, and worry. As we parked our car at the bottom of a hill, the Spirit impressed me to have my husband move the car a few car-lengths forward. My husband moved the car forward until I felt it was OK to park it. We went on to China Town. When we came back several hours later, we noticed the police were there by a totally smashed car, parked exactly where we had originally parked. We found out that a car at the top of the hill had lost its breaks and come down the hill and hit the car broadside. Of course, our car was just fine. It is always smart to hear from Yahuweh's Spirit, and obey right away!

"KAPUT" BUT NOT FORGOTTEN

My husband and I had gone to Germany after the birth of our second grandson. Our son was in the Air Force. We took a trip to Luxemburg. Our son was driving a friend's car, since his own had been wrecked in a very bad accident. On the way out of Luxemburg, the car made a loud noise and we pulled over to the side of the road and stopped. The car was kaput. The temperature was getting below freezing and the sun was going down, and besides that, it is illegal to stop on the autobahn. A couple of people stopped to see if they could help. They really tried, but it was to no avail. Then an older couple stopped, and we asked them to send a wrecker. It was getting colder, and darker. All that came out of my mouth to pray was: "Thank you Father; thank you Father." I said that over and over. I was tapping into a secret of His that He later explained more fully. After about an hour there, a wrecker came and towed us into Luxemburg city to a garage. My son called one of his superior officers who had become a friend. He was a born again brother. He came with another born again brother-friend from the Base at Spangdahlem, Germany. The officer took us to his home, where his wife fed us dinner. Then they gave us money to pay for the car repair. I had never known such real love in action from brothers and sisters in Messiah. I was in awe over it for years. In three days, the car was ready to be picked up. Their pastor went to get it, and even gave us more money to pay for the repairs. We had spoken at his church, so he got involved in our plight.

He never strands us. But, most people panic and grab on to somebody for help, before they give Him a chance to do what He does best. Don't panic! Boldly wait on His instructions, in peace. He says that He helps us through helpers He sends. Let your helpers be those that He chooses! When He chooses someone to help us, He knows them, and He knows they won't turn their back on us later on.

A PERILOUS TREK - A PROTECTIVE ABBA

I was in Uganda. I was going with a lady to her home village up above Sipi Falls, high up above Mbale, for a week of meetings. I knew that we had to leave early in the morning, but she kept fooling around with trivial things, even though I kept trying to hurry her up. I told her that if we did not get up the mountain quickly, the rains would stop us. We had hired a long-bed truck. The window on my side was broken. We headed up the mountain. As we got towards the area, the heavens opened up with hard rain and large balls of hail. And, we were on dirt roads. The hail was bouncing into my lap. We were on a steep incline. It was a sheer drop-off on the right side, and jungle on the left side.

All around, waterfalls were cascading down the mountains. We started to slide to the left. All of a sudden, about thirty men came to hold the truck up. I was about ten inches from the dirt ... we were almost totally on our side. This had happened before in going up a mountain in Uganda, so I just watched the dirt as it got closer and closer. They got the truck up-right, but then it started sliding to the right. They held it in place. About that time, another truck was sliding down the hill. Praise Him, it missed us. I had practice in this, so I was totally calm.

We got up to the village. The village was very remote. As we came into the village, we saw signs in English, Mt. Gerazim this, and El Shaddai that, and on and on with Hebrew names. When we got to our hostesses' house, and got settled into our stick-house room, we had tea. An old man, leaning on a cane, came to see us. I was introduced as having come from Jordan. He said, "Oh, you must tell us about our people. We hear on the short wave that there is trouble in Israel." Later on, the pastor of the church came to meet me. He said, "Above all things, you must tell us about Israel." The union of the Queen of Sheba and Solomon produced Menelek, who left Jerusalem and settled in Ethiopia. Did you ever wonder why the courier of Queen Candace from Ethiopia was reading **Isaiah 53**, when he encountered Philip in **Acts 8**? I was with many of this Bantu tribe in Kenya and Uganda.

BE OF GOOD CHEER!
ABBA GETS YOU WHERE YOUR GOING

During my nearly 400 flights in the last 30 years, I have had several airlines that stranded me--some because of mechanical failure, some because of being late arriving, making my next connection impossible, some because of bad weather. But, through it all, I was not stranded without help! Again: The word "forsaken" means to "strand along the roadside with NO HELP." He never forsakes us. **"In this world you will have tribulation, but be of good cheer, I have overcome the world." "And this is the victory that overcomes the world – even our faith."** (John 16:33b; I John 5:4b)

My papa requested that **I John 5:4b** be put on his grave stone. Ken's wife used to sing this song: "Ain't No Grave Gonna Hold My Body Down." Every time, upon visiting his grave, I would "hear" him sing that song from the eternal realm. When the resurrection of the justified dead takes place, and his soul-spirit body is restored to his natural transformed body, he will arise in victory, for he had victory before he died – he died in faith!

When my flight out of Tyler, Texas, in 2009, was so late leaving that it affected my flight out of Dallas to Tampa, my son was there to pick me up at D/FW and take me to his house nearby to spend the night. Then American Airlines put me in First Class for my return flight to Tampa. In going to Israel this time, the plane was delayed out of Tampa to New York. If the plane didn't come before they said it would, I would have missed my flight to Tel Aviv. I told them I could not sit so far back on the plane, first because of my sprained ankle, and because I'd need to get through Israeli security at JFK before getting on the plane to Tel Aviv. I sat in the wheelchair waiting, praying the plane would come early. The plane came early. They changed my seating all right – from 28 C to 1 A – First Class.

I've had some very close calls – as I wrote about in "Training Mission – A Day in the Life of Yedidah." But, when I am on assignment for Him, He even does the miraculous at times to get me where I am going. I tell more air-flight stories in Parts V and VI. In Part VI, I told about Abba literally backing up time for me, so that I could get to my bus in London on time and get to Wales on time.

One thing that has always amazed me is that no matter when I started on a trip, whether by car, plane, bus, train, or boat, I always get where I am going on time. I remember when Pastor Mark Kegohi came to Texas, from Kenya. Ruth and I were taking him to Kenneth Copeland Ministries. We were due to be there at 2:00 PM to get our tour. So many things happened to delay us – getting seriously lost, and having an enraged driver after us, and having to stop for several reasons. But, at exactly 2:00 PM, we drove up and parked in the parking lot of Kenneth Copeland Ministries.

I've had so many flights that left late and arrived early. His intervention, as I am about His business, has been a life-pattern. It has to do with exact timing. Abba respects those that do not waste time. He commands us not to waste time, but to "redeem it, for the days are evil." I guard time. I am disciplined. I do not waste time. Guarding time has to do with integrity and self-respect. Never tell someone you'll be somewhere at a certain time, and not be there. If you are supposed to be somewhere at a certain time, leave early. Being late as a habit is a sign of laziness, apathy, lack of discipline, or an "I don't care" attitude. It is those who are disciplined to guard time that Abba can use to be productive on His time-table.

I am a watchman. I record events by date and time. Ezekiel, the Prophet, was called to be a watchman, so he did the same thing. What if Abba was sloppy with His timing in regards to helping us? We are to emulate our Master! What if we are sloppy in performing our work-tasks in the secular work-world? We'd get fired. Because I have been astute to guard time, I can tell what time it is in the middle of the night, without first looking at the clock. Upon checking the clock, it is usually either right on, or within 1-4 minutes difference.

In studying end-time prophecy for about 48 years, watching and reporting, I have had to know His timing of events. Now, it is imperative that I know timing! Otherwise, I will not know what He is doing, and that would be disastrous for me, as well as for those that I teach, warn, and advise. My constant prayer is that He will make sure I am not a false prophet!

I travel almost exclusively alone to do what Father has called me to do. Of course, upon getting to where I am going, people meet me, or I have a rented place to go to. In all these places, He has given me protection from harm. And even though I've been in the midst of harm many times, the knowledge of His presence has been manifested so strongly that I have known I was not alone! Because I know His power to help me and my family, I have had boldness in many places by myself to help others.

A TYPICAL DAY IN THE LIFE OF THE "GOOD AND FAITHFUL"

I know this story is in Part VI, but here it is again with a few more details: In May 2001, after spending a week on the isle of Patmos, I had gone by ship into the port at Athens. I had reserved a hotel downtown near the Parthenon. I went to ancient Corinth by bus. The next morning, I was preparing to fly out to Amman. I went down to breakfast, and asked the waiter where I could get the bus for the airport. He said there was a strike, and all transportation was on strike. Even the Parthenon was shut down. I sat there stunned, not knowing what to do. I looked out the window and saw across the street, a man sitting in a travel agency. I went over to talk to him. He said that everything was shut down, even flights, except flights that only went out every 3-4 days. He checked my flight and saw that my flight, which went out every three days, was still OK. But, how do I get there?

He said there was a friend of his in a travel agency around the corner who knew a man who would take people to the airport. I went to that agency. He called, and the man said he'd take me at 3:00 PM. His price for the service was $20.00. I only had Jordanian Dinar. I was out of all other money. All the banks were closed, and as I went to the Parthenon and walked along the streets, I saw that all the exchange places were closed too. I walked up one street near the hotel, turned the corner, and there was an exchange place open. But, here I was in Greece. What are the odds of them exchanging Jordanian Dinar for US dollars in Greece? I looked at the list of currencies they offered. Number three was Jordanian Dinar. I really am telling the truth in all these details--not one exaggeration. I met the man at 3:00. He was a handsome Greek man driving a black Mercedes. All the way to the airport he leaned out the window waving his fist at other drivers and yelling. I noticed the other drivers did that too. But, he got me to the airport, and I plopped a $20.00 bill in his hand. As I got on the plane, after a week of doing what He told me to do there, I relaxed in my seat, and heard the familiar voice of Yahushua say: **"Well done, good and faithful servant.**" That's what we want to hear at the end of our earthly life! But, there is a high price to be paid for that!

THE VOICE IN THE BACKSEAT

Abba has let me know when one of my children was in danger. Abba would wake me up to pray, and give me a vision of what was happening. Later they would tell me what happened.

One day my youngest was on a two-lane road. All of a sudden she heard a man's voice from the backseat demanding that she pull over--NOW! She was so scared. She pulled over. Just as she did, two cars came racing down towards her, one in each lane, like crazy men. If she had not pulled over, she would be dead. She got out of the car and saw no one in the backseat. She called me shaking: "MOM I HEARD THE VOICE OF GOD."

TAKE THE WHEEL ABBA, I'M A BAD DRIVER!
A TESTIMONY TO A PERFECT DRIVING RECORD

This next story encompasses healing, perfect timing, and help along the roadside. I told this in Part VI, but I tell it here again in more detail, for it stands alone as an example of Abba's goodness to His servant. Abba sent me to Jerusalem to intercede for eighteen things at the Western Wall, the night of Yom Teruah, September 12, 2007. During that time, I had walked down the many stone steps going to the Wall from the Jewish Quarter, and back up. I had a brace on my knee, but it was a new type. It was not a wrap-around type, but a type that I pulled up over the knee. It had a little hole for the knee to move in. It braced the two sides but not the knee cap itself. The evening of the 12th, after returning from the Wall, I sat in my bed at Christ Church Guesthouse at the Jaffa Gate in Jerusalem and wrote: "The September 12, 2007 Report From Jerusalem." I was going to post it the day of Yom Teruah, the 13th, to all on my address list. The next morning I felt an urgency to edit the article and send it. Many on my address list understood the history-making turn of world events on that day. As I got ready to go downstairs to the courtyard, where the wireless service was the best, my knee popped forward and I fell onto the bed. I had torn tendons and ligaments that had not been torn before. I was stunned. I could hardly walk.

How was I going to go down to the courtyard with my heavy computer, and then to Tiberias the next day on the bus? I also had my suitcases with me from America, for I just came from the airport. But, having a strong will, I packed up the computer and hobbled downstairs to the garden courtyard to send the article. I had just paid for 30 minutes of wireless service, and was going to begin the sending process, when a man came to my table. He said: "Yedidah"? I looked at him and did not recognize him. I said "yes." He said, "It's John." I was perplexed. John who? He said: "We met at Grace's house in Florida when you had the meeting there." I exclaimed: "JOHN!" I said: "I'm sorry, you're out of

PART IX - Help Along the Roadside

context; I didn't recognize you. What are you doing in Jerusalem?" He said that Abba had sent him to Israel. He said Abba had directed him to stay at the Imperial Hotel, just around the corner. He had come to Christ Church for breakfast. The Word says that He "orders our steps" if we are walking daily in His path in obedience to Him! I asked if he could come back in 30 minutes and he said "yes." After sending the article, John returned. His first words to me were, "Is there anything I can do for you"? I laughed. I said that I had hurt my knee, and could he help me to the bus the next day. He said, "I'll help you to the bus, and I'll go with you to Tiberias if you want me to." I called John "my knight in shining armor." He was my gift from Yahuweh. Because the daylight savings time "fell back an hour," he was there an hour early the next morning. I arranged for a taxi to take me to the bus station. He helped me with all my stuff to the bus, put my things underneath, and then I told him "goodbye."

When I got to Tiberias, a nice taxi man was there to help me. I got to my new location to stay. Oh the perfect timing of His servants who flow in His will! Because I had hurt my knee, I stayed in the lovely apartment overlooking the "Sea of Galilee" for most of three months, and only ventured to the store when absolutely necessary to get groceries. I was "house sitting" for a lady who was in Canada, so it was a free stay. I wrote some of my best articles, as I looked over Lake Kinneret (Sea of Galilee). During that time, I got up to see the sunrise for six weeks straight. I wrote "The Sunrise Lessons" from that experience. What the Devil means for evil, Abba turns it for good!

We never need to fear anything. Abba is in control – IF we let Him have control of us. If we take control over our own life, He steps back. He will not help us if we try to usurp His authority over our lives. The wisest thing to do is to "die" to self-will, and submit to His leading. **Romans 8:14**: "They that are led by the Spirit--they are the sons of Yahuweh." So, it stands to reason that those not led by His Spirit are not His sons. Only those that come out of all worldly defilement can claim Him as their Abba (Father/Daddy) -- **II Corinthians 6:14-7:1**. It is very clear throughout the whole Tenach and Messianic Writings, that He is the Elohim of Light. As light cannot allow darkness in its presence by its very nature, neither can He allow sin in His presence. He has to be as exclusive as light is. But, in Him are no gray areas! He hates a mixture – so, as in **Genesis 1:4**, He divides the light from the darkness, and we have to take sides.

I will conclude my stories of roadside experiences here. There are many more to be told, but these are samples of some main ones. I hope you are encouraged by reading of my learning experiences, so that you might seek to know Him for yourself, so that you can write testimonies of what He has done for you, and share them with others who need encouragement. (**I Corinthians 1:3-10**)

PART X

STORM STOPPING MIRACLES

Another faith principle is to be found in Mark 4:35-5:1. It is the story of the storm at sea, and how Messiah calmed the storm. Mark 4:35: "...Let us pass over and go to the other side." Mark 5:1: "And they came over unto the other side of the sea, into the country of the Gadarenes." What happened in Mark 4:36-41? There was a severe storm on the Sea of Galilee. Messiah was asleep. Water was filling the boat. The disciples panicked. They woke Messiah up. He was quite disgusted with their lack of faith. He commanded the wind and waves to stop, which they did. Then He mildly rebuked the disciples asking them where their faith went. They were shocked. Who is this who can command the wind and the waves?

Since my 20s, I have taken this to mean that He gives His trusted ones authority, even over natural forces – IF those natural forces get in the way of His will being done! In such cases, I have commanded storms and hail, tornado winds, and other types of weather to stop for the purposes of ministering His Word, and He has always immediately stopped the hindering weather.

COMMANDING THE RAINS - A FIRST TIME EXPERIENCE

Back in 1967, I had written, and was to direct and be the pianist for, a Christmas play at Village Christian School in Sun Valley, California, where I worked as a second grade teacher. The play carried an evangelistic message. About 700 children were participating. The weather man predicted rain for that night, and the children would be standing outside a lot to come and go during the performance. I also knew unsaved parents would be there. It was an important ministry outreach. The theme was "Christ Was Born to Save", from an old English Christmas hymn we were to sing that night.

It was my first experience with commanding weather, but I prayed all afternoon, commanding the rains to stop. Just about two hours before the children were to line up outside the auditorium, the rains stopped. They did not start again until later that night after everyone got home. When it comes to His business, He will step in to stop storms, stop people, stop circumstances, stop wars, stop disease, stop death--stop all kinds of things so that His servants keep moving forward with His will! He is practical!

RAINS GIVE WAY TO THE SPIRIT

In 1997, in Uganda, I was high on a mountain, having a week long conference in a mud-hut village. It was storming and the people had to walk long distances over swollen rivers and streams, which were dangerous because logs would often come down the rivers swiftly. I commanded the rain to stop. The rains stopped, people made it safely, and many were saved and filled with the Ruach Yahuweh. Even former witchdoctors walked down from the mountains to be filled with Yahuweh's Spirit.

A CHICKEN SCARF AND THE RAINS THAT OBEYED

In 1998, my youngest daughter and I were in Bumbo, a remote village up in the mountains above Mbale, Uganda. The village was reached by crossing a stream on two wooden planks laid across the banks. There had been much flooding. We had to preach a meeting that next day out in the open air, and then go to another village to preach. It was 3:00 AM and I was asleep. The rains began. My daughter woke up and began to pray. I woke up. I felt a nice warm chicken cuddled up around my neck. How sweet! I laid there and prayed. Then we heard African women praying in the next room. They have no ceilings in their houses, so we all heard each other well. The next morning, the rain had stopped, we had our evangelistic meeting, and we were able to carry on. We crossed the stream OK in leaving the village.

A HUNGER FOR THE WORD - NOTHING SHALL STOP IT

In Uganda, I was having a series of meetings in a very remote area north of Mbale. It had been raining and the rivers were swollen. A man, simply known as Pastor John, had been preaching to witchdoctors and their friends up high in a mountain. It was a miracle that they got to me, because tree branches, some of them logs, came rushing down the streams and rivers, making the trek very dangerous. But, we prayed them through. John only had a "New Testament." He heard I was there, and he and the born again witchdoctors, forded the rivers, to come. He brought them to me so that they might be filled with the Spirit. One of the first things he told me was that daily they pray for the peace of Jerusalem. I asked him how he knew to do that. He said: It is just in us to do that. He had no idea of Psalm 122:6! I learned that these Bantu people were descendants of the Ethiopian Jews. I found them in many places in Uganda. There are several tribes in Kenya and Uganda who trace their heritage to Israel.

It is so common in third world nations for people to walk for many miles, even for days, in all types of severe weather, to hear the teaching of the Word, and to receive from Abba what only He can do for them. I get so angry at the lazy westerners who look at their watches after an hour of teaching, or fall asleep during the teaching. I talked to a man who went to China with Open Doors to teach the book of Matthew. Those meeting with him had come long distances. It was also very dangerous. If they were discovered, they'd all be killed. He said he taught for many hours, and was so tired. They brought him a mat, and he laid down on it and fell asleep. Two hours later, he woke up and they were still sitting there waiting for more teaching. He said he taught for as much as 18 hours a day, plus answered questions. Some walked from the north of China to the south to find one Bible.

ON ASSIGNMENT WITH ABBA
ANOTHER PICTURE PERFECT DAY

In 2006, Abba gave me a definite assignment to begin what would be years of intercession over the Gulf of Mexico, at the mouths of the main rivers of Texas, and from Corpus Christi to Key West. I went to Alaska, to the Ohio and Kentucky Rivers, and to the Atlantic Ocean. He took me to the Red River, the tributaries that came into Caddo Lake, and to the Mississippi River. He had me cover all the major exit points out of the U.S. But, initially, He said to do three trips to three locations, three days each, to the mouths of the four major rivers of Texas in the month of June. I finished June 30th.

The second trip was to go back to Houston, to Galveston Island, and across to Freeport. He assigned 1-2 friends to go with me on each trip. This second trip, I had asked Lori to go with me. Her husband, Norman, had agreed to let her drive their truck. But, that whole week before, Houston was totally flooded, and more storms were to come and more flooding. So, the night before we were to leave, the weather man said that Houston was forecasted to get more storms the next day, with more flooding. I said: "No! We will have nothing but white fluffy clouds, blue skies, and sunshine, with no flooding." But, Lori's husband was skeptical. Still, he did not cancel the trip. He knew me. The next morning on the 6:00 AM weather news, the lady covering the story was standing in Houston. She said: "We don't know what happened, but the rains not only stopped, the flooding has cleared out." I just stood there and smiled. We went and had three lovely days. But, I failed to pray about our exit (smile). We got into Houston from Freeport at rush-hour traffic, and the skies opened up and there was so much rain that it was a miracle that we didn't get in a wreck. It took us two hours to get out of Houston.

In 2010, Abba gave me a seven place assignment to take what Enoch gave to the fallen ones over 5,000 years ago, and tell them that the time of their judgment was near. He gave me six of the seven places, and surprised me with one. The logistics for these series of trips was horrendous. I was living in Panama then and it was harder to do the logistics from there.

The third assignment was to go to Tiahuanaco – about an hour's drive from La Paz, Bolivia. That was the hardest trip I have ever planned for. Yet, the hand of Abba was so strong on these trips. Tiahuanaco is the oldest known city ruins in existence, and is on the top of the Andes at over 13,000 feet. Just before Sharon and I went, the hotel sent her an update on the weather. It was March. They said that the weather during the two days of our stay was supposed to be below zero, icy, and with snow, making the roads impassable. I told my friend, "It will be above 40 degrees. I'm thinking Fahrenheit, not Celsius. I did not specify. We got there at 4:00 AM. The day dawned on a lovely sunny day with no clouds in the sky. We went shopping that afternoon. The next day we got up to go to Tiahuanaco, and it was gorgeous. I think it must have been 40 Celsius--hot. Abba has such a sense of humor! We went to Puma Punta.

Then our wonderful taxi man from the hotel took us all around the Bolivian side of Lake Titicaca. It was a gorgeous day from start to finish. The next morning we got up and went to the airport. Our plane was supposed to leave at 6:30. The captain came on the loud speaker and said that we had to wait an hour at least, because of all the foul weather that had moved in. My friend and I looked at each other and laughed. Fun with Father! That trip took us on seven different one-way flights in 4 days. I was staying in Panama, but had to fly out of, and into, Miami to get to La Paz. We got to Miami in just enough time to go through customs, and to get to our individual gates to go home. The captain came on and said: "There are dignitaries in the area; we have to wait about 30 minutes." I began praying in one of my prayer languages. In English, I said: "Abba Your dignitaries are here, and we need to get out of this plane." In ten minutes the captain began pulling the plane forward. He said: "If you look off of our right wing tip, you will see Air Force One." Abba's dignitaries got Obama to move out quick! He had come to visit the Governor of Florida. There is much more about this trip and the 7-point assignment (2010) in Part VI.

In November in Israel, 2012, I, and a family of six were going to do intercession across the North. The forecast had said severe thunder storms all that week. The Orthodox Jews had come from Jerusalem to the north to pray for rain, and wow, when they do that, Elohim sends rain! We were scheduled to go on Tuesday. It had been storming for days. It stormed on Monday. But, I told my friends that on Tuesday it would be sunny and lovely for us. On Tuesday it was sunny and lovely for us! On Wednesday it started raining again for more days. Abba makes sure His servants are cared for!

In 1999, I went to Russia from mid-September to mid-December. It was 30 below zero, and even the major rivers froze up. My translator was Russian born and lived in the area that Abba sent me. She said we would not be able to do much in the winter, because the roads froze over too, and often were impassable. She said it would snow day and night, and the temperatures dropped below zero. I told her that for the three months I would be there, every day would be clear skies, sunny and the roads totally passable no matter where we went. Well, being a traditional Christian she mocked that. Every day, for three months, I woke up and said to her: "Another beautiful day!" She got madder by the day. Each night it would snow, and the road crews would clear the roads. So, by morning, we were able to get out and do what Abba said to do.

EVEN THE VOLCANOES OBEY HIM!

I had horribly twisted my left knee, which stayed out of place just long enough to do a lot of damage. When I could get out of the apartment, I walked with a cane. While recuperating, Abba brought Jews to me. But, He healed me fast, and I was able to walk to places that opened up a large portion of eastern Russia for Jewish Aliyah, even up seven flights of stairs in one apartment building, several times. He is a great Healer! I remember walking back towards our apartment building one night with all my warm clothing on. But, my forehead was exposed. I felt it freeze. Not a pleasant feeling! But, there was not one day that was not clear and sunny the whole time I was there. PRAISE ABBA!

In March 2010, I was to fly into London, go to Wales to do intercession over Stonehenge, fly on to Germany, and then to Israel. Just a short time before I was to fly out of the U.S. for London, beginning around March 21st, the Iceland volcano Eyjafjallajokull erupted, spewing ash into the air over the UK and Europe. By April, all of Europe was shut down from the spewing ash. I held on, knowing my trip was ordered by Abba. But, the news was very negative. The Heathrow airport in London, and airports all across Europe were shut down, stranding many passengers for a long time. Then the air traffic controllers were not letting planes fly for days even after the ash was known to have lifted off. Less than a week before I was to fly out in early April, the airspaces were cleared and the planes began to fly again.

May 21st, 2011, I was in Israel. The Grimsvotn volcano, more powerful than the Eyjafjallajokull volcano, erupted, spewing ash towards Glasgow, Berlin, and London--the three airports I needed to fly through. I was to fly through Germany's Tegel airport, then to Heathrow, go to Wales, then take the train to Glasgow to get the plane for Stornoway, Outer Hebrides. All were shut down. I had only five days before I had to leave. I saw articles on the

Internet that showed people standing in line in Tegel waiting to rebook their flight.

I said: "OK Abba, You told me You would guide my travel by what You had seen (Psalm 32:7-8), so `put a plug in it' and stop that thing from erupting." I kept asking Him to plug it up.

I rely heavily on **Psalm 32:7-8** in the Artscroll *Tehillim*: King David said: **"You are a shelter to me; from distress You preserve me. With glad song of rescue you envelop me. [Yahuweh says] `I will educate you and enlighten you in the proper path to travel. I will advise you with what I have seen.'"**

The next day, the UK headlines told a perplexing story. For some reason, the volcano stopped erupting and was only putting out steam. But, the air traffic controllers still wouldn't let the planes fly. The day I was to leave for my trip, the planes started flying again. Oh the goodness of Yahuweh! He never leads us to strand us! He will not forsake us – i.e. leave us in the airport with no flight. Yet, we must be in contact with Him all the time, and use our authority on earth to bring His will into the earth. Mankind as a whole shut Him out, so His mankind, those that know Him as Abba, have to bring Him in. That's true intercession!

EVEN THE WINDS OBEY HIM!

One time I was supposed to fly from Miami to Panama. I was living in Panama at that time. A hurricane was coming across Miami on the very day I was to fly. The day before, I prayed: "Abba, turn the hurricane back East--back where it came from." The next morning, I saw that the Miami airport was still functioning OK. So, I went to check in at the Tampa airport to fly to Miami. As I did, I asked the man who checked me in how the weather was over the Caribbean. He said it was fine. He said: "Something happened last night that turned the hurricane east, and sent it back where it came from." I really worked hard not to laugh! Isn't Abba fun! People who live in their own self-created security boxes never know the thrill of having security in Him. Oh the joys of knowing Him well enough to lean on Him for all support!

In 1995, while we were living on Wind Chime Drive in Fort Worth, Texas, I felt strongly to stay up late to pray. Everyone else had gone to sleep. I did not turn on a light, but paced back and forth in the living room praying. About midnight, a terrific lightning storm began. Then I heard the familiar sound of a tornado. The winds increased in sound and intensity. I kept praying, rebuking the storm, and proclaiming that it would not harm us. The tornado sound (like a freight train rumbling across the tracks) grew louder and louder. The lightning and thunder grew stronger. But, I had peace. About an hour later, it was quiet and still again. I went to bed. The next morning, I went out to take a walk. I saw that a few leaves from a tree in our yard had blown off in the wind. But, all down our street I saw roofs that had been damaged or totally blown off, trees that had been uprooted, and damage of all sorts done to almost every home. A tornado, indeed, had gone down Wind Chime Drive, but we had only a few leaves in our driveway.

PART XI

STORIES OF PROTECTION AND RESCUE

WHERE'S MY CHILD?! - ABBA KNEW

One day our third child didn't come home from school. She was in the sixth grade at Wedgwood Middle School. I called the bus company--they said she didn't get on the bus. I called her friends. They said they had not seen her. I called the school. They did not answer. The school was in a bad neighborhood--drug peddling and rape were not uncommon in that area. I panicked! I had no idea where she might be. In my panic, my mind shut down--I couldn't think clearly. Father's Spirit cut across the panic in my head, and spoke into my eternal spirit. He showed me a vision of her sitting with her head cradled in her hands, hands on her knees, on the steps of the school. He spoke to my spirit: "She's sitting on the school steps, go get her." I was crying so hard. I said to Him: "You'd better be right." I grabbed my keys and drove to the school. There she was, sitting exactly as I saw her in the vision. She had missed the bus, and when she went back to call me, the school was locked.

I've written a lot on what happens when the mind shuts down. If we don't know how to live out of our re-born spirit, and hear Him in that "mind", we will be tragically hopeless when present-day technology is used, which can shut down the mind, and even blind and deafen us.

A VISION IN THE NIGHT

One time, the same daughter went via airplane to be with a friend in San Diego. She took a night flight and was supposed to arrive at a small airport at 3:00 AM. When it got to be that time, Father woke me up and let me see a vision of her. She got off the plane, and no one was there to meet her. She was very scared because there were some sleazy guys in the airport. Father had me praying for her for two hours, then at 5:00 AM, her time, He let me go back to sleep. I saw in the vision that she was scared and lonely and couldn't reach her friend by phone. The next morning, she called to let me know she was there OK. I told her what I saw in the vision. She said that was exactly what happened. Amber came to get her at 5:00 AM.

PROTECTION WITHIN THE FIRE

After I began going to Africa, I had an African American friend named Doris who became my prayer partner. One night, as I sought to go to sleep, I was attacked by demons severely. I began spiritual warfare. I looked up, and saw across the door of my room a white fire about four feet off the ground. I cried out:

"Fire of God surround me!" It moved all around me. I fell into a deep, peaceful sleep. The next morning, I called Doris to tell her about what happened. But, before I could, she said: "Wait! I have something to tell you." She said that the night before, she had been praying for me, and all of a sudden she said she watched her prayers take form, and turn into a wall of white fire and surround me. I told her my story. Zechariah 2:4-5: "`**Jerusalem is to remain un-walled. For I Myself am to her', declares Yahuweh, `a wall of fire all around, and for esteem I am in her midst.'** "

CAST OUT AND DELIVERED AT 3 FEET

In 1998, I was in Tanzania, teaching on the baptism into the Holy Spirit to born again believers. I was preparing people to receive Him. I was in an area where the people worshipped the black river god. They sacrificed animals to this god. Most of the born again ones had come out of witchcraft. If a person is born from above by the Spirit of Yahuweh, they cannot be possessed by demons--for possession by demonic spirits includes their presence in the spirit, soul, and body. When one is truly Scripturally born again, the spirit is perfected and set apart. It becomes a portal into the eternal realm of Yahuweh. But, after a person is born from above, demons, disembodied spirits of fallen angels, can still torment their mind and body, unless they receive deliverance.

In this place in Tanzania, there was much spiritual darkness. As I taught on the Holy Spirit, a lady got up and ran outside screaming, running all around the building. The other people didn't seem to think anything was out of the ordinary. They told me she had demons. When it came time for the people to receive the baptism into the Spirit, I set them in rows, as usual. There were about fifty of them. The pastors were ready to help. But, as the Spirit began to come down like a cloud upon the people, those with demons still tormenting their mind and body began to manifest the demonic presences. Some ran outside and threw rocks at passers-by. Some went violent. I was standing over by some benches, when a man came to do some harm to me. He had just testified of being saved and how much he loved Jesus. Five pastors were trying to hold him down. I stuck out my Torah finger and began commanding the demon to loose him and let him go. I had my son's video camera in my left hand. Having the mind that I do, seeing the humorous in serious things, all I could think of was, if my son's camera was harmed, he'd kill me. About three feet from me, the man dropped to the ground, and came up delivered. Many, after being delivered, came and melted into my arms praising Jesus. I can't say anything negative about His victories in my past when I used the name "Jesus", except now I know better.

Messiah was a Jew. His Name carries the Father's Name: **Yahu**shua—**Yahuweh. Yahuweh means**: I AM THE EVER-EXISTING ONE WHO BREATHES--**is Salvation**). Our Father has had a lot of mercy on our ignorance! That's why it is very foolish to criticize others who are not as far along in knowledge as we are! I've lived and worked a lot of my life in the Third World. Believers are dying for their faith in the One in Matthew, Mark, Luke and John, calling Him Jesus. My concern is for those who know His real Name and won't use it. That is breaking the third commandment--bringing His Name to nothingness. He says to use His Name, but many won't. Some won't out of religious superstition and fear. So, they mindlessly use pagan substitutes for titles, like "Lord," which in Hebrew is "Ba'al." Ba'al is the name for an ancient Canaanite god. Or they use `Adonai' for Lord, which comes from Phoenician "Adon," meaning Lord, but in Greek is the name of the god Adonis. Using these substitutes for His Name is no different from using the golden calf to represent Him. **(Exodus 32)**

We must not misuse His Name, or use it commonly. We must fear Him, and His Name! But, if one loves Him with all their heart, they use it with honor. Don't overuse it, but use it to praise Him! His name is the most powerful name in the universe, and Satan knows that. In rebuking Satan, Yahuweh uses His own Name, like in **Zechariah 3:2**. I call Him "Abba." It's like saying "Daddy" in English. I call Yahushua "Messiah" a lot of the time also.

NO FEAR - ABBA HAS MY BACK

While conducting one of my meetings out in Tanzania in 1998, in the bush country of the Serengeti Plain, about five or six rough-looking young men came in snickering and laughing and went and sat in the back row. I believe it was when I finished my teaching and called those forward who wanted prayer to receive "Jesus" that they started making noises and causing trouble. I walked calmly back to them, and got right in the face of the ring-leader, and just stared into his eyes. I told him that Jesus loved him and wanted to save him. He was scared. He started crying. Some of the others started crying too. They all received Jesus, and we had good fellowship with them afterwards. Now, I use Yahushua in speaking about the Savior!

This also happened at Bumbo. It was in a meeting we had before crossing the wooden planks and swollen stream to get out of that area. As I was preaching, to my left I saw young men causing trouble, and it was interfering with others who were listening. I did the same thing. I got in their faces, they got

PART XI - Protection and Rescue

scared, stopped their mischief, and listened. When I am encased in the power of the Spirit, I have boldness that is not typical of me.

Since age 20, I have faced gangs and been in many threatening situations. Like when I preached on the streets of Los Angeles' Skid Row late at night. But, I never had any fear of the threats of the enemy. I suppose it was because of my "schooling" for so many years in spiritual warfare, which began immediately after I was baptized into the Spirit in November, 1966. I have been in very dangerous situations, as you have read in the parts above. But, each time, Abba warned me ahead of time very strongly so that I could do spiritual warfare and escape death. Abba trained me in about every type of ministry possible, from age 6 to present.

In America, we don't see demonic manifestations very often, for we are too sophisticated and proper for such things. There is the deception--the demonic hides in respectability, in sophistication, in proper tact and cultural niceties. Yet, many of those who call themselves His people are demonized and act out in secret. Note: **II Corinthians 11:12-15.**

A WARNING VISION AND THE ESCAPE FROM DEATH

One night in Kisumu, Africa, a lady from America had her spiritual son staying with us. He was a local African, going to a local college. He was born again. He had a very evil brother who was a trouble-maker and also very demonized. In the middle of the night, Father woke me up dramatically, and fear gripped me. I knew this was life-threatening. He showed me a vision of a man coming through our front door with a knife and slitting our throats. I prayed hard, until Father released me and I went back to sleep. The next morning, the college student told us that in the middle of the night his brother had come knocking on the door. He wanted in. He looked through the peephole and saw that he had a knife. When he wouldn't open the door, his brother got violent and threatened to kill him and all of us. I've had other warnings like this to pray to avoid disaster.

THE POPGUN STORY

In 1974, when my son was three years old, a friend and I went on a visit to Gatlinburg, Tennessee. It is a very popular tourist town. That day it was flooded with people. I had bought my son a toy popgun, but wouldn't let him have it. He was mad at me. I let him hold it. I set him on a concrete ledge with other people, while I went to look inside a store that was close by. I was not gone more than a couple of minutes. I came out, and he had disappeared. I asked if anyone had seen him, and a lady said that he walked off crying. Talk about feeling guilty! I've never been so out-of-my-mind terrified in my life. There was a policeman at the corner directing four-way traffic, because the traffic lights were out. I ran out into the middle of the intersection and grabbed him. I was hysterical. The lady I was with, Joan, who had been in another shop, had my seven-year old daughter in hand. My little daughter said she was happy he was gone until she realized he really was gone. We laugh about that today, but at the time I was out of my mind with terror. She was very scared for her little brother. The policeman left all that traffic sitting still, and made a phone call to the chief of police. The Chief said that he'd been found and taken over to a shop called "The Trading Post." I found the shop, and there he was behind the counter, playing with his popgun. I couldn't be mad at him. I scooped him up in my arms and cuddled him. He was so beautiful, with long blond curls, and big blue eyes. He's a very handsome man today. All I could think of was that maybe a sexual pervert kidnapped him. We had just moved from California, where a lot of perverts kidnapped little boys. I thanked the man at the shop. He smiled and said, **"A nice young man brought him here."** I prayed for the nice young man to be blessed. Years later, I was so concerned about the salvation of my children in the time of tribulation. As I was pulling out of our driveway, the scene in the shop in Gatlinburg flashed before me. I remembered what the shop owner said: "A nice young man brought him here." Father spoke to me: **"He was an angel."**

AND HE SHALL RETURN

I had the trauma of seeing my son off to Germany. He had joined the Air Force. There were times that I was very concerned about my son's safety. I wondered if he'd return from Germany. Gulf War I had broken out in Iraq, 1991, and they were thinking of sending his squad to Iraq. He was in a special division that repaired the sites on the F-16s so that the pilots would bomb the enemy's installations at the desired place. One night Father woke me up. He instructed me to look in the Word. I got my Bible and went into the kitchen. He gave me this Word for my son, his wife, and their baby boy. He led me to **Jeremiah 42:11-13**. In the light of America being end-time Babylon, and the military under its control, this is very interesting: "**`Do not be afraid of the king of Babylon, of whom you are afraid. Do not be afraid of him,' declares Yahuweh, `for I am with you to save you and deliver you from his hand. And I will show compassion, so that he has compassion on you, and let you return to your own land.'** " It was addressed to me not to fear, and it was addressed to them about their coming home safely. I went back to bed and back to sleep. Yes, they were going to send him to

Iraq, but at the last minute ordered his special unit in Germany to stay in Germany.

HIS WORD IS TRUTH - ENOUGH SAID

One day I was praying for my children again, fearful of what might happen to them in the dark days ahead. I opened my Bible without looking where I was opening to, and I looked down to one marked verse. It read: **"I will save your children."** Enough said...

I have related some difficult things because many look at me now and think I've always been victorious in the Spirit. But, in the natural, I am as weak and frail as anyone else. But, because of His training, I also do not look back. One of my most favorite verses in the Bible is **Exodus 14:15**, regarding the crossing of the Red Sea: **"Speak to the children of Israel, and tell them to go forward."** [Refer to "Forward March"/February 2010]

Sha'ul says: **"I can do all things--through Messiah Who strengthens me." (Philippians 4:13)** Truly, in myself I am not strong. But, leaning on Him, I can do whatever He asks me to do! **II Corinthians 12:9-10**: "He (*Messiah*) said to me: `My grace is sufficient for you. For My power is perfected in weakness.' Most gladly then, I would rather boast in my weakness, so that the power of Messiah rests on me. Therefore, I take pleasure in weakness, in insults, in needs, in persecutions, in distress, for the sake of Messiah. For when I am weak, then am I strong!"

SHUTTING THE DOOR IN THE FACE OF ROCKETS

In August of 2001, I was in the office of Bethuel Dongo, my African Director in Kampala, Uganda. I had gotten my e-mails. One was from a lady who lived in Aqaba, but who was in the States for the summer. She wrote: "Do NOT go back to Aqaba. Something has happened there that I can't tell you about now, but it is too dangerous." I sat there and asked Father: "What do you want me to do?" He said: "Go back NOW!" I had to cancel two Pastor's conferences – one in Kenya, and the other one in Uganda. But, my Director and I went to the Egypt Air office in Kampala, and I changed my ticket to go back in 2 days.

Upon returning, it was about 120F. I sat on my balcony, drinking tea. I had just gotten back from the market. I saw all kinds of new people in Aqaba—big men with very big scruffy beards. They didn't look happy. But, I figured we had new people in Aqaba, that's all. I did not know that in looking at the Israeli border from my balcony I was looking down the nose of an Israeli rocket not far away. I prayed in tongues, primarily because I did not know why I was there. I was the only westerner in Aqaba, since all Americans and Europeans leave in the summer. A few days later, another lady came from Colorado. I asked her if she knew what was going on, and she said "No." I found out that Aqaba had been invaded by several thousand terrorists. They had put rockets on the border facing Eilat, Israel. Prime Minister Ariel Sharon had put rockets on the Israeli side facing Aqaba, with the threat: "If you don't get those rockets off the border, I'll blow Aqaba off the map." King Abdullah got the terrorists out. But, at the same time, Iranian Republican Guards entered the "West Bank" and Sharon sent in tanks.

The world's news media said Israel was being aggressive against poor Palestinians. At the same time, Iran sent 10,000 rockets into Syria, who got them to Hezbollah, and they sat all arrayed on the Lebanese border with Israel. Today there are over 60,000 rockets on the Lebanon border facing Israel, which are much more sophisticated... supplied by Russia via Syria to Hezbollah. So, Father needed me in Aqaba for intercession. Because of things like this, I was labeled a "risk taker." However, I never really take risks, I just obey my Abba.

Intercession opens the door for Him to be able to do what He wants done. **(Romans 8:26-27)** tells us that speaking in our prayer language of the spirit, opens the door for Him to pray through us His own will. It is always best to obey Father, even if He gives no explanation at the time! Intercession is not the church hocus pocus mysticism that stirs up demons. It is gate keeping--opening doors for His entrance, using His Word to proclaim in His Name. He has to thoroughly trust the true intercessor to only say and do what He says. The untrained don't know when to shut up. There has to be an intimate relationship between the servant and the Master for Him to trust a person. [Refer to: "Intercession: Knowing the Basics"]

Intercession isn't about "spiritual mapping," or finding "ley lines." It is about taking His Word, given by Him, going to where He says to speak them, and speaking with His authority backing. Otherwise it is just a game that stirs demons and reeks havoc on the spiritually immature. [Refer to: "Authority Backing"] A missionary friend to Albania once said: "If we do things the Bible's way, we'll get the Bible's results." Why can't people just go by how Messiah ministered, or the prophets, or the Apostles? Why do they have to get some modern big name to follow?

ZERO FEAR OF THE "SOUVENIR"

In the 1990s, I was on another missionary trip to the Navajo reservation with my church. I was out in the high desert of New Mexico, near what is called the "four corners." It was a warm day, and everyone was taking it easy. I decided to walk. I wanted to pick up driftwood as souvenirs for my children. I picked up one piece of driftwood, and it resembled a snake. Abba spoke harshly to me: "Put it down!" I argued that it looked like a snake ready to strike, which was symbolic of the desert. He yelled at me: "Put it down!" I dropped it. About five minutes later I saw a lovely piece of driftwood and bent over to pick it up. As I did, I heard a noise that I remembered I had heard on National Geographic nature programs--the sound of a rattlesnake. I froze in place, and then turned my eyes outward and just a short distance away was a rattlesnake ready to strike me. I did not move. I just said quietly, "Jesus! Jesus!" I then said: "Snake, stop your rattle!" I saw that it did. I was still bent over. I said to it: "You relax and totally uncoil." It immediately uncoiled. I slowly stood up, took several big steps away from it, and then began to preach it a sermon. I had zero fear the whole time. I went from there to the compound to tell the missionary what had happened. As soon as I got to the door of the compound, fear hit me hard. I have to laugh at that. When we're being encased in Abba's protection, there is no fear. But, afterwards, the flesh takes over and we react. Often Abba has to send His angels (His messengers) to help us. If we are on assignment for Him, He uses many means of protecting us. But, when we are dealing with powerful demonic spirits, He often sends His more-powerful angelic forces.

MY ANGEL WITH THE FUNNY HAIR

One hot early September afternoon, I was in my apartment in Jordan, taking a nap on my mattress on the floor, under a ceiling fan my neighbors had given me. As I awoke, I saw a young man standing by the right side of my office desk, resting his fingers on the desk. He had a very pale complexion, with chiseled features. He was wearing a white robe over white pants. His hair was what got my attention. It was combed forward from the center of his head, and then curled at the ends around his head. Very strange! As soon as he saw that I was awake, he flew over me about 12 inches and out the window. As he did, I saw his funny hair. I call him "my angel with the funny hair." I knew he wanted me to notice it, so that in the future, when I am in severe danger, I will recognize him, for he will be there to help me. I had so many dreams, visions, actual visitations and sightings in that apartment.

In the 2010 vision I had in Panama City, of the days of great turmoil in East Jerusalem, I watched myself escaping from bullet fire. I found an entrance into a tunnel. The floor could be reached by my going down a ladder. At the bottom, there was my angel with the funny hair. I wonder if he was one of the angels who flanked me during my most dangerous assignment at the Vatican, on Patmos, and in Delphi (July/August 2012). I was in the Jewish

Quarter in May of 2011, when gun fire broke out in the Kidron Valley.

THE ROCKS THAT NEARLY HIT ME

In the Fall of 2010, I was in the Kidron Valley when Arab children started throwing rocks at me, which almost hit me in the face. How many times has He shielded me from death? I will know in eternity.

RESCUED FROM THE DEPTHS

As a teen, I was in a car with other teenagers, who were going at high speeds down a hill, racing the car next to them. I jumped into a river of water earlier with them, and could not find bottom. So I panicked and started drowning. I was going down for the third time, when a boy jumped off a tree branch into the water and saved my life. How awesome it will be in eternity to see how many times we were rescued!

PART XII

MIRACLES OF HIS LEADING, CONFIRMATON OF HIS WORDS, AND OTHER ADVENTURES IN PERFECT TIMING

The word "mo'ed" means a "to-the-second appointment." Mo'edim is the plural. The seven festivals are called "Mo'edim." (Leviticus 23) They are the "mo'edim" of Yahuweh. They are eternal festivals. I have lived my life around these appointments that He scheduled, whether I realized it or not. As the need for them arises, they are brought into time at the exact second they are needed. I wrote an article entitled "Daily Flowing in His Perfect Timing"--a sequel to the manual "Faith Walk"--and one simply called "Led." I daily flow in His perfect will, thus flow in His perfect timing! This is my lifestyle. I am not any better than anyone else--I just know Yahuweh. You can too, but there is a high price tag for really knowing Him. It takes total death to self-will, selfishness, self-centeredness, selfish desires and hidden ambitions and agendas. It means totally emptying yourself of self-will, in order to submit to His will. Unless you are willing to do that, you cannot be a disciple of the Savior. (Luke 14:25-33)

Knowing the Creator personally means being wise enough to fear Him, and to obey Him. That means submitting our will, to take up His. As we are faithful, He trusts us more and more, and gives us harder assignments. He is the King of the universe. For Him to come to us, and seek our friendship, is very humbling indeed! Yet, His people so easily throw away this eternally valuable opportunity, in order to attempt to control their own lives, to satisfy the lusts of their flesh, and what their head reasons. It is tragic!

I arrived in Aqaba **April 18, 1999**. In 2007, I tried so hard to sublease my apartment, but Abba was releasing me from living in security in my own apartment. He was sending me more and more to the nations, and more to Israel. I fought Him – I tried to stay there, but He won! My dear friend Karen came to help me in March 2007. I knew I had to pack up and leave. I went to get my ticket on the same airline that she was flying out on. I did not think of the date. I just got a ticket the same day she was flying out. I was going to take with me almost all of my personal things from the apartment, and wow did I need help! She helped me move several large suitcases to Israel. One big one went to the Christian Friends of Israel in Jerusalem and the others went to Tiberias. After buying the ticket, the date jumped out at me: **April 18, 2007. Eight years to the day I arrived, I flew out**. Jordan was my "wilderness" experience. It prepared me to enter

His Land, and be a part of His end-time work there. Truly I came up out of the wilderness "leaning on my Beloved." (**Song of Songs 8:5**)

To begin to show you how He wants us to live a life of "mo'ed," I give you this story of how detailed His leading can be to get us to the right places, and the right people. He has woven my life in such a way, that I am continually mind-boggled at how He arranges for me to meet people, and to be led into what He wants me to do for Him. I am just a servant. But, the life of a bond-servant of the Master is the most exciting life anyone can live!

THE DAVIES STORY - DON'T HIT DELETE!

Here is just one example -- the complete story of meeting the Davies family, with whom I have done much intercession in 2011 and 2012, which also included meeting other families who were connected to them.

My friend, who posts my articles on **laydownlife.net** (my meeting him was a miracle mo'ed too), sends me e-mails from people who write to me, thinking the website is mine, and not knowing my personal communication e-mail address. One was from a man named John, who lived in Canada. He sounded very sweet. He had gotten my articles from someone else, and wanted to contact me. But, at that time, so many wanted on my list and I was skeptical about putting people on my private list that I did not know, so most got deleted. I started to delete John's e-mail, and Abba yelled at me: "NO!" I jerked back my hand. I said, "Ok, I won't." I wrote John back and found that he had a nice family. They were doing intercession across Canada.

We communicated back and forth, and I was very glad that I had not hit "delete." I was feeling in my spirit that Abba wanted me to do a couple of meetings while I was in the U.S. So, I wrote to those on my address list, and found that the largest group that wanted to meet with me was in Tennessee. So, I worked on that, getting three meetings. I had little money for air travel. One man, named Andrew, e-mailed me. He asked me to come to Pennsylvania. I told him I couldn't do it. He said he would wait on going to Ohio if I would come. I told him I couldn't do it. I went to delete Andrew's e-mail, and Abba screamed at me: "NO!" I said: "OK, I won't." But how was I going to work out a trip to Pennsylvania with a trip to Tennessee? But, I booked a multi-city flight. I had peace.

In the meantime, Andrew said something that set off red flags. It is funny now. He said a lady had told him about my friends in Panama with whom I stayed, and that he and his family were friends with my friends in Treasure Island. I thought: "Oh no, he's CIA and this is a trap." I am really not paranoid. I've just been in too many situations of betrayal, even almost to my death. So, I contacted these two friends. The one in Treasure Island said he and his family had stayed with them. The couple I stayed with in Panama said they had not met Andrew. However, they told me that he was a friend of the husband's brother, who had moved back to the US. So, it was the brother's wife who told Andrew about me.

This was too much. Andrew was going to Ohio to do garlic harvesting with the brother and his wife on his parent's farm. He said he's hold off going if I'd come. Well, I went. He had to drive two hours to the airport because he and his friends lived deep in Amish country. I found that two families had come from Canada to hear me, and one family from a neighboring state.

I've had people drive for hundreds of miles, some driving over two days, some 10 hours or more. In July of 2012, one couple drove 900 miles from Canada to southern Iowa, and one couple drove 1,000 miles from North Carolina. But, this was the first time I had some come from another country. As I sat there in this big living room, out in the country, Andrew introduced me to each family. He came to one family and said: "I think you know them." I was so shocked--it was John and his family from Canada--John, his wife, and four children. Andrew had done intercession with them in Canada. We had a packed three days of fellowship, and then I went to Tennessee where I had a packed three days of meetings.

There's more to this: I went to Israel in March 2011, and in early April went to stay with a lady who had a bed and breakfast in Tiberias. I walked in, and two families were there. They said they knew me from my articles. One couple was the head of a prosperous business/ministry in Israel—the very ministry that my Panama friends worked with. In fact, the lady from Treasure Island and her husband were in Israel at that time, taking courses from that same ministry. The lady of this couple had heard about me from one of the people who had invited me to speak in Tennessee. We started comparing notes of people they knew in Colorado too, and we knew several of the same people.

The heads of the ministry left. The other couple, Daniel and Carol, stayed for a week. Later, the same day, I got an e-mail from John in Canada. I told Daniel about them. He said that he and his wife had traveled with John and his family and they were the ones who had sent John my articles. I was so stunned--John had received my articles from a man I just met in Israel! I asked Daniel who sent him my articles. He said a lady named Jamie J. I was more shocked. Jamie and her husband had been friends for a long time. Jamie has sent my articles to lots of people. Daniel and

Carol had given John a travel trailer and van that they used to go across Canada. In the e-mail, John told me that he had sold this travel trailer and van because Father was leading them to cross Europe to Israel, backpacking and camping. Andrew had even traveled with them across Canada, for a while.

That week, Abba used Daniel to lead me to go to the Outer Hebrides. I was fellowshipping with Daniel. I explained to him how I had been doing intercession over the House of Israel/Ephraim/Joseph – the 10 northern tribes of Ya'cob – since 2006, for the return of a remnant to the Land, in preparation for Yahushua to return. Daniel told me about how the tribes left from the tip of the Outer Hebrides for America and Canada. I told him that Abba had been speaking to me since I first flew over the Outer Hebrides in 1992, on my way to Germany. During that week, I knew I was to go to the Isle of Lewis. Abba brought me information as I needed it. I wrote John about going there, and about what Abba had shown me through Daniel. Later, John said he and his family said they felt they should meet me in the Outer Hebrides, so that we could do intercession together.

In the last part of their trek across Canada, which I had encouraged them to finish, I received a lot of e-mails from John telling me of their adventures. They ended up at St. John's on the tip of Newfoundland--the most eastern part of Canada. Meanwhile, I had once again twisted my knee, this time very badly, while I was in downtown Tiberias. It took me six weeks to be able to walk normally. I went to Wales, where I stayed with a friend. Once together on the Isle of Lewis, we began making plans for our intercession for a remnant of the ten tribes of Israel to return to their homeland in Israel.

Our main day of intercession was very cold and bleak, rainy and bitter. We went by bus to the north-most tip, to go to the Lighthouse near the Port of Ness. I could not finish the long walk up the hill to the Lighthouse. It was bitter cold, and I was not prepared it. But, the Davies finished the work of the intercession, while I walked down to a little restaurant in town. I did not know how I would walk down that far, for it had begun raining, but the Davies asked a couple, who had driven to the Lighthouse, to stop and take me there. I think they were Jewish. Abba allowed me to see the top of the light house and the Atlantic, for which I am very grateful.

So, what if I had deleted John's e-mail, and Andrew's e-mail? What if I had not known the voice of Abba? Do you see how long it took just for me to share that one mo'ed? I've had a lifetime of them! The stores are all amazing, like this one!

HE BRINGS THE CONFIRMATION

It was two days before Gulf War II officially began--March 18, 2003. I had taught the Tenach since 1963. One chapter made me mad--I couldn't figure out what it was talking about--**Daniel 8**. But, on March 18, 2003, Father instructed me to read Daniel 8. I was in Aqaba at the time. I read it, and understood every word of it. It was about Gulf War II until the rise of anti-messiah. The details were in the news. Two days later, March 20th, 2003, the day Gulf War II officially began, a pastor-friend from Alabama came over to bring me some pie from his wife. He said that two days before, Father led him to study Daniel 8. I asked him what Father said about it. Yes, it was exactly what He had shown me.

In June, I met with a minister friend in Israel. I had just come back from intercession over the G-8 summit in Evian, France. He walked into the church where I was talking with some friends, and told me that in mid-March Father had given him Daniel 8, and proceeded to tell me what Abba had told me--same things.

You see, this is how He brings confirmation. We do not have to go looking for it. In fact, if we do, the enemy or our mind can steer us wrong. Know His voice... and life will be amazing! If the Spirit is the Teacher, then all who are taught by Him learn the same things. The whole week I was with Daniel and Carol, we flowed together in understanding because we were Spirit-taught.

If Yahuweh's Spirit is not the Teacher, then there are as many opinions and ideas as there are people. Thus, the religion of Christianity has about 5,000 denominations and organizations, with church splits being a common thing. There are over 350 English translations of the Bible – each one differing depending on the belief-system of the translators. This is NOT what Messiah died for! He died to bring us into Covenant with His Abba, so that His Abba could teach us by His Spirit. Yet, His people would rather go to a big-shot teacher than learn from "the Author and Finisher of our Faith!" Stupid--really stupid! It is amazing that Yahuweh uses the word "stupid" in reference to His children several times in the Word.

BOOKSTORE MO'EDIM

When I first went to China with Open Doors with Brother Andrew in 1994, they recommended that I read a certain book about the persecuted churches. I was saving all my money for the trip, so had no extra money for books. One day, as I was lying on my bed reading, His Spirit spoke loudly: "Get dressed and go to Joshua's Bookstore NOW!" I obeyed. I walked into Joshua's bookstore, and there to the right of the door was a card table with a sign on it: "All books $1.00." In the middle of the card table was the very book I needed about China. Abba is so personal!

Another time, while living in Texas, He instructed me to go to Half-Price Books. I was looking for the history of Israel, but only from the Bar Kokhba rebellion to Alexander the Great. As I stood in front of the Jewish section in the bookstore, I saw a book by my right hand that said *History of Israel*. I pulled it out and the whole title of the book was: *The History of Israel from the Bar Kokhba Rebellion to Alexander the Great*. I'm telling you like it was!

I spent eight years in Jordan watching the fulfillment of prophecy down to the last detail, regarding Edom, Mt. Seir, Sela – Petra, and the preparations for sustaining the remnant of His people during the time of tribulation. To do His will, Yahuweh has used the U.S., the E.U. and the U.N., the World Bank and the World Food Bank, as well as other investors, like the California Workers Pension Fund. I watched the beginning of the **Ezekiel 47** canal being cut, to facilitate the water flow when Messiah splits the Mount of Olives at His coming. It is a billion dollar project by the World Bank, to pump water from the Red Sea to the Dead Sea, to create a fishing industry, and create hydroelectric power. In 1999, Abba told me that the Gulf of Aqaba would be the only remaining International Port of the world when it was all said and done. In 2002, this was confirmed by the U.N.

In 2003, I was in Half-Price Books in Ft. Worth, Texas, with Karen. She had to leave to fix supper for her husband. I asked her if I could run into the clearance section just for a minute. She said: "OK." I stood in the clearance section and said: "Father, do you want to show me anything?" The books were all jumbled together with no organization, but they were all $1.00. I looked straight ahead and saw a thin paperback book titled *The New Middle East*, by Shimon Peres. On the cover was a picture of President Clinton, Yassir Arafat and Israel's Prime Minister Rabin, on the White House lawn on September 13, 1993. I stood in that bookstore and opened the book up to the middle, as I usually do. At the top of the chapter were the words "Aqaba Canal." I stood there and started reading all the plans of the world community back to the late 1800s in regards to making Aqaba the International Port of the world--the "Peace Port"--and how they were going to cut that canal. Now what are the odds of me opening to that information? I have had so many "coincidences" in my life, sometimes several a day, that I know it is not possible that they are mere coincidences! Abba guides the steps of His servants!

A RARE PRIVILEGE

In 1996, I was in Mongolia for three months with the English Language Institute summer college course. I've already told what

PART XII - Miracles of His Leading

Abba sent me to do in a previous part. During my time there, I met Paul Estabrooks. He had brought a team from Open Doors with Brother Andrew. I speak of this remarkable man in my part on China. He is one of those who orchestrated getting a million Bibles into China in one night, along with Brother David. He invited me to have lunch with him and his guests. I later had the rare privilege of standing outside the restaurant with Paul and the main translator of the Bible into Mongolian from New Zealand. I listen to them plot and plan how they would get Bibles into the Gobi Desert of Mongolia, where Buddhist priests will kill anyone found with a Bible. What a rare, rare privilege to listen to these two spies for the Kingdom of heaven! Abba has given me so many rare privileges like this.

NOT-SO "HO-HUM" IN THE DESERT

For three months, I was with a group called Practical Missionary Training in Arizona, on the Navajo Indian reservation. My assigned partner, Lorrine Prosser, and I, stayed in a medical missionary compound for part of our trip. One day, everyone had left the compound to go to town, except for a missionary nurse, a Navajo nurse, and me. It was still morning, when a truck pulled up and a man told us that a lady was having a baby and could not get to the hospital. We three jumped in a large van, and went to the hogan where she was. The lady laid down in the backseat with the Navajo nurse, and her mother got in the very back of the van. I sat up with the missionary nurse. We tried to get her there as fast as possible since she was near birth. We swerved through loose sand and got stuck. We could not dislodge the van in time. The woman began screaming. So, the nurse opened the side doors and there came the baby. I was an only child. I had never even held a baby until I held my own first child, let alone watch a baby being born. I stood there in awe. The baby boy came out a white child, but quickly the skin color turned to a lovely golden brown. Finally we got the van unstuck and got to the hospital. The afterbirth came out just after we got unstuck. All of this was a new experience for me.

But, again, I got to see something very rare. When we got back to the mission compound, my partner came and others with our group and asked: "Well how was your day?" They had a ho-hum day, and were shocked at mine. Throughout my life, I just happened to be in the right place at the right time. Don't you want that for your life? Again: "Daily Flowing in His Perfect Timing." It should be every believer's lifestyle!

On another assignment, Lorraine and I, and two other ladies with our group, were sent to the north near the Utah border, to live in hogans and dress like Navajos. We all stayed in one small hogan. We had to go to Utah to get water in rain barrels. We drank the water, used it in cooking, washed dishes, washed ourselves, and watered little trees we were trying to get to grow. I really learned a lot from this training!

THE BOOK IN THE ATTIC
ABBA GETS US WHAT WE NEED!

I had a class on Sunday evening at my church for two years. Dwaine and June were regular attendees. Dwaine worked for Lockheed. One Sunday evening he brought me a copy of a book that his boss had xeroxed off. He told me this story: His boss was an agnostic. He came that previous Friday morning to Dwaine saying cynically: "Your God kept me up all night." He was not happy. He said that he was going to sleep, when this gnawing thought came into his head that he had to find a book to give to Dwaine for someone else, because they needed it. He went looking for it, and after an hour ended up in the attic looking for it. He finally found it. Dwaine took the book and told his boss: "I know who it is for." It was a geologist's report as to what will happen when the Mount of Olives splits, and the whole Rift Valley Fault gives way. It contains amazing material that is also outlined in detail in the Bible. I memorized the scenario and every time I'd teach it, the anointing was so strong on me that I could hardly talk. One evening I was at a home meeting where I was teaching. Several were there from my church in Fort Worth. After the meeting, people stood around talking. One lady, a friend who also sang in the church choir as I did, a 5th grade school teacher, was talking to someone else. I overheard her telling the exact same scenario as I read about in this book. I asked her where she got that information. It was from another source, but exactly as the geologist in my book had reported. She had related that information to her students. Recently my son borrowed the book to do research on the video he was producing.

THE BOOK THAT FOUND ME

I was getting ready to write my mini-book, "The Foundation of Deception," which traces to the roots of Christianity. A young man at my meeting in Houston, Texas, said that a book was coming out early the next year called <u>Constantine's Sword</u> by James Carroll. He recommended that I check it for research. I looked for it at a bookstore after it was released, and saw it had been written by a Catholic. I put the book back. I wasn't going to read the history of the Roman Catholic Church written by a Catholic. Not long after that, a friend came to visit me. She gave me something in a Barnes and Noble bag. She said she was in this bookstore and asked Father what book I needed that she could buy for me. He directed her to the book she had in the bag. You guessed it--<u>Constantine's Sword</u>. I thanked her. But, when she left, I put the book on my desk. I laid down on my bed and stared at it. I asked Father what was in it that I needed to see. I grabbed it and opened it up to the center of the book. I began reading. I couldn't believe what I was reading. I was reading truth. It became my main reference source for my study, which searched to the roots of the Egyptian/Greco/Roman/Persian religion of Christianity--"The Foundation of Deception."

So many times, Father has placed books in my hands, or CDs or DVDs, that someone was led to send to me. This has happened several times lately. I just so happened to receive what someone was "led" to send me, and it was exactly what I needed to learn.

HE ALWAYS HAS A PURPOSE

As I told above, in 2006, while visiting at Grace Temple for my grandson's dedication, Pastor Nichols gave me two cassette tapes of two sermons by Billie Brim. He said that "the Lord" had impressed him to give them to me. I took them back to Israel with me. I listened to them in March. I took notes. Then I filed them with other cassettes. In March of 2007, Abba impressed me to re-listen to those cassettes. In doing so, He gave me revelation knowledge that launched me on a study that will go on into eternity. I learned about the last three 7-year cycles before Messiah comes, and "The Shmittah Year Prophecy."

ABBA KNOWS NETWORKING

I've told this story earlier, but want to give it briefly here, for without obeying Abba at each step, I would not have had the open door to Florida that I did. I moved with the family I stay with in 2006, from Texas to Florida. I knew not one person in Florida, but by the time we moved, and the furniture arrived ten days later, I knew about 100. As you've read in the precious parts above, my life, especially since 1986, has been one mo'edim after another, all leading to victorious things. But, actually, all of my life has been under His care for my education and wisdom.

In 2006, elders from Messianic assemblies in East Texas invited me to join them at a large Sukkot meeting in Oklahoma. I was to speak along side of a couple of very big-name teachers in Messianic circles. I really wanted to do that. Previously that year, I had spoken at an assembly in Alabama. On the last night of my meetings, the rabbi felt to call a couple who lived near New Orleans to come hear me. It was a long way from New Orleans to where he was in Alabama! They were going to a Monte Judah Conference the same weekend I was to speak in Alabama. They asked Abba, and He told them to come hear me. They obeyed Abba. What if they had not obeyed Abba? He uses His servants that He trusts to obey Him.

Thus, I met the couple from the New Orleans area. Both the husband and wife separately invited me to open their Sukkot in Louisiana. So, instead of being with the rich and famous big names, and lots of my friends, I obeyed Abba and went out in the woods with regular people (smile) – big names on Abba's list. The lady and her husband became dear friends. They had eight children. Knowing them opened up many meetings in Louisiana, in different places. Her husband died a few years back in a tragic accident. It really devastated me. But, Susan continued on. I just heard from her in an e-mail recently. She has been teaching Torah in several countries of southern Asia; in churches, in homes, and in India. I know He will keep her going in His service. She's dynamic!

After speaking at the opening of their Sukkot I met two ladies from Florida. They said that when I got to Florida, they would set up a combined meeting for me of several groups. On our way down Interstate 75, passing the off ramp to Ocala, on our day of moving to Florida, I called Tina, whom I had met at the Louisiana Sukkot. She said she had set up meetings for me. I told her I had ten days before I had to fly back to Dallas, to catch my flight to Jordan. Before the furniture even arrived, I had two meetings with a lot of people.

In that meeting I had met many people, some have become good friends. I had been doing a year and a half's worth of intercession over the Gulf of Mexico, on behalf of the remnant of His people, for the days of fleeing ahead. I thought there were no ports of any interest along the Florida Gulf Coast. I was in for a shock. As we came down Interstate 75, I saw a sign for the Port of Tampa. Then as we neared our turnoff for our new house, I saw a sign for the Port of Manatee. PORT OF MANATEE…WHAT? THE MANATEE IS A RIVER. I found out that it is the main U.S. Port north of the Panama Canal. In doing intercession over that, Father opened the door later on for me to do intercession over the Panama Canal in moving to Panama. Intercession is gate-keeping for the Master. Through it, we open portals for Abba's entrance!

Through meeting a lady in Florida, who became a super friend, I also met others and was led to be in Panama with them. One thing always leads to another if we are led by the Spirit. Never a dull moment! And we don't get bogged down with man-ministry stuff – wearing ourselves out pleasing the church, or a pastor, or a rabbi. His ways just flow.

IT PAYS TO INSTANTLY OBEY

In 2006, before leaving Florida to get my hook-up flight to Dallas for Jordan, I was making my bed, and Father said loudly and clearly: "Go call the airlines – NOW!" I know the value of

PART XII - Miracles of His Leading

instant obedience! I did, and the lady at the airlines told me that she was very glad I called because my flight had been changed. They did not have our new phone number. I was not going through Amsterdam, I was going through Paris. If I had not called, I would have missed my flight. Obey Him quickly! Isn't it intelligent to hear from Abba? He tells us things no one else can!

THE JOY OF THE TRANSFERRED LUGGAGE

This story in detail is in "Training Mission – A Day in the Life of Yedidah." I was returning from Israel in 2009, on my way to Panama. It was already a hard trip. Upon trying to check in with KLM in Tel Aviv, I found out from KLM in Tel Aviv that unless I had an exit plane ticket, Panama wouldn't let me in, and KLM wouldn't let me on their plane. So at 3:00 AM, I found myself at a ticket office in the airport purchasing a ticket out of Panama for America.

The plane coming into Amsterdam was very late. I did not have much time to transfer to my flight to Panama anyway, even if the flight had been on time. I had two heavy suitcases checked, and one carry on suitcase. If I got into Panama and the suitcases didn't arrive on time, I would have to wait two-three days at a hotel to get the suitcases because of flight schedules, and then fly to the north of Panama on another plane. So, I was looking at about $700.00 in expenses. I did not have money for that. The KLM flight attendants couldn't have been kinder. There was one male flight attendant that I thought might be angel. He was so filled with compassion. They tried to assure me all was OK, but I knew it wasn't. We arrived in barely enough time for me to transfer to my flight to Panama by fast-cart, but not for the luggage to be unloaded and re-loaded on my flight. It takes a good 40 minutes to unload and re-load or more, and we had a full flight, so there were probably over 500 suitcases, or more, to unload and transfer. I got to the top of the ramp, and a KLM agent called for a cart to take me to my next flight, or else I would have missed it. While waiting for the cart, all of a sudden Abba spoke: "**They are transferring your luggage NOW**!" The joy hit my spirit to such a degree that the whole flight I kept saying "YES!" "YES!" over and over, with "yes" gestures. I was so happy! I got to Panama, and of course, there were my suitcases on the baggage claim carousel.

There have been many times, when I would be delayed getting to an appointment ("mo'ed"), and yet, by His favor, I have arrived to the minute on time! I don't know how He pulls that off, but He does!

I have had hundreds of dreams and visions and prophetic words of knowledge and wisdom from Abba from a very young age. All have either come to pass, or are coming to pass. I hear Him well. I've heard His voice since age 4. But, He's had to work with me through the years so that I would be quick to obey and not doubt Him. I've learned! Many of the dreams and visions have been about present reality regarding myself, my family, others, or circumstances and situations. The "gift of the word of knowledge" (**I Corinthians 12:1-13**) is going to be much needed in the days ahead, accompanied by the "gift of the word of wisdom" as to what to do, and the "gift of discernment of spirits," to know what spirit you're dealing with.

THE STORY OF ROY AT THE WALL

I have told this story above regarding meeting Roy at the Wall in Jerusalem, December 2004, confirming all that He had given me for my article: "The Hebrew Names and Titles of the Creator of the Universe--the Father and Messiah of Israel"/January 2005." That was one of the most profound mo'ed, if not the most profound one I have ever had. So, here, I will re-tell it.

I had invited my friend Betty from Glen Rose to come to Israel in December of 2004. I had just finished writing a massive study on the Hebrew Names and Titles of Yahuweh and Yahushua. I thought I was finished. I wanted to get the article sent out to those on my address list before she came. But, Abba strongly said: "NO! Do not send it." I obeyed. She came and I taught her a little on Scriptural intercession in the garments of the High Priest, from **Exodus 28** and **Ephesians 6:10-18**. I especially taught her about the gold crown that the High Priest had to wear in order to be able to intercede for the people. On the crown was engraved in the gold: "Set-Apartness to YHWH."

On December 25th, a Shabbat, we had walked up to Hekal Shlomo – the Great Synagogue – to attend their service. Then I had taken her to the City of David. On December 26th, we went to the Western Wall. She had forgotten her souvenirs that she left in a sack at the checkpoint we had just come through, so she left to get it. Just as she left, a man came and said to me: "Do you know Yahweh?" I was stunned. In Jerusalem there are all kinds of weird people, so I did not reply quickly. But, I finally said: "Yes." He said, "I saw you walking down the steps and the Spirit told me to talk to you, that I had something you needed."

Roy was no weird person! He was down there every day to encourage the Orthodox Jews to use Abba's Name. Roy was ½ Welsh and ½ Jewish, had made aliyah, and was living in Jerusalem. Roy was in his late 60s I'd say, white hair, piercing blue eyes. He worked with a Messianic rabbi named Reuben who was in his 80s, who had researched the name of the Father and the Son for years.

Roy and I had the most glorious fellowship – the Spirit just leapt back and forth between us. Then just before Betty returned, he reached into his briefcase and pulled out a stack of notes. He said that the Spirit had told him to give them to me. Betty came back and I told Roy I would take her to the Temple Mount. He said, "Oh no, take her to the Temple Institute." I told him that since our fellowship had been so powerful, I'd do as he said. I went into the Temple Institute. In the large display case was the altar of incense – pure gold. But, just below it I saw the newly placed "crown" displayed—the very gold crown that I had told my friend about back in Aqaba. It was one of the great joys of my life to see it made for the coming HaGadal (High Priest – Yahushua). Awesome! I got back to Aqaba, and read the notes Roy gave me from Rabbi Reuben. I incorporated those notes all through that article He told me not to send. Those notes were confirmation that everything I had written was correct! Then He said "send it." How marvelous are His ways!

THE BIBLE CLUB

This is a fabulous story! It thrills me to tears just to write about it! When Abba wants something done, the hosts of hell cannot stop it! While living in Fort Worth, the third child, second daughter, had graduated from J.T. Stevens Elementary School, and was set to go to Middle School in the Fall. Many of the Christian parents whose children attended J.T. Stevens, put their children in private Christian schools, church schools, or home schooled them. I asked Abba about it, and He directed me to let her go to Wedgwood Middle School in Southwest Fort Worth. The reason why the Christian parents took their children out of this Middle School is because it had a reputation for gang activity, drugs, alcohol abuse, homosexuality among students, and rape. It was not in a good area, either.

I told about her missing the bus in a story above. But, on the first day of school, my daughter reported that she had a Christian Biology teacher who said he would not teach evolution. There were young people there who were outspoken about their faith. It was at the time when Burleson High School, just south of Fort Worth, had begun the "See you at the pole" event on the first day of school, where High School students would meet around the flag pole, hold hands, and pray over their school year. There were principles who actually called the police, who arrested the students, only to find out that the Supreme Court had approved it. I heard students saying that they considered it a privilege to be arrested because of their faith. The Supreme Court had also given High School Christian students the right to start their own Bible Clubs, IF they were student-initiated and student-led. This came out of a big Supreme Court battle, when a young girl wanted to start a Bible Club. Jay Sekulo, a Christian lawyer, took the case and won it. It was Sandra Day O'Connor who was the strongest advocate in favor of the Bible Clubs.

But, the Supreme Court said that children in Middle Schools were too young to make such decisions. That's a joke! They made decisions to rape, to take drugs, engage in drunken orgies, get into gang fights, and be homosexuals. But, to decide to have a Bible Club was too much for their pitiful brains. However, Abba thought differently! One thing Wedgwood Middle School had going for it was the Principal, Mrs. Younger -- a good woman!

One day, I was taking my daughter to school and Abba spoke the words of **Acts 18:9-10**: "**Be not afraid but speak and hold not your peace, for I am with you, and no man shall set on you to hurt you: for I have much people in this city.**" (KJV)

In saying "city," I knew He meant the school--those teachers who taught there and the students from Fort Worth. I also remembered it was from the book of Acts. I went home and found the verses. He let me know that He wanted to bring a Bible Club into that school, and that there were teachers there, like her Biology teacher, who also wanted to reach out to the students. Little did I know how many! So, I asked my daughter to ask her Biology teacher if I could meet with the Christian teachers and talk about a Bible Club. Now, remember, this was NOT approved by the Supreme Court. I did get government information on it, however. That's how I learned about Sandra Day O'Connor's part in opening up the High Schools. That afternoon, my daughter brought me the report. There were 28 Christian teachers at Wedgwood. They had been meeting for prayer three times a week before school to pray for the students. They were looking for some way to reach them without openly witnessing, which is against the law in public schools. Her Biology teacher was excited. I was invited to join them for their prayer meetings in different teacher's homes. So, I began going and praying with them, and encouraging them.

I went to talk to Mrs. Younger. She was excited about the possibility of having a Bible Club in her school. But, she said that there was a man who worked in the main office in Fort Worth named Mr. Ponder. She said he was not a nice man, that every time she proposed something good for the school, he vetoed it. The teachers knew of this man and how sadistic he was to Mrs. Younger. Somehow, it got out to the Christian students that I was working on starting a Bible Club. Their attitude was this: "If we have to put a cover on our Bibles, like we do on our text books, and sit out on the sidewalk, we want our Bible Club."

Mrs. Younger petitioned for a student-led Bible Club. It was legal in the sense that the Supreme Court had said that if a school had a Math Club, a Camera Club, or any kind of secular club, students could start a Bible Club – but that was for High School students. I remember our last prayer meeting together. The teachers were so discouraged. Mr. Ponder had not signed any papers saying they could have their club. I said to them: "Let's pray for Mr. Ponder's salvation." They thought that was a novel idea. No one had thought of that before (smile). So we prayed for his salvation. About 10:00 AM that morning, I took something to the school for my daughter. As I was talking to one of the teachers in our prayer meeting, the English teacher who had been in our prayer meeting that morning, came running up to me very excited. She said: "**Mr. Ponder is in Mrs. Younger's office right now, signing papers for us to have a Bible Club**!" That Bible Club became so popular with the students that it continued on year after year. I had parents tell me that the Bible Club saved their children from falling away from their faith.

When my youngest daughter was in Wedgwood Middle School, five years later, she was a cheerleader. I went to pick her up one day from cheerleading practice. While waiting, I saw a tall good-looking young man walking past the car, carrying a very large Bible. I rolled down the window and called out to him. He came over to the car. I asked him why he was carrying a large Bible. He smiled. He said he was the president of the Bible Club. I am crying now... I found out that year, the Wedgwood Middle School Yearbook had a full-page with pictures in it of those in the Bible Club. That was unheard of!

In writing this autobiography, I have had tears, and cried several times, but never in sadness because of anything negative or hurtful to me. I got rid of all the hurts years ago! I stopped being disappointed in people a long time ago! I am free. My tears are tears of gratitude for what my Abba has done!

I see the do-nothing so-called "believers" who do not know Him, going about their boring business and never knowing Him through their religion. They meet people every day who are on their way to eternal destruction, and they don't even care. They have their "treasures in earthen vessels", yet do not share it with anyone. Their lives are full of what they can do, or what man can do for them. They live; they die. And they just don't get it – that Messiah came to die so that we might be restored to a life of knowing His Father, and serving Him outside the systems of man. He has prepared such a wonderful eternity for those that obey His commandments, fear Him, and worship Him as their only "God" – their only "Most High," "Almighty" Creator! Yahuweh and

Yahushua Yahuweh, Father and Son, are totally outside the religious systems of man. To know Them, we have to go outside all religious systems of man also.

Since 2001, He has poured through me to write the articles. They are not mine. I often do not even remember what I wrote or the titles. I have to read the articles to see what I wrote. There have been times when I've "lost hours" while writing. One time, in Aqaba, it was very cold in the winter, and I began about 9:00 AM to write. I believe the article was "Preparation for the Inevitable." I stopped writing because my hands were so cold I could hardly type. I looked at the clock and it was 3:00 PM. I had not even had breakfast. I could not believe that I had lost six hours.

While writing "The Two Witnesses, The Bridal Remnant, The Forerunning Company, and the Fleeing Remnant," I was in another dimension, writing what He was giving me of the future. This has happened many times. I know it is all of Him, because when I read the articles, oftentimes I ask myself "who wrote this?" The re-born spirit is an open portal to the eternal realm. Often people ask me how I can retain so much information. I told them that the mind of the spirit is eternal – it can receive all that He has to tell us, and retain it. I do not go by the mind of the flesh--that mind has to use the brain to figure things out. I lean on His direction that He speaks into my eternal re-born spirit. Why not! We are born again in order to be eternal beings.

CONFIRMATION AND A SHOUT OF VICTORY

In 2007, when I finished writing "The Forty-Eight Hour Transition" – the sequel to "The Shmittah Year Prophecy" - I sat at my desk saying to Abba, I can't send this--my ministry will be over. He was saying to me harshly "SEND IT!" Finally I said "OK" and I sent it. I had written some things which I knew were of Him, but I didn't have any confirmation that they were correct. I'm not kidding! Less than ten minutes later, my daughter came with a package for me. For two years I had been trying to get a tape from Don Esposito entitled "Signs in the Heavens." That tape was in the package. I laid down and listened to it, coming up off the bed shouting with joy from time to time. Then I listened to Parts V and VI of "The Jonah Code Live" by Michael Rood, and lo and behold, the tape from Don and the DVD of Michael's said the same things--just what I had written in the article! "In the mouth of two or three witnesses, let every word be established." He is always faithful to confirm what He says. His variety is amazing! You can imagine I was shouting the victory. I rose up from my bed and wrote "The Three Levels of Daniel 9:24-27" by His leading, which was also confirmed by three witnesses.

2 DAYS IN ICELAND

In August of 2011, I knew that I had to get to Iceland to do intercession on Elul 1 (Hebrew calendar), to call a repentant Ephraim home, so that they might join with Judah for the end-time exploits, as per **Isaiah 11:12-14**. I booked tickets to leave that Sunday, giving me four days in Iceland to do the job of intercession. I booked a hotel that was near the sea at Reykjavik. But, as the day approached for me to go, Hurricane Irene hit the outer banks of the east coast of America, and began traveling north. On the day I was to fly out, Irene was to pass over Boston. My flight on Jet Blue to Boston was cancelled, so I could not fly out on Iceland Air as scheduled. My whole story can be read in "My Iceland Report", but to make a long story short, Jet Blue rescheduled me out of Tampa to fly Air Canada to Toronto. There was an Iceland Air flight out of Toronto that I could take. But my flight out of Tampa was so delayed that I missed my Iceland Air flight by 5 minutes. So I had to stay for 2 days in Toronto to catch the next Iceland Air flight. That would leave me two days to do my assignment—the eve of Elul 1 and Elul 1. But, upon getting to the Iceland Air check-in in Toronto, they said I was not in the computer. They had no record of my flight. I told them I had missed the previous flight by five minutes – and thought I had booked that one. They called for a manager. I told my story to her. She immediately printed me out a boarding pass. I really appreciate Iceland Air for letting me change my flight twice, with no extra charges!

I got to Iceland at 6:30 AM, not even knowing if the hotel was still available. But, the hotel checked me in, and did not charge me for the two days I was not able to be there. I was exhausted, but had a whaling boat trip planned, and a trip to the interior the next day. As I pulled back the curtains of my hotel room, I stood there amazed. I was facing the sea, looking west, to proclaim **Hosea 11:8-10, Jeremiah 31**, and other Scriptures He had given me. He said to go to the remote isles of the sea, and call for the remnant of a repentant and humble Ephraim to come home. The parable of the "prodigal son" in **Luke 15** speaks of Ephraim the prodigal returning to a loving Father.

In praying from that window, I saw that there was a bike/walk path down by the sea, and a bench to sit on. It was so cold. I didn't think I'd be able to get down there. But, when I returned from the tour of the interior of Iceland, I felt so wonderful that I just kept walking past my hotel entrance and down to that bench. For one hour I prayed, praised, and proclaimed from His Word. On the third day, after I arrived in Iceland, I flew out. I had no promise that Logan airport in Boston would be operational after Irene. I checked in with Iceland Air for my flight to Boston. The lady gave me my boarding pass to Boston, and another piece of paper that I thought was a wheelchair assistance ticket. I prayed across the Atlantic that I would get my flight in Boston to Tampa. I was pulling something out of my belt pack, and saw what I thought was the ticket I'd need for wheelchair assistance in Boston.

But, as I looked at it, my mind went blank. It was not something for wheelchair assistance, it was my boarding pass for my flight to Tampa. I could not believe what I was seeing. I had the answer to my prayers with me all along. I got to Boston on a lovely sunny day. On the plane, He tenderly said to me: "Go for it!" In other words, forget wheelchair assistance, just go to your gate by yourself. I did – and it was wonderful. I flew to Tampa-- no problem. Abba is so extraordinarily good! No matter what obstacles came in my path, I was there to do His will exactly on time! If we are in the center of His will, doing what He has told us to do as good servants that He can trust, no matter what comes in between, we will finish what we set out to do…by His mercy and favor! All praise to Him! Here are a few examples of being led by Him in new, and sometimes difficult and dangerous situations…

THE PSALM 3:6 STORY

In Jordan, there were many dangers. Every Friday, we'd have to stay inside, because we never knew when the men came out of the mosque whether they'd be ready to kill "infidels" or not. Sometimes there were riots, and buses from Amman would come with people all stirred up. On 9/11/2001, there was dancing and rejoicing in the streets of Aqaba because the twin towers fell and killed Americans. There were demonstrations against America and Israel. I lived just two blocks south of a main mosque. I heard the opening prayer, the hymn, the sermon, and always the screaming preaching. Then I would watch the men come out of the mosque fingering beads, like "rosary beads." I learned later that Islam is the offspring of the Vatican, to be used to get Jerusalem for the Vatican and eradicate the Jews.

!! DANGER !!
STATUS QUO IN THE LIFE OF HIS SERVANTS

One time the Jordanian police told us to stay inside because Hamas was coming to kill us. Another time, they put us on the roof of one of our people's houses for a week because thirteen Al Qaeda members were coming to kill us. They caught the thirteen in Amman, executed the leaders and imprisoned the others. That made CNN news in America too! A friend who heard it on CNN, told me that they said a group of American Christians were targeted for death. We were mostly Messianic, but what does CNN know?

PART XII - Miracles of His Leading

I really must say that as for dangers, I was put in more danger from betrayal by Americans I thought were friends, who came to visit me in Jordan, than by any gangs, tribal wars, or Muslim terrorists. When I was in China, I would walk from Kowloon, through dark allies in early morning before dawn and late at night, to and from the train station, and in other dangerous places smuggling Bibles into the restricted mainland.

Yes, many times my life was in danger. In my article "Betrayal," I tell of how betrayal almost led to my death and perhaps the deaths of other believers in Aqaba. I could have been killed many times in Russia, but it was the Christians who did the most harm. I tell you this because betrayal will be very common in the days to come, as foretold by Messiah Himself. In Russia I was arrested and almost imprisoned on two counts of breaking laws I did not know I broke – but He delivered me. You can read about this in the part above on Russia.

I had many miracles smuggling Bibles into Mainland China, as you can imagine. But, I was always in danger too. In Africa, the pastors were very good to me – they did not leave my side. They protected me from many dangers. In Mexico, Central and South America I encountered dangers. But, but some of the greatest dangers I encountered were on the back streets of Los Angles' Skid Row, in parks, and on boulevards in Hollywood, while preaching the Good News of salvation. You can read my many adventures in these countries in Parts V and VI.

The story of our risking our lives in Shanghai was amazing. Of course, in our risking our lives to get Bibles to the persecuted assemblies, we also risked the lives of those who came to get the Bibles. Taking Bibles to persecuted believers is illegal in China. Their "Three Self Government Church" prints a few Bibles. But, those who will not submit to the demands of the communist government, which so often violate the basics of the Bible, are considered illegal. Many spend years in prison for their faith.

Read the many stories of miracles in the section on China, Part V. Read the many miracles in 2003, in meeting Elaine, and how it led to miracles in 2004 and 2005 in Wales.

I have also suffered much from character assassination from evil people who hide behind a mask of spirituality in Christian or Messianic circles. The satanic nature behind these betrayals are beyond the nature of the natural human mind. They are so evil that most naïve believers do not even believe those that pass themselves off as Christians or Messianic are capable of such things. Therefore, they call the victim crazy, and justify the actions of the evil ones. I've had this happen many times. There are more dangers out there than physical ones. I've had a lifetime of education in the area of the demonic and have a powerful gift of the discernment of spirits. Abba has taken me deep into the dark kingdom, and I am very clear and knowledgeable about what we all are up against in the days ahead.

We have awesome promises from our Abba. One such promise He gave me while taking Bibles into Beijing, China: **Isaiah 41:10, 13**: **"DO NOT FEAR FOR I AM WITH YOU. DO NOT LOOK AROUND IN DISMAY FOR I AM YOUR ELOHIM. I WILL STRENGTHEN YOU. I WILL ALSO HELP YOU. I WILL ALSO UPHOLD YOU WITH THE RIGHT HAND OF MY RIGHTEOUSNESS."**

I have been writing a lot, as Abba has been showing me, about the end-time remnant that will do "exploits" in the face of the onslaught of the Beast during the tribulation time. (**Daniel 11:32**) This group has to be highly trained. They must know Him and trust Him implicitly. He must also trust them implicitly. They must work with Abba as a team... and obey instantly. Their training has taken a lifetime. I speak of this group as a forerunning company. They are united to prepare the way for Messiah. Within this group is the Bridal remnant. These people intimately KNOW Yahuweh. They intimately KNOW Yahushua. Again I shout the words of the Master: "Unless you forsake all, you cannot be MY disciple." The word "disciple" means a "taught one." We are a disciple of whoever teaches us. The taught one is not above his Master, but rather submits to learning how to emulate Him in every detail. To emulate our Master, to be changed into His image and likeness, with His character and nature, is impossible in our own strength. But, the Spirit of Yahuweh does it as we spend time in the Word, reading whole books to get continuity. Our transformation also comes while we are in daily worship, entering His Presence by the Spirit. If He is your Teacher, you will never be deceived!

The words of Sha'ul in **II Timothy 4:3-4** are for today: **"There shall be a time when they shall not bear sound teaching, but according to their own lustful desires they shall heap up for themselves teachers tickling the ear, and they shall indeed turn their ears away from the truth, and be turned aside to myths."**

II Timothy 3:1: **"But know this, that in the last days perilous times shall come."**

Then it lists how mankind will be saturated with the lusts of the flesh. But, the Greek word for "perilous times", simply means "raging insanity." I see this happening to the majority of Yahuweh's people--those who have allowed the Illuminati mind programming to take them over. Most live in fear, pride, dullness of mind, and deadness of spirit. We have indeed returned to the "days of Noah," when the Nephillim ruled the earth, and violence was everywhere (**Genesis 6**). The only safe hiding place is in the Presence of Yahuweh, hidden under His tallit. He is all Light. To hide in His Presence, one must discard all defilement – all darkness. (**II Corinthians 6:14-7:1**) "Defilement" means: "to be foul, contaminated, polluted, to be utterly pronounced `unclean' as a leper, impure, filthy and vile."

The message of set-apartness is the strongest message He has for His children today: "Come out from among them and be separate, and touch not the unclean thing, and I will receive you." All religion of man is defiled. Yahuweh is not in it--it is man-created. Therefore, we must come out and be separate if we want to be set-apart unto Yahuweh. Knowing Him and being led by Him is the only safe life.

I have met very few who are walking in the true life of the Scriptures as disciples and servants. Most are like the "foolish virgins" of **Matthew 25:1-12**, to whom Messiah will say: "Truly I say to you: `I do not know you.' "

Seek Them with all your heart, and you will find Them! **Jeremiah 29:11-13**: **"For I know the plans I am planning for you, declares Yahuweh, plans of peace and not for evil, to give you a future and expectancy. Then you shall call upon Me, and shall come and pray to Me, and I shall listen to you. And you shall seek Me, and shall find Me, when you search for Me with all your heart.**"

Read **I Kings 18**. Eliyahu had a contest with the worshippers of Ba'al (the Lord) on Mt. Carmel. Yahuweh won! This separation is coming to the whole world – choose sides! All in the middle will be spewed out of Yahushua's mouth at His return. The time of the spewing has come. The middle group will be spewed towards the kingdom of darkness. I have been in 37 countries, some many, many times, close to 50 times in Israel alone, on close to 400 flights, on 47 different airlines, written about 500 or more articles, and ministered to over a hundred thousand people; both person, and over the Internet. But, now, He is bringing me to the place where I must only minister to His small remnant that He is bringing together, those who will do exploits with Him in these last days. I am called to the "few" who seek to enter the "narrow gate that leads to life."

These are those who have little of this world's goods by their own choice, but they are following the Lamb wherever He goes. They have no personal agendas. They have no ambitions of their own to promote anyone but Yahuweh and Yahushua. The Spirit is orchestrating these people together to prepare for the days of the anti-messiah, in which they will work for the salvation and preservation of His people.

THE STORY OF THE GOLDEN CORD

April 21, 1992, I had a dream. I was standing in mid-air, wearing a long white skirt and a long-sleeved white blouse, holding a Bible, and preaching-teaching to an invisible/unseen audience. I had a gold cord around my waist. It was attached to a throne chair leg, inside His throne room. I saw the cord tied to the throne chair. All of a sudden, I heard a man's voice very rapidly counting backwards from the number 47--my age at the time. As he was counting, someone was pulling the cord around my waste – pulling me into the throne room. When he got to zero, I was inside the throne room.

In October, 2012, at the Temple Institute in Jerusalem, He brought that dream back to me. He later connected it to the changes that would happen after this autobiography, my "recorded history" as He put it, was finished. Of course, in 1992 I had no idea I would be preaching and teaching in cyberspace – via the Internet – to an unseen audience. I am to continue a while longer, but at some point, He will jerk on the cord and pull me to Himself. I know that.

As I wrote in Part VI, 2013: Near my time to go back to the U.S., in November, 2012, Abba spoke to me: "**When the recorded history of your life is finished, everything will change.**" When I returned to the U.S. in December, 2012, He said it like this: "**When the recorded history of your life is finished, your life will consist of what cannot be recorded.**" I understood.

It is now July, 2013. I am almost 69 years old. I see the changes. My autobiography is finished except for final editing. It will be put on electronic media. Now, as I see the finish line, I am spending more and more time in worship, prayer, intercession, and watching the final system of Lucifer beginning to rise. It is puffing up like a puff-adder (a large snake), but will quickly be deflated by Messiah!

As a young teen, I asked Abba not to let me miss anything He was doing. He has not let me miss anything. The reason it has taken me so long to write this autobiography is because of Part III. I never wanted to bring up the past that was so filled with sin and rebellion, deep hurts and life-threatening horrors. I wanted to only write good things to edify people. However, by writing the whole truth of my life, the bad and the good, I can show how Abba guides one that He will use in the days to come. So, I suppose reality is: THE GREATEST ADVENTURES ARE JUST

BEGINNING! The words come from deep inside my spirit, and are ever on my lips: "**THANK YOU ABBA**!"

"**To Him who sits on the throne, and to the Lamb, be blessing, and honor, glory, and power, forever and ever!**" **(Revelation 5:13b)** I conclude with the words, once again, from Steven Curtis Chapman's classic, "**The Great Adventure**"

The Great Adventure
---Steven Curtis Chapman---

Started out this morning in the usual way
Chasing thoughts inside my head of all I had to do today
Another time around the circle try to make it better than the last
I opened up the Bible and I read about me
Said I'd been a prisoner and God's grace had set me free
And somewhere between the pages it hit me like a lightning bolt
I saw a big frontier in front of me and I heard somebody say
"Let's Go!"

CHORUS
Saddle up your horses we've got a trail to blaze
Through the wild blue yonder of God's amazing grace
Let's follow our leader into the glorious unknown
This is a life like no other - this is The Great Adventure

Come on get ready for the ride of your life
Gonna leave long faced religion in a cloud of dust behind
And discover all the new horizons just waiting to be explored
This is what we were created for

(Chorus)

BRIDGE
We'll travel over, over mountains so high
We'll go through valleys below
Still through it all we'll find that
This is the greatest journey that the human heart will ever see
The love of God will take us far beyond our wildest dreams
Yeah... oh saddle up your horses... come on get ready to ride

(Chorus)

Come join me in the greatest adventure anyone could ever have!

Blessings to you as you continue your journey of faith!

With shalom, in His love,

Yedidah

Autobiography:
Began August 31, 2006; Finished July, 2013!

Final Edit:
Began April 16, 2013; Finished September 26, 2013!

P.S.: Below is a picture of me (smile) -- October, 2012... My son took the picture as he and his wife were in the ski lift behind me. We were descending from the top of Mount Hermon. Oh... just to be there on that mountain, about which so much Scripture is written...

AWESOME! It's a life like no other...

**REMEMBER ALWAYS
THE GREATEST MIRACLE OF ALL IS ABBA'S LOVE AND MERCY FOR US! HUMBLY, WITH LOVE, I PRAISE HIM FOR HIS OVERWHELMING LOVINGKINDNESS!**

www.ingramcontent.com/pod-product-compliance
Lightning Source LLC
Chambersburg PA
CBHW081836230426
43669CB00018B/2730